Praise for Poilu

"[Barthas's] notebooks . . . are among the great works of the war, deserving a place of mention with memoirs like Guy Chapman's *A Passionate Prodigality* and Ernst Jünger's *Storm of Steel.*"—Geoffrey Norman, *Wall Street Journal*

"One wonders why it took so long for an English translation—this is clearly one of the most readable and indispensible accounts of the death of the glory of war." —Nicholas Mancuso, *Daily Beast*

"Barthas's voice is unlike any other I know in the vast literature on the First World War. The translation is excellent, the grittiness of the text is captured beautifully, and so is the humanity of the man who wrote it."—Jay Winter, Yale University

"A revelatory book that brings the French experience of the Great War to life as you read. However much we may think the British and Americans suffered, their agony was shorter and less intense than the tragedy that overwhelmed the French nation in 1914–1918."—Peter Hart, author of *The Great War: A Combat History of the First World War*

"Ah, the notebooks of Louis Barthas! This book has profound historic value. It is also a genuine work of literature."—François Mitterrand, former president of France

"Louis Barthas' stunningly honest, graphic and gripping narrative has rightly made *Poilu* a classic trench memoir."—Douglas Porch, author of *The French Foreign Legion: A Complete History of the Legendary Fighting Force*

"There is nothing like this for the French experience of WWI, almost nothing from equivalent British and German perspectives. . . . I believe this will be a major contribution to the study of Third-Republic France, the French army, and the First World War: regularly cited, regularly assigned."—Dennis Showalter, Colorado College

"In Barthas' telling, the fighting men on both sides of No Man's Land shared a more natural bond with their fellows than with those career officers who pitted them against each other. Barthas' detailed real-time reportage captures instances of informal truces and slowdowns between combatants, as they tacitly aid one another in their shared struggle to survive the madness."—David Wright, *Seattle Times*

"Among World War I books being published in this centennial year of that conflict's start, none likely can connect readers more directly or vividly to the experience of those who fought it."—Alan Wallace, *Pittsburgh Tribune-Review*

"Barthas provides one of the best pictures of life in the trenches."—J.W. Thacker, *Park City Daily News*

Poilu

Poilu

The World War I Notebooks of

Corporal Louis Barthas, Barrelmaker,

1914–1918

Translated by

Edward M. Strauss

Foreword by Robert Cowley

Introductions and Afterword by Rémy Cazals

Yale UNIVERSITY PRESS/NEW HAVEN & LONDON

This work, published as part of a program of aid for publication, received support from the Institut Français. *(Cet ouvrage a bénéficié du soutien des Programmes d'aide à la publication de l'Institut Français.)*

Published with assistance from the foundation established in memory of Philip Hamilton McMillan of the Class of 1894, Yale College.

Yale University Press books may be purchased in quantity for educational, business, or promotional use. For information, please e-mail sales.press@yale.edu (U.S. office) or sales@yaleup.co.uk (U.K. office).

Designed by Mary Valencia.
Set in Adobe Garamond type by Integrated Publishing Solutions.
Printed in the United States of America.

The Library of Congress has cataloged the hardcover edition as follows:
Barthas, Louis, 1879–1952.
[Carnets de guerre de Louis Barthas, tonnelier, 1914–1918. English]
Poilu : the World War I notebooks of Corporal Louis Barthas, barrelmaker, 1914–1918 / translated by Edward M. Strauss.
    pages   cm.
"Originally published as Les carnets de guerre de Louis Barthas, tonnelier, 1914–1918 . . . Editions La Découverte, Paris, France, 1978"—Title page verso.
Includes bibliographical references and index.
ISBN 978-0-300-19159-2 (hardcover : alkaline paper)
1. Barthas, Louis, 1879–1952. 2. World War, 1914–1918—Personal narratives, French. 3. Soldiers—France—Biography. 4. France. Armée—Biography. 5. World War, 1914–1918—Campaigns. 6. France. Armée—Military life—History—20th century. I. Title.
D811.B361813 2014
940.4'D1244092—dc23
2013041264

ISBN 978-0-300-21248-8 (pbk.)

Frontispiece: Louis Barthas, circa 1914

A catalogue record for this book is available from the British Library.

Contents

Few documents from the Great War are as remarkable as the war notebooks of Louis Barthas, published in English for the first time in Edward M. Strauss's fine translation. They are special for a number of reasons. Their author left a record of four years of service at the front, an unusual span of survival. He was not an officer but a common soldier, a corporal, a man approaching middle age who in civilian life had been a barrelmaker from the Languedoc region of France, a wine-growing center.

Men in the ranks were not ordinarily chroniclers, and we'll never know what started Barthas on his singular project. He apparently began it as a diary, which over the war years came to fill many volumes. You have to suppose that he carried the most recent ones home with him, each caked with battlefield mud and chewed by rats, on his infrequent furloughs. He probably didn't want to risk leaving them behind, where they might be pilfered, inadvertently destroyed, or appropriated by the officers he so readily criticized and used against him in possible court-martial proceedings. (Some of those hostile superiors had seen to his brief demotion from corporal to private, on the flimsiest of evidence.) After he was mustered out in February 1919, Barthas began to assemble a narrative describing his time on the Western Front that would eventually run to nineteen notebooks. He would work on it after he finished a long day of barrel-making, fleshing out the original diaries with quotes from letters home, official reports and orders that he had kept, and accounts by fellow soldiers that he had written down at the time, as well as with ephemera such as postcards and newspaper clippings. Those sources he put together in the book you read here, one that is part diary, part memoir. The men in his squad encouraged their corporal's literary efforts:

"And you," said Ferié to me, "you who are writing about the life we're leading here, don't hide anything. You've got to tell it all."

"Yes, yes, everything, everything. We'll be there as your witnesses. Maybe we won't all die here," added the others.

"They won't believe us," said Mondiès, "or maybe they won't even give a damn."

Barthas was a natural writer, even if he had only one book in him; it did not come to light until the late seventies, when he had been dead for more than two decades, as Rémy Cazals recounts in his introduction. If I have any criticism, it is that Cazals is too modest about his discovery. There are few accounts of the experience of war on the Western Front equal to that of Louis Barthas; I sometimes think that it may be the best.

The barrelmaker was a keen observer who had a way with words and homespun images. Of an inept trench guide he comments, "The poor guy read his map like a carp reading a prayer book." Describing an overcrowded dugout, he remarks, "It was hot enough to hatch chickens in there." After a bombardment, he remembers "sharp, piercing sounds, first the whistling, sometimes like a cat meowing, then crashing down like a steady rain of steel." Of the corpse of a young and seemingly untouched German soldier, he observes that "death had brushed him with its wing, and preserved the smile which still marked his youthful face." There is a primitive vigor here. Think of an Henri Rousseau of the trenches. The perspectives are sometimes inexact but the compositions are true and original, and the colors always vivid.

Intelligent and obviously well read—circumstances had forced him to leave school early—stoic and forgiving (except of the officers he ridiculed as the "new noblemen of the twentieth century"), Barthas was a man who suffered much in return for little. The aging corporal was plainly popular with his squad mates, whom he regarded as a little family. Though he always did what was expected of him, he nonetheless refused to shed the blood of his German counterparts. He was a confirmed socialist who regarded them more as comrades than as enemies. But for all his good qualities, Barthas exhibited a countryman's lack of sophistication and prudishness—witness his shocked reaction to the "bare arms and shoulders" of Parisian women.

There are numerous accounts of the Great War by French officers with a literary bent, and not a few are memorable. But their war was different from that of Barthas. Even sergeants inhabited another world. As he says of his superiors, "To them, the soldier doesn't open up, is mistrustful, and any officer who will want to try, like me, to describe the strange life of the trenches will have never known, except by accident, the real sentiments, the true spirit, the clear language and the deepest thoughts of the soldier."

You would hardly grasp that perception from reading a book that has long been venerated as the most useful, indeed indispensable, study of the French literature of experience in the Great War, Jean Norton Cru's 1929 *Témoins— Witnesses*. Norton Cru's quirky but authoritative work cites 252 writers, sketching their biographies and their roles in the war, and evaluating their personal accounts, which run the gamut from letters and diaries to memoirs and novels.

He even ranks them. Norton Cru, a combat veteran himself, was a great man for lists. Almost all the writers he mentions were educated men from the middle or upper class; almost all were officers. He names not a single individual from the lower class, not a single one who was, in August 1914, a laborer. War accounts by such people apparently did not exist: in any assessment of Barthas' notebooks, can there be a fact more telling?

For a military historian, *Poilu* (I'll use Strauss's absolutely accurate title) is a treasure trove: pick your cliché. There was hardly a sector from Flanders to Verdun where Barthas didn't show up at some point in the fifty-four months in which he served. In that time he witnessed warfare making its fearsome leap into a new century. Within the framework of stalemate, we sometimes forget how much warfare did change on the Western Front. Barthas began his four years with night dashes across fields swept by rifle and machine gun fire to a single front-line trench and ended them in tunnels lit by light bulbs. ("Power stations in the trenches! But then they were thinking that the war would go on for years and years.") He took part in the infantry assaults of 1914 that still had the feel of charges out of the Franco-Prussian War, suffered the unimaginable rigors and dangers of the trenches (and those of their next evolution, fighting from shell hole to shell hole), sweated out artillery barrages that never seemed to end, prepared for poison gas attacks, was momentarily rendered wild-eyed and incoherent by the searing blast from a flamethrower, and went to ground in the deep dugouts and scattered outposts that characterized the undermanned defensive zones of 1918. He fraternized with his German opposites, seeing nothing wrong in doing so, and joined the mutinies of 1917, believing that they were justified. Louis Barthas was never less than an ideal soldier.

The late fall and winter of 1914–15 is a period largely missing from the histories of the Great War, those of the French especially. It was not one that they are proud of. They did their best to reverse their great victories at the Marne, the Grand Couronné, and, most recently, Ypres. While the British scraped the bottom of their replacement barrel and waited for their New Armies to take shape, the French expanded their leadership in the war. Their Western Front generals pursued what they called *la guerre d'usure,* "the war of wearing down," day after day sending men against the Germans and their plentiful machine guns, their thickening networks of barbed wire, probing for a new weak spot, an unturned flank to turn. The era of the breakthrough—*la percée*—was not to be. An angry former lieutenant, the novelist Jean Bernier, would later write of "the unpardonable offensives of that first winter" and of "the mud, and the rain, and the veritable jelly of corpses." Joffre, the French commander in chief, ruthlessly sacked generals who spoke their minds about what was happening. Of a planned attack, Marie-Émile Fayolle, then a corps commander, confided in his diary, "I believe it will be a bloody failure." The future marshal of France kept his doubts to himself. In the event, no word about the disasters leaked out.

Louis Barthas was one of the few who actually described taking part in those attacks, two of them on successive days, and his account didn't surface for six decades. He left a record of the patriotic madness that still seized both sides, and would do so for several months more. There is an almost cinematographic quality about his description of the attacks that initiated his ordeal on the Western Front. The date is December 16, 1914, and the scene is a railroad embankment in French Flanders outside a coal mining village called Vermelles, one of those otherwise forgettable places that briefly earned notoriety a century ago. Men in red trousers and dark blue greatcoats advance in the direction of what Barthas calls "the disagreeable tic-tac of machine guns." They flatten themselves against a faint artificial rise that offers little protection from machine guns firing from the upper stories of a neighboring village. Just as he arrives, out of breath—he never skimps the small details—"I saw one of those guys who had already taken cover there get hit in the back with a bullet. I'll never forget the sight of that hole, like it was made with a drill—a little whiff of smoke from burnt cloth, the man's violent somersault, a groan, and then the stillness of death."

When the troops spread out along the embankment refuse to budge, an officer yells out from the safety of a trench that if they don't move forward, he'll order them fired on. "Terrified, we crept a little farther along the embankment, like earthworms." An orderly approaches Corporal Barthas, carrying a message. "Hey," he said, "are you scared?" He had hardly spoken when a bullet pierced his chest and he pitched forward. "He didn't say a word. He just stuck out his hand to us. The guy closest to me and I both took it, but it was already motionless. He was dead."

There was more of the same the following afternoon. Finally, there was only one officer left standing. He called a halt.

The scene now switches a few miles south to a place called Notre Dame de Lorette, a long, five-hundred-foot-high hill that in 1915 witnessed some of the most brutal fighting on the entire Western Front. A chapel dedicated to the Virgin Mary, where pilgrims came to pray, crowned its summit. In 1914, the Germans, who had a knack for appropriating high ground, had established a considerable foothold there; the French spent the first nine months of the following year trying to evict them. Perhaps a hundred thousand men from both sides died contesting those heights. Firsthand accounts of the long struggle are rare, which makes Barthas' all the more noteworthy. But then, there were probably few survivors with the stomach to write about experiences ready-made for PTSD.

Today a national cemetery occupies much of the long hilltop. It is a rectangle of thirty-two acres with twenty thousand marked crosses crowding in on a nondescript white stone basilica and an adjacent observation tower. Low-walled enclosures surround grass-covered boneyards, containing the remains of another twenty-two thousand, all unknowns. There are cemeteries everywhere in the Artois: death is a major industry in this part of the world. Barthas called Notre Dame de Lorette a "charnel house." It would be hard to dispute that phrase. Once, years ago, I strolled from one end of the national cemetery to the other, occasionally glancing at my wristwatch. With scarcely a pause, my walk consumed nine minutes.

The British, who took over the sector from the French, were appalled by what they found at Notre Dame de Lorette (or Loretto, as the Germans called it). The original church had been pounded to smithereens. That was predictable. But the killing fields of the butte, which had not yet been cleaned up, were not. An Irish infantry officer, F. C. Hitchcock, described the place as it looked in October 1916:

> Passed numbers of skeletons on my way down the sunken road. . . . A rusty and twisted rifle barrel stuck into the ground, surmounted by the familiar kepi, indicated the grave of some unknown *poilu*. Skulls and bones bleached white lay strewn throughout rank grass. Twisted French rifles and equipment lay rotting everywhere. A skull was lying on top of Uhlan Alley communication trench. Some wag had stuck a derelict *kepi* on it in grim humour.

For all their losses in the year they contested Notre Dame de Lorette, neither side accomplished anything of operational, let alone strategic, value. Barthas was one of the thousands who took part in what must be reckoned as the consummate meaningless trench battle. By June 2, 1915, when he began his first perilous climb up those hideous slopes, he would have been wearing a new, but already muddied, sky blue uniform. (The characteristic ridged Adrian helmets, with the flaming grenade stamped in front, would not be introduced until midsummer.) "Right away," he wrote, "we found ourselves in a forest of cut-down, twisted, uprooted trees; in this inextricable mess we could barely follow the trace of what looked like a communication trench." Death was everywhere:

> Where the connecting trench joined in, an unfortunate fellow was stretched out, decapitated by a shell, just as if he had been guillotined. Beside him, another was frightfully mutilated. . . . I saw, as if hallucinating, a pile of

corpses, almost all of them German, that they had started to bury right in the trench . . .

"There's no one here but the dead!" I exclaimed.

Soon after, flames and "bitter smoke" filled his trench. "At my feet two miserable creatures are rolling on the ground, their clothes, their hands, their faces on fire." The Germans had unleashed a flamethrower attack. Barthas had arrived in a new world, the revolutionary zone of the industrial battlefield. "The time will come," wrote the German novelist Ernst Jünger (who also survived all four years of the war), "when the single unprotected rifleman will be ground between the millstones of machinery. . . . It is a question no longer of launching men en masse but machines."

Barthas' Artois ordeal wasn't over. He spent the fall of 1915 in the downlands to the south of the butte. The area had become trench warfare's Holy Land, dominated by shrines of lethality with names like the Labyrinth, the Pimple, and the Ouvrages Blancs, German defensive networks behind deep belts of barbed wire, with underground dugout shelters armed with machine guns that intersected one another in a kind of puzzle maker's maze. Behind them loomed the densely fortified slopes of Vimy Ridge. On September 25, the French launched a new offensive, which finally drove the Germans from Notre Dame de Lorette before it inevitably bogged down. Barthas' 296th Regiment waited in reserve. "At daybreak," he wrote, "we could see, to our horror, that in front of the trench and behind it the ground was covered with hundreds of French bodies . . ."

A deep change in the attitude of the ordinary poilu was becoming evident. Barthas—and he was not alone—openly spoke of "the incoherence of the high command." Common soldiers were increasingly reluctant to sacrifice their lives for remote commanders whose goals they no longer trusted or endorsed. Poilus, and not the men who led them, began to break off attacks on their own initiative. As the military historian Douglas Porch has written, "The sacrificial *élan* of the first year was gone, not to return in this war—or in the next."

The battlefield was changing, and so was the nature of warfare. In the spring of 1916, Barthas and his regiment found themselves at Verdun, holding the highlands on the west bank of the Meuse. As a colonel who ran the Verdun battlefield museum once told me, "People who speak about trenches here don't know what they are talking about." Men sheltered in, and fought from, shell holes. Artillery had become the weapon of choice. Shellfire rarely let up. The Germans, Barthas wrote, seemed determined "to pound us into marmalade." In this disjointed combat, you never saw your adversaries: "Our firing line was broken, with gaps of as much as four hundred meters between sections and companies. No one really knew whether we had Germans or French in front of us." The only human forms you saw were likely to be corpses.

Somehow, in "this monstrous avalanche of metal," this "veritable curtain of steel and fire," Barthas continued "cheating death." One day a heavy shell— what the poilus called a *marmite*, a "cooking pot"—burst almost on top of him. "I had just felt the death wind," he wrote. "Some say it's chilly; I found it hot and burning. It coursed through my whole body, from my rattled brain, to my heavy heart and lungs, all the way down to my rubbery legs."

In four years, that may have been the closest he came to being killed.

Through the last half of 1916 and all of 1917, Barthas served (with rare furlough breaks home) in the Champagne, the Somme, and the Argonne. The hard, dangerous life in the open remained a constant, but, for common soldiers of both sides, something had changed. The killing may not have stopped—if anything, death had become more mechanized and impersonal—but the desire to kill, along with the acceptance of your own death, had lost whatever attraction they once might have had. The sacrificial élan was indeed a thing of the past; a weary fatalism had replaced it, one that Barthas' narrative increasingly reflects. All that really mattered now was survival, live and let live.

Fraternization was a symptom of this new attitude. The Christmas truce of 1914 was the most famous example, with its football games between British and Germans that probably never happened. The British high command, which regarded fraternization as detrimental to the fighting spirit, made a strenuous, and mostly successful, effort to prevent a repetition. With the French and the Germans it was different, as the common soldier often took charge. Barthas (whose regiment had not observed the Christmas truce) first recorded an incident of fraternization in the Artois on December 10, 1915. Rain had been falling for days. "At many places along the front line, the soldiers had to come out of their trenches so as not to drown," Barthas wrote. "The Germans had to do the same. We therefore had the singular spectacle of two enemy armies facing each other without firing a shot." In their unofficial truce, soldiers "smiled, ex-changed comments; hands reached out and grasped; we shared tobacco, a can-teen of 'jus' [coffee] or pinard [cheap red wine]."

Barthas returned to the subject of fraternization in his account of life on the Champagne front in the summer of 1916. Unofficial meetings usually occurred where listening posts of the two sides were close. Barthas recorded the sight of "French and German sentries seated tranquilly on their parapets, smoking pipes and exchanging bits of conversation from time to time, like good neighbors taking some fresh air at their doorsteps." The practice was passed on from relief to relief.

Officers, who were often disliked by the men who served under them, tended to take a dim view of fraternization. At one point a lieutenant who had caught wind of the socializing came to the trenches to investigate. When a German sentry responded to the officer's attempt to lure the enemy into the open by "coughing loudly, speaking at high volume, and chuckling," the lieutenant grabbed a rifle and shot the man through the head. "Our sentries aren't doing their duty," the officer said to the dumbfounded corporal Barthas, who wrote: "As a result, the Germans blasted away at us all day long with rifle shots which tore our sandbags to shreds and made all surveillance impossible. We were quite lucky that none of our sentries had his head blown off."

Barthas also witnessed fraternization on the Somme that fall. His narrative makes it abundantly clear that the four-and-a-half-month struggle wasn't just a British battle—as it is usually portrayed. (The French actually captured more territory and suffered half the British casualties.) Can there be a moment more moving in this book than Barthas' description of an early morning attack that dissolves in an outburst of good feeling? The date was October 23, 1916, and his regiment had been ordered to take the German trench immediately in front of it. The French had dug attack trenches in No Man's Land to shorten the distance they would have to cross. In the fog and darkness one group had dug closer to the Germans than they had intended. But the enemy troops were apparently so fatigued that they heard nothing. Most of them simply raised their arms in surrender, shouting, "Comrades! Comrades!" The French took fifty-two prisoners. They also found a dead officer, his head beaten in, and, beside the body, the bloody shovel which one of his own men had wielded to dispatch him. "It seemed clear that, when he didn't want to surrender, his men had gotten rid of him."

For France, no interval of the war was potentially more ominous than May 1917, which followed the calamity of the Aisne offensive, where the French army lost more than a hundred thousand men attacking the highlands known as the Chemin des Dames. This, they had been assured by General Robert Nivelle, the commander in chief of the French army, would be the offensive that would break open the German defenses and win the war. The attack gained almost nothing. Troops mutinied and refused to return to the front. They demanded more pay, more and better food, more leave, and no more vain bloodbaths. The Russian Revolution was beginning, and in the manner of the Russians they formed Soldiers' Councils and marched, arm in arm, singing "The International," that universal anthem of the working class. It is generally assumed that these mutinies had taken place mostly in the sector of the failed offensive—though new evidence makes it clear that the disturbances were more widespread than that.

The notebooks of Louis Barthas are part of that new evidence. Barthas and his regiment were at the time stationed in the Argonne, long a quiet sector. That made no difference to the present mood of the French army. "A wind of revolt blew across almost all the regiments," he wrote. He went on to describe demonstrations near Sainte Menehould that were indeed mutinous, as well as the near killing of a general who attempted to order the regiment to return to the front. Barthas himself was offered the presidency of a "soviet" that "would take control of the regiment." A mere corporal would replace the colonel in command: that had to be an indication of the respect with which other poilus regarded him. "Of course I refused. I had no desire to shake hands with a firing squad, just for the child's play of pretending we were the Russians." He did, however, write a "manifesto" protesting the delay in furloughs.

Though the mutinous activities resulted in a relative handful of executions and other severe disciplinary measures, the French army did listen to the mutineers' most pressing demands. General Henri-Philippe Pétain, who replaced Nivelle, saw to more frequent leaves, better food, an improved medical service, more sanitary and comfortable rest areas, and, most important of all, a scaling back of costly offensive actions. But as punishment for its too-overt protests, the French high command dissolved Barthas' regiment and merged it with a Breton unit, the 248th Regiment, thought to be more reliable. Barthas himself would end the war as an infantry instructor, teaching tactics to Breton recruits. His new role probably saved his life. Open warfare always kills more men than the stationary combat to which he had become accustomed. Barthas was fortunate to miss the war of movement that characterized 1918.

Still, how did he manage to survive four years in which he was so constantly under fire—in the words of the old Socialist, "fifty-four months of slavery"? Fighter pilots have a phrase for that singular capacity: "situational awareness." According to a British aviation authority, Michael Spick, situational awareness is "the mysterious sixth sense that enables a pilot to keep track of everything happening around him in the middle of a confused dogfight." Men who can handle sudden change—and foresee it—survive. Louis Barthas spoke in much the same language. "Throughout the course of this war I had, on many occasions, a mysterious intuition, an instinct about the imminence of danger. At this very moment, from the very bottom of my being, a voice told me that it was time to flee." He talked of fellow soldiers who didn't listen to his warnings, men who moments later would be, in his phrase, "pounded into marmalade."

Infantrymen, too, can be blessed with situational awareness. Like Louis Barthas, they are the survivors.

Robert Cowley
Military historian and founding editor, *MHQ:
The Quarterly Journal of Military History*

Translator's Note

I undertook this translation at the suggestion of my friend Rob Cowley, founding editor of *MHQ: The Quarterly Journal of Military History,* on which we worked together in the mid-1990s. I'd commented to Rob that firsthand accounts of the First World War from the French side available to English-speaking readers were quite rare, and that the available histories, memoirs, and novels were virtually monopolized by English writers (and a handful of Americans) as well as by Germans (Erich Maria Remarque, Ernst Jünger). I had asked Rob to recommend a French memoir of the First World War that, in his opinion, deserved to be translated for English-speaking readers but had not been, and which I might undertake. He immediately replied: Barthas! After sampling the French text in its 1997 paperback edition, I contacted the French publisher, La Découverte, and the editor of the Barthas *Carnets de guerre* [War Notebooks], Professor Rémy Cazals of the University of Toulouse, and learned that, to their knowledge, nobody else was working on a translation.

Further encouraged about the worthiness of the project by several of the Great War's leading historians—Jay Winter at Cambridge and Yale, Robert Doughty at West Point, Leonard Smith at Oberlin, and later Hew Strachan at Oxford and John Horne at Trinity College Dublin—I got to work, part-time, over the next decade, cheered on by my family—wife Anne, daughters Louisa and Ellie—and by friends such as James Bednarz and Stella Paul, Peter Carry, David D'Arcy, Robert Farré, Jacques and Anne-Marie Guy, Leigh and Eleanor Hoagland, and Professor James and Pat McPherson. Rob Cowley has provided unflagging and cheerful support and encouragement throughout the process, as have Professor Cazals and Delphine Ribouchon at La Découverte in Paris. I've enjoyed the professional collaboration with Chris Rogers, Jeff Schier, and Christina Tucker at Yale University Press, and with Bill Nelson on the maps.

As the centennial of the war's outbreak in 1914 approaches, I am proud to make this remarkable account of one Frenchman's experience in the First World War accessible to readers of English. I dedicate this translation to the memory of my parents—Francophiles late in their lives—and to the teachers of French language and history who inspired me at Shady Side Academy in

Pittsburgh, 1964–68 (T. C. Adams, Miles Charest, Jack Cousins, Don Moisdon), and at Princeton University (Robert Darnton, André Maman).

Louis Barthas was meticulous about chronicling personal names and place names, calendar dates, weather, and times of day. There are occasional inconsistencies and variants in his manuscript. Alternatives are offered in the translated text and on the maps. The terms "communication trench" and *boyau* (plural *boyaux*) are used interchangeably, meaning a trench leading to the front lines (see note 5 to 2nd Notebook, p. 395).

Introduction to the
English Translation (2014)

Rémy Cazals

Louis Barthas does not belong to the category of history's "Great Men," whether civilian or military. A simple barrelmaker (in French, *tonnelier*) by trade, in a village of the Aude *département* in the Languedoc region of France, he never sought promotion above his rank of corporal in the army. He accomplished no earth-shattering deed which would have brought him great renown. All he did was write about his experiences in the First World War—1,732 manuscript pages, resulting in a big book which has now become a classic: *Les carnets de guerre de Louis Barthas, tonnelier, 1914–1918.* This book brought him to the French nation's attention. Now its reach is international, with translations into Dutch (1998) and English and Spanish (2014).

The Life of Louis Barthas

"Do you know a work about the life of Louis Barthas?" asked an enthusiastic reader after the first edition of the book came out in France. Apart from the very complete autobiography of the war years, we know little about his life, but enough to place his testimony in its context.

Louis Barthas was born on Bastille Day—July 14, 1879—in the town of Homps. His father was a barrelmaker and his mother a seamstress. The family settled in Peyriac-Minervois, in the same département of the Aude. Louis was an excellent pupil in school, ranking first in his district in the exam for the *Certificat d'études primaires* at age thirteen. He did not advance to the level of secondary education, but he had acquired solid, fundamental knowledge and an openness of mind which led him to further his education on his own. This shines through clearly in the *Carnets de guerre,* with numerous allusions to history, literature, and even classical Greco-Roman mythology. A proud and dedicated craftsman, he became a militant trade-union activist and secretary of the local branch of the Socialist Party, where he worked side by side with his boyhood friend Léon Hudelle. Hudelle had been to university, and in 1914 had become editor in chief of the regional daily newspaper *Le Midi Socialiste,* which Barthas read regularly. At the time of mobilization, in August 1914, Barthas had the rank of corporal in the army reserves, while Hudelle was an officer. (On the front lines, Corporal Barthas and Captain Hudelle called each other "*tu*" for "you"—highly uncommon practice between an officer and an enlisted man). At that time Barthas was thirty-five years old and married, with two sons, Abel (age eight) and André (age six). Brought up in the Catholic church, he lived according to Christian precepts though he did not attend religious services.

In the mobilization of August 1914, men of Barthas' age belonged to the reserve Territorial Army, which explains his initial posting to Narbonne while the younger reserves and regulars went right up to the front lines. Corporal Barthas escorted some of the very first German prisoners of war in the opposite direction, to the fortress of Mont-Louis in the Pyrenees, which allowed him a day trip into Spanish territory: crossing a simple stream took one from a world at war to a land at peace. The mass slaughter of the war's first months tore huge holes in the ranks of regiments fighting on the front lines, and reinforcements were levied from the older reserves. Louis Barthas arrived at the Western Front lines in the Artois, northeastern France, on November 8, 1914. He was not evacuated to the rear until April 1918, completely worn out. It was his luck to escape the two terrible phases of the "war of movement" (August–October 1914 and April–November 1918), but he lived through the whole period of trench warfare—in the Artois up to early 1916, to Verdun that May, then in Champagne and on the Somme, and in 1917 on the right flank of the ill-fated Spring Offensive (the Chemin des Dames), then in the Argonne. All in all, he spent fifty-four months under the colors, forty-one of which were in an infantry regiment right on the front lines, as a corporal (and even some time as a private, being summarily broken in rank). To be clear, let us note that the infantry suffered the army's heaviest losses, to the order of 22 percent killed (versus 6 percent for the artillery), and bore the most severe hardships, as recounted throughout the narrative. Let us furthermore note that a corporal lived amid the twelve or fifteen men of his squad, that he shared their daily life and knew their most intimate thoughts. "The squad," writes Barthas, "is like a little family, a center of affection where deep feelings prevail, of solidarity, mutual devotion, intimacy, and from which the officer and even the sergeant are excluded. To them, the soldier doesn't open up, is mistrustful, and any officer who will want to try to describe the strange life of the trenches, as I'm doing, will never have known, except by accident, the real sentiments, the true spirit, the clear language and the deepest thoughts of the soldier."

After the war, the corporal went back to his life as a barrelmaker in Peyriac-Minervois, in a renowned wine-growing region. The final page of his notebooks tells us that, from then on, he savored all the little pleasures of peacetime, as a survivor and as someone who had truly suffered. A postcard from the postwar years shows Louis Barthas, with his son Abel as a barrelmaker's apprentice, and some friends on the village square. The outbreak of a new war, twenty years after the peace treaty of 1919, was heartbreaking for the socialist pacifist who had just turned sixty. Abel, himself a socialist, joined the Resistance and became mayor of Peyriac-Minervois at the Liberation. Louis Barthas died on May 4, 1952.

The person pictured on the postcard has faded away. But he left behind, for his family and for posterity, a veritable treasure: his manuscript.

The Life of a Manuscript

In his analysis of three hundred eyewitness accounts written by combat veterans of 1914–18, the critic Jean Norton Cru[1] posed the same question to each one: Is the author truly qualified to speak as an eyewitness? The months Barthas spent at the front and in the trenches vouch for him. Our corporal belonged to the category of "notebook *poilus* [French infantrymen]," those who sought to keep a written record of their experiences. Furthermore, he was considered by his own comrades as their spokesman. "You, who are writing about the life we're leading, be sure not to hide anything," his buddy Ferié told him. Just like Gayraud, another comrade, everyone knew that he was writing the "true story" of their "doleful calvary." In the summer of 1917, at La Harazée in the Argonne, not far from the home of Académie Française member André Theuriet, Barthas noted: "In the shade of a linden tree, I've written these lines while sitting on a stone bench where perhaps the gifted writer himself wrote those books which tell about the surrounding countryside." He truly wrote his notebooks "right on the spot."

Like many other veterans of the trenches, Louis Barthas sought to do battle against what they called "stuffing the brain with rubbish" [*"bourrage de crâne"*], the lies put forth by wartime propaganda. His testimony had the mission of truth-telling. It was addressed to posterity, even if that notion was never concretely defined. It was a cry of protest for dignity. Jean Norton Cru was right to say that a genuine eyewitness account should be subjective: here is what I saw, what I felt, what I was told. That of Barthas is of steadfast, consistent honesty. Pacifist that he was, he could well have embroidered his account of the Christmas cease-fires of 1914. But, that night of December 25, entrenched in the second line, he simply noted: "In fact, something unusual happened at the front line. You could hear songs, clamors, numerous flares were set off on both sides, but no firing at all." He subsequently described other scenes of fraternization and tacit cease-fires which he himself experienced firsthand.[2]

This is not the place to recount the corporal's full testimony. Its richness is for the reader to discover in the pages that follow. Let us just note here that Louis Barthas' capacity for reflection permits him to rise above the mud of the trenches, to comment on the infantryman's war: "In a war like this one, combat meant mostly being a target for shells. The best leader wasn't the cleverest tactician, but rather the one who knew best how to keep his men alive." The capacity, too, to reflect upon and judge a society which propelled its young men into "the accursed, infamous war, which forever dishonored our century and blighted the civilization of which we were so proud."

A survivor, demobilized on February 14, 1919, Louis Barthas found himself back home with his pocket diaries—mud-stained, chewed by rats, as described to me by his son Abel in 1978. He needed to "clean them up," a good schoolboy's reflex which other veterans recall sharing. Relying on letters and postcards he sent home to his family throughout the war, filling up the same hundred-page notebooks he had used in the schoolroom, the barrelmaker undertook his written narrative every evening after the day's work was done. The truthfulness of the author's genuine experience of war is immediately apparent, and concrete evidence backs it up, as related below. The few postwar amendments are clear, and in no way detract from the narrative, whether it's a reference to an author whom Barthas considers a "*bourreur de crâne*" (Henri Bordeaux) or to the death of a comrade, or to the subscription undertaken to build a *monument aux morts* [war memorial] in Peyriac.

With the close of the nineteenth and final notebook, how to reach the "posterity" to whom this testimony is bequeathed? At the end of the First World War, the world of a village artisan and that of book publishers were hermetically sealed off from one another. It would not have entered the mind of a barrelmaker to submit his manuscript to a publishing house the way professional writers did (such as Henri Barbusse, Roland Dorgelès, Maurice Genevoix, et cetera). The notebooks therefore sat in the back of a drawer, and son Abel Barthas kept them as well. Abel's son Georges became a teacher of drawing and sculpture at a lycée in Carcassonne. He consigned the notebooks to a colleague, a teacher of history, who read to his students passages of Louis Barthas as part of his coverage of the First World War. Hearing about this, I had some excerpts published by a local historical society, the *Fédération audoise des œuvres laïques*. I then sounded out the Paris publisher Maspero, with whom I was working on another book. François Maspero, to whom I wish to pay homage in these few lines, could immediately see the extraordinary quality of the manuscript, supported by the author's style, humor, spirit, and convictions. He enthusiastically agreed to take the risk of publishing a lengthy book written by an unknown author on a subject unlikely to draw a huge readership.

The Life of the Book

The bet paid off. Four thousand copies went on sale in France on November 11, 1978 (exactly sixty years after the war's end). A second printing followed quickly, before Christmas. Since then, *Barthas* is a book that has remained—and been constantly replenished—on bookstore shelves. The publishing house La Découverte succeeded François Maspero; *Barthas* came out in paperback in 1997 and received a newly designed cover in 2003. Counting all editions, one hundred thousand copies will have been printed by 2014—a key symbolic milestone and anniversary. Among its many admirers has been the late president of France, François Mitterand. On a visit to the Aude he was given a copy. On a subsequent visit he made the following comment: "Ah, the *Carnets* of Louis Barthas! This book has great historical value, and it's truly a work of literature as well."

The reactions of veterans of 1914–18 to the book's first edition were not systematically surveyed. But the many letters of support included one from Jacques Meyer, himself author of a book about the daily lives of combatants.[3] Auguste Bastide, a veteran whose political views were far from those of Barthas, nevertheless wrote me: "[The story] of the trenches, and really of the whole war, is described in a way that is simple and totally authentic by Louis Barthas, barrelmaker. This book is a marvel, a veritable fresco of '14–'18 by a poilu who lived through it. This book is so fine and so true that I cried several times while reading it." And again, from Adrien Béziat: "I read this book from beginning to end in one day. I'll read again, often, because it represents a whole period of my life. . . . I find myself in the same situations, because I (like Barthas) was an infantryman and I had a tough time of it, as they say." Or the widow of Fernand Tailhades: "See what Barthas writes. They were equals. They both say the same things."

I won't list the many historians who have welcomed the book by Louis Barthas. Their opinion is exemplified by this quote from Pierre Barral: "Its quality and its originality, which immediately strike every reader, place it among the narratives recognized as the most reliable, and thus give it a value of the first order."[4] The few people who have sought to discredit the barrelmaker's story are thwarted by the way it corresponds with newly emerging pieces of evidence. The *Journaux des marches et d'opérations* of the successive regiments in which Barthas served confirm the accuracy of his dates and facts. The account of Léopold Noé, who also served in the 280th Infantry Regiment in 1915, is often identical. On September 23, for example, after having heard the patriotic speech by a colonel announcing an upcoming offensive, Barthas wrote: "An impressive silence greeted the colonel's final words." Noé: "A sad silence followed the end of his speech." The two men in the trenches tell of the December floods which obliged the French and Germans to come out in the open, which led to scenes of fraternization. Many other soldiers in the same sector, as well as a medical officer at a field hospital, have left accounts which confirm these episodes. The collection of photographs belonging to Captain Hudelle illustrates the life of the 280th Regiment in the Artois, particularly around Vermelles—the same life as described in the corporal's notebooks. In various archives, researchers have found letters from Barthas to the government minister Marcel Sembat (complaining, on behalf of his comrades, about the poor quality of bread), to social-work agencies on behalf of young soldiers without families, and even to the Socialist deputy Brizon, requesting pacifist brochures to distribute and discuss among his front-line comrades.[5]

Finally, the publication of the barrelmaker's *Carnets* marked a key date in the historiography of the Great War. The book's own inherent power and the publication of excerpts in numerous textbooks have motivated a number of teachers and ordinary readers to undertake research among veterans, including notebooks, diaries, and letters home from the front. And publishers have followed. Some, reluctant to take risks, have reissued the accounts which Jean Norton Cru deemed the most reliable, or have brought into print the unpublished accounts of intellectuals (Jules Isaac, Robert Hertz, Étienne Tanty, etc.). But this flowering includes the work of ordinary combatants: workers, artisans, farmers, rural schoolteachers . . . the shelves of bookstores and libraries are now full of such works.[6] As a forerunner, Barthas' book has led to the discovery that "ordinary people," even without officers' stripes on their sleeves, participated in history and, even without diplomas or degrees, knew how to bear witness to it.

At that same moment in December 1915, after the floods which brought fraternization between Frenchmen and Germans, Louis Barthas wrote: "Who knows? Perhaps some day, in this corner of the Artois, they'll raise a monument to commemorate this spirit of fraternity among men who shared a horror of war and who were obliged to kill each other, against their wills." One can easily understand that building such a monument was out of the question for a long time. But on November 11, 1992, Marie-Christine Blandin, president of the Nord-Pas-de-Calais *région,* finished her speech with this very quote from Barthas and proposed the construction of just such a monument, "on this ground where, seventy-seven years ago, in the space of a few short hours, humanity triumphed over folly. Life won out over death." This was still too early, and the idea fell victim to vigorous opposition. Christian Carion, producer of the film *Joyeux Noël,* which brought to life the 1914 Christmas truce among Germans, British, and French, revived the idea in 2005. Meanwhile, an active association in Peyriac-Minervois installed a Peace Garden and a monument to Louis Barthas. The book has itself become a "monument" in its multiple editions and in the number of other publications it has initiated. Plays and documentary films have drawn on the *Carnets* of Barthas. They have been a source of inspiration for the filmmaker Jean-Pierre Jeunet, shooting scenes in the trenches for his film *Un long dimanche de fiançailles* (A Very Long Engagement). Jeunet gave copies of the *Carnets de guerre de Louis Barthas* to the whole cast, to put them in the right mood, and everyone came back to him saying, in so many words, "God dammit, I never imagined it was like that!"[7]

Introduction (1978)

Rémy Cazals

Documents, even written documents, that can constitute popular memory are perhaps more numerous than we might think. A small organization in the *département* of Aude, [southwestern] France, the *Fédération audoise des œuvres laïques,* has taken on, among its many missions, seeking out such documents and making them known. In the course of two years it has brought out, from the cupboards where they slept, some remarkable documents, notably the written accounts, day by day, of schoolchildren in a village in the Corbières [mountain range] under the Occupation, and then the war notebooks of Louis Barthas, socialist militant of a village in the Minervois [wine-growing region north of Carcassonne].[1]

The original manuscript of Barthas consists of nineteen schoolboy's notebooks (*cahiers d'écolier*), each from eighty to a hundred pages, written in pen and, for the most part, in purple ink. The notebooks are abundantly illustrated by postcards sent by the author from the front to his family, and by other cards or photos found in German trenches after their occupation by French infantry. The family of Louis Barthas has given us some information about the author, now deceased, and on the writing of the notebooks.

We present these specifics here, briefly; the work speaks for itself, and does not require a lengthy presentation.

Louis Barthas was born on July 14, 1879, in Homps, in the département of Aude. He therefore was thirty-five years old at the time of the declaration of war in 1914; he was married, the father of two boys, Abel (eight years old) and André (six). From a modest family, he was an agricultural laborer at first, then a barrelmaker (*tonnelier*) and owner of several plots of vineyards. He settled in Peyriac-Minervois.

In order to write—very properly—the hundreds of pages of war memoirs, what education did he have? In fact, he left school with a *certificat d'études primaires.* But let us make clear that he ranked first in his district and won the *Prix du conseil général.* Thereafter he was an avid reader, eager to learn, curious about everything, assiduous reader of Victor Hugo, Émile Zola, Anatole France, and even Karl Marx and Jules Guesde. For Louis Barthas soon subscribed to socialism and to militant trade-unionism [*syndicalisme*]. In Peyriac-Minervois, he participated in the creation of the *syndicat des ouvriers agricoles* (agricultural workers' union). A member of the Socialist Party, he was active in the Minervois alongside his future army captain in 1914, Léon Hudelle; Dr. Ferroul, of Narbonne; and Jean Jaurès, deputy from the Tarn.

In one of his notebooks, he writes: "I will always be faithful to my principles as a socialist, a humanitarian, even a true Christian." Louis Barthas was a Catholic, but not an observant one. Tolerant, he became anticlerical due to the opposition of the Church to syndicalism and socialism. It was this Christian socialist, syndicalist, pacifist, and antimilitarist who remained under the colors from August 4, 1914, to February 14, 1919—that is, for four and a half years, mostly on the front lines, as a corporal in the infantry (and even some time as a simple private, after having been broken in rank for political reasons).

From the first day, he kept his notebooks, and his comrades soon knew that he was writing down "the story of [their] Calvary." He wrote on whatever paper he had, on various pages sewn together with thread; his son has seen these first-draft notebooks, which were spattered with mud, gnawed by rats. At the same time, he sent numerous letters and postcards to his wife and his children, asking that they be preserved. The notebooks, letters, and cards then helped him, once demobilized, to properly write up the nineteen school notebooks (*cahiers*). He took on this task as soon as he returned home. It was his evening work, a duty to which he devoted himself: to put down what he had witnessed.

Was Louis Barthas a good witness? Around 1930, a scholar, himself a war veteran, Jean Norton Cru, brought out two books, *Témoins* (Witnesses) (1929) and the more accessible *Du témoinage* (1939).[2] In these works, a scrupulous analysis established the fanciful character of certain successful works, and defined the qualities of a "good witness" (*bon témoin*). Louis Barthas possessed these qualities: he really knew the life on the front lines; his daily notes permitted him to not give himself over to his imagination; he knew how to see, showed himself to be curious about everything around him, noted things down with precision, reflected, and sought to understand.

Louis Barthas is a good witness. But do we need any more witnesses? We already know that the infantry was mainly cannon fodder, that the poilus lived in the mud, among rats and lice, that the attacks launched by Joffre in 1915 were criminal acts (throwing infantrymen in front of enemy machine guns without artillery preparation), that fraternization between Germans and Frenchmen took place along the front lines, that mutinies broke out in 1917, etc. It's true. But with the accounts of Barthas, we are there! One remarkable account, among many others: that of fraternization between flooded trenches; it ends up in Occitan [the dialect of southwestern France].

Louis Barthas isn't the only good witness. Before him, a great number of war memoirs have appeared, including high-quality ones. Jean Norton Cru quotes extracts from them, and Jacques Meyer has used them, in addition to his own, to write the *Vie quotidienne des soldats pendant la grande guerre.*[3] But Barthas becomes an extraordinarily precious witness because he is an ordinary witness: a simple corporal, a barrelmaker in civilian life. Jean Norton Cru felt that no one above the level of captain really knew what trench life was like. Even among the good witnesses, most were lieutenants, or at least sergeants. "Among the two or three hundred authors studied by Norton Cru, only two or three were not *bacheliers* [graduates of French lycées who had earned the *baccalauréat* certificate] when they wrote about the war. At least two-thirds had the *licence* [first-level university degree] or an equivalent degree and education. Two of them wrote their doctoral theses in the trenches."[4] One can immediately see the interest in an eyewitness account by a manual laborer, a corporal, living for a long while in the midst of his squad. As Barthas wrote, "The squad is like a little family, a center of affection where deep feelings prevail, of solidarity, mutual devotion, intimacy, and from which the officer and even the sergeant are excluded. To them, the soldier doesn't open up, is mistrustful, and any officer who will want to try to describe the strange life of the trenches, as I'm doing, will never have known, except by accident, the real sentiments, the true spirit, the clear language and the deepest thoughts of the soldier."

And that Barthas comes from Peyriac-Minervois is also of particular interest: his squad, the "Minervois squad," speaks and thinks in Occitan.[5]

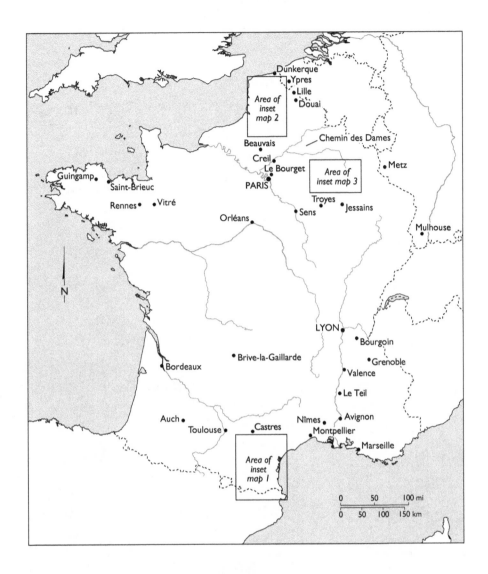

France, 1914–18

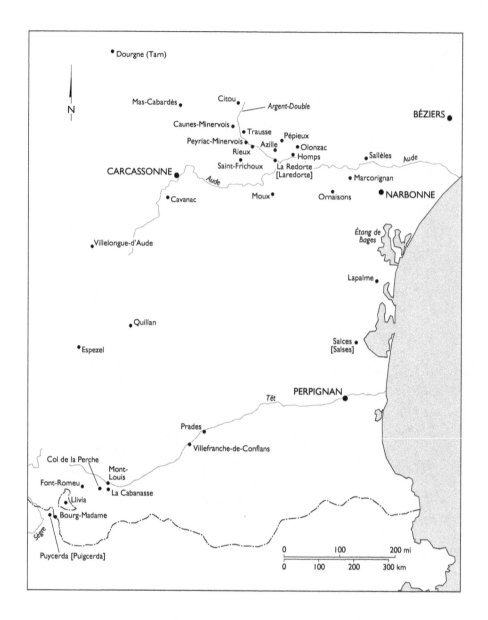

Inset map 1: Midi-Pyrenees

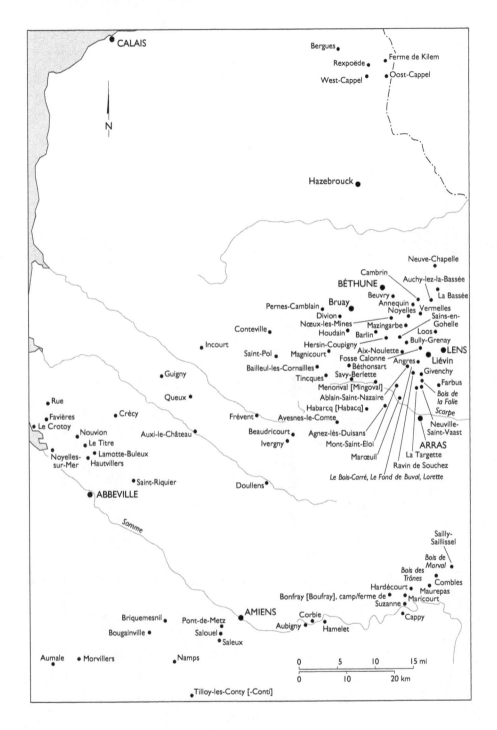

Inset map 2: Flanders-Artois-Picardy-Somme

xxxi

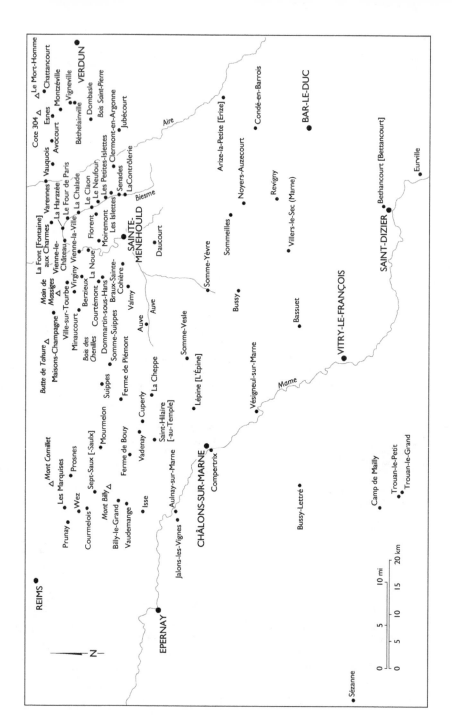

Inset map 3: Champagne-Argonne-Verdun

REIMS •

ÉPERNAY •

Sézanne •

N

0   5   10 mi
0   5   10   15   20 km

△ Le Mort-Homme
Chattancourt •
VERDUN •
Montzéville •
Cote 304 △   • Esnes   Vigneville •
Avocourt •   Dombasle •
Vauquois •   Béthelainville •   • Bois Saint-Pierre
La Harazée   Le Four de Paris   • Clermont-en-Argonne
Varennes •   △   Jubécourt •
Ville-sur-Tourbe   La Chalade
Vienne-le-   Le Claon •   Les Petites-Islettes •
Château •   Virginy Vienne-la-Ville •   • Senades   • LaContrôlerie
La Font [Fontaine]   Florent •   Les Islettes •
aux Charmes   La Noue •   Moiremont •
Main de   Minaucourt   Courtémont •   Braux-Sainte-
Massiges   △   Berzieux •   Dommartin-sous-Hans   Cohière •
Maisons-Champagne •   Somme-Suippes •   Valmy •
Butte de Tahure △   Bois des
Chenilles   • Suippes   SAINTE-
MENEHOULD
Les Marquises •   Mourmelon •   Ferme de Piémont •   Daucourt •
△ Mont Cornillet   Sept-Saux [-Saulx] •   Ferme de Bouy •   Auve •   Auve
Prunay •   Prosnes •   Vadenay •   Cuperly •   Somme-Vesle •
• Wez   Mont Billy △   Saint-Hilaire   Somme-Yèvre •
Courmelois •   Billy-le-Grand •   Issé •   [-au-Temple]   Lépine [L'Épine] •
Vaudemange •   Aulnay-sur-Marne •   La Cheppe •   Vésigneul-sur-Marne •
Jalons-les-Vignes •   CHÂLONS-SUR-MARNE
Compertrix •

Aire

Biesme

Marne

Arize-la-Petite [Erize] •
Condé-en-Barrois •
BAR-LE-DUC •
Noyers-Auzecourt •
Sommeilles •   Revigny •
Eurville •
Villers-le-Sec (Marne) •
Bethancourt [Bettancourt] •
SAINT-DIZIER •
Bussy •
Bassuet •
VITRY-LE-FRANÇOIS •
Camp de Mailly •   Trouan-le-Petit •
Bussy-Lettré •   Trouan-le-Grand •

xxxii

Poilu

Garrison Duty:
August 2–November 1, 1914

General mobilization. Departure for Narbonne.

August 2, 1914. A broiling hot August afternoon. The streets of the village all but deserted. Suddenly, a drumroll. Probably a traveling merchant setting up shop on the main square, or maybe some acrobats announcing their evening performance.

But no, it's not that. When the drum falls silent, we hear the voice of the town clerk, the *commissaire* as we call this unique embodiment of local authority. So we lend our ears, expecting to hear the reading of a new decree about rabies or keeping the streets clean.

Alas! This fellow proceeded to announce the most frightful cataclysm to afflict humanity since the Flood. He announced the greatest of all scourges, the source of all evils. He announced the general mobilization, prelude to the war—the accursed, infamous war, which forever dishonored our century and blighted the civilization of which we were so proud.

This announcement, to my great amazement, aroused more enthusiasm than sorrow. Unthinking people seemed proud to live in a time when something so magnificent was about to happen. Even the most indifferent didn't doubt for an instant that victory would be prompt and decisive.

Wouldn't Austria shatter into pieces at the first shock of a Russian attack?

And wouldn't Germany be ground to bits between France and Russia, like a nut in a gigantic vise?

Everyone got ready, at a fever pitch, as if they really feared not getting there in time before the victory was complete. A few headed off even before their appointed departure dates.

We saw extraordinary things: irreconcilable brothers suddenly reconciled; mothers-in-law and their sons-in-law, who the day before would have been smacking each other and pulling each other's hair out, now exchanging kisses; neighbors who weren't speaking, now engaging in the friendliest of dialogues.

There were no more political adversaries, insults, injuries, hatreds—all was forgotten. The first effect of the war was the accomplishment of a miracle—peace, concord, reconciliation among people who hated each other.

Would this fraternal spirit last? The future will tell.

On August 4, the third day of mobilization, about half the mobilized men of the village embarked at the train station, accompanied by almost the whole population.

Everyone showed courage, whether true or false. There were only two women whose nerves were so sensitive that they fainted away at the sight of their sons or husbands leaving.

At this time I was only just recovering from a serious illness, an erysipelas[1] of the face which had sapped all my strength. On August 4, the date set for my departure, it was all I could do to walk around my bedroom. I wasn't in any condition to march on Berlin!

The *gendarmes,* alerted to the impossibility of my departure, would hear nothing of it. I had to leave, just like everyone else. I no longer belonged to myself, I belonged to the fatherland, like a soul condemned to Satan's power.

My family went crazy. In this situation, my political opponents who held the reins of municipal power, forgetting that I had done everything I could to oust them, went out of their way to pull me out of this mess. One of them took my father in his automobile and went to find the prefect of the Aude *département* who, hesitating, handed me over to the mercy of my recruitment commander, who responded that I had to join up as soon as I could.

A few days later, feeling strong enough to make the journey, I left for Narbonne[2] to join the *dépôt* of the 125th Territorial Regiment[3] installed in a former Capuchin[4] monastery whose monks had been asked a few years earlier to go chant their daily offices in Spain.

A mob of soldiers filled Narbonne, dressed half in mufti, half in uniform. No one knew where to billet all these people running around with a purposefulness that disconcerted the military authorities themselves, who expected to have to deal with hundreds of slackers and deserters. But everyone stepped forward obediently to put their liberty in chains, to stoop beneath the yoke of militarism.

Garrison duty

Narbonne—It's my first night there, curled up in a confessional booth of the former Capuchin church where we were all piled in.

Narbonne—Crowds of soldiers filling up hotels, cafés—and the coffers of the shopkeepers.

Narbonne—The departure of 80th *Active* [Line] Regiment for the frontier on August 7th, the 280th Active Reserve Regiment on the 13th, both in the midst of indescribable enthusiasm.

During the night of the 12th–13th it was the turn of the 125th Territorial Regiment, which left for Morocco. In spite of the void left by the departure of these three regiments, the streets were just as packed with *pantalons rouges* [red trousers].[5]

Why call up, in the same week, on the same day, ten times more soldiers than were necessary, and bring normal life to such a sudden halt?

Wouldn't it have been simpler, more sensible, to call up each reserve class as needed? But no, the mistrustful military flung itself upon the public like a beast upon its prey, and clutched it to itself in the iron grip of discipline. Who knew if these people, so docile, wouldn't regain their senses and their strength, once the initial shock had passed?

That's why they called up everyone, from the beardless conscripts to the old codgers of the R.A.T., at the risk of not being able to house, feed, and clothe all this vile rabble.

We were kitted out in old, patched-up, filthy, ragged, cast-off clothing. Weren't we dazzling! As for food, that was even worse: having nothing or almost nothing to eat, we emptied our purses into the pockets of hotelkeepers, lousy cooks, and other tradespeople.

But we didn't complain too much because, at first, the discipline wasn't too rigorous. We still thought we were free men. But that couldn't last. We were soon subjected to the dictatorship of one Manival, named *commandant* of the different regimental depots of the city.

This paragon of militarism started out by confining us all to quarters all day long, obliging us to nibble on bad and meager food, and at night the doors opened only very late and then closed pitilessly at first call.

Day and night, patrols hunted those who tried to escape into town. I won't take the time to recount all the little irritants, the bothers, the big and petty tyrannies to which Manival subjected the garrison. That would take too long. This big striper was just right for running a prison hulk, not free men—but then we were no longer free, I forgot to say.

Meanwhile there was one fellow who defied Manival's authority, his orders, his instructions, with boldness and scorn. This man was known widely throughout Narbonne as "Falet," especially by the police, who picked him up almost daily, drunk on the sidewalk, after he had been amusing passersby with his songs, skits, and pantomime. He spent more nights in the town jail, sleeping off his wine, than he did in his barracks bunk, if he even had one.

The war had made Falet a soldier, but a drunk he was and a drunk he remained, all the more because, right then, wine was selling for almost nothing and was even given out for free at the winegrowers' association.

A drunk thrives on liberty, open space, fresh air. It was clear that our disciple of Bacchus wouldn't be content to stroll in the little garden where the monks had come to read their prayer books and where a few stunted pines grew. That's why he usually missed the roll calls and the drills.

In vain was he consigned to barracks. In vain were the sentries at the gates declared responsible for his whereabouts. Falet slipped between them like a needle, and disappeared.

One day, right under the captain's nose, Falet took off for the hills, or rather into town. I had the bad luck to be posted on guard duty, so the captain gave me the order to pursue the escapee and to bring him back into military custody.

Here I was, with four fellow guards, in pursuit of Falet. But he seemed to have sprouted wings. Our pursuit had no result other than attracting a bigger and bigger crowd of delighted street urchins, shouting, "You'll find him! No you won't!" We had to come back to the barracks empty-handed.

That night Falet held court in a café and made as much racket as four men. An officer told him to pipe down. Falet didn't take it well; he insulted the officer and even threatened him with a bayonet. The officer called in two policemen, who hauled Falet off to a dingy cell of the 80th Regiment.

The terrible Manival would no doubt have had this unlucky fellow shot out of hand, but Falet had earned the sympathy of the public, who saw him as a harmless and easygoing drunk. Furious to see his despotic authority held in check, the *Narbonnais* dictator made a public notice in his orders of the day, flaying the conduct of Private Assens,[6] who was sullying the uniform which, at the front, his comrades were covering with glory, holding him up to everyone's scorn, nailing him to the pillory, et cetera.

Never had anyone piled such honors on Falet. They made him a celebrity. He was let go, but far from repenting, he continued to do honor to the local vintages, which made him the frequent guest of Commandant Manival in the prison of the Montmorency barracks, as you can imagine.

I mentioned that I arrived at Narbonne in a pitiful state of health. If I bring it up again, it's to point out the welcome I got from the *majors* [medical officers] whose help I sought.

There were two doctors in the reserve units at Narbonne itself. In no time they had sent back to the ranks a hundred sick men who paraded in front of them. You can understand that they weren't generous to me, despite my gaunt appearance.

"Well," they said to me, "you had a mortal illness, you pulled through, and you still have the nerve to complain, and waste our time?"

"But I still need some care," I insisted, "I still can't digest anything except milk."

"Enough. Who's next? Don't let us see you back here." That's how they sent me away, and how they sent away almost everyone who was sick.

The guy behind me showed a suppurative wound on his stomach. "That's nothing, it will scab up," they said without even examining the wound. "Next!" And so forth.

That very day this fellow and I went to report these facts to Ferroul,[7] the sympathetic mayor of Narbonne, and asked for his help. When he heard what we had to say, he angrily crumpled up a piece of paper on his desk and threw it to the floor, but said nothing. What good would a protest of his have done, in this time of fever, of madness, when all of France was up in arms, in a state of siege?

Of course he lavished on us what care he could, freely, as he did to all the soldiers who came to him for help.

Soon Manival was putting us through long drill sessions, day and night. It was a relief when we were assigned to duty at the powder magazine, the firing range, the railway station, et cetera.

The firing range was on the banks of the Étang [lake] de Bages, and on shooting days our bullets chased the fishermen away.

A detail of four men and a corporal stood guard, day and night, at the cabin where they kept the targets, and also kept watch over the embankment behind the targets to keep bullet collectors away. The twenty-four hours of guard duty in this spot should have pleased me greatly, due to the peace and quiet, the wide-open space, the splendid view, the fresh air. But what made it very unpleasant was the company of millions of tiny, sharp-tongued mosquitoes that, as soon as the last ray of sunlight stretched across the lake, surged from the gorse and the bushes and attacked our poor skin, which nature had made so tender and sensitive.

We had to light brushfires, the smoke from which kept them at bay; it was the only weapon at our disposal. That wasn't all. When you wanted to lie down on the five filthy mattresses which the military authorities had so generously provided, or simply on the planks of the camp beds, you had to be completely overcome with fatigue so as to fall asleep before feeling the stingers of legions of famished ticks and lice, which infested these quarters, boring into your skin.

Back at the barracks, the fleas had multiplied so quickly since our arrival that sometimes you had to resort to bunking outside, under the pine trees in the garden, at the risk of catching a head cold or a stiff neck.

Duty at the railway station was more interesting, due to the variety of sights and sounds one could see there during the first few months of the war. The trains came and went without interruption, trains with Italian laborers heading home, refugees, war materiel, horses, and troops who adorned their railway cars as if they were going to a party, these unknowing ones.

How many bellicose, bragging inscriptions scrawled in chalk on the railway cars! One quickly saw the frivolous, childlike, presumptuous spirit of the French soldier. How many insults addressed to the Kaiser, to the Germans, that the officers should have erased if they had any sense of propriety or dignity.

Then, one day, came the arrival of the first trainload of wounded men. I was on duty at the station when the first such train rolled in.

What emotion! What a crowd! What enthusiasm! This was a big event. An hour before the arrival, something like twenty thousand people massed around the station, barely held back by a full company of soldiers which had to be reinforced.

Only the volunteer stretcher-bearers had the right to enter the platforms. To earn this envied privilege, local big shots and high officials signed up as porters.

Finally, at 9 in the evening, the train bearing the wounded flesh entered the station. At the sight of the first stretcher emerging from the waiting room, there was mass delirium. The crowd applauded, wept, stamped their feet, pushed, seeking a closer look, and finally broke through the cordon of troops which could only yield.

By midnight the last automobile had long ago taken away the last of the wounded, but a dense crowd still waited in front of the station. Who knows? Maybe another train was coming in.

Alas, in a week all the hospitals in the city were overflowing with wounded, and the authorities had to call upon the civic devotion of people willing to take care of wounded men in their homes. Oh, the inconstancy of enthusiasm, the fickleness of the mob. Barely a week after the first train arrived, indifference had already set in, hearts became blasé. There was no longer anyone curious enough to witness the arrival of wounded men, ever more numerous, who sometimes were billeted right at the station because there was nowhere to send them.

Really, there were too many of them. They were becoming bothersome. They should have waited until the first ones were healed. The hell of a nerve!

By then everyone had his own situation to be sorry about, before having any time to pity others. Each family was in anxious expectation, uncertain about the fate of a loved one. Death began to choose its victims.

Next came the passage of the first German prisoners, on their way to Castres or Perpignan. The crowd, alerted, had packed the railway crossing at the Avenue de Carcassonne, where a footbridge across the tracks threatened to collapse under the weight of spectators who crowded it, jammed onto the steps like amphitheater seats.

The length of the wait didn't daunt the crowd. Finally the train appeared, and the engineer, to be nice to the crowd, slowed his speed considerably.

Spirits at this moment were overheated to the highest degree, by the acts of savagery (true or false) that the hate-mongering newspapers laid upon the Germans.

That was an extenuating circumstance for this crowd, which indulged in scandalous demonstrations while the convoy passed by. It was a clamor of imprecations and curses. Fine gentlemen brandished their canes, lovely ladies threatened with their silk parasols, urchins threw stones, the most fervent pulled out their knives and leaped onto the tracks, meekly resisted by the sentries, and even after the train had departed the crowd still called out to the Germans, who must have gotten a fine idea of French culture in general and Narbonnais courtesy in particular.

But soon this ferocious hatred diminished, once there was proof that they didn't massacre all the prisoners they took and that even, unimaginably, these barbarians cared for those who were wounded.

This discovery boosted spirits, and from then on the passages of prisoners stirred up little more than curiosity, which diminished over time to the point of complete indifference, and even pity on the part of sensitive folks, more numerous than one would have thought.

Besides, the curiosity of the crowds was distracted by various other spectacles. First of all was the stop at Narbonne for a few days of a magnificent Algerian division. We couldn't get enough of admiring the bearing, the parades, the marches of these Zouaves,[8] these proud, showy infantrymen in their unique outfits.

What a difference compared to us, decked out in our overcoats, either too big or too short, patched-up old trousers, misshapen caps. There was plenty to be jealous about, plenty to envy! The Narbonnais had eyes only for these exotic Africans.

And what a colonel they had! It gave us goose bumps just to look at him. High-strung, tough, hard-looking, he struck fear in his men like the plague.

On the beautiful Promenade des Barques, the Canebière[9] of Narbonne, I was walking one day with some comrades when this terrifying personage, whom we hadn't noticed, bounded across the avenue and asked us, indignantly and angrily, why we hadn't saluted him.

"But colonel," we stammered, terrified, "we didn't see you."

"Ah, you didn't see me," cried this madman, crossing his arms and looking at us like a sparrow hawk eyeing a little wren. "Well," he said, with a scornful look at us, "I can only feel pity for you." And then he disappeared.

Two days later, I was posted as an orderly at the post of the weekly adjutant, at the barracks of the 80th Regiment, when a vibrant bugle call shattered the air. It was the regiment of Zouaves, heading out on maneuvers. At its head, slim and proud on his horse, rode the famous colonel.

Those who had ventured out beyond the gate saluted him. Those who had stayed inside considered themselves exempt from this duty by distance, because the gate was back a good bit from the road. But the sharp eye of the colonel saw the offense committed against his lofty personage and, turning his bridle, he rode into the courtyard and took down the names of the delinquents, whom he sentenced to six days in prison.

I believe that this colonel would have had us salute him a kilometer away, if he dared.

A few days later the Zouaves and their colonel embarked for the front.

Good riddance! But we pitied the poor Zouaves being led into battle by such a brute. Not many were lucky enough to get back to Algeria, I'll bet.

Several days afterward, more sensational news stirred up public curiosity, nothing less than the imminent passage of a vast army of Hindus who had landed at Marseille.[10]

What confirmed the truth of this unbelievable news were the rigorous security and surveillance measures put in place along the railway line. Almost all the available soldiers in the depot were deployed, for five whole days, so as not to leave one meter without surveillance.

And the famous Hindus indeed passed through, stopping for a few hours at Narbonne station for a meal break. But very few Narbonnais were able to satisfy their legitimate curiosity, since access to the station was strictly prohibited.

For what reasons did they keep the crowd away from these warriors who had come from so far away to fight on our soil?

It seems that there were fears that gawkers would make fun of their costumes, their habits, their prayers, etc., which was quite likely, given the impertinence of our southern character.

Their favorite dish was goat meat. They slaughtered the animals themselves, at the station, but before killing them their priests had to bless them, which involved many prayers, genuflections, and benedictions.

They also ate certain grains, of which I had a taste. These had no flavor to speak of.

At the end of the meal, they lit a big pipe which they could have called the squad's pipe, because in each group every man took a few puffs and then passed it fraternally to his neighbor.

> *Mont-Louis. Incidents in the journey. The brutal "porpoise."*
> *A Catalan welcome. The "merry men."*
> *The Germanophobe medical officer. Puycerda.*

On October 2, 1914, I was part of a detachment of 25 men assigned to escort a convoy of German prisoners from the Narbonne station to Mont-Louis,[11] where we would remain as prison guards.

Thanks to this assignment we were going to be able to breathe the pure air of the Pyrenees, and we left the Capuchin convent, and the myriads of fleas whose living prey we had been, with no regrets.

At 4 in the morning we were already at the station, although the train bringing the prisoners wasn't due until five.

The station was already in a near state of siege, and the old softy who exercised the function of stationmaster was under great pressure. Guards were everywhere, instructions were flying back and forth, civilians were chased off the platforms and herded into the waiting rooms. If they had been expecting a trainload of madmen or cannibals, or dangerous criminals, they wouldn't have taken more careful precautions.

Finally the long-awaited train arrived. It had hardly stopped before we, in groups of six, hoisted ourselves into the carloads of prisoners, with bayonets fixed to the barrels of our loaded rifles, as if mounting an assault. The escort got off, and we took its place.

The Germans were seated on benches running along the sides of each freight car. We sat on planks in the middle, since the prisoners weren't so polite as to offer us their seats. Silent, peaceful, they acted like good little children, smiling at us, no doubt looking to earn our good graces.

The train had only just started up when we were not a little surprised to hear the "Marseillaise" being sung, in a voice without the slightest accent, by one of the prisoners. It was an Alsatian who gave us this surprise. The others listened, indifferent and impassive.

From that point the Alsatian joined easily into our conversation, served as an interpreter, and we shared with him our meals, which were a bit more substantial than what the prisoners had to eat.

Soon we were riding alongside the Mediterranean, "the big blue." At this very moment the sun rose, seeming to leap right out of the waves. This was a magic spectacle, an apotheosis of colors, of rays and reflections, quickly succeeding the gray tints of dawn.

Instinctively the Germans leaned toward the open door of the freight car, to take in the view of this enchanting scene. We didn't push them back. We were indulgent and a little proud of how they admired our blue lake, our beautiful sun of the Midi.

Further along we passed through a large estate so filled with game that the noise of the train flushed out whole companies of quail, squads of rabbits, columns of guinea-fowl, pheasants, etc. Frenchmen and Germans crowded at the open door of the car, marveling and pointing at all the fleeing beasts and birds.

From then on a détente existed between guards and captives. The prisoners dared to chat among themselves in low voices and even to hum and sing a few songs, with melodious airs but rude and guttural words, proof that nature had created two categories of larynx, one for the French, the other for the Germans.

At the station at Salces [Salses] there was a stop. A marine infantry non-com climbed onto the step of our wagon, looked around, and then pounced on a German and grabbed his distinctive "baker's cap" with the clear intention of appropriating it. But the German saw right away what was happening. He quickly clamped his hands on his head and held on to his headgear with all his might. "Will you give it up, dirty *Boche* [slang for a German]?" said the marine sergeant, raising his fist and bringing it down once, twice, three times into the face of the German, who was pale with rage but who didn't let go of his cap. His neighbors tried to lend their aid, but the *marsouin* [literally "porpoise"; slang for a French marine] ended up victorious and ran off with the cap.

This all happened so fast that we couldn't intervene. In my role as corporal, *chef de wagon,* in charge, I said to this brutal visitor, "If you want trophies, go find them on the battlefield. Get out of here." But a non-com, from a colonial regiment no less, has no dealings with an infantry corporal, and a Territorial one at that. That's why it was just as if I hadn't protested at all. I then asked a comrade to go ask the lieutenant who commanded the detachment, but when he brought him back the thief had disappeared, off into the countryside.

Now the victim wept hot tears of anger, shame, and regret over the loss of his headgear, but one of us made him a gift of a *bonnet de police* [fatigue cap],[12] which was disdainfully refused. Finally, upon our insistence, the German accepted it, more as a duty than in goodwill.

At Perpignan there was a newspaper famous for its jingoism. Its exaggerations played right into the worst prejudices of its readers, and right now exacerbated the hatred for the Germans, who were nothing but "monsters with human faces."

Of all the southerners, the Catalans are the ones with, as we say, "the blood closest to the head," ready to fly off the handle, to demonstrate with enthusiasm and fire their most extreme sympathies and antipathies. These aren't faults; they are characteristics of their race.

So this newspaper, having learned the date of our passage, didn't waste any time in announcing it as an event of the highest importance, in terms which persuaded the Catalans that it was their patriotic duty to come and shout their hatred at these disarmed soldiers.

From Perpignan, at each level crossing, at each station, a furious crowd awaited us, spewing imprecations and curses upon the uneasy prisoners. The women were the most extreme. They tried to climb into the cars to spit on the prisoners, and some threatened them with knives, clubs, and stones. There's no doubt that if the prisoners had been handed over to them, they would have had a rough time of it.

In contrast, to us Frenchmen they brought grapes, figs, and other fruits, and they filled our canteens with wine, the good, rich wine of Roussillon.

"Just don't give any to these murderers," they said to us.

But once the train started up we wasted no time in sharing all of it with the prisoners. This act of camaraderie made up for the odious demonstrations against disarmed enemies.

At Prades the crowd extended along both sides of the track. The cars were opened only on one side, so half the crowd, disappointed to be on the closed-up side, protested so violently that, to prevent regrettable incidents, we had to open the car doors on both sides, which made our guard duty even more difficult, to fend off the waves of enraged patriots, especially the women who predominated.

At the station of Villefranche-de-Conflans we changed to the electric railroad. Recently built, climbing up into the Pyrenees, this line followed the valley of the river Têt, rolling along the bottom of deep gorges or climbing along the flank of a precipice, twice crossing the valley on bridges which were perhaps unique in France, one a suspension bridge, the other one made of stone. We all felt sensations of fright and vertigo, and were gripped with ecstasy before the grandiose beauty of these mountains, these rocky cliffs, these valleys, woods, and waterfalls.

Now all was calm and solitude, no more howling mobs. The villages were few and far between, peopled with inoffensive shepherds and peaceable woodcutters.

The track that we were following, which ran right up to the Spanish frontier, had been inaugurated a few years earlier in a tragic fashion.

The engineers and other notables had taken their places in the very first train coming down from the Pyrenees, when for one reason or another the brakes didn't work, or weren't strong enough, and the runaway train picked up a dizzying speed and ended up jumping the tracks and tumbling all the way to the bottom of a precipice. One can imagine how the travelers felt, nearly all of whom met their deaths. The Mountain had claimed its revenge for being conquered by the intelligence and boldness of Man.

At noon we got off at the station of La Cabanasse, which served the village of Mont-Louis, perched at the summit of a rugged, long ridge which seemed to climb right up to the clouds.

Mont-Louis itself is dominated by high mountains, from which one could enjoy a grandiose panorama, but I never made the ascent because my legs couldn't take a climb lasting several hours. I contented myself with the panorama which was spread out all around us. Below the fortress, at the bottom of a deep valley, flowed the river Têt, which tumbled wildly through rocks and waterfalls. Then, on the other side, ran the only road which goes to Spain from this side of the Pyrenees.

This fortress had been built by Vauban, and right down to the smallest detail you could see the art, the genius which had guided its construction, still valid right up to the development of present-day artillery. Mont-Louis was a redoubtable stronghold, utterly impregnable to assault.

A first ring of walls encircled the village of about a thousand inhabitants, and a second enclosed the barracks, casemates, magazines, etc. In ordinary times one company occupied the fort. Now we were going to guard six hundred prisoners there, which was a dangerous imprudence given the proximity of the Spanish frontier (about twelve kilometers away), and also given our weak number, about a hundred, and no other troops between us and the border.

The Germans moved about freely, in daylight, through the courtyards of the fort. It would have been simple for them to overwhelm us and escape. Not to do so showed that they weren't driven to seek their freedom. It's true that they couldn't know that, at the border, only a few customs agents stood guard, not for them but for smugglers.

A few days before our arrival, Mont-Louis had been the scene of grave incidents.

By a capricious decision of our high command, all the *joyeux* [merry men] in France—reservists assigned to disciplinary battalions of [French] African army units—had been assembled at Mont-Louis for mobilization. They made their way there but, for reasons unknown to me, soon after they arrived they mutinied, pillaged, vandalized whatever they could, then burst through the gates and spread through the village, terrorizing the inhabitants.

It took the arrival of a detachment of troops from Perpignan to reestablish order. Soon they were all sent back to Africa.

They were refused the honor of going to the front, of dying for the fatherland. No one had confidence in them. It remains to be seen if these "merry men" felt humiliated or, to the contrary, relieved to be so far from the fields of honor.

You could still see the results of the looting. What was especially heartbreaking was to see with what brutality and greed they had broken into and rifled the footlockers of the young soldiers of the garrison who had packed them with their personal belongings, in haste, right when they were heading off to the front: clothing, letters, souvenirs, etc.

Anything of value had disappeared. The rest lay scattered pell-mell throughout the rooms.

The Boches, treated as barbarians and bandits every day in our newspapers, were paschal lambs beside our terrible *Zéphirs* [whirlwinds] from Africa.

Our German prisoners showed themselves to be quite docile, and there wasn't the slightest incident on their part during my stay at Mont-Louis. They didn't have too much to complain about during their captivity: not much work, pretty good lodging, bedded down and fed about the same as we were. They could indulge themselves at the canteen, one hour a day.

Nevertheless some of them weren't satisfied with all that. They monitored our mess teams carrying back our leftovers to the kitchens or to tubs of greasy water, and stuffed themselves with the remainders of inedible portions, tendons, fat and gristle, gnawed bones, etc.

Some of our men amused themselves by throwing out the windows pieces of bread which fell into the mud, where ten hands grappled to seize them.

Among the prisoners were ten or so from Alsace-Lorraine who spoke French more or less fluently. They were introduced one day to a general who had come to Mont-Louis on an inspection tour.

This general naïvely thought that he was doing them a great honor by granting them permission to enlist in the French army. But at this proposition the Alsatians and Lorrainers, or those pretending to be, grimaced and refused, claiming that if they joined up on our side, they wouldn't be able to return to their native lands when the war was over.

"What?" cried the scandalized general, "they doubt our victory? Well, let's treat these people just like the Boches they are!" But thanks to the service they could render by their knowledge of the two languages, they had a privileged situation from then on.

To keep the prisoners busy, they were obliged to carry out military exercises, war games, and drills. It would have been smarter to have them do some useful work.

What a difference between their drill-field maneuvers and ours! The command to "attention" transformed them into marble statues. Their ranks and columns were as straight as a rule, they pivoted on a compass point, and all their movements were automatic and geometrical.

When, each evening, our guard changed, the Germans mocked the awkwardness and irregularity of our to-the-right-march and our pitiful presenting of arms, so much so that the captain made us assemble behind a building which blocked the prisoners' view of us.

Then, to improve our skills, unlike the Germans, we had to drill outside the fortress, open to the biting winds, which chapped our lips and chilled our throats.

The snow started to fall heavily during October, and we shivered in our rooms in spite of the stoves stuffed with firewood cut by prisoner work details in nearby forests.

One fine day we took a little march to the Col de la Perche,[13] from which the road descended the opposite slope of the Pyrenees.

During the [French] Revolution a furious battle took place here. It seems that the Spanish tried to grab what didn't belong to them, and they were severely thrashed for doing so.

Near there was the enclave of Llivia.[14] By the Treaty of the Pyrenees, Louis

XIV, eager to establish a foothold on the other side of the Pyrenees, demanded the cession of thirty villages of the Spanish Cerdagne, but in the list of these villages Llivia was forgotten and remained Spanish. A neutral road links it to Spain. Its inhabitants can bless this omission which deprived them of the honor of being subjects of Louis XIV but which spared their great-grandchildren the sacrifices and the horrors which the present ignoble war would have imposed upon them.

From the Col de la Perche, along a mountainside and the edge of a wood, you could see the sumptuous hotel of Font-Romeu, built by the railroad company, the *Compagnie de chemins de fer du Midi.*

The capitalists could come here and breathe the extra-pure air, which would have done more good to the families of workers piled up in airless hovels in the cities, but in order to come and vacation in this hotel, furnished with every modern comfort and excessive convenience, you had to have a big, bulging wallet and be able to live, play, get fat, and have fun upon the sweat of others.

In these enthusiastic times, the frontier wasn't guarded. Why should it be? The French who lived in Spain rushed into France to enlist. It was even thought that suitably trained Spaniards would come over, too, but they didn't appreciate the purity of our cause and egotistically stayed home.

Our bosses were so trustful of us that they granted us leave, on Sunday, to go spend the day in Puycerda,[15] the first Spanish locale across the border. Taking advantage of this incredible liberty, one Sunday I took the electric train and descended the other slope of the Pyrenees all the way to Bourg-Madame, the last French village. The railway went no farther, since the Spaniards weren't rich enough to continue it, but Puycerda was barely a kilometer away.

At the customs post the *carabineros* politely asked us to leave our bayonets with them, which they would give back to us when we returned. That was the only formality required to have the right to tread the soil of hospitable Spain.

Near the post a river, the Sègre, divided the two nations. It was Louis XIV's ambition which made this little stream the border.

Puycerda is a pretty little town beside a little lake. The wine was good, tasty, and very inexpensive at the "*posada* d'Aragon," where for a modest price you could have an excellent meal, and then puff away on some detestable cigars and cigarettes while strolling around town.

It was a fine autumn Sunday and happiness was in the air. Young men and girls flocked to numerous dance parties, where you could hear loud music from the organs, accordions, or guitars.

This made our hearts ache. Over on our side nobody thought about having fun anymore. The war dominated everything, and spirits were burdened with anguish and worry. And all this joy, these appeals to pleasure and love, shocked us.

Come to think of it, the Spaniards would have been silly to share these sentiments with us. Had we been overcome with gloom in France when our neighbors were being massacred in Cuba or in Morocco?

At the posada where I had lunch, I struck up a conversation, half in French, half in Spanish, with my neighbor at the next table, and I asked him what he thought about this war. He gave an extraordinary answer: "When there's war in Spain, everybody who can get away heads for France. The French do exactly the opposite: the ones who live here leave Spain and go home to fight." And this Spaniard didn't try to explain; he evidently thought that we were no more intelligent than they were.

Keep in mind that the Spaniard has all the characteristics of what one calls a good soldier: sober, durable, sharp, valiant. But he doesn't have a warrior spirit, and his proud and independent personality doesn't bend well to the odious yoke of discipline. That's why my luncheon companion was so baffled.

I didn't visit Puycerda again, because my departure for the front was near, but I don't want to end the story of my stay at Mont-Louis without saying a word about the medical officer whom we had there, the *major,* and about his attitude toward the prisoners who needed his enlightened care.

Someone had discovered in the back of an infirmary locker a container of cod liver oil which had gone rancid. Even in its prime it's not a very savory drink. Think about how going rancid might improve it! For as long as it lasted, this oil was administered copiously and generously to the Germans who presented themselves at sick bay. The grimaces of these fellows brought joy to the *major* and his staff. If the sick man came back the next day, that was truly an exception.

One day they vaccinated the prisoners against smallpox. The *major* had a field day wielding his scalpel. Some fainted dead away, while those who could bear it squealed as if their throats were being cut.

One morning, when I was present at sick bay, a prisoner showed up with a badly swollen cheek. The *major,* to take care of him, took up his pliers and his scalpels and went to work on his jaw and his molars. The unfortunate one, stricken with terror, ran away howling, the *major* burst into laughter, and to push the farce even further he had the German seized by the guards and hauled back. Terrified, the prisoner had to have his painful jaws worked on with care as tender as you could imagine.

One evening, when I was on guard duty, the prisoners called out through the bars of a casemate: one of their comrades was very sick, they said. Escorted by four fellow guards and carrying a lantern and a ring of big keys dating back to Vauban, I made my way into the casemate and saw that a dozen Germans were grouped around the sick man and had piled up blankets over him to keep him warm. They begged me to find the *major,—Herr Doktor saniter,* they said, trying to be understood.

Five minutes later I found, in a café, the medical staff corporal, who was none other than Edouard Durand from my hometown, Peyriac. He was willing to leave his card game and to run to find the *major*, even though he said he knew this would get him a kick in the teeth.

Sure enough, the *major* told him that he wasn't going to bestir himself for a Boche, and that if the prisoner "croaked" all that was needed was to haul his carcass to the dung heap.

With a bit more humanity, my comrade Durand went back to the infirmary and made a cup of tea that was brought to the sick man. That didn't keep him from "croaking" three or four days later, at the infirmary where at last they had finally brought him.

No one would want to write about such an attitude on the part of a doctor who might hate the Germans, but should be able to overcome that hatred and fulfill his duty. His mission is to care for those who suffer, whoever they might be.

While we were at Mont-Louis, the depots in the garrison towns emptied rapidly. At the end of October, two reserve classes, the youngest of the Territorial Army, one of which I belonged to,[16] were assigned to leave for the front to reinforce the two regiments from Narbonne (the 80th and the 280th), which had just been decimated.

Ah, how extravagant our generals were with the lives of others!

Departure from Mont-Louis. Perpignan. Last farewells. En route to the hell of the front.

On October 30, 1914, thirty of us Territorials from the [conscription reserve] classes of 1899 and 1900 left Mont-Louis to rejoin our depot at Narbonne.

A thick blanket of snow covered the ground, a cold wind chilled our bodies and our hearts. Henceforth we were destined for sacrifice. We were going to follow the stations of the cross, on painful marches along which our dead bodies would litter the path. A ray of sunlight would have diminished our melancholy, our sadness, but this storm which shrouded the surrounding mountains in fog dampened our flagging spirits.

At noon sharp, we filed into the courtyard where the prisoners had shoveled a path for us in the snow. These fellows, massed under the vaults of the fortress, saluted us all. Was this derision or mockery? I looked at them, but no, their faces were grave. They were saluting gladiators descending into the bloodstained arena. They honored the victims who were going to suffer and die.

Our captain accompanied us as far as the station at La Cabanasse, in spite of the lousy weather and the very bad condition of the road. We knew he didn't do it willingly. By his haughty attitude, so cold in his dealings with us, he had lost our sympathy. He felt obliged to give us a little speech which had no comforting effect on us. It really wasn't worth his catching a cold to come as far as La Cabanasse.

At eight in the evening we arrived at Perpignan, where we had to wait a couple of hours. What a difference in temperature! Here, not the slightest trace of snow. In this corner of France, privileged in its climate, there was still the sweet warmth of autumn.

All Perpignan was out on the streets, and an enormous crowd jammed a square and adjacent streets. From moment to moment, you heard applause, cries of anger, of fury, one after the other. Sometimes the crowd was convulsed with mad laughter. What were they looking at, these gawkers, instead of quietly going home to their beds?

I approached, and found myself outside the offices of the famous jingoistic newspaper of the Pyrenées-Orientales [département]. Every ten minutes there appeared, projected in luminous letters on a screen on the building's façade, the news headlines which would appear in the newspaper the next day. You can guess that everything was exaggerated, blown up, and the slightest event was presented as a great drama. Despite the fact that, at this point, everything was going from bad to worse, the situation was presented as excellent. The Catalans were letting their heads get stuffed with nonsense, just like the vulgar Parisians.

In the station a big billboard caught our attention. It read, "Here we give out wine *à l'œil* [for free]" and instead of the final word there was a gigantic *œil* [eye]. Free wine—was this possible? It's true, this was a gift from winegrowers for soldiers passing through. You could fill your stomach as well as your canteen, bottles, et cetera.

Each cask of wine bore the name of its proprietor and the vintage, and you could pick from among the most famous wines. This was heaven for even the most sober soldier. To tell the truth, at this time the price of wine was very low, and this tempting and beneficial billboard would soon disappear.

At three in the morning we entered the Montmorency Barracks in Narbonne. The dictator Manival certainly knew about our arrival, because it was on his orders that we were coming, but nothing was prepared for our reception. I don't want to say that we were expecting drums and bugles in our honor at the station, or that the barracks would be all decked out. We would have been happy with a mug of hot coffee upon our arrival and a comfortable spot to spend the night, even if it was planks to stretch out on. But even that was expecting too much. We had to start getting used to suffering.

Manival hadn't deigned to take the trouble to alert the authorities about our arrival. We had to go into town to seek out the battalion adjutant, a grumpy, bilious Corsican who showed up in a furor at being bothered this way. Without a care about waking up everyone, since he already was up, he had the buglers on duty call out all eight company sergeants in the depot. It took three bugle calls for all the sergeants to turn up. Think about what kind of welcome they gave the newcomers. The Corsican dealt us out haphazardly to each NCO [noncommissioned officer, or non-com].

With three other comrades I was led into a billet already full of sleepers sprawled out pell-mell on scraps of straw, and we succeeded in spending the night in this pile of ticks, fleas, and lice, which the barracks by now was well provisioned with.

The next day, November 1, at five in the afternoon, a reinforcement of 700 men from the first three classes of the Territorial Army left for the front to re-join the 280th [Réserve de l'Active] Infantry Regiment, which had been deci-mated near Béthune.

Manival wanted us to clear out with this detachment. Luckily we didn't have enough time to get kitted out and equipped. But we were alerted to be ready to leave the following Wednesday. As this was on a Saturday, we rushed to our company command posts to request 24-hour furloughs for the next day, to go home and embrace our families one last time, but alas, under the fallacious pretext that the Sunday furlough requests had to be submitted to the Grand Inquisitor Manival by no later than the Thursday before, this satisfaction was denied us.

A condemned man is granted the opportunity to see his loved ones, one last time. But we didn't get that. We weren't supposed to get all soft in the heart, right when we were heading out.

There was no thought of leaving, in any case. The railway station was under a state of siege: an NCO at every ticket window, others at the access points to the platforms, warnings posted everywhere.

But nothing could stop me. With a couple of comrades, scorning the warn-ings of Manival, we headed out of Narbonne on foot and caught the outbound train at the next station, Marcorignan, and so I had the pleasure of spending the next day in the midst of my family.

To the Killing Fields:
November 4–December 14, 1914

Last good-bye. Departure for the front.
Arrival at the 280th Infantry Regiment.

Our departure from Narbonne was set for Wednesday, November 4th. I was part of a detachment of fifty men going to reinforce the 280th Infantry Regiment, which was operating near Béthune and La Bassée in northern France.

As sad as that journey was, if I live a thousand years I will never forget the tiniest memories, the smallest details.

My wife was determined to come to Narbonne and to stay by my side until the very last minute, bringing with her my youngest son, six years old, my dear little André. Out of pity they allowed wives whose husbands were leaving to stay in the barracks courtyard until the last moment.

Here we are at the fatal hour. The bugle calls us to assembly. I kiss my loved ones a final time, I clasp them to my heart, and I ask my wife to leave, to disappear, to not come to see me off at the station, since that would wipe out whatever little bit of courage I had left, I told her.

Too overcome to answer me, she goes away slowly, pulling by the arm my child who seems to understand the gravity of the separation and lets out a heart-rending cry, "Papa!"

How this cry from my own flesh and blood, this cry of nature, bowled me over! Poor little one! Will I ever see you again? I asked myself, breaking up.

But I had to pull myself together. You couldn't march across town with your eyes full of tears, like a crybaby. We all put on steady, serious faces. Manival gave us an escort of some drums and bugles, and we attracted a big crowd along our way.

But it was no longer the enthusiastic, delirious crowd which attended the first departures. They threw no flowers, sent no kisses; they didn't deafen our ears with hurrahs and bravos.

That's because it was no longer the short, clean, joyous war announced at the start by the lying newspapers. France had been invaded. We were at the threshold of winter, and the war looked to be long and the outcome doubtful.

The sentiments of the crowd had changed. On many faces you saw pity. Women wiped their eyes. Everyone watching us was grave and silent. Just as when a column of condemned men goes by, many uncovered their heads.

In the freight car where I took my place, I threw my pack in a corner and, a bit dazed, my mind empty of any thoughts, indifferent to everything, I crouched in a corner, eyes closed so I wouldn't see anything, reduced to the level of a beast of burden.

The journey was long and painful. At Nîmes the train was put on a siding, but we couldn't get off because it could leave at any moment.

It wasn't until the next morning that we left Nîmes. We had shivered all night long in our freight car, but no one dared to complain. What about the martyrs whom we'd be joining at the front? Weren't they suffering in the mud and snow, perhaps without any shelter at all?

In the afternoon they made us get down at Le Teil and offered us a meal break. We didn't quite take seats at the station's dining room and enjoy a succulent repast. The day's menu was a hunk of bread, a mug of bouillon, and a cup of coffee.

Through the station gates, we could see women and children rushing up with baskets of fruit, boxes of chocolate, jars of preserves, containers of wine, etc.

We were touched. This reminded us of our passage through Roussillon, when at each station pretty Catalan girls brought us wine and fruit. But alas, they weren't giving anything away for free anymore. The flame of generosity, of enthusiasm, was already extinguished. Human egoism, snuffed out for a moment, reappeared everywhere. If you wanted any fruit or wine, you had to dig into your pocketbook.

That night we were at Lyon, and after many stops by the next evening we were at Le Bourget. We stayed there for twenty-four hours, lodged in our uncomfortable cattle car, without the tiniest distribution of food. We didn't dare wander off to find something to eat, out of fear of a sudden departure. It was only at nightfall that the train headed out, to the north.

The next day, as the sun rose, we were at Saint-Pol[1] in the Pas-de-Calais. To warm us up a bit, a mug of coffee would have been most welcome. We had plenty of coffee tablets and sugar in our food reserves, but how would we boil water when the train was about to pull out?

Someone had the idea of asking the engineer for some boiling water, from which we made an excellent pot of coffee, right on the spot.

On November 8th, at 9 in the morning, we arrived at the end of our railway journey.

Ironically, the station where we disembarked was called Barlin. On the sides of our freight cars you could read, among other inscriptions, written in chalk: "Death to Wilhelm! On to Berlin! On to Berlin!"

Alas, we were only one letter away from Berlin—one letter, and a thousand kilometers.

It was at Barlin that I heard, for the first time, the sound of cannon at the front. I turned my head in that direction, instinctively, like a beast turns toward where he senses danger. In the fog, all I could make out were these pyramid-like hills, which they said were slag heaps. We were in coal-mining country.

Then we headed out. Around noon we reached the important center of Nœux-les-Mines[2] where we had a long halt. At nightfall we arrived, exhausted, at Noyelles, where we were supposed to meet up with the 280th Infantry Regiment. But we were the victims of an error. The regiment was at another village, called Annequin. We were told that, thanks to the fog, we were lucky, really lucky, because two kilometers outside Noyelles the road was wide open to the Germans, who could sweep it with their shells and their bullets.

This information didn't do much to reassure us. We wasted no time turning back. Finally, completely worn out with fatigue, we arrived in the dark of night at Annequin, where the reserve companies of the 280th Regiment were located.

The village was totally abandoned by its inhabitants, with good reason, because bullets whistled along the streets, and everywhere you could see houses pulverized by shells.

They led us into the schoolroom, where we immediately bedded down on a bit of damp straw. During the night we were shaken awake by nearby explosions which rattled the schoolhouse.

We were frightened by all this racket. But there was no reason to be, because it came from a battery of our own 75's,[3] which had moved up near the school to fire a few shells.

The German counterbatteries responded with several timed-fuse shells of their own, and the shrapnel from them splattered on the roof like hailstones, breaking some of the tiles.

Some of us fled, terrified, out into the dark of night. Others crawled and burrowed under benches and tables piled up in one corner of the schoolroom.

Daylight appeared like deliverance to us, like the end of a nightmare. In the morning they assigned us to companies. I asked to be assigned to the 21st Company, which was commanded by a fellow *Peyriacois,* Captain Léon Hudelle.[4] But the *capitaine-adjutant-major* responsible for these assignments, a haughty and bad-tempered person, paid no attention. To my great disappointment I was turned over to the 22nd Company, and alerted that at nightfall I would have to join my company up on the front line.

The Vermelles sector (Pas-de-Calais). First night in the trenches.
First visions of war. Annequin. Interrupted trip to Béthune.

When the morning fog cleared a little, I headed out to the east, to have a look at the lines of trenches, hardly two kilometers away. But all I saw were dikes of earth, swellings, all vague and imprecise.

Not a cannon shot, not a rifle shot, total silence. You really had to use your imagination to convince yourself that you were right at the edge of the volcano, that thousands of men were watching, ready to kill each other.

I was right at the confines of civilization. Two kilometers away, men had plunged backward twenty centuries, into the midst of the barbarism which reigned in those distant times.

My spirits were sunk in these gloomy thoughts, and I was just about to re-trace my steps when I saw, heading toward me, three dwellers of the trenches.

I looked at them with horror. They were covered in mud, from the tips of their shoes to the peaks of their képis, as if they had just waded through a sea of muck. Their hands, their faces, mustaches, eyebrows, hair, all covered with viscid mud.

But what was most bizarre was that these refugees from the age of the cave-men made signs to me! They called me by name. I was stupefied. They shook my hand, embraced me. Only then did I recognize three Peyriacois comrades: Gabriel Gils, François Maizonnave, and Louis Jordy.

They had left Narbonne on October 31, barely five days ahead of me, and they were already unrecognizable! In such a state!

We all had tears in our eyes. In a few words they sketched out their sad fate. Every night you had to attack, patrol, or dig. The machine guns drove you mad. You had to lie in the mud for hours at a time. Daily rains, no shelters, badly fed—such was their sad fate, and such was going to be mine.

Having heard about the arrival of reinforcements in the village, they asked to come on work detail to see if there was someone of their acquaintance among the newcomers. They found me along the way.

At 6 in the evening, with five comrades, we left Annequin, guided by an orderly. The darkness was complete. Our guide gave us prudent advice: "Do just as I do," he said. "When I drop, you drop. When I hit the ground, you hit the ground, no matter where. If I run, you run like hell." All of this signified that we were in the midst of great dangers. Our fears were fully justified. We had to cross open country, where bullets whistled, because at this point in the war the machine guns on both sides fired almost without interruption, all night long and often all day long. Cannon fire was relatively weak.

We crossed a prairie which would have been better called a marshland, then a field of sugar beets through which we stumbled because we couldn't see them.

They hadn't yet had the time or the idea to dig *boyaux* [communication trenches] leading up to the front lines.⁵ Because of that, each relief party or work detail was marked by an accident, often a mortal one.

Then we followed a railroad track along which a train couldn't have gone five meters without derailing. The shells had dug holes, twisted the rails, torn up the ties, knocked over the poles, and in the darkness we collided with all these obstacles, to the detriment of our poor, damaged legs and knees. Every minute we asked our guide if we would be arriving soon. Dripping with sweat, breathless, we could do no more.

We barely covered more than two kilometers, but no subsequent relief treks seemed longer or more painful than that one.

All of a sudden we found ourselves in a narrow, muddy ditch. We had arrived. This was our bedroom for the first night. We wouldn't be assigned to squads until the next day.

Five days of travel in a cattle car, one night of terror in the school at Annequin: the successive emotions we went through had completely broken us with fatigue.

Without a care about the cold, about the bullets which whistled above us, about the proximity of the enemy, about passersby treading on our feet and legs, we slept a deep sleep, rolled up in our flimsy blankets.

Even so, in the night I was awakened by the sound of picks and shovels, right nearby. I carefully raised my head above the parapet and asked these nocturnal workers what kind of work they were doing.

"Can't you see that we're burying the dead from the last assault?" a rough voice answered.

This response made me shiver with fear, to think that there were dead men all around me, and they were being buried under just a couple of shovelfuls of dirt.

A few hundred meters to the right you could see fire lighting up the landscape with a lugubrious clarity. It was a haystack that the Germans had set on fire to illuminate the landscape, since the use of flares had not yet become commonplace.

At the first hint of dawn, we were handed a mug full of iced coffee, a piece of meat, and bread splattered with mud. That made up our whole menu for the day.

Once daylight had fully arrived, I wanted to have a look at my surroundings. Despite the bullets, hidden behind a clump of bushes, I caught sight of a pile of ruins on my right. That was Vermelles, a big mining town upon which our artillery concentrated its fire in order to dislodge the Germans. On my left, a veteran showed me Givenchy [-lez-la-Bassée], which marked the end of the sector held by the English. Behind me, I was surprised to see that Annequin was so close, since last evening the trip from there had seemed so long.

Around Vermelles there were a large number of haystacks of straw or sheaves of wheat, which the Germans used as flaming torches every night. They husbanded them well besides, because a month later, when they pulled back, there was a large quantity left over.

Here and there were shapes, dark gray masses around which crows were circling. These were German and French corpses, awaiting their entombment, and they would keep on waiting until the German pullback of December 7.

During the day we got the good news that the 22nd Company was being relieved that very evening, at 8 o'clock, to have two days' rest at Annequin. If our bosses had cared more about saving us from needless fatigue, they could have kept us in the village [Annequin] for another 24 hours, which would have allowed us to recover from our journey. But nobody had thought about that.

The return to the village was just as hard, and even longer, than the day before. The machine guns never ceased firing, forcing us to await a calm moment to get across certain stretches of ground. There was one particular piece of open field, a real devil's den, upon which a machine gun had its sights fixed. One by one we passed between the bullets, and it was an astonishing fate that, by the evening, we had only one man wounded. It took us an hour and a half to get to the village, where we were billeted in the church, still intact. Only a few windowpanes were broken, and the openings were stuffed with cassocks and other bits of ecclesiastical ornament.

The church of Annequin, built when the village had neither mines, nor *corons* [miners' red-brick row houses], nor taverns, was tiny, and we had to arrange ourselves pell-mell like a flock of sheep. As for myself, I had a bit of high-altar step where I didn't sleep too badly, thanks to my great fatigue.

But why, instead of dispersing us in the still-intact houses of the village, did they pile the whole company into this isolated church, stuck out in full view beyond the first houses, upon which one big shell could have fallen and wiped out almost all of us?

And that very night shells did fall, all around the church, but didn't explode. Call it a miracle, or sheer luck. Later on more shells fell on the church, and one of them claimed some victims among the civilian population attending a service there. This took place after the German withdrawal, the following December.

The next day I visited the village of Annequin, and saw for myself, sadly, the anger, the cupidity, the spirit of vandalism displayed by those who had pillaged the town—Frenchmen, alas, soldiers like us, from companies who came there one after another, for periods of rest.

Even leaving out those who were looking for food or drink, why break down the doors of locked rooms, why force open cupboards? Why toss to the ground, trample, break, and sully all the linens, utensils, beds, furniture, etc.?

You would have thought that a band of wild *apaches*[6] or burglars had swooped down on the village.

The most sacred things—portraits, diplomas, religious paintings, souvenirs of first communions and marriage certificates—were strewn pell-mell through the garbage.

Yes, war is a moralizer. It inspires noble sentiments and lofty virtues. There are people who have dared to write about and to talk about this monstrosity.

In the presbytery, the priest, before he departed, had locked up the sacred objects: chalices, crosses, incense burners, etc., in a cupboard with an inscription saying that the house and everything in it were at the disposal of the soldiers, but to please respect this cupboard.

That didn't prevent some *poilus* ["hairy ones," slang for French infantrymen], suspecting perhaps that there were a couple of good bottles of wine or other tasty liqueurs inside, from plundering it and stealing everything inside, without the slightest compunction.

Later on, when the curate returned, he protested in a letter he wrote to the regimental colonel, and which was read to us at assembly. I recall this passage: "[He] knew that when the regiment was fighting in Alsace [occupied by Germany], at the very start of the war, men were punished with prison terms for stealing a simple apple or pear, but in France itself how could we tolerate such looting, such a profanation. . . ."

One of my comrades, who had come from Mont-Louis with me, now found himself with me again in the same squad. His name was Courtade, an excellent and valued companion during those first hard weeks of war.

We learned that the city of Béthune was only six kilometers away. We decided to go there that afternoon to pick up some provisions, given the inadequacy of our food supplies.

The German cannons would have made an easy mouthful of this city, but they respected it, fully expecting to take it any day. While waiting, daily life went on there just like in Carcassonne or Perpignan.

We went along a wide paved highway, the kind you hardly see anywhere else but the rich regions of the North. After having gone three kilometers we reached the mining town of Beuvry, which the Germans had been bombarding. We were dumbfounded to see that the inhabitants paid hardly any attention to it, and quietly went about their errands. The Germans invariably bombarded only a single part of town—one deserted by its residents, of course.

The road went right through this part of town, and a long line of vehicles of every kind was lined up along it, patiently awaiting the end of the bombardment, interrupting our journey. Some pitiless gendarmes held up all traffic.

At Beuvry we found all kinds of provisions. With our rucksacks filled, we made our way back to Annequin, postponing until later our visit to Béthune *la noire* [black Béthune].

When, back with the company, our comrades learned about our escapade, they were surprised by our boldness. Had our absence been noted at assembly or roll call, we would have faced a court-martial. It was only the most head-strong who risked leaving camp during their rest days.

"But then we might as well let ourselves starve to death," I cried out.

Then, with lowered voices, they let me in on a secret. Every day, a soldier from the company went across the fields into Béthune and came back in the evening with a big bag full of whatever his comrades asked for.

This man left camp and the trench, flouted the military code, risked a court-martial, to earn a couple of *sous*. He was never denounced or discovered.

The two days of rest quickly passed, and on November 12, at 6 in the evening, we were on our way to the trenches.

It's not my intention to recount every one of my trips to the front lines. I've only made note of those which are most vividly engraved on my memory by the fatigue and the sufferings which they brought me. The number isn't small.

For every eight days in the front-line trenches, my section spent four in reserve, and we had just made ourselves at home after groping our way along little holes dug into an embankment. My friend Courtade and I burrowed into one of them, squeezed by necessity into this uncomfortable berth. Rolled up snugly in our blankets, we spent the first night like that. We had to spend four hours each of the next four nights digging a trench.

The embankment where we were dug in ended at the railroad track, which I have already mentioned. At the angle of the two embankments our commandant, Lianas, was installed, a man of great courage but who was as careless about others' lives as he was of his own.

He had made himself a little cabana which was like a palace to us, compared to our rat hole.

At this place the railroad track was also on an embankment about two meters high. To keep from being seen climbing it, a narrow trench cut across and underneath the track. Once on the other side, you were protected from enemy fire. Well, the commandant absolutely prohibited anyone from crossing the track by using this trench. Day and night, work details and relief units had to move up along and across the track, fully exposed to enemy fire. Too bad if the bullets whistled, and too bad if they sometimes claimed unlucky victims.

After heavy rains a swamp had formed, which washed over the embankment at one point. They built footbridges out of branches, which we had to use, all the same . . .

But, you might say, why did this commandant persist in risking his men's lives so carelessly?

Perhaps he wanted to get us used to hearing bullets whistle past our ears, so they wouldn't bother us when we went into combat, someday.

One night, on relief duty, an officer who was unhappy with the racket with which we were making our way along these passageways, thinking that we weren't keeping quiet enough, found nothing better to do than to keep us there, lined up for ten long minutes, in spite of the bullets landing around us.

If I had to, I would say that this officer had taken too big a dose of *gniole* [hooch], which took away his common sense, as an extenuating circumstance.

After spending four days like this in reserve, we moved up in dark of night to the front lines. To get there we had to cross three or four hundred meters of open ground, crisscrossed by enemy bullets. You'd have thought we were crossing a firing range on the day of a target shoot. They didn't need any more goads to spur on the laggards.

It was with a gasp of relief—ten, twenty gasps—from our heaving chests that we tumbled into the trench—the kind of trench we dug before the Germans showed us just how to make them.

A wide, shallow stream at the bottom. No protective barbed wire. No parapets, no loopholes. No firing step. No trace of a shelter for us. And yet this trench, so poorly equipped, which would have made the Romans of Julius Caesar smile with pity, seemed to us a precious refuge.

To our right, a stream, its sluggish waters spreading out to form a swamp separating us from the neighboring company. To our left, a large stretch of unoccupied trench, abandoned to the determined efforts of a German battery to fire on it day and night, as if it were an important strategic point.

Right away I saw that our half-section was completely isolated, with no possibility of falling back in case of attack or bombardment. This bit of trench could have been our grave, "our glorious tomb," as the newspapers of that time would have called it.

My comrade Courtade and I spent the night side by side, in a trance, in such darkness that you couldn't have seen an elephant two paces away. We were always seeing Germans rising up, coming like fierce assassins to massacre us without pity. Perhaps twenty times during the night, the sentinels sounded the alarm, and we all blasted away like madmen.

That night seemed endless to us. Finally daylight appeared, and we felt as if we'd been delivered from a terrible danger. But another enemy arrived: the rain, against which we had no defense at all. We didn't yet have any tents!

This wasn't a fine, soft rain—a good winter rain we call it at home—but a driving rain, pounding us with big, fat raindrops, so that you thought that God was unleashing a second Deluge to extinguish the madness of his creatures.

My friend Courtade and I managed to unearth a German overcoat splattered with congealed blood and, draping it over two broken rifles which we stretched across the trench, we'd gotten ourselves a shelter which made others envious. A precarious shelter, however, from which dripped multiple streams of reddish-brown water soaking through the cloak, falling on our hands, our necks, our clothes.

And the rain kept falling, all night long. The walls of the trench crumbled, and in spite of the distinct slope, in certain spots the water accumulated, dammed up by the landslides. The stream at the trench's bottom grew larger as the waters expanded, creeping toward us in a vast lake. The sentries no longer kept watch, seeking refuge from the flood and the collapsing walls. Some abandoned the trench altogether; others went to work digging individual holes for themselves, which collapsed almost immediately.

What a cruel night! How long it was before this November day broke, dirty and foggy, bringing us no sunlight but, instead, more rain, still more rain. When it stopped, we had to clean up the landslides, let the water run out. We warmed ourselves by the vigor with which we wielded our picks and shovels.

The next night the sky cleared up, as if a curtain had been lifted, and we saw the most sublime spectacle man can ever admire: a sky luminously sprinkled with stars, and a resplendent, radiant, silvery moon.

But alas, at the same time the temperature plummeted, as if these faraway worlds were sending us an icy wind. Our overcoats and our soaked blankets stiffened with the frost; our feet were numbed with cold. I had to take my shoes off, despite the formal prohibition, and rub them vigorously with a little brandy kept in reserve, then wrap them in the driest corner of my blanket. At daybreak the ration team couldn't serve us the *jus* [coffee] we so impatiently awaited. It had frozen in the containers, en route to us.

Worst of all was the thirst which tortured us, in spite of the cascades of water falling from the sky. At this date, *pinard* [cheap red wine] wasn't part of the poilu's daily fare. We had to be happy with a mug of jus brought up each morning. This was insufficient to staunch our thirst brought on by dry, spicy food and by a form of "trench fever" which we were all suffering.

One day, our containers were completely dry—the only dry things around, by the way. That morning our mug of jus was transformed, according to the laws of nature, into a block of ice in the ration team's container. We were assailed by a thirst so terrible that we could hardly move our tongues. Courtade and I agreed that, at all costs, we had to get some kind of liquid to quench our unbearable thirst.

To do that, we had only to take a few steps to reach the stream which ran along the bottom of the trench. But at the very thought of contact between our lips and this water a horrible disgust seized us and tightened our hearts.

It wasn't simply that the water was dirty, where we were, which bothered us. It was just that we had seen, the first day, among the bushes and reeds along the banks, the same stream's water gently bathing and flowing over dead bodies, both French and German.

You can easily understand our disgust. And still our comrades resigned themselves to drink this water. The sufferings of thirst are much greater than those of hunger.

Risking court-martial and a firing squad for a canteen full of water, my buddy and I quietly slipped out of the trench, following along it at first to our left, the side which wasn't manned. It was already badly damaged by the shell-fire concentrated on it, and after the heavy rains it was completely impassable. Bent double, splashing along in mud up to our knees, we moved forward. At one point, no more trench at all, or hardly any. We had to crawl. But the Germans spotted us, and a volley of bullets splattered around us.

A moment later, safe and sound, there we were at the point where the narrow passage crossed the railroad tracks, and near where our terrible commandant, as dangerous to us as the Germans were, kept watch. But luck favored us. We passed by unnoticed, and soon, not without feeling the whistle of a few bullets in places where the machine guns were constantly aimed, we arrived at Annequin. There we could fill our mouths, our gullets, our stomachs. We could drink until we were full. This well water wasn't exactly clear, but it was fresh, and how delicious it was to us!

It is clear that, if war brought on bitter physical sufferings like cold, hunger, thirst, sleeplessness, it also brought on an equally high degree of satisfaction when those sufferings were relieved.

Someone who has never been at war cannot appreciate, like someone who has, just what it means to have a good fire, a good bed, a good meal. That's one small benefit.

Back to our sad situation. The return from Annequin to the trench took place with the same fatigue and unpleasantness, but without incident or mishap. We got back to our muddy stream without our escapade having been noticed.

The last day, in the afternoon, with overcoats and other effects taken from wounded or dead men, we fabricated sorts of puppets or scarecrows which we stuck on the ends of our bayonets.

What was this masquerade all about? Nobody told us. We didn't get any explanation until the evening.

As usual, before the moon rose, the Germans ignited a haystack in front of Vermelles, a gigantic torch which lit up a half-league all around.

Suddenly, with a signal fired by a 75, the whole French line unleashed an angry, crazy fusillade. After a few minutes they gave us the order to agitate our carnival mannequins, to simulate an attack from our side. The Germans, alerted by the fusillade, had to believe that we were sprinting toward them, and responded with a violent salvo in their turn. This made for quite a pretty concert.

This was our command's goal, to get all the Germans up and alert in their trenches, because right away the batteries of 75's concealed in the slag heaps behind us unleashed an infernal surprise volley of shellfire onto the enemy positions.

That night was quite lively all through the sector, and we hardly got any sleep at all, as you can imagine.

Finally, the evening of the next day, we happily departed from this bad spot. In spite of everything, we hadn't had anyone killed or wounded. But two hours before we headed out, one of my good comrades from Mont-Louis, Private Cau from Lapalme (Aude), took a bullet right through the head. He was the first man to be killed in front of us; it was the first blood we saw flow, and it affected us painfully.

We buried him beside the trench, and after a last look at this tomb which marked our passage in this sad place we sprinted at full speed across a German machine gun's firing range.

This time we were lodged in abandoned houses, very comfortably as if we were the proprietors, and we could warm ourselves with coal that we could take from the mine.

From the hell we'd been in, it seemed like we had two days in paradise. Nevertheless, inconsiderate bullets would smack the walls, and we had to block up the windows with mattresses. Sometimes a salvo of shells would trouble our repose, but what was that compared to our sojourn at the front line?

Except for a few skirmishes, up to the end of November the sector was fairly calm. Besides, the weather was very bad—sleet, rain, snow—making any serious military action impossible, which didn't bother us at all.

Our relief assignments to the front were not quite as hard. We began to set up little shelters where we could dig between watch details. Finally they distributed tent cloths, one for every three men, without telling us that we had to either draw lots and let each man have it for a day, or share it among three of us.

Taking Vermelles, December 1–7, 1914

On December 1 we were at rest, dispersed in the corons of Annequin where we had installed ourselves like proprietors. It was around midnight that the order came to hoist our sacks and get ready to depart.

Clearly we weren't heading back to the rear. Something was in the works, and it looked like it was our turn to fill up the next day's dispatches from the front.

Soon a company officer came and climbed up to the attic of our house. Through the dormer window he fixed his binoculars on Vermelles. He was willing to share with us a bit of intelligence.

They were going to attack the Château de Vermelles, right at the entrance to the village, which the Germans had transformed into a fortress. Depending on how this operation went, a general attack would then be ordered.

For several days our sappers had been digging an underground gallery in order to blow up the château with a mine. The explosion was set to go off at noon, exactly. The bombardment and attack would commence immediately afterward.

To witness such a spectacle, trembling at the thought of becoming actors in it ourselves, we scrambled to the windows. Some clung to walls, others perched on rooftops.

At the appointed hour, we saw the château disappear in a cloud of smoke, and a muffled detonation could be heard.

Right away our batteries, brought up into close range during the night, unleashed a rain of hellish fire onto Vermelles. The spectacle evoked the scene of Sodom and Gomorrah and the rain of fire, stones, and sulphur which destroyed them.

Profiting from the unpleasant surprise effect all this must have had on the Germans, our neighboring regiment, the 296th,[7] went on the attack, preceded by a detachment of skirmishers whom they had fueled with alcohol to excite their warrior spirit.

The attack was only partially successful. The château and its park indeed fell into our hands. But when they tried to penetrate into the town itself they ran into solid defenses: barricades, trenches which cut across streets, crenellated walls that the Germans, once they recovered, defended fiercely. A new effort was necessary. They had done enough for one day. Not in numbers killed, mind you; that wasn't part of the equation. But a sustained attack by infantry alone was impossible.

This all lasted barely three quarters of an hour. We were called down from alert status, and to see the joy which was so evident on all our faces was proof that each one of us, egotistically, had wished for the operation to fail so that we wouldn't have to participate in it. Decidedly, we were pretty sorry soldiers. But each one put his own skin first, no matter how little it was worth at the moment, ahead of all the houses and all the coal in Vermelles.

In the afternoon of the same day, I was attached to the 21st Company, sought after for its Peyriacois captain, Léon Hudelle. I joined the 13th Squad, composed uniquely of men from Peyriac and vicinity. It was the *Minervois* squad.

I was welcomed joyfully by my comrades, and we were placed under the command of a corporal from Toulouse, whose deputy I became. The next evening we went up to the front line in relief of another company. This time we were on the opposite bank of the stream.

Captain Hudelle had already brought up a big quantity of timbers from the

Annequin coal mine, which were used to build both individual shelters and others big enough to lodge a whole squad.

The next day the captain himself took me to see all the improvements which he had so intelligently undertaken in his sector. In the course of this tour he pointed out an abandoned trench. "Take a look," he said. Eyes wide with horror, I saw a lugubrious tableau: On both sides of the trench, uncovered by earth slides, appeared skulls, feet, leg bones, skeletal hands, all mixed up with rags, shredded packs, and other shapeless debris.

"But this is a charnel house," I said, recoiling in disgust.

The captain told me how, some time earlier, one of his company's sections had moved up in the night to dig this trench. The men had worked energetically because they knew that, the next day, they would be manning the same trench. It was in their best interest to dig it deep, as soon as they could.

At daybreak, in the fog, our men saw silhouettes of skirmishers advancing upon them.

The sentinels called out, "To arms! To arms!" Soon a few shots rang out, but immediately the assailants cried, "Don't shoot! We're English!"

Indeed they wore the caps of our allies, and given their close proximity there was nothing unreasonable about our encountering an English patrol or work detail lost in the fog. The firing ceased immediately.

But alas, it was the Kaiser's cutthroats, in disguise. Leaping into the trench with savage cries, they massacred the occupants. Some of our men tried to fall back to our lines, but they were cut down before reaching them.

A few owed their lives to hiding in the water, in the high grass of the marshland.

A schoolteacher who was now in my squad, Monsieur Mondiès from Pépieux (Aude), one of the escapees, had to spend several hours crouched in the freezing water. Brought back to Annequin by the captain to dry out his effects, he found in his pocket a fish which he kept as a souvenir of this miserable day. His skin had turned completely black; then later it dried out and returned to normal, just as happens after certain illnesses.

Meanwhile the colonel ordered the 21st Company to retake this trench the very same day, no matter the cost (easy for him, who didn't risk the slightest scratch). Not to avenge our dead, because their number was likely to double. Not for the value of the terrain we had lost, which wasn't worth ten francs. No, it was for our so-called honor and pride, and in reality because it could constitute a black mark against the further advancement of our big bosses if this trench were not retaken.

The captain insisted on artillery support for the attack. He himself went to Annequin, to the observation post set up at the top of a slag heap, and pointed out to the artillerymen exactly where to direct their fire.

At 5 p.m. a battery opened up a terrific bombardment, with mathematical precision, right onto the enemy trench, which had no protective shelter to offer since it had just been excavated.

Once night had fallen, a patrol sent out by the captain crawled forward. Emboldened by the silence they encountered, they arrived at the trench, and found it stuffed with corpses. There was only one wounded German, who was taken away.

The trench was reoccupied. They tossed out the dead bodies to both sides, front and rear, and covered them insufficiently with the earth they shoveled out while deepening the trench. But the steady rains uncovered the bodies, little by little, and they had to abandon the trench. A signpost at its entrance bore this lugubrious inscription: "Tranchée de la Mort" [Trench of Death]. In truth, there were only dead men there.

After a surprise like this, the captain demanded rigorous surveillance and the utmost vigilance. And as is always the case in military life, we went from one extreme to another. The men were exhausted from long hours on guard duty.

On December 7, at dawn, we noticed an abnormal slowing of the usual fusillade from our adversaries. Then came complete silence.

Were we being led into a trap?

Patrols carefully inched up to the German positions, which were discovered to be empty of occupants.

During the night our neighbors had given us the slip and evacuated Vermelles and the surrounding trenches.

They hadn't left in order to please us, but because they found themselves in an extended salient, exposed to our enfilading fire from two directions.

It was a simple straightening of their lines. But our striped-sleeve big shots, excited by this easy success, believed that this was the great German retreat getting under way, as announced daily by Hervé[8] in his newspaper.

That day we were at rest in Annequin. We all sprang into action, rushing in every direction. We quickly loaded all the caissons, all the vehicles. We packed everything up in feverish haste.

"Be sure to bring everything, don't forget anything," our captain told us. "We're not coming back to Annequin." At noon the march forward—the pursuit, if you will—would begin. Victory was spreading its wings over us. Warfare in the open was starting up again. This day, our battalion would be marching in reserve, but they promised us that we'd have our turn.

As the noon bell rang, we left the village with no worries about being seen by the enemy, who was no doubt far away, as far away as Lille.

Soon we passed by our trenches, henceforth useless, which we marched past in triumph. In front of us we could see scouting patrols. From a gloomy, gray sky the rain started to fall, and our marching turned to slogging.

Right away, a few volleys of shells fell upon the first columns, no doubt from artillery covering the German retreat. But soon we heard the disagreeable tic-tac of machine guns. We noticed then that the Germans had posted themselves along the crest of an elevation above the plain, in front of the village of Auchy-lez-la-Bassée. We were in the presence of strongly organized positions, ready for action.

Who saw any humor in this? We surely did not, stuck in the middle of a swampy plain where we could hardly stick our noses in the air without hearing a couple of bullets whiz by, looking to hook onto us in their dizzying trajectories.

All was indecision and confusion. Night arrived quickly, and with it more wind and rain.

In an abandoned trench we crawled into dugouts, but the spaces were far from being snug. We didn't count on getting a meal that evening. On a day when victory is won, a soldier doesn't ask for bread, it's true, but glory on the battlefield has never filled anyone's belly.

Chilled to the bone, soaking wet, caked with mud up to our ears, we asked how many hours, days perhaps, we were going to be staying there. The blessed voice of the company's cyclist called out in the darkness that the 21st Company would be heading back to Annequin to finish up its three days of rest.

We departed without a look back, but the night was so dark that we slid, fell down, stumbled constantly into shell holes filled with water or into boyaux and invisible trenches. We scattered, we lost our way. It was now that the storm unleashed all its power and reached its climax.

We wondered if the night would be long enough for us to reach Annequin, even though it was only three kilometers away.

Finally, around midnight, in a state you can imagine, our squad made its pitiful entrance into the village, where at least we could warm ourselves, dry out, lie down on clean straw, and relax. But we could imagine what suffering was felt by those who spent the night out on the plain transformed into a lake, or up against the embankment of the Vermelles-Béthune railway, where our front line was established.

So ended this day of glory and victory. It sure was sweet, our victory.

For several days the daily communiqué from the front had been disconcertingly banal. Nothing to sink your teeth into, for the bedroom strategists, the journalists, the oglers, all those who held up the daily dispatch as gospel truth.

Well, at last, what a windfall! The taking of a town of four thousand inhabitants! Therefore, triumphantly, the next day's communiqué announced to France and to the whole world: ". . . . after a brilliant combat, the town of Vermelles and Le Rutoire fell into our hands. . . ."

Of course, we couldn't admit that we had simply occupied a position abandoned by the enemy who had fallen back on another, even stronger position.
"To conquer without peril is to triumph without glory."[9] But what to think
about that qualifier "brilliant" inserted into the dispatch?

It's like saying that after any combat, no matter how brilliant it may be,
there are no heads or chests riddled with holes, or bellies burst open, or flesh
torn off in strips, shredded, or crushed. What cynicism, what an attitude on
the part of those who wrote these dispatches, to dare to say "after a brilliant
combat"!

The day after, we took our turn occupying our new front lines. We passed
through Vermelles for the first time. One would have thought a cyclone had
swooped down on the place and knocked it flat. We were very impressed by
this spectacle, but later on I saw other towns and villages in the same state or
worse, including some where you didn't see anything left at all.

Two kilometers from Vermelles we set up camp in an embryo of a trench.
All night long we had to either stand watch or get to work. No one could rest
or lie down. But who wanted to stretch out to sleep in the mud?

Immediately the Germans set fire to a hundred haystacks. The whole horizon was ablaze. It looked like an immense city being devoured by flames. We
were quite discomfited by the clouds of smoke which the wind brought down
upon us.

Why did the Germans burn these haystacks instead of carrying them off?

Did they have too many of them?

Were they expecting a tougher response from us?

I don't know.

In the morning some heavy downpours put out these fires, but the smoke
got even worse, and mingled with fog to make the night seem endless.

All day long we could work without being bothered, walk around in the
open, do chores without being seen. But it seemed like the Germans had the
eyes of lynxes. They spotted a squad of our company heading toward Annequin to pick up some mine struts and beams, and they chased them along with
machine guns. Thanks to the clumsiness of the machine gunners only one of
our men was wounded.

Night arrived early, and so did the accursed rain. It fell in torrents until the
next day, without a break. It was enough to make us envy the frogs and other
amphibians which could live indifferently both on land and in the water.

Once my guard duty was over I could crouch down with my Peyriacois friend
Gabriel Gils, under a little shelter we had made with three shovel handles and
a tent cloth on top, which drew off the rainwater like a skimmer. Others sheltered themselves as best they could under a bit of planking, or blankets, or

knapsacks. Only the two schoolteachers, demoralized, discouraged, showed no initiative to take up the struggle against the elements. They endured this glacial rain planted squarely in the trench, passive as beasts of burden, they said.

They could really have said lower than beasts of burden, who would not have stayed immobile for hours on end in this torment.

On December 12 they came to relieve us from this sewer, and we were billeted on a farm near Annequin.

Coming into the courtyard in the dark of night, we forgot about the inevitable pool of water which was common in all the farms of the North, hidden under a covering of straw and dung. The result of this oversight was soaked feet, legs, or bottoms for most of us. But what the hell, who cared if we were a bit wetter than we had been? And we soon found straw to stretch out and dry out on.

The day after next, in the afternoon, we assembled for roll call. Once the usual platitudes and banalities were out of the way, the sergeant-major, with the same indifferent voice he would have used to tell us about an exercise planned for the next day, told us: "Tomorrow, at 5 a.m., the 21st and 24th Companies will go on the attack. Departure this evening at 6 p.m." And that was all.

The sergeant-major had already disappeared. We stood there, dumbfounded, staring at each other, some understanding nothing at all, others comprehending very well that this spelled a death sentence for some of us, those whom fate would choose.

Some officers who took their jobs seriously would have made a point of giving us some information and some comforting words, but none of ours took the trouble to make this effort.

After we'd eaten our evening meal, without much of an appetite, they assembled us for the departure. They were generous enough to give us two-hundred-fifty cartridges per man, and parsimonious enough to give us rations for two days.

The captain asked for forty volunteers to march in the vanguard of the company, on the attack. That was the same as asking for those who wanted to commit suicide. There was not one volunteer.

But one section had to be first. We proceeded to draw lots, and one section—not mine—was designated.

In the night, we left Annequin like a gang of evildoers up to no good. We followed the railway line, which shellfire had put into a miserable condition. You couldn't go four steps without tripping, stumbling, getting hung up in splintered ties, pieces of broken rail, uprooted telegraph poles, without a bit of moonlight. After two hours of marching, dripping with sweat, scraped, scratched, bruised, we stopped and set up a position in a former German trench. There we waited for dawn.

To cover about three kilometers, they made us leave fourteen hours earlier. At the height of winter!

There were in this empty trench some dugouts, which were immediately taken by assault. As for me, among the last to arrive, I couldn't find a spot in any of these dugouts or anywhere in the trench. Overcome with fatigue, I rolled myself up in my oilcloth raincoat and my blanket, and I sat down next to a tree with its branches stripped of any leaves. The *bise* [wind] blew through it, and to the sound of this bitter music I fell asleep. My thoughts immediately flew off to my distant home, to where I could re-create the happy hours of yesteryear. Suddenly a hand roughly grabbed my shoulder. I woke up with a start and was terrified, thinking that a Boche was surprising me and grabbing me. But no, it was my Peyriacois friend Gabriel Gils, who was looking for me to tell me that the attack order had been countermanded, and a new order was sending us back to our village.

A false alert? A last-minute reprieve?

We didn't look for an answer. So two hours afterward we were snoring away in bed in our previous billets.

Massacres:
December 15, 1914–May 4, 1915*

But alas, we hadn't gained anything by waiting.

By the next evening at 8 o'clock, many of us had already bedded down, some were writing letters or playing cards by candlelight, others were singing, when an orderly appeared and cried out in a voice that immediately got our attention: "Here are the orders. The regiment is relieved. You're going to have some rest at Mazingarbe. Departure at 4 in the morning. Blankets rolled up horseshoe-style on your knapsacks."

That brought an explosion of joy. We cried, we applauded, we laughed. So as not to be late, the eager ones rolled up their blankets right away, even if it meant shivering all night long.

At 3 a.m., impatient to leave, we are already on our feet. Finally the sergeant bellowed "Shape up!"

We lined up in front of the farm, along the road. But what does this mean? Here they are, distributing the two-hundred-fifty cartridges per man, just like they did the day before. Someone explained that it was to lighten the company's truckload. But that only half-convinced us.

Here they are again, distributing rations for two days. Is this also to lighten the regimental truckload? If not, it's a little strange to give us so many provisions just to go to Mazingarbe, barely six kilometers away.

Finally they order us to the right, by fours, and we could see where we were headed: along the railroad track that we'd followed the day before yesterday.

The officers told us that the attack was set for dawn. There was our rest; yes, eternal rest for those who would give their lives there.

But why this ridiculous comedy, this loathsome trick? What did they fear? A revolt, perhaps?

They gave us too much credit if they thought we'd offer any protest on the way to the slaughterhouse. We were no longer citizens, but beasts of burden.

*Dates of original notebook; however, the narrative does not extend beyond December 1914.

At dawn we were in the first line of trenches, occupied by smartly dressed, peaceful-looking Territorials.

How we envied these grandfathers! How we wanted to be their age, with their white hair, to be exempt from attacks.

I lifted my head above the parapet and saw only a vast plain of sugar beet fields.

At about eight hundred meters you could barely make out where the ground rose, but we couldn't see any evidence of the enemy. At sixty meters to our right was the rail line that we had followed and which led on to Auchy-lez-la-Bassée. We could see the first red-roofed houses of the town, five or six hundred meters away.

There was a long wait. Day had broken. We hoped for a counterorder that would take us back to Annequin. It didn't seem possible, even if we were commanded by madmen or criminals, that we'd be made to advance in broad daylight, in open country, across such a great distance.

During this time, the wildest rumors flew, to boost our morale: according to one, our own ferocious Hindus[1] lurked in the fields right in front of us, with their famous cutlasses in their teeth. On the other hand, it was unlikely that there'd be any of the enemy out there to meet us, since the Territorials strolled around peacefully in the open every day, without drawing a single enemy rifle shot. The war must be over in this corner of Flanders.

In brief, this affair seemed like a peaceful occupation of abandoned trenches.

What mean-spirited, miserable tricks by our bosses! They lied to us shamelessly. The truth was—and I got this right from the mouth of our Captain Hudelle—that we were really and truly sacrificed. For three days our regiment was to undertake a series of attacks in order to draw in the enemy forces and mask an English attack on La Bassée and a French one on Arras.

The attack order stated, in writing—Captain Hudelle put it right in front of my eyes, the next day—that we needed to "attack whatever the cost, paying no attention to losses. The section leaders are responsible for the execution of this order."

This barbarous order which led us to the slaughterhouse wasn't signed. It was anonymous, like a simple note to a servant. The scoundrels who wrote it were also cowards!

Oh *patrie* [fatherland]! What crimes were committed in your name!

Suddenly the order came to fix bayonets. A shiver ran through my whole body. I, whose sensitive heart bleeds and wails at the slightest suffering. I, who often turned my foot away so as not to step on an ant, a little insect. I'm going to be thrown into savage, hand-to-hand fighting, without mercy, against unhappy victims of fate just like me!

Ah, it was too horrible. I cast a glance at my comrades. They seemed not to understand what was expected of them. Like unconscious beings, they were there, quiet and tranquil like actors waiting in the wings to go on stage. As to our two schoolteachers, one had taken in a strong dose of alcohol and seemed to be concentrating all his energy on not falling asleep. The other smoked cigarette after cigarette, like a madman. Alas for him—they were the last cigarettes of a condemned man—this was his last day!

It was 8 in the morning. Our batteries of 75's immediately opened up a violent barrage on the enemy lines. It impressed us, but it was utterly insufficient to protect our attack. After a few minutes, the fatal word "Forward!" came down the trench.

We thought we would climb out of the trench all at once and move out in a line, like skirmishers, elbow to elbow. But no, they'd figured out something better: From the main trench, another narrow trench extended forward about fifteen meters, at the end of which were a few crudely dug steps. We were going out single file, that way.

With no volunteers around, the section that fate placed first in line started right out. Our section came next.

With the great distance and a light fog that the pale sun hadn't completely burned off, the Germans didn't see anything at first. But hardly had twenty men gotten out before one machine gun started clattering, then two, then three. Bullets started smacking the lip of the trench like hailstones, making us pull down our heads. In the squad that went ahead of us, one man was shot right through the shoulder, spurting so much blood that he was surely going to die without immediate attention. But no stretcher-bearers were in sight, and you couldn't stop your march forward to take care of even your own brother.

Passing in front of, or rather stepping over, this first moaning, wounded comrade, we had to splash through his blood, which made quite a nasty impression on us.

Even the stupidest understood that we were going to our deaths, without the slightest hope of success, simply to serve as living targets for the German machine gunners.

Our leaders might as well have been in the pay of the Kaiser, having sold out to the enemy. If they had been, they wouldn't have acted any differently, drawing us into an ambush and getting us massacred.

The German machine gunners were in too much of a hurry. If they had waited a few minutes before firing, the whole company, the whole battalion would have been out of the trenches, and by that evening you would have counted the dead in the hundreds.

But the Germans were scared stiff, and went crazy with their machine guns. Only two sections of our company got out.

At the entrance to the forward trench, our Captain Hudelle, upright, pale, face frozen, watched us march past. When our squad passed in front of him—the "Minervois squad," he called it—he didn't even recognize us. His thoughts, his spirit, were far away from this sad spectacle.

Some may be surprised that the captain wasn't at the head of his men. *Noblesse oblige*—stripes do, too, you would think—but now they had come up with this: the colonel marches with his reserve battalion; the commandant, with his reserve company; the captain, with his support section; and the section chief with his relief squad. It was left to the corporal to march at the head of his squad. The sergeants took up the rear, to move along the laggards and shoot them down with their revolvers, if they felt they needed to.

That day, I wasn't in front of the squad, but in the line, being the second, or "honorary," corporal. The top corporal was regular army, a young guy from Toulouse.

As soon as each of us left the trench, we took off at full speed and flattened ourselves against the railway embankment.

This slightly elevated slope protected us only imperfectly from the bullets fired from the windows and rooftops of Auchy, by machine guns we could see. Just as I arrived at the slope, out of breath like after a long run, I saw one of those guys who had already taken cover there get hit in the back with a bullet. I'll never forget the sight of that hole, like it was made with a drill—a little whiff of smoke from burnt cloth, the man's violent somersault, a groan, and then the stillness of death.

Crazed, I started to run, bent double, vainly seeking a more sheltered spot along the embankment, all this in the middle of a steadily growing hail of bullets.

Now we were all stretched out, immobile, along two or three hundred meters of railroad track. But from the trench behind us the captain cried out, "Forward! Forward! In a skirmish line! Advance!"

We crept forward a few meters. The captain, urged on by the commandant, was getting impatient. Barely half of the company had gotten out of the trench.

From the trench a rough voice threw out to us a terrible threat: "Tell Adjutant Col (the section chief) that if the section doesn't move forward, we'll fire on it!"

Terrified, we crept a little farther along the embankment, like earthworms. Up in front, they tried to form a skirmish line, but those who left the slope to do so were immediately struck down, riddled with bullets.

Just then, an orderly, with a folded-up piece of paper in his hand, moving as low to the ground as he could, came near me. "Hey," he said, "are you scared?" He had hardly said the last word when a bullet went through his chest. He fell forward, his face in the dirt, then rolled over on his back in a final convulsion.

In a few seconds I saw the pallor of death spread across his face, his eyes cloud over, and a bloody dribble appear at his lips.

He didn't say a word. He just stuck out his hand to us. The guy closest to me and I both took it, but it was already motionless. He was dead.

The brutes who commanded this assault finally seemed to understand that, since we didn't have skin like a hippopotamus, it was impossible for us to advance into a hailstorm of bullets. With his raspy, piercing voice, Captain Hudelle called out to us to try to get to another trench, one that I hadn't noticed. It began about as far out as I was, and extended toward the enemy lines. But from where I was it was about eighty meters away from the embankment. I could be killed eighty times before reaching this refuge. And if I got there, I might find it filled up with earth, or too shallow, or filled with water.

But I couldn't stay in this situation any longer. Lying on this cold, wet ground we were shivering, but that was only a minor detail. We would have been happy to stay put if the Boches weren't chewing us up with their machine guns. We weren't protected enough from their field of fire, and we were just like silhouetted targets for them. From time to time a bullet would strike home, leaving a man dead or wounded.

The corporal of my squad, the little guy from Toulouse, had a shattered arm. He had enough strength to crawl back to the trench we had left from, leaving a bloody trail behind him. From number two corporal I was now number one. But where was my squad? Only one who was part of it, Ferié from Peyriac, whose family lived in the countryside outside town, was stretched out behind me, his head between my legs.

We took counsel, hesitating to leave, since of those who had tried to get back to the safety of the trench, several hadn't made it. But a bullet that looked explosive to me landed in the ground a few centimeters from my head, splattering my face with mud.

"Ferié, old friend," I said, "I think that if we want to see the church tower of Peyriac again, we need to clear out of here."

So there we went, dragging ourselves across the sugar beet field, with my knees and elbows crying out for mercy.

When I'd gotten about twenty meters, I couldn't go any farther. And to think that safety was right there, just a few steps away!

I suddenly made a desperate decision: I got up and ran, or rather I thought I was running, because my legs were like lead and I could barely move forward.

A machine gun crackled, a salvo of bullets tore up the sugar beets around me. Private Thomas, from Sallèles d'Aude, who was crawling in a furrow, cried out wildly, "You're crazy! You're going to get me killed! Get down!" I was only four paces from the shelter, from my goal. But the advice was right, for him as well as for me. I flung myself down. The machine gunners thought I was dead and stopped their damned machine.

I was disappointed to see that what we thought was a trench was just a series of rifle pits, spaced out from one another, where German sentinels no doubt had kept watch at night.

Only one of these pits, where a man could barely flatten himself out, was unoccupied. With one leap I reached it and collapsed into it in a heap, mentally and physically wiped out. I was saved!

Meanwhile Thomas from Sallèles, seeing that I was going to steal this pit to which he was also headed, rose up at the same time as I did and fell onto me at top speed, right in the middle of a new crackling of bullets.

Thomas was big and fat. He hadn't had enough time to get thin. With his warrior's gear he weighed about a hundred kilos.

There are those who complain about tight living quarters. I'd like to see them there, curled up, head down, in a hole of barely sixty square centimeters, weighted down by a hundred-kilo heap!

In fact I was suffocating, and if in a supreme effort I hadn't been able to throw Thomas off I was going to die in this hole, with no glory, no beauty.

On my knapsack I had a spade, Thomas had a pickax. Flattened out and after strenuous efforts, with these two tools we succeeded in making a little protective parapet. Our neighbors in other holes did the same, and we were able to link up with them, digging our own little trench from which we could scoff at the Kaiser's machine gunners.

A latecomer who crawled up asked if there was room for him.

We had barely answered yes when, fooled by a moment of calm, he rose up and dashed toward us. But alas, he was riddled with bullets at the very moment he was stepping over the parapet.

And this other one—why is he advancing so slowly, and why does he stop? But we recognize him. It's the schoolteacher, Izard, from my squad.

He tells us that he's wounded in the belly and that he can't go any farther. I think that an explosive bullet has torn his guts to shreds.

Poor Izard, in his cruel agony he didn't offer a word of complaint. When someone asked him if he was suffering, he didn't want to make us sad, and he answered, "No, I'm not suffering, but I'm cold." It was the cold hand of death that was already upon him.

Someone rolled up a blanket in a ball and threw it out to him. He could grab it and spread it out over himself.

Another soldier who was crawling up suddenly leapt up and fell right in the middle of us, but we were frozen with horror. This man had almost no face left. An explosive bullet had blown up in his mouth, blasting out his cheeks, ripping out his tongue (a piece of which hung down), and shattering his jaws, and blood poured copiously from these horrible wounds.

We opened several packs of bandages which we wrapped around what was left of his face, to try to stop the hemorrhaging; he displayed an incredible energy and willpower, and didn't show the slightest weakness, right up to the evening when we were finally able to get him to a first-aid station.

Meanwhile someone recognized this soldier: "It's Gachet. He's from Corporal Barthas' squad." The wounded man affirmed with a nod of his head that indeed he was Gachet.

I hadn't recognized a man from my own squad. But would his own mother herself have recognized him, like that?

In a rage at seeing the Germans firing explosive bullets, some comrades pulled out bullets from their casings and reloaded them with the point down; it seemed that was all that was needed for them to expand on the slightest contact.

That's the way that war, with the reprisals it provokes, annihilates every sentiment of generosity in the heart of man, taking him back to a primitive state.

Finally, darkness and fog spread out over the bloody plain. The machine guns fell silent. We could show ourselves openly.

We thought that, with night falling, we would see stretcher-bearers, medics, warrant officers, rushing out to care for the wounded and to take them back. But those folks didn't bother themselves for so little. It is true that we were afflicted, in the 280th Regiment, with a chief medical officer who was a real executioner—more about him later.

No, we had to bring back our own wounded comrades, carrying them on our backs or on a pair of rifles serving as a makeshift stretcher.

Our captain was indignant. "For the honor of the army," he said to us, "don't say a word about this scandalous business."

He was wrong. We should have shouted it so loudly, so strongly, so high, that the whole of France would hear it, and quake with rage to know that, the very night after a long-planned combat, we abandoned our wounded on the battlefield, with no help.

We had rushed over to schoolteacher Izard, but he was in a coma. All around him his blood had soaked the earth. We shook his hand for the eternal farewell. He didn't recognize us. Two comrades carried him on two rifles back to the first-aid station, where he expired almost immediately.

When we got back to Annequin, where we buried him, we all gathered thoughtfully at the grave of the schoolteacher from Espezel, which we decorated with greenery. I was picked by the squad to write a letter of condolence to his widow, for which she thanked us sincerely.

But let's not look ahead. Let's get back to our sad situation. Each one sought out, in the protecting night, his comrades, his friends, his bosses, the survivors of his squad. We greeted each other with emotion, eager to show our cloaks and knapsacks riddled with bullet holes.

Our joy was so great at finding Gabriel Gils from Peyriac safe and sound that we threw ourselves into each other's arms, weeping.

Since we had sensibly equipped ourselves with two days' rations—a few biscuits and a piece of boiled beef—they didn't bring us anything to eat or drink, that day or the next. Those who had something left in their knapsacks shared it fraternally with others.

They made us work all night to dig a front-line trench as far out as the farthest had gotten in the attack, and then a trench connecting the new one to the original one, from which we had left.

To motivate us, they told us that if the connecting trench and the new trench were deep enough to keep us safe, then we wouldn't attack.

This was an odious lie, a rude trick to get us to work harder. But we still had faith in the word of our bosses, and for twelve hours, from seven at night to seven in the morning, we worked diligently to finish the job.

Only those at the front since the start of the war were skeptical. The schoolteacher Mondiès told us: "You don't know them. You'll work until you drop, and then you'll attack all the same."

The next morning, December 17, numb with cold, worn out with fatigue, we were stretched out in the connecting trench which we had just dug in this long, cold December night.

Near me was Private Second Class Jordy, with whom I'd spent three years of military servitude [compulsory military service], lived in the same room, tramped the same terrain in maneuvers, undergone the same abuses from a loud, cantankerous adjutant.

Jordy was from Azille. He had even lived in Peyriac for a time. While he was there, I was a candidate on the Socialist slate in municipal elections. Jordy, fervent pacifist that he was, had openly promised me his vote.

But my political opponents in Peyriac made the naïve Jordy believe that the alluring post of municipal grave digger was going to be vacant and that, if he voted for them, the keys to the cemetery would be his, the day after the election, "But only on condition," they told him, "that you don't vote, even for your pal Barthas."

Jordy went back on his word; he sacrificed me, he didn't vote for me. But he didn't get to be the grave digger of Peyriac, either. They just laughed at him.

Today, all that was forgotten. It was with mutual, heartfelt joy that we found each other in the same squad.

The day before, Jordy had found himself in the path of a German bullet that plowed right into his back. The bullet entered his knapsack, and by all the laws of ballistics it should have passed right through Jordy and come out in front.

But two centimeters before entering his body, this bullet slammed up against a tin of coconut candy, and could do no more than ricochet off and depart through the side of the knapsack.

Jordy couldn't wait to give this marvelous news to his lawfully wedded wife Adrienne (we all knew each other's wives by their first names). And wouldn't you know it, in a few days Jordy got from his wife a little parcel containing a dozen tins of coconut candy, of all sizes and flavors. There was menthol, vanilla, lemon, something for every taste.

Jordy, stunned, gaped at these cans while we all held our sides laughing at the sight of his amazement. "I think," he said, "my wife is going crazy."

But the next day a letter from Adrienne explained this elaborate package. Having read in her husband's letter that a tin of coconut candy had saved his life, she naïvely believed that there was some mysterious substance in coconut that deflected bullets. In her letter she told how she went to all the shops in Azille, and was sorry that she couldn't find more tins of coconut candy.

But now I need to take my thoughts back to this gray December morning, to focus on the memory of this time of damnation.

All of a sudden, in a big hurry, an orderly rushed up, tossing out these terrible words: "Put on your knapsacks, get ready, we're going to attack at 3 this afternoon!"

We looked at each other, stunned. What! Was this going to start again? We were going to relive the frightful hours of the day before, see blood flow again, hear the cries of pain, the moans of agony, and by nightfall perhaps be a cold cadaver abandoned on this gloomy field?

We felt revolt rising in our whole beings before such a fate, such cruelty on the part of those who disposed of our existence so indifferently.

Our captain [Hudelle] passed by. I followed him, to get some details. "Barthas, my friend," he said, "it's serious. Yesterday only two companies attacked. Today it's a big deal, the whole regiment has to march. The orders are more severe than yesterday about getting the men out of the trenches."

These words that I reported back to my comrades threw them into consternation. Jordy had a sudden attack of colic, and soiled his pants.

"I'm going to say goodbye to my loved ones," said my friend Gils, and this example was followed by almost everyone. It was touching to see all these men, as if condemned to be executed, with their hearts far away from this sad place, absorbed in writing their last words and farewells to their mother, wife, sons or brothers.

Some were so shaken that their hands trembled and they couldn't write their addresses in a legible hand. I offered to my friend Gils and to other comrades the service of writing for them. I was as demoralized as they were, but I had better control of my nerves.

At ten minutes to 3, they had us hoist our knapsacks, for this early in the war they were intelligent enough to have us go into battle with all the heavy baggage of an unhappy trooper. I don't think that the warriors of the Middle Ages, clad in iron, were more weighted down than we were.

Sublieutenant Rodière was no doubt keen to win his second stripe. He was a volunteer. He seemed to me highly excited, and the strong smell of alcohol wafted through the trench as he passed by. He brandished a German bayonet, and whacked it against the parapet two or three times, saying, "You see, I'm going to kill the Boches with their own bayonet."

Alas, a quarter of an hour later he was dead, his head shattered by a bullet the moment he peered out over the trench.

At five minutes to three they had us fix bayonets. Our artillery opened up. The German guns, all but silent the day before, immediately responded with violence.

After just five minutes of preparation, and just with our 75's, the attack was launched on a broad front. Immediately the German machine guns went wild, mowing down those who, pushed out of the trenches, couldn't go to ground behind any kind of shelter.

Beholding this spectacle of horror, I thought about the paintings of battles which cover the walls of our museums or which illustrate the pages of our French history books, where you'd see leaders resplendent on horseback, banners flapping in the wind, bugles, drums, cannon, all arrayed, sounding, beating, animated with an intoxication, with heroic frenzy.

Today, where are our great leaders? Or even our little ones? Holed up in a bunker, ear stuck to a telephone.

The regimental flag? Safely stowed in a sturdy cellar in Vermelles. Two bullets scorched it and left holes in it at the start of the war, near Mulhouse, where it was almost taken by the enemy. That was enough glory.

The buglers? The drummers? Musicians? Useless. They're good only for putting on concerts at rest time. Now they're stretcher-bearers, orderlies, batmen.

Meanwhile, our company finding itself right at the front line, our captain declared that he wouldn't move until the other companies caught up with us, and he repeated this twice to the commandant, who gave the order to attack immediately, no matter what. By the way, that's the motto of the 80th and 280th regiments, posted on the walls of the Montmorency Barracks in Narbonne: "Forward, no matter what!"

An orderly brought up the order to attack immediately. This time it was serious. For Captain Hudelle it meant his stripes, his reputation for courage, his honor, even his life.

But, placed between his duty to obey and his conscience as a leader responsible for the lives of his men, he didn't hesitate to refuse the commandant's order.

The decision of our captain saved the lives of several of us, since on December 17 the 21st Company had insignificant losses, while others were very badly mauled.

But a few steps from where we were, a singular drama was unfolding at the 24th Company, where our commandant was.

The captain of this company, who had just arrived four or five days earlier from a Zouave regiment, protested against this attack organized against all common sense and doomed to certain failure, but, instructed to obey, he hurled himself forward and was struck down after a few steps.

In the trench, the men trembled, wept, pleaded. "I have three children," cried one. "Mama, mama," said another, sobbing. "Have mercy, have pity," one could hear. But the commandant, out of control, revolver in hand, cursed and threatened to send the laggards to the gallows. To a lieutenant who cried out in pain with a shattered thigh, he said, "Shut up! Don't discourage the men!"

Spotting a couple of men crouching behind a fold in the ground, a few meters from the trench, he ordered them to advance; seeing that they didn't budge, he threw himself toward them, threatening them with his revolver. But suddenly he toppled over, his head pierced by a bullet.

Commandant Lianas was dead.

The battalion adjutant, F. Calvet from Peyriac, alerted Captain Hudelle, the only one remaining of the battalion, that he had to take command. Captain Hudelle immediately halted the attack. We all sheathed "Rosalie"[2] in her scabbard, and took up picks and shovels, which we wielded all night long.

Those who recovered the commandant's body claimed that his revolver wasn't loaded. Some believe that this officer sought death in a moment of madness, caught between his duty as a leader, which required him to execute inhumane orders, and his conscience as an honest man terrified by such a frightful responsibility. Had he thought that his death would stop the assault, would put an end to the killing? Some thought so.

Whatever it may be, he took with him to his tomb the secret of his final thoughts.

May he rest in peace!

The next day we took a moment of well-earned rest in the trench, warming ourselves in the pale rays of a December sun, thinking how good it was to be over with these futile assaults, when Captain Hudelle came by, inspecting the work we had done. We were chatting a bit, when an orderly came up and gave the captain a sealed envelope. It contained these words: "Today, same attack order as yesterday. The time will be given later on."

This bad news, which spread like wildfire, provoked grumbling and protests. We weren't shy about saying that we were commanded by murderers, butchers, and that the general and the colonel should put themselves at our head instead of hiding in the rear, otherwise we weren't marching.

The commandant of the 4th Battalion, de Fageoles, declared to the colonel that he wouldn't take responsibility for an attack launched in such conditions. He had the courage to ask that the general himself come and take stock of the situation.

And General "X"[3] came. He recognized that Commandant de Fageoles was correct to prefer advancing our trench lines at night, rather than getting ourselves massacred by advancing in open order, in daylight.

The attack didn't take place, and that was the end of these murderous assaults. What was their result, from a strategic point of view? It appears that our leaders were satisfied with them. They had reason to be! We had drawn a good bit of artillery fire upon ourselves, but that didn't keep the combined French-British attack at La Bassée and Arras from failing completely.

These attacks took place according to a general plan of our headquarters staff. A daily order from General Joffre[4] himself was made known to us, saying that the hour had arrived to throw the hated enemy out of France.

Joffre was a little too presumptuous and too much in a hurry. He shouldn't have let them enter in the first place. At the same time, to excite our hatred, our patriotism, they read us a daily order from a Bavarian general, ordering the massacre of all Frenchmen taken prisoner.

We can presume that these orders were not carried out to the letter, since 400,000 French prisoners[5] went into captivity.

What was even more striking was that our little business was represented as a clear success: "We moved forward five hundred meters and we held firm to the conquered ground," claimed the dispatches, daily orders, and citation statements. So as not to tarnish our glory, they didn't add that we didn't push the Germans back one centimeter, that they had made us simply, stupidly walk right up to the mortars, mines, grenades, and it was worth it, wasn't it, the sacrifice of those whose bodies were fertilizing this corner of Flanders.

There were some individual decorations in our company. I won't talk about them except to mention some of the common themes: "Part of a group of forty who volunteered to attack from a trench . . . etc." Not one of those who were decorated had the courage, the shame to refuse with the greatest disdain these ridiculous *Croix de Guerre,* these lying citations, these burlesque congratulations.

Up until December 23 they put us to work without relief, day and night, digging parallels and communication trenches, in spite of the rain and the cold. Sometimes at night German patrols loomed up. We thought they were full-fledged attacks, and mad panics ensued, volleys which stirred up neighboring sectors and provoked artillery salvos on both sides.

Sometimes there were false alarms given by jumpy sentries who mistook bushes and shrubs waving in the wind for pointed helmets.

One night my section, which was working out ahead of the front line, fired away for more than an hour at shadows which we saw advancing for two hundred meters along the railway, and these shadows responded just as violently. A reserve section rushed up to reinforce us, and the fusillade doubled in strength. But it was an error. It was an advance outpost of our own company which we had taken for a German patrol. The outpost was happy to be able to take shelter behind the railway embankment, and we ourselves were in a rather deep communication trench. Otherwise the company would have wiped itself out.

These were days of forced labor, without sleep, without shelter, not even a bit of hole in which to ward off the rain a little. Our feet turned blue from the cold. They were sore, and they swelled up so much that we couldn't take our muddy boots off. Each night we were sentenced to dig a bit of trench which the next day would be our campsite. When they finally came to relieve us, we were haggard, skinny, dirty, muddy, so much so that we couldn't even recognize one another.[6]

Toward the Lorette Charnel House:
May 4–June 2, 1915*

First Christmas at war. Accursed month of January.
Battle for Béthune.

On December 23[1] they led us up to trenches where the occupants who had preceded us had the bright idea of setting up shelters for two or three men each. There was even a bed of straw in each one.

We could finally stretch out, take our shoes off, and not be on constant alert. When you're miserable, the slightest comfort and the tiniest well-being become a big deal, a stroke of good luck.

During the night of December 23–24, ten unpatriotic Germans came to enlist as prisoners within our lines. In the 17th Company this was a big event, since these were the first prisoners taken by the regiment.

The following night was the holy night of Christmas Eve. As soon as night fell, we were huddled in our holes, enjoying the thought of sleeping until dawn, when at about 9 o'clock a harsh voice passed the order to get out of our holes and to hoist our packs with all speed.

In fact, something unusual happened up at the front line. You could hear songs, clamors, numerous flares were set off on both sides, but no firing at all.

Two hours later, the alert was called off. We had no explanation of what had happened until the next day. I yield the pen to someone who can speak with more authority than I can, our captain [Léon Hudelle], who tells about this curious tale in a book.[2]

On Christmas Day, without any respect for the holiness of the day, they put us to work digging a big shelter where the whole squad was supposed to make itself happy. Useless work, at least for us, for that very evening we had to go up to the front line, after just forty-eight hours of "rest"—and what rest!

There were five more days and five more nights of vigil and hard labor, without rest, without sleep, paddling around in the mud, bending under a rainstorm or shivering when the bise of the North froze the ground solid.

*Dates of original notebook; however, the narrative begins in December 1914.

On January 1, 1915, at 6 in the evening, we came back to Annequin after seventeen days in the trenches, during which we couldn't shave or even once wash the dirt off our hands.

We came to this village for just two days. There wasn't even time to wash our clothes and dry them out. Both days were spent in distributions of equipment, drills, roll calls. We wondered with growing fear if this repugnant life was going to last much longer.

Yet even during these two days we had some fun. We ate and drank what the *Narbonnais* had been generous enough to send us, to celebrate the New Year. But on January 2 we were back on the muddy path to the uncomfortable trenches.

What that month of January was like, what we suffered through, I won't even try to describe. I would never have thought that the human body could withstand such trials. Almost every morning there was dry, white frost which formed icy stalactites hanging on our beards and mustaches and refrigerated our feet. Then during the day or the night the temperature would rise and the rain would fall, sometimes in a downpour, filling with mud and water our trenches which became rushing streams, irrigation canals. It was enough to make us wish to turn into frogs.

To do battle with the sleeplessness, the fatigue, the cold, the thirst, the hunger, the men took to drinking poison—the harmful alcohol which the rationers brought from Annequin, where the merchants sold it for twenty-five or thirty sous per liter.

You can imagine what precious liquors were in this dubious mixture. Some got to the point of absorbing a liter a day; the most sober were happy with a quarter or a half-liter. If the military authorities hadn't called a halt to the traffic, three-quarters of the drinkers would have gone out of their minds from it.

On January 23 we were going to take a break in Vermelles, for the first time. Bullets whizzed by on the outskirts of town, which was in full view and range of German batteries, but by some twist of fate it was quite exceptional that any German shells were fired on Vermelles. Each time we came there for rest we enjoyed complete safety, even though there were batteries of our 75's hidden within ruined houses.

No house stood undamaged. The least deteriorated were requisitioned by the big shots with three or four gold stripes on their sleeves; those which were half-demolished became the property of lowly adjutants and lieutenants; and finally those missing three-quarters of their roofs, or a floor out of two, became the customary camping ground of a squad.

The first night, the whole 21st Company piled into a ballroom from which the dancers had long ago departed. My squad, being the last one in, had to take our places in the only space left: the balcony where the orchestra played, rather high up. With no ladder we had to get up there by means of acrobatic tricks. In this balcony five or six musicians would have been quite comfortable, but it was a bit narrow to serve as a berth for sixteen sleepers. Fear of crashing down on those below kept us from getting a good sleep ourselves, which I greatly needed.

The next day, following the law of first-come, first-served, we took possession of a house which appeared quite comfortable to us.

It was a house of well-to-do blacksmiths or saddle makers, whose workshop was still filled with tools. It ran along the road, with a courtyard in the middle and the residential part in the rear.

The Germans had occupied this lodging, the roof of which had been almost all blown away by shellfire. All the furniture was still in place, hardly damaged at all.

The cellar was our bedroom. The Germans, having drunk all the wine, had covered the ground with three layers of bottles carefully laid on top of each other, to draw off the dampness, then a thick layer of grain sheaves on top to make a soft bed; they brought down pillows and mattresses from the house, and the walls were covered with bedsheets.

You sleep well in the bed of your enemy, they say, and on the morning of January 25 we were sleeping like dormice when all of a sudden, at 6 a.m., a sudden and violent cannonade was unleashed. The rapid fire of 75's installed in our immediate neighborhood shook the house.

Quickly, we got up and by instinct hoisted our packs, eager to know what was going on.

It was a German attack on the 295th Regiment, which was on our left, in front of Béthune. The Kaiser, who was himself present, it seems, was launching a surprise attack to take this important town.

January 25 was Kaiser Wilhelm's birthday, and the German army wanted to mark this date with a glorious deed. Unfortunately for them, and fortunately for us, word of this attack had gotten around, and appropriate dispositions had been made on our side.

The first news wasn't so good. The 295th Regiment, our neighbor, had held its ground, but farther to the left the English weren't fully committed to defending terrain which wasn't their own, and fell back precipitously. A gap opened up, but a battalion of Territorials from the Gers [département, southwestern France; prefecture (principal town) is Auch], in reserve at Givenchy [-lez-la-Bassée], put up a lively resistance and, counterattacking with a ferocious energy, retook part of the lost ground.

Béthune was saved! But it was mainly our batteries of 75's set up in Vermelles which broke the German attacks.

Each time that the Kaiser's subjects poured out onto the Lille-Béthune road, they were hit on the flanks, literally mowed down. It was a massacre, pure carnage. The next day, some from our side went out to see this sad spectacle of thousands of chewed-up, broken bodies. You could still hear the moans and plaintive cries of those who were dying.

I had no desire to go see such a scene of horror. It would have given me several nights of nightmares.

On January 31 we came to Annequin for four days' rest. Squad by squad we were going to quietly reclaim our customary billets, but we were very badly received by the townspeople, a large part of whom had returned. They accused us of having looted and pillaged their houses, and called us by the worst epithets. Not feeling especially charitable ourselves, we put the blame on the English, who were occupying a part of the village. This lessened the inhabitants' resentment toward us a bit, but we now had to camp out in quarters suitable only for pariahs from the trenches.

The next day, on guard duty at the police station, I was watching two hundred reinforcements march past, sent by the Narbonnais purveyor Manival, when I had the happy surprise of seeing a fellow Peyriacois, Louis Allard.

This Narbonnais contingent immediately received its baptism by fire. Either by fate or by plan, the Germans unleashed a volley of timed-fuse shells, which damaged a couple of roofs and brought some inoffensive tiles clattering down onto the terrified *Audois,* who hit the ground and cowered along the walls, terrified; but all they suffered from was fear, as no one had the slightest scratch.

Before they headed up to the front lines, our captain had the generous idea of offering to our Peyriacois comrades an ample feast. We were reaching the end of it, a glass of precious benedictine in our hands. Deeply moved, we were offering a toast in honor of our distant Peyriac, when a mighty explosion shook the house; walls crumbled, windows shattered into shards of glass, pieces of metal and wood penetrated the furniture.

It was a monstrous shell which had just landed beside the road, at the corner of the Annequin cemetery, which was across from the house. For a long time afterward you could see a big hole where there had been three tombs, whose occupants' remains had been pulverized. Some bits of them had no doubt landed on our dinner table, along with all the dust, powder, and mud.

In fact, this shell had killed only men already dead, and had waited until the end of our meal. But it was likely to be followed soon by another one, less inoffensive, so we scattered as quickly as we could.

On February 4, along with our new comrades, we returned to the muddy trenches. There we found our comrade Mondiès, who hadn't joined us in the rest period, having gotten a spell of punishment duty.

At the start of the war, our top leaders had turned logic on its head, in coming up with a new way to punish wrongdoers without putting them in prison. They ended up with this bit of nastiness: Someone being punished had to stay up on the front lines when his company rotated back to the rear for a rest, for the same number of days as he would have served in jail.

He was compelled to do the same work details and guard duties as the front-line troops. But the replacements themselves generally didn't go along with this, and let the punished man have a bit of rest on his own, as best he could.

This barbarous procedure was finally ended and replaced by the disciplinary units. How comfortable the gloomy, damp prisons and barrack cells would appear to soldiers in peacetime if they thought about the suffering and the danger faced by unhappy poilus subjected to hideous, brutal, and despotic wartime discipline.

Our friend Mondiès, a true antimilitarist, professed the most absolute scorn for his murderous firearm, the rifle, and treated it so negligently that he was slapped with eight days of prison.

Our trench duty got much better. We were two days on the front line, two days in reserve, and four days at rest in the rear, once at Annequin and the next one at Vermelles, still deserted by the *Vermellois,* who were kept at a distance by the bullets and the shells.

Luckier were the inhabitants of Philosophe, barely one kilometer from Vermelles, who continued their comings and goings as if nothing were happening. But it was said that the owners of the coal mine and the château there lived on the other side of the Rhine, which explained everything.

In the deserted, grassy fields between Annequin and Vermelles you would see a flock of sheep appear each day, peacefully led by an old shepherd (who perhaps was disguising his age) dressed in an ample old cloak.

We were amazed by his carelessness, but who was going to challenge an old man who already had one foot in the tomb?

Nevertheless this fellow turned out to be a spy, no doubt a German who carried out his villainous job until the day when the English, less trusting than we were, sent him off to spy in the next world. They had finally noticed that whenever one of their own batteries was put into place, the sheep came to graze nearby, arrayed in such a way that the Germans could fix their sights on the battery. Be on the lookout for the howitzer shells which soon came tumbling down.

While we were in this sector, our side installed, with much effort, some large-caliber artillery pieces well hidden among the pyramid-shaped slag heaps of Annequin. But as soon as these pieces were put into place, even before firing a shot, they were destroyed by a violent bombardment directed right onto the slag heap.

The false shepherd perhaps had something to do with this, but our cannon builders couldn't have asked for anything better.

On February 20, while at Annequin, we were supposed to move up to the front line that evening, but in the afternoon there was a violent hailstorm, whipped up by a great wind, filling the communication trenches with hailstones. When, in the evening, we had to wade into these trenches filled with the icy water of the melted hail, you can imagine the lovely soaking our feet, legs, and knees got. And we were drenched in sweat! There really was a God for the poor poilus, who kept them immunized from bronchitis, head colds, etc.

Arriving at the front line with a comrade, I was going to occupy our usual little cabin, but alas it had collapsed. No shelter for me to crawl into after my hours of guard duty.

In a neighboring dugout, they had a bit of a fire going, and they allowed me to warm myself up there. Otherwise I feared that I would die from the cold, that very night.

Two days later, with my squad, we went to the Vermelles coal mine to gather up timber. At the point where the communication trench opened onto the railroad track, feeling a bit tired, I stopped and decided to wait for my comrades on their return trip. Here were found some shelters which the commandant of our battalion had caused to be made with lots of pick-and-shovel work and plenty of requisitioned mine props. But once a few shells fell in the neighborhood, the commandant had bravely taken off and had other shelters built elsewhere for himself and his entourage. Manpower and materials cost nothing to the big striped-sleeve types.

Planted in front of the entrance of one of these abandoned shelters, I was trying to figure how much it had cost in wasted effort and fatigue, when a shell, a 105, arrived like a thunderbolt, brushed past my head, burst through the roof of the shelter and exploded inside. If the roof had offered enough resistance to cause the shell to explode, I'd have been done for, my head blown off. I got off easy, with just a big scare, but you can see how death hung right over our heads, ready to mow us down when we were least expecting it, even in sectors considered calm.

Of course, in the routine of trench life, this was just one small incident, and if I'd been guillotined by that shell they'd have thought it perfectly natural.

On March 23, the 21st Company finding itself at rest in Annequin, the captain had the bright idea of sending us to visit Béthune, famous among gourmets for its macaroons, but also a very important mining center.

A distance of barely six kilometers separated this city from Annequin, but our legs were in such bad shape and we were so tired that in the evening, upon our return, we were as exhausted as if we had had a long march.

When we got to Béthune, they made us traverse the city and go to a vast enclosure where we were held like prisoners, all day long. They didn't trust us enough to give us a few hours of liberty. However they did authorize each squad to designate two men to go into town to look for provisions for themselves and their comrades.

From that day on, access to Béthune was forbidden for companies. I don't know the reasons for it, but I suspect that it's for the same motives that, throughout the war, they kept poilus away from cities, so they wouldn't be shocked by the multitude of *embusqués* [shirkers] they saw, that they wouldn't frown at the sight of the excess, the luxuries, the coquettish attitudes and the attire of many of the women, and, at least in appearance, the almost universal gaiety, the seeking-after of entertainment, pleasure, amusement—all of which were insults to the soldier's tragic fate.

Béthune, despite the proximity of the front lines, continued its active life. This would last until the day that the Germans, despairing of taking the town, made it undergo the fate of Verdun, Reims, or Arras.

During these four days of rest, a few shells fell on Annequin and claimed victims among soldiers and civilians. I noticed for the first time that, in front of a house where someone had died, they placed a spray of flowers in the form of a cross, with a laurel branch in the middle.

Easter Day found us back in the trenches, where nothing distinguished it from any other day, except for a Mass which was said ten meters from our front line, at "La Cuvette" [The Washbowl].

This "washbowl," so named by the poilus, was a depression in the earth of about a hectare, in the form of a circle, surrounded by a protective parapet two or three meters high.

If you were safe from bullets there, you weren't safe from shells. But in this place, well known nevertheless to the Germans because they had occupied it at one time, I never saw one shell fall.

All around, elegant cabins had been built, with grassy lawns and flowerbeds. These were officers' quarters.

On this field we had assemblies, we made up barbed-wire emplacements, we worked with wood, and we even played rugby. The Germans would have been blind not to see the ball fly into the air and sometimes land way out ahead of the front line, in the barbed wire where a bold player would go out to get it, testing the courtesy of the Germans, who never fired on the players.

On Easter Day they improvised an open-air altar on the slope of the "Washbowl," with our front line running right behind it. A chaplain said Mass, which was sung by the officers and especially Lieutenant Cordier, whose booming voice must have reached German ears.

The commandant and almost all the officers of the regiment were present at this service, and all the soldiers who weren't on guard duty were authorized to attend it.

I say almost all the officers, because most assuredly our Captain Hudelle was absent, taking every opportunity to show his antipathy toward anything religious.

But this time his anticlericalism went too far and made him commit an error which his adversaries could later use against him, to reproach his sectarianism.

His company was in reserve, in a support trench. At the very time that the Mass was taking place he ordered a roll call, and imposed two days of "prison" on about thirty who weren't there.

Commandant Garceau, who had himself given the authorization for everyone to go to the "washbowl," begged and pleaded with our captain to lift these two-day prison sentences. But the captain wouldn't budge and kept the sentences, which were fictitious in any case, because when we stood down to rest periods the punished men did not stay in the trenches, as the inhuman regulations of that time would have required.

The captain said to one of the punished men, Corporal Gleizes, that he was punishing him for being absent from the trench without authorization. But the corporal replied to him sharply, "Captain, there's no use in hiding it, we were punished for going to Mass. We know it."

To wipe out the bad impression left in the company on this occasion, Captain Hudelle offered up, for May Day, at company expense, a bigger meal than usual, and at his own expense some cakes and cigars. On the package made up for each squad was a label inscribed: "To the non-coms and soldiers, on the occasion of May Day, the holiday of workers who suffer and who yearn to be set free."

This gesture by our captain didn't arouse the slightest enthusiasm, didn't stir any souls, didn't awaken the conscience of any soldier. We had lost any sentiment of dignity. We felt like we had been taken down, in our morale, to the level of beasts of burden.

Who, indeed, could dream about social emancipation or universal fraternity when the here and now was so gloomy for us? We were caught up in the claws, in the straitjacket of militarism, doomed to a hideous death or long months and years of unknown suffering.

We had lost all faith, all hope. We were miserable wrecks.

On May 4, we were back on the front line. It was 11 p.m., a dark night, completely calm.

My squad, the Minervois squad, stood watch, forming a link in the immense chain which stretched from the North Sea to Switzerland. Men were stationed twenty meters from each other. From the middle of the sector we were observing, a sap about thirty meters long ran out toward the enemy lines.[3] At the end of it two sentinels watched and listened; it was a listening post. In the main trench, at the entrance to the sap, a third sentinel was in place.

The two poilus stationed up at the listening post, Mondiès and Ayrix, finding the time long and the hours monotonous, decided to have some fun at the expense of their comrade who was at the entrance to the sap.

They came running back, pounding their feet and rattling their bayonets in their scabbards to give the illusion of bigger numbers. They ran past, wild-eyed, flying by their sleeping comrade, crying out in a desperate voice, "Gils, Gils, the Germans are coming!"

Toward the charnel house of Lorette, 4 May–2 June 1915

Terrified, the Peyriacois Gils believed them. Thinking that his final moment had arrived, he instinctively recalled the heroic act of the Chevalier d'Assas[4] and, mustering all his strength into one supreme effort, shouted, "To arms! To arms! The Germans are here!"

Immediately, to the right and to the left, sentinels pick up the cry of alarm: "To arms!" Rifle shots crackle; the Germans reply; white and red flares light up the sky.

The cannon sounds. The fusillade grows, extends as far as Vermelles, and at Annequin the alert is given to the companies at rest.

In the trench, those who were sleeping quickly pour out of their holes. Some leap to the parapet and start shooting like madmen, without knowing where, while others, considering the loss of the trench less important than the loss of their lives, prudently and promptly beat a retreat through the main communication trench.

At the moment when my friend Gils' cry of alarm burst forth in such a resonant and desperate voice, I was having a chat, thirty meters away, with the Peyriacois Louis Allard, who had stepped down from his firing spot at the parapet, given the prevailing calm.

We had so little expectation of an attack on such a dark night that we were dumbstruck at first, but soon we heard the sound of pounding footsteps coming closer. Shadows rose up a few paces away. There was no doubt that the Germans were pouring into the trench. With one leap of my long legs I was up on the parapet, but Allard had neither the time nor the presence of mind to do like me. He was knocked over, trampled. Once the avalanche had passed, he got up, having been completely ground down.

But it wasn't the Germans. It was simply Frenchmen who were running like hell.

Retreating along the communication trench, they collided with a section of reinforcements who were heading up rapidly. The officer at their head, revolver in hand, made them turn around. Without the intervention of Capt. Hudelle they would have been court-martialed for abandoning their posts.

The racket didn't let up. Two machine guns set up at the center of our company were the only ones which were silent. They couldn't operate. There were plenty of inquiries, reports, and sanctions about this afterward.

But here is our captain [Hudelle] arriving, bare-headed, enraged, whose booming voice dominates the tumult: "What's going on? So what's going on?"

No one knew anything, no one replied. I approached and, in a low voice, explained that it appeared to be a practical joke which got out of hand, but that since Peyriacois were involved we should try to fix things up.

Things got fixed up, in the end, without any unfortunate results. But what a racket, what a waste of powder, what turmoil this false alarm provoked!

On May 6, we came back to Annequin for four days of rest. The next morning we were put to work digging trenches around the houses, to serve as refuge in the likely event of bombardment, because a big Anglo-French offensive was imminent. Batteries of big-caliber guns installed around Annequin fired range-finding shots, ambulances appeared in large numbers, all signs that a new massacre was in the works. What role were we going to play in this bloody drama? We had no idea, and we lived in a fever of anxious expectation.

On May 7, at 6 in the evening, a shell knocked off a corner of the church tower. Another gravely wounded our good Commandant Garceau, who was unfortunately replaced by a man despised by all the soldiers: Commandant Nadaud.

At dawn on May 9, while all of nature was coming to life in springtime splendor, a frightful rolling of thunder suddenly burst forth. Hundreds, perhaps thousands of cannon opened fire onto the German positions, from Arras all the way north to the Belgian border. This lasted all day; like every storm it had its pauses and its unexpected surges. That evening we learned that, to our right, the French had seized several villages: Ablain-Saint-Nazaire, La Targette, Neuville-Saint-Vaast. On their end of the front, the English had more meager booty, taking only the village of Neuve-Chapelle.[5]

In the center, our division had to stay at the ready and wait until the enemy was sufficiently pushed back on both wings before we marched.

From a purely military point of view, though not a humanitarian one, the results of this first day of massacre were satisfying. But from the next day on we were hurling ourselves against masses of German reserve troops supported by formidable artillery, and all our efforts to exploit the successful surprise of the first day were in vain.

Common sense and simple reason warranted staying with what we had gained and preparing another surprise effect elsewhere. But try telling that to our ignorant generals, who, for weeks and months to come, would pursue a struggle of attrition, of wearing down, which consisted of taking and retaking, ten times, twenty times, a sunken road, a ravine, a trench, a cemetery, a sugar mill, etc.

The Noublette Wood, the Lorette Plateau, the Souchez Ravine, the muddy plains of Neuville-Saint-Vaast, all became human charnel houses where almost all the army corps took their turns bringing their tribute of human flesh.

For us, the day of May 9 passed in relative calm, as much as could be had in our uncertainty and in the middle of such a racket.

That day, my squad was on guard duty between Annequin and Cambrin, where the two villages practically touched each other. We had two duties to carry out. The first was to arrest civilians without passports. The second, more interesting, was to prevent the entry of alcohol, that poison which the poilus unfortunately were crazy about.

We therefore had to be especially rigorous in our searches of women suspected of concealing forbidden liquors on their persons. We generally let old women pass by, but we invariably stopped all the young ones, and made full use of our prescribed mission in patting down the round and protruding parts of their anatomies.

Some of them slipped through our hands and escaped, thumbing their noses at us and saying *Baï té fa rasa,* a southern expression they had learned which meant "Go get a shave."

The guard that we mounted against alcohol was useless and ridiculous. In fact, anyone who had reason to avoid us could do so by crossing the fields and backyards at twenty different points which no one was watching. Alcohol flowed freely into the gullets of poilus and even more into those of the officers who, while lacking in other examples for us to follow, always provided this one.

Regarding passports, a little incident took place which brought us much laughter despite the gravity of the circumstances. A hundred meters from our checkpoint, our comrade Jordy blocked the road, as a sentinel against smugglers and spies. Jordy was a zealous and enterprising soldier but, barely literate, his ignorance sometimes led him to commit blunders.

On the way from Annequin a *charcutier* [hog butcher], a neighbor of ours, came up with his horse and wagon, a fat pig majestically planted on it.

The charcutier displayed his passport and wanted to continue on his way, but Jordy, just following orders, refused entry to the horse and pig because they were not equipped with passports.

Jordy didn't recognize any difference between bipeds and quadrupeds, between citizens and animals.

The charcutier had to come to the guardhouse to request my intervention. To much laughter and catcalls, Jordy, sheepish and confused, had to let the pig, horse, and charcutier pass with impunity. The charcutier had no hard feelings. That evening he invited Jordy to drink a tankard of wine with him as recompense for his zeal in watching out for the security of Annequin.

That afternoon, a misshapen piece of steel fell like a thunderbolt against our guardhouse door just when, by good fortune, we were all inside. It was a fragment from a French 150mm cannon which had exploded not far from us. The same day another cannon blew up at a nearby battery. Our cannons were becoming decidedly as dangerous for the bombarders as for the bombardees since, as you can imagine, these explosions claimed victims.

To wrap up this day of emotions, we saw a French airplane hit the ground right between the two front lines. That night one of our patrols courageously went out to bring back the aviator, but he was burnt to a crisp, the airplane having caught fire when it crashed.

The next day, no order having arrived for us to participate in the battle—about which no one appeared particularly upset—we made our customary trip up to the front-line trenches to relieve the battalion which was there.

We saw right away that our trenches had been heavily shelled, and in this relief we counted three dead and five wounded in our battalion. This was next to nothing—except for those who got hit—compared to the slaughters on the nearby battlefield, where daily fusillades and cannonades raged.

Not far away, one afternoon we watched the "superb, magnificent" assault (to borrow military terms) of a regular infantry regiment which, with "irresistible élan," almost reached the village of Loos, taken later by the English.

But violent counterattacks pushed our guys back to where they started. The regiment was almost wiped out, along with a supporting regiment, the 281st from Montpellier, in our division.

On May 15 we were informed, to our great surprise, that the next day we would be relieved from the sector by a Scottish regiment.

Four days earlier the English had already relieved the regiment to our left. Fed in the trenches exclusively with biscuits and preserves, they came to our trenches to gather up scraps of bread off the ground or to scrape up the bit of leftover ratatouille left on our plates. In exchange, they gave us tobacco and cigarettes, of which they had plenty.

280th Regiment, 1915. Farewell, English!
Farewell, Annequin! Nœux-les-Mines, Mazingarbe.

It wasn't without regrets that we left the Vermelles sector, one of the quietest on the front for the past few months. These regrets were brought on mostly by apprehension about what they were going to do with us.

And then, where would we find another sector kept up as nicely as this one?

Even at the front line, each group of two, three, or four men had its own little *guitoune* [dugout] where, after hours of hard labor or guard duty, you could stretch out on an armful of straw and warm yourself up by a crackling fire fed with mine timbers which the Germans were kind enough to leave behind at the Vermelles coal mine.

Sparks, flames, and smoke poured out of hundreds of little chimneys, day and night, in front of the eyes of the Germans, who tolerated it because they did exactly the same on their side.

Back on the second line, the scene was even more picturesque. Some of the guitounes were veritable villas, with materials and furniture taken from demolished houses in Vermelles.

In my squad they had built a real house, with a door, windows, dining room, table, chairs, mirrors, camp beds, and a large fireplace.

Each time we came back to the same place, and we were always relieved by the same units, which made the men feel like they were constantly improving their quarters.

A few planks, a sheet of metal, some tarpaulins, and a little earth on top, and here's your roof. The ugly *Minenwerfer* mortars and their heavy projectiles were still unknown in this sector.

We had been working not for the King of Prussia, but for *Messieurs les Anglais*. We were assured that our allies would come and attack in our place. They were therefore most welcome, and we were quite happy to leave the scene.

The relief took place in a driving rain the night of May 15–16. While passing through Vermelles we were enjoying a mug of coffee or broth when a volley of 105mm shells crashed down around us, just as if the Germans had guessed our presence there.

Our company had only one man wounded. Each of us had flattened against a bit of wall or stretched out in the mud at the first whistling sound of a shell.

This way of saying good-bye by the Germans seemed in very bad taste to us. We left "Vermelles the dead" as quickly as possible, where we seemed to have overstayed our welcome.

Soon after we passed through sleeping Annequin. Some *Annequinoises* would no doubt have awakened if they knew we were marching by. Reconciliation was now complete, soldiers and civilians had gotten to know each other. Friendships, intimacies had been created, idylls had been launched, knotted, and even broken in various ways. Some had even led to marriages by *Monsieur le Maire* [Mr. Mayor].

At dawn, we arrived at Nœux-les-Mines, an important mining town. They didn't go to any expense of greeting us, despite the fact that the 280th Regiment had, for the past six months, been making a rampart of its bodies out in front of the village.

Our company had as its billet the stable of a dirty, worn-out old farm. A quarter of us couldn't even find a place to put down our packs and all our gear, which we had to leave outside.

Decidedly, we had been better housed in the trenches. There was plenty for us to envy the Scotsmen who had taken over our comfortable guitounes.

Some of us perhaps consoled ourselves in knowing that the officers and non-coms were marvelously installed in a spacious house nearby. In the hope that remorse would incite the striped-sleeve types, once they were settled and rested, to get us some kind of shelter for the following night, I killed some time by visiting the cemetery which was right next to our farm.

I wouldn't like to say that in the North they have less reverence for the dead than elsewhere. But to see these cemeteries surrounded by a ragged hedge, or by nothing at all, you can't help but get an impression of negligence, abandonment, indifference. After all, closing the place up with a high wall might appear superfluous, since the dead aren't going anywhere. But it seems to me that one can't be indifferent to the place of infinite rest being at the mercy of incursions by dogs, cats, and the indiscreet curiosity of passersby.

A simple strand of wire which I stepped over without effort, and there I was in the cemetery of Nœux. It was vast, big enough to bury two or three generations of inhabitants. But it was going to have to be enlarged very soon, because it was filling up every day with poor little soldiers dying at the first-aid station before they could be evacuated. In this season of offensives, five or six came to the cemetery each day.

I attended the burial of this day's batch. It was quickly done, like a boring chore. Territorials whom the war had turned into grave diggers excavated a long ditch and put the coffins in, right next to each other for best use of the space, shoveled dirt on top, a little cross with a name and a number, and that was it.

And the team of Territorial grave diggers in the ditch continued its work, under a leaden sun which made the air stuffy and hard to breathe, because there had to be space for those coming tomorrow, and the day after, and all the days to come, in this sinister ditch.

I pulled myself away from this sad spectacle, which was nevertheless a banal scene of the war, and I came back to our billet where, to my surprise, I saw everyone getting ready to leave.

Great, I said to myself, they've finally found us better lodging. But I was soon disappointed to learn that we would be leaving Nœux-les-Mines in an hour.

After seven consecutive months of trench duty, after a long winter of hard suffering, we thought we might have merited a good month of rest. But that wasn't the impression of our big bosses, because the very day we were supposed to leave for rest, we had to make a half-turn back toward the front, and after an hour's march we arrived at Mazingarbe-les-Brébis, welcomed at the entry to the village by a volley of flares.

This big village, very near the front lines, still had almost all it inhabitants, even though the shells sometimes claimed victims.

We stayed there for about two weeks. Since we couldn't do exercises or drills by daylight, right under the enemy's nose, they had us doing maneuvers and forced marches at night, to keep our legs from getting rusty.

Furthermore, every other day each company was on alert, packs hoisted, ready to leave for the front lines at the first signal.

It was at Mazingarbe that they took away our red trousers and dark-blue overcoats and dressed us in new sky-blue uniforms.

We underwent no less than five inspections while they were figuring out exactly where to position the regimental patches, sewing and unsewing them so many times until the colonel himself made this important decision.

Our new commandant, his lordship Nadaud, by his dirty tricks and his rigorous application of discipline, made us regret the loss of his predecessor, who had been so good to us.

Just like in a city under siege or in enemy territory, we risked jail time for venturing into the streets before the evening meal. Too bad for you if they saw you leaving a grocer's with a piece of cheese—a patrol would snatch you up as if you'd stolen the cheese, and you'd be dragged off to jail.

Every day, at sick bay, there were many who were truly ill, and those who were not, as at any sick bay. The commandant became furious when he saw people testing the aversion he had against early-evening promenades. He then found a way to improve the sanitary health of his battalion, by imposing a week in the guardhouse for those went to sick bay and were found to have nothing wrong with them.

For having forgotten to punish four men in his company who didn't pass medical inspection with a grade of "medical consultation justified," our Peyriacois Captain Hudelle saw himself slapped with a week's jail time. I admire him more for this punishment than for all his battlefield commendations.

I think the time has come to say something about our *chef-major,* our chief medical officer, "our undertaker," as the poilus called him. We weren't sure if he had ever set foot in any sort of medical school, because he never recognized anyone truly sick presenting himself at sick call, except for a few times when he observed that they were in utter agony.

One of my comrades who was in treatment in the evacuation hospital of Nœux-les-Mines heard these words from our chief medical officer: "I don't want to see anyone from the 280th Regiment unless he's dead."

At sick call, we were always greeted with insults, verbal abuse, sarcastic remarks or, when he was in a particularly good mood, with jokes and hilarities in the worst possible taste.

Because he and our captain didn't get along, he took it out on us, because he didn't dare take it out on the captain.

"Ah," he said, "you're from the 21st Company. Wait here, I'll take care of you myself." And even if you had Asiatic cholera or leprosy, he'd mark you "not sick."

It would take a whole book to tell everything that this executioner, this torturer, carries on his conscience, assuming he has one. I am just going to mention a couple of incidents which I myself witnessed.

There was in my squad Private E. . . . who fell ill. Not officially recognized as such for three days, on the fourth day he was told: "I can see that you're sick, all right, but you're in this war to die. What does it matter whether you die from a bullet or sickness? Get out, and don't let me see you again."

The sick man decided that there was no use in trying that again, and, without wanting to or being able to eat anything, he begged us to leave him alone to croak in his hole.

It must be said that, to appear at sick bay, you had to go about a kilometer to the rear, and along this kilometer you had to follow the railway line in full view of the Germans. Except for foggy days, you had to walk crouched over if you were short and on all fours if you were tall, crawling along on your long legs, sticking close to the meager embankment so as not to be caught by a bullet sent either purposely or haphazardly.

The first-aid station was in a tollhouse, two-thirds incinerated and half-demolished. The latter part of the building, without ceiling, without roof, no door, no windows, was the antechamber, the waiting room, where the sick, seated on debris or half-burnt rafters, waited for the *major* to come up from the cellar and begin his sick call in the second half of the house, which was still standing.

In my capacity as corporal-of-the-day, I often attended these sick call visits, where you could hear statements like these: "You say you have a bad heart, that it's beating too fast? It's when it stops beating that you have something wrong with you. Get out. Nothing noted. And you? No appetite? You'd like a purge? Get out of here. There's nothing better than the air of the trenches for the appetite."

And to me, one day when I had a sore throat: "Gargle with warm water and a few drops of tincture of iodine. Get lost!"

"But, *Monsieur le Major,* the tincture of iodine?"

"Find it yourself," he said, raising his voice and frowning. "We need to keep the tincture of iodine for those who are sicker than you."

As for Private E. . . ., who was suffering in the trench without any medical attention, here is what we did about him. We went to bring our good Lieutenant Cordier, commanding the company, up to date about him. He was indignant, and told us, "Bring this man to the dressing station and leave him there. They'll be obliged to take care of him."

The sick man was therefore carried to the dressing station, where the *major,* although furious, had to have him evacuated just to get him out of the way. I have no further news about him.

Later on, in my squad, there was a soldier whose name I will give because I'm sure he won't object: Lados. The cold had swollen his feet so that they were cracked all over; they formed one big wound. The *major* was content to prescribe warm baths, something impossible in the trenches. He then exempted Lados from work details, saying, "You can stand guard at the parapet."

At each change of guard we witnessed this scene: Private Lados, two hours early, heading out, his feet wrapped in rags and sandbags, hobbling on two crutches, dragging himself up to the front line where, as you can imagine, they let him take it easy.

At one sick call visit, two of his toe nails came right off in the fingers of the *major,* who said, "You still have eight, which is more than you need to walk with."

On the day of a big offensive, you could hear the *major* shouting like a madman at the stretcher-bearers, "These are just dead men, dead men that you're bringing me."

This executioner thought that they were making him waste too much time with men who were too gravely wounded.

You never saw him any place that was too heavily bombarded, and he never went out to take care of wounded men, saying, "Why risk the lives of healthy men to take care of those who are dying?"

In these circumstances, a wounded man could count himself lucky if he had friends, real friends, to take care of him and to bring him back to the rear.

But let's leave this *major* behind, this sad character who isn't worth the ink I've used in talking about him. In spite of numerous denunciations, protests, and petitions sent to high places, and a veritable indictment sent to Senator Maurice Sarraut,[6] we had to endure this slaughterer, this hog butcher with sleeve stripes and medals, until the day he got a promotion, which freed us from him. He went to ply his evil attentions at a distant hospital. They surely didn't linger too long a time there, in that hospital, the unlucky sick or wounded.

Our squad was billeted on a farm on the outskirts of the village. Under the covered passageway which linked the courtyard to the road, there were two pigsties, vacated by their usual tenants, where half the squad set up house. The other half settled in up above, once inhabited by rabbits and now by a multitude of rats who pounced on our musette bags, ravaged our knapsacks, came running and chasing each other at nighttime, dancing a farandole on top of us, obliging us to wrap our heads in our blankets and risk suffocating, to protect our noses and our ears.

I occupied the corner of a balcony by which the rats came and went, with no respect for my person. I was finally forced to yield the place to them and go spend the night on a cart in the middle of the courtyard, preferring to suffer the chills of a springtime night to contact with these nibblers.

This village, instead of being called Mazingarbe-les-Brébis, should have been called Mazingarbe-les-Rats.

This was no longer a nice little country village. It was a little mining center with a mixed-up population, then consisting of many refugees from the La Bassée and Loos regions who lived in discomfort if not in outright misery.

We took our meals by squad, in a primitive fashion, from cooking pots set up on big stones arranged in a square against one of the walls of the farm's courtyard.

From the first day there, the enticing aroma of our meals prepared southern style by our clever cook, Terrisse, attracted two kids, aged seven, two brothers who told us their lamentable story. They were from Loos, father mobilized. With their mother they had fled the German invasion, the avalanche. They had fled to Mazingarbe with no resources. The mother was then in a hospital in Béthune. They lived on charity, sleeping in an old abandoned house on a pile of old cloth bags.

During our sojourn in this village they always had their ration of soup or ratatouille, and they left the billet only to do errands for our cook.

The soldiers came to love these two lads, because they all were grown-up kids themselves. We were full of affection for these little castaways.

One day, a neighbor woman who was going to Béthune took them to see their mother, who had just died. Despite the fact that the poilu's purse was usually not very well stocked, we took up a collection in the squad, each soldier contributing his meager coin, so that the orphans could put a bouquet of flowers on their mother's grave and buy some provisions for this little journey.

What became of these shipwrecks in the frightful storm? I don't know, because we had to leave them behind when we departed, despite their moving supplications. "Take us along," they said, "We'll be good, don't leave us behind."

This separation made us think of those who had children, who perhaps would never see them again, because at this time there was no talk of furloughs, but rather of *guerre à outrance,* war to the bitter end, and continued offensives.

The inhabitants of the farm where we lodged had given us a very bad welcome from the first days, refusing to lend us a few utensils to augment our kitchen supplies, such as plates, pots, pans, etc. What's more, a kid of twelve years was always hanging around us, spying on us, watching our every move and gesture.

We soon had an explanation for this lack of hospitality. A few days before we got there, some *chasseurs-à-pied* [light infantrymen] who preceded us at this farm had seized some harmless chickens and ducks, not to mention the mysterious disappearance of a few dozen eggs.

From that came an understandable mistrust directed at us. Nevertheless, good relations didn't take much time to establish themselves. We helped out, not with the poultry, but working in the vegetable garden or in the fields. Then, once they saw how clean we were keeping the billet and how careful we were not to commit any depredations, they thought better of us than they did of the chasseurs-à-pied.

When we left, everything in the farm was laid out for us to take, and when we shook hands with these worthy folks we could see their eyes were moist.

The good humor, the lively communication, the happy spirit of southern sociability had won over these northerners, who were instinctively cold and mistrustful, but who deep down were good and honest.

Our sojourn at this farm was troubled only by a single accident. One evening we were just about to enjoy a good potful of string beans. Our Sergeant Baruteau was already holding out his mess tin when he let out a loud cry and fell to the ground, unconscious.

Completely surprised, we wondered what had hit him. We finally noticed that the casing of a shell fired at an enemy aircraft had struck the non-com on the back, raising an ugly contusion.

Luckily we were standing along a wall with an espaliered pear tree. The shell fragment had first hit a branch of the pear tree, which had slowed down its velocity. Otherwise our sergeant would have been killed outright, without having enjoyed a taste of the string beans, a rare treat in those times.

During the night of May 29–30 we left Mazingarbe, replaced by the English, who took up positions there. We weren't sure of the direction in which we would be heading. At six in the evening, the grenadiers left for the trenches in the "Ouvrages Blancs" [White Earthworks]. A battalion headed out for the front, soon afterward.

Our battalion left around midnight, doubtless following the other one. Upon leaving Mazingarbe we could see the front right nearby, a true volcano lit up by flares of every color. In the continual rumbling of cannon fire you could distinguish the crackling of machine-gun fire and grenades going off.

This was the terrible Lorette sector. Without a doubt they were going to throw us into it. But at a crossroads it was to the right—that is, to the rear— that the battalion turned. What a sigh of relief; how light our packs felt, how short the kilometers felt—kilometers which, alas, we would have to retrace, in the opposite direction, three days later. But not knowing this, we let ourselves rejoice boundlessly to be able to flee this fiery furnace.

The morning of the next day, May 30, at about 5 o'clock, we halted on the downward slope of a smiling valley, at the bottom of which was spread out, half-hidden in the greenery, a good-sized village where we would be billeted, Houdain, watered by a pretty little river, the Lavée.

At the end of the road, halfway down the slope overlooking the village, was the church, a place of devotion which attracted the faithful every year from twenty kilometers around. What brought them were a few scraps of human bone which I saw the next day, sealed up in a glass jar on the high altar.

These were the bones, it was said, of John the Baptist. I would like to have known how, from the banks of the River Jordan, they ended up in this church in the Pas-de-Calais, but no one could satisfy my curiosity.

Stretched out in ditches along the side of the road, lying on dewy grass, we patiently awaited word of our assigned lodgings.

We had to wait quite a while. The time hadn't come to figure out where to put these vulgar poilus. But for *Messieurs les officiers* it was a different story. For each one they had to find a comfortable bed and a bedroom worthy of welcoming him. No officer could ever share a bunk with a soldier without dishonoring himself.

Finally we entered the village, and our section was led to a sheepfold which had been abandoned because it was no longer inhabitable by sheep. Built of straw and wattle, it looked like it would collapse at the slightest puff of wind. Luckily there weren't any vigorous winds blowing there.

In spite of the risk of collapse, and the drafts which blew through the building like a dozen ventilators, we installed ourselves the best we could. To make things worse, the sheepfold was at the end of a road crisscrossed day and night by autos and trucks of all kinds, which paraded with a thunderous racket, making any sleep impossible unless you were deaf as a woodcock.

But what had we come to Houdain to do? It certainly wasn't someone's pious plan to come here to venerate the precious relics of John the Baptist, as venerable as they might be. Had we come for a nice long stretch of rest, to take a little vacation in this charming valley? That idea was soon corrected.

During the morning of June 1, the order came to leave that evening for the front. Our big rest was finished. It had lasted two days.

At about 5 o'clock in the afternoon, we left Houdain and followed, in the opposite direction, the same road we had taken the day before yesterday.

This incoherence by the high command cost our poor legs fifty kilometers. But the fatigue of others didn't count for anything.

At 11 at night we arrived at Sains-en-Gohelle, at the company town of the coal mine, a vast agglomeration of several hundred charming little red-brick houses, each one surrounded with a pretty garden and a courtyard.

But these lodgings weren't for us, who arrived like intruders. At this late hour no one was waiting up for us, nothing had been prepared to welcome us. Waiting for daybreak, the companies clustered along the streets which separated the ranks of *corons* [miners' red-brick row houses].

This didn't suit everyone's taste. An almost-Peyriacois comrade, from the neighboring village of Trausse, made the grave mistake of saying in a loud voice what all of us were quietly thinking. It was comrade Paul Comps, who cried out, "I think we're commanded by a gang of . . ."

This statement, sacrilegious to discipline and militarism, reached the ear of a non-com who probably thought the same as Private Comps but who felt it was in his best interest to report these words to the captain. The captain leapt to his feet in indignation and did his duty in leading the delinquent before a court-martial, which condemned him to two years in prison and separation from the regiment.

That taught him to keep his thoughts to himself.

The next day, at roll call, they announced our departure for the trenches that very evening. We stayed in bunches along the avenues. No use seeking out comfortable billets. Some nice ones surely awaited us, where we were going.

The Lorette Charnel House:
June 2–July 2, 1915

1915. Lorette sector. The armored shelters of Aix-Noulette.
Appalling visions. Massacre of the 21st Company.
Death of Commandant Nadaud.

Lorette—a sinister name, evoking scenes of horror, gloomy woods, sunken roads, plateaus and ravines taken and retaken twenty times, where for months, night after night, we cut each other's throats, massacred each other incessantly. We made that little corner of the earth a human charnel house, by the criminal obstinacy of our top brass, who knew quite well that nothing decisive would come from this petty style of fighting a war, these nasty little attacks. But they imagined that in this war of attrition, this cruel game, the Germans would be the first ones to be worn down.

"*Je les grignote* [I'm nibbling away at them]," says paunchy old Joffre—a phrase that the press picks up like a rare pearl, and this futile, bloody offensive dragged on for several months.

On June 2, 1915, at 8 in the evening, resigned, sullen, without enthusiasm but without useless complaining, we set off for the trenches, which weren't very far off.

Traveling a few kilometers from Sains-en-Gohelle we arrived at the mining town of Bully-Grenay, which still had almost all its inhabitants, even though it was close to the front line of trenches. The mine still operated, thanks to the Boches, who no doubt didn't want to destroy it so they could make use of it later. But the area around the train station and the road we headed down were often bombarded.

After a few hundred more meters we reached the nearly deserted village of Aix-Noulette, the last vestige of civilization. From here on, all was desolation.

At the entrance to Aix we followed a large boyau, which led us to a branch of a sunken road near the little ruined village of Noulette. We had to stay here for three days, in reserve. This was no doubt to get us used to the cannon's roar, the musty smell of rotten flesh, the fat venomous flies, the ticks, the worms, the rats, everything unclean and impure that swarms and flourishes in a charnel house.

Along the embankment of the sunken road, the engineers had carved dugouts covered with sheets of iron, each meant to hold a dozen men at most—but where forty of us were piled up.

Of course, you couldn't lie down, or hardly even crouch down with your legs curled up, and you couldn't move without provoking howls of complaint from your neighbors. You couldn't get out of this stuffy hole without stepping on feet, legs, and knees, and what little air there was inside was poisonous. It was hot enough to hatch chickens in there. To make things worse, legions of fleas and ticks climbed up the straw, which covered the floor, and onto our legs, our arms, our backbones, leading to uncontrollable itching.

And to think that, before the war, I pitied the poor gypsies who camped outside our village. I won't feel sorry for them anymore, no matter how shabby their wagons might be. Their fate is enviable, compared to what we went through.

But why, one might ask, didn't you go outside, to be more comfortable? Well, sure. An accursed German battery had sighted its 105's right on this road, in enfilade. If someone ventured outside, even hugging the embankment, it would unleash a blast from a 105, and sometimes a volley. These gunners weren't stingy with their shells. Even without any strollers on the deserted road, they would toss a few shells over, just to remind us how vigilant they were, always ready to yank the lanyards.

During the day, a shell hit the entrance to the bunker next to ours, wounding five soldiers, one mortally. That night, the German guns ceased firing, so we were put to work on various tasks. I got the order to take my squad and dig some latrines, deep along the embankment of the road.

Captain Hudelle came to see us and told us not to take this ridiculous task as a joke, and that we needed to be finished with it by dawn.

"But it won't be forty-eight hours before these latrines are filled up by shellfire," I said, "and they're too far from the dugouts. Guys will want to go somewhere closer, in a shell hole."

"It doesn't matter," said Hudelle, "it's an order. If it's not finished by tomorrow morning, you'll keep working on it in the daylight."

"It must be that old cow Commandant Nadaud who gave that order," said the *ravitailleur* [rationer] Terrisse.

"The smarter they seem, the stupider they turn out to be," said the gravedigger candidate of Peyriac, Jordy.

"You know the fable of the animals who were sick with the plague," said the schoolteacher Mondiès. "Well, our bosses won't all die of it, but they'll all get sick, not with the plague but with stupidity.[1] As for me, I'm not lifting a shovelful of dirt," he added.

A sergeant came and requisitioned three men from me, to take some materials up to the front line. They came back in the daytime, exhausted.

Then I had to supply a man to go help a sailor posted in the woods with a Gatling gun. Lapeyre, from Citou, volunteered for this mysterious mission.

At midnight, Terrisse, escorted by his sidekick Ayrix, headed off with his food containers and his portable kitchen, for Aix.

You'll understand that the work on these latrines hadn't made much progress by the time the protective, nocturnal darkness began to dissipate, so we prudently made our way back to our stuffy hole.

An hour later a sergeant appeared:

"Corporal Barthas, take your squad and finish the latrines immediately!"

"Is it the captain who gave you this order?"

"Yes, because the commandant insists that the work be finished."

The whole squad groaned.

"Well, sergeant, I refuse to risk human lives for such a ridiculous, unimportant task."

The sergeant left, fuming. Five minutes later he came back, even more in a rage. The captain, when he heard about my refusal, had ordered the sergeant himself to make my squad finish up those damned latrines, sending men out two by two, taking turns.

The sergeant forced me to pick out the first two, from the 13th Squad. They were the two Peyriacois, Allard and Gils, who refused right away, arguing that they were sick. Under threat of being sent immediately to the care of that angel of death, the medical officer Torrès, they took up their picks and shovels to continue their latrine digging. But soon the shells started falling on the road, and they dropped their tools and rejoined us in the shelter.

For the rest of the day they didn't bother us anymore about those latrines, and for good reason. We had to leave, that very evening, for the front lines, to relieve some units which had been sorely tested. That was why our reserve duty was cut short.

Before leaving, I went to shake the hand of the Peyriacois Joseph Jammes, who was in the 22nd Company, occupying armored shelters like our own. I didn't see him again, as he was wounded the next day.

At 9 at night we left this suffocating, lousy hellhole with few regrets, and made our way to an even worse place. But you could say that our section was privileged, because we went up there in reserve. Right away we found ourselves in a forest of cut-down, twisted, uprooted trees; in this inextricable mess we could barely follow the trace of what looked like a communication trench.

Suddenly a volley of shells struck the woods, with a frightful racket. Clutching the ground, trembling with fear, we were sure that our final hour had come, all the more because, right in front of us, we heard the cries and moans of wounded men. It was like being in a calm in the midst of the most furious storm. Why not take advantage, and flee?

How long the minutes are, in times like these! Finally, after having gone back and forth more than ten times about why we weren't going forward, we resumed our march.

A hundred meters farther, still in the woods, we relieved the section which had been waiting impatiently. Right when they were leaving, shells exploded above our heads, and one of their men was killed outright. Our section, just arriving, already had six wounded.

They advised us to watch carefully, to not shoot, to not even speak, so as not to reveal our positions, and to hide ourselves completely by day.

That's what you call being in reserve—lost in the woods, and surrounded by Boches on all sides!

We spent the night without incident, crouched in hiding behind the trunks of fallen trees. At dawn we ceased our vigils; everyone sought out a hole, a shelter, a refuge in which to hide. We let the cannons do the talking.

Why are we wandering around like this, far from any help, in a wood occupied by the Germans? Scattered like we were, a Boche sergeant with four men could have rounded us up as easily as scooping up snails.

Along a small slope we found two shelters, side by side, made from tree limbs and planks, in which the 13th Squad had found refuge—pretty miserable shelters, which kept out the sunlight and the man-eating flies.

That day, June 5, was one of the bloodiest days of this futile battle of Artois.

The French communiqué of the following day claimed that our artillery had fired 500,000 projectiles. I can speak for those who lived through that hell, when I say that the German artillery gave us back just as many.

A million cannon rounds in twenty-four hours! On just a few square kilometers of territory.

Of this fantastic number of shells of every caliber, maybe 50,000 or 100,000 fell right in the woods where we were.

Explosions filled the air, without ceasing. Strange, sharp, piercing sounds, first the whistling, sometimes like a cat meowing, then crashing down like a steady rain of steel.

We stayed, for the whole stifling June day, flattened out next to each other, with spirits numbed, our brains gripped with extreme nervous tension. From time to time, from shelter to shelter, we called out to each other, asking if anyone was wounded.

It's truly a miracle that, in the midst of this avalanche of iron, none of us had the slightest scratch.

No matter how skeptical you might be, it's times like this that make you wonder if some mysterious, supernatural force isn't watching over us.

My memory of this day is spotty, and I have only a few vague recollections of it. First of all, a dead French soldier a few steps away from us. Lying on his back, he looks like he is sleeping. This sight bothered us, and in spite of the danger, Allard went out to throw a blanket over the body.

A moment later a huge explosion, right nearby, woke us up from our torpor.

A shell had just dug an enormous hole, exhuming a corpse and blasting it into pieces, which immediately drew thousands of ravenous flies.

Oh, those flies from the Lorette charnel house, which reached back way behind the front lines. What intense disgust they inspired among all of us. They got into everything—canteens, mess kits, pots and pans—swarming incessantly all around us, whether we were alive or dead, like bees going from flower to flower.

At twilight there was a slight letup. We hadn't seen each other since morning. What has happened to our comrades? We hear the voice of our young Sergeant Darles, calling us. We have to hoist our packs and follow him, we're rejoining the company. There's nothing to bother us anymore. Under our own artillery fire, the Boches have abandoned the woods, which I'm told later is called the Bois Carré [Square Woods]. I wasn't able to appreciate its geometric shape, whether it was square, round, or rectangular.

The fellow who guided us said that, at three in the afternoon, our 21st Company had attacked, with Captain Hudelle at the head of the troops. The Germans—from the Imperial Guard, if you please—were as stunned as raw recruits, and thirty-two of them were taken prisoner, while others scrambled away from the Frenchmen bursting into their trenches.

We struggled to keep up with the sergeant, but it wasn't easy. No natural cataclysm could have wreaked the frightful chaos which we saw in those gloomy places.

We left the woods, and entered a labyrinth of communication trenches, filled up in many places by shell blasts.

Suddenly, without warning, a couple of timed-fuse shells burst right over our heads. Sergeant Darles had an arm pierced by shrapnel; streams of blood gushed out of it, and he ran off howling, out of his mind. Our guide, also wounded, disappeared too. We were left to wander aimlessly through the deserted trenches. We came across the body of a fellow from our company, trampled to death—I learned the next day—by a gang of cowards barreling through the trenches in a mad panic.

At nightfall, we rejoined the company. Standing in the middle of the trench, Captain Hudelle, victor over the Imperial Guard, conqueror of the Fond de Buval, crowned with glory, stopped us. I was about to shake his hand and congratulate him, but in a dry voice he said to us: "Where are you going like that?"

"But isn't it by your order that we've come up here?" I said, puzzled.

"Not at all!" he replied, in a lousy mood. "Who brought you here?"

"Sergeant Darles. But he was wounded on the way here, and took off. Aw, what the hell! Since there's a misunderstanding, we'll rejoin our section."

Since there weren't any more Germans in the wood, I was thinking, that will make for a quiet night in comparison.

"Not so fast," said the captain, annoyed. "Stay here, there's work to do. To-night you're going to dig a communication trench to link this trench to the one we've taken. So that tomorrow, you hear, we can move around these trenches without being seen."

So we went to work, but what an awful night it was. The bombardment continued, as heavy as that during the day. We were dazed, blinded by the lightning flashes of cannons and shells. Maybe a hundred times that night we threw ourselves to the ground when shellfire spattered around us.

What a contrast: such a storm in the midst of calm, of the serenity of a glorious summer night!

Daybreak. The sun rises, indifferent to the field of horror. Everywhere we see nothing but cadavers and shapeless human remains, pasturage for the rats which were more courageous than the crows, whose fear kept them away.

Captain Hudelle didn't look very happy about our work, even though one could move along the trench, at a crouch, without being seen. He urged me to continue the work, but I maintained that the men were literally exhausted by what they had just accomplished, and he didn't insist.

"Anyway," I said to him, "neither Poincaré[2] nor General Joffre is going to be coming to the Fond de Buval trench, today."

That afternoon, an ugly rumor ran along the trench: At 3 p.m. the 21st Company was going on the attack, once more.

In the face of energetic protests from our captain, who claimed that his men were exhausted, Commandant Nadaud came up to the front line, his pipe in his mouth and his cane in his hand.

With a map before him, he asked, "Where is this trench that you took yesterday?"

"It's right here—You're standing in it!" replied Hudelle.

Squinting at the map, the commandant said, "I thought you had gotten farther than that. Today you must get up there, on that crest. Let's go, Hudelle, I'm ordering you to do it."

Real courage, for a leader, isn't blindly executing every order that's given to him. It's refusing to execute that order when his conscience tells him to, to save human lives from being sacrificed uselessly.

In a calm but firm voice, our captain declared that he wasn't going to make his men advance, having asked a supreme effort from them the day before. It was another company's turn to attack today.

During this confrontation a frightful bombardment opened up, and a shell falling right onto the trench wounded Captain Hudelle in the shoulder and Commandant Nadaud in the thigh.

At the commandant's orders, just one section had gone over the top, out of the trench, but it was immediately hit by machine-gun fire, and those who survived had to flatten themselves in shell holes until nightfall.

At quarter to three, our section chief, Lieutenant Col, had us hoist our packs and make ready to head for the front line, fifty meters away, once the attack was launched. Up ahead were the shock troops; our job, in the second wave, was pursuit.

We noticed that Sergeant Baruteau was missing. "I know where he is," I said to the lieutenant. "Go get him!" I was told. I had spotted him a little bit to the rear. Stretched out in a little shelter, a niche in the sandbags, he was sleeping like a baby. I grabbed his shoulder and gave him a shake, saying, "How can you think of sleeping at a time like this—we're about to attack! We've hoisted our packs, and the commandant is right there!" Sergeant Baruteau got up, pale, haggard, like a condemned man whom the warden is awakening the morning of his execution. In fact, he could see himself in front of a court-martial and a firing squad for hiding at the moment of attack.

We were hurrying back to our section when, from a communication trench to our right, a stampede of shirkers from a neighboring regiment made us turn back, like it or not. They were shouting, wildly, "The Boches are here! They're coming!" Right at this moment the cannon fire seemed to have reached its paroxysm, which made their terror even worse.

Panic is contagious. Followed by Sergeant Baruteau, I fled with all the speed that my long legs could muster. Soon I was exhausted, out of breath, and I had to stop. But the memory of my trampled comrade, the day before, spurred me on to the extreme limit of my strength.

We passed through a connecting trench where individual holes had been dug in the side walls. I stuffed myself into one of them, and the sergeant did the same. The many shirkers passed by and lost themselves in the woods where we had been the day before, and several were killed or wounded by shellfire.

I was very surprised not to see the Germans right on their heels. But this was just a mindless panic which, for some of the shirkers, had its epilogue in a court-martial. A corporal from our company got as far as Béthune, where he was arrested. The judges were willing to attribute his conduct to a momentary lapse of reason, and he got off with a light sentence. Less fortunate was a soldier from our regiment, who hid for several days in the Bois de Noulette. He was condemned to death, and legally murdered by twelve French bullets at Bully-Grenay.

It was said out loud that, for the case of this unfortunate trooper, the judges were inclined to be indulgent, but our odious new captain, Monsieur Cros-Mayrevielle, from Carcassonne, acting in the function of police chief, demanded the strict application of the military code. But I don't have any proof of this, since the public wasn't admitted to this parody of justice.

Meanwhile we weren't without worries about what might come from our own absence at the time of an attack, and we quickly rejoined our section, when along the route, or rather along the trench, we met up with an unfortunate fellow who had gone mad and was being carried by four of his comrades. Oh, those haggard eyes, that convulsed, terrified, grimacing face, which had lost all human expression. What horrible scenes had those eyes seen, so that madness invaded the brain?

To live in such a frightful nightmare—is that where we were all going to end up?

We rejoined our comrades, who still had packs hoisted and bayonets fixed, awaiting specific orders to move up. At this moment a ravitailleur arrived with two jerricans of hooch, to give out immediately. Each of us held out our canteens, but many sniffed at it with distrust; this unexpected distribution just before an attack appeared suspicious. Jordy declared that "this smells like a pharmacy," and Tort, from Rieux, said, "It's ether!"

Mondiès watered the ground with the contents of his canteen. "It's poison!" he shouted angrily. "They want to make us crazy. But for two sous' worth of *gniole* [hooch], they're not going to make a killer out of me!"

But here's a runner from the front lines, dispatch in hand. We assail him with questions: "What's going on? Have we attacked?"

"Yes," he gasped, "I think we went out, but the captain and the commandant are wounded. I'm on my way to the first-aid station to get a medic."

Hearing these words, I threw my pack on the ground and ran toward the front line, to find out how seriously my friend Hudelle was wounded. In the trench I met a soldier from the company who was dragging along a wounded man.

"What the hell are you going to do up there, in the trench? It's terrible!" they told me.

I kept running, but before getting there I ran right into Captain Hudelle himself, who was heading to the first-aid post with the help of *caporal-fourrier* [quartermaster-corporal] Faurie.

His jacket had been torn in many places by shell fragments, and blood flowed from his left shoulder. In a few words he sketched out the scene which I described above—his clash with the commandant who, wounded in the thigh, couldn't leave the trench.

I offered to accompany him to the first-aid station, but he told me not to bother, since his wound didn't appear to be serious.

"You'll come back to the 280th," I said to him.

"Yes," he promised, "I'll do whatever I can."

But he wouldn't come back. Once healed, he rejoined the 80th [Regular] Infantry Regiment. Besides, at the first-aid station, he met our Colonel Poujal, who told him brutally, "Well, you're wounded, you're lucky, you're going to a battalion of chasseurs-à-pied."

That would teach our captain—for punishing men who missed a roll call to go to Easter Mass, for being so bold as to celebrate the First of May, for wanting too much to keep his men alive.

Before leaving, Captain Hudelle paid a hundred francs for an extra ration of wine for the men of his company.

Saddened to take leave of my friend Hudelle, I reached the trench which the Imperial Guard had held, just a day ago. Yes, it was horrible. Let's say, first of all, that it didn't look at all like a trench. Daily bombardments had turned it into a volcanic crevasse, a gaping fissure in the earth, very deep in certain spots, very wide or narrow in other places. There were even places where you couldn't see any trace of a trench anymore.

Where the connecting trench joined in, an unfortunate fellow was stretched out, decapitated by a shell, just as if he'd been guillotined. Beside him, another was frightfully mutilated. I took a couple of steps to the left. I saw, as if hallucinating, a pile of corpses, almost all of them German, that they had started to bury right in the trench, which had been made quite wide at this point.

At the entrance to the connecting trench, leaning on the slope, was a young German who looked like he was asleep. There was no visible wound. Death had brushed him with its wing, and preserved the smile which still marked his youthful face.

"There's no one here but the dead!" I exclaimed. Retracing my path, I headed to the right, where I finally found some living souls, with haggard eyes, leaning on each other in threes and fours like frightened beasts, silent, not even looking around. They seemed indifferent to the fierce cannonades, which hadn't ceased.

But what is this? Has Hell opened up under our feet? Are we right at the rim of a furious volcano? The trench is filled with flames, with sparks, with bitter smoke, the air is unbreathable. I hear hissing, crackling, and alas, yes, the cries of pain. Sergeant Vergès has scorched eyes. At my feet two miserable creatures are rolling on the ground, their clothes, their hands, their faces on fire, like human torches. And in the trench everything is on fire—blankets, tent cloths, sandbags. The Germans had just fired some sort of incendiary liquid on us.[3] What's more, a pack of signal fuses has just ignited, and that's what's causing the most noise, the most sparks, the most smoke.

My two arms protecting my face, I flee from this Hell, my senses completely overturned. I rejoin my squad. They tell me that my eyes stared vacantly, wildly, and that I spoke incoherently, but that didn't last, and I quickly got out of it.

Lieutenant Col sent us up to reinforce the front line. My squad took a position on the right of the communication trench, and another one was on the left.

At the middle of the place we occupied, sitting up against the slope of the trench, was our Commandant Nadaud, wounded in the thigh. He looked like he was really suffering; he didn't say a word.

The medical-officer-executioner Torrès had decreed that the stretcher-bearers wouldn't come to fetch any wounded from our trench, even at night—it was too dangerous. Too bad for anyone who fell. He'd be lucky if he had a devoted friend to carry or drag him to the first-aid station. Lucky too if he had a good comrade to staunch his wound, because you wouldn't find a nurse or a medic there to do it.

For the commandant, and for him alone, a medic came up to do a quick dressing. I have to say that before he left, he took the time to look at the other wounded around him. Then he headed off, promising the commandant that he would come back to get him, as soon as night fell.

Commandant Nadaud was detested by his men, so his sad fate left them indifferent. Nobody paid any attention to him. Only Sergeant Faure, consumed with ambition for an adjutant's stripe, made any effort for him, no doubt in hope of getting compensated for it. He pulled blankets from packs to make the wounded man more comfortable.

Once the commandant fainted. The sergeant asked if anyone had any peppermint schnapps or *eau de mélisse* [nonalcoholic lemon-and-orange-flavored drink]. No one answered. Furious, the sergeant dug through packs and confiscated a flask of schnapps from Jordy—Jordy, whom, not a week earlier at Houdain, the commandant had wanted to throw into prison for a week for not having jumped to salute him quickly enough. That night, the medic and two stretcher-bearers came and took the commandant away. While the bearers were putting him onto the stretcher, the medic, visibly frightened, crouched down next to me in a sharp angle of the trench. "What are those smaller explosions right nearby?" he asked.

"Those are grenades which the Boches are throwing at us. They're hiding in shell holes."

"The hell they are," said the medic, less and less reassured, "and that's pretty dangerous, isn't it?"

"We've had a few wounded by grenades. Rives almost had his head taken off by one." (That's Rives the roadworker, from Mas-Cabardès.)

The medic didn't want any more of this, and he urged the stretcher-bearers to get moving. I'm not sure if he even waited for them. He had asked me for someone to hold up the wounded man. I had given him Gabriel Gils, the strongest of the squad, and I told him under my breath: "Take your time. Don't hurry back. Find a hole somewhere and stick yourself in it. As long as you're back here by daylight, that's fine." In fact he didn't reappear until dawn.

As for the commandant, he died the next day.

"Good riddance," said the ravitailleur Terrisse.

That was his funeral prayer.

The Lorette sector. At the Fond de Buval. A lively night.
The Fosse aux Loups. Second bloodletting.
The death of schoolteacher Mondiès, from Pépieux.

A few days later, the medic who had come to take care of Commandant Nadaud was decorated with the Croix de Guerre, for going to the aid of a wounded officer under fire. That was fine, but it is worth noting that the medic was following orders. And if he got a Croix de Guerre for staying such a brief moment in this trench, what did those who actually took that trench deserve to get, not to mention those who had to live there, work and fight there, day and night?

This was a tragic night. Bombs and grenades rained all around us. We could hardly answer back, because we had only a very small supply of these devices, and not many of us knew how to throw them.

There were continual alerts—true or false—and an excessive waste of cartridges. All this to kill nothing more than a rat, since I don't think we were dealing with more than a handful of daring Boches who had crept up to throw bombs at us.

One moment, Tort, from Rieux, called out to me in a half-crazed voice: "Barthas! There's a Boche heading toward us, there, a few steps away!" Indeed, despite the darkness, I could make out a man bounding toward our trench from one shell hole to another. He was no doubt coming to toss some grenades right at us. Instinctively Tort and I fired our rifles at this character who could have only the worst intentions for us, but in the darkness we couldn't aim properly and we missed him. He could have at least taken fright and turned tail, but no, at two paces from us he stood up, his bayoneted rifle at full length, and launched himself right into the trench, between Tort and me. We were dumbfounded. But what a surprise—this wasn't one of Goethe's compatriots. It was a soldier from our company, Delsol, from Homps. He explained to us that he had been part of the platoon which had gone out on patrol. He had to wait in a shell hole until it was dark, then he tried to reach our lines, lost his way, and reached our trench by chance, where he almost got himself shot or skewered by us.

About midnight the cry went up, "To arms!" It looked liked the Boches were counterattacking, to retake this fine trench for the Kaiser.

As for me, I didn't see a thing, but all of us blasted away pell-mell from the edge of the parapet. The guy next to me, Argence, from Quillan, had his wrist shot through, right when he was firing. The blood spurted out like a fountain and I was covered in it. The wounded man thought he was a goner, and started to scream bloody murder. I yanked off his cravat and squeezed it around his arm as hard as I could. The hemorrhaging stopped, and he was able to reach the first-aid station. I don't think he exaggerated when he said later on, in a letter home, that I had saved his life.

Lying stretched out on the ground at our feet, moaning and unrecognizable, were the two soldiers we had seen in flames. Their skin was completely black. One died that night. The other, delirious, sang the songs of his childhood, conversed with his wife and his mother, spoke about his village. Hearing this, we all had tears in our eyes.

"They're worse than murderers," cried an anonymous voice in the dark, "to let these guys die without giving them a bit of care."

"Ah, if we weren't all cowards," said a well-known voice, that of Terrisse, "those who wanted this war would be here in our place. Then we'd see!"

"It's too late now," I chimed in. "It's before things start that we need people to see clearly. Let's hope that those who get out of this will remember that, at least."

"And you," said Ferié to me, "you who are writing about the life we're leading here, don't hide anything. You've got to tell it all."

"Yes, yes, everything, everything. We'll be there as your witnesses. Maybe we won't all die here," added the others.

"They won't believe us," said Mondiès, "or maybe they won't even give a damn."

In vain we put the dying man alongside the trench wall so he wouldn't get trampled. He kept rolling right into the middle. Worn down by fatigue and the need to sleep, I slumped down for a moment. I was leaning on the dead man, and the dying man was leaning on me. I slept between a corpse and a near-corpse. It didn't bother me at all. In the face of certain trials, the heart loses all sensation.

I was pulled from my sleep by the arrival of a soldier from another company, who was looking for his brother who, someone had told him, had been killed. Leaning over the burned soldier, he couldn't tell if it was his brother. "Joseph! Joseph! Answer me! It's Pierre, your brother, calling you!" But it was in vain. He was speaking to someone who had lost his mind.

The company no longer had any officers. The only one left, Sublieutenant Col, had just missed being buried alive by a shell which filled up the trench where he'd been crouching. With much effort, very badly bruised, he dug himself out of the sandbags which had collapsed all around him. Unfortunately for him, he didn't have the slightest scratch, and he hadn't lost a drop of blood. Here's how it was for him: You're squashed flat as a herring, all your ribs are broken, and you don't even get a look of pity. But your skin gets a little scrape, and you lose a few drops of blood—not enough to fill a thimble—then you're a hero, a martyr, you've paid your debt to the fatherland, you're crowned with glory and honor.

The colonel frowned when he heard about Sublieutenant Col's mishap, and he suspected that he faked this accident. So Col had to stay in the trench at the Fond de Buval. The next day they took his command away, and transferred him to another battalion.

The fate of the 21st Company was now in the hands of Adjutant Caminade. He was an old lifer of a non-com, a hard-bitten maniac who had just earned his lieutenant's stripes that very night. Revolver in hand, he blocked the way of anyone who was seized with the understandable desire to escape from the trench.

He did such a good job, and kept us so busy, that he scared off any desire on the part of the Germans to try to retake the trench by a surprise attack. Thanks to him, all the wounded were evacuated.

At the first-aid station, the medical officer–executioner Torrès shouted, "But they're just bringing me dead bodies, dead bodies. Don't bring me any more!" Fine words for the wounded to hear.

When Caminade heard about this, he said he would send Torrès even more dead bodies, to make him even madder.

By daybreak, all we had left in the trench was the blackened, unknown soldier, still delirious, but the cool of the morning must have calmed his fever because he was almost quiet.

The mess crew brought coffee and we savored it with delight, when the dying man called out to us, "And what about me? Aren't you going to give me any?"

We all looked at him, dumbfounded. We expected him to step over into the next world at any moment, and then we would toss his body over the parapet. And here he is, claiming his share of juice!

He drank three mugfuls, and also had a slug of hooch, which livened him up a bit. I ran up to Adjutant Caminade, who, thinking that I was making a break for it, leveled his revolver at me.

"Hey, no kidding," I said, and I told him about this resurrection. He assigned four men to carry the poor devil to Torrès. I don't know what became of him.

June 7 was rather calm compared to the days before. First came some good news: We were going to be relieved the next night. Then the bad news: We had to attack, at three in the afternoon.

"That will be an attack by ghosts," said Mondiès. In fact, we looked like ghosts—haggard, ragged, skin the color of dirt—worn out by several nights without sleep, by tough work details, by the anguish which gnawed at all of us, by bad food, by thirst which burned our gullets. Yes, we looked like ghosts who had risen from the grave.

Sure, the cooks and ration squads did their best to bring us decent food. But try eating a square meal when the air is polluted with the odor of rotting flesh from the hundreds of cadavers which surrounded us, putrefying in the hot June sun. Almost all of us wore a strip of cloth with a little sack of camphor under our noses, and a handkerchief in front of our faces to keep the flies away.

You'll understand how we gulped down our food, and swilled our drinks. All we asked for was some kind of beverage, or just plain water. And this last day we had a nice surprise: with great effort and at much danger to themselves, moving around in the open, they brought each section a keg of beer. As a barrel-maker I was assigned the task of tapping our keg, and finally we were really able to quench our thirst.

As for the announced attack, it didn't take place. Our bosses realized, just in time, that our strength in numbers was insufficient for us to have any chance of success. That consideration alone is what made up their minds. Finally, to our great joy, our relief was announced for nine o'clock that evening.

At the appointed hour, and even before, we were as ready as we could be, but all through the night no one showed up to relieve us. Caminade was furious; he sent runner after runner, but no one could find any trace of the other battalion of the 280th which was supposed to replace us. Finally at dawn, just when we were beginning to give up hope, our replacements, who had gotten lost and wandered around all night, arrived to deliver us.

We didn't go far, about a kilometer back from the front line, to a place called the "Fosse aux Loups" [Wolves' Ditch]. It was nothing more than a wide, steep-sided stretch of road which the German artillery spotters hadn't yet fixed their sights on.

Indeed, when you left the furnace of the Fond de Buval, any place would seem like a garden of delights. All the same, exposed to a scorching sun, without any shelter, you couldn't miss the fact that the slightest comfort was lacking.

When we complained that there weren't any shelters for us to sleep in, Caminade mocked us, saying, "My little ones, here the nights aren't made for sweet dreams. I've already gotten my orders. We're on work detail every night." Caminade could make fun of us, all right; at the end of the road there was a nice dugout where he could snore away to his heart's content.

That's what they call being at rest. Each night we went out with our picks and shovels, through artillery barrages, to repair the day's damage to the trenches caused by shellfire. It was convict's work, and we grumbled about it but someone had to do it. At all cost we had to maintain the trenches leading up to the front lines, so that the ration squads, stretcher-bearers, and relief units could get through. To encourage us they told us that soon we'd be heading to the rear for some real rest. But once again they were deceiving us. On June 11, at nightfall, we headed back up the road toward the sinister Fond de Buval.

This time, we were a few hundred meters to the left, toward Angres. We didn't gain much from this shift in position; we were in the same hellhole.

At night, we stayed in squads at the forward listening posts. By day, due to the violent bombardments, we left only a few sentries at the front line, and each squad went to safe ground as best it could, fleeing the shellfire like hunted animals.

On June 13, at dawn, the 13th Squad had just spent the night at the front line, repairing an earth slide, and we had just installed ourselves in a rather deep stretch of the communication trench. We didn't have anything to do until evening, when we would have to go back to our ditch digging on these roads to Calvary, or occupy some listening post at the farthest limit of our lines.

Around us was complete solitude. Frightened by the number of our casualties, the bosses now left only a few scattered squads in the forward zone, simply to provide surveillance, abandoned to whatever our fate might be.

The men of Squad 13, after having ditched all their gear, set about writing, reading, sewing. A few had already stretched out and dozed off, when suddenly a couple of shells exploded nearby. We didn't pay them much attention. "Here come the wake-up snacks again," someone said.

In a brief instant, new explosions, this time closer at hand. Like beasts who sniff danger in the air, some of us stood up right away. We knew that these weren't your cheap, run-of-the-mill shells, but perhaps 150's, just one of which, well aimed, could wipe out our whole squad.

Three or four minutes passed, and then in the distance we could hear the dull thuds, like the sound of a gong, of shells being shot from their cannons, which then landed loudly about eighty meters from where we were, a few seconds later.

Had some German artillery spotter found us and pointed us out to his idle gunners? It's possible. Our opinions were split: some wanted to get out right away, others thought that here at the end of the trench we were safe.

But throughout the course of this war I had, on many occasions, a mysterious intuition, an instinct about the imminence of danger. At this very moment, from the very bottom of my being, a voice told me that it was time to flee.

"Everybody pick up your gear and get ready to move out. Stand up! Get a move on!" I cried out to those who didn't answer my first appeal. I had never given orders with such vehemence. Seeing that the whole squad was ready, I waited for the next sound of firing. It arrived like thunder, then the shells crashed down thirty meters from us. Chunks of stone, of iron, of earth whistled over our heads. Great vaults of black smoke obscured the sunlight. No doubt, they were after us. They were doing us quite an honor.

"Head to the right," I shouted. "Save yourselves! Hurry up! Let's go, move out!" Like the captain of a sinking ship, I had to be the last one to leave. When you accept a promotion, even as slight as that of corporal, you have to accept the responsibility and step up to the task at hand, even at the risk of your own life.

My friends Gils and Allard yelled to me, as they fled, "Mondiès doesn't want to come! Go get him!" The schoolteacher from Pépieux was at the other end of the squad. In three bounds I was on him. Tort was still there, urging him one last time to follow us. When I appeared, Tort took off.

Mondiès, hunched over, was quietly writing a letter, just as calm as if he were at his desk in the schoolroom, in front of his class. It seemed to mean nothing to him that a battery of heavy-caliber guns had trained their sights on him.

"Well, you're crazy, Mondiès," I said to him, "You want to get yourself blown to pieces?"

"What the hell," he said, "Maybe you'll get killed where you're going."

"No," I begged him. "They've been moving steadily in this direction, each time they fire. The next one is right in line with the one before. It'll land right here! Come on!"

Mondiès shook his head, and continued to write. Right across from him crouched a soldier from the other squad, the 14th, which formed the half-section with ours. He was called Laffont, from Cavanac. A tailor, he was sewing his overcoat. Why, for his own sake, hadn't he followed his own squad, instead of staying with us? I have no idea. I asked him if he didn't want to follow us. "No," he said. "If Mondiès stays, I stay."

In the face of such stubbornness, I had to save my own skin. Already the others, dragging their gear, bent double, were out of danger. I had hardly gotten sixty meters when I heard the frightful detonation of the shell, which landed right where we had been. I barely had time to hit the ground, to avoid the blast of the explosion. Then, getting up, I bolted for the spot where the squad had stopped.

A few more salvos landed, and then the Boches turned the mouths of their cannon elsewhere.

The habitual cannonade lit up the crests. The ravines and the woods were filled with whiffs of black, gray, greenish, and white smoke, which mixed as they floated up in the air, and made an increasingly opaque fog, forming a halo around the sun.

The layers of air were shaken by a hundred thunderclaps sounding at once, and in the midst of this rumbling you could distinctly hear the shells bursting in the Fond de Buval, resonating like a death knell which echoed through the ravines.

But after a while you ignore it, and there were those who slept, snoring away, dreaming to the sound of this infernal music. The shells had to be landing right next to you before you would get excited about them.

Meanwhile we were very worried about what had happened to our comrades

Mondiès and Laffont. As for me, I reproached myself for not having the will-power and the energy to make them follow us. Nevertheless my conscience couldn't really hold me to blame. But they could be lying wounded out there, needing our help.

I asked for a volunteer to come with me. Ayrix, from Narbonne, stepped forward. He was illiterate, and Mondiès had written his letters home to his family. With pick and shovel we made our way back to the place from which the shells had chased us. When we were twenty paces from it, we found a musette bag torn to shreds, with only a notebook intact inside. It belonged to Mondiès, the only memento of his which I could send to his family.

As for the place where Mondiès had been, the trench was completely filled in. In spite of the risk of being spotted by the Germans, we excavated a bit and uncovered a boiled, shriveled head and a képi which, by its distinctive shape, we recognized to be that of Mondiès. With big drops of sweat rolling off our foreheads, our limbs trembling with emotion, Ayrix and I threw a couple of shovelfuls of earth onto this head out of which all the life and intelligence had been so brutally torn, leaving behind just a shapeless mass.

For some time Mondiès had a premonition of his fate. The very day before, he had written a despondent letter to his family, we learned later on.

Private Laffont, buried by the same shell, was pulled out that evening by his own squad. His body showed no trace of the slightest wound. He had been struck down by the concussion of the blast.

Night having fallen, the 13th Squad went to work digging out the body of Mondiès and burying it properly, but hardly had we gotten this done when we were called to man a forward listening post.

An engineer team arrived just then, to put the trench back into shape. We asked them to watch out for our comrade, but they didn't pay any attention. Instead they thought it proper to dig right alongside, so that the next morning when we came back we saw that they had piled up on top of the body all the dirt they had dug from the trench. We did everything we could to save it from oblivion. We stuck on top of it a rude cross made of two pieces of wood, next to which we planted a bottle, neck down, containing a piece of paper with his name written on it. But we knew that a couple of shells landing nearby would soon make an end of it, and the name Mondiès would live on only in our memories.

At the forward post where we had just spent the night, a fatal accident had occurred. The whole half-section was there, two squads; while one squad rested, the other stood guard. Around midnight, a shell landed near the for-ward post, and a man from the 14th Squad took a piece of shrapnel in the heart and fell dead without saying a word. We hardly knew him; he had arrived with the latest reinforcements. It was his first, and last, front-line duty. The war was over for him.

On June 14, the Germans concentrated their fire right on the zone where we were. Several times we had to flee violent bombardments, running here and there like the damned chased by devils. At one point I proposed that we go to the forward post where we had spent the night. "Maybe," I said, "there's less shelling up there."

Only two comrades agreed to go along with me. But we were no safer there than anywhere else. The artilleries of both sides fixed their sights on the front lines; their shells intermingled right among the forward posts.

When we arrived, the three of us were surprised to see a man on his knees, a rosary in his hands. It was Corporal Marty, of the 14th Squad. Highly devout, he had come alone to await death in repentance and prayer. He too had a premonition of his imminent death; his days were numbered.

At nightfall, the whole squad got together again. While I was up at the forward post, a shell had wounded Ferié in the leg. Having staunched his wound with his own supply of bandages, he made his way to the first-aid station. In him the squad lost a steady, thoughtful soldier, on whom you could count in any situation. Robust and courageous, he was a hard worker. I was sorry not to be able to shake his hand when he left.

Finally, at ten o'clock that evening, the first battalion of chasseurs-à-pied came to our relief. After six hours of marching, we reached Barlin-les-Mines at 4 in the morning on June 15. There, they billeted us by squads in the red-brick houses of the miners, who gave us a decent welcome.

Angres-Lorette sector. Barlin-les-Mines. Sains-en-Gohelle. *"Halt, verda!" A shell lands in the midst of the 13th Squad.*

We didn't come to Barlin in order to rest. It was only to fill up empty places in our ranks, to restore ourselves with powerful reinforcements waiting patiently for us.

It was the army of retreads and peacetime auxiliaries whom they were bringing up to take their turn at being massacred. In our company we needed a hundred men, because nearly half the company was missing at the first roll call.

They didn't make a deal about the total number of losses for the whole regiment, but almost all the companies had suffered as many as we had, if not worse.

We spent only twenty-four hours at Barlin, just the time necessary to incorporate the new recruits and to equip them with cartridges, grenades, tools, field kitchens, etc., and during the night of June 15–16 they brought us back up to the firing line.

At dawn, they halted us at the workers' quarters of the mines at Sains-en-Gohelle. In the streets of this neighborhood they made us form up in clusters, as if they had no idea what to do with us. We had to stay in place for several hours, prohibited from wandering off.

In a neighboring company, a man was bold enough to criticize, out loud, this uncertainty of our leaders, and cried out, "I think we're being led by idiots." A tattletale sergeant brought these irreverent words to the attention of Captain Barbier, commanding that company. The soldier was arrested and brought before a court-martial, which gave him a suspended two-year prison sentence and transferred him to another regiment. This was Private Paul Comps, from Trausse.

Finally we received the order to billet, by squad, in the corons of the miners, but at high alert, ready to move out at a moment's notice. This seemed inconceivable to us, given our state of extreme fatigue. But our big bosses, in their blind and stupid presumption, believed that the German front facing us would melt away, and we had to be ready for pursuit.

Sains-en-Gohelle, a few years ago, was nothing but an insignificant little farming village. Now there was, surrounding the mine, a vast estate with hundreds of quaint little houses lined up, all identical, surrounded by spacious gardens, separated by wide lanes. It presented the vision of the "new city" dreamed of by the socialists.

But, as I explained to my comrades, these habitations were the property of a few arrogant capitalists, and in order to live there you had to be a wage slave in the mine.

Despite the town and the mine being in full view and in close range of the German artillery, no shells had been falling on Sains-en-Gohelle.

While we were there, a big-caliber one did fall, nevertheless. Why this one shell, and not two, three, or a dozen?

A question which only the German gunners could answer.

On June 24, the regiment got orders to move up to the trenches. The 13th Squad was back to full strength. To replace the wounded comrades Lados and Ferié and the dead Mondiès, we welcomed Privates François Ventresque, from Rieux-Minervois; Favier, from Saint-Frichoux; and Pélissier, from Lapalme. At about 11 p.m., we reached our reserve position. It was a communication trench built up with mine timbers and earth, which was fine, but you couldn't stretch out to sleep without being trampled by the dainty feet of the poilus passing by in large numbers, because this boyau was the route of access to the front lines.

We were available for all kinds of work details, and half the night had not passed before we were called up for some sort of nocturnal task. On June 25, a violent storm having unleashed a torrential rain onto our trenches, the following night was completely devoted to bailing out the water with shrimping nets, an exhausting chore.

To relieve us from these fatiguing duties, on June 28 at 8 p.m. they sent us up to the front line, about seven or eight hundred meters away. A distance which we could normally cover in a half-hour; this time, it took us five hours!

Had the Germans been warned about this relief, or was it a simple coincidence? Whatever the cause, the communication trenches that we were following were bombarded heavily, until midnight. It resulted in halts, pullbacks, gaps in our column. Our half-section was lost, mixed up with other units which were no more sure of where they were going than we were. Nevertheless we were lucky enough to finally reach our company, deployed at the front line.

They positioned us a bit to the rear. Since it was our turn to be reserve, they were considerate enough to let us rest that night, stretched out on the ground in the boyau.

The three *bleus* [rookies] of the squad were completely exhausted. The artillery barrages which we had to cross, the shells falling nearby, the blinding bursts of flares, the constant drumming of bullets, the explosions of grenades at the advance posts, all this had completely terrorized them.

And the old hands amused themselves by frightening them all the more, by making them crouch down, scramble along, hit the ground, while repeating, "This is nothing. You haven't seen anything!" The three unfortunate ones had to be wondering what it would be like when something big happened.

When day broke, we saw with horror that we were in a place completely overturned by recent bombardments. Here and there, broken rifles, shredded knapsacks, shapeless debris, and alas, some dead bodies, all made a tableau which was hardly reassuring.

At about 3 in the afternoon, a big shell landed in the boyau, brushing right past two Peyriacois, Gils and Allard. The ground trembled, and we saw a huge bunch of earth thrown up more than four meters into the air. With failing hearts and frazzled nerves, we awaited the brutal explosion which would tear us all to pieces, but all that landed on our heads was a harmless shower of pulverized earth. The shell hadn't exploded, which happened sometimes, and it plowed deep into the ground. Half the squad, seized with fear, had fled, and soon came back. It was no safer anywhere else than where we were.

In the boyau lay a fully loaded haversack which no doubt belonged to the poor soldier, yesterday full of life, today frightfully mutilated, whom we saw a few steps away.

Rolled up on top of this haversack was a good pair of corduroy trousers, which I appropriated without scruple. The time for wasting materials had not yet arrived, and my own trousers were torn in many places, so right there I undertook an exchange of pants.

Then we opened the haversack. Perhaps we would discover the name of its owner. Indeed, it contained a pile of postcards and letters, all in the name of Laboucarié.

What? Laboucarié was dead! The poor bastard! Everyone in the regiment knew him. He was famous for all kinds of eccentricities, his colorful clothing, the songs he made up and sang in the cabarets, always arousing wild laughter.

Fulfilling a duty, we gave the letters and his military papers to our rationer, Terrisse, to give to the sergeant-major of the 23rd Company, to which the dead man belonged. The sergeant-major was quite surprised, because at this very moment Laboucarié was in the bloom of health, as much as one could be in the trenches. When questioned, the walking corpse had to explain how his haversack had fallen into our hands. He was forced to admit that he had abandoned the trench after a violent bombardment. That was all it took for him to be sent up for a court-martial.

From that day on Laboucarié had it in for me, for two reasons: first of all, for having brought all these troubles upon him, and then for having taken his corduroy trousers.

Back to our precarious situation. That night, the 13th Squad was called out to dig a trench where the front line no longer existed, having been completely obliterated by bombardments. We had to reestablish it, for at least a hundred meters. It had been the scene of combats, of attacks and counterattacks, and the ground was strewn with corpses and all sorts of debris. We had to put our picks and shovels to work in the middle of a charnel house.

When they heard what kind of work we had to do, the three replacements, newcomers in our ranks, grew faint with fear. I took it upon myself to leave them behind, in our redoubt. At night, their absence would easily pass unnoticed.

At 9 p.m. about forty of us followed Sublieutenant Malvezy, who deployed us along the line we had to trace. It was a very dark night, when maps and compasses were of no use; instinct alone was our guide. But it guided us falsely, this time. Those who were right up front with the lieutenant ran smack into the German trench. We knew about it only when the enemy sentries, probably more frightened than we were, shouted in their guttural voices, *Halt! Wer da?* [Who goes there]? *Halt! Wer da?*

For us it was pandemonium, mindless flight, with no one having any idea where the French lines were. Bullets whistled around us, some grenades burst. We plunged into shell holes, but they got crowded fast. Everywhere men were flattened on the ground. Our squad had scattered.

"Hey you, over there, what company?"

"And you—What about you? Are you in the 21st?"

These questions went unanswered, because they were all addressed to dead comrades. What a slaughter! I speak for my fellow survivors of the 13th Squad— my friends Tort, Allard, Gils—when I say that nowhere, not even at Verdun, did we see such a deadly harvest of souls, than in those few minutes.

And all this virile youth—why was it sacrificed there? To take, or retake, a few lousy square meters of shell holes!

How long were we going to stay in this graveyard? Wouldn't this alert un-leash a bombardment which could last all night? An uninterrupted rain of shell-fire? Luckily, nothing of the kind took place. Soon, all was calm. We rallied, and took up the work that had been assigned to us.

The next morning, the only one missing from our squad was our pal Tort, about whose fate we all worried. But later in the day we had the pleasure of seeing him arrive back, with all his limbs intact. When all hell had broken loose the night before, he had leaped into a shell hole where other comrades had al-ready sought refuge. He saw right away that he was surrounded by dead men. Terrified, he bolted like a madman, and landed in a trench full of Moroccan *tirailleurs* [sharpshooters], who were ready to cut his head off, without a second thought.

This day was marked by violent bombardments on our lines. Slumped in our boyau, we were completely numbed by the incessant rolling of thunderbolts. In the 21st Company there were men wounded and killed; among the latter, a comrade named Bigou.

It was with real joy that we went up to the front line that evening; joy to be getting away from that accursed boyau, joy to not be going to work on the trench we'd begun the night before.

In the latest offensive, the French had reached the village, but a counter-attack had pushed them back to the point where we were. In the plain beyond Angres you could see, uninterrupted, the corons and the high smokestacks of Liévin and, farther on, those of Lens.[4]

That night and the next one, July 1, passed without incident. I noted that we were in front of Angres, just a few hundred meters away.

In this sector there were no listening posts. Sentries were posted three or four paces from one another. By half-section, one squad was on guard, the other rested.

During the night of July 1–2, our trench was going to be bloodied. In our half-section, fifteen men were going to be killed or wounded, in the following circumstances.

The Accursed War, the Charnel House of Lorette, the Slaughter of September 25, 1915: July 1–September 27, 1915

That night, July 1–2, the 13th Squad was supposed to take its turn up front, at the firing trench, from midnight until daybreak. The 14th Squad had the shift before us, but at about 9 p.m. their corporal, Marty, from Narbonne, said he wasn't feeling well and asked if he and I could switch places. I was happy to oblige.

At midnight, the 13th Squad took its post on the firing line. Our three newcomers were awestruck. They couldn't believe that they were only fifty meters from the Germans. They didn't dare raise their heads above the parapet. We did our best to calm them down.

By that time Corporal Marty was feeling better, so he urged me to take a break and get some rest. He would go up front with my squad, in my place. I stretched out at the widest place in the boyau and had a nice, restful sleep, blissfully unaware of the footsteps of passersby. Suddenly I was yanked awake by a terrible explosion, followed by cries and moans.

In the smoke-filled trench a man stumbled by, waving his arms in the air, groaning, then collapsing a few steps from me.

It was Corporal Marty. "Help me, don't leave me," he cried. I lunged toward him. In the light of a lamp which a comrade held up for me, I took a sharp knife and cut through his greatcoat and his shirt, revealing a horrible wound along his left side from which blood gushed in torrents.

With a cold-bloodedness which I never thought I had in me, I staunched the hemorrhaging for the time being.

Right then a medical officer and two stretcher-bearers rushed up. It was our section chief, Sublieutenant Malvezy, who had gone to get them and had practically dragged them up by force.

I have to congratulate this officer for his devotion to duty. I can forgive him for some of the little vexations which he brought upon all of us, and me in particular, later on.

The medical officer sought to examine the wound, but poor Marty flailed around and cried out even louder—fifty meters from the Germans, who, in the calm of this July dawn, must have heard everything.

"Shut your goddamned mouth," said the medical officer, brutally. What sweet words of consolation when one is on the verge of death, with a shattered body, far from loved ones.

"My poor children," cried Marty (he had three of them), "I'll never see you again." Then, praying with all his faith, he called upon the Virgin Mary and Saint Theresa, who, he had told me many times, was the protector of wounded men.

But alas, no miracle occurred. Death struck down the true believer just as blindly as the unrepentant atheist. Poor Marty expired before he could reach the dressing station.

In this war, you see how the tiniest circumstances, the most fortuitous co-incidences, can make the difference between life and death. If at 9 p.m. Marty hadn't been suffering from a headache, each of us two corporals would have taken his turn at the firing line with his own squad. It probably would have been me whose skin would have been ripped open by a jagged piece of metal.

Poor Marty! So complacent, so good, so gentle. Destiny willed that you would die in my place. Forgive me.

But I didn't have the time to grieve or to contemplate this death. Blood poured from other men's wounds. They had just found Private Favier, lying inanimately. We brought him back to life. His blood flowed from multiple wounds. He was unconscious, and already had the death rattle in his throat.

I ran in pursuit of the medical officer, the *major,* who had prudently fled these dangerous places. I led him to the unfortunate Favier. The *major* felt his pulse for a few seconds. "He's finished," he said. "There's nothing more to do."

Before he left, we got him to promise that his stretcher-bearers would come pick up Favier. But it took our sublieutenant going to the first-aid station to get the stretcher-bearers to come take poor Favier, who died just as he arrived at the field hospital at Hersin-Coupigny.

Favier, who had arrived with the latest reinforcements, fell mortally wounded the first night he was on the front line. He had shown great terror in the face of bombardments, and we had to reassure him with encouraging words when we ourselves had much need of being comforted.

When he climbed up to the firing step to take his turn at watch, I had to stay near him for a little while. There was no loophole for observing, and in order to do his job of surveillance he had to stick his head above the parapet. Favier couldn't get used to it. He crouched down each time he heard a bullet whistle past. I suggested that he fill up a couple of sandbags and pile them up to make a crenellation, behind which he would be better protected. The poor guy had listened to me. When we picked him up in the communication trench, at the place where the big shell had fallen, he was holding a sandbag in his arms.

I was perhaps the unwitting cause of his death. If I hadn't suggested to him the idea of filling sandbags, he wouldn't have been at the most dangerous spot. Poor Favier. You too, please forgive me.

Now that dawn was beginning to lighten the night sky, those of us who were safe and sound could help the other wounded. First of all was my friend Tort, who, seated on the firing step, was moaning and groaning enough to break your heart, saying that he had a shattered leg. Upon inspection, all we could see was a tiny scratch on his heel, from which not one drop of blood had flowed. We teased him for being such a crybaby, but it turned out that he did have a little piece of shell fragment in the bone, which brought on gangrene, and they had to amputate his leg a few days later.

After spending a month wavering between life and death, he was sent back to his village, Rieux-Minervois.

Tort was forty-one years old. How many there were, ten or fifteen years younger than he was, who had never laid eyes on a trench!

The Peyriacois Gabriel Gils, at the moment when the big shell hit, was obeying a call of nature a few steps behind the trench. He got a shell fragment in his back, which he will keep his whole life, as a souvenir of this tragic night.

A few days later, this fragment brought on a pulmonary congestion, which put his life in great danger.

Jordy, formerly of Peyriac, got a shell fragment in a knee, on which I put a rudimentary dressing.

Sergeant Baruteau, who was sleeping while sitting on the firing step, had his legs torn up. Other soldiers from the 14th Squad, sitting or lying on the firing step, were also wounded.

In all, this one shell claimed fifteen or so victims. Once again, I had been warned in a way by this kind of instinctive intuition, which I had already felt several times previously.

Like all who were not standing watch, I went to find a spot to sleep on the firing step, but a sudden idea came to me to stretch out at the bottom of the trench, although I risked being trampled by the boots of passersby. But shell fragments couldn't reach me there.

The Peyriacois Allard had a close call. A fragment struck and shattered the hilt of his bayonet, which he had on the ground right beside him. It should have been on the end of his rifle. This infraction of the rules may have saved his life.

Meanwhile, out of all these wounded men, none dared to go to the first-aid station. With a brute like [medical officer] *Major* Torrès on duty, you couldn't go up to him with a simple scratch. We all knew what he sometimes said to the wounded and the sick: "Even if you came to me holding your head in your hands, I wouldn't pay any attention to you."

But on the other hand, when they would bring him a man who was too gravely wounded, he would burst into a rage because his medical skills would be useless and he'd be wasting his time.

To leave the front line, without being evacuated or medically "recognized," risked a court-martial. Oh, we were doing just fine, under the boot of militarism.

But we couldn't keep all these wounded in the trench with us.

Sublieutenant Malvezy took it upon himself to convey them to the nearest field station where, by a lucky chance, Torrès was nowhere to be seen.

And after a flurry of handshakes and embraces, as these would no doubt be definitive separations, we parted company with saddened hearts. The wounded disappeared at the turn of the boyau, hobbling along and helping one another.

Into a shell crater we threw torn-up equipment, shredded knapsacks, broken rifles which littered the ground. With our shovels we got rid of the blood-soaked mud upon which swarms of flies had descended. Now the trench was clean. Nothing remained to remind us of the frightful drama of the night before.

Soon the ravitailleur Terrisse arrived. He had left early in the evening, and knew nothing about what had happened. He ran into me first. When he saw me with blood splattered on my face, my hands, all over my clothing, he went pale and staggered against the side of the trench.

"Did something bad happen to you?" he said.

I told him all the details about what had happened. Then he gave us our rations, which we ate with an appetite that you can imagine.

At ten in the evening, the 281st Infantry Regiment from our division came to our relief, and three hours later we arrived at our billets at Hersin-Coupigny.

1915. Angres-Lorette sector. Bully-Grenay. July 14.
The "Tranchée Carbonnière."

Hersin-Coupigny is a big mining town. Yesterday it was a village. Today it is almost a prosperous city, as long as the Germans don't reduce it to ashes. It's within the range of their cannons, which from time to time send over volleys of shells.

We were lodged in a dance hall, a place of pleasure changed into a human stable. But even in the worst stable there's a bit of straw. In ours, we had to lie on a brick floor.

At the cemetery at Hersin we gathered around the grave of our unlucky comrade Favier, who had gotten some rest—the biggest rest you can get—before we ever did.

Three days later, we went to camp in the corons of Sains-en-Gohelle, and the next day to Bully-Grenay. We were like the Wandering Jew, condemned to wander ceaselessly.[1] We were going from Purgatory to Hell and from Hell back to Purgatory.

The village of Bully-Grenay, right at the threshold of the trenches, was bombarded daily, but how could we complain when the inhabitants didn't flee? If their houses collapsed, they settled in their cellars or took refuge with a neighbor.

During one of our stays there, a whole family, except the father, was wiped out, but this catastrophe wasn't enough to incite the inhabitants to leave.

At Bully, the 21st Company received a small number of replacements who were apportioned among the squads. In the 13th we got two strapping lads who knew nothing about the trenches except what they'd seen in the illustrated newspapers.

The squad also got reinforced with a priest, the Abbé Galaup, who had been expelled from France by the Laws of Separation,[2] and had come back from Egypt, where he'd been teaching in a religious school, to defend his homeland which had exiled him. Now that had merit.

But we lost the Peryacois Allard. He got a job as a driver, which his age (41) entitled him to.

On July 10, at 9 in the evening, we left Bully and went up to occupy a second-line trench for four days.

The bombardments had noticeably diminished. It was almost a sector for rest. But on July 14, all that was spoiled. To remind the Germans that this was our national holiday, at three in the afternoon our artillery unleashed a violent cannonade upon the opposing trenches. We would have done better to leave the Germans alone, because they replied in kind, not on our artillerymen, which would have been logical, but on us infantrymen, who had nothing to do with it.

Stuck out there all by ourselves, the 13th Squad occupied a section of abandoned trench. In an instant, the shells began to rain down around us. Not having any shelters to seek refuge in, I thought it most prudent for the squad to immediately leave the position. Only Father Galaup, as we called him, refused to follow. On his knees, resigned to his death, he was reciting the Act of Contrition.

It was in vain that I told him the story of the schoolteacher Mondiès, who died because he wouldn't follow the rest of us. This headstrong abbé didn't want to know anything about it, and stayed there by himself. As for the two other newcomers, they were terrified, completely lost. They didn't know where to take themselves.

When we came back we noticed that shells had fallen near our position, and one had landed right in the middle of the trench.

Father Galaup was safe and sound, and still praying. "Now it's to thank God for saving my life, a real miracle," he said.

Thunder mixed its voice with the cannon fire, and soon the rain came down in sheets, finally appeasing the rage of the artillerymen.

In the company, there were only a few wounded, and one soldier was killed in his hole and buried at the same time, by a grave digger shell.

The rain didn't stop. Night arrived, but our relief did not. Packs hoisted, we waited, silent, immobile, dripping with water, attentive to the slightest sound of footsteps.

Finally, at 10 in the evening, our replacements arrived. They had gotten lost in the darkness, in the communication trenches transformed into sewers.

And we got lost, too. We slogged along for six hours through water and mud, covering maybe fifteen or twenty kilometers, while there was only one kilometer as the crow flies to reach the third line, where we had just spent four days.

At daybreak we came out into a long, narrow field, surrounded by the network of trenches.

This was the "Tranchée Carbonnière." They should have called it "Cimetière" [Cemetery] because every day they buried the dead of the sector there.

Despite the large size of the field, it risked becoming too small to hold both the living and the dead.

It will be a macabre surprise for those who come back here to cultivate their fields and find cemeteries instead.

We were very disappointed to observe that there were no shelters at all. We camped out in the open, under the sun and the stars; life in the outdoors, in the fullest sense of the word.

With our shirts soaked with rain and sweat, gripped with cold, some yielded to their fatigue, and even fell asleep curled up on their packs or lying in the mud.

The newspapers constantly praised the care and attention of our commanders toward their men. For the months that the Tranchée Carbonnière had been used as a reserve position, no one had thought to put up a couple of shelters.

Nevertheless there were some of them, occupied of course exclusively by officers, these modern-day noblemen. As for the soldiers? In the mud!

However, not all philosophically accepted their fate. A good-sized group gathered in front of the shelter of our provisional company commander, the crazy Sublieutenant Caminade. Shouts and protests burst forth, a few daring souls called for the singing of the "Internationale,"[3] the supreme cry of revolt for the poilus.

Hearing this racket, the famous Caminade burst from his hole in anger. "What is this all about?" he said. "You're complaining, and you're not wrong to do so, but what do you want—we're at war!"

And with this cynical word, which excused so many inexcusable things during the war, His Honor Caminade disappeared back into his hole, where he could rest while the sergeant of the day handed out work details.

As for me, I had to head out with a crew of twenty men to take water to Bully-Grenay, about two kilometers away by communication trench.

This wasn't such a pleasant chore, with two men carrying a fifty-liter keg of water suspended from a pole. How many curses arose when we had to make a sharp turn, or when we got stuck without being able to go forward or backward, or when the prickly barbed wire hanging over the top of the trench forced us to walk at a half-crouch, or when we had to make our way through narrow passages, right on top of each other. What an accursed chore, which made the communication trenches seem interminable.

For three nights, we were employed hauling heavy beams and rafters from a mine, about seven or eight kilometers from the front line. The mine was called the Fosse Calonne [Calonne Pit], and was bombarded day and night with high-caliber shells, fragments from which reached us.

Since we were so loud in our demands for shelters, we were now building them. But they were for our successors.

At the Fosse Calonne there was enough lumber available to furnish a whole town. The Germans also knew about this precious resource, and they were jealous. That's what brought on these frequent barrages, which made the neighborhood very dangerous.

Up to this point, no chief had wanted to risk his men's lives to collect this wood. Caminade risked ours, without the slightest scruple. But at least we had no one wounded, and when we moved on from the Carbonnière we left behind some good-sized shelters, almost completed.

On July 18, at one in the morning, our battalion arrived at Hersin-Coupigny, to spend seven days of rest. Clearly they were spoiling us.

We were billeted by squad, in the corons of the miners. Each coron had a little enclosure for storing coal, doing the wash, etc. That was our lodging. It was tight, and we had to sleep right next to each other, "head to feet" as they say rudely. But that was a minor detail, and we were worn out by our night march, so we slept late, until about nine in the morning.

Once we had rested and cleaned up a bit, the two oldest veterans of the squad, Ayrix and Lapeyre, invited me to go with them to the end of the road that met the main road passing through the village. At this crossroads the company's field kitchen had set up shop, in the open air.

I was ready to follow my two buddies when, all of a sudden, I was overcome by an indefinable sensation of worry, anguish, fear. I was sure of it; this was the imminence of danger which I was feeling.

Dogs know when their masters are about to die, and they know when they themselves are going to die, I'm sure.

The schoolteacher Mondiès, and many others whom I've known, have sensed their imminent doom.

Many have escaped death, guided by intuition that they didn't even know they had. Everything may depend on the degree of sensitivity of our nerves, or how impressionable they are.

But on this day, I thought that my intuition must be wrong. What danger could land on me? We weren't in the sinister Fond de Buval. We were in a calm and peaceful village. The street was bustling with activity, children were playing, housewives were gossiping at their doorsteps, non-coms flirted with pretty blondes.

I held back from telling my two comrades what I was feeling. They would have made fun of me. But I didn't follow them, with the excuse that I had something to do.

But to flee this unknown danger, should I stay in the cantonment or go away from it? I followed an impulse to go into a shop where postcards with scenes of Hersin were for sale. Up until now the censors had prohibited them from being sold.

With Private Ventresque I went into this shop. We picked out a couple of scenes (some of which appear in this notebook), and we were on our way out when suddenly a series of explosions could be heard. A volley of powerful, timed-fuse shells had just fallen on Hersin. Next to the shop was a little court-yard with a skylight roof; a big shell fragment shattered it, producing a shower of broken glass.

The terrified shopkeeper and her family fled down a staircase into the basement. If we'd been of a more larcenous mind, we could have helped ourselves to plenty of treats in the shop, but we rushed back to our billet.

There we learned that three powerful shells had fallen right onto the crossroads where our field kitchen stood. The four cooks were critically injured. The kitchen had its chimney knocked off, and the cooking pot was blown apart. We would go hungry that day.

Ayrix had such a serious wound to his arm that it had to be amputated.

Lapeyre was badly wounded in the leg. A shell fragment had sliced off, as neatly as a pastry slicer, a piece of his calf as big as a chestnut, and the blood poured out like a fountain. In all, the company had twelve wounded men, all of whom had been standing around the field kitchen, chatting away.

Very luckily, less than a hundred meters away was a military hospital where the wounded were taken quickly and given immediate attention.

The next day, when we went to this hospital for news of Lapeyre and Ayrix, we found the doors locked. Because of the bombardment they had evacuated all the wounded during the night and closed down the hospital.

Therefore, of all the veterans of the 13th Squad, I was the only one left still fighting, along with rationer Terrisse. All the others were killed or wounded. When would my turn come?

Until the end of August we shuttled between Hersin, Sains-en-Gohelle, Bully-Grenay, and the trenches. Gradually the sector quieted down, and we wouldn't have traded this corner of the front for any other, for fear of falling into a bad spot.

On August 27 we were in Sains-en-Gohelle, and we had to go up to the front line that evening. But during the day a dramatic counterorder pulled us out of the sector altogether. Our departure was set for 2 a.m.

We passed through the sleeping towns of Hersin and Barlin, the village of Mesnil, which had been completely destroyed by an exploding ammunition dump, and the big mining center of Bruay. Next came Division, and then, fairly worn out by an eight-hour march with only a mug of coffee in our bellies, we arrived at Camblain-Châtelain.

Three days later, at noon, we boarded railroad cars at the Pernes-Camblain station, our musette bags filled with indigestible biscuits and cans of *singe* [monkey-meat], enough for three more days. Where the devil were they taking us in such a hurry?

The train departed, heading north. We passed by Hazebrouck, and at 8 p.m. we disembarked at the station of Bergues, six kilometers from Dunkerque.

We were hoping to be billeted in this good-sized town of Bergues, but to our great disappointment we crossed it without stopping and forged ahead into the dark of night across an endless plain, the plain of Flanders.

The road seemed interminable. We marched and marched. The packs grew more and more terribly heavy on our shoulders. Finally we stopped at a village. At the entrance was the usual sentinel who observed us parade by. Passing him, I asked him the name of the village. He threw me back a tongue twister of a name, but it mattered only if we were halting there.

But this wasn't to be our stopping-place. The wandering battalion launched itself once again onto the vast plain, shrouded in darkness.

To make things worse, the weather turned rainy, and more and more laggards fell further behind the column of march. In the darkness you could hear murmurs and shouts. The officers played deaf. They knew that the men hadn't had anything warm to eat or drink since morning, and they themselves had plenty. Those who were being paid had no right to complain.

At the head of our column marched our new commandant, named Leblanc.

He was small, thin, and scrawny. A wag had baptized him *Quinze-Grammes* [fifteen grams; "half-pint"], which was an immediate success. He would never be called anything else by the irreverent soldiers.

It was he who was leading us. But the poor guy read his map like a carp reading a prayer book.

Leaving the village we had just crossed, we should have turned left, but he had us go right. That was his big mistake.

He should have gotten information from the ridiculous watchwoman. For once in her life she could have been of some use. But no doubt his dignity wouldn't permit it. He would have had to admit that he couldn't make sense of his map and compass.

As a result, in the middle of a rainstorm, around one in the morning, we found ourselves in a field where the road we were on ended.

I heard the commandant admit, pitifully, "I think that we might be lost." He was still not entirely convinced of it.

He send scouts out, left and right, to find a farm where he could seek refuge with his officers. As for us, he generously granted us the liberty of sleeping in a muddy field, to await the coming day.

We discovered nearby a big barn which Providence seemed to have placed there just for us.

It's true that it was open to the elements on all four sides, the roof resting upon four old posts stuck in the ground.

Nearby were some haystacks. In the blink of an eye they were pillaged, and in less than a quarter of an hour the sound of heavy snoring emanated from the barn. Practically the whole battalion was camped out there, the men burrowed into a thick bed of hay.

I don't recall sleeping better my whole life. But I do recall being roughly shaken awake by angry voices which showered us with curses. These were the voices of the owners of the hay, expressing a rightful rage. But not one sleeper budged. We offered in opposition the strength of our inertia. Only a few voices, with accents of the Paris *faubourgs* [working-class neighborhoods], responded with classic, disrespectful wisecracks: "Shut up, you old stove! Take a hike! To the showers!"

Soon our commandant Leblanc appeared, white with rage, and obliged us to put the haystacks back in place, calming somewhat the irascible Flemings.

Three hours later we arrived at the village of Oost-Cappel, neighbor of West-Cappel. We were lodged by units in farms, spaced two or three hundred meters from one another.

Our unit was assigned to the Kilem farm, in an old sheepfold. A dilapidated, hole-covered partition separated us from the pigpen, where four or five noisy and quarrelsome piglets kept jarring us awake with their sharp cries.

The Reverend Father Galaup, a bit less resigned than Job on his dung heap, cried out with his hands joined in prayer, "Lying on the hard ground in a sheep-fold is nothing. Jesus was born in a stable. But it's this foul odor that makes me sick, and this coating of pig-shit slurry spreading all over the floor, turning our straw bed into a stinking manure pile."

In fact, after three nights I couldn't take it anymore, and I went outside and found a spot under a threshing machine in a barn.

We also suffered from a lack of drinking water. It's not that there was a drought; to the contrary, torrential downpours came frequently. But the next day there wouldn't be a trace of the rain.

I prefer our sunny South to this Flanders which, although fertile, lacked the green ribbon of our streams and rivers, our capricious waterfalls, and the oases of our springs of fresh, bubbling water.

To remove the dirt from our hands and faces each day, they had to bring water in kegs. As for our shirts and our clothes, we had to wash them in ponds, which are a feature of all the farms of northern France. The water in them is generally dirty and polluted. The pigs, cows, and horses would refuse outright to drink it. These beasts were lucky enough to be immune to typhoid fever and other pernicious diseases.

Sometimes in the evening we would go to the nearby village of Oost-Cappel, despite the prohibition which had been issued.

The border followed the road which cuts right through the village, so that half of Oost-Cappel is French and the other half is Belgian. The only difference you notice was that the shop windows on the Belgian side were piled high with pyramids of tobacco packets and cigar boxes, freely for sale. It was a paradise for the smokers and chewers, because the prices were laughably low.

Every morning we went out on elaborate field exercises and long marches. The afternoons were given over to obligatory games of football, parallel bars, races, etc. Even the grandfathers of 40, 43, or even 44 years old whom we had among us joined in willingly.

Some of a more morose spirit wanted to stay out of such childish games. But our new captain, Cros-Mayrevieille, made them do calisthenics instead, running wind sprints without taking breaks, so that they would appreciate the appeal of these games. The choice was theirs.

At that time the farmers were harvesting the hops. One day one of our bosses had the bright idea of issuing an order at roll call authorizing us to help harvest the hops that afternoon. We would be paid one sou per kilo. It was enticing; we would fill our pocketbooks. But alas, our maladroit hands couldn't gather up enough for more than seven or eight sous an afternoon. It was small change, but it kept us out of our captain's clutches.

To win the favor of the Flemish girls, the young poilus posted themselves alongside them and helped them fill their sacks. And these young people, carefree as they have always been and always will be, sang, laughed, flirted, and embraced, indifferent to the dull roar of cannon fire which sounded over toward Ypres.

For me, as an old papa, every afternoon I went to the aid of two old folks whose poverty obliged them to come from several kilometers away to gain their livelihood, a pretty meager one even counting the few sous which my help added to their earnings.

One morning, coming back from the stupid daily drill, Sublieutenant Malvezy, chief of our section and commander of the Kilem Farm billet, stopped me at the entrance to our sheepfold, our sleeping quarters, and in a roguish manner ordered me out into a nearby field.

Sublieutenant Malvezy was, before the war, a simple employee of the Aude departmental tramways. He hadn't earned his stripes by some gallant battlefield exploit, destined to be inscribed in the history books. No, he had earned them in the Narbonne garrison. To fill up vacancies, they had promoted to officers some sergeants from older conscript classes who were growing stale in the garrison. They didn't want to promote the ones who were at the front, because they were too friendly with the enlisted men. They were afraid that these non-coms wouldn't have enough authority over the men when they had to send them to their slaughter.

That's how the roadworker Malvezy became our section chief. Not meanspirited, but swollen with pride, he was always getting back at us for the lack of respect we showed him, by little vexations.

When we were a little ways off, he told me, in the tone of a schoolteacher reprimanding a student, "Corporal Barthas, I'm not happy with you. It appears to me that you're giving antimilitarist ideas to your comrades. You're demoralizing them, instead of boosting their morale. I was a Socialist too, but now we all have to do our duty."

"Excuse me, lieutenant," I replied forcefully, "can you tell me where and when I have not done my duty? What words are you accusing me of having said to my comrades?"

Without answering my question, Malvezy added, "And your squad isn't marching very well. Today, in the assault at Rexpoëde (a laughable assault) your men were the last ones to arrive!"

"Hold on, you know well that the tailor Moulis is crippled with rheumatism, and that little Pélissier excretes blood every day, Father Galaup has a hernia as big as a sugar loaf, Terrisse has asthma, and old Chapman has a son in the trenches and is going nuts about it, and you want me to force these poor devils to run, to jump, to do more than they're able to do? No, never, and if it's these lousy corporal's stripes that you want, take them from me whenever you'd like. They don't mean anything to me."

"Fine," said Malvezy, "I'll talk about it with the captain."

"Talk about it with General Joffre if you want to," I said, as I headed off.

There was evidently a snitch among us whom we had to watch out for. Our suspicions fell on Sergeant F. . . ., who from that day was ostracized by the 13th Squad.

From then on Malvezy showed no ill will toward me. To the contrary, he seemed to want to remedy the injury he had done to me, or thought he had done me.

He was going on leave a few days later, and since there was no sergeant present in the section there had to be a corporal named to take over the command in his absence. I was quite surprised when the sublieutenant, calling me forward, told me that it was up to me to command the 4th Section. Was he making fun of me? But no, this was serious, and despite my excuses I had to, willingly or not, take on the military command of the Kilem Farm. Decadence and grandeur!

While we were at rest in Belgium, we received reinforcements from a regiment which was less battle tested than the 280th. Of course, they sent us not the elite, but the rejects. In the 13th Squad they assigned us Privates Chapman and Lefèvre, both from Calais.

The first was tall, scrawny, old, and constantly in a funk about his oldest son, who was in the trenches in an assault regiment.

The second was a sailor, robust, stocky, clever. He would have made a good soldier if it weren't for his weakness for the *pinard* [cheap red wine], or for any fermented drink, which led him often to drunkenness.

On September 12 we changed our billet. We went about five kilometers to a farm between Oost-Cappel and Rexpoëde.

Every day now was taken up with marches and grand maneuvers directed by the famous General Niessel,[4] a brawler who dreamed of nothing but combats and assaults. We didn't know what it meant that we were being assigned to this saber rattler. He was quickly baptized *General Tenglandi* [Occitan dialect expression meaning "I'm going to beat you up"].[5]

On September 20, in the afternoon, all the non-coms and corporals who had been sent for two weeks of training in handling grenades and other advanced— that's to say, more homicidal—weaponry at Souix suddenly came back. This signified that our vacation had come to an end.

In fact, the order for departure was set for that very evening at 11 o'clock. At assembly, Private Lefèvre, whom no one had seen since supper, was absent. We finally found him dead drunk, beside a pond. You can imagine the trouble this drunkard gave us in getting him to follow us all the way to Bergues, where we would embark for a destination unknown to any of us.

We arrived there at 1 in the morning. We stacked our rifles in the streets, with orders not to wander off since we would be leaving at any minute.

This minute arrived at 7 o'clock. For six hours we languished, stretched out on the pavement, doing everything we could think of to stay warm, because a whitish sleet was falling, something that we had never seen in the Midi this time of year.

Who had given this stupid order, to leave eight hours early to catch a train only six kilometers away?

Finally, around 7, here we are embarking for an unknown destination. Near the station we saw some big holes. Two months ago the Germans, testing things out at the same time as they were bombarding Dunkerque, had sent, postage-paid, a gift package of fourteen enormous 450mm shells, fired from a distance of 37 kilometers.

Passing by Vercqueil we could hear a hellish cannonade. They told us that three British armored trains were firing on La Bassée, Lens, and Liévin.

At 11 a.m. we halted at Saint-Pol. This was our "unknown destination." Right away, packs on our backs, here we are heading out along a dusty road, in torrid weather, to arrive later that afternoon in the little village of Ecoivres.

Our section was badly housed. A dark, cramped, and filthy compound. Facing us were three pigpens, two of which were occupied by quadrupeds, the middle one of which was empty. I set myself up there, with a comrade. We didn't do too badly, despite the grunts of our neighbors and the huge rats that devoured the contents of our musette bags during the night.

The farm folk weren't very welcoming. They padlocked the pump at the well, which made it very difficult for us to get water to drink and to shave with. Boy, did our bosses take good care of us!

On September 23, at four in the afternoon, the regiment was assembled and massed in a square in a meadow. Our Colonel Poujal announced what we already knew, that a general offensive was going to be unleashed, that at this moment the Russians were falling back, but while most of the Germans were bogged down in Poland we would crush them on our front.

"And now," he cried in a loud voice. "Forward! No more hernias! No more weak hearts! No more aches and pains! Nothing but the will to win! *Vive la France!*"

This patriotic nonsense didn't arouse the slightest enthusiasm. We hadn't forgotten the horrors of the last offensive of Lorette. An impressive silence greeted the colonel's final words. Only the undertaker Torrès smiled. He nodded his head as if to say, "Yes, let the herniated, the weak-hearted, the sciatics come to me. They'll get a nice reception!"

The next night, at three in the morning, in rainy weather, we left Ecoivres and headed in the direction of Arras. As morning came, the weather became hot and heavy, which made the march even more tiring. We crossed the little town of Avesnes-le-Comte, and at one in the afternoon the regiment stopped to encamp in the little village of Habacq, twelve kilometers from Arras. At least half of our unit was still in the rear. The road was packed with laggards. Nobody bothered them. You knew that the docile sheep would arrive at the slaughterhouse on time.

We could hear a violent cannonade all along the front. You couldn't make out individual cannons firing. It was more like an uninterrupted roar, like in a violent storm when the single claps of thunder, close together, form a continuous rumbling sound.

They called the corporals to the company office.

"How many men in your squad?" asked the officer.

"Fourteen, chief."

"Well, here, take these fourteen cutlasses; give one of them to each man."

"These are arms for murderers, not for soldiers," I exclaimed.

"It matters little to me," said the officer, pushing me out the door, "and keep your opinions to yourself."

No, I won't keep these reflections to myself, and I'll explain it to my comrades, the way it was clearly told elsewhere, that they were for finishing off the wounded and for killing prisoners.

"Well, my cutlass won't be used for such crimes," I told them, and right in front of everybody I tossed mine up onto the roof of an adjacent house.

Almost everyone got rid of theirs, and no one asked what happened to them. Only Sublieutenant Malvezy, in the 4th Section, our wild Tatar, took the biggest cutlass and carried it ostentatiously hooked to his belt.

Before supper our officers got orders to "stuff our heads" about how an incalculable number of cannon were pounding, clobbering the German front, destroying everything from the North Sea all the way to Belfort. All the French, Belgian, and English troops would rise up at the same time and rush out in pursuit of the few miserable Boches who had escaped being massacred by our artillery.

Our division didn't have the honor of being in the first wave. Its role was pursuit, capturing the fleeing enemy, and the next day we'd be drinking an aperitif in [German-occupied] Douai, the regiment's objective.

This time it was for real. Open-field warfare was beginning again. It was so certain that they gave us squares of white cloth to attach to our packs, so that our airplanes and our artillerymen could better distinguish us from afar. In brief, they were telling us that it was going to be a picnic.

Next came a generous distribution of grenades, cartridges, biscuits, tools, sandbags, etc. Twenty times were the corporals called to the distribution centers. At ten in the evening, we were stuffing our packs and our musette bags, and at one in the morning the 280th Regiment headed off to the trenches in complete silence. Everyone was thinking about the anguish and suffering he would be going through, either once again or for the first time.

After around two hours on the march, we arrived at the village of Marœuil, six kilometers from Arras. We crossed this half-demolished little town, and they made us stack our rifles in a field beside a blasted factory where they made corduroy cloth.

A little river, subsequently sadly renowned by the terrible combats which bloodied its banks, ran across the field. This was the Scarpe, which flowed slowly and quietly, but with difficulty, through the plain of Arras.

They warned us not to leave our groups or dismount our equipment. Our dash to Douai, in pursuit of the fleeing enemy, was imminent.

Dawn rose on this historic day, September 25. A gigantic battle was about to be engaged, across an immense front. Millions of men, whole peoples, whole races, were going to clash with each other. Thousands of fiery mouths of guns had been spitting lead and steel for three days, without ceasing. In the final hours before H-hour, the fateful minute, the cannonade reached its climax, making the earth tremble, shaking the air, gripping our souls with an uncertain terror, with a fear that we couldn't put aside.

There was no "sun of Austerlitz,"[6] but rather heavy showers which fell intermittently, without our having the slightest shelter under which to keep ourselves out of it. There were fine shelters in the village, but only the officers found refuge there.

Right behind us, on the other side of the river, on a railroad track, an armored train with naval guns began firing right at daybreak, with a clockwork regularity as if at a target-shoot. At each detonation it seemed like our guts and our brains were going to burst.

During all this, bits of encouraging news were circulated, to inspire our warrior spirit and our patriotic zeal.

In Champagne they were making marmalade of the Boches. On our left, the English had taken Loos in a single grab. In front of us, the first enemy line was captured in one bound; now they were going to attack the second line. Watch out, our turn was coming soon! In fact, at noon, the blast of a whistle brought us all to our feet. This was the signal for us to start in pursuit. Our legs were going to work!

As we left the village, near the cemetery, we entered a wide and well-built communication trench, studded with recent shell craters. We stepped over busted canteens, torn-open and shredded packs, broken and twisted rifles. These were worrisome paving stones. We tramped cautiously through the black mud. This boyau was a bad place for a stroll. Each one of us, feeling oppressed and pessi-mistic, marched forward silently, with our heads down.

The bombardment was angrier than ever. Across the whole front the cannon fire rumbled, the machine guns let forth their chilling, murderous rat-tat-tat. The great battle was engaged; Death was reaping with great sweeps of his scythe.

Meanwhile, ahead of us, the forward momentum of our troops, having crossed the front line, was stopped by the fierce resistance of the Germans.

Luckily our General Niessel had a brilliant idea: Since we couldn't make the Germans leave with cannon blows, let's make them flee out of sheer terror, and immediately the order was given to climb out of the trenches and to march across the open country, bayonets fixed to our rifle barrels.

The whole division was there. It was a true forest of bayonets marching forward. And that wasn't all. The division's cavalry squadron rushed forward in a furious charge, came back, and circled on a hill around a clearing, to give the impression of greater numbers.

But it did no good. The Boches stood their ground in their trenches, des-perately, as if they were fighting on their home ground. Some timed-fuse shells exploding here and there over our heads made us crouch down in the commu-nication trenches, without waiting for the authorization of the stupid General Niessel (whom, for my part, I didn't see at all that day).

They made us stop in an old, abandoned trench, where the whole regiment dug in. This was an historic trench: We were in what had been the German front line at the time of our May offensive, when the nearby villages of Neuville-Saint-Vaast and Ablain-Saint-Nazaire were retaken. Would we be in this trench for a day, a night, an hour? No one knew.

General Niessel, right then, gave an order which was terrible for the rear-echelon shirkers. Orderlies, cooks, rationers, etc., received the order to rejoin their units. That's how the 13th Squad was reinforced with the Peyriacois Fran-çois Maizonnave, who carried out the precious duties of assistant cook and ratio-ner at the officers' mess. Niessel wanted everyone to get a share of the glory, but if you saw the terrified and discomfited faces of these slackers, you would see that they'd have a thousand times preferred to stay with their pots and pans.

And night fell. We wouldn't be enjoying an aperitif in Douai, as they had promised us. Instead we had, for free, some nice refreshing showers, because all night long a cold rain fell, in torrential downpours, and without any shelter for us to dry out in. We were resigned to getting soaked right through our shirts.

You have to have lived through nights like that to appreciate, on a winter night, a well-lit room, a good fire in the fireplace, and a warm, soft bed. Thoughts of those enviable things played upon our imagination.

If we suffered so stoically, without raising useless complaints, don't let anyone tell you that it was because of patriotism, or to defend the rights of peoples to live their own lives, or to end all wars, or other nonsense. It was simply by force, because, as victims of an implacable fate we had to undergo our destiny. Each one of us was caught up in the wheels of a formidable machine. At the slightest hint of revolt we would be ground to bits. Having lost our dignity and our human conscience, we were nothing more than beasts of burden. Like them, we were passive, indifferent, and dazed.

And my comrades in the squad, what did they say? What were they thinking in this gloomy night, in the icy rain? Father Galaup couldn't read his breviary, but he fumbled with his rosary beads in his frostbitten fingers. We talked, and he told me that he was offering his sufferings to God in penitence for the expiation of his sins, and he was sure that this would shorten his time in purgatory. This man was almost happy in his suffering. I envy him, because I doubt that some invisible being, in this opaque night, is out there tallying up our sufferings and taking exact note of them for the hereafter.

I turn toward Lefèvre, and I envy him, too. Having drunk a bottle of pinard to the last drop, he's sleeping, even snoring, desensitized in the sleep of drunkenness.

And that one who's sobbing, that's Chapman. He thinks only about his son who was in the attack today in Champagne. Is he dead, wounded, or alive right now? That's his whole thought, and he's indifferent to everything else, his own suffering and the dangers he himself faces. I try to comfort him, but he doesn't even hear me.

And poor Pélissier, from Lapalme: small, sickly, scrawny, a wreck, he is slumped in the boyau, without the strength even to speak.

The Peyriacois Maizonnave does nothing but rage all night long against Niessel. And the others who didn't spend the last winter in the trenches don't dare to complain, understanding what the veterans have suffered before them.

Only the rationer Terrisse slept. He had the rare ability of being able to sleep in any kind of place, no matter what the circumstances. And yet this night, the deaf themselves could not have slept. Barely a hundred meters behind us was installed a battery of big artillery pieces which fired all night long.

The whistling of the shells overhead kept our nerves on edge. The shells seemed to rush by, right above our trenches, making us duck our heads instinctively. Finally we got used to the noise, but we were also kept awake all night long by the lightning flashes from the cannons' mouths as the shells were fired.

At about 1 a.m. they summoned the rationers to head to the field kitchens to get our supper, but in this dark night the cooks were looking blindly for the rationers and vice versa. The result of this game of hide-and-seek was that the men with the food didn't arrive until just before dawn, more soaked with rain and sweat than the miserable meals they brought us. The loaves of bread were transformed into loaves of mud, the coffee was cold—very little comfort after such a bad night.

The morning of the 26th was rainy, but around noon the weather improved. They took advantage of it by restarting the carnage all along the front.

Packs hoisted, all kitted out, we awaited orders, just like the actors in a theater waiting their turn to go on stage.

At 4 p.m., we had a visit from Commandant Quinze-Grammes, his acolyte *Capitaine-Adjutant-Major* Cros-Mayrevieille, and the battalion's adjutant, the Peryriacois François Calvet. Except for the non-coms, no one saluted them.

Their uniforms and effects were dry and spotless. "The bastards found some kind of shelter to keep themselves in," said Terrisse. He had spent half the night in rain-soaked terrain, and couldn't hide his ill humor.

My countryman Calvet stopped to give me a handshake, but at this moment an orderly, with dispatch in hand, all excited, asked where he could find the commandant.

We shuddered. This scrap of paper no doubt held our destiny. In fact, the commandant read it out in a loud voice, and I caught a few snatches of significant words:

". . . Our troops have taken the trench of Les Tilleuls. The 280th Regiment will take the communication trench at La Targette . . . the attack on Farbus will be pushed to the limit . . ."

"Pushed to the limit . . ." That meant: Pay no attention to losses; take this village, whatever the cost. Too bad for those who left their hides there. That's war!

General Niessel was just doing his job by sending us to the killing fields.

A quarter of an hour later, the 280th Regiment made its way up through the communication trenches to the front lines. We passed through the ruined village of La Targette; then we got caught up in an entanglement of trenches, crossing and recrossing the same places without finding the right path.

We came upon men, isolated or in small groups, heading to the rear. Most gave no response to our questions. Others exclaimed, "The poor guys, the poor guys . . ." or "It's horrible, frightful." They seemed half-crazy.

Nobody had heard anything about Farbus. We began to think that this village existed only in the imagination of General Niessel.

Soon whole battalions and companies were getting mixed up in an inextricable confusion, and the regiment didn't reach the front lines until one in the morning, in a state of extreme fatigue. For nine hours we hadn't taken the packs off of our afflicted shoulders.

There was a long halt. Most of the men were falling down and immediately going to sleep, when our Colonel Poujal ran into another colonel, twenty steps from where our squad was.

We heard our colonel cry out in a loud voice, ". . . Nevertheless, I have a direct order from General Niessel to attack Farbus tonight!"

"But that's insane!" exclaimed the other colonel. "Our division has been wiped out without taking the second German line, and you're planning to go take Farbus, somewhere out there, who knows where? The best thing for you to do," added the colonel, "would be to fall back on Neuville-Saint-Vaast, about fifteen hundred meters from here."

What can one think about this General Niessel, who sent his regiments out in a night like this, so dark that you couldn't see a cow at two paces, to attack a village in the rear of the enemy lines?

Were we in the hands of a dangerous maniac, a total madman, completely unbalanced in the head? How reassuring!

The regiment did fall back on Neuville-Saint-Vaast, where we arrived at dawn. Since 4 o'clock the previous afternoon we had been tramping around in the muddy trenches. Fourteen hours to cover a trajectory which, in a straight line, would have taken an hour and a half!

The Bloody and Futile Offensive
of September 25, 1915:
September 27–November 15, 1915

The Neuville-Saint-Vaast sector. The offensive of September 25th.
Second attack on Farbus. Surprises and panics.
Our haughty captain gets slapped.

Neuville-Saint-Vaast was nothing but a pile of ruins. Our section was lodged in the cellar of a lawyer's house which everyone who passed through Neuville knew well. This dark and humid cellar was filled with all kinds of unspeakable waste and gave off a sickening odor. With our entrenching tools, each one of us cleared a spot to lie down and rest after our little stroll of more than twelve hours in the trenches.

In the afternoon, my friend Gayraud, the colonel's barber, the pride of the 13th Squad to which he still nominally belonged, paid me a visit. The squad is like a little family, a center of affection where deep feelings prevail, of solidarity, mutual devotion, intimacy, and from which the officer and even the sergeant are excluded. To them, the soldier doesn't open up, is mistrustful, and any officer who will want to try to describe the strange life of the trenches, as I'm doing, will never have known, except by accident, the real sentiments, the true spirit, the clear language and the deepest thoughts of the soldier.

So that he would always have his barber at hand, the colonel had named Gayraud his personal orderly. In this spot, he knew all the inside news, which he hastened to tell us. Knowing that I "was writing" the true account of our dolorous calvary, he brought me precious bits of intelligence that even the superior officers didn't know.

This time, the ex-barber from Villelongue didn't bring very uplifting news. General Niessel wasn't going to let us get moldy in this unhealthy cellar. But it wasn't because he cared about our hygiene—that wasn't what mattered.

That evening we had to attack the fatal village of Farbus once again. To prevent a repeat of yesterday's confusion, the runners carefully reconnoitered the connecting trenches leading to the front lines. Our regiment was supposed to move out at 5 p.m. The exact timing of our attack was kept secret from the men until the very last moment, for morale purposes. In reality they didn't want to give the soldiers time to organize any sort of resistance to orders. Our officers couldn't believe that, in the twentieth century, free men would allow themselves to be led to the slaughter, without knowing why or how.

At 4:30 they brought up the evening meal. We weren't used to being served so early in the day. "That's nice, now they're really spoiling us," someone said. We had hardly gulped down the last mouthful when, to everyone's stupefaction except mine, the officers ordered us to hoist our packs. Ten minutes later, by way of three different connecting trenches, the regiment moved briskly up toward Farbus, where we would be unleashed like a rushing torrent, flanked to the right and the left by the other regiments of the division.

But we had hardly gone five hundred meters when we stopped for a good while. What was going on? At the crossroads of two connecting trenches, where we had arrived either too early or too late, we had to make way for another battalion to pass ahead of us.

We took off at a run, then halted, then pulled back. Then we were crammed into a dead-end trench, to let the units which were being relieved make their way back to the rear. For several hours it was like this: halts, pullbacks, spurts ahead. Night fell, and so did the rain, in torrents, soaking us to the bone and filling the trenches, turning them into muddy morasses. What a pretty sight we would make when we finally got around to attacking this damned Farbus.

All of a sudden we all shuddered, as a lively fusillade burst over our heads, followed by cries and shouts. What happened? Had we finally reached Farbus?

No. It was like this. Without realizing it, the 23rd Company, which preceded our own [21st], had gone past our forward listening posts, into no-man's-land, and fell right into a German trench and a welcoming hailstorm of bullets.

Evidently that all went according to plan. Out of fear that we wouldn't attack, they decided to push us beyond our forward positions without telling us. Once we were right on top of the Germans we would have to take care of ourselves and make the best of it.

This crude trick could have had grave consequences, and it shows the villainous mentality of our leaders. It did nothing to raise their prestige in our eyes, or to diminish the mistrust which they inspired in us.

The men of the 23rd Company hit the ground, until the hail of gunfire subsided; then they came rushing back in disarray, throwing the whole regiment into a confused panic. There were plenty of dead and wounded in that company.

Around midnight, our company found ourselves in a completely collapsed trench where all the dugouts, even the deepest ones, were caved in. This had been the German front line which our troops had taken on September 25th. We spent the rest of the night there.

At daybreak we could see, to our horror, that in front of the trench and behind it the ground was covered with hundreds of French bodies. Complete lines, entire ranks of foot soldiers had been mowed down. This was the price paid for an advance of four or five hundred meters—something like one human life per square meter. While our dispatches sang about our victories, they could have been bordered in black.

That day I was exploring a communication trench nearby when I was surprised to find myself in the presence of a German, seated, apparently wounded, who gave me a terrified look. "Kamerad, Kamerad," he stammered. I approached him and saw that he was badly wounded in one leg and had an eye swollen shut. I gave him a couple of sips of peppermint schnapps, which comforted him both physically and mentally, because I think he was expecting a bayonet thrust instead of a helping hand.

I went to find my comrades, who ran up. The prisoner was revived, fed, refreshed with a hefty swig of pinard, and led along the trench. Well, what do you know—this was the 13th Squad's first prisoner. You wouldn't have believed the astounded look he had on his face.

Just then our commandant, nicknamed Quinze-Grammes, passed by, and said to me, "What's all the fuss about?"

"It's a wounded German we found in a communication trench. If you want to have a look, he's right over there."

"I'm not interested," said Quinze-Grammes, who continued along his way.

What was one more wounded German to a stripe-sleeved big shot like Quinze-Grammes?

The stretcher-bearers said that they would take care of the German wounded only once all the French wounded had been taken away. From a humanitarian viewpoint this was grossly unjust, but from a French viewpoint it was perfectly logical. As it happened, before nightfall the wounded German and several of his comrades whom we had snagged in the communication trenches were taken back to the dressing station.

At 4 p.m. the order came to hoist our packs. Were we going to relieve another unit? Were we just moving from one place to another? Or were we mounting another attack on this phantom village of Farbus which we had been straining our eyes to glimpse, all day long?

We first followed the main trench to the left. Then our section alone entered a deep, narrow boyau, heading forward.

Had there been hand-to-hand combat here? Had wounded and dying men dragged themselves to this spot?

Whatever had happened, there were numerous bodies of Frenchmen and Germans, whom death had surprised in every conceivable pose: lying, kneeling, crouched down; the boyau was narrow, and we were forced to step on corpses. What a horror that was!

All of a sudden, right in front of the head of the section, came a burst of grenade blasts, followed by furious cries, shrieks, moans. Voices yelled, "Fall back! It's the Boches! Run like hell!"

Our boyau ran right into the main German trench. We had come up against a German advance party that proceeded to massacre, with hand grenades, those of us who were at the front of the column, who had been moving along imprudently, expecting to relieve a squad of fellow Frenchmen.

Our leaders must have known that we would bump into the Germans. Why not warn us? Why not give us the chance to take every precaution which would apply to an advance into a dangerous boyau?

Well, it was always the same reason. They feared that we would refuse to go forward. That we would confront their orders with our passivity, with the strength and power of our inertia.

When our leaders had to sink to such stratagems to get their troops to march, it shows that there is no reciprocal confidence, that there is a complete divergence of interests. The bosses are interested only in chalking up a success, to make it worthwhile. The men, who have everything to lose and nothing to gain, who don't know why they're there, who are looking only to escape any danger they can and to save their skins. It's human nature.

In the narrow boyau filled with the sounds of massacre, our column was slow to execute an about-face. Each terrified soldier tried to clamber out of the trench and make his way back through the brush, across open country. I tried to do the same, but the weight of my pack prevented it. I couldn't even unbuckle the strap to get it off me. I was finally able to get rid of it and to get out of the trench, one of the last to do so before the Germans swept through the trench.

Night was falling, and I could make my way in the open, without being seen. I arrived at a trench occupied by the 108th Infantry Regiment. The soldiers, alerted by our cries, had fixed bayonets and were ready to open fire.

"Hurry up," they called out to me, "get out of our line of fire!"

They told me what had happened, and showed me the way to the trenches occupied by the 28oth.

After ten minutes, I arrived at the entrance to the boyau. At this point the trench was quite wide, like a sunken road. Our cowardly captain, Cros-Mayrevieille, was there.

"It's shameful, what happened out there," he cried, "Get back out into the trench." But nobody budged. If Captain Cros-Mayrevieille had put himself in front of us, we all would have followed him.

At this moment, Agussol, an epileptic who for some time had shown signs of mental weakness but whom we had kept with us all the same, lost his mind. Hearing that we were being ordered back into the trench where we had had such a frightful time, he advanced on the captain and swung an empty musette bag at him, by the straps, smacking him in the face and knocking his spectacles off. Then he charged off into the trench, shouting and singing the verses of a battle song:

"The air is pure, the road is wide/The bugler sounds the charge . . ."[1]

He disappeared into the falling night, and then all was silent. The next day we found his body, riddled with bullets, along the boyau.

Once again we made our way along the dark corridor. This time a team of grenadiers was at the head of the column, lobbing grenades continuously as we advanced. No more Germans; they were no doubt waiting for us in their trench. Someone decided it was a good idea to halt about fifty meters before reaching it, and we waited for orders.

From this moment, the daily rain began to fall, and continued all night long in heavy downpours. The attack was postponed until the next day.

We spent a miserable night there, without any shelter at all, soaked to our shirts, shivering with cold. We envied the poor dead men who littered the boyau; they at least weren't suffering anymore.

Each squad took turns standing watch at the head of the column. Around midnight, our Sublieutenant Malvezy, who wisely kept to the rear of the section, passed us a note which we read with Sergeant Faure, by the light of an electric lamp. It was an order to move up in the boyau.

The men started to protest violently at word of this order. They didn't have any spirit of adventure. They weren't curious at all. The sergeant was perplexed. I suggested that he respond this way: "The men ask that the section chief lead them at the head of the column."

He scribbled down these few words, and the note was passed back, from hand to hand, to the prudent Malvezy, who decided not to press the matter any further. He would have to earn his second-lieutenant's stripe on his own; we weren't going to earn it for him.

At first light we yielded our place, without much pleading, to another section which came to relieve us.

We weren't going far in reserve. Only back to the nearest trench, practically at the entrance to the boyau where we had spent such a miserable night.

In a corner of the boyau we discovered a German officers' shelter where we set up lodging.

In this shelter there were some illustrated German newspapers. In one of them our Joffre was depicted sleeping on a bed. Sweat dripped from his body in the form of great drops of blood that he had caused to flow in vain and futile offensives.

Another showed Joffre on horseback, advancing at the head of a vast army which is halted by insurmountable tangles of barbed wire protecting a German trench, where only three or four machine gunners stand guard, bottles of beer under their arms, enjoying a snack while firing their machine gun, producing a pile of slaughtered Frenchmen.

We were all set to spend a comfortable night in this shelter, which would have brought us some well-earned rest, but the butcher Niessel had decided on another attack, that very afternoon at five o'clock.

We made our way up the "Boyau des Morts," where we had just spent such a disagreeable night. There was a long wait, as usual; then the order came to fix bayonets. We passed from hand to hand the order from Commandant Quinze-Grammes, telling the officer of the lead section to report back every ten minutes about what was happening. How curious he was, our commandant, and how prudent, too.

This aroused the anger of the men, who, without scruple, unfolded and read the note. "Let him come up here himself, to see what happens. Let him get out of his hole," cried rough voices.

One soldier, I don't know anymore who it was, tore the note to pieces, to the approving laughter of those watching.

Each one had come to the same resolution. We would not attack. We would not move out from the boyau. The word went from the front to the rear and back again, at least twenty times: "Pass the word. We're not attacking."

Some may call this cowardice. But mounting an attack against sturdy, well-defended trenches, protected by thick barbed-wire entanglements, without the slightest artillery fire beforehand—wouldn't you call that criminal?

Along the whole front the offensive had failed lamentably. Only Niessel persisted in wanting to attack, day and night. If he couldn't take Douai, he wanted Farbus, no matter what the cost, so that they could say, "Here is Niessel, the conqueror of Farbus!"

Beside me, Father Galaup told me that if the order came, saying "Forward!" his priest's conscience would compel him to go forth, even if he were the only one.

"I have one favor to ask you," he said. "If I'm killed in the attack, I beg you not to leave me unburied out there. Nothing horrifies me more than the thought of being prey to the rats and the crows."

I promised him nothing. "Do you seriously think," I answered him, "that if you're crazy enough to go out there on your own, we're going to risk our lives to go pull your body off the barbed wire?"

Bothered by this, the holy Father Galaup thought a moment, then asked me: "Would you give me a counterorder to come back to the boyau after the order comes to attack?"

"Sure, if that's what you need. I'll even grab you by your coattails and haul you back into the boyau," I promised him.

His conscience would be clear, his responsibility disengaged. Having reconciled his patriotic priestly duties with the desire for self-preservation, he went back to clicking his rosary beads.

Night had fallen, and still we awaited the order to attack. We were in a state of nervous expectation, which only those who have experienced can know what it's like.

Private Viale in my squad hurt his hand while opening and closing the breech of his rifle. The blood flowed, and Sergeant F. . . ., the one who had denounced me as an antimilitarist, accused him of having wounded himself on purpose and hauled him before the captain. Despite Viale's vehement protests he was sent back to the squad.

It was 9 p.m. We'd been waiting for four hours, bayonets fixed, for them to pronounce the two terrible words, *En avant!* [Forward!]

What did this long wait mean? No one knew, but along came our friend Gayraud, making his way up the boyau, to rejoin the 13th Squad and, guessing our deep anxiety, determined to tell us what he knew.

"There's some good news," he said. "The 23rd Company, who were supposed to launch the attack, refused to march. Their captain, Darnaudy (from La Redorte), and the section chiefs went to explain the situation to the commandant. They're telephoning to the colonel and to Niessel."

But the general demanded that the attack take place, making Captain Darnaudy responsible for it being carried out. Therefore he threw himself over the top, all alone, and fell at ten paces from the trench, gravely wounded. (He had an arm amputated.)

The attack was finally postponed to another time, and we put Rosalie [slang term for bayonet; see note 2, 3rd Notebook] back into her scabbard. They passed out picks and shovels to us, and we spent the night digging a communication trench. We didn't want to attack? So have us dig a trench, no matter where. That will teach us to play games when we're supposed to be marching to massacre.

At daybreak, our commandant Quinze-Grammes sent the battalion adjutant, the Peyriacois François Calvet, to check on the work we had done. He had barely entered the trench when a stray bullet tore up his right shoulder quite badly. One centimeter closer and there would have been one less Peyriacois in the world.

Our pal Calvet was hardly bothered by this. "My wound might save the lives of others," he said, "because before I'm evacuated I'll say in my report that this boyau is in full view of the Boches and open to enfilading fire."

We had worked ten hours for nothing, but this thought of Calvet's showed a generosity of spirit that many others, in the emotion of being wounded and the joy of getting out of these bad places, would not have had.

They sent us to take twenty-four hours of so-called rest in the front-line trench, and what rest! Work details, all day long, and at night the company got orders to bury the dead who lay between the lines since the assaults of September 25–26.

The dead men were divided into lots, and we drew for them by squad. For the 13th Squad I drew a lucky hand. We only had six corpses to get rid of, and they were very close to the trench. We got the work done quickly. You pushed the cadaver into a shell hole, tossed a few shovelfuls of earth on top, and on to the next one. As corporal I had to take off each one's identity tag. Some had it on their wrists, others hanging around their necks, or in a pocket— what a chore! To dig through a dead man's pockets, pat him down, and with a knife or scissors cut the cord or the chain which held the identity tag. It seemed like a profanation to us, and we spoke in whispers as if we were afraid of waking them up.

The squad that had to take care of the corpses in the boyau itself, the ones we had been tramping over for three days, took all night to accomplish its lugubrious task, digging out the half-crushed, broken, collapsed bodies, mixed in with dirt, musette bags, knapsacks, which for many formed a single, blood-soaked, muddy mass.

And when this work was done, we didn't even have a drop of water for washing our hands. We had to rub them with dirt to clean them a little bit. But our initial repugnance softened; living in filth, we became worse than animals.

The next morning, October 1, our section went to take up its post in the same boyau. Each squad took the up-front position in turn. The 13th had to be there from seven p.m. until midnight. A simple barricade of sandbags was the French border, at this point. We had the bad luck that, during our turn at guard, the order came to move this barricade forward. Maybe it was so that they could say in the next day's communiqué that, in Artois, we had made forward progress.

Were the Germans nearby? How far ahead were they? Wouldn't they fall upon us, massacre us during our work, in this night which was so dark you couldn't have seen a cow at two paces, even with eyes like ours, habituated more to a nocturnal life than one by daylight?

"We need a volunteer," I said, "to be a lookout, a couple of paces ahead of us." But it was truly frightening, this dark, mysterious trench where we knew there were Germans up ahead. At first nobody offered his devoted service, but then the abbé Galaup accepted this dangerous post and waited out there, alone, as a sentinel while the barricade was being erected.

At four the next morning we were relieved, and sent back to a reserve position near the ruins of Neuville-Saint-Vaast. That night we could finally bed down in individual holes dug into the slope of a sunken road which led into the village.

Since September 25 we had only one hour of sleep at a time. Seven consecutive nights of watch, of work, of burying the dead . . .

Meanwhile, the 13th Squad, despite its ill-fated number thirteen, came back from these skirmishes without having lost one man. But the next day Private Guerard was wounded by a stray bullet in the leg, carrying a load of water from Neuville. The stretcher-bearers who came to pick him up told us that the regiment was losing, on average, ten men a day, killed or wounded.

But if we had listened to that clown Niessel, and attacked like mad the way he told us to, it's likely that we'd have lost a hundred men a day, instead of ten.

In the night of October 4–5 we were sleeping soundly in our holes when we were rudely awakened by cries of "To arms! Alert! Everybody up! Hoist your packs. Two men from each squad take grenades, two more take cartridges, two more for rations. Let's go, on the double!"

"My God," the abbé Galaup asked me, "what's going on now?"

"Well, it must be some business of Niessel's, we'll see," I replied.

In fact, we soon learned that a general attack was to be launched at daybreak. At 2 in the morning we were posted up near the front line, in a communication trench so narrow that we could neither sit nor crouch down.

The rain came down in torrents. It seemed as if they had forgotten about us there. Around noontime, our bosses remembered that we hadn't had any food since the meager supper of the evening before, and generously authorized us to eat our rations.

Those who had jackals' teeth could nibble at their biscuits, already gnawed on by rats, which we carried in our packs, and that was all. They weren't giving chocolate yet, and we couldn't eat beans, rice, coffee, and sugar, since our bi-ped stomachs weren't able to digest these foods uncooked.

It was just to make fun of us. All we could do was to tighten our belts a notch, and everything would be fine. Under the lashing downpour which addled our brains, emptied our minds of all conscious thought, we waited, immobile and silent.

An almost total calm reigned. No volleys; an occasional cannon fired to break the silence, but it was muted, deafened by the fog, resonating like the ringing of a distant gong.

Finally, around five in the afternoon, I heard someone say, "Pass this note to Corporal Barthas." Vaguely worried, I wondered what someone would want from me in this ditch. But as soon as I cast my eyes on this note, I was reassured. It was our good comrade Gayraud who was sending us some inside news about the situation, in a few sentences scribbled down in haste: "The 5th Battalion was supposed to launch the attack but its commandant (de Fageoles), judging success to be impossible, emphatically refused to attack, despite the anger and exasperation of Niessel. The attack didn't take place. We're going to pull back to Marœuil."

It wasn't our own cowardly commandant Quinze-Grammes who would have dared resist the terrible Niessel!

Soon our torture came to an end. For fifteen hours we had been at a half-crouch, our limbs stiffened by such long immobility, but our joy gave us wings and legs to carry us, half-dead with fatigue, to Marœuil, at 9 in the evening after three and a half hours of marching.

We wandered around the village for an hour, searching for some sort of billet, since no one expected our arrival.

Our section ended up bunking in a hovel half-demolished by shells, but nobody complained. It was so bad where we had come from that we all slept at least as soundly as Niessel in his château, if not better.

We spent four days of rest in Marœuil. One evening I attended a religious service at the church, honoring Saint Bertilde or Bertille, whose relics drew pilgrimages to Marœuil, because this saint had the reputation of healing illnesses of the eyes.

A bad region for eye doctors, with a competitor like that!

A few days earlier, a big shell had fallen on the church and exploded in the choir, pulverizing everything except the glass reliquary containing the saint's bones. Miracle? Accident?

Of course, for the curate of Marœuil, there was no doubt; this was a genuine miracle. At the service I attended, he affirmed that this was the third time these relics had escaped complete destruction: during the Hundred Years' War, the Revolution of 1789, and now in 1915.

On October 9 the 280th Regiment received the order to move back up to the front line, since you can imagine that Niessel wasn't going to let us have six months of rest. At seven in the evening we were already assembled, ready to move out, when a counterorder arrived, and to our great surprise they sent us off in the opposite direction, away from Neuville-Saint-Vaast.

At the end of an hour and a half march we could see some lights twinkling in the dark. We were arriving at the village of Agnez-lès-Duisans, where we were to be billeted.

Our *fourrier* [quartermaster] told us that the 21st Company was going to be lodged in the outbuildings of the château where Niessel had installed himself as lord of the manor.

This news made us happy. Certainly, we thought, a campsite right under the eyes of the division's general must be equipped with all the comforts we could desire. But how great was our disappointment when they stuck us in a stable, with a thick layer of manure covering the whole floor!

A hundred men would have had trouble lying down in there. They were piling up 250, and we also had to make room for fifty sappers.

In vain I looked all around for a barn, a pig sty, any sort of shelter suitable for spending the night. I found nothing. I was forced to go back to the stable, where we arrayed ourselves as best we could, one on top of another, in every position. We could hardly sleep at all because someone was always coming in or going out, which couldn't be done without trampling on someone and provoking angry shouts, complaints, and threats from those being stepped upon.

As soon as day broke, a large number of us went out into the courtyard and started into vigorous calisthenics to battle against the bitter cold. We made quite a racket, like true southerners who never lose their petulance. We thought about nothing but Niessel sleeping comfortably in his fine bed, and that we were troubling his sleep or his profound strategic meditations, or his love-making, because it was said that Niessel and the pretty lady of the manor . . . but that was none of our business.

Suddenly a door of the château burst open, and the general appeared, bareheaded, with an angry scowl, and cried out in an irritated voice: "Would you please shut up, or I'll have you sent to the trenches right away! Go back to bed and get some rest!"

He was talking to us just as a master talks to his dogs. He was granting us permission to go to bed, without deigning to think about whether there was any place to do that.

The next morning, the general was in a better mood. He came into the courtyard with packets of one-penny pencils which he handed out to some baffled soldiers, telling them, "Here, fellows, distribute these to your comrades."

"This distribution of pencils doesn't tell me anything worth knowing," I said to my comrades in the squad. "You'll see that Niessel is preparing some sort of unhappy surprise for us."

In fact, at 10:30, we had barely finished our meals when the order was given to leave immediately for the trenches. Along the way, the officers told us that the 280th Regiment was going to support a divisional attack.

When we had passed beyond Neuville-Saint-Vaast, the Germans unleashed a violent barrage upon us. We fell back upon Neuville in hasty flight.

Ah, they'll say, those southerners, always ready to turn tail. But in our ranks were Parisians and Bretons, and I noticed that they scampered along as quickly as we did.

Commandant Quinze-Grammes and the *Kronprinz* [nickname for Captain

Cros-Mayrevieille (see note 6, 9th Notebook)], at the moment that the firing began, were passing in front of a big shelter, where they immediately sought refuge.

When calm returned, they sent out their servants (or I should say their orderlies) to gather us up. This wasn't easy, since we were widely scattered.

The attack took place, but two sections of the 281st Regiment who went over the top from the trenches were immediately cut down by machine guns.

In spite of repeated orders from Niessel, no one else wanted to go out.

At seven in the evening, our company went up to reinforce the 281st Regiment. We occupied a communication trench which was badly damaged by shellfire. We had to spend the night in the open, despite frequent volleys of shells which the Germans haphazardly sent over onto our lines.

Another bad night to be engraved on our memories.

The next day, October 12, at 9 p.m. we went back to the front line, relieving the 281st Regiment.

Arriving at the firing line, we noticed assault ladders placed every ten meters along the parapet. This sight made us shiver, just as if we were walking past the gallows.

In our trench were the remnants of a German heavy artillery battery, completely wiped out by our own artillery: shells, equipment, and German corpses, all buried together.

Night and day, they put us to work excavating the dugouts in this strongpoint.

Right behind and in front of the firing line there were large numbers of dead, in proportion of about one German for every twenty Frenchmen. The latter belonged to the 50th Infantry Regiment.

This advance had cost us dearly. Seven or eight hundred meters, which didn't really gain us anything. We were facing enemy trenches which were just as solidly defended as the ones which we had taken.

Under cover of the thick fog which covered the landscape each morning, some of us went out to find rifles, revolvers, et cetera. A few of the less scrupulous went through the pockets of the dead men.

One morning Corporal Cathala, of our company, out in the open on such a mission, was hit by a bullet which wounded him gravely in the thigh, leading to a subsequent amputation. He dragged himself back to the trench, where they staunched his wound. He was lying on ground soaked in his own blood.

All of a sudden, here was General Niessel, whom we saw often in the trenches at daybreak—when all was calm.

"Ah!," said the general, "Where was this corporal wounded?"

We couldn't tell him that he had been pilfering the pockets of dead men. So we said it was at an observation post.

"Find me the captain! Are you satisfied with this soldier's conduct?" he asked our captain [Cros-Mayrevieille], nicknamed the Kronprinz, who had quickly appeared on the scene.

"Yes, very satisfied," stammered our captain.

"Very well. He will be commended, and will get the Croix de Guerre and the Médaille Militaire."

And that's how Corporal Cathala became a hero.

The abbé Galaup was haunted for some time by the desire to find a German rifle with a saw-toothed bayonet attached, to take home as a souvenir.

The Germans had one of these in each squad, in case it was needed to cut a branch, saw up a wooden plank, etc. Of course they would occasionally put it on the end of a rifle, to cut through a thorax or a belly. It served double duty.

Father Galaup, in search of this combination weapon-tool, went out into the fog each morning, at the risk of intercepting a bullet along the way.

One day, he told me that if I wanted a revolver and a nice pair of binoculars, he would point them out to me. The next day, accepting this offer, I went to the place he indicated, where an enormous shell had exploded right in the middle of a group of French soldiers mounting an assault, decapitating and frightfully mutilating a dozen men, who were now nothing more than bloody scraps.

I spotted the binoculars and the revolver on the ground, still in their leather cases. I quickly grabbed them and fled, appalled by the horrible scene.

With the help of these binoculars, the abbé Galaup ended up finding the object of his desire, a precious saw-toothed bayonet at the end of a rifle held by a dead German, a few paces from the trench, tangled up in a mass of barbed wire.

You'd have to be crazy to want to go out, even at night, to look for a weapon like this, risking nine chances out of ten to be killed for a bayonet, even a saw-toothed one. Probably no man in the regiment would have attempted it.

Well, this priest tried it. The following night he crept out, succeeded in getting his fascinating bayonet, and came back without arousing the attention of the Germans. But while he was coming back he lost his way and stumbled upon a listening post of a neighboring company, where two sentinels fired on him but missed.

At the very moment that he got away from this post, a 105mm shell fell right onto it, killing the two sentinels.

The abbé Galaup offered profound thanks to Providence, which favored him in this rash enterprise and kept him safe from such serious dangers.

Meanwhile, Lieutenant Malvezy cast envious eyes upon my new binoculars, and brazenly proposed that I exchange them for his own, which weren't worth forty sous. I refused. He insisted; I refused even more emphatically. He didn't waste much time exacting petty vengeance on me.

On October 17, at nine in the evening, a shell burst about thirty meters from our position, right in the trench, killing outright two unfortunate rationers bringing food up for their squad.

One of them was my poor comrade Vieu, from Mas-Cabardès, who had come up as a replacement in July. He was attached to my squad at first, but after a while he was transferred to the 18th Company, where his brother was a rationer for officers. This brother was also killed, a short time afterward. These were two good, sincere Socialist militants from Mas-Cabardès. The war had positive results for the capitalist bourgeoisie!

During this stint at the front lines, our neighboring company, the 18th, was sorely tested. They had a score of killed or wounded, while our company only had three wounded. That was because we were so close to the Germans that their artillerymen didn't dare pound on us, in fear of hitting their own trenches.

One day Father Galaup was firing the German rifle he had picked up, out of his loophole, like a madman. I warned him, "Who lives by the sword will die by the sword."

The Germans, who had gone for many hours without firing a single shot, began to reply to Father Galaup's fusillade. They soon discovered the loophole from which the rifle fire was coming, and right away a bullet passed through the narrow opening and shattered the wrist of the fighting priest before going through his helmet and grazing his forehead. He was taken to the first-aid station and then evacuated to Royaumont,[2] from where he sent us greetings and best wishes.

The last day of this front-line assignment, at dawn, General Niessel came up to the trenches. He stopped first at the neighboring company, the 18th, which my squad was in contact with. I heard him chewing out a sentry who had made no sign of respect to his august personage.

"In the trenches," he cried, "I don't require a full, rule-book salute, but at least take a deferential attitude."

It must be said that, away from the trenches, the general didn't fool around when it came to the exterior signs of respect. He required that you salute when his staff car went by, whether he was in it or not.

On this occasion, Commandant de Fageoles, who was also making his morning rounds, came face to face with Niessel.

At sight of the commandant, the general exploded in anger. He clearly had not pardoned him for refusing to have his battalion massacred at the regiment's last assault.

"Look at the Boches, commandant, what work they've done over the past two weeks, and we've done nothing! Nothing! And I mean to change that. Every day I want a detailed report on all the work that's done, and I'll come verify it myself."

At a humble interruption by his interlocutor, Niessel shouted so loudly that the Boches must have heard him:

"I'm not asking for your advice, I'm giving you an order!"

Then, getting more and more worked up . . .

"And tell your men that we have to get the Boches out of here. We have to attack, if not today, then tomorrow. You'll get the order."

If it was up to him, it wouldn't have dragged out much longer.

And then, casting a scornful eye on the ragged, muddy, dirty men who had gathered around him out of curiosity, he said, "Look at these outfits, you'd think they were a bunch of militiamen. I could have done more with a section of my old Zouaves than with your whole regiment!"

Brusquely the general turned to me and said angrily, "Have you passed the word that I am here? It's been twenty minutes, and no one has come to meet me."

"Excuse me, general. I told my sergeant that you were here."

"So that's how your captain takes care of business. We'll go have a look."

But as for me, I couldn't go have a look, which was too bad. Our captain, Master Cros-Mayrevieille, had to take the heat, according to his rank. This devil of a general mistreated his officers like simpletons, with no regard for their stripes.

The same day we learned that, contrary to the wishes of General Niessel, the offensive was being halted everywhere, and that furloughs and leaves were going to begin. What a sigh of relief! What a weight fell from our shoulders. In spite of our fatigue, our joy gave us such wings—or such legs—that we arrived at Marœuil at one in the morning, having found neither the road too long nor our packs too heavy.

Starting the next day, each company had to form a section specialized in throwing grenades. It was understood that preference would go to young, vigorous men.

In our section, Sublieutenant Malvezy, who was assigned to choose the grenadier-section's corporal, quickly chose me, despite the fact that of the four corporals I was the eldest. That was no doubt to teach me a lesson for having finer binoculars than his own.

I could have complained. But I told myself that up at the listening posts, where the grenadiers would be located, I would be more favorably posted—more exposed to grenades and to surprise attacks, but less exposed to shells and mortar rounds, than I would be farther to the rear. So I left my good comrades in the squad, and joined the grenadier section.

The next day of our sojourn at Marœuil they put us to work in the front lines, digging a boyau. Heading out at 6 in the evening, we arrived back at 4 in the morning, worn out because we'd had to cover twenty kilometers in all. They called that being "at rest." There was one of us who didn't come back, having been killed outright by a stray bullet. Nobody wept over him. Who deserved to be mourned—him, or us?

During the day we kept busy by tossing stones instead of grenades, from morning to night, along the banks of the river Scarpe, to build up our throwing arms. But by the end of four days we had all wrenched our shoulders out.

On October 23, at 6 in the evening, we went to billet at Agnez for four more days. This time we were lodged not at Niessel's château but at another one in the middle of the village. They bunked us in piles of hay with, for our pillows, bunches of straw where legions of ticks and fleas swarmed.

This château was a true nest of shirkers, for the whole division: telephone operators, stenographers, stretcher-bearers, gendarmes. All of these folks naturally occupied the best spots, and looked upon us with visible disdain.

One afternoon, General Niessel summoned all the sergeants and corporals for a conference about our role in the trenches during the upcoming winter campaign.

We were assembled in a schoolroom. The general welcomed us with a big smile, all jolly and perky. This was no longer the terrible brawler who dreamed only of cuts and bruises, assaults and combats.

"Well," he said with a twinkle in his eye, "you're all good, sturdy fellows. With men like you we can get something done. I like the way you look and how you handle yourselves."

After this flattering preamble, the general told us, "You know that, this coming winter, we're not going to let the Boches sit comfortably in their holes. We're going to bother them all the time, and here's how . . ."

And in front of a blackboard, chalk in hand, Niessel explained to us, for two whole hours, how to dig an approach trench to take a listening post or a trench, how to get close enough to the enemy to throw grenades, wham-bam-bam, and he concluded each sentence with the words, "It'll be easy."

In fact, it looked easy, even too easy, child's play. You'd hardly know that we were talking about killings, throat cuttings, massacres.

Then Niessel deigned to thank us for our (required) attention and headed off to his château, persuaded no doubt that he had excited our warrior spirit and patriotic sentiments.

How wrong he was!

Neuville-Saint-Vaast sector, 1915. Discipline on the march.
The grenadier section. The Tranchée du Moulin.

On October 25, before we went back to the trenches, it was decided that, in order to get us back into proper disciplinary shape, we would take a long march during which the rules would be observed strictly.

With Sergeant Lasserre, head of the company's grenadiers, being away on furlough, I was promoted (against my best wishes) to be temporary head of what was called the "elite" section; it was actually the one to which each squad had sent its biggest malcontents.

In spite of rainy weather, we set out at noon, the grenadiers in line of march. Expecting to meet Niessel, the scourge of officers, our captain declared that he was insisting on perfect marching order as we passed through Agnez-lès-Duisans.

It was our bad luck that, as we came out of our encampment, three or four trucks in a row crossed our path and cut the company's grenadier section in two. There was a gap of about fifty meters separating the half which had gone ahead from our half, which was left behind.

I begged my grenadiers to pick up the pace and catch up to the rest of the column, before the captain saw what had happened.

Some ran, others galloped, but half continued at the normal pace. The result: indescribable disorder, and here is the captain who looks back and gives us a furious look. I tried to explain that our column had been cut by trucks crossing, but this only exasperated him. For a full half-hour he put us through close-order drills, making us repeat the same maneuvers four, five, ten times, me along with the men.

Finally, he himself got tired of giving us orders, and he let us alone and went off to bother other sections or the whole company.

It was a steady stream of whistle blasts, moving from route pace to cadenced pace, forming squares, et cetera . . . all accompanied by fastidious run-through of the manual of arms.

With his horse he made us keep the left side of the road wide open. We had to keep to the edge of the road, even if there were big puddles or mud holes, all because it was written in the rule book.

Passing through the village of Montecourt [Montenescourt, southwest of Agnez-lès-Duisans], the grenadier section came back into his good graces. We seemed to have paraded in an impeccable fashion, while the others had marched like a bunch of firemen. To reward us, he let us march at a normal, walking pace, while the others had to step briskly at a cadenced pace, with arms shouldered.

It was the grenadiers' turn to have some fun. Not all of them, however. For example, Grenadier Segueil, who got four days in prison for being so rash as to puff on his pipe which he kept hidden in his left hand when we were marching at cadenced pace. This was not to be believed, and the captain was pitiless. Likewise for another who couldn't hold his tongue, forgetting that at cadenced pace you're supposed to be quiet as a carp.

On October 28, at five in the afternoon, we headed out again, accompanied by cold downpours, to occupy reserve trenches near Neuville-Saint-Vaast.

We were drenched by these steady rains, slipping and stumbling along al-

most impassable roads and paths in the dark night. They finally stopped bothering us with their stupid rules and marching orders.

Cursing, grumbling, complaining, each one of us marched along, dragging
himself forward as best he could. To arrive where? In gloomy boyaux, full of
mud, where we argued with each other over half-collapsed holes which our
predecessors had dug. Only the officers had halfway-decent shelters at their
disposal.

A few slabs of sheet metal, some planks placed across the top of the trench
and covered with earth, would have been enough to give us a shelter, if not
comfortable, at least sufficient to protect us from the glacial wind and the
downpours. But no. There, like practically everywhere else, nothing had been
planned for, nothing had been ordered, by some colonel or other or by Generalissimo Joffre, to shelter the human cattle against the bad weather.

Two days later, at nightfall, our company went up to occupy a second-line
trench called the "Tranchée du Moulin" [Trench of the Mill].

There had indeed been a mill in the vicinity. But I spotted only the remains
of it three days later, a few bricks sticking out of the earth and mud.

The miller will have a fit when he comes back!

At the emplacement occupied by the grenadier section, there was only a single shelter for all of us. It had been dug by the Germans, who started digging a
mine there. Unfortunately our advance had interrupted their work, and all that
was left was a staircase with about forty steps dug into the earth. At the bottom
was a shallow, narrow corridor where, because so little air got down that far,
candles wouldn't even stay lit.

There was so little room that we had to leave our weapons, rifles, and packs
outside on the firing step, at the mercy of the rain and any larcenous souls.

Those who find their bedrooms not spacious or comfortable enough should
consider whether forty men were comfortable on this narrow, muddy, slippery
staircase, where every moment someone was either going up or coming down,
and there wasn't room for two slightly overweight men to pass each other.
Luckily we were all pretty thin.

The opening of this cave faced the enemy, and it was quite possible that an
errant shell could come bouncing down the staircase and make a bloody grenadier omelet. But we didn't give this a second thought; we were familiar with
mortal danger.

Besides, we weren't gathering any moss in this dead-end spot. On the captain's behalf, morning and night, an orderly came and put us into work details.
We had to carry out our chores in the rain; since we had arrived at the Tranchée
du Moulin it rained almost without stopping.

On November 2 it really came down in torrents. The trenches were transformed into open sewers. That day, at nightfall, in full deluge, I received the

order to put all the grenadiers to work cleaning out the boyaux which led to the front lines, all through the night.

A stupid, senseless, barbarous order. To work in a night of opaque, tomblike darkness, in icy water, in mud, on a task which was hopeless as long as the rain fell. It was too much, and the men declared that they didn't want to work.

I scribbled a couple of lines on the back of the written order brought by the orderly, telling the captain the reasons why we would do better to wait for the rain to stop.

A half-hour later I received another note, this one a veritable ultimatum ordering me to begin work immediately. I was responsible for the execution of this order, and the captain himself would be coming up to see that it would be carried out.

By the light of an electric lamp, I wrote my response: "Captain, I know the limits of work, of effort, of fatigue which one can ask of a man. My conscience won't allow me to go beyond those limits. Either grant me that, or give my command to someone else."

A minute later the orderly, soaked to the skin by these multiple excursions in the trench transformed into a canal, brought me the order to present myself before the captain, immediately.

The captain was installed in a deep shelter, a dozen steps below ground.

Seated at a little table, he was enjoying a peaceful game of cards with Lieutenant Mouret.

To the side a brazier threw off lovely warmth, and an aide was heating up the teapot. What a difference between these officers' situation and our own!

"Corporal," the captain said dryly, "by order of the commandant, you have to put your men to work all night long, to keep the boyaux passable up to the front lines. Go to it!"

"Captain, as long as the rain is coming down in torrents, I'm not going to have my men out there working, because their efforts would be useless, and all their fatigue, their suffering, would be for nothing. And besides, they wouldn't obey me."

"I repeat, it's the commandant's order!"

"And I repeat that this order can't be carried out. Please give the command of the grenadier section to another non-com. It's not for me, a simple corporal, to be in charge."

The captain stood up, in a rage.

"Corporal Barthas, for the last time, I'm demanding that you execute this order. I'm holding you responsible. I'll come to see for myself. Now get out of here!"

A quarter-hour later, after almost stumbling and drowning in the torrential rain, I found myself in front of the narrow entrance to our staircase, where everyone was so tightly packed that anyone who went out wouldn't find a place again.

Completely soaked, I was shivering, my teeth were chattering. Was I going to die of cold, of exhaustion, in this gloomy boyau?

To my physical distress was added moral distress. This order to put men to work, to throw them out of their shelter, into the mud, the gloom, the storm, the icy water, these forty men already frozen right through, filled my head with storms of rage, of hate-filled anger against these inhuman orders.

My decision was made. I would defy the captain's and the commandant's orders. The men would stay in their shelter. But maybe tomorrow I would be arrested for refusing to obey an order, and dragged before a court-martial. They could even be scoundrels enough to have me shot, as an example.

No, not that. They won't get me. Crazy thoughts invaded my brain. Before dying I would go back to the captain's lair and skewer him with my bayonet like an ill-behaved beast. Then I thought about how, at the bottom of the staircase, candles wouldn't stay lit, and no one dared go to sleep down there, preferring to pile up on the stairs. Well I would go down there, and by tomorrow I would likely be asphyxiated. That would be a nice, painless death, the end of this cruel life. The thought of my loved ones didn't hold me back. I had long ago given up any hope of seeing them again.

I made my way down the narrow staircase, stepping on and slipping on feet, legs, backs, bellies, provoking angry growls and grumbles directed at me.

Finally I got to the bottom. I had my pack with me, and I took off my dripping clothes and wrapped myself in my blanket, as if in a shroud and, stretched out on the damp ground, abandoned myself to the sleep of the dead.

Around midnight, someone roughly shook me awake by the shoulders. "Let me die in peace," I cried out.

"Are you crazy?" said the captain's orderly. "Here, read this paper." And by the light of an electric lamp I read that the captain was demanding that I give an account of the work accomplished so far.

On a scrap of paper I wrote that the men were at work on such and such a trench. I knew that the orderly was a good comrade and wouldn't betray me.

At daybreak, the rationers left for La Targette where the field kitchens arrived to distribute coffee, hooch, and breakfast. The staircase emptied out, and the men shook themselves awake in the trench, the rain having finally ceased.

The men knew that I had refused to make them work at night, in the rain. With scoops and shovels they went to work with a burst of energy and enthusiasm.

Around 10 o'clock the commandant and our captain, booted up to their bellies, came to pay us a visit.

The captain looked at me with a suspicious eye.

"So this is what you've done since last evening," he said to me, "with forty men!"

He didn't press the matter further, and that's how I got out of this scrape.

The steady rain brought on landslides which uncovered many French cadavers alongside our trench, which had been taken on September 25. They had been tossed out of the trench and insufficiently covered with a bit of dirt. It wasn't unusual to be grabbed, while passing, by a skeletal hand or a foot sticking out of the trench wall. We were so blasé about it that we paid it no more attention than to a root we might trip upon in our path.

Finally, on November 6, at 6 o'clock in the evening, the 281st Regiment came to relieve us, to pull us out of this hell-hole, and we went back to Agnez until the 13th.

There were daily downpours, but at the slightest sign of clear weather, of course, we were sent out on the usual, stupid exercises which started up again.

On November 13, at nightfall, we left for Marœuil, and stayed there six days, in reserve.

During the day I had washed out my shirt, which was thick with lice, and I now was looking around the courtyard of our cantonment for a sunny spot in which to spread it out to dry. I noticed, for the first time, in a corner, an old carriage dating back to the Restoration or even the First Empire. Under this carriage was an old piece of cloth which I pulled out with a stick. What did I find inside but two plump hens, which some shameless poilu had no doubt sacrificed that very morning and was awaiting nightfall to take them away.

I quickly alerted my fellow grenadier Segueil. He was a sly rascal who affirmed that, since in wartime we were permitted, and even ordered, to kill, it was a minor peccadillo to wring the neck of a duck, hen, or rabbit. Furthermore he was an excellent chef who could teach a cordon-bleu a thing or two.

In spite of the continual coming and going in the courtyard, it was child's play for Segueil to take charge of these two hens and spirit them away in his knapsack and musette bag.

That evening in Marœuil, in a house half-demolished but with its kitchen intact, Segueil skillfully cooked up the two birds in mess tins, and with two other comrades we enjoyed an excellent repast, savoring a double pleasure: that of a good meal, and the delight of having outsmarted a thief.

Each night at Marœuil we had to go dig or clean out boyaux leading up to the front lines.

They were long and tiring, these starless, moonless nights, which a thick fog made even gloomier.

To improve our routine in the trenches a little bit, they gave us hardly anything to eat, back in the rear. Try working or marching all night, and keeping your spirits up, on an empty stomach!

And meanwhile, nice and warm, with full bellies, our officers drank, sang, enjoyed themselves in the village. It was revolting—and it ended up leading the men to revolt.

At 6 in the evening came the usual assembly, called by the officer of the day (or rather the evening). Only the grenadier section didn't move; everyone claimed to be sick. Called out individually, many got scared and declared themselves cured. The others were sent before the medical officer, a worthy disciple of his predecessor and former boss Torrès. It was Doctor Colombiès, from Dourgne (in the Tarn [département, southwestern France, adjacent to the Aude; principal town is Albi]).

We had already digested our meager pittance, but he was still enjoying his supper with the battalion officers. He stood up, furious at being bothered like this. "Ah, here are the laggards who don't want to work! We'll see about them," he said.

Of course, not one was accepted into sick bay. Headaches, colic, back pains, et cetera—all were met with the same answer: "Not accepted."

Refusing to work, now that was serious. Prison for sure; perhaps a court-martial. Only one, Private X, persisted in claiming to be ill, and went to bed. The rest left, but in a sign of protest they crossed the village singing the "Internationale," which will always be the hymn of the oppressed, the unfortunate ones for whom it is an expression of discontent and of hope.

The Neuville-Saint-Vaast Sector:
November 15, 1915–February 29, 1916

Rebellion. Attack on a listening post.

That evening of revolt, I had been assigned to guard duty at the police station, so I had not been able to take an active part in this movement. But I was suspected of being one of the instigators of it, and they were looking for the first opportunity to get rid of me.

The next day Private X was hauled before the battalion's two dictators, our captain and Commandant Quinze-Grammes, who told him that they were going to make a good example of him and introduce him to the court-martial judges of our corps.

But the recalcitrant patient responded vigorously that, with the insufficient food we were being given, neither he nor his comrades could undertake such fatiguing work.

The two partners, fearing that this business would end up bringing them bad luck, gave him only eight days of prison, a very light sentence, and spoke no further about this incident, which will never appear in any official history of the war.

On November 19 we were supposed to move up to the trenches at nightfall, but, due to the thick fog which covered the landscape, we left Marœuil at 11 in the morning.

A few hours later, we settled into a boyau leading to the front line.

Settling in consisted of depositing our things onto the firing step and waiting to be called up for some more or less appealing chore.

There wasn't anything even close to a shelter in the position occupied by the grenadier squad. This total indifference by our bosses about the lowly troop of beasts of burden which we had become no longer surprised anyone.

Our General Niessel even prohibited us from digging individual shelters into the trench wall, because that might compromise its solidity.

He also expressly forbade us from seeking shelter in mine shafts or in trenches leading to listening posts, "so that the men can get out fast enough in case of an alert," he said.

This communication trench was enlivened by the presence of four of our *crapouillots* [trench mortars] which the German artillerymen had targeted. Big craters could be seen in front, behind, and even right in the middle of the trench. This was quite reassuring!

At night, the lucky crapouillot teams abandoned their pieces and went back to the rear to sleep. We took advantage of their absence by piling into the two entrances of the big shelter they had dug for themselves. These folks stayed in one place for several months. But we, the Wandering Jews of the trenches, stayed only three or four days in the same spot.

Each night we had a work assignment which was far from interesting. We had to bring up heavy rolls of barbed wire wrapped around wooden sawhorses.

What a chore! Sometimes we needed twenty men to get this burden across a trench or a crater, or to untangle the barbed wire from that which was already there and which darkness kept us from seeing. It could take us half the night to cover sixty or eighty meters.

Once we got to our destination, we heaved the sawhorse over the top of a slope, and it rolled noisily down into a ravine, on the other side of which were the Germans who certainly heard all the racket. But they never fired a shot. This was reciprocal; we rarely fired at each other's work details.

How many thousands more victims there would have been without this tacit accord, dictated not by our bosses but by reason and common sense!

Once the work was done, we returned to our gloomy trench, with skin torn, scratched, and punctured by the spiny barbed wire, without counting the multiple rips and tears in our greatcoats and trousers.

On November 22nd, with no regrets, we left the crapouillot trench and its nocturnal chores, where we had torn up our hands and our legs, and I went with my grenadier team to occupy a listening post installed behind a barricade in a trench which we held in common with the Germans.

This was a listening post which was fixed up in accordance with recent instructions from General Niessel. For this he deserved congratulations, because this was the first time that one of our big chiefs showed the slightest concern about protecting the soldier from intemperate weather and battlefield dangers.

First of all, a piece of sheet metal across the top, for the sentinels. Then a screen of metallic mesh, farther to the rear, to ward off bombs and grenades. Finally, a dugout, seven or eight steps deep, where between watches the men could, if not lie down, at least rest and shelter themselves.

In this forward post you couldn't show any curiosity about the surrounding landscape, because as soon as you stuck your head above the parapet it would be shot full of holes, like a kitchen strainer.

Instead, to survey the territory, we had to use "periscopes." In spite of the care we took to conceal the upper mirror behind a tuft of grass or a clump of dirt, crack!—three times bullets shattered the periscopes.

From morning to night, German snipers, with fingers on the triggers, had their sights trained on our forward post, and on us. We didn't even know the exact position of their own forward post, it was so well hidden.

On November 25, at 5 in the morning, I was carefully making my way from the forward post to the trench and from the trench back to the forward post, battling the cold and keeping my feet warm, and just when I reached the post, two grenade detonations almost knocked me over. They had just gone off, right at my feet. I was surrounded by smoke and flames, but I escaped with just the ends of my mustache singed. But the two sentries, Vialle and Roques, weren't so lucky; gravely wounded, they cried out that they were going to die.

Hustled immediately to the first-aid station, they were stabilized and evacuated.

A third sentry, Private Pestel, a Parisian, had his nose slightly scorched. He too went to the first-aid station, but he got a few drops of tincture of iodine on his nose and came right back to his loophole, greatly disappointed.

A few days later, Private Pestel was written up in these glorious terms: "As a sentinel, he returned to his post after having his wound looked after, refusing to be evacuated."

How he must have laughed, Private Pestel, when he read these lines in the citation which Sergeant Faure, whose batman he was, had put him up for.

But who had thrown these two grenades? Our own belief was that they had exploded in the hands of the two sentries, who had mishandled them imprudently. Besides, in the daylight, we could see when we cleaned up the debris that the fragments were from the same model of grenades that we had at the forward post.

Nevertheless we decided, with one accord, to say that we had been attacked by German grenades. They were already charged with so many crimes that one more on their record wouldn't blacken them any worse than they already were.

That made everyone happy: the wounded, who were treated as heroes instead of being punished for their clumsiness; all our bosses, from the grenadier-sergeant all the way up to crazy General Niessel, happy in the knowledge that his elite men didn't fall back one inch in the face of an avalanche of German grenades; finally, the headquarters and Joffre himself could delight in being able to adorn their meager next-day's dispatch with the lines "In the Neuville-Saint-Vaast sector, grenade attacks on our forward posts were repulsed."

I alone encountered unpleasant results. The famous Sergeant Faure said loudly to the captain, "It's not astonishing that this forward post was surprised. Corporal Barthas must have been sleeping."

This nasty insinuation gave the captain the idea of launching an inquiry. What luck, if they could profit from this opportunity to get rid of me by sending me before a court-martial!

But this time they didn't succeed. Lieutenant Malvezy, making his rounds, had stopped to chat with me a moment before the "attack" occurred. Sergeant Marc and my grenadier Sergeant Lasserre had likewise spoken with me between four and five that morning. They attested to it spontaneously, vigorously, at the risk of alienating the captain and the commandant, who then had to leave me alone.

This affair of the grenade attack was the object of dispatches and reports which, from hand to hand, must have arrived under the eyes of Joffre himself. They were written according to our bosses' imagination, because neither my comrades nor I, who commanded at the forward post, were ever asked to give anything like accurate information. That's how the history of this war will be written.

That same day, at one in the afternoon, we were relieved by the 281st Infantry Regiment and arrived at Agnez at nightfall.

The lice. A deluge. A collapsed shelter.
Six hours in the water. Bogged down.

We had six days of rest at Agnez-lès-Duisans. With heavy rains each day forcing us to stay inside our billets, our primary occupation was hunting lice. Each of us carried thousands of them. They found a home in the smallest crease, along seams, in the linings of our clothing. There were white ones, black ones, gray ones with crosses on their backs like crusaders, tiny ones and others as big as a grain of wheat, and all this variety swarmed and multiplied to the detriment of our skins.

And these lice bore in as well on the tough skin of a rude peasant as on the soft skin of an effeminate Parisian. They made no distinction among levels of society. To get rid of them, some rubbed themselves all over with gasoline, every night; others carried sachets of camphor, or powdered themselves with insecticide; nothing did any good. You'd kill ten of them, and a hundred more would appear.

This all came from the repulsive filthiness of our bedding, which was hardly ever changed, and the difficulties we had doing laundry. The cold was so pervasive that as soon as anything was washed, it froze solid. Where could we thaw it out and put it out to dry?

One day, Private Carrère asked the captain if we could get our straw changed, but he didn't even deign to respond; he showed his generosity by not punishing the soldier.

What did it matter to the officers if we were devoured by vermin? They had a clean bed and money with which to keep the dirt away.

After five days spent hunting lice, on December 1st we went back up to the lines, just as lousy as when we arrived at Agnez.

Torrential rains had fallen the previous two days. There's no point in describing the condition of the trenches.

What painful steps we had to take, on these relief marches. Jesus fell three times in climbing the Stations of the Cross. How many times did we fall, slip, stumble, in these trenches transformed into open sewers of mud and water?

Having left Agnez at nine in the morning, it was not until seven in the evening that the squad was able to reach its position in a reserve trench.

We spent the night piled up in a rather solid, deep shelter, but it was a little too tight for comfort. You had to be half-dead with fatigue to fall asleep so jammed together, soaking wet with rain and sweat, all jumbled up with one another.

And I thought, as I listened to the snoring of the sleepers and became numb with sleepiness, that there are people who can't sleep because their beds are not made just right, that there's a fold in the sheet, that the pillow is a little too high or a bit too low . . .

The next day, my friend Ventresque and I benefited from the hospitality of a neighboring shelter, occupied by telephone operators. One evening, we were already dozing off when they came to take us for a work detail.

Two hours later, when we came back, we saw with horror that an enormous mound of earth had collapsed onto the very spot where we had earlier been lying. If not for this work detail, we would have been buried alive. They wouldn't have needed a grave digger to bury us.

A big shell had fallen onto the shelter a few days earlier, leaving a big crater which filled up with rainwater, which seeped into the ground, causing the landslide. Now the water was rushing into the shelter in multiple streams, and we had to struggle for several hours to dig out our blankets, our weapons, all our gear, and to seek out a slightly drier spot.

Another landslide might occur. But where else could we get out of the rain?

Despite our working day and night to keep the trenches in shape, they became more and more impassable. Some rationers met horrible deaths there, buried in mudslides. We worked for four hours to dig out a medical officer from the 296th Regiment. He was lucky that we were close enough to hear his cries for help.

What was curious and terrible was that underneath a thin layer of water or liquid mud there was a much thicker layer, which grabbed onto you like cement, holding tight onto feet and legs like a vise.

Those who complained the loudest were the signalmen, the rationers, the couriers. In ordinary times they were envied because they were exempt from duty at forward listening posts or work details. But now, having to head out, sometimes by themselves, they could get stuck and not be able to get out, and be forced to wait for hours until someone came along and helped them.

General Niessel had the courage to come up and see for himself the state of the trenches, and made his way as far as the front lines, despite having to walk in certain spots with water up to his belly.

This fact is worth noting, because it contrasts with the attitude of certain section chiefs, who never left their dugouts even to obey calls of nature.

The general, in his orders of the day (or the night), gave us plenty of encouragement and ordered that, once we got back to our encampments, we were to be left alone.

So that we wouldn't be blockaded by floods, he ordered brought up to the trenches piles of reserve foodstuffs, cans of preserves, cookies, etc.

On December 7 our section got orders to go occupy a shelter about a hundred meters to the rear of the front line, along the Mercier boyau which led there.

We left at four-thirty in the afternoon, figuring that we'd be at the Mercier shelter in a half-hour at most, figuring that the distance would be only about five or six hundred meters. But here we were, after fifteen minutes, at a crossroads of communication trenches, and we had to wait a full hour for the 23rd Company to pass by as it headed up to the front lines.

Then came our terrible enemy, the rain, which started coming down in torrents, flooding the trench.

We barely reached the second-line trench, the famous Tranchée du Moulin, which we had occupied in an earlier relief. We followed it for two or three hundred meters. It was occupied by the rest of the company. We envied our comrades there, even though the water was starting to enter their dugouts. We had strength enough to laugh at those whose shelters had collapsed and who were vainly trying to shore them up.

Now we got beyond inhabited places. Silence. Solitude and gloom. We've entered the Mercier trench. The rain redoubled in strength, and we moved forward with more and more difficulty, one step forward every five minutes, until soon we halted completely.

We learned with anguish that a number of soldiers from the company ahead of us were stuck in the mud. We had no idea how long we would stay here.

All of a sudden we heard laughter, songs, happy shouts. Dumbstruck, we learned that we were in front of the shelter of our captain and the company's officers.

They were completely indifferent to our distress.

"If they can't pass along the trench, then they should go on top of it," said our unsympathetic Cros-Mayrevieille.

That was a cruel joke, because we were in the middle of a forest of barbed wire. Some sought refuge by the steps leading into the captain's shelter, but that officer, pitiless and cruel, chased them away, and inside the well-lit, well-heated shelter, laughter and songs began again. This was too much. This gaiety was an insult to our sad lot.

Rough voices cried out, "Enough! Enough! Scum, crooks!" and other invectives like these.

This resulted in silence inside the shelter. One never knew how far anger could push someone. A couple of grenades could come bouncing down the steps. The idea of throwing them wasn't foreign to some of us.

We finally reached the place where those who had gone before had such difficulties. They had left behind one unfortunate fellow whom they couldn't disengage. We made some vain efforts to pull him out, almost to the point of pulling his arms and legs out of their sockets. Seeing that we too were abandoning him, he begged us to put him out of his misery with a rifle shot. We promised that we would come back and get him in the morning, and we left him with a shovel so that he could try to save himself.

While we were trying to dig out this poor guy, our comrades in the squad ahead had disappeared. We called out to them, and got no answer. Were they already that far away, or had they all drowned?

No one wanted to be at the front of the line. That's how frightening this dark trench was, transformed into a canal. We could hear big chunks of earth crumbling into the water. But we couldn't spend the night like this. We had to keep trying to reach the shelter.

With a shovel in one hand and my electric lamp in the other, I launched myself ahead, into the sewer. My comrades let me go about ten paces ahead, then some of them risked following me. I was an old veteran of the trenches, because this was the second winter that I was slogging through the mud. Except for the rationer Terrisse, who had stayed back with field kitchens, the squad was made up of reinforcements who had spent the first winter safe at home.

I led my comrades with the advice that my experience had taught me.

"Walk with your legs spread as wide apart as possible. Walk on your toes, not flat-footed. Take small steps. Don't stop!" I called out to them.

Finally I heard voices—not celestial ones, but human. I could see a light. We were saved. Here was the Mercier shelter.

It was half-past midnight. We'd been slogging for eight hours, through the water, through the mud, in this December night's stormy weather which had soaked us through and through.

Bitterly cold, we would have given anything for the chance to warm up around a good fire, to stretch out upon a bit of straw, but these sweet things were unattainable dreams for us.

We spent the night cleaning out the flooded shelter, and scraping off the carapace of mud which covered our shoes, our trousers, our greatcoats.

Barely half the section reached the shelter. It was only the next day that the laggards rejoined us. Out of fear of drowning or sinking, they had preferred to spend the night, an interminable December night, in the trench!

And again we had to go back to rescue some, especially those whose legs were too short. Some left their shoes in the mud. Others had wrenched hernias for themselves. The strange thing was, not one of us came down with a cold.

Neuville-Saint-Vaast sector. The Mercier shelter. Human fraternity. The deserter Gontran.

Our principal occupation was to keep the Mercier boyau open up to the Tranchée du Moulin. As a new twist on the torture of the Danaïdes,[1] we weren't condemned to fill up a bottomless barrel, but instead to clean out the water and the mud which kept coming back as a result of the daily downpours.

I suggested to Sergeant Faure, who commanded the section, the idea of digging a stretch of communication trench in a straight line to the Tranchée du Moulin. This would have avoided a big elbowlike curve and numerous sharp detours which the boyau made.

Digging it less deep, and in earth less turned over and moved around, we could certainly keep it practicable with less effort.

This idea was submitted to the captain. He in turn consulted the commandant about this weighty matter. The prudent Quinze-Grammes took it to the colonel, who spoke about it with the general, who hesitated because of the effect it might have on the symmetry of the sector!

Meanwhile it became more and more necessary that something be done, because the Mercier boyau was disappearing into a virtual lake.

In this period the situation of the front-line troops was truly lamentable. In certain places the trenches had completely disappeared under water. Almost all the dugouts had collapsed. Our section was lucky enough to have a dugout which was still intact and where, when our work was done, we could stretch out on the cold, damp ground.

But one night, when the rain came down in torrents, the tide invaded our dugout and cascaded down both sets of steps. At the height of the storm, some of the men had to devote all their efforts to building a dam, which the water then broke through at three or four places. We spent the rest of the night battling the floodwaters.

The next day, December 10, at many places along the front line, the soldiers had to come out of their trenches so as not to drown. The Germans had to do the same. We therefore had the singular spectacle of two enemy armies facing each other without firing a shot.

Our common sufferings brought our hearts together, melted the hatreds, nurtured sympathy between strangers and adversaries. Those who deny it are ignoring human psychology.

Frenchmen and Germans looked at each other, and saw that they were all men, no different from one another. They smiled, exchanged comments; hands reached out and grasped; we shared tobacco, a canteen of *jus* [coffee] or pinard.

If only we spoke the same language!

One day, a huge devil of a German stood up on a mound and gave a speech, which only the Germans could understand word for word, but everyone knew what it meant, because he smashed his rifle on a tree stump, breaking it into two in a gesture of anger.

Applause broke out on both sides, and the "Internationale" was sung.

Well, if only you had been there, mad kings, bloody generals, fanatical ministers, jingoistic journalists, rear-echelon patriots, to contemplate this sublime spectacle!

But it wasn't enough that the soldiers refuse to fight one another. What was needed was for them to turn back on the monsters who were pushing them, one against the other, and to cut them down like wild beasts. For not having done so, how much longer would the killing go on?

Meanwhile, our big-shot leaders were in a furor. What in the Lord's name would happen if the soldiers refused to kill each other? Our artillerymen received orders to fire on any assemblies of men which were pointed out to them, and to mow down indiscriminately both Frenchmen and Germans, just like when in the ancient circuses they slaughtered wild beasts who were too intelligent to tear each others' throats out and devour each other.

Furthermore, once the front line was established again, for better or worse, it was forbidden under penalty of death to leave the trench. Any act of familiarity with the Germans had to cease.

It was over. What we really needed was a second biblical Flood, a universal deluge to stop the war, to appease all the anger and the bloody madness of our leaders.

Who knows—maybe one day in this corner of Artois they will raise a monument to commemorate this spirit of fraternity among men who shared a horror of war and who were forced to kill each other against their wills.

Meanwhile, in spite of the ferocious orders, friendly contact between Frenchmen and Germans continued, particularly at the listening posts. In the 21st Company, Private Gontran, from Caunes-Minervois, even paid a visit to the German trench.

He had gotten to know the German captain, a good family man who always asked about his own children and gave him a few cigarettes.

Whenever Gontran stayed too long, the captain pushed him out of the German trench, saying "Let's go, on your way."

Unfortunately for Gontran, one day when he was making his way back from the German trench he was spotted by an officer of his company—none other than Lieutenant Grulois, who said to him, "I've got you now. You'll be shot at dawn. Arrest this man."

Nobody moved. Everybody stared stupidly. Gontran, maddened by the officer's threat, scrambled up the side of the trench, crying out *Béni mé querré* [*Viens me chercher:* in the Occitan dialect of Languedoc, "Come and get me"]. In a few strides he made it to the enemy trench, and he didn't come back.

That very evening a court-martial composed of the superior officers of the regiment and presided over by the colonel met in the dugout of our commandant.

In five seconds, Private Gontran was condemned to death in absentia.

After an investigation, Lieutenant Grulois was put under arrest for being too zealous in frightening the guilty party and causing his desertion. Corporal Escande, from Citou, and the soldiers of his squad barely escaped court-martial for not firing on their deserting comrade as he fled across no-man's-land.

On December 13, after working all the preceding night to make the communication trenches practicable, we were relieved, and at 8 o'clock in the evening we arrived at Agnez.

The next day a reinforcement of a hundred men arrived from Narbonne. They were scattered across the regiment's companies.

This contingent included four Peyriacois: Adjutant Calvet, who came back healed of his wound, and three "ex-auxiliaries," Julien Chiffre, Louis Richardis, and Maurice Badou, who came to seek their share of glory at the front for the first time.

The latter three, by a stroke of good luck, were assigned to my half-section. Their faces fell when they saw us still covered in mud right to the tips of our mustaches and our hair, stained the color of dirt, looking more like cadavers than living men.

We got the sensational news that the regiment was being dissolved, no doubt due to the incidents of the latest relief.

The whole division would be going to the rear to reorganize. Our departure from Agnez was set for December 19.

We were going to leave the Neuville-Saint-Vaast sector, which we had occupied since September 25, for good.

1915. Toward new destinies. Dissolution of the 280th Infantry Regiment. Review by General d'Urbal

On December 19, at 7 in the evening, in a chilly bise which blew under a gray sky, we left Agnez-lès-Duisans, with few regrets on my part. I had left a pint of blood there, not from wounds—May the god Mars spare me!—but sucked out of me by legions of lice.

We covered the journey on foot. We had to loosen up our legs, which had stiffened after three months in the trenches. Unfortunately for me, like for many others, the more I walked, the wobblier my legs got, and soon it seemed like I was carrying a load of lead on my shoulders, so heavily was my pack weighing me down. We were marching steadily. It was noon. The time for a break had passed a moment ago. The company, at a fork in the road, had left the column and was proceeding by itself, under the orders of our Kronprinz, perched on his nag.

A few timid cries of "How about a rest break?"—quickly suppressed by the section chiefs—must have reached the big ears of the captain, but he appeared not to hear them. He was serious, lost in thought, careful. His mind was no doubt seeking the solution of some thorny strategic problem, or perhaps, more prosaically, he was thinking about whether he would find a comfortable bed, a well-stocked table, and pretty ladies at the next cantonment.

Perhaps he was also thinking back to that old rule that he had imparted to us one day theoretically: that a rest stop might be a custom, a favor, but it was not a right for a soldier on the march.

The captain certainly had cold feet, and his dignity prevented him from dismounting, so it was all the more urgent for him to arrive at the cantonment.

It was there, no doubt, that he would have a legitimate reason to put this old rule about rest stops into practice.

Adding to our bad luck, this route started to climb up a long and narrow ridge which lost itself in the fog up ahead.

Soon, the stragglers came to a halt. The captain, lost in his meditations, continued on for a while without noticing that he had pulled far ahead of the company. A zealous sergeant brought it to his attention. Turning around, he hurled himself at the laggards, ordering them to rehoist their packs and threatening to punish them if they didn't arrive at the cantonment along with everyone else.

It was at Beaudricourt that we were going to be billeted. Despite the "beau" in the name of this little village, I didn't notice anything particularly pretty about it.

The billet assigned to our section was actually quite rough: a loft which one reached by a worm-eaten, rickety, puny ladder.

This loft was missing some of its planks, and others had rotted through, so that you'd be both imprudent and foolhardy to venture forth in the dark without a light.

The earthen walls were full of holes. The rain, the wind, the snow poured in through the cracks, and we had to resign ourselves to sleeping under our tent cloths, just as if we'd been outdoors. But while the storm raged in these dark nights, we were far from complaining, and we felt sorry for those who had replaced us in the muddy trenches of Neuville-Saint-Vaast.

At assembly, it was announced that two regiments of the division were being dissolved. They didn't say which ones, but we all understood that the 280th was condemned. It was no worse or better than any other, but it was from Narbonne, the "red" city of the Midi, and had to pay the price.

If the brass hats thought they were afflicting us and humiliating us by dissolving the 280th, they were hugely mistaken. It made no difference to us. Our fate wasn't changing.

It must be acknowledged that, all the same, they did think carefully about our southern sensitivities. They decided that whole battalions would be kept intact and shifted, ours to the 296th Regiment from Béziers² and the other to the 281st Regiment from Montpellier [both southern cities, in the département of Hérault, next to Aude].

Finally, as a supreme favor which, in the minds of our leaders, would console us in our disgrace and alleviate our sadness, they kept our badges of the 280th in place for awhile.

As if that meant anything to us, to have one number or another on our badges!

Big news was announced: General d'Urbal,³ commander of all the armies of the north, was coming in person to review our regiment and to salute our now-useless flag.

This news threw the striped sleeves into consternation. Our captain, above all, was at loose ends. He loaded us up with inspections of our belongings, our weapons, our shoes. For forty-eight hours, with brushes and needles and thread in hand, we hardly had time in the day to get something to eat.

Up to this point, I hadn't seen any good reason to decorate my sleeves with the two woolen stripes signifying my corporal's rank. I attribute it to the captain's myopia that he never noticed it. But during one of his inspections, with all our trappings of war, his eye fell unluckily upon my private's sleeves.

This man, who was obsessed with stripes, stood for a moment, speechless, amazed. "Why don't you have any stripes?" he asked.

"I've never had them. Everyone knows I'm a corporal."

"Listen here, if your stripes aren't sewn on by tomorrow, you'll be sorry!"

"Captain, I don't have any stripes."

"Sergeant-major! Give this man some stripes."

"I don't know how to sew."

The captain threw me a furious look, and headed off. I thought that this argument had gotten me off from obeying this order. But the next morning, as soon as I got out of bed, the company's tailor—or rather the tailor of the company's officers and non-coms—came and sewed some superb black stripes onto the ends of my sleeves, the indispensable signs of prestige necessary to impose authority upon the nonstriped rabble.

A review can't happen without a parade, and a captain's standing is compromised if his company doesn't parade correctly when it passes before the august personage for whom it is parading.

Our captain, desirous of being noticed and of perhaps earning a compliment to his vanity, consequently drilled us rigorously.

All morning long, the day before the review, by sections, we paraded along the widest—and the only—street of the village, twenty times, maybe thirty times. He was stationed at the end of the street, and each time we passed him we turned our heads sharply toward him, fixing our eyes upon him just like he told us to. In return we got a flash of sunlight reflected off his oversized eyeglasses and a grimace of unhappiness, because he was far from satisfied with our performance.

Lunchtime delivered us from this slogging through the puddles in the road, the principal cause of our sloppy parading.

Finally, the great day dawned. It was December 23; a regiment of France was going to disappear in an apotheosis of glory.

The regiment assembled in a big field, one kilometer from the village. Not one curious spectator, not even a little kid. Decidedly, in this part of the country, they weren't fond of military parades.

We waited for two full hours. We spent the time getting into position, shifting, lining up, and blowing on our fingers to keep them warm.

Finally, General d'Urbal arrived. I will keep silent on all the usual goings-on of any military review.

The general had the good taste to find everything just perfect, and even more than perfect: uniforms, speed, parade, etc. With a stentorian voice he gave us a speech in which we heard ourselves called a superb regiment, magnificent. What touched us most was that we would get a few days of rest.

Then the general approached the flag, his naked sword in his hand.

"Flag of the 280th," he said, "I salute you. Off you go to the Invalides, alongside the glorious standards of Austerlitz, of Arcola, of Jena."[4]

The flag dipped, the bugles sounded across the fields, the moment was solemn.

The next day's report said that, at that moment, a shiver went through the ranks. I shivered, too, but it was from the cold.

The next day the battalion left Beaudricourt and joined the 296th, of which it was henceforth part, at Ivergny, which was only a half-hour away.

This time, the section was billeted on the ground floor. In this particular building we couldn't be lodged anywhere else, because there was no upper floor.

It was nothing but a lousy stable with a few scraps of rotten straw for us to lie down on.

One door, one window, no air, but a few drafts. No sunlight got in, but the rain penetrated through gaps in the walls. To tell the truth, we missed the rickety loft of Beaudricourt.

This day, December 24, was a sad Christmas Eve, gloomy and rainy. One thousand nine hundred sixteen years ago, Jesus was born in a stable. Like him, we made our beds there, but at least he had a bed of straw which wasn't like ours, filled with lice.

On Christmas Day, the rain fell in torrents. It was bad luck, since it was already a day of rest. The rain is a blessing to the soldier when it exempts him from a day on the drill field, but that did no good this time.

The captain made the most of this day of rest to inspect our *sabots* [wooden shoes], yes, the sabots which the soldiers had bought for themselves and for which they were reimbursed according to the captain's whims.

For him, this was an opportunity to show his ugly side. You'd have thought that he was paying for them out of his own pocket. He generously awarded four francs for sabots which had cost twelve or fifteen.

My comrade Ventresque had bought a fine pair of sabots, but he had left one of them behind in the mud of the Mercier boyau by pulling his foot out too vigorously.

The captain, in the face of this embarrassing situation, scratched his ear, then his nose, as if a huge sum were in play, and finally declared that once Ventresque presented the complete pair to him, he would be paid. Leaving the proprietor of the one sabot in a state of disappointment, he moved on.

He had done well by the fatherland. He had saved the Treasury a hundred sous by stealing them from a poor soldier!

Artois, 1915. Ivergny. Hersin-Coupigny. The sick man in bed. Queux.

On December 26 the rain ended and, what do you know, we spent the day on the drill field, and the next one too, but on December 28 at 8 o'clock in the morning we suddenly left Ivergny in trucks and, after four bone-jarring hours of bumps, leaps forward, leaps backward on pot-holed, muddy roads, we arrived at Hersin-Coupigny, our old resting place when we were in the Lorette sector.

The inhabitants recognized us and gave us a nice welcome, but what were we going to do here in this village? We certainly weren't here to pay a friendly visit to the *Hersinois* and their womenfolk. Certain indiscretions informed us that we were going to rejoin our new division, which was holding the Loos sector.

Nothing abnormal about that, but what was far from appealing to us was knowing that we were incorporated into a so-called elite, shock, or attack division, consisting of the 114th and 125th Regiments.

Was this an honor or a penalty, an homage or a punishment?

To assuage the worries growing inside of us, it was confirmed that this division was going to be relieved and sent back to the rear, for rest. They always tried that.

The day after we arrived, the band of the 296th Regiment gave a concert on the town hall square, at around four in the afternoon. A couple of shells landed near the train station, and four poor Territorials busy unloading a freight car were mortally wounded, alas. The concert went on, all the same, and the unfortunate ones, transported to the nearest dispensary, could give up their souls to the lively or languorous rhythms of a polka or a waltz.

No matter that our departure was imminent; the day after our arrival we were out on the drill field again. As usual, our rest break was devoted to calisthenics and footraces.

By squads, we ran from one end of the field to the other. Woe to those at the end of the pack. The sergeant of the day, notebook and pencil in hand, took their names down for work details, without noting the menacing invectives of the captain.

Lucky were those to whom nature had granted long legs, like me, or who were young and supple.

The Peyriacois Babou, little accustomed to this kind of sport, made such a violent effort to not be among the latecomers that he wrenched a tendon in his heel, so that to get back to Hersin he couldn't keep up with the company, and I had to accompany him and help him along.

Two days later, when we had to go meet the trucks which were awaiting us between Hersin and Barlin, his leg was swollen as big as a sandbag, and he couldn't get out of bed. ("Bed" is understood to mean a thin straw pallet upon which the soldiers had lain for a few weeks, and was practically transformed into a manure pile.)

And so Babou, following the customary practice, had to go to sick call while still in his bed.

[Medical officer] *Major* Colombiès, worthy successor to the hated Torrès, arrived in a very bad mood at being so disturbed at the moment of departure. After a quick glance at the leg, he cried out, "What? Is that why you bothered me? Let his comrades help him a bit. If he doesn't want to walk, they should just give him a couple of kicks in the butt!"

The end of this sentence was heard by the whole company, assembled in the street. A murmur of indignation ran through the ranks, and a voice cried out loud, "That's shameful, language like that."

The captain jumped up, as if a swarm of hornets had attacked the fleshiest part of his Don-Quixote-like person. He jumped up not in indignation at hearing such words unworthy of a French doctor, but in anger at hearing the murmurs which greeted them.

The *major* promptly disappeared, and order was restored. Two strapping fellows took turns carrying Babou on their sturdy shoulders, to the stunned looks of the townsfolk. The rest of us carried his weapons and his gear, and we proceeded to the trucks with the wisecracking stretcher-bearers carrying their litters folded up on their shoulders.

And then there we were, riding along, bouncing and jostling on the roads of the Pas-de-Calais. It was January 2, 1916. A driving rain followed us on our journey. We crossed the coal-mining country with its major centers, its corons, its mines, its slag heaps. We passed through Bruay, Saint-Pol, Frévent. We'd have liked to stop and billet in these small towns, so tempting with their well-lit, well-stocked shops, their welcoming bistros, their attractive, smiling women who gave us friendly greetings as we passed by. But these places were too good for us; they were reserved for the embusqués, the slackers of every category who crowded these rear echelons.

At about three in the afternoon, the trucks pulled up near the village of Queux, where we were going to rest awhile.

We had to leave Babou by the side of the road, in the rain, and come back and get him with a wheelbarrow.

Our half-section was lodged in a makeshift billet, with no straw. It's true that they distributed a bale of straw to us, the equivalent of a handful per soldier, but we unanimously agreed to give it all to Babou, whose leg was still swollen and purplish and who couldn't move from the corner where they put him.

The next day, *Major* Colombiès—the same one who spoke about healing sprains with kicks in the butt—came to see the sick man, accompanied by the captain. The latter still pretended not to recognize Babou, his old schoolmate. Apparently when you get three gold stripes on your sleeve, you can't shake hands with a simple private second class. The greater interest of discipline won't stand for it.

As for the *major,* he had no doubt learned that he was dealing with more than just some vulgar peasant, and he judged it prudent to be seen as being a little more polite.

That didn't keep Babou from telling him what he thought, and protesting against the ill-mannered statements of the evening before, in scathing words.

"All right, calm down, calm down," the *major* told him, "we'll take care of your leg, and if it's not better in two or three days, we'll evacuate you."

Then he got the best care possible. Massages, frequent warm baths, but nothing did any good, and three days later he was evacuated. He would never come back, because once he was at the hospital he was transferred to the auxiliaries as a truck driver.

One evening, coming back from the drill field, I learned that I was to depart on home leave that very night. This news, while long awaited, stunned me. I became completely pale, I couldn't swallow a mouthful of supper, and I feverishly prepared my departure.

Finally I was going to see my loved ones, my home, my village, after having given up this joyful prospect so many times as death brushed so close to me.

Artois, 1916. First home leave. The return. Hautvillers.

On January 10, at 2 in the morning, I went with a dozen other leave takers eight kilometers from Queux to take the train at the station of Auxi-le-Château.

The next day, at 10 in the evening, I jumped down onto the platform at the station at Moux [Aude, approximately twenty kilometers east of Carcassonne]. I breathed in with delight the air of my birthplace. In truth, this air was a bitter, cold bise which was blowing down from the Montagne Noire [mountain range north of the Minervois region]. But it seemed to me to be as sweet as the softest summer breeze.

The sky was gloomy, the night was pitch-black, the road was muddy, but no promenade was ever so exquisite as the fifteen kilometers that I had to cover to get to my village.

Finally I approached it. I had reached the edge of the little plateau, "La Serre." Still a little valley to cross, and I arrived. I stopped, full of emotion, a short distance away. I noticed the flickering of electric lights marking the place occupied by my village.

It was among these lights, in a lodging the threshold of which I would soon cross, that a mother, a father, a wife, and two children anxiously awaited the arrival of the absent one. I felt as if I could see them watching for my arrival, trembling at the slightest sound of a footstep in the street, because along the way I had been able to alert them by telegraph.

Of course, I'd have to leave in six days, perhaps forever, those whom I loved so much. But for now I abandoned myself to the delirious joy of seeing them again after fourteen months of absence.

A half-hour later I was in the arms of my family. As long as the days of suffering were, the days of happiness seemed just as short. These few days of home leave soon ran out, but they will stay fixed in my memory as one of the greatest and rarest pleasures of this long war.

I noticed that, in the rear, a blissful optimism reigned, an absolute confidence in a prompt and victorious end to the war. This was the nefarious work of lying newspapers; the unanimous cry was *Jusqu'au bout!* [To the end, whatever it takes!]

What blindness! What folly! In vain did a few wounded men and leave takers who were not embusqués try to combat this disconcerting enthusiasm, this stupid attitude, but nothing did any good.

Only the mothers and the wives trembled, suffered, prayed, but in silence, muffling their sobs. You couldn't tell by the number of saddened faces and tear-reddened eyes that we were at war.

These observations made the departure even more bitter. We had the sense of being sacrificed, and that our indescribable sufferings weren't being understood and in no way troubled the soft quietude of life on the home front.

On January 21st I had to tear myself away from the arms of my weeping loved ones and take the sad road back to the front. I had two traveling companions. One was my friend Allard from Peyriac, a veteran of the 13th Squad and survivor of Lorette who was joining his new regiment of Territorials, where his age had earned him a spot.

The other was Private Sabatier, from Rieux, in the same battalion as mine. Illiterate, ignorant, and simpleminded, not understanding even French,[5] Sabatier would not have been able to get back to the front without me.

By the time we arrived in Toulouse, the train of returning leave takers had already departed. The railway employees compelled us to take the express train to Paris, which was just about to pull out. This obligation made us suspicious, and we were right. They wanted to rid the Toulouse station of the mob of soldiers, but then at each station they would empty out a car or two. Our turn arrived: A conductor very politely asked to see our leave papers, as if to verify them; then, when the train stopped, he told us to get off, and warned us that our papers were being held in the stationmaster's office until the next evening, when the next leave takers' special train would be coming along.

So there we were in Brive-la-Gaillarde, stuck for twenty-four hours. Since it was the same thing every day, the hotel keepers flocked to the station to offer their hospitality (at a price) for the night to the disoriented leave takers. We had no choice but to spend a night in a hotel bed.

The next day we visited Brive like dutiful tourists, taking in its churches, its museums, the Corrèze River, and the statue of Marshal Brune.[6]

That evening, at 8 p.m., we piled onto the leave takers' train, which deposited us the next morning at the Gare du Nord in Paris.

At nine that evening, we got off at the Abbeville station. It was in this vicinity that our regiment was at rest, or, rather, on a big training exercise.

My comrade Sabatier and I were uneasy about getting off at the Abbeville station, which was reserved exclusively for the British army. While we were looking for a way to escape from the station into town, some English policemen caught us and hauled us before the stationmaster.

This was a French lieutenant-colonel, who heaped us with invectives and threats for being so bold as to get off at this station.

In vain I pleaded that, in the middle of the night, I couldn't just get off at some little country station, where we might not even find a place to sleep. This fellow's anger didn't lessen. I wondered what he was going to do with us, when

Sabatier, who hadn't understood a word of this heated conversation in French, spoke up in our southern dialect: "Say, can a guy get a drink somewhere around here?" He followed this pronouncement with his customary long burst of laughter.

The stationmaster, at first struck dumb by this loud and disrespectful outburst, leapt from his chair and shouted in an angry voice, "Shut up, you!"

But Sabatier wouldn't be deterred. "Hey, are we in France, or with the Boches?" he shouted back.

At a gesture from the stationmaster, the policemen rushed in and grabbed Sabatier, who wanted only to go into town.

We were locked up in a baggage storeroom. Two turns of the key, and there we were, imprisoned.

Well, it wasn't exactly warm in that room, but we were indoors, and that was something to be appreciated by those of us who had been in the trenches. We stretched out with no ceremony upon a bench. But at 2 in the morning the English police came to wake us up and ordered us to follow them.

A train was in the station. They pushed us onto a car and closed the door, standing guard outside it until the train pulled out.

We'd been told to get off at Noyelles-sur-Mer. A half-hour later we were on the platform of this station, which had no shelter to offer passing poilus other than a frigid waiting room without a fireplace.

All the benches were already occupied by sleepers. We had no recourse but to stretch out on the cement floor. Fatigue pushed me into a deep sleep, but the cold fought back. The latter won out, and I had to pace back and forth to keep warm.

I had the thought of going to take a look at the sea, which I thought would be right close by, but I learned from an early-morning passerby that it was more than a league away. I postponed my seaside visit to some other occasion.

Finally, daylight arrived, and the hour of departure for the departmental tramway which we were to take was approaching. This tramway dropped us at Nouvion [Nouvion-en-Ponthieu], where vague directions led us to hope that we would find our regiment. From Nouvion we had to cover only four kilometers on foot to Hautvillers, where our battalion was encamped, just six kilometers from Abbeville.

Starting the next day, to cure our homesickness, we went into training, and the day after that we went to the camp of Saint-Riquier to do a complicated maneuver, twelve kilometers from Hautvillers.

This was a day of thick fog. We spent a good hour moving back and forth, from place to place. Finally we took up a position in a rough trench, and shivered there for a half-hour. Then we went back, the "enemy" being judged to be "in flight."

And for all that we covered twenty-four kilometers, and risked soaking ourselves to the skin.

On February 1, at daybreak, the regiment left for Noyelles-sur-Mer to embark—not on board the Channel Squadron, but onto railway cars.

We passed through Abbeville, Doullens, Saint-Pol. A few stations after this
last town, we got off. It was 6 in the evening. On the façade of the station I
read "Tincques." At the previous station they had unloaded all of our encampment gear and supplies, since that was only one kilometer from the village
where we would be billeted, Bailleul-les-Cornailles. Why make us get off at the
next station, which forced us to undergo two hours of night march? I'm still
wondering.

Perhaps, some felt, it was so that they could make things nice and comfortable for us by the time we got there. But alas, we were going from bad to worse.
How much worse is for anyone to judge.

Artois, 1916. Bailleul-les-Cornailles (Pas-de-Calais).
Theft of hens and ducks. The corporal's pocketbook.

The billet assigned to our half-section was a ruined stable, with neither door
nor windows, long in disuse and filled with all kinds of garbage. A fetid odor
wafted out of this redoubt, arousing in us a profound nausea.

Nevertheless there were fine barns in the village where there were bountiful
supplies of straw. I discovered one of these shelters, and with a couple of comrades dug under two or three meters of straw to escape the view of the proprietors, who would be sure to complain.

The next day our captain, despite his desire and his orders that we make the
best of our assigned billets, had to bow to our emphatic complaints and get us
more suitable quarters.

And the training exercises started up again with intensity. In rain or wind, in
cold or snow, we had to go out. By night and by day, one-quarter of the company was standing watch, for nothing, to no useful purpose, simply because
that is what was called for in field regulations.

If the guards weren't guarding anything, they still had to be on the lookout
for visits by the commandant or the captain. Woe to them if the proper honors
and signs of respect weren't paid, following prescribed etiquette, or if they
didn't have their uniforms just right or the exact passwords at hand.

This often resulted in a few days in prison for the sentry, and sometimes for
the corporal who was responsible for the guard post.

Never was the mean, narrow-minded, hateful spirit of the captain more in
evidence than during our stay at Bailleul-les-Cornailles. In the 21st Company,
the number of those being punished for such infractions became so great that

the field police station couldn't hold them all, and those guarding them were so vexed that they had to complain.

Our captain was authorized to set up a special billet for those being punished. Numbering around thirty, they were parked in a kind of hangar, under the eyes of a guard detail. They came out only for exercise and various work details.

There were also general measures of repression which, being of a generous mind, I won't call acts of cowardly harassment.

Among other displays of meanness and spitefulness, he made us turn out for roll call in full campaign gear and undergo rigorous inspections in which someone would always be slapped with a few days in detention.

One day, at assembly, the colonel reminded us that the wearing of képis was strictly prohibited. This applied to corporals and privates first class and second class. Non-coms and officers were, as before, authorized to wear their képis decorated however they wished.

The captain had, for a long time, been a stickler about this proscription, and we didn't dare show up without our ridiculous fatigue caps on our heads. Only a headstrong Parisian, recently arrived in the company, dared to sport a magnificent képi, as fine as the captain's own, complete with stripes and braids. His name was Vacher. The following dialogue ensued:

The captain: "Vacher, you've heard this before. Get rid of that képi immediately."

Vacher: "This képi is mine. I bought it, and I'm going to wear it."

The captain became pale with rage, red with anger, then greenish-purple. His face turned all the colors of the rainbow, like a chameleon. What! A simple soldier, a private second class, dared to defy him, and the colonel, and regulations! If he were in worse physical shape, he might have had a heart attack, right on the spot; he had every reason to. But the dialogue continued:

The captain: "If I see you again with that képi on, you'll get a week in prison."

Vacher: "When the officers and non-coms stop wearing theirs, then I will, but not before."

And Vacher kept wearing his képi, with no further bother. But the captain never forgave him for this act of defiance, and less than a month later he found a way to get rid of Vacher by dragging him in front of a court-martial. But that's getting ahead of the story.

One day, a Sunday, we noticed soldiers from a neighboring company hoisting their packs hastily and assembling in a meadow. What did this alert signify? The men we asked said that they were leaving the village; they knew nothing more.

It was only a false alarm. Someone had stolen a pair of ducks in the billets occupied by this company, and the captain had resorted to this trick, figuring that the culprit wouldn't abandon his web-footed spoils.

Indeed, the packs and musette bags were searched, and the guilty party nabbed. The ducks lay headless at the bottom of his musette bag.

For not having been content with the standard mess offerings, this poilu was hauled before a court-martial, the outcome of which I don't know.

This harsh example didn't do any good. In the part of the village where my company was quartered, two plump hens soon disappeared from a henhouse without leaving the slightest trace.

On this occasion, our captain wanted to show that he was as clever as his colleague from the 16th Company. He repeated the ruse, but the thief, having learned from the misadventure of the duck-napper, made sure that he had hidden away his ill-gotten gains. Careful examination of our packs and musette bags revealed no telltale feathers.

The captain, greatly disappointed, demanded silence and, calling us to attention, said: "Will the chicken thief identify himself?"

Silence.

"Will those who know who he is, denounce him?"

Again, silence.

"Fine. The owner of the hens will be compensated with funds from the company's mess kitty, that's to say, with your own money. Each of you will end up paying two or three sous, so that one of you can enjoy eating chicken and toasting your good health."

To tell the truth, we would have happily paid double or triple to keep the captain from finding out the thief or thieves.

Three days later, another alert, another inspection, this time turning our pockets inside-out, all without the slightest result.

What had been stolen this time?

We soon found out. The captain told us:

"Someone has stolen the corporal's pocketbook. It had 150 francs in it, of which a hundred was the company mess kitty, sent to you by your families or paid in by you for the purchase of extra food. Since we can't find the thief, it's you who will suffer the consequences. This sum will be considered as already spent on food—but you didn't get to eat any of it."

That was too much. The corporal claimed that someone had stolen the money from him. But maybe he lost it, or spent it himself. And what did this matter to us? Let the corporal and captain figure it out between themselves, however they liked. Ultimately the captain is responsible to us for the money he is holding for us, which is meant for our benefit.

Shame, honesty, loyalty—these elementary feelings should have led our well-off captain to make good this loss out of his own pocket. He found it easier to make us pay for it ourselves, to the detriment of our bellies, rather than his purse.

And this guy had been to law school! What a judge he would have made!

Nevertheless, this ruling went so much against common sense that it was welcomed with grumbles, and the incorrigible Vacher shouted, "We've already been starving—now we're really going to feel it!"

The captain pretended not to hear, and declared dryly that, for better or worse, that's how things would be.

One night, a poor fellow completely demoralized by such discipline fled the village and reached the neighboring woods. The next day, rather than going out on field drills, we went on a search for him, and were happy to have this diversion from the daily routine.

The fugitive had meanwhile reached Saint-Pol, where, distressed, he turned himself in. Our captain showed himself to be magnanimous. The flight was attributed to an episode of dark depression, and he slapped the naïve deserter with just fifteen days in prison, on principle.

On February 21, 1916, the regiment left Bailleul-les-Cornailles for Béthonsart (Pas-de-Calais).

Artois 1916. Bois de la Folie sector. Béthonsart. Mont-Saint-Eloi.

They were really spoiling us this time. To cover the ten kilometers which separated us from Béthonsart, they used trucks to haul us.

But we got there too quickly. The troops which were occupying the village hadn't left yet, so while we awaited their departure we stood shivering for two hours in a field outside the village.

The next day the captain called us together, sergeants and corporals, to tell us that shortly we would be going to occupy a sector near the ill-famed Bois de la Folie.

The division which was holding this sector considered itself an attack division, and hadn't stooped to do fortification work. We therefore couldn't expect to find any shelters in the trenches we would be occupying. This made us grimace, but the captain was all smiles, certain that he would have a fine shelter for his precious self.

Then we learned that the trenches were honeycombed with mines.[7] We had to start getting used to this mine warfare, to the idea that one morning you could see the earth open up right under your feet, like a volcano. There would only be the minimum number of soldiers on duty on the front lines. The captain kept smiling, with the knowledge that it wouldn't be him who would head out to the observation posts and risk getting blown to bits.

Finally, he wrapped up his harangue by saying that he was counting on the energy of us non-coms to get the most work possible out of the poilus, in fortifying the sector.

The temperature had dropped sharply, and on February 23, as we left Béthonsart on foot, the snow started falling heavy and thick, slowing down our march, stinging our faces, sticking to our clothes. It was whipped up by a violent wind, freezing and transforming into icy stalactites which hung from our beards and mustaches.

The regiment was going up to the front line. By luck our battalion stayed back in reserve at Mont-Saint-Eloi, where we arrived at nightfall, more exhausted than if we had covered thirty kilometers, when only ten kilometers separated Béthonsart from Saint-Eloi.

Our company was quartered in some newly built barracks. They were the first we had seen, a symbol, finally some belated recognition by our ignorant headquarters that we were now fighting trench warfare, a war of fixed positions.

Blinded up to that point, hemmed in, their narrow minds refusing to accept any warfare other than one of constant movement, an untenable dogma, the military upper caste considered everything that had happened since 1914 as provisional, fluid, changing from one day to the next. They refused to improve the lot of the fighting man in this new kind of siege warfare.

How much suffering, exhaustion, sickness, injuries, and deaths would have been spared, if only we'd had bosses with some basic common sense!

It was with great joy that we took possession of these barracks, where we were at last sheltered from wind and snow. But alas, the cold, that terrible enemy that cuts through barriers and walls, easily penetrated our clothes and our damp blankets, and we shivered, all night long, packed tightly against one another, because there wasn't the slightest spark of a fire in there.

The next evening, right when most of us had bedded down, they told us we had to give up the barracks to troops who were coming back from the trenches. This was only right, but it was bothersome for us to go out in the night, at the edge of the village, looking for lodging among houses more or less demolished by shellfire.

The best my squad could find was a hovel with its roof three-quarters torn off. In the dark of night we had to rig up a shelter with our tent cloths, under the remaining corner of the roof which was just barely holding on, who knows how. The snow kept falling, right into our shelter. We couldn't even think about lying down. With a few beams and planks pulled from under the rubble we made a nice fire, which was quite an accomplishment considering that the wood was damp and the wind and rain tried their hardest to put it out.

The fire won out over the battling elements, and we spent the night crouched around it, thinking about the evening's orders which had proclaimed that, thanks to careful planning, the soldiers weren't suffering from cold or rain this winter.

The next day we cleaned up and improved our quarters a bit. As stealthy as a band of *apaches*,[8] we stole a hay bale from a neighboring barn, despite the proprietor's vigilance, and so we had some comfortable bedding.

We spent four days in all at Saint-Eloi. The bad weather made field exercises impossible, so we amused ourselves by visiting the historic towers of the Abbey of Saint-Eloi. In earlier days these towers dominated the plains of Artois, but now the German howitzers had transformed them into piles of rubble.[9]

But we couldn't hang around too long in this area, because now and then the Boches had the habit of lobbing a few shells onto the ruins. The whole surrounding neighborhood had been obliterated.

We watched the installation of large-caliber artillery batteries at the top of Mont-Saint-Eloi. This was no mean feat, hauling these steel monsters up rutted pathways where horses, men, and cannon were slipping, sliding, and getting stuck at each step forward.

Not far from our billet, three cemeteries spread their long lines of little crosses along the slope.

Toward the Hell of Verdun:
February 29–April 26, 1916

Each morning they brought a few dead bodies up there from the field hospitals in nearby sectors.

There was nothing sadder than watching a raw-boned nag hauling an old tumbrel upon which two, three, or four cadavers were trundled along, hastily wrapped in grubby tent cloth, with their legs, still in mud-splattered boots and puttees, hanging off the back of the stubby wagon.

A chaplain in his cloak, accompanied by a soldier-seminarian, followed behind, and made up the funeral party with three or four old Territorials transformed into grave diggers, with picks and shovels on their shoulders.

So went to the field of honor those whose fate, as the song says, is worthy of envy.[1]

On February 29 our battalion left at 6 in the evening for the front lines, to relieve one of the battalions up there.

The weather, which had started to improve during the day, turned bad that evening, and we were greeted with some very nasty downpours on our trip to the trenches.

Leaving the village, we had to cross a swampy plain along duckboard paths over a stretch that was several kilometers long.

Marching on slippery, muddy planks, in bad condition, was very hard, and more than one of us pitched headlong into the snow or the mud. And watch out if such an accident occurred when the pathway was crossing a ditch or a shell hole or a pond—then you'd get a complete dunking.

We reached the Béthune-Arras road. This was as close to the front as the field kitchens could get, each evening.

Once we'd gotten across this road, through an inextricable jumble of vehicles and all kinds of equipment, we plunged into a network of communication trenches which were fairly well maintained by the reserve companies stationed along them, sheltered as best they could be.

But once we got past the second line, the trenches were in lamentable condition, and our feet and legs were soon soaked and frozen.

Then we stopped, and they left us there for a good long while—or rather a bad long while. Our feet grew numb once they reached a certain level of cold. Our patience was at its limit. Occasionally someone would let out, "Why aren't we advancing?" But no response was heard. Finally, Vacher cried out, "Since things are this way, I'm going back, and I'm spending the night in the first shelter I come across. If you're not all cowards, do as I do!"

And with that, he headed off.

We took counsel, and all agreed that we couldn't spend the night standing in mud up to our knees, stuck in a boyau where a frigid wind was blowing. We decided that if, in the next ten minutes, no order came to pull us out of this sewer, we would follow Vacher's lead.

But soon after we came to this decision, we heard the voices of our section chief and the sergeants, coming to "reconnoiter."

A third of the section went right to the outposts, where you had to stay eight hours out of twenty-four. The rest of us were led a little farther along, to a place where a bit of firing step could be seen along the trench wall.

We were invited to install ourselves here. This narrow shelf was our resting place when we came back from eight hours on guard duty at the outposts.

We were too many to fit along the shelf. There wasn't even room for us to stow our packs.

And throughout the dark night, the snow swirled around us. Overcome with fatigue, with cold, how comfortable to us seemed the memories of the ruins of Saint-Eloi, the stable at Queux, the horse barn at Ivergny. How delightedly would we have stretched out at any one of those places!

It was clear that staying where we were until daylight would mean a slow death from the cold. Death would have been deliverance, the end of harsh suffering, but the terrifying mystery of death is such that we flee from it, we find a sudden burst of energy when it gets too close to us.

One of us who had gone to explore the vicinity discovered a mine shaft. We piled into it. The engineers were digging at the far end, and men from the reserve companies were dragging sacks full of earth to the entrance.

We stretched ourselves out along the tunnel, which was too narrow and badly lit. The workers trampled on us, or let their sacks drag across us. But we put up with it all, too happy that they tolerated us being there, through compassion, solidarity, and fraternity which united all the martyrs of this disgusting war.

Our captain wasn't moved by any of these fine sentiments, and when he learned that we had the audacity to seek refuge in this mine tunnel, he prohibited us from going back there because we were bothering the workers. Better for us to die of cold, outside; it didn't bother him, he had a fine shelter.

So we were forced to install ourselves along the shelf in the boyau, with a few poles upon which we stretched our tent cloths, a fragile roof which stopped neither the wind nor the rain nor the cold. That is where we came to relax during the leisure time we had between daily and nightly work details and guard duty at the outposts.

You couldn't even think about lying down, or sleeping sitting up. The terrible cold which reigned throughout the night obliged us to head frequently to a place where the duckboards weren't covered with water, to stamp our feet furiously in order to struggle with frostbite, keeping our feet from swelling up, turning blue, and cracking painfully.

To do battle with the cold, instead of giving us more fortifying meals or an extra ration of pinard, our captain could himself find nothing better to do than to send us on work details, nonstop. This hard work consisted of ridding the trenches of water, mud, and snow. But rain or snow fell every day, almost without stopping; the sides of the trenches caved in, and the water bubbled up in thousands of little springs, between the edges of the duckboards.

You had to say that the captain's remedy did some good. The men who would complain about suffering from the cold had only to try slogging twelve hours out of twenty-four in freezing water up to their knees, and then they would see how effective it was.

Luckily the sector was calm. One could truly say that the Germans had compassion for us. If they had bombarded us in these shallow communication trenches, with no shelters, they would have made a nice marmalade out of us.

And so by their carelessness, their fatuousness, their negligence—let's say no more about the generals who succeeded each other in this sector, and their commanding general who should have known all about it—a part of the front, stabilized for more than a year, hadn't a slab of sheet metal or a simple plank of wood to protect the soldiers from a downpour between two shifts of guard duty or two work details.

And the engineers, instead of building useful shelters, spent day and night digging mine tunnels, at great expense and involving two months of Herculean efforts, to blow up a bit of trench where, in most cases, no one was present.

And to think that, every day, courts-martial condemned those imprudent enough to have dared to utter a doubt about the final victory, or say something in protest against the ignoble, worldwide killing.

The crime of *lèse-militarisme* had replaced the crime of *lèse-majesté*.

What punishment would these inhuman generals deserve, the artisans of defeat, for ruining, spoiling, exposing to suffering and death so many precious souls?

At the outposts, which were nothing more than bits of sap[2] sticking out from the front trench line, the men stood guard for four daylight hours and four nighttime hours. Then they went back to stretch out on a firing step, or to clean out the trenches. In my capacity as corporal, I had to spend twelve hours out of twenty-four on guard duty. It's true that I didn't have to keep watch right at the loopholes. That made up for the extra four hours I had to serve.

Night and day, "listeners" from the engineers came up to the outposts, to find out how far along our neighbors were in their own underground excavations. When questioned by us, these "listeners" always reassured us that it was way off to our left that the Boches were digging. To those on our left they said it was to the right, that's to say right under our feet.

They were following good advice by deceiving us like that. Everyone was reassured.

In fact, during this time there was only one mine explosion, on March 13 at 5 in the evening, in the sector next to ours, in front of Neuville-Saint-Vaast. It was our side which blew it up, but the Boches responded with a bombardment which probably caused more damage on our side than our mine had on theirs.

And our captain, what became of him in his deep shelter, where a well-fueled stove threw off plenty of soothing warmth, day and night? He had the good company of his friend the commandant, Quinze-Grammes, because the shortage of shelters forced them to bunk together.

This shelter, with two staircases going in and out, was as busy as an anthill. Orderlies, messengers, couriers, signalmen, quartermaster-sergeants, all piled up on the steps of these muddy, narrow staircases, but those who were privileged enough to stay there were greatly envied by those who were only visiting.

On the front line there were a few individual shelters, a couple of mine tunnels, and some listening posts which had been started. Despite the constant danger of being buried there, alive or dead, by a mine explosion, those on front-line guard duty decided to stay out there and seek refuge, once their shifts were over.

The captain was against it, but in vain. Furious at being defied, he prohibited the rationers from bringing any food up to the front line. Those on guard duty were therefore obliged to make the difficult journey back to the second line if they wanted to eat.

One can imagine the desire which the sentinels had for a cup of coffee in the morning, to warm them up a little. You had to see the joy painted on their faces at the sight of the squad's rationer making an appearance.

Thanks to the captain's orders, all that was over. They had to wait for their relief, later in the morning.

The temperature, rather than improving, turned frightfully cold. Gusts of snow alternated with downpours of rain. We had to give up trying to get the water out of the trenches, and it was fifty to sixty centimeters deep in certain places. In order to get through, some of us took off our shoes, and rolled up our trousers like crayfishermen. Others wrapped their legs and feet in several sandbags. But how could you keep from getting soaked, and getting bogged down in mud from head to foot?

All this unprecedented suffering exasperated the soldiers. A spirit of revolt began to stir. At last, this was all just too much.

One evening, at 8 o'clock, I was up at an outpost with three sentinels, in utter darkness, sheltered precariously from the drifting snow by a barrier of frozen earth which we had built up during the day.

The men had been looking at their watches with a flashlight, at least twenty times. At last, 8 o'clock. The relief crew would be coming. But a quarter of an hour passed, then a half-hour, three-quarters of an hour. No one showed up.

I couldn't leave my post until midnight. But the three others declared that they were going to abandon me if I wouldn't go back to find their replacements.

I calmly took off my shoes, rolled up my trousers, and launched myself into the canals which led back to the second trench line, in temperatures five or six degrees below zero. As I passed by the next outpost, I found out that their relief hadn't arrived, either. What was going on?

But at this outpost, they had accepted things philosophically. The sentinels were no longer on watch. With a couple of old planks, some sandbags and tent cloths, they had made a little cabin where they now crouched, dozing off, overcome with fatigue.

I made my way back to the second line, and after a dozen slips and falls and as many collisions with the trench walls and shrapnel shields, I found the sergeant of grenadiers who was in charge of these two outposts.

Dumbfounded, he told me that he had sent the relief detail up at ten minutes to eight. So we had to get to work and find them. This game of hide and seek, in such a place and in such darkness, would be no child's play.

I suggested that the men could be in the mine tunnel which we had discovered the first day. Indeed, that's where they were, these twenty rebels. To the sergeant's curses they replied that they were all too sick to go on duty.

They felt no shame about leaving their comrades to freeze at the outposts. Nothing doing.

The sergeant could hardly bring himself to report what happened to the captain, who was also stupefied but recovered quickly.

"Bring them here to me!" he said.

One by one they descended into the shelter where the commandant, who was also sputtering with rage, held court, and the captain in a rough voice said, with no preliminaries, "You claim to be sick?"

"Yes."

"Fine. The *major* will see you. We'll take you to him. If you're not diagnosed as sick, it's a court-martial for you, with the charge of desertion of your post in the face of the enemy. Get out of here!"

The rebels went out, but not one of them dared to submit himself to the *major*'s diagnosis. All of them, terrified by the captain's threat, which they knew was not a bluff, took up the path, or rather the streams and water-filled ruts, which led right to the outposts.

Worried about the hints of rebellion, the captain himself went to the outposts that night and each night thereafter, his legs protected in high waterproof boots.

He didn't come to comfort or encourage the frozen sentinels. He was trying to find fault with their vigilance, and to do so he crept up like a wolf and suddenly snapped on his flashlight.

On March 3, at 7 in the evening I was in the trench, at the turnoff to the boyau leading to the outpost. I was on the lookout for the coffee man, who had promised to supply us despite the captain's prohibition. I heard footsteps, no doubt announcing his arrival. But alas, it was our captain. I saluted and stood aside, thinking that he was heading for the outpost, but in a harsh voice he addressed me: "You should be a little busier than that."

"Captain," I replied, "what do you mean?"

"I mean that I want to see everyone hard at work. How many sentinels are there on guard duty?"

"Since it's getting dark, just one. The other two are at rest."

"Oh, they're resting, are they? Get them here right away, with shovels."

"But captain, we haven't had any coffee and, besides, we cleaned out the boyau and the approaches to the trench as best we could, just this morning."

"I've had enough of your excuses. Put these two men to work in the trench right away!"

"Captain, I don't think you know the danger there is letting yourself be seen in this part of the trench. It's in full view of the Boches, in enfilade of a machine gun. The last company here had several wounded. Yesterday Private Delile, moving along at a crouch, had his helmet shot right through. . . ."

"Enough! All you have to do is obey orders," the captain cut me off.

"I also have to obey my conscience."

There we were, eye to eye—he exasperated, I defiant.

"Yes or no, Corporal Barthas. Will you obey me?"

"Captain, I would do what you want, in dark of night, or in thick fog. But while it's still daylight, I'm not going to risk the lives of my men needlessly."

"Fine. You'll be punished." And he went away, furious.

Two days later, I was at the outpost. Happy news had reached us: We were being definitively relieved from the sector by the English, starting that very evening at 8 o'clock. This haste to relieve us was explained by the bad news from Verdun. The English were extending their front to make French troops available for reassignment.[3]

By five in the evening, with blankets rolled up and tent cloths stowed, we eagerly awaited the arrival of the "Tommies."

But here is the sergeant of the day, with a paper in his hand. He tells me, in a sad voice: "Barthas, I have some bad news to tell you."

I grew pale. Perhaps it's illness or death of a loved one, announced by telegram. "What is it?" I said with anguish.

He held out the paper to me, and I read: "Corporal Barthas is broken in rank and assigned to the 15th Company."

I let out a breath. So that was all! I tore off my stripes and tossed them into the mud. I felt a sense of deliverance from remorse, liberated from chains. By accepting a rank, however minor it may be, one took on a bit of authority, of this odious discipline, and one was in some way complicit in all the misdeeds of this loathsome militarism.

As a simple private, I recovered my independence, my freedom to criticize, to hate, to curse, to condemn this same militarism, the cause of this ignoble, worldwide killing spree.

Sergeant Marc had the assignment of conducting me immediately to my new company. It was only this change which saddened me, because it meant losing some fast friends and good comrades which are made only over time. Since we were being relieved that very evening, I asked Sergeant Marc if he could get the captain to postpone my reassignment to the next day, so that we wouldn't have to make our way through the labyrinth of flooded, barely navigable trenches at the same time as the relief was taking place. The sergeant, who was equally uninspired by the prospect of this promenade, hastened off to present my request to Captain Cros. The captain flew into a rage, refused my request, and insisted that the sergeant carry out the order immediately. If there had been any gendarmes around in the trenches, I'm sure he would have had me clapped in handcuffs and hauled away.

This refusal vexed me, and my hatred for the captain would have grown worse if there were room for it to do so. I shook the hands of the saddened sentinels, and after two hours of sloshing around, Sergeant Marc and I reached the command post of Lieutenant Breton, of the 15th Company, who immediately assigned me to the first squad at hand.

That same day, a corporal had been broken and expelled from the 15th Company. The reason: having said to a soldier who was being evacuated with frostbitten feet, "You're lucky, you."

This corporal had forgotten the currently fashionable watchword: "Keep quiet, watch out, enemy ears are listening."

And in my own company the captain had made other victims. One snowy day Private Vacher had the unfortunate inspiration to go eat his soup while sitting in a shelter occupied by a machine gun officer, right next to our captain's shelter. The machine gun officer, spotting Vacher, warned him about the standing order to keep the stairways clear. But Vacher had the bad manners to reply that he wasn't in the way, sheltering himself for a while. The officer, who'd been praised in the newspapers for voicing sentiments of fraternity between the ranks, defied this reputation by threatening to punish Vacher if he didn't clear off, in a tone which you wouldn't use when putting a dog out. Vacher answered back, and raised the stakes by calling the lieutenant a "toilet seat" and a "blockhead." He could have gotten into big trouble for these disrespectful words, but the officer felt remorse the next day and decided not to pursue the matter, in which he hadn't played such a fine role.

But the captain, when he heard about this affair, didn't take it so lightly. He had Vacher arrested and sent back to Saint-Eloi, where he was handed over to the gendarmes. A little later we learned that he had been condemned to two years in prison by a court-martial.

For comparing an officer to a toilet seat: one year in prison. To a chestnut pan: the same. Vacher was lucky to have stopped there. A few more epithets like these and he'd have ended his days in hard labor.

At 9 in the evening we were relieved by a battalion of our own regiment, the general relief by the English having been postponed by five days.

At 11 that evening we were in Saint-Eloi, where the field kitchens offered us a quarter-liter of bouillon and one of coffee. But it was at Béthonsart that we would be billeted. What a road to get there! And in what weather! The thermometer that night dropped to 10 degrees below zero. Gusts of swirling snow blinded us. The road was slippery because the snow froze as soon as it hit the ground.

Soon our ranks were all jumbled up. The battalion was nothing more than a straggling mob of human rags, leaning on sticks to ease our cold-ravaged feet. Most of the men didn't arrive until the next day. To see this disorganized band, in dark of night and in such a snowstorm, brought to mind a vision of the retreat of Napoleon's *Grande Armée* in Russia.

Luckily I had in my cartridge box a flask of 90 percent alcohol which I nipped at, along the way. Thanks to this, and an almost superhuman effort of willpower, I kept up with the leading group of my company, commanded and guided by Sublieutenant Séverac.

Finally, here is Menonval [Mingoval]. Two more kilometers and we would be there. But how long it takes to cover these two thousand meters. We thought we could do it in one effort, in a single bound, but fatigue obliges us to call a halt.

What was hardest was that, despite the clarity of the snow which allowed us to see quite far, we couldn't see anything on the horizon which looked like a village.

We soon started out again, since the cold didn't allow us to take long breaks. But the plain still stretched out before our anxious gazes, as in those vast Muscovite expanses. We were utterly discouraged and messed up.

Finally, we ended up reaching a village. But there's a train station in it, and the railroad doesn't go to Béthonsart. The station was right alongside our road, and on the signboard we read the name "Savy-Berlette."

We had lost our way. Our discouragement was extreme. It didn't lessen when a railroad employee told us that we were about five kilometers from Béthonsart . . .

Artois 1916. The only relief (continued).
Magnicourt. Conteville. Incourt. Guigny.

Derisive whistles were heard, directed at our commanding officer. This sub-lieutenant wasn't a bad fellow, but too meticulous, a stickler about everything, and he didn't have the sympathy of his men. This was a good opportunity, or a bad one, depending on your viewpoint, for this to be made known.

Scattered in the darkness, concealed by the thickly falling snow, just try to find out who is whistling. The soldier who is certain of impunity sometimes can become unjust and cruel.

Of course, mistakes can happen. Anyone can miss a turn in the road when the snow is swirling around, blinding you, and obscuring the road ahead and its borders. And nobody else noticed that we had taken a wrong turn.

In general, I have a strong aversion against those who wear gold stripes, who display a bit of authority, of despotism, of the militarism which had us all in its sharp claws. But this time I didn't at all approve of the attitude of my comrades, because they didn't stop at whistling. They hurled all kinds of the rudest imaginable insults upon this officer.

Others called out to him, "Go learn to read a map! To the schoolhouse! Do you need a lantern to show you how to get there? You don't deserve to wear those stripes—you should give them up."

The officer didn't say a word, and, after being shown the road to Béthonsart by the railway employee, he gave the order to head out. Those followed who wanted to, or who could. I don't know how I found the strength to get to this village. The human body sometimes seems to be an inexhaustible source of energy, even if it means that legs, loins, and haunches demand an accounting later on and remind us with sharp pains what excesses had been asked of them.

When we arrived, we were counting on a quarter-liter of *jus* [coffee]. We'd been promised it, but the field kitchens hadn't arrived yet. In a big shed they had spread out a little straw. I collapsed in a corner and, rolled up in my blanket, slept like a log.

It was 6 in the morning. Since 9 o'clock the night before we'd been marching, covering thirty kilometers in frightful weather and roads. In my company, only about thirty of us had arrived together. The others straggled in during the course of the day.

At noon someone shook me awake, to eat a bit of soup, but then I fell asleep again. My nerves were unwound, and I was like a marionette with broken strings; I couldn't even stand up.

The next day my feet felt a little less painful, and I summoned the strength to go to Menonval to find my pack, still in the care of my former company, which was then billeted in this village.

I took advantage of this opportunity to find out the reason for the punishment which the captain had inflicted on me. I expected to read a masterpiece of literature. After all, he had a law degree! And had held a staff post at the ministry!

The sergeant-major agreed to show me the register of punishments, and I read: "Barthas, class of . . . etc. . . . . charged with carrying out an order, he said to his men, 'Just look like you're working.'" That seemed stupid to me, "neither fish nor fowl," as they say. Surely Colonel Douce must have been curious for other explanations for my being broken in rank. But then colonels aren't expected to have dealings with corporals; that might risk diminishing their standing.

I was just about to slam shut this libelous book where my name was forever inscribed for indiscipline, when I noticed that the charge was accompanied by the following amendments, signed by Commandant Leblanc: "This corporal sets a bad example; he is unfit to serve as a non-com; there are a good number of candidates in his company who could replace him, to good effect. In consequence, I have the honor, colonel, to ask you to reduce him in rank."

These lines wounded and infuriated me. Take away my stripes because I lack military spirit, for my socialist and antimilitarist opinions—so be it. For me, that would be a badge of honor, just like the Croix de Guerre is for others. It would be evidence of fidelity to my principles, in a time when so many had denied theirs. But the words "setting a bad example" were just too much.

I immediately decided to file a protest with the colonel. But then I reflected that my poor stripes were hardly worth the trouble of stirring up a fuss, screwing up the whole hierarchical structure. And further, wouldn't it be satisfying for those who had taken them from me, to see how hurt I was by losing them?

But in the 13th Company all my comrades begged me to protest, to give a humiliating lesson to the captain. Corporals offered to turn in their stripes in an act of protest. Deeply moved, I dissuaded them from doing this. Finally, when I left for Béthonsart, all hands were stretched out to me, and I saw tears welling up in the eyes of comrades, some of whom were with me since Mont-Louis.

All these promises of support truly touched me, and this fortified me to resolve to ask for a hearing with Colonel Douce. From victim I would turn accuser against Captain Cros, for having forced men to work in a trench exposed to machine gun fire, without it being absolutely necessary.

I had to postpone my request for a hearing. The regiment was dispersed, the colonel was still at the front lines (not at an outpost), and finally we were pulling up stakes and shifting back and forth to make room for the English.

On March 8, in lousy weather always threatening to snow, we left Béthonsart and went to encamp at Magnicourt. The course was a short one, only seven kilometers, but very hard, since everybody's feet were more or less afflicted by the cold.

The next day, twice the distance to cover, and twice the suffering. The regiment encamped at Conteville.

That evening I took a little walk by myself. I noticed, at the end of an empty courtyard, a little house with doors and windows wide open. I boldly entered this seemingly abandoned lodging. The ground floor consisted of a single, darkened room. At first I couldn't see anything, but once my eyes grew accustomed to the darkness I was not a little surprised to see a human body stretched out on the ground, covered with such miserable rags that it left parts of the body naked.

I quickly approached the body, and once I touched it I realized that it was a plaster statue dressed in beggar's cloths. Then I saw a door leading to a small chapel, and an inscription above told me that I was the guest of St. Benedict, and that this hovel was where he had lived and died in piety, zeal, and penitence. One was invited to send a wish or a prayer to this influential saint, which would surely be answered.

I wanted to ask that all the cannon, rifles, and other murderous devices be hurled into Hell, but I thought it would be useless. St. Benedict wouldn't have done that, no matter how highly placed he was at the Lord's right hand.

It's curious how often you come upon shrines to saints in the Pas-de-Calais. One would think that a good portion of the inhabitants of Paradise came from this very département.

The next day we had to get back on the road and scratch out twenty-three kilometers, this time, to get to Incourt. We arrived there hobbling along, leaning on sturdy sticks like a bunch of old men.

I call upon those who have taken a walk with a simple blister on the heel or the ankle, to think about our suffering, with feet that were nothing but one whole blister, or even worse, one whole chilblain.

The name Incourt seemed to mean that it was "un-short," and indeed the houses of this village stretched for almost two kilometers along the road. It was a big disappointment to think that we had only a few more steps to reach our encampment, and instead it took a half-hour to get to it, at the farthest point in the village.

The next day, again on the road. We wondered what our goal was, where we were going, but in vain because no one told us anything. That day we encamped at Guigny.

This village was so little that some sections—mine included—couldn't find any room in it, and we had to use our own tent cloths for shelter, which wasn't too comfortable. In the night, the cold chased us out from under them. As for me, I sought out a little space in a stable, where I slept like a blessed soul, despite the risk of catching a few kicks from the cows who were sleeping there.

Finally, March 12 was supposed to be our last day of marching. But they told us that it would be a long and hard one, so they took two packs away from each squad. That way, after each rest break, by turns, two soldiers in each squad could march without carrying anything.

1916. Artois. Picardy. Crécy. Le Titre.
Lamotte-Buleux. Favières. Le Crotoy.

Along the way we passed through Crécy[4] and the famous battlefield, an episode of the Hundred Years' War.

Just one monument placed in the town square of Crécy reminded the passerby of this historical fact. Today this would only be a minor skirmish, a raid, compared to the titanic battles of the current war.

After the battlefield we had to cross an interminable forest. Who knows if these centuries-old oak trees hadn't been witnesses to the precipitous flight of the king of France and his companions?

Finally, at three o'clock in the afternoon, our battalion arrived at its cantonment in the village of Le Titre. But three days later they moved us to the neighboring village of Lamotte-Buleux.

The squad I was in was lucky enough to be lodged with sturdy farm folk who also ran a roadside tavern, where the tables and chairs were at our disposal for taking our meals.

In the barn, a soft bed of fresh straw was heavenly for us. Of course, the drills began right away, and no doubt at the orders of our commandant they became long and intensive.

One day we were surprised at our exercises by the unexpected arrival of Colonel Douce. Lieutenant Grulois, nicknamed *Gueule-de-Bois* ["wooden mug," slang for hangover], who commanded our company, obsequiously rushed up to the big boss.

"How many hours of drilling are these men doing?" asked the colonel.

"Eight hours," replied Lieutenant Grulois, afraid that it wouldn't be enough, "with ten minutes rest each hour."

"Eight hours!" exclaimed the colonel. "I would be completely wiped out after that! Lieutenant, less drilling, and more rest."

And he disappeared.

After this visit, our rest breaks were ten minutes longer. That was ten minutes less of getting wiped out, as the colonel had said.

One night, I was yanked out of a deep sleep by the noise of the door opening, and here was our landlord, lantern in hand, who approached us.

"What's going on?" I asked him.

"I need two of you to give me a hand."

"Right away," I said as I got up and shook my neighbor awake.

If he wasn't already a priest, my neighbor was training to be one. Steeped in devotion, he had little to do with us except the most strictly indispensable relations and conversations. He spent his free time in the company of the battalion's curates, monks, and seminarians. Galin was his name.

But what was this peaceable duty we were recruited for? There was no enemy outpost around here to be raided. It was simply to lend a hand to a cow who was having a hard time calving.

Modestly I confessed my inexperience in these matters. The abbé Galin's inexperience was no less than my own, but as a true disciple of Christ he couldn't refuse to help his fellow man. Besides, our landlord assured us that our role couldn't be easier and required no serious apprenticeship.

As if he knew the dismal fate which awaited him in this world, the little veal-calf had gotten his rear legs and his hindquarters out, but he obstinately refused to get the rest out. That's what we had to get him to do.

The farmer tied a rope to the legs of the newborn. Galin and I were asked to pull on the rope while the farmer took care of the cow.

But we had to act with care and a certain dexterity, which we lacked completely, in order to coordinate our efforts with the mother's contractions. We had to work with nature, and not force it or abuse it. But you don't become a midwife of cattle in just a day.

Despite our best intentions we must have pulled too hard, because once the horned baby finally got his nose out he seemed to be in miserable shape.

In vain they gave him a swig of hot rum, and a brisk rubdown, then they rolled him in a basket of straw as soft as a duvet. But nothing did any good. The little calf died, right away.

These good folks wanted to thank us nonetheless for our troubles, and they invited us to drink a bowl of mulled wine. I accepted with pleasure, but Galin refused. Thinking that he didn't like wine, they offered him a little glass of excellent rum, but he refused it quite obstinately.

These people were dumbfounded. For a poilu to refuse a glass of wine was extraordinary enough, but to turn down a glass of rum, that went beyond anything a Picard could imagine.

But once Galin had left, I explained that, he being a priest, and the next day being Sunday, the day of communion, he couldn't risk his soul's salvation by swallowing even a drop of water, midnight having been rung a few moments before.

The farmers were astounded to learn that they had recruited a clergyman to help their cow to give birth. They felt a vague remorse at having tempted a minister of God and placing him at risk of mortal sin.

One evening, while we were eating our supper in the main room of the tavern, our section chief pushed the door open and told us, in few words, to be ready for departure at 6 the next morning.

The officer could have waited until the end of our meal, because the news threw us into such a troubled state that we could hardly touch the heaping platter of beans which, just a moment before, we were all set to devour.

We knew that, at Verdun, it would be nothing like this. We were even surprised that they gave us that much time to rest up.

Home leaves were completely suspended from the time we left Saint-Eloi.

Two kilometers beyond Lamotte-Buleux, the road forked. One way led to Noyelles-sur-Mer, our point of embarkation. The other way led to the plains of Ponthieu [region of Picardy, principal town is Abbeville]. That will explain the efforts we made the next day to see which direction the head of the column would take. We let out a big sigh of relief when we saw that the vanguard turned its back on Noyelles. That meant we weren't leaving for Verdun, the very name of which froze us with dread. Any other destination did not matter to us, and immediately joy and gaiety spread through the ranks in the form of songs, laughter, jokes, and lively conversation.

The whole division was on the move. It was assembled in an immense field for a big rest break, because the march was long and hard. Then the regiments and battalions dispersed to their respective cantonments.

We were on the shores of the English Channel, near the mouth of the Somme. Our battalion was billeted at Favières, two kilometers from Le Crotoy, where I made my way the next day, a Sunday.

Le Crotoy is a pleasant seaside resort right at the mouth of the Somme. One regiment of the division was billeted there. At low tide hundreds of soldiers went fishing for shellfish and shrimps in the sand of the beach. The little town was quite lively.

The next day, to exercise our legs, we carried out a long march by Rue along the sand dunes of the seacoast.

And then the next day, April 3, we once again took the road for Lamotte-Buleux.

What had we come to Favières for? It certainly wasn't to breathe the restorative air of the Channel for three days.

But we didn't waste any time trying to solve the mystery of this strategic maneuver. To tell the truth, we weren't unhappy to be returning to Lamotte-Buleux, which we reached at around two in the afternoon.

That day we had an oppressive heat, coming right after some rather cold temperatures, and we hadn't left Favières until 8 in the morning, which meant that we endured the strongest heat of the day.

At the last rest breaks, in the shade of each and every tree, you'd see a laggard lying, out of breath, dripping sweat. There were a hundred of them from each battalion.

Once we arrived, they asked for a list by company of the men who weren't able to keep up. It was, so they said, to put together a category of slackers, of men who had to be watched. Some clever ones detected an advantage to being put on this list. Who knows, maybe you'd be exempt from carrying a pack in the next march, or maybe you'd be sent back to the divisional depot for a rest. I knew some who were left off the list, and others who hadn't fallen by the wayside but who got their names on the list all the same.

But the next day, at assembly, here is what they read out to us: "The men who couldn't keep up with the column yesterday evidently need more training. As a consequence, until further notice they will go to drills in campaign gear, with full packs. The others won't have to carry their packs."

And that's how, for once, the tricksters got themselves tricked.

The long sojourn we had in this village was such that a great intimacy built up between the poilus and the inhabitants, especially among the ladies. Some idylls were kindled; there were some amorous adventures which became tied and untied. As for me, a loving and faithful husband, I won the affections of a lady of Lamotte.

But alas, for her and for me. The snows of sixty-five winters had colored her hair, and this lady was a poor old hag living with her husband in a shack at the far end of the village.

The husband, worn down by the years and by rheumatism, lay moaning in his bed. His wife used up her last reserves of strength making sure that her bits of field didn't go fallow, as well as a rather large garden surrounding the thatched cottage, three-quarters of which were choked with thistles and other weeds.

I observed all this one day, when I was on my way to guard duty at the village's exit points, this useless and ridiculous guard duty which they had set up according to established practice.

Except on Sundays, this guard duty was a sort of relief for the poilus; in exchange, you could cut out twenty-four hours of drills or parades. Only the four hours of night duty you'd pull could perhaps be wearisome for those who couldn't appreciate the charm of solitude, of nocturnal silence, of contemplation of a starry sky, etc.

It's true that, at this time, stinging April showers often troubled the poetic moonlit vigils. Then you would seek refuge in the clever little sentry boxes which the wicker workers had fashioned out of the boughs of the Crécy forest. But if the downpour lasted, you'd be chased out by the raindrops and find better shelter behind a wall. It was during one of my breaks between guard duty shifts that I picked up a tool and went to working, spading the old lady's garden.

"But monsieur," said the old lady, "you're working for nothing. I'm too poor to pay you anything."

"Don't worry about that, grandma. I'll stop by every day when I'm off duty, until your garden is in good shape and your potatoes are planted," which she despaired about getting done in time.

In fact, four or five days later, the work was done. The old lady didn't know how to express her thanks. She picked out for me the best apples in her cupboard, and I had to accept a coffee one evening. The old man wanted to be at the party, too, so we took our coffee in the sickroom.

As coquettish as any daughter of Eve, the old lady showed me her portrait at age twenty, and the old codger smiled impishly, as if to say, "You see, we were young once, and we were carefree in those days."

And I had to listen to the tales of their young love. They were about to be married when the war broke out—the war of 1870, that is. He went off in the *Garde Mobile.*[5] Once peace was signed, he hurried back to Lamotte to find his fiancée, but the Prussians were still occupying the region and the village. The marriage was put off. From morning to evening he was at her house, attending to her every need. One day, they were having a cozy tête-à-tête at home, which they hardly ever left, when a rude and insolent *Interoffizier* [probably *Unteroffizier,* corporal] burst in. He claimed that he needed some information, but his true purpose was to harass the lovers. He went so far as to try to kiss the young woman, right in front of her fiancé.

Evoking these distant memories, the old lady turned red with indignation, as if she could still feel the lips of the Boche.

But the story isn't finished. The young man—now an old codger, nailed to his bed—had to defend the honor of his Picard blood, and to avenge the outrage he slapped the German on both cheeks.

The non-com dashed out more quickly than he had come in, but he came back a moment later with a squad of policemen who seized the unlucky fiancé and dragged him off to jail, under a rain of blows and kicks.

The cantonment's commander was a captain who inspired real terror among the inhabitants for his severity, his brutal discipline. He decided to set an example, to make it known that whoever dared to raise a hand against a German non-com would be shot the very next day.

He had no idea of the circumstances which brought on this incident. But luckily for our pair of young lovers, he was billeted at the home of the town's mayor, who told him the whole story.

The terrifying officer summoned the young girl, the heroine of the story, to his office. She presented herself, fearful and faltering. There also appeared the ungallant non-com, who was forced to confess his misdeeds.

The next day they released the young Frenchman who was expecting to be shot. Three days later the village was delivered from German occupation. And our two young folks got married, loved each other, and had many children, now either dead or living far away. And they remained there, at home in the poor thatched cottage, from which only death would take them away.

I took advantage of our stay in Lamotte to try to see the colonel about my punishment. I submitted my request for a hearing at my company's office. I waited patiently for a week, and I made the request again.

The next day Commandant Leblanc had me summoned and received me in a very ungracious manner.

"Why do you want to talk to the colonel?" he asked.

"Commandant, sir, it's about my punishment."

"You know full well that if Captain Cros has punished you, he had good reason to do so."

"That's not my opinion."

"So you are persisting in your intention to protest this matter?"

"Yes, commandant, sir."

"You know, I won't support your request for a hearing."

"Commandant, I'm sorry, but I will persist all the same."

"Fine. Go to it."

"Commandant, may I go there right away?"

"Certainly not. You'll wait until the colonel asks for you."

Three days later, an orderly handed me a note, upon which I read: "Corporal Barthas will be presented to me when I visit the encampment at Lamotte-Buleux."

In fact, the colonel, who was based at Le Titre, did pass through the encampment a short while later, but he didn't have me summoned.

Hey, what was going on? Simply this: the commandant and the captain, fearing troubles for themselves on account of my appeal, could find nothing better to do than to intercept my request, and the colonel's reply was a fabrication to make me wait patiently and then to lose patience, to put me off through failure.

What can you call the conduct of these two stripers? Counterfeiters, liars, cowards?

Decidedly, I said to myself, it was easier to obtain an audience with the Sun King Louis XIV, in the olden days, than it was today to approach a simple colonel. Seeing, or rather not seeing anything happening, I decided to write directly to this Olympian personage, in spite of the rigorous rules which applied to those who didn't strictly follow the sacrosanct hierarchical channels.

I made sure to mention that I was going outside the prescribed procedures because I hadn't been able to reach him through the regular ways.

Things now moved quickly. That very evening Lieutenant Breton, commanding the 15th Company, had me summoned and told me that he was being asked to present me himself to the colonel, the next morning.

The next day, April 10, I made my way to Le Titre. After an hour's wait in the courtyard of the château which sheltered the colonel, Lieutenant Breton and I were brought inside. Vestibules, corridors, staircases, everything shined with fresh wax and polish. There were carpets everywhere.

Orderlies, batmen, chambermaids, all looked at me in a way which signified, "Where is this filthy poilu going?" Muddy, too, with my clodhoppers leaving a nasty imprint on the parquet floors and the carpets.

Finally they opened a door for us. We entered a room where Colonel Douce, alone, leaning against the marble mantelpiece, received us like a judge receives an accused man.

After an inquiring look at my humble person, he said to me in a rough voice, "What are you asking for?" I told my complaints against the punishment which had been inflicted upon me, and I handed him my written appeal which he read in full.

When he finished reading it, he was silent for a moment.

"Nevertheless," he said, "according to your commandant and your captain, you're a pretty lousy soldier."

"Colonel, sir, I have no punishments on my record, neither during the three years of my military service, nor during the current campaign. And as I have spelled out in that paper, I've done my duty in every situation, and I can, if you want, give you statements from irrefutable eyewitnesses. If I refused an order that Captain Cros gave me, the whole company will attest that it would have exposed the men to certain death, uselessly, by making them work in daylight in a trench enfiladed by enemy machine guns."

"But then," said the colonel in a softer voice, "how do you explain the bad marks in your record?"

"Colonel, sir, I can't say, but it might be helpful to know that Captain Cros has some friends in my village who are political adversaries of mine."

"Fine. You're dismissed. Lieutenant, stay here."

And these two personages discussed the fate of my two humble corporal's stripes.

That afternoon, in a large fallow field, our company was conducting an exercise. At the far end of my section, deployed as skirmishers, I was crouching with my comrades in the high grass when we spotted, riding toward us, two horsemen whom we recognized as the colonel and our commandant, Quinze-Grammes. The latter looked quite exhausted and worn out. He normally seemed to have all the difficulty in the world staying balanced on his horse, but today it was truly laughable. He was making the most comical efforts to cling to his nag, which was having trouble keeping up with the colonel's mount. One would have said it was Sancho Panza trying to follow his master, Don Quixote.

The two cavaliers turned toward us, and we could see from the liveliness of their gestures and the sounds of their voices that a spirited discussion was under way. They came right past us without seeing us, and we could hear their words clearly, proving that I was the topic of their conversation. It was the commandant who was saying in his nasal voice: "You know, colonel, sir, this corporal has very extreme socialist ideas."

But right then the two officers spotted us, and the colonel, quite surprised, changed the subject: "This terrain would be good for a battalion to maneuver in."

The next day, I learned from the colonel's aide—who was from Homps, and who was killed on *Cote* [Hill] 304 at Verdun a short time afterward—that Commandant Leblanc (Quinze-Grammes) and Captain Cros (the Kronprinz[6]) were harshly lectured by the colonel. What made him the maddest was that they had blocked my requests for a hearing. He ordered them to restore my stripes to me at the next promotion ceremony. That meant little to me, but I was satisfied by the stroke of bad luck which these two interesting characters had encountered.

That didn't keep Captain Cros from being promoted to *capitaine-adjutant-major.*

This news brought great rejoicing to the 21st Company. The men were beside themselves with joyous exclamations (in Occitan): "No more Kronprinz!" "'Four-Eyes' is gone!" But our own joy turned into consternation throughout the battalion, because now he'd be wielding his petty tyranny over all of us.

The useless functions of capitaine-adjutant-major had been abolished by a superior officer less stupid than the others, but then they were restored by some idiot at headquarters.

The next few days, at the daily assembly, it was nothing but prohibitions, orders, punishments, threats. Beforehand we had enjoyed a state of relative liberty at our cantonments. The good times were at an end.

In the main hall of the *mairie* of Lamotte-Buleux, where once the daily affairs of the village were decided, under the gaze of Marianne[7] who symbolizes
all the freedoms, our new tyrant had established his headquarters, his *Kom-
mandantur.* From daybreak he was right there, booted, gloved, girded in his
English getup. His first duty was to pay a visit to the prisoners locked in the
firehouse; he counted and recounted them with scrupulous care. Then, with his
chronometer in hand marking the official time, the time of the Paris longitude
to which all watches would be set, he went about his tasks, verifying departures, assemblies, work details, units going out on exercises, etc.

Each day a whole company, armed with long brooms made of branches so
abundant in the nearby Crécy forest, scoured the streets of Lamotte, with shovels, spades, rakes, wheelbarrows, tumbrels, sweeping, scraping, scouring, until
the appointed hour when the work detail was completed. A few dry leaves or an
overlooked sardine can would be enough to put him into a furor.

Would that there had been a Courteline[8] in our battalion. He would have
made Captain Cros-Mayrevieille into a legendary character like Adjutant Flic!

Around noon, during a break in the exercises, he would convoke the small-
fry of the stripers, the sergeants and the corporals. And fixing his glasses on a
book as thick as the Old Testament, he would interrogate them on the mys-
teries of military theory.

In the evenings he was no less busy. He would sneak up on the sentinels
guarding the exits from the village and the police posts. He would burst into
the taverns to collar some poilus who might be quenching their thirsts outside
of authorized hours, pursuing petty thieves in the billets, sending home those
who were walking around in greatcoat and police cap when you were supposed
to be wearing jacket and helmet and hood or even not supposed to be out at
all, because there were set times of day for these getups, and patrols of non-
coms made the rounds to enforce these rules.

This was becoming idiotic. Here is how the heroes, the saviors of civilization, the defenders of the right and the good, etc., are being led. It was a return
to the dark past, the age of feudalism, of ancient slavery.

On April 8, a big maneuver took place on the Crécy battlefield. I don't know
if they wanted to re-create the to-and-fros of the [medieval] battle, but we spent
all day tangled up in the forest, tramping through dense thickets, our faces
lashed by branches and our legs scratched by brambles.

At a crossroads I witnessed an altercation between Captain Cros-Mayrevieille
and Lieutenant Cordier, commander of the 14th Company. I caught these words
on the fly:

Captain: "I gave you this order."

Cordier: "No, you didn't. You're lying."

Captain: "Watch your language!"

Cordier: "What? Watch my language? Watch how I knock your glasses off your nose!"

Captain Cros was particularly fond of his glasses, and even fonder of the nose which held them on his face, because he quickly sped off on horseback, to the great joy of all who were watching.

1916. Toward the furnace.[9] *Revigny.*
Villers-le-Sec. Noyers. Condé-en-Barrois.

On April 15, after the morning meal, the regiment took the road to Noyelles-sur-Mer to embark on railway cars for a destination officially unknown, but everyone had the sense that we were going to Verdun, where the gigantic battle continued without interruption. Therefore you heard no singing along the ten-kilometer route which took us to Noyelles.

Nevertheless some of us clung to the vague hope that we were going to re-join our corps in the Oise [département, north of Paris]. Others said they had tips that we would take up a sector in Champagne.

At 7 that evening, with forty piled into each of the cattle cars, and with no straw or benches, the train took us away. Even the colonel didn't know where.

Stacked one on top of another, without even being able to stretch out our legs, which accordingly cramped up, we spent a very bad night indeed. At 7 in the morning, we passed through Le Bourget. At noon we were at Sézanne, in Champagne, and we still kept heading east.

At 4 in the afternoon, the train entered the station at Vitry-le-François. At this point we still didn't know our destination, but we would soon find out. If the train took the direction of Châlons, we'd be going to Champagne, which was very calm at that moment. If we continued on toward the east, there could be no more doubt—we were going to Verdun. Alas, that's exactly where we were headed, and at nightfall we disembarked at the station in Revigny.

Revigny was a pretty little town, now half-destroyed. Three months earlier a Zeppelin had been shot down there.[10] No doubt to stretch our legs after twenty-four hours of immobility, they sent us off to encamp twelve kilometers from Revigny. It was a moonless night, but starry, and the North Star told us that we were turning our backs on Verdun. What did that mean?

Besides we were a good distance from the front lines, because the breeze brought us only the very slightest grumbling from far away, where the horizon sometimes lit up with imprecise flashes of lightning.

While passing through one village, a brief order ran along the column: "Attention! The general!"

In the village square, beside his automobile, General P. . . . watched the regiment parading by. When I passed near him, he called out as he stomped his foot, "But these men are sleeping! Will you look at that!" The general was right.

All the men were dozing off. But he was wrong to reproach us, because he had traveled first class, then in an automobile, while we, jumbled together like a herd of animals, were obliged to pace off the kilometers heavily weighted down.

We arrived around midnight in a little village where my section was billeted in a shed with half-demolished walls. For bedding, some scraps of straw and hay, of a very doubtful cleanliness. We arrived just in time, because the rain soon started to fall, forcing me to change places three times to escape the bothersome drain spouts.

The next day it kept right on raining. I read the name on the signpost at the village entrance: "Villers-le-Sec, Marne." [Villers-the-Dry]. It should have been called "Villers-le-Mouillé" [Villers-the-Wet].

The next day, April 17, we rested, because the day after we had to begin our approach to Verdun.

The Germans had occupied Villers-le-Sec for a few days, but according to the inhabitants they weren't guilty of any serious depredations. The farmer's wife with whom I was billeted was still complaining that a uhlan[11] had threatened her with his revolver. He had discovered some chocolate, sugar, and other delicacies hidden under the good woman's bed, and he wanted to confiscate them, but she protested so energetically that this uhlan, who in truth was not very ferocious, did not press the matter further.

I know Frenchmen who, if they'd been in Germany and in a similar situation, would have had fewer scruples and would have taken possession of the chocolate from under the bed without any hesitation, and of the woman too, as part of the deal, if she'd been young and pretty.

At the corner of a little square, while walking around, I saw a crowd gathering, and ran over. At first I could see nothing very unusual: they had formed a circle around a brownish, greasy mass, containing what were clearly pieces of bone. What then was this?

Someone explained to me that in August 1914, after the terrible struggles which took place in this region, the Germans, masters of the battlefield, gathered up all the dead—their own, and ours—and made an immense funeral pyre which they doused with gasoline and lit. For several days the wind carried the hideous odor of grilled flesh for miles around.

No one knew how, but this shape which I had before my eyes was a piece of what remained when the sinister bonfire burned out.

On April 18, at 8 in the morning, we left Villers-le-Sec. As if to mock us, the rain fell in a heavy downpour. Each of us protected himself as best he could; most had English raincoats which the "Tommies" had sold or traded us. Others improvised hoods with tent cloths. All of a sudden I thought I heard wrong: they passed down the order to remove our raincoats, right at the moment when the rain was heaviest. This stupid order came right from our famous capitaine-adjutant-major, the Kronprinz.

He was no doubt recalling, with perfect timing, that a circular had gone around a few days ago, prohibiting the wearing of raincoats which weren't the color blue, the only one allowed (no doubt at the instigation of a supplier).

Captain Cros-Mayrevieille wouldn't have given it a second thought, without the idea of avenging himself for the affront that Lieutenant Cordier, commanding the 22nd Company, had given him in the forest of Crécy.

I've already said that Lieutenant Cordier had equipped all the men in the company in khaki-colored raincoats. Preventing us from using these raincoats made this act of generosity completely useless, and enraged Lieutenant Cordier, whose principal and perhaps only fault was being too quick-witted. That was reason enough for the Kronprinz. Letting a thousand men get soaking wet was secondary for him.

Himself wrapped in a sky-blue foul-weather cape, he rode alongside the flank of the column, pitilessly ordering the removal of the offending raincoats. Those who had put their packs, canteens, haversacks, and other gear on top of the raincoats were obliged to halt and fall behind a kilometer or so while they arranged their attire.

At noon we arrived, still in the rain, at the village of Noyers [Noyers-Auzecourt], in the Meuse, where the regiment would be billeted.

This village was filled with rear-echelon slackers who had been ensconced there for more than a year. There were hundreds of them: signalmen who were guarding a substantial amount of communications gear, destined to be installed in conquered territory. You could see stacks of telephone and telegraph poles, piles of porcelain fixtures, and rolls and rolls of enough wire to link Paris to Berlin . . . once we got there.

While waiting for that, the main task of the slackers was to go fishing in the river, to pass time carving on artillery shell caps, and to flirt with the ladies of Noyers.

Our untimely arrival troubled the peace of these pacifistic soldiers, and we had a tough time finding something with which to shelter ourselves, so we had to wait in the rain for someone to make room for us.

My section was lodged in the attic of a tumbling-down old house, inhabited by poor folks, a woman with five or six children, not counting the three others who were out in front, defending this dump.

The floorboards where thirty of us were lodged were half-rotted away, and we feared that at any moment we'd all go crashing down onto the ground floor.

We didn't get any straw, and I was considered a lucky stiff by my comrades for having found, in a nook, an armful of dried pea plants to stick under my backside.

In 1914 a skirmish had taken place in Noyers. The church was grazed by a shell, and in the adjacent cemetery a few soldiers, both French and German, rested fraternally partnered in death.

The day after our arrival we rested. We expected to depart at any minute, but no order came down, that day or the next day. That afternoon, despite stormy weather, they sent us out to do field exercises.

But Noyers is surrounded by prairies which the recent rains had transformed into swamps. We covered several kilometers without finding suitable ground for maneuvering with dry feet. We almost got lucky enough to escape this need for exercise, but nevertheless ended up finding a bit of ground less soggy than the others, and the exercise took place, despite the water which sometimes submerged our shoes.

Meanwhile the clouds piled up in a worrisome way, and thunder was heard, but this had no effect on the lieutenant who was commanding us and who waited for the first raindrops to fall before ordering our return to camp. The result: a complete soaking, with the bonus of a lashing, stinging sleet, all very disagreeable.

Soaked through to the bone, we reached the first houses of Noyers, savoring the thought of dry underwear and shirts on our skins, when we saw our old acquaintance Captain Cros-Mayrevieille (the Kronprinz) running toward us, waving his arms for us to stop.

What did he want, this animal? His timing was perfect. A murmur, or rather a groan, ran through the ranks.

As if he were announcing sensational news, the captain explained to our lieutenant that army headquarters, after what were no doubt laborious studies, had decided that henceforth we could march in columns of threes, instead of only in fours, twos, or single-file, as military theory had previously set forth. All that had been missing was threes, and this highly regrettable omission was now rectified. Our enthusiastic capitaine-adjutant-major couldn't wait to try it out on the first unit which fell into his hands.

Cursing under our breaths, we did a left-face, then counted out one, two, three, then the lieutenant commanded, "To the right, by threes, march!"

The movement, with childlike simplicity, was executed perfectly. The captain, dumbfounded and beaming, asked our lieutenant to repeat this maneuver frequently and to get us used to marching in threes. Then he left us to return home in peace.

On April 25 we carried out a marching exercise during which we went through the village of Sommeilles, entirely burned down and razed. All that was left was the blackened carcass of the church.

The newspapers had told how in 1914 the Germans, exasperated by the fierce resistance offered by a tiny rear-guard unit, avenged themselves atrociously on this village, which they pillaged and burned, and on its inhabitants. It was said that people were shot, children were raped and killed, women's breasts were cut off. But I have to say that, of the inhabitants of the region whom I questioned about these matters, none could give me precise information.

On the ruins of the houses they had built cozy little wooden habitations, painted in bright colors, garlanded with climbing flowers, all in an unexpected, charming, and picturesque appearance.

In these devastated places where I expected to find only lugubrious silence, I heard the song of a young girl, the laughter of a child, a dog barking, a cow mooing. Sommeilles was arising from its own ashes.

The next day, April 20 [*sic*], we had to leave Noyers for good. Up to this time the weather was cold and rainy, but now we were afflicted on our march by a beating sun which made the kilometers seem interminable, especially the last ones.

Nevertheless we were passing through a smiling landscape: pretty little villages—although some showed damage—green prairies, charming groves, shady ravines, and sometimes alongside the road clear springs bubbled up, where we eagerly filled our canteens. But it wasn't to admire the beauties of this corner of Lorraine that large numbers of soldiers were lined up along the road, whom the weight of their packs and the stifling heat had obliged to halt for awhile.

Our Kronprinz didn't calm down. Heat, fatigue, sickness, age, all those were negligible to him. To succumb, at the limit of your endurance, was to be a bad soldier, to display bad spirits. Except to drop dead, a soldier shouldn't quit the ranks, like a convict forming a link in a chain gang.

Reaching the end of my own capabilities, it wasn't without pleasure that we arrived at the object of our day's march: Condé-en-Barrois.

The Verdun Charnel House:
April 26–May 19, 1916

1916. Toward the furnace. Condé-en-Barrois.
Jubécourt. Bois Saint-Pierre.

Hardly had we unloaded our packs in the big threshing barn where our whole company was billeted when, by order of our unsympathetic capitaine-adjutant-major, a thorough roll call was carried out in each squad. Those who were missing, which meant those whom fatigue had forced to fall out en route, had to be called to medical inspection by the sergeant on duty, as soon as they staggered into camp.

Those who weren't deemed to be sick had to be hauled off, without delay, to the jail which our battalion's *capitaine-adjutant-flic* [*flic* means "cop"] had set up next to the police station.

If our old *major* [medical officer]-executioner Torrès had been on duty, there'd be as many in prison as there were laggards. But we had at this time a good and decent *major* who excused everyone, thereby canceling out the petty meanness.

That evening, despite our limbs being worn out with fatigue, my friend V. . . . and I went out to buy a couple of bottles of good Meuse beer, and we looked for a quiet corner in which to enjoy them in an interminable game of *manille*,[1] of which we were fanatical players.

At the edge of the village, next to a fine-looking house, was a shady garden where we set ourselves up quite comfortably on a grassy green lawn.

Our game hadn't been going for five minutes when a captain suddenly turned up and headed toward us, looking furious.

Dumbfounded, we wondered what crime we had committed. Well, it was having come to play cards right under the window of our colonel's lodging. What audacity for a couple of simple poilus! Louis XIV noticing a trespasser strolling across his lawns at Marly[2] would not have been more scandalized than was our colonel, who had us chased away from the garden *manu militari* [by

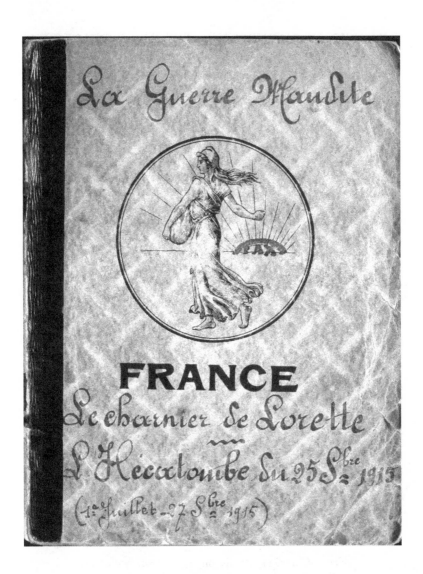

"La Guerre Maudite" (The Accursed War).
6th Notebook cover: July–September 1915.

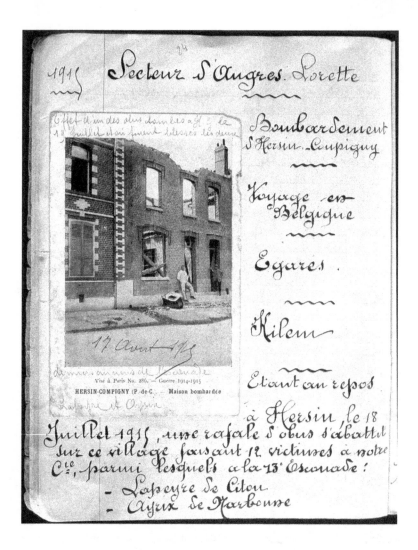

Hersin-Compigny, Artois, July 1915: "A volley of shells fell on this village, costing us 12 victims" (pp. 101–2).

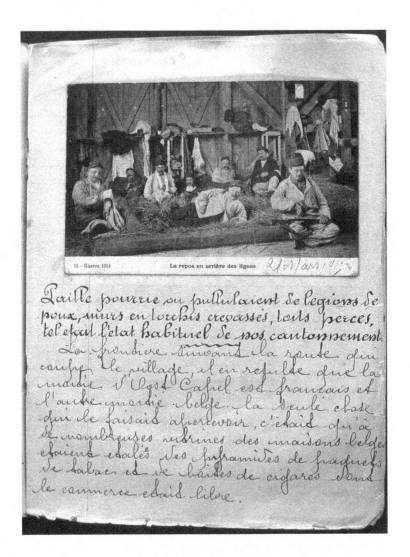

15 - Guerre 1914   Le repos en arrière des lignes

Rest in the rear, 1915: "Rotten straw swarming with legions
of ticks . . . the usual state of our billets."

The Mort-Homme . . . to the left bank of the Meuse, Verdun,
May 1916: "Position occupied by my squad" (10th Notebook).

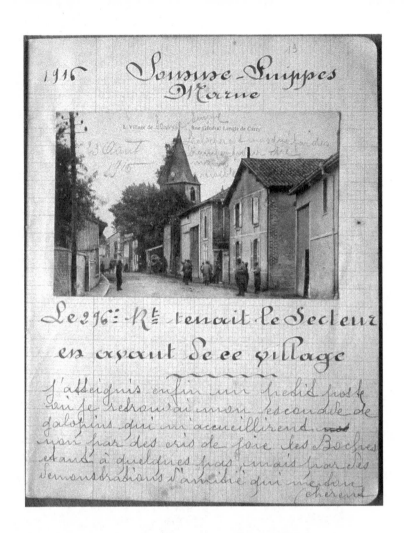

Somme-Suippes, Champagne, August 1916: "The church steeple
is masked by branches to make it invisible" (pp. 233–34).

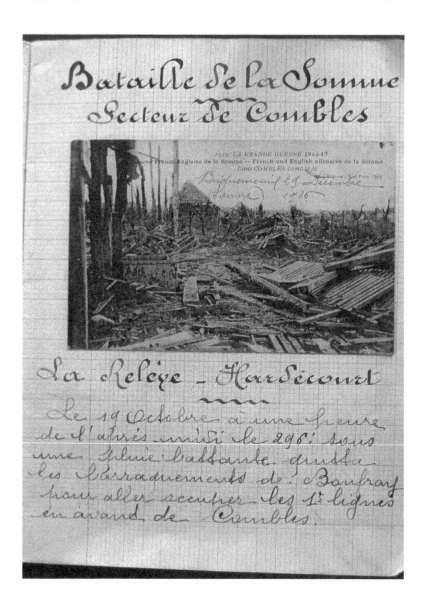

Battle of the Somme, Combles Sector, October 1916 (p. 258).

Carte
trouvée
dans une
tranchée
allemande
prise le 23
Octobre 1916
en avant de
Combles

Bataille de la Somme
(Octobre 1916)

carcasses de maisons étaient enco
debout mais pas pour longtem
sans doute car chaque jour les
obus allemands s'acharnaient su
ces ruines
Après avoir dépassé Combles
nous quittâmes la route et à trave

Combles, October 1916: "Card found in a German trench" (13th Notebook).

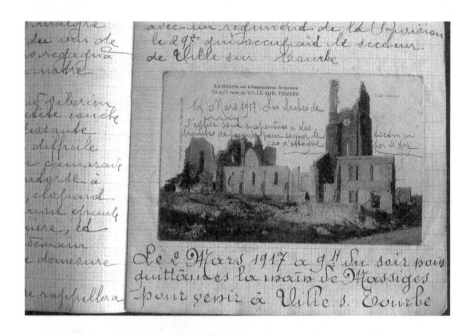

Ville-sur-Tourbe, Champagne-Argonne, March 1917: "The church bells, hung in trees . . . sound the tocsin in case of a poison-gas attack" (p. 302).

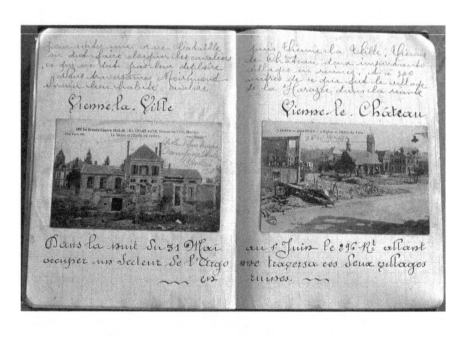

Vienne-la-Ville and Vienne-le-Château, Champagne-Argonne, May–June 1917: "Two good-sized villages in ruins" (p. 328).

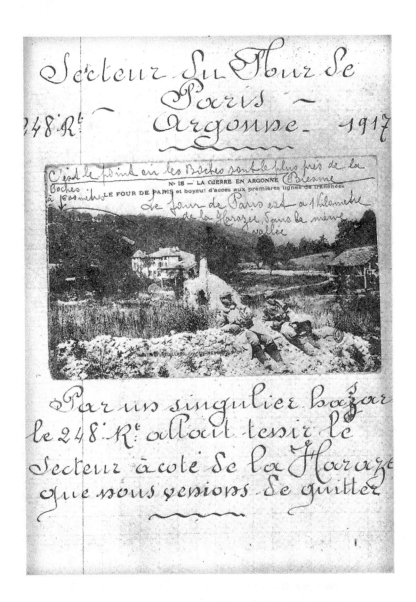

Le Four de Paris, Argonne, June–December 1917:
". . . where the Boches were closest . . ." (pp. 329 and 407n4).

Le Neufour, Biesme River valley, Argonne, February 1918:
"The cabin where I'm staying" (marked by cross on postcard) (pp. 360–61).

Paris, en route to Peyriac, September 1918:
"I visited the Palais des Invalides . . ." (p. 378).

! Peyriac-Minervois (Aude) — Place du Bourguet

Peacetime, circa 1920s: Peyriac-Minervois (Aude), town square.
Louis Barthas is second from left, wearing an overcoat (pp. xx–xxi).

force of arms], not without noting down our names and serial numbers and warning us that a severe punishment would teach us to pick another spot to play our game of manille. Having consumed the contents of the bottles, we made our way sheepishly back to our billet. On our way we passed the *estaminet* [roadside tavern] to turn in our empty bottles and get back our half-franc deposits for each one. But in front of the door a big crowd had formed. The reason was that the doors and windows were shut tight, under the apparently false pretext that there was no more wine or beer.

Nevertheless, some thought that local slackers were enjoying themselves inside.

From the crowd, growing more and more irritated, came invectives directed at the besieged inside. Some stones were even thrown against the shutters.

At a moment of calm I approached the door to explain that I wanted to turn in some empty bottles, but it was the wrong thing to do. From the window above, a bucket of water cascaded onto me; at the same time a stone from the crowd whizzed by my head. I was caught between two fires, or rather between water and stone. Some in the crowd had taken me for a slacker looking to get inside the place, while others inside took me for a bold besieger launching an attack on the estaminet.

Fed up, I left my bottles behind—I never saw them again—and I fled from the brawl.

The dumping of the bucket of water had been the signal for a mass attack on the door, which was barricaded with tables and chairs. Those inside put all their weight behind it, but the door started to crack and buckle when a cry went up, "Here come the police!" This was true, and nothing more was needed to put to flight all the players and spectators of this siege.

A few minutes later I reached my billet and sought out the farthest corner to lie down in. Along one wall, numerous sacks of oats had been piled up. I perched myself there, happy to have found such a nice spot. But once the brouhaha of two hundred men packed in there had quieted down, and the last candle of a few manille players had been extinguished, it was as if an order or a signal had been given. All along the wall, the roof beams, the ground, brushing up against me, nibbling, gnawing, with little yelps of joy, along my legs, across my body, my face—all the rats of the neighborhood, gathering for their daily feast.

In vain I tried to frighten them off by turning on my flashlight, and swinging a club back and forth. No sooner had I turned off the flashlight and set down my club than an even bigger mob swarmed to the feast. Defeated, I had to move and lie down on a beam along one wall.

But why didn't the owner of these bags of oats realize that, in a fortnight, he'd be left with only a handful? I stopped wondering when, the next day, a neighbor told me that these oats had already been requisitioned and paid for. So if they went into the mouths of rats or of horses, what difference did it make?

Condé-en-Barrois marked the farthest point of the German advance in this region, in 1914.

Five uhlans, on a reconnaissance mission, had been shot down as they entered the village, on the bridge. The inhabitants had all fled. They told me that a [French] soldier of the naval infantry [marines] put on civilian clothing, set himself up in a wine wholesaler's shop, and sold all the pinard at a deeply discounted price—all was profit for him—so that the next day, in combat in a nearby wood, the men of the German unit were in such terrible shape that they either were massacred or fled shamefully.

The profiteering of this wine dealer in disguise was uncovered and he was shot without trial the next day. A small drama, beside the larger drama of four years of killing.

From the day after our arrival there were, as could be expected, daily field exercises, but on the next day, a Sunday, there was a concert by our regimental band on the public square, to the rhythm of high-caliber artillery from Verdun. There were football matches and other games for the sports-minded and the idle. For everyone there were showers.

The installation of these showers didn't match modern standards of comfort. In a little old hovel open to all the winds of April, we had to slog through the mud to get a sprinkle of rather cold water, which came out of a container set up on the roof, filled with buckets of river water that medical orderlies passed up a ladder, in a bucket brigade.

Many of us balked at the risk of catching a cold by undergoing this kind of shower, which was surely beneficial only for madmen. But inexorably discipline was brought to bear, in the person of our capitaine-adjutant-major: stiff-necked, haughty, all decked out in his field outfit, he cast a suspicious eye on those who were getting dressed, lifted up their helmets to examine whether their hair was wet or not, and went away only to survey the arrival and departure of the sections, which had to come and go in the best possible order, sometimes having to redo their march at the wave of his hand, signaling "to the right by fours" or "line left."

On May 3, at 6 in the morning, the 296th Regiment made its way to Arize-la-Petite, about twelve kilometers from Condé, to take part in a review or, rather, a sensational ceremony. It was the awarding of the *Grand-Croix* of the *Légion d'Honneur* to General Pétain,[3] the self-proclaimed savior of Verdun, at the hands of Generalissimo Joffre himself.

The whole division, including the 114th and 125th Line Regiments,[4] the engineers, the artillery, with all their flags and their bands, was assembled there.

Despite the grandeur of the spectacle, not one local inhabitant came to have a look.

They figured, with good reason, that the time would be better spent plowing a few more furrows in their fields.

It took at least an hour for everyone to get assembled in a big prairie transformed into a *Champ-de-Mars* [literally "field of Mars," a place of assembly for military exercises], and we had to line up a good twenty times. We were still getting the alignment just right, each try having been deemed imperfect by the division's general, when automobiles appeared around the corner of the road, stopped, and disgorged people whose képis and sleeves sparked in the sun, if not from glory then at least from the reflection of golden stars and stripes.

Immediately the bands struck up "Aux Champs" and the "Marseillaise." They had us present arms; it was a solemn moment. Joffre and his followers passed by on foot, two paces from the division's front ranks.

Fate having placed me in the front rank, I was at last going to see Joffre, this demigod, this superman, this genius—Joffre, the hero of the Marne, but also the man of Charleroi.[5]

He came close. Without moving my head (which no doubt would have brought down a severe punishment) I shifted my eyes, I saw him, and I was disappointed.

Joffre was nothing like a thunderbolt of war. He paraded in front of the men with a vague expression, absentmindedly; he seemed not to see us. At the same time, his face had an air of good fellowship.

His task completed, the future marshal addressed the generals and the colonels, and said something like this:

"I am proud to review such a fine division. It is going to occupy a difficult sector, but lately the enemy is showing a little less bite. You will have some losses, as your predecessors have . . ."

The awarding of the Grand-Croix and other decorations went off according to the customary ritual. Then we formed ranks for the parade. It was far from impeccable; our battalion maneuvered in a particularly deplorable fashion. Our commandant, Quinze-Grammes, and his crony the *capitaine-adjutant-major* Cros-Mayrevieille, utterly helpless, couldn't get us disentangled from the 125th Regiment, in whose midst we were stuck. But Joffre, as a good prince would, closed his eyes, or rather turned his back so as not to see, and appeared to be absorbed in a discussion of strategy with his generals.

Once the parade was completed, Joffre, Pétain, and their beribboned entourage piled into their automobiles and headed off for Bar-le-Duc, where they no doubt gathered around an ample table to celebrate this Grand-Croix won by the blood of thousands of poor devils.

Meanwhile, slowly, heavily, under a scorching sun, in a cloud of dust which our marching feet stirred up, we returned to our respective encampments where a meager *rata* [ratatouille, stew] awaited us.

Two days later, the cannonade was more violent than usual. That day, May 5, the Germans attacked and took Cote 304 [northwest of Verdun], held by a division of our army corps.

At 6 that evening we were eating our soup when some news went around, killing our appetites. The order had just been given for the regiment as well as the whole division to depart in auto transport at 7 p.m.

One hour later we piled into trucks which carried us off into the night.[6]

One time we had a stop. They turned off the headlights on the right, and a little farther along they turned off those on the left, and finally at the first glimmer of daylight they got us down from the trucks. We had arrived.

They've given so much praise to the truckers of Verdun who advanced so boldly toward the line of fire, but you'd be right to praise the cautious prudence of those who were transporting us. They dropped us near Clermont-en-Argonne, in the valley of the Aire, at least thirty kilometers from Cote 304.

We were half-asleep, stiff from several hours of immobility. In order to wake us up and get our limbs loosened they had us proceed along slippery, muddy roads which twisted and turned across the fields and led us to Jubécourt, a little village, tranquil up to this time, but where a catastrophe had occurred five days earlier. On Sunday, April 30, an enemy air squadron had come and dropped bombs on the village. Houses had collapsed, fires had broken out, and in the midst of this noise one could hear the cries of the wounded and the moans of the dying. In telling these stories the inhabitants still trembled with terror; many had already fled. There were a hundred or so victims, of whom about thirty had died. A non-com and a private had fled into the fields, but a Boche aircraft had chased them and, strafing the ground, cut them down with his machine gun.

Hardly had we arrived at Jubécourt than the rain started to fall in abundance. We learned that the 114th and 125th Regiments were ahead of us, and had the assignment of retaking Cote 304.

We had to await the call to go to their rescue. By 8 in the evening, no such order having arrived, we were authorized to bed down.

With no better billet at hand, I set myself up rather badly in the corner of a stable, where I was sheltered from the rain but not from the kicks of a bad-tempered mare who was nursing her young colt and whose horseshoes nearly dislocated my knee.

A few pieces of bread which I offered earned her good graces, and I could lie down with no further problems and even sleep peacefully, despite this sword of Damocles suspended over my head.

A comrade who approached imprudently without the proper olive branch of peace in his hand—that's to say, without a few pieces of bread—was kicked in the ribs and had to be evacuated, which he wasn't sorry about, despite all the glory that we would grab without him.

The next morning the rain had stopped. When we left Jubécourt the sky was clear and sunny.

At eight kilometers from Jubécourt we reached the Bois Saint-Pierre [Saint-Peter Woods], which the regiment entered and where we then bivouacked.

With tree branches and our tent cloths we organized impromptu shelters for the night to come. At nine in the evening, right when the winds, rains, and lightning flashes of a violent thunderstorm reached their climax, there was an alert. In the dark of night, in a torrential rain lashed by a wind which twisted the plaintive oaks, we had to hoist our packs and get ready. Panic-stricken, men looked in the gloom for some lost object or other, a rifle, a pack, cooking utensils, pots and pans. Then came the roll call. Some who were asleep or too widely scattered didn't hear the call to arms and didn't join us until the next day. They weren't punished; they arrived just in time for the sacrifice.

Once we got out of the woods we could advance only very slowly. Artillery batteries, caissons, wagons, interminable lines of all sorts of vehicles were crossing each other and passing each, all in the midst of the shouts, curses, and threats of their drivers.

We had to halt perhaps a hundred times, and it took us all night to cover the eight kilometers which separated the Saint-Pierre woods from the Béthelainville woods, where they had us halt.

At nightfall they brusquely ordered us to leave; our battalion was going to encamp in reserve, at Béthelainville.

This village was only partly destroyed. Nevertheless the inhabitants had prudently taken off, except for one poor old fellow who couldn't bring himself to die far from the church tower of his birthplace.

Despite finding ourselves at the mercy of an enemy bombardment, we took up quarters happily in the barns, where we rested up from the preceding nights we had spent in the rain.

But for the past two or three days I'd been doubled over with terrible pains in my belly. I made my way to sick call. Without even looking at me, the *major* [medical officer] gave me an opium pill and asked me not to come back, saying that he too had a bellyache and continued to do his duty all the same.

As I insisted that I hadn't been able to eat hardly anything for three days, he generously had me swallow two pills instead of one and sent me off with the word "Go!" which signified that I was not to return.

At the eve of each day of carnage, they tried using lies to counter the depressed morale of the soldier.

According to self-proclaimed reliable sources, and from encouraging notes passed around, the division was going to be relieved; we weren't going up to the front line; the rationers were giving us only two days' worth of food; and other tales which bolstered our confidence and chased the anguish from our hearts.

But these illusions were short-lived. On May 11 our battalion got the order to head up to the front line. Departure was set for 8 in the evening.

Each of us had to carry 250 cartridges, grenades, reserve rations, flares, assorted tools, etc.

Weak, still suffering, I had to make a superhuman effort to keep up with my comrades, who lightened my load as best they could. Many times a cold sweat soaked my temples, and it looked like I was going to fall over. A few swallows of eau de mélisse fortified me. Along the route I threw away everything: food, cartridges, grenades, tools. Boy, if our Kronprinz had seen me!

We passed through Vigneville and Montzéville, in ruins, and at about eleven at night we set ourselves up in a trench about one kilometer to the right of Esnes, fifty meters from a windmill. Its walls, riddled by shellfire, were still standing.

There was, at this moment, a relative calm. All night long they brought forward pieces of sheet metal, planks, and tree branches to cover up this trench and hide us from the view of aircraft, just as had been recommended to us.

We were going to fill up our canteens at the mill, next to which a pretty little spring bubbled forth.

1916. The Defense of Verdun. Cote 304.

As day broke, I looked out upon this famous, nameless hill. Our trench lay at the foot of it. For several months the hill had been disputed as if it had diamond mines on its slopes.

Alas, all it contained now were thousands of shredded, pulverized corpses.

Nothing distinguished it from neighboring hills. It seemed to have been partly wooded at one time, but no trace of vegetation remained. The convulsed, overturned earth offered nothing but a spectacle of devastation.

All day long we stayed close to the ground, huddled in this covered trench, suffering from heat and lack of air. The Boche planes hadn't spotted us, so we weren't bombarded by howitzer fire. We waited impatiently for nighttime, when we could walk around and breathe at our leisure. But at nightfall our company received orders to go forward and occupy a trench a couple of hundred meters ahead.

Separately, by squads, we made our way there. The terrain had been much more heavily bombarded than what we had seen farther to the rear, at the mill at Esnes. I think that the strategic necessity which brought us there was simply to provide more security and peace of mind for our colonel, whose deep dugout was right nearby.

But what had the 114th and the 125th Regiments of our division already done to retake Cote 304?

The official army dispatches, and even the least jingoistic newspapers, depicted the fantastic charge of these two superb regiments, hurling themselves forward with an irresistible élan, handing this little volcanic mountain over to tearful Pétain and Joffre.

The truth was altogether different. After a prodigious expenditure of all sorts of projectiles, these two regiments moved forward and reconquered, or rather simply reoccupied, some positions they had previously lost, because the Germans had pulled back to their own lines without waiting for the assault.

Which isn't to say that the losses weren't substantial on our side.

In brief, things were as they were before May 5: the French on one side of the hill, the Germans on the other, the crest once again a neutral zone blasted by the two artilleries.

At the summit, the Germans still held a redoubt which an Algerian division hadn't been able to take. This was very bothersome for us.

That division held the slope adjacent to the Forêt d'Avocourt, and our division held the slope facing the sinister Mort Homme, its grayish mass looming on our right, no less desolate than Cote 304.

Their task completed, the 114th and 125th Infantry Regiments made room for us, and headed back to breathe the fresh air of the Bois Saint-Pierre. Our regiment, the 296th, had the mission of once again consolidating and fortifying the French positions.

The trench we had just occupied was about halfway up the slope. At its entrance, on what was left of a sign, I read the words "Rascas Trench."

In reality this wasn't much more than a miserable boyau dug, in one night, by troops who were hanging on there and who, the next day, were pulverized by howitzer fire.

There, human flesh had been shredded, torn to bits. At places where the earth was soaked with blood, swarms of flies swirled and eddied. You couldn't really see corpses, but you knew where they were, hidden in shell holes with a layer of dirt on top of them, from the wafting smells of rotten flesh. There was all sorts of debris everywhere: broken rifles; gutted packs from which spilled out pages of tenderly written letters and other carefully guarded souvenirs from home, and which the wind scattered; crushed canteens, shredded musette bags— all labeled 125th Regiment. I was easily able to replace the munitions, rations, and tools which I had cast off during the march up to the front.

The sight of this gloomy tableau suggested to us that the next day, once the Boches spotted our presence there, they would pound us into marmalade.

All night long we were put to work, making the boyau practicable and habitable. At the first light of dawn, to our great joy, the sky was covered with low-hanging clouds which enveloped Cote 304 with an opaque veil, masking us from the enemy all day long.

At any moment, with no evident pattern, the Boches fired salvoes of shells. Pressed into the deepest recesses of the boyau, we didn't have any wounded that day.

That night, our battalion had to go up to occupy the firing line. At the appointed hour we headed out, following the Rascas boyau, which soon was no more than a muddy ditch, collapsed in places.

Why, and how, had the order come for us to stop in this place?

Some botched-up relief schedule, no doubt. Or a designated path which was no longer there.

We were crouching down, so as not to catch a stray bullet or shell fragment passing by. And if this weren't bad enough, a heavy rain started to fall. It didn't take long for the water to fill the ditch, and to submerge our shoes. Our helmets were transformed into drain spouts. Little waterfalls ran down our packs onto our hips, off our shoulders and along our arms. We didn't know what, or whom, we were waiting for. The night was pitch black. Were they just going to leave us stuck in this sewer?

Finally we moved out again. Soon, no more boyau. We had to cross over an entanglement of barbed wire, fence posts, shredded sandbags, dead bodies, all sorts of debris. Some of us got lost, or got stuck on the prickly barbed wire which you couldn't see in the dark of night, which grew even darker after each shell burst.

Our company split up. One section stayed in reserve, as an honor guard for our commander Quinze-Grammes and the Kronprinz, who had gone into a fairly deep shelter dug by the Germans.

Two other sections went up to reinforce other companies on the firing line. The 4th Section, to which I belonged, was sent to observe on the slope of Cote 304 facing the Mort Homme.

Everything was sinister in these places, but this place was even worse, if that's possible. At the bottom of the ravine, where the *ruisseau* [stream] des Forges flowed, shells of every caliber, fired by both sides, fell without respite. This dark abyss seemed like a volcano in constant eruption, and there we were, hanging right on its rim.

Our mission consisted of maintaining liaison, by patrols, with the troops who held the facing slopes. But these patrols took place only on paper, in fictional reports. In reality, the patrols had ceased after three days—there was no one to send out on patrol.

The morning after our arrival, curiosity led me to inspect the immediate surroundings of our emplacements. We were still protected by a veil of fog which the May sun would soon dissipate. Just then, in a shell hole, I saw the body of a soldier, thickly encrusted from head to toe in dried mud.

"Well," I said, "here's a dead one already." And I poked him with my foot, to make sure he was no longer among the living but had entered the realm of Pluto.

The reply was a protest: "Leave me alone!" And in this grumbling I recognized the voice of my fellow Peyriacois, Edouard Durand, who was in the 4th Section with me.

Stupefied, I asked him how he had gotten into this comatose state.

He told me how, tangled up in a jumble of barbed wire, he couldn't get himself loose until nightfall, after much trouble, and then he couldn't rejoin our section, which had disappeared in the darkness.

After having wandered around for hours, he finally was able to rejoin his squad at daybreak.

"But," I told him, "don't stay there, immobile, all soaked on the damp ground. Get up, and shake yourself off!"

Overcome with fatigue, he didn't budge.

"One way of croaking is just as good as another," he said. And I wasn't able to pull him out of this state.

Besides, his half-section had left us, to go who knows where, and I didn't see my comrade again.

Only two squads of us stayed, to cover a gap in our lines of several hundred meters. It's true that, right above us, a French machine gun section was installed in a rather solid, well-hidden dugout. But one morning we saw, to our horror, that this emplacement had been completely destroyed in an avalanche of big shells. Machine guns, and machine gunners, had disappeared!

We were alone, quite alone—thirty men with Sublieutenant Lorius, abandoned, sacrificed in this den of cutthroats.

Our firing line was broken, with gaps of as much as four hundred meters between sections and companies. No one really knew whether we had Germans or Frenchmen in front of us. Some of the gaps were heavily bombarded, and no one could hold them.

That evening, Sergeant Fontès got the mission from Sublieutenant Lorius to take with him a "courageous" fellow and, that night, to reconnoiter and to find out who was up ahead of us: subjects of the Kaiser, or of Poincaré.

Sergeant Fontès couldn't find one volunteer in the section who sought to earn the label of "courageous."

Each one had a perfectly good reason to invoke: One had blisters on his feet, another had rheumatism, yet another could prove that he been in the latest patrol. Young men begged off because of weakness, old men out of exhaustion.

Finally, reluctantly, Sergeant Fontès turned to me—the ex-corporal who had been busted in rank for his advanced socialist ideas and his pacifism. He spoke to me not as a superior, but as a comrade and even as a friend.

I accepted, but with conditions that took a lot of the shine off my apparent zeal. I demanded to be exempt from three nights of outpost duty, patrols, and chores.

With nothing more than a rifle, a bayonet, and two packs of cartridges in our pockets, the two of us headed out. A sliver of moonlight shone the way for us, across a terrain as pockmarked as a kitchen strainer. In some places the ground was worked over, slashed and overturned as if by a recent earthquake. Any living thing had been snuffed out.

After covering a few hundred meters of this chaotic terrain, our senses were able to discern the limits of this immeasurable horizon of nothingness. We thought we were lost in the middle of an immense desert. It was impossible for us to tell from where we had come and where we were going. Crouched in a shell crater, we sought in vain to orient ourselves by flares, or by the sound of artillery batteries firing.

All of a sudden the jumbled sound of voices reached us. Anxiously we listened: a German patrol? A French work detail?

But we soon picked out a few emphatic *Macarels* and *Noun de Diou* and other sonorous curses which could come only from natives of the banks of the Garonne [river in southwestern France] and the Mediterranean.

It was a providential ration detail from my old company, the 21st, Captain Hudelle's, which was just passing by us.

These men gave us precious information, and told us that a segment of the French front line was about two hundred meters ahead of us.

"So," I said, "Any losses today?"

"Well, we're starting out nicely," they said, "Cabanel the barber got killed. Sergeant Laflorencie is mortally wounded. Some others, too."

The most terrible accident had befallen my former section. Three of my old pals, fooled by either a moment of calm or their own bravado, decided to make up a game of manille, without finding a fourth hand. No sooner had the cards been dealt than a 105mm shell fell right in their midst, blasting them to bits. Only Corporal Larche was able to cry out, "Oh my God, my God!" The other two unfortunates were Corporal Peyre and Private Courtauly.

If I had still been with them, wouldn't I have been tempted to take up the fourth hand of this fatal manille game? And right now wouldn't I be blown to pieces, like my luckless comrades? It gives me chills just to think about it.

Our buddies told us that two or three hundred meters in front of us we'd find scattered remnants of the 22nd Company. To cover this distance we had to tumble into a crevasse, a kind of twisted corridor which linked one shell hole to the next. This was the front-line trench, or rather a segment of it, which the soldiers, silent shadows, dug out and extended while others, flattened against the slope, immobile, seeming to sleep with rifles at hand, burrowed into the darkness.

Right when we arrived, bullets whistled around our ears, and a cry and a death rattle were heard in the trench. A fellow just had his skull shattered by one of these bullets fired from a machine gun on the slopes of the Mort Homme.

Sergeant Fontès got our patrol order countersigned by Lieutenant Cordier, who commanded this company. The command post was no more than a shell hole half-covered by a wooden plank. This done, we made our way back to our own emplacement, guided only by the instinct developed in us after long months of nervous tension—the same instinct which leads a wild beast back to its lair.

We had hardly gotten back, at about 9 p.m., when bursts of machine gun fire were unleashed upon Cote 304, which was thrown into turmoil. Our little corner wasn't too badly pounded. To the sound of this infernal music, dead tired, crouched in the trench, I fell asleep as easily as in my own bed at home when I drifted off to the sound of raindrops on the gutters.

At dawn, I awoke to a cold and damp sensation on my knees, which stuck out from the little excavation I had dug in the side of the trench, my little bed-chamber. It was the rain which was coming down in buckets, and which would fall all day long.

But far from complaining, we rejoiced. No sun meant no German airplanes overhead, no "sausages"—it was a truce, a rest. We were free to walk around, to chat, to stick our noses out of our holes, to get some food brought up from the rear. This was a blessed rain. We would have been happy to spend all our time on the firing line in water up to our necks. But on the morning of May 16 a cool breeze swept the sky clean of clouds, and a bright sun rose.

It didn't take long for several enemy airplanes to make their bothersome droning heard, and they circled over Cote 304 and the Mort Homme all day long, like birds of ill fortune foretelling a great storm.

Naïvely we thought that our own aviators would arrive and chase these interlopers away. But no such luck. Today, and every day after, they came with impunity, in total freedom, swooping back and forth at low altitude, scouting out and scrutinizing the emplacement of our positions.

This reminded our Colonel Douce: "When we were in Artois, they told us that German airplanes were being shot down every day over Verdun. Now that we're here, the daily communiqués say that's what's happening in Artois."

As a result, we were condemned to complete immobility. We had to conceal anything that would reveal our positions: tools, arms, mess kits, packs, everything had to disappear, and ourselves, too, under penalty of receiving an unannounced avalanche of shellfire.

In the afternoon, the German batteries—well briefed, no doubt, by their aviators—opened a rolling fire on Cote 304, lasting at least two hours.

How many tons of projectiles fell on this hill?

Our brains were shaken by the nearby explosions. Stunned, we expected to be pulverized at any minute. It was just a matter of being caught in a salvo.

Finally the hurricane of iron and fire gradually let up. Then came intermittent but almost regular barrages which landed haphazardly.

Heartened by this relative calm, five or six of us gathered under a thin sheet of corrugated metal, which would protect us from only the smallest shell fragment, but which gave us the illusion of perfect security.

We talked about the next furlough coming up, the overdue relief we were waiting for, our homes where our loved ones would shudder to know what a hell we were living through. Sometimes, when the storm raged too loudly, we had to interrupt our conversation, and pick it up again where a nearby explosion had cut short a sentence.

Suddenly a shell, with a harsh and brutal hiss, cut right through our sheet of metal as if it were a piece of paper, and burrowed into the slope of the trench without bursting.

Did we faint dead away? No. Once the first few seconds of shock passed, there was an outburst of laughter all around. Why the laughter? Who can explain the reason for it?

Was it the relief at escaping great danger? Was it what someone was saying, that was interrupted? Was it a kind of nervous reaction?

At midnight, with three comrades under the orders of Corporal Cazelles, we went out to occupy the outpost which was almost at the bottom of the heavily bombarded ravine.

While two men kept watch, the others went to work clearing away the many landslides caused by the latest bombardment of the boyau, or remnant of a boyau, which linked the outpost to the position occupied by our half-section.

Did the Boches hear the sounds of our tools? Or the noise of our irrepressible southern voices which we couldn't muffle? Had our outpost been found out?

Whatever the reason, all of a sudden a volley of small-caliber shellfire fell all around us with a crackling like fireworks. What kind of devilish device was this, which we hadn't encountered before—and never did again afterward? Doubtless it was some new kind of rapid-firing cannon which the Germans never used again (too bad for them). The firing lasted about thirty seconds, which seemed interminable, then started up again. These packets of shells tore up the earth all around us, whistled, farted, shot off showers of sparks and flames, and stirred up a storm of iron fragments, chunks of dirt, and stones.

Flat on our bellies with our noses in the dirt, we were terrified, disconcerted by this new way of scaring and killing people.

To tell the truth, these shells did not turn out to be excessively murderous. We realized it when, once things calmed down, we discovered that none of us had suffered the slightest scratch. But it's certain that these shells would have had a much more fatal effect on troops in the open.

We thought we were through with this vexing alert and we were laughing at our earlier fright when, click-clack, here is that satanic farting again, forcing us once again to dig our noses into the dirt. This time it didn't let up, which led us to think that they had chosen our listening post as the testing ground for this new device.

Here we are, prostrate on the earth like a bunch of Mohammedans. When our southern nerves—quickly enraged, but just as quickly calmed—restored our capability to speak, our good Corporal Cazelles, behind me, his head between my legs, made it clear that we should probably come to some sort of decision.

Corporal Cazelles held me in high regard, no doubt because of the prestige of my former corporal's stripes. He asked me, ahead of anyone else, what opinion our precarious situation brought to mind. I advised him that we should flee these inhospitable confines without further delay. The others, consulted as a formality, agreed, and we set off at a slow crawl, like a troop of slugs. But our mothers had taught us to walk on two legs, so it took us an hour to cover the hundred meters which separated us from our half-section. Our elbows, knees, and bellies were sorely afflicted by the disagreeable crawling on the damp earth soaked by the preceding day's rain.

Looking ahead to the next war-to-end-all-wars, they should train the school-kids, every day, to crawl on their bellies. Some day, or some night, the knowledge might come in handy.

We finally got out of the test-firing range of these new devices. A sonorous snoring that could come only from our buddy Sabatier told us that we were back among our comrades.

But once we were out of danger, Corporal Cazelles was suddenly overcome with scruples. He had abandoned the listening post under his charge, while everywhere else at Verdun the order was to resist without ever taking one step back.

In this massive, frightening void of gloom, where now no French soldier stood guard, he could see the whole army of the German Crown Prince rushing to the attack. I reassured him that as long as the Germans were firing into the ravine they wouldn't be taking a stroll there. Let's look after our own comrades. That's what's important.

At this moment, our ration teams arrived. Each night they went to pick up our meals, our letters and packages from home, at the field kitchens which were advancing, not without risk, on the road between Vigneville and Esnes.

A shot of hooch could set aside our little nighttime cares. Right then the snoring of Sabatier ceased. A 420mm shell falling right next to him might not have awakened him, but the one word "hooch," or just the smell of it, got him up right away.

The ration teams gave us the comforting news that our relief would come up the following night. Soon the first indistinct glimmers of dawn scattered the protective shadow which surrounded Cote 304, and like owls we sought shelter in holes scraped out of the slopes of the trench. We brought our comrades up to date about our nighttime adventures. They burst out laughing at our fright, but they didn't laugh for long. On several occasions our trench was assaulted by the same diabolical devices we had encountered. One of us saw his mess bag disappear. Another had his canteen half-melted. A howitzer shell exploded right beside the parapet. My neighbor, who had piled his cartridges in a mound beside him, saw them scattered as if blown away by a demon, and several of them went off.

And that happened without the slightest warning. You only heard these little shells being fired, and their snakelike hissing, after they had already exploded and their black smoke was already dissipating.

This was an ordeal. We would have preferred a violent bombardment, which would eventually come to an end, to this rain of little farting shells which fell on us indiscriminately, seeming to come right out of the earth.

And to make it worse, as I have already described, all of us, one after the other, suffered from an epidemic of intestinal disorders. The resulting diarrhea sure cleaned us out, but inopportunely. As soon as one of us got over it, his next-door neighbor was afflicted with it, and had the bad luck to have to climb out of the trench and head for the shell hole which served as a latrine. Of course we did this only as a last resort, at the last moment of agony, stretching our guts until they were about to burst.

One of us was surprised in the latrine by one of these sudden fusillades, and collapsed into his own excrement.

So as not to expose oneself to similar incidents, some used sardine or "monkey-meat" cans as chamber pots, so as not to have to leave one's hole in the ground. One even sacrificed his cast-iron dinner plate.

We soon had other pressing reasons not to move. On that day, May 17, from noon to 4 in the afternoon, the Boches unleashed upon Cote 304 one of the most terrible bombardments that I heard and saw throughout the whole war.

A thick cloud of smoke mixed with dust, marked with black smudges or by the vivid green left by bursting flares against the sun's rays, burned our eyes and parched our gullets, while the stench of sulfur or of I don't know what, mixed with the lingering smell of rotting flesh, grabbed us by the throat.

Like the waves of a raging ocean, the salvoes of iron and fire marched forward, retreated, advanced again, submerging Cote 304 in a torrent of shellfire.

And to think that we were only one small link in Verdun's chain of defense. To our right, at Avocourt, and to our left towards Chattancourt, the cannonade went wild.[7]

And on the other side of the Meuse, at Damloup, Fleury, the fort of Vaux,[8] it was even worse.

Behind us, did our own artillery respond? I cannot say. In this immense cacophony, we couldn't even tell whether our trench was being assailed by these little shells which caused so much comical fright. In a noisy concert performance it is always the brasses which drown out the sound of a little flute.

The boyau leading to the command post, still in rather good shape in the morning, had been razed, almost completely leveled. Of the other one that led down to the outpost in the ravine there was no longer a trace. Just our little corner, where we cowered, terrified, seemed to be protected by an all-powerful, invisible hand. We still hadn't had any wounded or killed.

I was by myself, at the far end of our little stretch of boyau, crouched in a little hole, when a big shell landed like a thunderbolt just three or four meters in front of me. The violence of the blast tore away the tent cloth which I had arranged in front of my hole, to keep out the sun and the flies, and tossed it who knows where. As for me, I had the sense of being knocked flat, and for a few seconds I couldn't get my breath. I had just felt the death wind. Some say it's chilly; I found it hot and burning. It coursed through my whole body, from my rattled brain, to my heavy heart and lungs, all the way down to my rubbery legs.

Cheating death one more time, I scrambled out of my shell hole and sought refuge in the dugout of our section chief, Sublieutenant Lorius, twenty meters away. He welcomed us as comrades, but going there was admitting to being afraid, which is tougher than one might think for a native of the Aude or the Garonne [département, southeastern France, adjacent to the Aude; principal town is Toulouse] to admit, even when, like me, you feel like you've already got one foot in the grave.

The collapse of my shell hole was an excuse which safeguarded my reputation for courage. Sublieutenant Lorius, seated philosophically in his shelter like Diogenes in his barrel,[9] smoked cigarette after cigarette. To calm me down, he offered me a Valda *pastille*[10]—a lozenge to heal colds and bronchitis—which was better than nothing.

The dugout of our amiable section chief was a bit of tunnel entrance dug one day by the Germans when they had taken or retaken this part of Cote 304. Unfortunately they didn't have the time to finish it, and it had only four steps going down.

Other soldiers nearby, emboldened by our presence and fearful of being buried alive in their own foxholes, came to the shelter. I remember Corporal S. . . ., each time a shell whistled overhead, dipping his head and his shoulders in an instinctive movement, like a condemned man who sees the executioner brandishing the axe over his head.

Our sublieutenant finally told him that it wasn't worth the trouble to scrunch your head down each time, as if the shell was coming right down on us. "We don't need you to scare us all stiff," he said.

Sublieutenant Lorius wasn't one to stay put. Forced immobility at the bottom of a dugout was intolerable for him. He often headed out to visit other section chiefs, sometimes quite far away, or Lieutenant Breton, who commanded the company. He came and went, all alone, with an extraordinary insouciance and an absolute scorn for danger. In an instant, he took off, abandoning his shelter to us.

This bombardment cost us three wounded—two in the head, one in the legs. At nightfall there was a moment of calm, and we profited from it by getting our gear ready for the long-awaited relief. But when the lieutenant returned he told us that the relief was postponed by twenty-four hours. The reason was that at 2 a.m. the Moroccan division on our left was supposed to attack an outcropping of Cote 304 that the enemy had transformed into a fortified stronghold. They didn't want our attack's preliminary bombardment to fall on the columns en route to relieve us.

The delay of our relief, as justified as it was, made us grimace with irritation. Wasn't this a death warrant for some of us who had already undergone bombardments every day? And it was with much apprehension that we awaited the hour of the attack.

It seems that the commander of the Moroccan Zouaves, leading the attack, gave his men an odious order: "My friends, I have no orders to give, but you already know what I expect you to do in an attack . . ." He meant taking no prisoners. This was reported to me by eyewitnesses. The language was unworthy of a Frenchman. And the Germans, when they would advance and see the fate reserved for those who fell into our hands, would resist to the last when they saw themselves surrounded. Or they would massacre those of us who fell into their hands. That's the way they killed those who were at one of our first-aid stations: the medical officer, the orderlies, the wounded, some of them finished off with blows from rifle butts.

On both sides they fought like cannibals, with a cruelty perhaps greater than in the long-ago times of the barbarian invasions. *Vae Victis!* [Woe to the conquered].[11] It was bad luck for anyone on Cote 304 who fell, still alive, into enemy hands. All human sentiment was banished. I myself saw a lieutenant fire on German stretcher-bearers carrying a wounded man. To a soldier who had the courage to criticize this misdeed, the officer replied, "Aw, hell, the Germans would have done the same."

At the appointed hour the attack was launched, and, by surprise, the Zouaves seized the outcropping without much resistance from the enemy. But the red rockets traced their bloody furrows across the night sky, and here is Cote 304 once again transformed into an erupting volcano, with high-caliber batteries zeroing in on the point of attack and, at the same time, sowing destruction everywhere, except our little corner, intact like an island in the middle of a stormy sea.

The bombardment rendered the strongpoint untenable for the Zouaves, who had to pull back with heavy losses. The commander and all the captains of the battalion of Zouaves were put *hors de combat*. It was Captain Barbier of the 23rd Company of our regiment who took under his command the remnants of this battalion.[12]

Captain Barbier was built like Hercules. Professor of something or other in civilian life, he had, in spite of his teacher's degree, like so many other officers, a narrow and singular conception of his role as chief—a warped conception, which made them see in the soldier an inferior being to be treated without respect, like a shepherd treats his sheep, a huntsman his pack of dogs.

This Captain Barbier wasn't liked by his men, whom he led rudely, cursing them scornfully, insulting them and punishing them for anything and everything. In the regiment he was nicknamed "the Brute."

At the same time, we couldn't reproach him for any lack of courage. He was right up at the front line, tossing grenades with remarkable strength and skill.

In fact it was he who organized all the front lines, filled in the gaps, installed outposts, established a more or less continuous front. Our commandant, Quinze-Grammes, and the Kronprinz, both cowering in a shelter a few hundred meters to the rear, had left the command of the battalion to him.

On the morning of May 18, when Captain Barbier saw the Germans batter the Zouaves and retake the outcropping, he got really excited. He sent men and work details out in every direction, looking for boxes of grenades, cartridges, flares, et cetera.

Around 10 a.m. a few groups of enemy soldiers probed our lines. They were quickly halted by a couple of fusillades, but Captain Barbier lost his head and demanded reinforcements from the commandant.

The latter had only three sections of our company at his disposal, and he sent up one of them. A half-hour later they had to send up another one. Only our half-section remained, now completely isolated and linked up with the commandant's C.P. [command post]. But the men were ready, packs hoisted, all set to march at the first call of Captain Barbier, which wouldn't be long coming.

The colonel, much impressed, sent us a company from the reserve battalion. All of this took place in broad daylight, right under the noses of the Germans. The smoke from the thickly falling shells prevented them from seeing what was going on as they destroyed, in the blink of an eye, anything that was moving on the earth's surface.

To make things worse, a battery of our 75's, firing too short, dropped shells onto our own front line. Signals, flares, phone calls, nothing worked. This was really irritating, just like some other times since we had arrived in the sector. Our artillery couldn't succeed in regulating its fire, and cost us victims almost daily.

This day, a [French] 75 shell fell right on top of Captain Barbier's precarious shelter, killing outright a Zouave officer.

The captain, brandishing a revolver, cursed and swore that he wanted to kill the first artilleryman who came into his sight.

As for our half-section, it was lying flattened out in a section of boyau, ready to spring forward across open country to reinforce our front line—a prospect that hardly gave us any pleasure.

Suddenly here is a big 105 shell which explodes so close that the boyau collapses, burying Jalabert and Sabatier, who didn't like this game at all and waved their arms and legs around like a couple of devils in a chapel, to try to get out of there.

After a minute of stupor we started to go to their help when, boom!, here's a second shell coming along, which by a singular fate blasts away the big chunk of earth which had smothered our two comrades, freeing them and leaving them without a scratch.

Jalabert rushed off like a madman, but Sabatier, shaking himself off like a wet dog, declares in a cheerful voice, "What do you know—my pipe is busted!" To appreciate this you had to know that Sabatier's pipe was stuck in his mouth eleven hours out of twelve. The commission evaluating reparations for wartime damages will have to include Sabatier's pipe on the lists it draws up.

But here's an orderly running up. Sublieutenant Lorius must immediately assign someone to serve as liaison with the command post.

Liaison duty on Cote 304, the day of an attack—that's no sinecure. But I volunteered immediately. I wasn't ignorant of the dangers I would be running, but if I had to be there I would a hundred times rather die with a dispatch in my hand than with a rifle which had just killed a fellow workingman like me, a brother in misery and suffering. No, I'm not going to perish with that on my humanitarian, socialist conscience.

Five minutes later, I was in front of the liaison shelter, fifty meters from that of our two old friends Quinze-Grammes and the Kronprinz. It was a lousy shelter, a simple staircase with a dozen steps around which stretcher-bearers and orderlies were already crowded. At the bottom, a little square of ground where four crazy cardplayers were busy in a game of manille.

The medics and stretcher-bearers were idle until nighttime, when they could go out and bring back the wounded.

With not even a square inch of space available on the steps, I had to stay on the threshold between the shelter and the boyau which led to it. Right then a reinforcing company passed by, the men's eyes haggard, their dirty faces dripping sweat, sunburned, dropping to the ground at each passing shell which rained down sixty or eighty meters away, beyond the emplacement to which they were headed.

Where were the journalists who cynically affirm that our soldiers stormed up Cote 304 and the Mort Homme furiously, enthusiastically, singing, men whose chiefs couldn't hold them back? They weren't there that afternoon to see the lamentable parade of human wrecks, a flock of sheep headed for the slaughterhouse. But at least sheep are unaware of their fate. Right up to the moment of their death they're probably thinking that they're heading out to pasture, in a nice meadow.

The men passed by, singly or in little groups, stopping, hiding, terrified of entering the fiery furnace. Some of them stayed until nightfall at the shelter's threshold. Nobody bothered about them. Others hid away in a half-collapsed shelter right next to the commandant's C.P.

But at one point *Capitaine-Major* Cros, sticking his nose out, noticed the latter and ordered them to rejoin their company. But they categorically refused. "We won't move up to rejoin them until nightfall," they said.

The captain, not disposing of any means to make them head out—gendarmes didn't venture this far forward—rapidly disappeared back down into his hole.

Two little signalmen, seated next to me on the first step of the staircase, hearing the *capitaine-adjutant-major*'s voice, couldn't keep from expressing themselves at his expense: "Christ almighty, what an idiot!"

"What's he done to you, then?" I asked them.

"No sooner is the telephone line broken, which happens twenty times a day, and he sends us out to fix it, no matter how violent the bombardment. He won't allow the slightest objection, but with the coldest tone sends us away with an impatient 'Get going!' which won't permit a reply."

Understandably, the signalmen had disappeared from the commandant's dugout and instead came to hide in our "liaison" shelter, waiting for a moment of calm.

When, order in hand, an orderly or the battalion adjutant (Calvet from Peyriac) appeared at the shelter's entrance, there was a poignant silence. What company's number was being called? Wasn't this a death sentence for him who was leaving, alone, for the front lines, a deadly assignment on its own?

He who was called sometimes went pale, but without hesitation plunged ahead and sometimes never came back.

Later I read a book by Captain Henry Bordeaux, an Academician, *The Last Days of the Fort of Vaux*,[13] where there is plenty of whitewashed nonsense. He wrote about liaison runners; if one fell, another took his place. Those who were left were always at the ready; they even offered their services before their turns came along. In other words, this Academician would say that they would be happy to go get themselves killed. In ordinary times a liaison's job was a lucky one, and no one turned it down. In a nasty sector they still had to do their jobs. But to say that they jumped to the head of the line—that's too much.

I found my countryman, the Peyriacois Julien Chiffre, haggard, his features drawn, who by a miracle had escaped certain death at least ten times. "Today," he said, "was the worst ever." He confided to me that, in despair of getting out alive, he had just said confession to a stretcher-bearing priest, and then stayed on his knees in prayer. I tried to boost his morale, affirming my own good hope of leaving this place alive. "The relief will be here tomorrow night; have courage, hold on until then," I told him.

At this moment any hope seemed like an illusion, the cannonade reaching a new level of violence. The dispatches reported that this afternoon the aviators flying over Cote 304 couldn't see it through the thick cover of smoke, pierced by flashes of lightning.

As for me, no one called for me, no one asked for me or bothered with me. I still wonder why they had made me come there.

At nightfall, a signalman informed us that the colonel, comfortable in his shelter, wanted to let our battalion have twenty-four hours more, but, he said, the commandant and the *capitaine-adjutant-major* cried out, on the telephone, that that was impossible, that the exhausted men couldn't hold on anymore, et cetera. In the face of such energetic protests, the colonel granted our relief for the next night.

The order of relief stated that, once replaced, each unit had to make its way immediately back on its own to the Bois Saint-Pierre, the battalion's assembly point.

At 11 at night, the liaison from the relief unit arrived. We could now head out, but we had to await our bosses, Quinze-Grammes and the Kronprinz, who didn't seem to be in any hurry to get out of their holes while the cannonade still raged.

Crouched around the shelter, making ourselves as small as we could, we were eager to go but no one dared to leave.

Some timed-fuse shells exploded above our heads, and a piece of shrapnel hit my helmet. Those shells generally announced the imminent arrival of even more dangerous armor-piercing shells. The fear of this caused a couple of shadowy figures to break off from our group and disappear into the darkness.

I suggested to my friend Chiffre, sprawled beside me in the same shell hole, that I had had it with the company of the commandant and his partner-in-crime, and was ready to head out myself. Together we took off with all the speed that our heavy loads and our state of exhaustion would allow. By following the regular route of the relief units and the work details, in ten minutes one could be at the base of the hill, at the mill of Esnes. But at this moment all was madness. A veritable curtain of steel and fire blocked the road.

The only way through was to make a long detour to avoid this monstrous avalanche of metal. My comrade, worn out and sick, let me lead the way through the darkness and obscurity, across all sorts of obstacles which blocked our way. Tree trunks, branches, shattered weapons, barbed-wire defense lines, half-deserted and three-quarters-filled trenches, and dead bodies everywhere. A frightful solitude reigned in these places where twenty savage combats had been contested, an unthinkable human charnel house. But we were indifferent to these horrors, thinking only of getting out of this macabre place. That wasn't easy, because we had to clamber over big bunches of barbed wire which grabbed our trousers and the tails of our greatcoats, like invisible hands grabbing us and holding us back in this hell. Sometimes we had to crawl along on our hands and our bellies to make our way through.

My friend Chiffre, afflicted with chronic bronchitis and incipient asthma, huffed and puffed behind and had to stop every now and then. I used these pauses to reconnoiter a pathway ahead. Bothered by this, he called my name, fearing that I would abandon him.

Of course the howitzer shells rained down on these slopes, forcing us to throw ourselves to the ground as soon as the violent, sinister whistling announced that they were heading in our direction.

To guide us in our flight, we turned our backs on the flares and rockets which marked our front line. Each step forward took us farther to the rear. There was no need for a map or a compass. It didn't matter where we ended up.

Here and there appeared other shadowy figures, fugitives like ourselves seeking the road to safety. All of a sudden an imperious voice behind us called on us to halt. And at just the right time! In the middle of a salvo of shellfire, a minute lost could be fatal, so we played deaf. After a second summons which we also ignored, we heard the jumble of footsteps coming toward us and suddenly someone jammed the barrel of a big revolver right under my nose, crying out in a terrible voice that if I took one more step I'd be a dead man. Another stranger was shaking Chiffre by the collar as if to strangle him.

Christ, had we run into a couple of madmen? There were plenty of examples of those who had lost their wits altogether in places like Cote 304.

But I soon recognized that I had in front of me the young Sublieutenant Roques of the 23rd Company—that of "the brute," the terrible Captain Barbier.

Sublieutenant Roques represented a common type of young officer: brave, courageous, well-trained, but immature, play-acting, filled with pride, treating the men like children, sometimes having fun with them but, in a quick mood swing, capable of meanness and petty vexations. In a word, just as likely to commit dramatic acts of egotism and cowardice as acts of heroism, depending on the circumstances (and the amount of hooch consumed).

Outraged by this highly impolite way of stopping people, I hoisted my Lebel rifle and replied to him, "You've got your revolver, I've got my rifle, so what do you want to do now?"

Seeing us moving downhill at all deliberate speed, he had figured that we knew where we were going, and he had wanted us to wait for him and his orderly so that we could guide them along, too. He swore, besides, that he had no intention of using his revolver on us, but just like Captain Barbier he wanted to shoot down the first artilleryman he ran into—which he didn't do, nor would he have.

Soon after that, we met up with a poilu completely draped in armor made of platters, canteens, and cooking pots and pans. It was a conscientious rationer, transporting all of his cooking equipment. We were joyfully surprised to discover that this peaceable warrior was none other than our fellow Peyriacois, Paul Alpech.

Finally we reached a road. We hadn't yet put quite enough space between the mouths of German cannons and our worthy selves, but here we felt at least we could breathe a little.

At the end of our strength, we collapsed against the slope alongside the road. The night before we hadn't gotten rations, and our mess kits, our canteens, and our stomachs were absolutely empty. Exhausted and famished, we wondered if we'd be able to pick up the march again, when all of a sudden we sniffed the tempting aromas of coffee, of bouillon, of garlic wafting their way into our nostrils.

The darkness had kept us from seeing, a short distance away, some field kitchens, awaiting in complete silence the arrival of ration teams. I immediately headed for these providential food carts.

The 296th Regiment in Champagne: May 19–July 12, 1916

By a happy stroke of luck, these field kitchens belonged to the 142nd Territorial Regiment. A long-standing friendship united this regiment to our own, further strengthened by a winter of great danger and suffering (1914–1915) shared in the plains and the swamps of Vermelles and Givenchy, in Artois, when we were side by side.

They welcomed us like brothers and offered us as much food and drink as we wanted. As for me, I wolfed down a plateful of codfish and salad, the plat du jour. These Territorials definitely didn't deprive themselves of anything. While we were savoring a second quarter-liter of coffee, Sublieutenant Roques sprang up, still brandishing his revolver. His state of confusion was still at an early stage. He spotted a poor devil of a rationer who was arriving loaded down with canteens and mess tins. Pouncing on him, Roques stuck his revolver right between his eyes, crying: "You're an artilleryman, aren't you? You're going to pay! Speak up! You're an artilleryman, right?" The rationer, baffled, dropped all his pots and pans, and sputtered that he was a Territorial.

"Well, consider yourself lucky to have gotten off so easy," said the officer to him, finally holstering his pistol and wandering off, whistling a popular tune.

The Territorial had to believe that he had just met a madman or a sick practical joker.

The three of us from Peyriac, well rested, strength regained, and informed of our whereabouts by the Territorials, headed down the road to the Bois Saint-Pierre. Soon we ran into some groups, or rather some disorganized gangs, from the 296th Regiment. Men from different companies were all mixed up. Each one marched, or rather dragged himself, along as best he could, stopped to rest, headed out across fields, lingered in villages he passed through: Montréville, Vignéville, Bethelainville [variants, respectively, of Montzéville, Vigneville, and Béthelainville].

What a miserable picture! Seven days of insomnia, fatigue, thirst, anguish had transformed these sturdy men, these superbly disciplined companies, into ragged troops of laggards, of sickly, moribund figures, who nevertheless displayed an air of calm contentment for the joy of simply being alive.

At the summit of a hill, we paused at the foot of a spring which bubbled clear, fresh water beside the road, where each passerby paused to quench the feverish thirst which consumed him.

We took one final look back at Cote 304 and the Mort Homme, which stood out in the rosy horizon of dawn.

As if from two erupting volcanoes, clouds of smoke rose up from each of the two hilltops, and the flames of explosions burst forth like jets of incandescent lava.

From where we stood, we could look down on our artillery batteries hidden in the nearby ravines, valleys, and woods, firing away with all their guns. It shook up this whole corner of the Argonne. What did this insane bombardment signify?

Were the Boches launching a fresh attack on Cote 304 and the Mort Homme?

Our curiosity wasn't strong enough to make us go back and find out. A few shells landed on a nearby hill, spurring us along our way.

At Béthelainville, someone showed us a connecting road which would save us a kilometer in distance. But we came upon several crossings in the road and we couldn't pick the right one, so we had to cover at least two kilometers more.

At the edge of the Bois de Béthelainville [Béthelainville Woods] we reached the main road. There was a large gathering of stragglers, and some officers were trying to regroup their units, with varying degrees of success.

Suddenly two men on horseback appeared. It was our old friends, Quinze-Grammes and the Kronprinz. Seeing all these people in headlong flight, the Kronprinz scowled even more grimly than he usually did when he was angry.

Good God, what was the world coming to if we let soldiers do what they please instead of forming up properly—it was the end of everything! Good thing we had spent so much of our rest time in close-order drills, with ranks as tightly formed as he could make them.

It wouldn't have surprised me if he had tried to take this shapeless mass of men "in hand," as he liked to say. But he restrained himself.

Meanwhile Quinze-Grammes, always on the lookout, scanned the four corners of the horizon, fearing the appearance of an enemy airplane squadron in search of prey on which to drop its murderous bombs.

Despite the fact that the sky was crisscrossed not by aircraft but only by inoffensive larks and swooping swallows, he curtly ordered us to disperse into the Bois Saint-Pierre.

Like a couple of medieval knights returning from the field of combat, covered with glory, our two leaders, proudly mounted on their steeds, rode off at a gentle gallop, followed at a respectful distance by their aides—or should I say, their pages.

To reach the Bois Saint-Pierre, the road made a big curve as far as Dombasle. I had a vivid recollection of the principle of elementary geometry, that a straight line is the shortest distance between two points. Applying this principle, I cut across the fields, all the while astonished that this brilliant idea had occurred to me alone. My astonishment lasted only a brief while.

My two traveling companions had rejoined their units: one in a liaison group which arrived at the edge of the woods before we did, despite our starting out ahead of them; and the other in a core group of his company which was at the big assembly point.

I was therefore traveling on my own, cheerful, unattached, free of any duties for an hour or so, taking great gulps of fresh air unpolluted of any harmful ingredients, savoring all the real and imagined liberties which made me forget how tired I was.

But what was this shimmering I saw, these sparkling rays of sunshine reflected in the field ahead of me?

Well, it was a big stretch of marshland which blocked my route. That's why no one else had headed across this field, except me—who considered myself more clever than anyone else!

But let it not be said that any sort of marshland would halt the forward progress of a hero of Cote 304. So I pushed on resolutely, smiling at the panic of legions of toads and frogs who fled, terrified, at my approach.

Suddenly my forward foot got stuck in a gooey patch of thick mud. I quickly yanked it back so forcefully that I fell right into the water.

Now I wasn't smiling anymore. This incident made me feel like beating a hasty retreat. It would be worth the extra effort to escape safe and sound from a frightful danger, rather than getting mired in a toad hole. But just a short way ahead I could see the greenery of the Bois Saint-Pierre. I pressed on, not without taking some prudent measures: frequent soundings with my walking stick, and numerous small detours.

How bizarre Mother Nature was, I told myself, in the distribution of her treasures. In the Somme and Pas-de-Calais [départements], you had to figure on four or five cable lengths of rope to get a bucketful of muddy water out of a well. Here in the Meuse [département], there was water everywhere, and you didn't even know where it came from. Scarcity in one place, overabundance in another; it was hard to understand. What I did understand was that it took me a large number of broken, zigzag lines, instead of one long straight one, which had lengthened my route considerably before finally reaching the firmer soil of our Promised Land, the Bois Saint-Pierre.

As I arrived, I met a poilu dragging himself along slowly, leaning on a long stick like a shepherd's crook and limping like a dog whose leg had been broken. Surprise: it was a Peyriacois, my friend Edouard Durand, corporal in the same section as mine. The natives of the banks of the Argent-Double[1] surely do have a hard life, but this fellow had received a blow on his knee from a stone kicked up by an exploding shell, and also had a half-dozen blisters on his feet.

We had finally made it, after twelve hours or so of marching. Alongside the road, each straggler rejoined his own company, stacked his rifle, and stretched out on the mossy ground.

After having unburdened myself of all the trappings of a modern warrior, I was just about to do likewise, when Lieutenant Breton, commanding our company, waved me over. I was hardly in any presentable condition, all rumpled and splattered with sticky mud from head to heels. But I had to approach my boss, expecting with utter indifference some sort of reproach on account of my tardy arrival or my sewer worker's appearance.

Well, yes sir, that's just what it was. All Lieutenant Breton wanted to do was to congratulate me immediately for my courageous conduct on Cote 304!

Surprised and confused, I mumbled that I hadn't done anything extraordinary. "No, no," he said, "Lieutenant Lorius reported to me that you volunteered for a perilous reconnaissance, replacing a courier on the very day of our being relieved."

Fierce antimilitarist that I was, to be congratulated as an exemplary soldier was almost as painful to me as a wound would have been. But adding it all up, for my future well-being it would be better that my bosses had esteem and consideration for me, which would help wipe out the warnings and black marks which Commandant Leblanc and Captain Cros had amassed next to my name.

A moment later, we saw a bicyclist arrive, huffing and puffing from his rapid pace, a mysterious envelope in his hand, asking for the commandant.

The latter was sitting under a big oak tree, right nearby. His household staff was bustling around, setting up a splendid meal for him.

The commandant read the fatal note and stood speechless; over his shoulder, Captain Cros-Mayrevieille read it, too, and made an indecipherable grimace; I could see no good coming out of any of this; there was something ominous about it. It was nothing less than an order from Colonel Douce, ordering us to take the road back to Cote 304 immediately. The Germans were once again massing for an assault, and our two front-line battalions were poorly positioned.

To set out again, when a quarter of the battalion hadn't arrived yet; to redo twenty kilometers under a leaden sun, with the cheerful prospect of returning to that hellhole; all this was too much. There was murmuring; some declared that they were going to lie down and would have to be carried up there. But the great majority greeted this news with a dumb silence, apathetic, not seeming to realize the gravity of the order.

The commandant ruled that we would leave in an hour, once we had eaten our supper. We ate without any appetite. Having dreamt of a restorative siesta, and now thinking that soon we would be reliving the hours of nightmare, making the superhuman effort to return to such awful places, didn't do much to stimulate our appetites.

Suddenly, a cloud of dust rolls down the road and stops in front of us. It clears away, and a handsome automobile appears before our eyes. On the hood and the sides are painted a square with red stripes: it's a divisional staff car, and from the door which an orderly hastens to open descends our divisional general, General Andrieu.[2]

His face radiates joy. At the sight of him, the commandant and the capitaine-adjutant-major interrupt their repast and rush up to their big boss, bowing and saluting, grimacing with smiles. "I bring you good news," the general calls out. "The division is relieved!"

Embarrassed, the commandant puts the colonel's message in front of him.

"Oh, the devil," the general says, scratching an ear. "This is serious."

He took a look at us, a look filled with pity, then got back into his car, saying, "I'm going to Corps headquarters in Bar-le-Duc. In an hour you'll be all set."

This hour was, for us, an hour of anguish; the anguish of a condemned man who is awaiting his final judgment of life or death.

At the end of three-quarters of an hour, we were all fixing our gazes on the dusty road bleached almost white-hot by the sun. Like Sister Anne, we saw nothing coming.[3] The road was hopelessly deserted.

Perched on an outcropping, one of us pointed out a cloud of dust in the distance which was approaching at breakneck speed. Two or three minutes later, the divisional staff car pulled up a few paces from the commandant. This time, no general. The driver, by himself, carried the precious piece of paper which contained the definitive relief order from the division.

Following the ironic military expression, in an hour the "fresh" troops, in spite of the torrid heat that day, would be arriving, and the same vehicles which were bringing them up to the slaughterhouse would carry us away to our places of rest.

The companies awaiting these providential vehicles stacked their arms at the edge of the woods. Men slumped over right on the spot, so great was their fatigue, abandoning themselves to a heavy sleep, indifferent to the scorching rays of the sun.

Captain Cros-Mayrevieille, catching sight of this, gave the order for everyone to get back into the woods. He made a point of browbeating those who didn't hop to it quickly enough. It was enough to melt your heart: this man, so egotistical, so hard on the others, so indifferent to suffering elsewhere, now displayed the kind attentions of a mother. The only thing missing was someone to point out how ridiculous it all was!

But our siesta didn't last long. Soon the well-known whistle of the commandant was heard, and we had to hoist packs and move out. There was a moment of worry. Was this some terrible counterorder? Luckily not; but we had to go as far as a village, the name of which I didn't ask, to get to the trucks.

Someone had figured out that it was better to save on a few liters of gasoline, which cost money, and instead add to our fatigue, which cost them nothing.

Whoever gave this order had no thought for the amount of suffering and weariness which he was imposing on us. These several kilometers of marching opened up the scrapes and blisters on our feet, and the straps of our packs cut painful furrows in our shoulders.

Finally the liberating vehicles arrived, and disgorged onto the roadside clusters of soldiers who silently examined our cadaverous faces, our untidy uniforms, our coatings of mud, our shaggy beards, all of which made us look like highway robbers.

They posed few questions, as they looked at us and listened to the incessant rumbling of the cannonade in the distance. Even the stupidest among them understood where they were going and what was awaiting them. They surely envied our lot, and on our side we surely pitied them. But to each his turn, and to each his destiny.

The trucks carried us off in the direction of Bar-le-Duc, which we passed through at five in the afternoon, nearly twilight. We saw tall smokestacks profiled on the horizon; they were the steel mills at Saint-Dizier. We halted two kilometers from the city, at the village of Bethancourt [variant of Bettancourt].

The 15th Company was billeted in a dilapidated barn, largely open to the breezes and quite filthy. But it looked like a palace to us, compared to our uncomfortable lodgings on Cote 304, and we enjoyed a calm and restorative sleep with no fear of falling shells.

The next day, early on, General Andrieu himself came to bring us the happy news that home leaves would start up again, after having been suspended for three months.

And that very evening the first leave takers headed off to get the train at Saint-Dizier, to the envy of everyone else.

Leaving for home was a moment of rare joy, of consolation, of happiness, awaited with feverish impatience. You forgot everything else, whether the sufferings of days just past or the bitterness of having to return to the front.

Oh, you would have to pay a high price for the poorest poilu to give up his leave.

The next few days, amazingly, they left us alone. It was the first time that we could really rest and get cleaned up, which we sorely needed.

In the evenings, with a couple of comrades, and despite the strict prohibition which had been set on us, I went into Saint-Dizier, an industrial city of 16,000 inhabitants. Like everywhere else in the rear, life went on calmly and peacefully as if it were the year 2000 and Cote 304 were as far away as Mount Sinai.

When I say that they left us alone, I have to make an exception for the inevitable inspections by our maniacal commandant, who couldn't find complete satisfaction and an undisturbed sleep without being assured that the latrines were properly installed, by the rules, at the minimum width and depth.

What we had to eat meant nothing to him. But where we deposited the vestiges of the kitchens had, for him, a capital importance.

Similarly, he couldn't sit still until he had come to check if the squad's lantern was hung on the correct crossbeam, or if a full bucket of water was at the door in case of fire. But drafts of cold air, filthiness of billets, absence of straw for sleeping—those were secondary for him.

Of course, he went on his inspection tours only when he was sure that he had, for his own precious person, a comfortable lodging and a soft bed.

Nevertheless, this man was more irritating than terrifying, and he inspired only a modest fear in us.

The next day after our arrival at Bethancourt, he visited the billets of the 22nd Company, followed by his shadow, the capitaine-adjutant-major. He spotted among the soldiers a poilu in shirtsleeves who seemed to pay no attention to the presence of these two eminent personages, and who was in the process of shaving before a basin of water.

Offended by this disrespectful attitude, the commandant sharply reprimanded this undisciplined fellow. He'd be sorry that he did so.

The soldier was a hothead in normal circumstances, and a sorehead when he was a little out of sorts, as was the case today.

Insolently looking the commandant up and down, from head to toe, he lashed him with a stream of scornful phrases: "You little runt, you little ragamuffin. It's out there, on the front lines, that you should come visit us, and now on the first day of rest we have, you show up and bother us. On Cote 304, you didn't even dare come out of your hole. Now get out of my sight!"

The commandant was as stunned as if a 250-caliber howitzer shell had landed at his feet. The capitaine-adjutant-major staggered back, clutching at the spectacles which he could barely hold onto his nose. Both raging with anger, they ordered Lieutenant Cordier to immediately draw up disciplinary charges against this rebel, and then departed, no doubt wondering if this unprecedented act wasn't one of the signs of the end of the world, which the Holy Scriptures describe so vividly in terms of abomination and desolation.

The outcome was that Lieutenant Cordier, in all good conscience, wrote up a report about this soldier, emphasizing the courage he had shown on Cote 304 at every opportunity, always volunteering for the most perilous missions and positions.

The commandant was floored.

"I asked for a list of charges," he said, "and you give me the text for a medal citation."

"I'm just telling the truth," Lieutenant Cordier replied with vigor.

And the soldier got out of it with no punishment at all.

The next day, the two inseparable striped-sleevers scoured the main streets of the village of Bethancourt, assuring themselves that their prescriptions for good order, proper attire, etc., were being observed, and that their assignments to the sentries were being carried out to the letter. There had of course been patrols and rounds carried out as part of this surveillance, but as time passed they could be sure only by checking for themselves, firsthand.

Grave and serious, they arrived in front of the town hall, where the police station was located. At the door was a sentry, who was none other than the sometime-Peyriacois Sabatier, he who had been both buried and exhumed by shells on Cote 304.

He was worrying deeply about when he could next treat his gullet to a bottle of wine or beer. The battalion's two big shots passed in front of him, and cast a blatant look at his greatcoat, where three buttonholes were empty of buttons, and at his trousers covered with rips, still splattered with the glorious mud of Cote 304.

But the two officers stopped short, dumbstruck: the insolent Sabatier hadn't seen the need to take his pipe out of his mouth—a brand-new pipe, the old one having been blasted to bits and torn from his mouth, up there, by a shell's blast.

That was already a grave misstep for a sentry. But the imprudent Sabatier took things even further, to the crime of lèse-majesté, by not saluting his bosses with his rifle. He took no more notice than if the village constable had strolled past.

This was too much. Violated discipline required vengeance. The commandant approached the guilty party and severely demanded:

"Since when do you not pay your respects?"

Without rousing himself, Sabatier stretched his arms out toward the sun, which was hiding behind a cloud, and called out in a booming voice:

"Oh, sorry. The sun has gone down."

"What are you saying?"

"I'm saying that on Cote 304 we never saw you. Here we don't salute anymore."

This incoherent language was perfectly clear to our two partners, who fled as if they'd been slapped.

The lowliest, most ignorant private was reproaching them for the cowardice they had shown on Cote 304.

It was long ago that they had lost the esteem of their men. Now they had earned their scorn.

From that point on, Commandant Quinze-Grammes, his dignity wounded as deeply as it could be, shrank from our view and soon would leave us. He lost all his appetite. In vain did our friend Richardis—yet another Peyriacois; they wormed their way in everywhere—who took care of the gastronomic needs of the two partners, draw upon all of his extensive knowledge of the culinary arts; in vain did he outdo himself in the preparation of sauces and cakes, applying the precious secrets which contributed to the lofty reputation of the Hotel Richardis in Peyriac.

In vain did he conjure up aromas which would have tempted the nostrils of the most demanding gourmets. Quinze-Grammes, faced with these treasures of the table, made a frown which pulled his mouth farther and farther down on his face, and with a voice which came out of his nose, said disdainfully:

"Is this what there is? I don't want any. Give me a soft-boiled egg."

The cooking, seasoning, and presentation of this egg weren't handed off to the first dishwasher who came along.

So "Vatel"[4] Richardis, in person, watched over the boiling of the egg, to the exacting tastes of Quinze-Grammes, and made sure that no more or no fewer than the precise number of centigrams of salt went onto it.

His comrade, the Kronprinz, didn't lose his appetite over so small a matter. He eagerly devoured both his portion and that of Quinze-Grammes.

Meanwhile, what had happened to the regiment's two other battalions, left in the furnace of Verdun? The most alarming rumors were spreading, and they turned out to be true.

On May 23, the debris of these two battalions joined us at Bethancourt. I watched their lamentable parade, and I noted the almost complete disappearance of the 24th, 23rd, and 19th Companies, where there were hardly any men left, except those who hadn't been up on the front lines. In other companies, the sections were reduced to the size of a squad.

What had happened after we left? From the soldiers of various companies whom I questioned, it was difficult to come up with an exact indication. But what was clear was that after furious bombardments the Germans had attacked in compact bunches and occupied some of our trench lines, capturing or massacring the occupants. The skin of our commandant must have crawled at the news that the Germans had gotten as far as the shelter where he had been.

Stretcher-bearers, telephone operators, and orderlies had all pitched in, keeping the enemy back with volleys of grenades.

There was desperate resistance by certain units, and acts of true heroism which broke the efforts of the assailants.

Therefore at assembly on May 24 there was an avalanche of congratulations, and we heard many statements like this one: "Regiment of brave men, who preferred to be chopped to pieces right there rather than yielding an inch of ground."

To future newcomers to the 296th Regiment, to whom they will keep repeating these fine phrases, they'll hold back from telling them that the poor devils who were there, those "brave men," could do nothing else but stay there; for any who would have been tempted to save themselves, there would have been a firing squad.

There was naturally a cascade of Croix de Guerre distributed, as always, according to the whims of the officers, who began by giving them to each other.

For these, the company commanders had to present a list of those most deserving. Lieutenant Cordier responded with these noble words: "All my men did their duty. To reward a few would be to do an injury to the others. That's an injustice to which I will not subscribe."

One can understand that Lieutenant Cordier, by manifesting such independence of heart and character, was far from being in good standing with the two ridiculous dictators of our battalion, who avenged themselves upon him and his company by petty vexations.

By reliable intelligence, I learned that the total number of killed, wounded, and missing from the regiment went as high as 1,050. That, it seemed, was sufficient for us not to be sent up to the front again. I truly believe that, with one more week, we would all have stayed there forever.[5]

Not one Peyriacois had even a scratch. You would have said that a mysterious hand had protected them. But what hand?

On May 24, we were duly informed at assembly that field exercises would be starting up again. Wasn't it urgent that this dangerous spirit of indiscipline which was starting to manifest itself be checked?

To bring everyone back to a strict conception of his duties, there was surely nothing like a few sessions of bayonet drill, of basic training singly and by section, supplemented by a few excursions across rugged terrain, from which one would return with shirts dripping with sweat.

Commandant Quinze-Grammes had already drawn up a training program in which not one paragraph, one article, one subsection of theory had been left out. We'd get something out of it! We were being treated like raw recruits.

But the next day, rather than heading out onto the training ground, we had to get ready to depart. An order which came from the mysterious and invisible high reaches of headquarters enjoined the 296th Regiment to embark for an unknown destination.

We had to leave Bethancourt by six in the evening. We all thought this meant embarking at the Saint-Dizier station, right nearby, but to our stupefaction we took the opposite direction.

The route that we took looped its way across countryside rich in vegetation: fields with a variety of crops, filled with fruit trees; grapevines lined the road. But most of us were insensitive to the beauties of the landscape, and we paid more attention to a gathering of menacing clouds which ended up unleashing a terrible downpour upon us.

And still we marched. We passed through several villages. Night was falling. Where were they leading us?

At about 10 in the evening, we arrived in a pitiable state at a station, that of Eurville.

They left us by the side of the road, soaked with sweat and rain. Then we loaded onto trains: the officers in first- or second-class carriages, we as usual in cattle cars, packed so tightly that we had to take turns sitting down. I spent half the trip holding onto a ring which hung from a crossbeam, just to keep my balance.

At one stop, I read on the station sign, through the slats: "Saint-Dizier."

So they had imposed upon us a long, hard march, soaking us to the skin, having us stand shivering for two hours at night in front of a station in the middle of nowhere—just to come back to Saint-Dizier!

Who gave this idiotic order? Who burdened us with these wearying and useless sufferings?

There's a lawful punishment for whoever beats an animal with brutality. But there is no sanction, no punishment; there is complete impunity for these jerks for whom we serve as toys, as punching bags.

1916. Commandant Leblanc's misadventure.
Cuperly. Vadenay. The camp at Châlons.

We passed by Vitry-le-François, and at daybreak we went through Châlons-sur-Marne. At the station at Saint-Hilaire [-au-Temple] there was a brief halt. Commandant Leblanc took advantage of it and went to the toilet. Was he constipated? Or did he linger to examine these restrooms—a subject about which he was very knowledgeable? I can't set straight anyone who reads these lines, but the outcome was that when Quinze-Grammes stepped back onto the station platform, our train had disappeared.

At the station at Cuperly they had us get out of the train. This was the end of an ordeal. Now we could relax our arms and legs, loosen up our shoulders and our flanks, after twelve hours of being piled up in cattle cars too small for the number of men they contained. This was a great relief, a blessing. It's true that a fine, thick rain was falling, and that the wait in front of the station, with arms stacked, really lasted a bit too long.

What were we doing there, anyway, instead of proceeding to our next encampment?

Well, the reason was that the commandant alone knew where our battalion had to be. He was stuck in the lavatories back at the Saint-Hilaire station, and he had to arrive in order to reveal to us the site of our next billet—a secret which he had kept to himself like a state secret, which he had not revealed even to our friend François Calvet, the battalion's adjutant, nor to his *eminence grise,* Captain Cros-Mayrevieille.

When the news of his misadventure spread through the battalion, it brought on a general outburst of laughter. He himself arrived sooner than we thought he would, brought by an automobile which a providential fate carried to Cuperly.

Almost immediately, the bleating of a hoarse goat was heard. It was the whistle of Quinze-Grammes giving the signal for departure.

A half-hour later we took possession of our barracks, hidden away in the clearings of a forest of stunted pines; a road—from Cuperly to La Cheppe— and a river—the Noblette—cut across our encampment.[6]

What the hell! It was in this place of exile that we had come to rest on our laurels. We, whose glory, according to what the newspapers said, eclipsed that of all the heroes whose exploits history had recorded!

One would have had to be leprous, scabrous, vermin-ridden, to be put in quarantine, to be driven to a place as isolated, as desolate, as rude as this was.

It's true that we should have been flattered to find ourselves in the place where, it seems, the terrible Attila was crushed after a horrendous battle, a thousand years ago. But human ingratitude is such that no memorial, not even a stone, recalled the memory of this battle where the fate of our nation was played out.[7]

As for comfort in the aforementioned barracks, they left much to be desired: for bedsteads, rough planks trampled over all day long by our muddy feet. For pillows, our packs.

It's a good thing that our shoulders and our sides were toughened. We would have appreciated an armful of fresh straw upon which to rest our sore bodies. But at this time straw was a luxury which only officers could afford—and the horses of officers.

One day, at assembly, a whole panoply of heroes was rewarded with a profusion of decorations and sleeve stripes of every variety.

I was named a corporal, once again. That left me completely indifferent, but since the stripes were given to me in defiance of the wishes of the commandant and the capitaine-adjutant-major I could only rejoice at their annoyance.

They gave me command of the 6th Squad—a phantom squad, consisting of one barber, one drummer, one orderly, and other staff employees whom you saw only at mealtimes.

The only man fit for combat duty and who showed up with me at inspections and drills was a schoolteacher named Dartigues. He never offered any excuses, and was as unerringly phlegmatic as any son of England. His face manifested an attitude so stupid that it sometimes disconcerted and disarmed our section chief, Adjutant Toulzan, who thought him hopeless.

Once he had swallowed his meal, our pedagogue disappeared as if by magic, and then at roll calls and departures he would reappear at the last minute, but in what attire! Puttees undone and falling around his ankles; in greatcoat when he was supposed to be in jacket, and vice versa; his cap stuck on his head like a nightcap when the others wore helmets; his necktie twisted to the side; his pack with its straps going every which way, from which blanket, mess tins, billycans, tools, all hung down, hooked and roped on just enough so that they wouldn't fall off.

Chewed out by the adjutant, he was sent back morning and night by the corporal or the sergeant on duty; his name was always at the top of the work-duty roster, but he led a taciturn existence, indifferent to everyone and everything, living apart from his comrades.

Had the war clouded his brain?

Was he a poker face making fun of us all?

Was he a philosopher, whose spirit soared in realms inaccessible to common mortals, and whose body was simply vegetating here on earth? What a mystery!

As you might well imagine, the field exercises had begun again. Watch out when you were under the orders of Lieutenant Grulois, nicknamed Gueule de Bois ["wooden mug," which is slang for hangover]. He led us to a large clearing in the woods, where the sections trained separately.

There was no point trying to fool around with this jail warden of a lieutenant. From the shade of a pine tree he kept us all in his sight, and no false movement or faulty order escaped his notice.

At a signal, a whistle blast from him, a movement or a command had to be done over and over again until it was perfect.

It was my turn to take command of the section.

Dartigues, always either distracted or not paying attention, sometimes understood a complicated change of direction or an assembly, but I always ended up no better or no worse than anyone else.

This was a relief whenever the lieutenant said, "Someone else take charge!" You couldn't ask to be knocked back down in rank.

One day, the regiment received a reinforcement of two hundred men from the conscript class of 1916. What an aberration, to pour such young folks into a regiment in which many of us were 35 to 40 years old and more. The 296th Regiment indeed became an active-duty, regular regiment.

Maybe they thought that the insouciance, the innocence, the enthusiasm of these young ones would shake off the apathy and the inertia of us veterans, just like a bar owner pours a bucket of new wine into a cask of old, stale wine to refresh it.

During the night of May 30–31, we had a visitor whom we would have gladly missed: a Boche pilot flew his airplane over and dropped some bombs on the camp. Thanks to his clumsiness, there were no victims.

On June 1, the battalion left the camp and went to billets in Cuperly, just a few kilometers away. We were finally returning to civilization.

We spent all day setting up, hastily digging deep latrines in anticipation of the inevitable visit of Quinze-Grammes. But all was in vain. The next day, without knowing why or how, we moved three kilometers to the village of Vadenay. We got, from a dozen different garrison towns, reinforcements in batches of twenty, thirty, forty men, and the regiment was quickly brought back to strength.

We thought we'd enjoy a nice long rest, but on June 5 we got the unhappy news that the next day, at 6 in the morning, we were heading up to the trenches.

After a march of four hours, across an arid plain which was none other than the Camp de Châlons,[8] we arrived, at 10 in the morning, at the little town of Suippes, completely abandoned by its inhabitants.

Many of the houses were still intact, but once in a while bombs from airplanes or shells from howitzers would blast one of them to bits. Only a few slackers occupied the town.

Our company was billeted, or rather stuffed, in too-tight quarters. We complained, but they stopped our complaints by kindly alerting us that we would, that very evening at 8 o'clock, get to know our new sector, which we reached around midnight, dead-tired.

The sector was calm, and compared to Cote 304 it was a vacation spot. But what spoiled the pleasure of occupying this peaceful sector was that it had recently seen a poison-gas attack, which had claimed many victims, and we feared another attack. We were going to live or die with this nightmare.

Our section being in reserve, we occupied deep shelters, with two entrances, which made us ecstatic. This was the first time we had seen anything like this. Inside them, nothing to fear from bombardments—but it wasn't the same for that accursed gas.

We had no more than mediocre confidence in the precautions taken. At the entrances of each shelter, there was a stick of wood, some straw, and some gasoline, to be lit in order to dissipate the murderous cloud. There were special grenades to disperse the gas by their explosions; exploding canisters full of water with bisulfite to make the gas cling to the ground.

But it wasn't enough to have these things there. What was needed was a detailed organization, with each of us having an assignment to carry out in an emergency. We should have been paying attention to the upkeep and the readiness of all these items.

In reality, only the officers who consistently occupied the same shelters could take such useful precautions.

The sections changed positions every night or two, so that the men had no taste for keeping themselves ready for a gas attack at any moment.

So the water went stale in its containers, the canisters rusted and became unusable, the powdered bisulfite disappeared, the gasoline was used by the poilus to light up their shelters, the wood and the straw got soaked in the rain and the dew. Nobody knew, in case of a gas attack, just what we needed to do and where to hide ourselves away in the shelters. Everything was left to chance.

All we could do was put ourselves into the hands of Boreas, the god of the winds, in hopes that he would favor us. To do so, at each shelter or outpost, the clever poilus had installed tiny windmills to serve as weather vanes.

When a light breeze blew across the Champagne, we observed the movements of these little windmills with no less concern than a sailor watches the needle of his barometer move toward or away from the word "Stormy."

But after a few days we got used to this danger, like all the others, and we didn't attach any more importance to it than we did to an imaginary danger.

The next night our half-section went up to the front line to reinforce the outposts, which were manned by squads of no more than three or four unlucky men, always the same ones obliged to be on watch night and day, almost without interruption.

For some reason or other, two-thirds of the effective strength of the companies had been exempted from outpost duty and assigned to the rear.

Around the command posts of commandants and captains, you'd see more and more strapping young fellows carrying out vague functions: orderlies, cooks, aides, signalmen, rationers, tailors, barbers, etc., all bowing and scraping before the officers, these new noblemen of the twentieth century who, in exchange, pulled them out of the first circle of this new Dante's Inferno: the trenches.

With my squad of three men—including the taciturn, mysterious Dartigues—I could do no more than reinforce an outpost occupied by a squad of two men.

The night before, a shell had scored a direct hit on this outpost, wounding five occupants, one mortally.

Thus we were not very reassured to be occupying this outpost, so evidently targeted by the Boche artillerymen. But whether out of humanity or in order to conserve ammunition, they left us alone this night and the next several.

On June 15, at 3 in the morning, a battalion of our regiment came to relieve us, and after a four-hour march we encamped in barracks called the "Ferme de Piémont," [Piémont Farm] in the Camp—or rather the desert—of Châlons.

Our rest was brief. On June 20, at 8 in the evening, we were marched up to the trenches to carry out some work upon which an impenetrable mystery hung.

They split us up as we got close to the front lines, in the middle of a pine forest called the "Bois des Chenilles" [Woods of the Caterpillars], I don't know why because I never saw one specimen of this creature there.

The next night, with three sturdy comrades, I was ordered to put myself at the disposal of the railway station at Chenilles. This station, in a clearing eight hundred meters from the front line, was filled with all sorts of entrenching materials brought up every night by the narrow-gauge Decauville trains.[9] But the locomotive prudently stayed at one station farther up the line, and the freight cars were hauled up at great effort by some thin and skeletal horses.

The Chenilles station chief, a big-bellied slacker who never left his lair, had plenty to say to everyone, in full voice, gesticulating with an air of importance no way inferior to that of station chiefs in the biggest stations in Paris. He chewed me out because I was late, and didn't let us go until around midnight without paying us a simple thank-you.

The weather was stormy, the night terribly dark, and in our haste to get to our shelter before the menacing downpour we got lost in a maze of footpaths. I remembered the story of *Petit-Poucet* [Tom Thumb][10] and climbed up a pine tree—not to see if there was a light on the horizon, but so that the line of luminous flares would give me the general direction of north.

We renewed our march on tiptoes. I was at the front of the line, which doesn't have any particular merit but which explains my great surprise and terror when two harsh and ominous voices roared out: "Halt right there! *Qui vive?* [Who goes there?]" And as lightning flashed I saw the points of two menacing bayonets advancing toward my chest. At a second flash I saw two faces as black as the finest ebony, but hardly reassuring.

So, there were man-eaters, cannibals, in the Bois de Chenilles, right in the middle of Champagne!

"Comrades!" I cried out. "We aren't Boches! Please, let us pass!"

Ah, yes. Let us pass. That's all we needed to say to not be skewered on bayonets. But we had to take the long way around.

After some discussion among themselves, these blacks who spoke French so well told us that they were from Martinique. There were quite a number of them in the regiment next to ours, and they were able to give us helpful directions for getting back to our shelters.

Our shelters, where each of us had a wire-mesh bunk, an innovation which seemed to us an unaccustomed luxury.

The supplier of that wire mesh—yet another one who will make his fortune! The war is not an equally cruel scourge to everyone.

The next night they sent us up to the front line to help with some mysterious works. It consisted of digging shallow, projecting trenches with no more than two or three steps at the end. You didn't need to be a wizard to figure out that these were shelters for preparing an emission of asphyxiating gas. Soon this was Polichinelle's secret,[11] and everyone added to it: we were going to launch these gases along the whole Champagne front; the gases we had launched up to now were nothing but simple insecticides, but these new ones would strike down the Boches to a depth of twenty kilometers. Already in each regiment they were forming teams of "courageous" men to go explore, after the emission, the places where this breath of doom had passed. Special gas masks would be issued to them at Suippes, Mourmelon, and Châlons, and experiment after experiment would be carried out on the harmfulness of the gases and on the effectiveness of the gas masks.

Near to the shelter where I was working, some of the Martiniquais were standing guard at the parapets. They displayed a silent and melancholy air, distracted, their spirits far, far away, no doubt across the immense ocean.

I interrogated some of them to get to know their state of mind. They had hardly any martial spirit, these poor devils shivering in the chill of nighttime.

They had been infused with hatred of the Germans, and they were persuaded that if we were conquered their own land would be prey to the Germans and they would fall into a frightful slavery.

They therefore accepted their fate as inevitable. Their brains had been stuffed to make cannon fodder out of them.

One night, returning from work, we found the shelter surrounded by thirty or so very young men—volunteers, or forced conscripts from the classes of 1917 and 1918 not yet called up.

Skinny, beardless, and with insolent looks and talk full of the cheekiness of a Parisian Gavroche,[12] these were what they called "seasoned" guys, despite the fact that some of them had the faces of girls or of kids of fifteen.

Some came right out of reform school; others, as delivery boys, had neglected to hand over to their bosses some money from a client; some, employed by the post office, had had the indiscretion to peek into the content of private letters. One of them had found nothing better to do than to kidnap a young miss of fourteen whose folks didn't want to give her to him in marriage.

Finally, there were those who, young as they were, had been convicted as pimps, and they proudly showed off the letters, packages, and money which their faithful "hens" sent to them.

To these kids precocious in vice, they had opened the prison gates in exchange for enlistment for the duration of the war. This was offered as a form of re-habilitation.

In reality, it was a strange deal: to pardon them for stealing, they sent them out to kill. How's that for restoring the soul.

Among them were a number of unfortunate orphans who, to free themselves from the tutelage of Public Assistance, had enlisted. They had been snared, dazzled by life on the front lines as depicted in the newspapers, and now they came to live out fantastic adventures and gather up stripes and medals with ease.

All these recruits were assigned to the 15th Company, and a sergeant, list in hand, presented me with a dozen of these hard cases, whose corporal I now became.

The barber, the drummer boy, the signalman, etc., and the enigmatic Dartigues were taken away from me, to reinforce some other squad.

I furrowed my brow at this news. Why had they chosen me to command this young band of budding *apaches?*[13] They'd bring me nothing but bad luck, all sorts of nasty surprises.

Did they take me for a firm-handed type, and were they counting on my toughness to bring them to heel?

We'll see what happens. For now, having escaped the severe discipline of a penal battalion, they acted astonished to be at the front, almost right on the front lines, and they sang and danced with an almost childlike joy, to the bafflement of their indulgent elders.

Let me hasten to say that these young rascals always treated me with respect and, I'd even dare to say, affection. It's true that I didn't use a rough manner. I reprimanded them as a comrade, as an older brother rather than as a superior in rank. I took an interest in their fates, writing applications for charity awards for these disinherited ones, and I succeeded in finding *marraines de guerre*[14] for them or getting grants allocated to them.

And these poor little guys, many of whom would have only me to weep over their deaths, in exchange for my solicitude to them, took on a true and touching attachment for me.

Meanwhile, the works having been completed, we left the Bois des Chenilles during the night of June 29–30, and after a long march we came to our billets in Cuperly.

This wasn't a rest period for us. From dawn to dusk we had nothing but long exercises, maneuvers, and marches in a withering heat. It made us miss the trenches.

This pounding and bashing came at the orders of the firm-handed colonel sent to the 296th Regiment, it was said, to shape us up, or to get us back into shape, because evidently someone had noted a slippage of discipline in the regiment.

This was Colonel Robert.[15] This terrible fellow stuck his nose into everything, watching, surveying firsthand to make sure that the numerous rules he issued each day at roll call were being observed.

What bothered him most of all was seeing the tail flaps of our uniform coats even a centimeter out of place, when they were folded back.

Even if you were a hero, brave as could be, or as smart as anyone, you were nothing but an idiot, a good-for-nothing, if you showed too much of the pocket underneath the flap.

He rushed up to companies leaving for or coming back from exercises just for this kind of inspection. In preparation, our officers and non-coms spent every day making sure everything was just right.

You'd have thought we had a lunatic, a maniac, a nut case in charge. We wondered what he would do with us once we got up to the front lines.

Back to my new squad of hooligans, brawlers, troublemakers thinking mainly about having a good time at someone else's expense. They were hungry as young wolves and poor as church mice, so I had to scramble to get them extra bread rations from some mess corporals of my acquaintance.

My Peyriac buddies Richardis and Maizonnave, who were cooks at the officers' and non-coms' mess, gave me a heads-up when there were some leftovers in the kitchen or a platter or casserole to scrape off.

I had to make small advances or loans against their meager pay to buy a bottle of wine or some writing paper or other small items.

On July 4 a tragic accident took place in Cuperly. At daybreak a horse-drawn artillery wagon with five gunners riding on it was crossing the railroad tracks when a passenger train arrived at exactly the same time and smashed the wagon and its squad to bits. Three of the poor devils were horribly injured and died almost immediately; two others were gravely hurt.

That same day, wrapped in tent cloth, the three dead artillerymen were buried without any ceremony to speak of—these weren't heroes who died on the field of honor—in the little cemetery which surrounds the church.

This accident went almost unnoticed. We were hardened against any emotion. We cared only about our own fates. War is the best teacher of egoism.

But tragedy for some is often profitable for others. Thanks to this sad accident my twelve young brigands could finally satisfy their appetites. The dead horses were cut up by the butcher Jalabert—from my old squad—and the meat was distributed to the companies. My pal Jalabert secretly passed along to me, for the 15th Squad, a platter and two haversacks full of pieces of meat from the choicest cuts.

Imagine how my young brigands jumped with joy at the promise of such a feast! We unanimously decided to transform this meat into savory steaks, cooked nice and rare. We passed the hat to buy some oil. In a skillet without a

handle which someone found by lucky chance, a choice slab of meat was soon
grilling away, letting off an aroma which flared the nostrils of the ravenous and
impatient customers. One of them poked the steak with the point of his knife
to see how it was cooking, and knocked over the skillet. The slice of meat fell
into the fire and was transformed into a hunk of coal in less time than it takes
to tell the tale. There was a howl of rage against this clumsy fellow, and if I
hadn't intervened right away he would have gotten quite a lesson for having
been in more of a hurry than the others.

But that was just a brief delay. Eight times the skillet was loaded with meat
and its contents swallowed down as soon as it was cooked. The fellows were
finally satisfied, which they hadn't been in quite a long while.

Right at this time a complete reorganization took place in all the infantry
regiments. The battalions were reduced to three rifle companies. The fourth
company of each battalion was dissolved and replaced by a machine-gun company; the dissolved company's men were dispersed into the other three companies. All that to explain that my Peyriac buddy Paul Alpech came into my
company and my squad.

This valuable reinforcement was just enough to bring some good order among
our hooligans, always ready to quarrel and exchange blows with each other.

Good old Alpech was designated the squad's cook, because while we were
at rest the field kitchens were also resting and we were on our own for food.
Alpech was the classic type of cook, and he brought to the exercise of his culinary functions an importance and a solemnity which you couldn't help but
notice.

Back from exercises at the end of the day, the famished gang rushed to the
patch of ground where the cooking pot bubbled away on two big rocks, and
everyone dipped his bread into it, under pretext of seeing how the bouillon was
cooking, to the great despair of Alpech, who threatened to throw off his apron.
Granted the widest powers by me, he armed himself with a fishing rod, which
earned a respectful fear from the rascals once it had whipped the ears of a few
of them.

One day, at assembly, the sergeant-major read out: "The 15th Company will
designate a corporal to go on a training assignment to learn about the new trench
cannon."

The prospect of getting out of Colonel Robert's clutches for a few days
could only inspire the enthusiasm of the company's sixteen corporals and cause
them to raise their hands—both hands.

But in vain did the sergeant-major and Lieutenant Breton repeat the demand;
none of the corporals budged. The reason was that, six months earlier, a corporal had gone off on a training assignment for the *crapouillots* [trench mortars].

But when he came back he stayed a foot soldier, just like before. All he got was the nickname "Crapouillot," which made him mad as hell.

New to the 15th Company, I didn't know this, and I shot my hand up into the air. What worse could happen to me?

Two days later, along with a dozen privates, corporals, and sergeants, I headed off to the Ferme de Bouy [Bouy Farm], the training center for the Fourth Army, where they would reveal to us the secrets of this brand new engine of destruction.

The Ferme de Bouy is only six kilometers from Cuperly, right in the middle of the Camp de Châlons. In peacetime it was a horse farm for remount stallions, but today it was a center for perfecting all kinds of legal ways to kill people, to cut them down more quickly, in the largest possible number, all to save civilization from peril.

Grenadiers came there to learn from crazy Captain B. . . . how to toss grenades fast and far.

Bomb throwers, snipers, machine gunners came in teams to the Ferme de Bouy to spend ten or twelve days.

This made the place a slacker's haven for instructor officers and non-coms and their entourages of orderlies, aides, cooks, messengers, secretaries, etc.

There was a whole garrison there, the divisional squadron, resting up for the last great day of the final pursuit, or the triumphal entry of our general as his escort into Strasbourg or Berlin.

The very evening of our arrival, I went into the village of Bouy with my comrades, and there I saw Russian soldiers for the first time.[16] They occupied the neighboring sector, took their rest in the nearby village of Mourmelon, and in spite of the strict prohibitions given to them they wandered around the area in the evenings. There was an order given in the region, prohibiting their being served any alcoholic beverages, including the sacred pinard.

12th Notebook

The 296th Regiment in Champagne:
July 13–August 29, 1916

Nevertheless you could tell that the Slavic soldiers I met in the streets of Bouy had had something other than tea, their customary beverage, to drink. They zigzagged in a manner which was dangerous to their equilibrium, and some of them, gesticulating, singing, stopped women and girls in the streets, kneeling comically before them to give them what was no doubt an elaborate declaration of love, in the form of raucous sounds interrupted with hiccups.

Indulgent and amused, the men and women of Bouy formed circles around these harmless drunkards.

I'll pass over without comment the next day, July 14 [Bastille Day, the French national holiday]. Only a supplemental ration of pinard and a slightly better bill of fare, which was more than made up for in the following week, barely distinguished this day from any other.

We didn't even get any extra rest. In fact, our training course, which could hardly be postponed, began that very day.

They introduced us to this new homicidal engine. Most of us couldn't hold back a frown of disdain. It was a minuscule cannon, a 75 in miniature, a child's toy. Its shell was barely bigger than a hen's egg.

The instructors waxed elegiac about this cannon, praising its precision, its rapidity of fire, and the penetrating power of the shells.

This was the 37mm cannon, intended to destroy machine-gun nests, observation posts, etc.[1]

I will spare the reader the various exercises, test firings, and lectures on theory which transformed us into brilliant cannoneers in twelve days. And to think that the old farts at headquarters claimed, before the war, that two years were insufficient time to make a perfect artilleryman!

After the war they will be capable of picking the topic up again.

The daily lectures on theory pretty much limited themselves to stuffing our heads with what is a point, a line, an angle. After the hundred times or so which our instructor's repeated it, we ended up knowing that a point is the intersection of two lines and a line is the limit of two planes. As for the definitions of various angles, a thousandth, and various other geometrical expressions, a dozen brains out of thirty refused to record in their gray-matter cells these too-monotonous words.

A comical note was provided by a corporal from the 114th Regiment who could never pronounce certain words correctly. For example, when it was his turn he called out *tir de capacité* ["capacity fire"] instead of *tir d'efficacité* ["efficiency fire"].

In vain did the poor fellow make a violent effort to say it correctly, but when he was halfway through, his tongue would make a wrong turn and the command would come out as "tir de capacité" to everyone's pitiless laughter. Only I didn't laugh, because I was afflicted by a sudden and untimely indisposition. I completely lost my appetite, and for two days I had all the trouble in the world standing up on my two legs, my eyes reddened and burned, spots broke out on my throat, a lip swelled up; I no longer looked like a Christian. I should have gone to sickbay, but the irritated instructor-lieutenant said that I would have to travel several kilometers to find an infirmary and a medical officer, and given the short stay I'd have at Bouy I'd be better off "sticking it out to the end," according to the expression in fashion then. And that's what I resigned myself to do, with the local water of dubious potability being the only thing my stomach would accept.

One evening, feeling a little better, with my gastronomical equipment having shown some hints of an appetite, I decided to try the journey to Mourmelon-le-Grand in order to provision myself. They said it would take about a half-hour, it was on the other side of a bare hill. But behind this hill there was another, then two or three more, and finally it took me more than four hours to reach Mourmelon, where I arrived in a state of complete exhaustion.

The presence in this village of Russian troops and a number of support services of the French army made this locale quite lively.

By unexpected luck, I found a restaurant where they squeezed every bit out of your pocketbook but where I could, to my great benefit, get served two eggs, a salad, and some fruit.

By the end of this frugal meal, twilight had fallen, and I hastened to take up the road back to camp. But I was held back awhile by the spectacle of a Russian regiment leaving for relief on the front line.

The men marched in ranks of ten or twelve, as wide as the roadway. They had a slow pace, and at the lead of their officers they intoned hymns borrowed from religious settings like canticles.

At the front of the companies little Russians of ten to fifteen years kept the pace and sang their heads off, mixing their shrill voices with the deep ones of their elders, whose adopted children they were; they carried out the functions of couriers, cyclists, drummer boys, pot scrubbers, etc.

Once I got back on the road, night enveloped the deserted steppes of the Camp de Châlons with an opaque darkness, and despite having noted a few landmarks on my journey there I got lost and soon, completely at the end of my strength, I passed out on the ground.

With no sense of suffering, like a lamp which goes out at its last drop of oil, I lost all thought of earthly things, and I felt myself slipping into the oblivion of death.

But perhaps I was destined for a more glorious end, one worthy of envy, as Victor Hugo said[2]—like, for example, being pounded, shredded, asphyxiated, blown to bits in a cloud of smoke.

The coolness of the evening revived me, and at about eleven o'clock, after many rest stops and detours, I arrived back at the barracks where we were lodged.

My absence had gone almost unnoticed due to incidents which had occurred during the evening.

At Bouy, in a tavern, a quarrel had broken out between some soldiers from the 296th Regiment and some grenadiers and soldiers from some other regiments.

The reasons for it were the same as always: antagonism, indeed hatred, between the Midi and other parts of France.

These sentiments, always regrettable in their latent state, sometimes came to the fore when a few bottles of wine heated up the heads of the descendants of the Visigoths and those of the Franks.

Usually these were limited to unpleasant insinuations, sometimes rising to the level of insults, but this time it was more serious. There were fisticuffs exchanged, even clubs wielded, if you please, and blood flowed; one of the "Franks" was literally knocked out while two "Visigoths" from the 296th had their faces pounded into marmalade.[3]

A general brawl had ensued, and in the barracks where we slept on a single long camp bed there was a storm raging in the air, even though the most passionate combatants belonged to another billet.

As an isolated minority, we were subjected to stupid provocations, insinuations, mockeries, shouted insults, and stone throwing. We met all of this with scornful silence and went to bed; but they burst in and started jumping and dancing on the boards of the camp bed, and forced us to get up. In the face of this harassment we picked up our blankets and went to sleep outside, under a beautiful, starry July sky.

On July 21, the eve of our departure, all the regiments of the Fourth Army sent to Bouy a whole slew of commandants and captains, summoned to witness the new formation of combat companies, composed of teams of grenadiers, machine gunners, bomb throwers, 37mm cannons, etc.

General Gouraud, missing an arm and a leg, chief of the Fourth Army, was there.[4] He looked quite no-nonsense, this general; around him swarmed officers bedecked with ribbons and medals who made themselves as stiff and attentive before their chief as they would be arrogant toward a subordinate.

Our demonstration drills of attacking and defending a trench were crowned with success, as they always were on maneuvers. Our firing onto targets which we'd carefully plotted out the night before were naturally deemed to be marvelous in their precision.

All those present were astounded, or pretended to be. Then we listened raptly to the warlike thunderings of General Gouraud.

The pope delivering a sermon at St. Peter's could not have been listened to more respectfully than the general was, by this crowd. I could hear a cricket singing. Amazingly, I actually heard a few bits and pieces of the speech; a simple corporal couldn't make his way up to the front row and plant himself right under the nose of such a lofty personage.

The rifle was obsolete, he said, and would have to be relegated to the museum of prehistoric arms. We weren't killing men one by one anymore; let's talk about grenades, bombs, flamethrowers, machine guns, etc. With all that at our disposal, we'd soon have the Boches on the run.

General Gouraud was sure of it. Besides, in a confidential tone, he repeated the words of the Spanish ambassador in Berlin, that if the French knew the state of exhaustion and discouragement of the German people we would be waving banners of joy. He must have been very well informed, this ambassador, or else he was making fun of us.

At the end, the general said the Battle of the Somme was at full force and that the Fourth Army "would soon be taking its turn and claiming its share of glory." We didn't doubt the accuracy of this promise.

The officers applauded, displayed a real enthusiasm about leading us, and then disappeared, carried off by automobiles in every direction, while we, under a leaden sun, made our way back to the Ferme de Bouy, painfully dragging our cannon along.

The next day, July 22, we left the Ferme de Bouy to rejoin our regiment which, since the 17th, had been on the front lines near the Butte de Tahure.[5]

A truck took us to the train station at Saint-Hilaire-au-Temple, the train took us to Suippes, and then our own legs took us to the divisional depot not far from Somme-Suippes, where we arrived after the evening meal was over. And since the offerings there weren't very abundant, we didn't even have any leftovers for our supper, nor a corner to lie down in. I had to sleep under a cart.

That doesn't say much about the hospitality at the divisional depot.

Our Lieutenant Lorius had led us to believe that, as guardians of the secrets of manipulating this new cannon, our persons became precious, and that they would no doubt keep us at the depot to preserve us from the numerous risks of a soldier's trade.

No such luck. The commandant of the depot handed down the order for us to rejoin our respective units at daybreak the next day. As badly fed and lodged as we were at the depot, we'd have rather spent a few more days there. But the next day at dawn we set out on our way, a journey with no charms across the desert of the *Champagne pouilleuse*,[6] which a few clumps of stunted pines weren't able to enliven.

At nightfall I finally reached an outpost where I found my squad of hooligans, who welcomed me not with cries of joy—the Boches were a few paces away—but by other displays of friendship which touched me.

Worn down with fatigue, I stretched out on the outpost's firing step, hoping that the Boches wouldn't pay us a visit that night, given the impossibility of my defending myself, or clearing out, or keeping up if they hauled me back with them.

By half-section, the two squads spent twenty-four hours watching our neighbors across the way and twenty-four hours in a hole in the front line. This would have been fine if the reliefs had taken place at dawn or at twilight. But instead they took place at midnight. So we all had two nights split in half, instead of one full night's sleep.

But someone had said "midnight to midnight," just as easily as saying "noon to noon." Who was responsible for this? A colonel, a commandant, a captain? These people lived too close to us, and too far away; too far to bother with such small details, they could sleep as much as they wanted. But if a lowly private feels tempted to fall asleep, he has the prospect of a court-martial to keep him wide awake.

What kind of nonsense was this, to put a whole squad into an outpost, which was simply the front end of a sap, where we were all piled up on top of each other. One shell, or a mortar round, or a simple grenade could have killed all of the occupants.

Couldn't they have put two sentries on duty, and the others a little bit to the rear, in a shelter, where they could have mounted some resistance to an attack?

But let's not be too demanding, when we've been at war for only two years; everything can't be perfect. And after all, if a mortar round kills two men or a dozen, what difference does that make? Back there is the divisional depot which can disgorge "brave men, eager for the honor of coming up to the front line," as the newspapers said. We weren't yet having manpower shortages. Lord knows we'd have a victory before that happened.

Therefore at midnight they came to relieve us, and five minutes later we were at the rest-shelter dugout, not very deep but with two entry points. The floor was laid with planks, which might appear to be a luxury; these planks served us as mattress and pillow; this was a comfort, considering that up to now we had slept on the damp earth.

For those who envy us this well-being, it needs to be said that legions of lice and fleas had already chosen this floor as their domicile. Furthermore, these rough planks, simply laid next to each other by a clumsy carpenter on uneven ground, were like piano keys, so that when you were lying down and a comrade came into the shelter, you wouldn't be surprised to have your shoulder, your head, or your flank be bounced up while your other shoulder or flank sank down.

One would think that, once we got to the shelter, all we did was unpack our blankets, stretch out under them, blow out our candles, and revel in a well-earned sleep—while lice and fleas jammed their suckers into our bodies.

But the fear of poison gas was like a new sword of Damocles hanging over the heads of the trench dwellers, from which came the necessity of mounting guard duty by a watcher who would be relieved each hour, in front of the shelter. This was easier said than done. Nobody wanted to be first; everybody came up with a reason which appeared irrefutable, leading to endless palaver.

Our squad had the bad luck of being closest to the crossroads of communication trenches leading to the outpost.

There was set up a periscope, the upper mirror of which was affixed to the top end of a fake tree trunk which rotated in all directions. It allowed us to admire the charming lunar landscape which surrounded us.

There were also signal flares, and also the shelter of the section chief, who slept more peacefully when he knew there was a sentry in front of his abode, a sentry which my squad had to supply, night and day.

Furthermore, we were always available for work details at anyone's pleasure. It was rare that two hours went by without a "liaison man" or the sergeant coming and pulling you from your sleep to tell the corporal to furnish one, two, or three men to go resupply our grenades, bombs, flares, cartridges, sandbags; sometimes the corporal is sent along, too.

You can understand how the choice of these men for work detail didn't happen without protests or complaints by those who were designated.

Each night we also had to send out a work detail for water for the command post of the captain or the commandant. There weren't any "Wallace fountains"[7] in the trenches, and we sometimes had to cover some kilometers to reach the terminus of the *tacots* [narrow-gauge railroad trains] which brought up the water in kegs.

The poilu often doesn't have a drop of water to quench his thirst, but *Mes-*

sieurs les officiers and even their orderlies, the rationers, and other do-nothings are keen on doing their daily ablutions with plenty of water.

Of course, the poilu coming back from outpost duty would much prefer taking a snooze to hauling a barrel or a big keg of water on his shoulders, in gloomy communication trenches where he would sometimes lose his way, but if he grumbled a bit, or even a lot, he obeyed all the same.

Add to this the fact that, each hour, the sentries on duty at the periscope and at the shelter's entrance came in to wake up their relievers a good ten minutes early, and the latter, knowing what was coming, turned a deaf ear to them, so obliging themselves to be summoned three and four times, with increasing loudness, so that everyone was forced to wake up as well.

During the day you couldn't think of getting any shut-eye. There was coffee, meals, letters to read and write, work details, and the boyau and dugout area to keep in a state of propriety in anticipation of an inspection or of the colonel passing by, or a general, which hardly ever happened but which our captain was always anticipating.

This first night, after establishing the roster of sentries and picking a work detail for "duckboard duty," I thought I might try to get some sleep. Not so fast! I was almost immediately awakened by a rough, surly voice at the top of the stairs, passing the order to "the corporal" to come up to the surface "as quick as it takes to say these words."

It was Lieutenant so-and-so from Company such-and-such who was making his rounds, and he had just surprised the sentry at the periscope, a young Breton, fast asleep on duty, perhaps dreaming about his peaceful Brittany and his pretty little Breton girlfriend, whose picture he had so proudly shown me as soon as I'd arrived.

The situation was serious. The officer could have easily held me responsible for it. The guilty party was right there, overwhelmed. He could have claimed that, even if he had succumbed to sleeplessness and fatigue, those most guilty were perhaps those who either didn't know how, or else didn't want, to give men like him sufficient time off for sleep. But the poor boy didn't think to claim extenuating circumstances. He might have made things even worse.

Timidly I invoked his young age, his fatigue, his status as an orphan, and finally that he was at this post more as an orderly than as a sentry. But the officer cut short my pleading. "We'll see about that," he said dryly as he left.

This was not a minor infraction, as the next day the military hierarchy got word of the call for punishment brought by this officer.

What! A front-line sentry who couldn't resist sleepiness? What exemplary punishment were they going to inflict on him? Prison? But all the sentries were likely to fall asleep in order to get out of the trenches to where there was shelter from shells, poison gas, lice, cold, rain—no matter how dark and gloomy the prison cell.

The only suitable punishment was death. Nevertheless he was not stood up and shot. They were not so ferocious at this point. Or rather they wanted his death to fit into their plans.

Getting ready to launch a poison-gas attack, for which we had recently dug some earthworks, they set up in the regiment a "free" section, charged with going out and exploring the German lines right after the emission.

Would this gas strangle the Boches halfway, or three-quarters, or all the way? Or would it just make them sneeze? That's what we needed to know. A dangerous curiosity, because we couldn't expect much of a welcome. And we could be asphyxiated by our own gas, in spite of the special gas masks they gave us (of always-dubious effectiveness).

These men were to be sacrificed, in a sense. Those being punished for some grave infraction of discipline were chosen automatically. There were also some volunteers, lured by the promise of home leave, or a Croix de Guerre, or stripes on their sleeves.

Maurice Yver went to bolster the number of these volunteers, and left the squad for the moment to go off for training in this famous "free section" near the colonel's command post.

He was also favored with two weeks of prison, for the principle of it, the rest being no more than a means of rehabilitation.

The next day, at midnight, our squad headed out to occupy an outpost which was different from the one where we had been the night before. At daybreak the sentry who was watching the periscope, which was hidden behind a high clump of grass, signaled me frantically to come up. I looked in the mirror and was stupefied to see a German's head reflected in it—a neck like a bull's, a big square head, a thick red mop of hair, a bestial look—all enough to give you nightmares.

This apparition was coming out of the earth, barely four or five meters from us, into our own barbed wire which surrounded our outpost, without the slightest shovelful of disturbed earth to indicate that there was any sort of trench or excavation around him.

Evidently this was not a mirage; the Germans must have dug a subterranean passage, carrying back to the rear the dirt they removed.

The sentry took a grenade and was about to toss it at this intruder, looking at me for approval.

I held his arm. I will always be faithful to my principles as a socialist, a humanitarian, even a true Christian, even if they cost me my life, of not firing on someone unless in legitimate self-defense. And was it in our interest to break the neighborly relations which existed between our two adjoining outposts?

"If this *lascar* is poking his head up only out of curiosity," I said to my comrades in a low voice, "that's all the same to us. If he is coming to check out our position in order to send over a couple of grenades, we'll open our eyes so that he doesn't show us his big square head again, or we'll make it round for him."

The following night passed without incident, but it was a very black night. The wind rattled the barbed wire and the rats danced a wild farandole out there. The daylight apparition of the big square head, the discovery of the underground passage emerging so close to us, all this impressed my little rookies, and on several occasions they started to toss grenades and take potshots; their imaginations made them see big square heads on all sides.

Each time I had to call a cease-fire. It risked raising a general alarm in the whole sector.

On July 26 at 11 p.m., we were relieved, and seven kilometers to the rear we took possession of some barracks set up in a pinewoods clearing. This was "Camp A."

The landscape had nothing to commend it, right in the midst of the "lousy Champagne": some scraggy pines, bare clearings, ravines and valleys with no streams or meadows; in normal times only a few misanthropic crows and solitary rats inhabited these places, as sad as the confines of the desert.

These barracks enclosed two big camp beds, one superimposed above the other. The first who entered took, by right, the ground level, and I, being among the latecomers, had to install myself on the top story, or rather the top shelf.

To get up there required a vigorous effort of the forearms. The young rookies scrambled up like cats; as for me, I could haul myself up only with the help of an obliging neighbor.

Apart from that, and the freezing-cold nights and broiling-hot days, it could have been worse.

A few hundred meters away, at the bottom of a ravine, were the ruins of the "Maison Forestière" [Forester's Cabin] made famous by the fighting around it during the 1915 offensive.

After the war, the forester who occupied it could also take on the additional job of cemetery keeper, to take care of the grave sites which spread like vineyards along the slopes of the ravine.

The whole "lousy Champagne" isn't worth one drop of the precious blood which was spilled to conquer this bit of desert.

At the bottom of this ravine I saw, under a sort of hangar covered with foliage, a row of half-hogsheads, each with a big, wooden spigot.

Was this a wine merchant boldly setting up shop, within range of shellfire? No, this was a watering post, and these kegs were more often empty than full.

They didn't give out water to just any passerby. Only a regular work detail, with a non-com bearing a written order, could come and partake of it.

Although you could quench your thirst there, you couldn't get water to clean the mud and the lice out of your clothes. For that you had to bribe the Territorial on guard duty in front of the barrels, or distract him, which could be done only at night, if at all.

Well, you didn't need a hundred-franc note, or even a tenner, to purchase the Territorial's compliance. For me, all that was needed was a three-sou cigar to get him to turn his back while I filled a canvas bucket, which was all I needed to do my laundry.

In this camp there was no way to get anything to eat. The food cooperatives were only in the planning stage, and the truck gardeners didn't risk coming up this close to the front lines.

A jug of coffee, a jug of wine for a drink, the meager company mess for food, that was all. We were in the same state as an army under siege, except for Messieurs les officiers who, through their rationers, lacked neither the necessities nor the luxuries.

Certain desert animals have the gift of finding water, I don't know how many leagues away. Similarly, the poilu could sniff out pinard at a great distance. From early on they could discern the wine of the merchants of Suippes, Somme-Suippes, and other places.

Right away you'd see poilus heading out, with a dozen jerricans suspended from their shoulders, in search of the precious liquid. But alas, at every turn of the pathway or at each crossroads the vigilant policemen—real head-knockers—would pitilessly send them back, after having carefully taken down their names and serial numbers.

And each day, at roll call, there'd be a torrent of prison days raining down on those who were naïve enough to think that, fighting for the liberty of peoples, they could have the liberty to go buy a jerrican of wine or a piece of cheese.

A corporal from my company, having decided to go to Somme-Suippes, thought himself clever enough to make up a false authorization which he signed, by his own hand, with the name of the company commandant. But the gendarmes who stopped him got suspicious and sent this permission slip to the division, which sent it to the colonel, and finally to the captain, and the trick was discovered.

This corporal was in a real mess. No one talked of anything less than a court-martial, breaking in rank, forced labor. I don't know how he pulled himself out of it.

But this zeal in carrying out such a rigorous and absurd duty irritated the poilus, who went out in groups and administered some hard knocks to the gendarmes with stout clubs.

But these reprisals went too far. One day they found two gendarmes swinging from the branches of a pine tree, with their tongues hanging out. From this moment, the poilus could go get food in the neighborhood without worrying about a thing.

Far up the chain of command, they were moved by this incident. At roll call, for three days straight, they read and reread a note from the *général-en-chef* praising the tough and thankless job that the brave gendarmes carry out, earning the respect of all.

The officers couldn't repress the guffaws and sarcastic comments which welcomed this reading. "If they find their jobs too tough and thankless," said a voice, "then they should come up to an outpost one time."

It's too bad that the generals didn't attend, incognito, the readings of their notes to the troops. They would soon be edified about the judgment brought upon them and their flowery words by the soldiers in their good common sense.

We spent only four days at Camp A. The last day a couple of shells landed two or three hundred meters away. It's clear that the Germans weren't just trying to bust up a few pine trees; they knew about the camp, and it was just a miscalculation in their aim which kept us from having some casualties.

On July 30, after the evening meal and in a suffocating heat, we went up to the front line as reserves, near the tragically famous "Trou Bricot."[8]

There was no shortage of shelters. In fact, there were too many to choose from. Before our 1915 offensive, the Germans had installed their reserves there, and you could still see the emplacement of a monumental water pump protected by a reinforced concrete shelter.

We saw near our shelter a mine crater where a battalion could have been hidden.

There had been quite a struggle for control of this crater. Debris of all kinds, grenades, barbed wire, broken weapons, all attested to it. But each of us passed by indifferently. It was only an insignificant episode, a tiny detail in the great drama.

These places in particular were infested with rats, who came, according to their habits, to rob our haversacks, and at nighttime to drag their muzzles, their paws, and their tails across our sleeping faces.

You can imagine the disgust which these detestable rodents inspired in us when we learned that they lived in a nearby cemetery for German soldiers.

Each grave site was honeycombed with their burrows, and the sickening odor which escaped from this cemetery left no doubt that these rats were devouring the cadavers, once the contents of our haversacks and the various castoffs of a troop stationed nearby ceased to be enough for their nourishment.

By day, they dwelt among the dead, and by night, among us—the living. What charming neighbors!

Day and night, teams of men took turns going up to the front line, putting themselves in the hands of the engineers for mine-tunneling duty.

Others more qualified than I will someday tell the story about these mines, with their damp, narrow, gloomy subterranean communication trenches. Perhaps they will calculate what amount of work they involved, how much effort, how much fatigue, suffering, and sleeplessness.

Will they be able to add up the staggering bill? The Canal des Deux-Mers[9] probably will have cost significantly fewer swings of a pickax.

When it was my turn, I went up with my squad to this project worthy of a team of convicts. Our task consisted of transporting heavy loads of construction material—planks, beams, crates of powder—up to the mine entrances, then working right behind the miners, filling up sacks with stones which they dug out and dragging them back to a landing from where a wagon pulled by a winch lifted them up and away from the mine entrance, where others disposed of the contents by spreading them out at nighttime, outside the trenches.

There were stretches of tunnel where you couldn't pass through without bending over and walking on your knees. Dripping with sweat, worn out, the men passed the sacks from one to another, which sometimes took twenty minutes to reach the mouth, because some of the galleries were several hundred meters long.

One night, with my squad, I found myself about fifty meters underground when, relayed from mouth to mouth, the terrible cry of "Gas alert!" reached us. The result was a headlong flight to the mine's entrance, but in the haste and confusion the few candles which lit our way were blown out or knocked over, and I found myself alone, with two or three laggards, in the deep gloom, lost in the labyrinth of galleries.

If there really had been a gas attack, we could have made our acts of contrition; this mine would be our tomb, the gas would certainly sweep right through it.

Luckily this was only a false alarm, passed along in the sector as an exercise and an experiment, and soon some engineers came and found us. But almost all of the soldiers from my squad had profited from this incident by escaping all the way to the Trou Bricot. As a result, I couldn't finish the work that had been assigned to me. The pitiless officer of engineers made his report, and if I didn't lose my corporal's stripes it was, so Lieutenant Breton commanding the 15th Company told me, because of my brilliant conduct on Cote 304. I have already recounted my exploits there, which are far from worthy of being passed along to posterity.

On August 4, at 8 in the evening, the 15th Company went up to the front line. It was almost with pleasure that we returned to the outposts; this delivered us from work in the mines, and from the company of the cadaver-eating rats.

On August 6, in the evening, my squad occupied an outpost for the second time. A total calm reigned over the Champagne front, in harmony with the serenity, the sweet warmth of this summer evening. Half of the squad stood watch at the loopholes, while the other half dozed on the firing steps.

To struggle with sleepiness, I did the hundred paces from the outpost to the front line, recalling that August 6 was the date of the local festival in my village. I conjured up the memory of the crowd pouring in from nearby villages, the dancing beneath the plane trees, the illuminated booths, the happy young people. All this was the image of peace; now, back there in the village, there was no festival, no dancing. Silence, sadness, mourning, and anguish had replaced joyfulness.

I was brusquely pulled out of my reveries by frantic cries, which seemed to come from the neighboring outpost to our right: "To arms! To arms!"

Immediately some grenades burst, red flares lit up the sky, and in less than five minutes cannon, trench mortars, bomb throwers, machine guns, everything that was in the trenches was spitting fire, lead, iron; death was unleashed, in a fury.

Once the first few minutes of stupor had passed, my little rookies got control of themselves and, like madmen, threw their grenades in all directions and fired all their cartridges.

So what had happened?

We didn't find out until two days later, by reading the communiqué in the newspapers: The Germans had tried, by surprise attack, to seize some of our outposts and penetrate into our lines, in the sector of Tahure and Cote 193, without great success.

But at that moment, isolated in the night in the middle of this raging storm, which reminded me of the bad days of Lorette and Verdun, and in the uncertainty of what was going on, we weren't without worries. Profiting from a relative moment of calm, two courageous Parisians volunteered to go to the section chief's dugout and the reserve squad's post; after a few minutes they came back, terrified: "We're lost," they cried. "The Boches are in our front line."

"Shit," I said, "they're going to gobble us up right away. But did you see them, or hear them?"

"No, but in the emplacements of the support squad there was nobody, and everything was dumped in the middle of the boyau—dishes, pots and pans, jerricans. Who else would have tossed all that onto the ground, other than Boches passing through there? They probably took all of our guys prisoner."

Indeed, these weren't reassuring signs. In case of attack the outposts were supposed to fall back, so we abandoned our post, moving with infinite precaution, grenade or loaded rifle in hand. But here, at a turn in the boyau, by the sudden light of a flare, we saw, sticking up above the height of the boyau, glinting bayonets, and right at the angle appeared a hand brandishing a revolver.

There we go, we thought in anguish, we've fallen in among the Boches just when we're trying to get away from them. With a strangled voice I instinctively let out the cry *Qui vive?* [Who goes there?] But, surprise, at the same time, in a voice no less strangled with fear than mine was, the same cry burst forth, in the purest Languedoc accent: "Qui vive?"

Well, what do you know? It was the voice of the pastry chef from Narbonne, our adjutant Toulzan, at the head of two reserve squads.

Having sought refuge in a dugout more solid than their own, at the support trench line, and worrying about our fate, they came to see what had happened to us, fearing to find the Kaiser's minions in our place.

As for the trashing of our cookware, the culprit was simply a mortar round landing in close proximity.

The rest of that night was agitated by bombardments and fusillades. We were in a constant state of alert, but in our case we never saw the silhouette of an enemy.

Two days later, our 6th Squad went to occupy outpost number 10. This was nothing more than a barricade in a former communication trench linking German lines. It was there that the final assault wave of the first great Champagne offensive had ended, after the flux and reflux of the last attacks and counterattacks.

Six meters from our barricade, the Germans had established their own. A few strands of barbed wire thrown in between, which one could have crossed in four bounds, were all that separated the two peoples, the two races, from exterminating each other.

There was even a covered passageway which reached as far as a meter from the German sandbags. From there, you could have stuck out your arms and shaken hands.

On learning that they were sentenced to spend twenty-four hours in an outpost like this, rear-echelon slackers or good bourgeoisie, no matter how patriotic, would have felt their hair stand on end, and wouldn't have wasted any time making up a last will and testament before entering into this death trap.

But imagine their astonishment, their stupefaction, to see the calm and tranquility which reigned in this area. Some smoked, others read, some wrote, a few squabbled, without lowering their voices one note.

And if these patriots, these slackers, had lent an ear, they would have heard the Germans coughing, spitting, talking, singing, etc., with the same lack of ceremony.

Their stupefaction would have changed to bewilderment if they had seen the French and German sentries seated tranquilly on their parapets, smoking pipes and exchanging bits of conversation from time to time, like good neighbors taking some fresh air at their doorsteps.

From relief to relief, we passed along the habits and customs of these outposts. The Germans did the same. Even if the whole Champagne burst into flames, not a single grenade would fall in this privileged corner.

During the day I had come to reconnoiter the somewhat tangled road from this outpost, which was stuck at least four hundred meters away from the place where the rest of the section was located.

Our section chief found himself there in conversation with a "Fritz" who spoke fairly good French. He was saying that they were mostly Poles in his regiment. They wouldn't surrender, because the Germans would take it out on their families and their property. But this Pole suddenly indicated that someone was coming along the boyau, and he dropped down, calling out *Vive la Pologne! Vive la France!*

Sometimes there were exchanges of gifts, like packets of tobacco from the Régie Française [French government tobacco monopoly] which went to fill the big German pipes, or delicious German cigarettes which came over to the French side.

We also exchanged lighters, buttons, newspapers, bread.

Here was a crazy business of commerce and intelligence with the enemy, which would have stirred up the indignation of the patriots and superpatriots, from the Royalist Daudet to Clemenceau, the gunman of Narbonne, by way of the chameleon Hervé.[10]

It's a matter of taste. Some will consider this sublime, others will call it criminal. It depends on whether you place the ideal of Humanity above or below the ideal of Patriotism.

You can be sure that this gesture of fraternity occurred in more than one place, in fact wherever the proximity of outposts allowed it. And our big bosses, our leaders, had no illusions about it. If the trenches had been closer together, if they hadn't been separated by prickly barbed wire, hands would have reached out everywhere, proof among a thousand that this horrible war had been unleashed counter to the consent of the peoples.

By whose pen will the next generation, struck with stupor, disconcerted by this universal sanguinary madness, learn about these acts of fraternity, which were like a protest, a revolt against the mortal fate which set, face to face, men who had no reason to hate each other?

For the honor of our generation, of civilization, of humanity, may those who follow us have the truth revealed to them. For some it will be a comfort, for others an example, a lesson, a warning about the danger of launching a new war.

That same day, from the outpost of a neighboring company, a sergeant eager for promotion saw what was happening at outpost number 10. He wanted to throw a grenade at the German sentry who, without mistrust, stuck his head above the parapet.

This sergeant was prevented by the outpost's occupants. Furious, he went off and denounced these acts to the commandant, who notified Lieutenant Breton, who was in charge of our company. He in turn called for our section chief, the ex-pastry-chef Toulzan.

"It appears that your section," he told him, "is up to some dirty business. They're chatting it up with the Boches, is that true?"

Our adjutant, knowing that at the very least his stripe was at risk, swore that nothing abnormal was going on. But he warned me to keep my guard up for the next twenty-four hours that I was occupying the outpost, because it was probable that we would be closely watched by the big chiefs, who would be ferocious, pitiless, if they found us in flagrante delicto in conversation with the enemy.

It's certain that a clever command could have profited from this opportunity to gain specific intelligence about the sector: the likelihood of poison-gas attacks, the plans for blowing up mines, or attacks, or various positions. All that would be needed would be a few liters of pinard or a few quarts of hooch, which the Germans lacked, to loosen their tongues.

But no one would have dared suggest this to our bosses. This would have been admitting the start of fraternization with the enemy. A firing squad could well have been the response to such a suggestion.

It's as if, in the time of the Inquisition, a poor fellow had confessed that he had just had a conversation with Satan.

Given the incidents of the day, it wasn't without some apprehension that I took charge of this outpost, and I recommended clearly to the sentries that they not show themselves, that they not reply to calls or conversations made by our neighbors; they stay silent and vigilant. At the same time, I asked little Marcel, a Parisian as wily as a ferret, to keep a lookout to the rear, in case we ourselves were being watched.

I was comforted by the presence of Peyriac's Paul Alpech, who as a rationer was exempt from guard duty but who, considering the circumstances, told me that he would keep watch all night long and make sure that my recommendations were followed.

An hour went by, and the summer night covered the Champagne with a darkness which heightened the clarity of the legion of stars filling the sky with their tiny, silvery pinpoints. My spirits wandered off, far from the melancholy present; I contemplated this mysterious spectacle, and I asked myself, how many stars are there? A billion? Ten billion? Even without counting those which you can't see, and those you can only see a hint of.

And to think that, put together, all those numberless points of light give off less warmth and light than one ray of sunshine. Even the moon made them look pale and outshone almost all of them.

And I told myself than all the hundreds and thousands of acts of war, of honor, of glory which people will celebrate in the history of this monstrous war won't have the same value as one single discovery useful to the good of humanity, or a single invention by one savant.

And I had these dreams as I moved along from one group of sentries to another, stationed at every ten paces along the boyau. Not a rifle shot disturbed the silence. In the distance you could scarcely hear the rumble of vehicles on the roads, or the huffing and puffing of the little putt-putt trains, when all of a sudden young Marcel, who was watching the "French" side, arrived all out of breath and warned me that an officer, Sublieutenant Lorius, armed with a revolver, had posted himself forty meters away.

The whole squad was alerted; the four sentries who were at the end of the boyau, facing the German outpost, turned a deaf ear to the persistent whistles which a "Fritz," no doubt annoyed, made to call them. Not receiving any response, he sat on the parapet with a comrade and sent pipe smoke wafting toward us, doubtless peeved at our sulky silence.

Eight or ten paces away from the group at the barricade, young P. . . . was on watch, a Gascon who was always boasting about how much more courageous he was than the others.

As I passed near him he cried out, "Corporal, the Boches, the Boches! They're right there, in the wire!" At the same time he threw a grenade which I heard land with the same dull thud that a stone makes when it hits someone's shoulder or back. But either because of the clumsiness of the thrower or the bad quality of the grenade, there was no explosion.

The Gascon had, I believe, in his confusion forgotten to arm the grenade by striking it on his knee or another hard part of his body. He was already grabbing for a second one, but I stopped his arm and said to him, believing that he hadn't seen anything at all, "But wait! Where are they, the Boches?" Climbing up onto the firing step, I looked across the parapet and was quite astounded to see a human form, tangled up in the mass of barbed wire, apparently crawling toward our position.

To tell the truth, this nocturnal rambler could have found a more comfortable spot for his little walkabout. To come right up under the noses of the French and German sentries who could have easily seen him, he had to be either crazy or drunk. "Qui vive?" I said in a half-whisper. There was no response, but the intruder still approached, vigorously shaking the wire; now he was only three paces from us.

"Qui vive?" I said again, now really alarmed, as I raised my rifle to my cheek and the sentry brandished a grenade. But this time an angry voice came back: "Leave me alone. Don't worry about me."

It was the voice of Sublieutenant Lorius, of our company. A minute later he jumped into the trench, revolver in hand. His breath stunk of hooch, and he was in a high state of excitement.

"Who threw the grenade in my face?" he said.

"The sentry did his duty," I replied.

"Yeah, it's true, you're right," he agreed between hiccups, "but you're lucky I didn't catch you talking with the Boches. I was ready to kill you on the spot."

"Well, lieutenant, you can see for yourself that there's nothing wrong, and that we're keeping good watch at outpost number 10."

But the lieutenant worked himself up into a rage once again. "I have to kill somebody tonight. I'm going to kill a German sentry. Show me where they are."

The little Gascon had the clever idea to point to a mound of earth sticking up opposite the German outpost, saying: "They're over there."

The officer squinted uselessly into the darkness. Holstering his revolver, he stalked off, muttering inarticulate and incoherent phrases and threats.

The rest of the night passed by for us in painful recollection of this incident, which could have had a much more tragic outcome.

As daybreak approached, the Germans called out to us. There were three of them, including a very young fellow, with cheeks as rosy as a Fräulein, and they asked us if we had any coffee to drink. They told us that, the day before, our artillery had killed two of their comrades. But I hastened to bring this conversation to an end. We told them about last evening's incident, and said that they should keep from showing themselves, as we were being so closely watched ourselves.

The Germans, deeply moved, thanked us profusely before disappearing behind their sandbags. One of them clasped one hand in the other and cried out: "Frenchmen, Germans, soldiers, all comrades. Officers . . ."—and here he raised a clenched fist—"No!"

Oh, how right he was, this German. It's true that you shouldn't generalize. But how many of our officers were more distantly separated, more morally estranged from us soldiers than were the poor German devils, who were being led to the same slaughterhouse despite themselves.

To the corporal who came to take my place, I recommended that he be careful. But he wasn't careful enough, because the next day he was broken in rank, an indulgence they granted from the weakness of their case against him.

He had committed the crime of not firing on the German sentries who showed themselves for an instant.

The day after, with my squad, I went up to occupy outpost number 9.

Three sentries stood guard at the end of a sap which then wandered off toward enemy lines. What was the utility of these three sentries, stuck way out in this place where you couldn't see ten paces in front of you?

Nobody seemed to know. A little farther along in the sap the Germans had also posted a couple of sentries. They were too far apart to carry on a conversation, but not too far apart to observe each other through the loopholes, which were simply gaps in the parapet sandbags. Little by little both sides became more confident in the reciprocal interest of not firing upon each other, and they ended up showing themselves without challenge, exchanging a wave of camaraderie, a smile, a friendly look.

Among those who haven't suffered through the crisis of the trenches, many won't be able to understand this tacit entente, this fraternity of adversaries whom they thought were always on the alert, fingers on the triggers. But they should think seriously about the fate of men whom a long, common suffering of dangers has brought together, by the strength of an irresistible instinct of human nature.

Isn't it true that, among people facing death on a ship battered by storms and in danger of sinking under the waves, all rancors and hatreds seem to abate and disappear?

Where are we, on the road of human progress, that we have to plead extenuating circumstances for such a natural thing?

But we've gotten far from outpost number nine-and-a-half, as this emplacement of three sentries was designated on the sector map.

During the next day, around eight in the morning, the dreadful and dreaded Lieutenant Grulois—Gueule de Bois ["wooden mug," slang for hangover]— came to call on us. It was he who had just surprised my successor at outpost number 10 and had him punished for the aforesaid reason.

He cast a suspicious look at us, and without a word he headed toward the group of three sentinels.

He started coughing loudly, speaking at high volume, and chuckling, in order to incite the German sentries to show themselves. In fact, one of them was intrigued enough to stick up his head. Then the French officer took a sentry's rifle and, aiming slowly, carefully, and in a most cowardly way, sent a bullet right through his head.

As a result, the Germans blasted away at us all day long with rifle shots which tore our sandbags to shreds and made all surveillance impossible. We were quite lucky that none of our sentries had his head blown off.

And to think that this lieutenant was the most decorated officer of the regiment!

"Our sentries aren't doing their duty," he said to me severely. He no doubt was convinced that he had just carried out a most noble act.

Should one complain about, or blame, or excuse, or curse those whom nature has granted such a perverse and unfeeling mentality!

On August 12 our section went into reserve, eighty meters back from the front line, in a support trench for a week.

Our main daytime task consisted of making *hérissons* [hedgehogs] which, come nightfall, had to be thrown out beyond the outposts.

For the uninitiated, I'll explain that hérissons were prickly bundles of barbed wire wrapped around four iron ingots bound together in the middle.

In making these hérissons you risked tearing your sleeves, your trousers, or your skin, and in pushing or tossing them around the outposts you risked catching a bullet on the fly, or being caught by a grenade.

I'll never forget how my little rookies, far from balking at this night work, didn't manifest the slightest fear, and insisted that I stay down in the boyau, not wanting me to expose myself without absolute need. "You're the father of a family," they said to me, "stay down, we'll do just as fine without you."

One night we got an alert. Men from the so-called free sections, operating in no-man's-land, came back through the squads, having been summoned to the colonel's command post. Orderlies and messengers rushed in every direction, bearing orders.

What was going on?

The wind was in our favor. They were going to launch against the Boches the famous poison gas, for which we had been preparing for so long.

Nobody within my hearing was particularly happy about this operation. There was going to be a big bombardment, on both sides, and from what the patrols told us we might have to occupy certain enemy positions.

While waiting, our section was going to occupy a jumping-off point in a part of the trench with no shelter at all in which to protect ourselves from the likely bombardment.

Soon we learned that the time was set for midnight, the hour of crime. But you could say that the wind was guilty of collusion with the enemy: at ten minutes to midnight, the wind was blowing too hard.

They postponed the business to two in the morning. But by that time the wind had stopped blowing altogether, to the point where it wouldn't have moved a candle's flame.

The order came down to go back to our dugouts. A reprieve of 24 hours was granted to the Kaiser's subjects who were swarming throughout Champagne.

Then the next night a strong mistral was blowing. They had to postpone the emission once more. But the Boches were happy to wait for the night of August 15–16 for a wind which was neither too strong nor too weak. Without the slightest respect for the holiness of the day,[11] all the dispositions were made ready for eleven o'clock that evening.

But here we are at ten-thirty, when the wind suddenly turned from south to north. It would have been suicide for us to launch a gas attack.

If Boreas, the god of the winds, hadn't been high up on Olympus, beyond the reach of the military authorities, he would have been indicted for thereby betraying the cause of righteousness and civilization.

Headquarters was furious at these setbacks—or, rather, blowbacks. In contrast, the poilus, who had nothing to gain by this emission but the risk of a violent bombardment, were delighted that the sector stayed calm and peaceful.

Finally, during the night of August 19–20, our company went for a week of rest at Camp I, two kilometers in front of Somme-Suippes.

Camp I was made up of barracks which contained, as furniture, a kind of floor to lie down on; that was all. Primitive man at least had tree trunks or big boulders to sit down on; for eating, they had a hearth; for sleeping they had dry leaves and some moss to lie on. This was rough comfort, to be sure, but we would have been very happy with it in our relative nakedness.

Furthermore we were all completely infested with ticks. So it was with pleasure that we went to Somme-Suippes to take showers in a model bathing facility paid for by Her Majesty the Empress of All the Russias, if you please!

We had never been showered and disinfected like we were in this imperial installation. While we were in the showers, our effects passed through a superheated brazier, where ticks of every generation, from those who had not yet burst from their eggs to the old, black, hairy ones, were smothered without reprieve.

This was a memorable day. After many months this was the first time we didn't feel the slightest itchiness.

It was enough to make us call out, *Vive la Czarina!* Despite my revulsion for tyrants, thanks to her we were going to spend a couple of restful nights.

One night out of two the companies went up to work in the trenches, sometimes at the front lines, from which we were a dozen kilometers away. The next day, after having made the twenty-four-kilometer round-trip, and having done seven or eight hours of work, the men came back exhausted. "What a galley slave's life," they said. "Boy, if we ever get through this . . . ," proclaimed others. Some were in such despair that they didn't even have the strength to complain.

I was lucky to get out of this forced labor, since I found myself on assignment every time my turn came up.

One afternoon we had a military parade. It was the occasion for awarding Croix de Guerre to those who had won them, more or less deservingly, at Cote 304. Our company had the honor of handing out the "honors." Our capitaine-adjutant-major, our old friend the Kronprinz, had the duty of pinning them on the chests of all these worthy soldiers, in the name of the Fatherland, of the President of the Republic, of the Generalissimo, etc.

The Kronprinz seemed quite moved, weighted down by such a great honor. He had the company form up in a square and ordered a musical salute. But we had present only one bugler, who had a cracked instrument, and a drum with a skin so worn that it sounded like an old cauldron.

The salute was sounded all the same, amid outbursts of laughter which this cacophony provoked. The rite was carried out, and if the ceremony lost some of its grandeur, that's too bad.

The Kronprinz turned a severe look upon us, and began the reading of the exploits accomplished by each awardee. As he fastened the Croix de Guerre onto the recipient's greatcoat and gave him the traditional accolade, the "kiss of the fatherland," the bursts of laughter came forth once again. Really, these poilus had no respect for anything, but this time there was good reason.

You would have thought that this was the first time he had ever embraced a fellow man. Apart from his obvious repugnance at placing his lips on the leathery skin of the poilus, he was so nearsighted that the visor of his cap kept him from approaching the patient's face, and his big spectacles got hooked on the awardee's nose and fell to the ground, or his own nose, of a prodigious prominence, got tangled in the poilu's mustache or beard or collided with his helmet.

The officers themselves couldn't keep from smiling; it was as much a vaudeville show as it was a solemn ceremony.

The captain, alone, did not smile, and fled the scene as soon as he could, haughty and stiff.

One night, all the circumstances appearing favorable for the launch of a gas attack, we were put on alert. But at the last minute, as a result of either the force or the direction of the wind becoming doubtful, the gas wasn't launched in certain places, while in others it was. The result was mediocre. Among the engineer troops who handled the equipment, several succumbed.

On the Boche side, some of our patrols reported that trenches were filled with dying men who were yielding up their souls to God, but little Yver, who was part of the 296th regiment's reconnaissance, swore to me that he and his comrades had stayed concealed between the lines and then made their way back after having made up and memorized a phony report crafted by the head of the reconnaissance team. That made our big bosses happy, satisfied by the effectiveness of the gas, as well as the scouts, who all came back at such little risk.

Our Colonel Robert showed his skepticism, however; he sent the "volunteers" back to their companies without giving them Croix de Guerre or stripes or home leaves.

The gas containers which were not emptied that night were buried deep in the ground, because it appeared that after a certain time they would lose their toxicity. We would have to find stronger insecticides to chase away the Boches who infested our soil!

Suddenly the rumor spread that our division would be relieved. On August 28 the relief of front-line units began.

While the replacement troops were passing by, heading for the trenches, a violent storm broke out, followed by a deluge of biblical proportions.

How pitiable were these men, bent double under this onslaught of rainfall which further drenched their sweat-soaked bodies!

We urgently awaited our own relief. Would it take place in similar weather? We were no doubt eagerly awaited in the Somme, where the battle was raging.

But no, it was a month and a half before we got there. For now we would have field exercises and big training maneuvers for the open-field warfare which our high command, as blind as ever, believed to be imminent.

To shelter the troops from the storm in the many camps which were lined up just to the rear of the trenches—there was plenty of room—would have been an act of humanity, of common sense, of simple duty on the part of the bosses. It would involve just a little bit of consideration for the health, for the physical suffering of their troops.

But in wartime, rain doesn't matter. Even if hailstones as big as your fist had been falling, the relief would have kept going all the same. Too bad if those who got through it would later suffer from aches and pains, rheumatism, sore backs—it was for the Patrie!

On August 29, in the course of the morning, our battalion left Camp I. We were leaving Champagne, a relatively quiet and restful sector, to go to a place of horror, to know once again the bad old days of Vermelles, Lorette, Verdun.

We left joylessly, but after having marched four kilometers we had the pleasant surprise of finding a truck convoy which carried us to the village of Lettré.

This village had 32 inhabitants in peacetime and 28 when we arrived. You can imagine how comfortably our battalion would be quartered in such a small place.

They told us that we would be leaving soon, but while we were waiting, no doubt so we wouldn't get bored, our daily exercises were undertaken right away.

Our captain being away on leave, it was Lieutenant Gueule de Bois who took command of the 15th Company. It would take too long to recount all the injustices, petty crimes, inspections, and punishments which he afflicted upon the company.

This character would have been the ideal commander for a chain gang of convicts.

No one dared to venture more than fifty meters from the encampment, for fear of missing an assembly, an unscheduled roll call. No one dared to laugh, to speak freely, to make the slightest noise, for fear of attracting his Nero-like gaze.

The Somme Offensive: In the Blood-Soaked Mud: August 29–November 1, 1916

No one dared to rest, or even to lie down, outside of the appointed hours, for fear of being observed, because this odious character was always worming his way into the midst of groups, mixing in quietly, suspiciously looking to pick up a few shameful statements or opinions.

The daily reading-out of orders took at least a full hour. He would pick three or four squads at random for roll call, just to make sure nobody was absent.

If he heard someone whispering, he'd form the company into a square and make the guilty party stand in the middle and say out loud what he had whispered. If the blabbermouth stayed silent, then it would be work details and punishments for all of us.

There was always something, and usually several things, to present: arms, tools, or other items, all of course perfectly clean and in good shape; he checked each one personally.

Not far from Lettré there were several good-sized villages, but you had to have a damn good reason to get authorization to go to any of them.

One evening, nonetheless, I took a jaunt to Bussy. The category of rear-echelon slackers on duty there seemed to me to be the only thing worth commenting on.

They were the Russian interpreters, that is to say Frenchmen who had the unhoped-for good luck of speaking Russian and were promoted to officer's rank in a day's time. They waited in this village for the Russian troops arriving in France to ask for their services.

On September 1 the 37mm cannon team was formed, and I was assigned to the 4th Machine-Gun Company.

It was with regret that I had to quit my little *bleus* [rookies], to whom I'd become quite attached. But I wasn't leaving them altogether, since we'd still be in the same battalion.

On September 4 we left Lettré, without much regret, and after a rather hard march we came to billets at Trouan-le-Grand, which the width of a river separated from Trouan-le-Petit; we were near the Camp de Mailly, where the Russian troops were stationed at this time.

At Trouan you could see the traces of a combat which had taken place, the inhabitants told us, on September 9, 1914.

Starting the next day, without even having the customary day for getting settled in our new billets, the training began, or rather continued. But what a change for me! I could scarcely believe it. No more roll calls and parades; the hated field exercises were nothing more than distractions, a few brief series of maneuvers with our cannon, a few breaks for talks about theory, and that was it. We quickly learned that it was not much more than strolls through the countryside and nice siestas in the shade of the bushes.

I have to say that our commanding officer was a far cry from Gueule de Bois. He treated us like comrades, and he spared us plenty of work details, dangers, and stretches of boredom. He had only one fault. (Who doesn't have one?)

Sometimes too strong a whiff of wine or booze reached his nostrils, and when that happened, watch out! You had to be careful not to cross him or contradict him. He was like a champagne bottle with the cork three-quarters of the way out, which something makes explode and all the bottle's contents burst out.

But if he lashed out and injured someone with too sharp a reproach, he was the first to apologize and admit his mistake.

This officer was Sublieutenant Lorius, the same one whom a sentry from my squad almost dispatched with a hand grenade. He never made the slightest reference to that incident, ever again, nor did I. He was a former non-com from an artillery regiment who was enticed into the infantry because of a desire for a gold officer's stripe.

From dawn to dusk, the regiment was subjected by the terrible colonel to an intensive training regime, across the Mailly steppes. Men came back exhausted, saying that they missed the trenches—which is saying a lot!

In the evening we'd hear the songs and the prayers performed in unison by the Russians at the Camp de Mailly. The men would assemble at attention, as if for an inspection. That astonished us. Some of us made our way over to the camp, just to watch this unbelievable spectacle.

On September 14 I had the great joy of obtaining my second home leave, seven months after my first one. In the night of the 16th–17th, having come on foot from the station at Moux,[1] I had the pleasure of seeing my loved ones, once again, and forgetting for a few days, too quickly gone by, the hard reality, the primitive life of the trenches, so far from civilization.

On the morning of the 24th I had to pull myself away from the sweetness of family life, to take the rough road back to the front lines.

I was going to leave on the tram from the village of Trausse, three kilometers away. My wife alone accompanied me; my dear little ones had preferred to kiss me goodbye at the house, which troubled them less there than at the tram station.

From the station I could see, once again, all my relatives busy at work, harvesting a nearby patch of grapevines, and I wondered if next year I could come and be there with them, this frightful war being over, to help my poor father in this rough work.

Here and there amid the vines laden with fruit which the gentle sun was ripening, appeared groups of grape pickers, gloomy and silent. There were only children, women, and old men. When would the joyful harvests return, in which young people contributed their laughter, their games, their songs?

I departed with a heavy heart, pulling myself away from those who, without thinking, without any special interest, without any hypocrisy, love you with all their hearts. I was going back into the realm of the bitterest egoism, to die amid the indifference of all who surround you.

The next day, at dawn, I was at Orléans. A few minutes later I took the train to Champagne. It was so crowded that I had to scramble up to a lookout post, and at five in the evening I got off at the mustering station of Jessains, where they told us that the regiment had left for the Somme; at eight that evening we embarked for the mustering station of Creil. Nobody complained about the length of the journey; it was that much more time to enjoy in liberty and in safety.

Twenty-four hours later I got off in Amiens. Traversing the city, I went to the Saint-Roch station to wait for the departure of a train which was supposed to leave at seven in the morning; it was then nine in the evening.

Several hundred leave takers filled the station and spilled out onto the sidewalks, worn out by the fatigue of a long voyage. I did the same.

What an idea, I thought, to call this station Saint-Roch. He was a saint from where we come from; there were even relics of this great saint in a chapel in a village near Peyriac, the same place [Trausse] from where I embarked on my return trip. It seems that he had protected the village from a number of scourges. I prayed to him to protect me from catching a nasty cold in this chilly autumn evening.

I was stretched out next to some young fellows, Belgians [who had fled their country when it was invaded, now reaching twenty years of age] in the conscript class of 1917, called to the colors at Rennes. They were waiting for the same train as me. Like me, they would no doubt have preferred to be lying in bed somewhere, rather than on the sidewalk. While we weren't enthusiastic about it, we didn't complain, which wouldn't have done any good anyway.

The next morning I got off at the station of Namps, and after covering ten kilometers on foot I finally discovered the regiment in the village of Tilloy-les-Conty.

In view of the part we were to play in the Somme offensive, the regiment was subjected to an intensive training program. There were field exercises in full campaign gear, from morning to evening, signifying a return to open-field warfare, as if they had not yet seen the negative results of this bloody offensive.

On October 6, trucks carried us toward the front, but it was not our turn yet, or maybe we needed a bit more training; they dropped us off at the village of Hamelet.

At the entrance to the village we encountered a column of German prisoners. Some cynics maintained that they were placed there on purpose, to boost our confidence, so that seeing them would encourage us.

Every evening we could witness the tragic show which the front lines of the Battle of the Somme put on for us. The sky was crisscrossed with flashes, illuminated, lit up with meteoric bolts, sudden bursts of light, all accompanied by a deafening, continuous rumbling. We felt like we were watching a gigantic volcano, seeing the sinister reflections of hell itself.

"It's just like Verdun," said the veterans, worried, "but there will also be cold, rain, and mud!" The young ones were terrified before this frightful tableau, just right for inspiring horror of war and filling the soul with terror.

On October 9, after the morning meal, we left Hamelet to the tune of a lively polka played by the regimental band. A funeral march would have been more appropriate.

Our route followed the valley of the Somme, but here and there marshlands had overflowed. Sometimes the road had to climb the steep hillside and then come back down a little farther ahead, resulting in much fatigue from following this roller-coaster course.

At nightfall we arrived at an immense camp, and they piled us into barracks where we went to bed pell-mell on the hard, damp floor.

This was the camp of the "Bonfray Farm." No symmetry, few barracks built yet, but all sorts of shelters in tent cloth, or made from planks, busted-up crates, tree branches and trunks, etc. Some English officers were installed in elegant cabins which spared no comforts.

This camp, where thousands of English recruits learned the noble profession of arms, covered several hundred hectares of terrain. It was a veritable human anthill; on the roads which crisscrossed the camp passed innumerable convoys of automobiles, trucks, heavy caissons, all sorts of vehicles, relief columns, ambulances, etc., day and night.

They had put down railway lines which were hauling heavy shipments of materiel, munitions, foodstuffs, etc. All sorts of goods were warehoused and piled up, everywhere. To see this intense life, pulsating, without a break, made you dizzy. Your eye couldn't see the limits of the camp. Your ear took in and identified the different sounds, the jumble of noises, which mixed with the rolling cannonade in the background.

Near our barracks some monstrous English artillery pieces, on platforms and on rails, fired hundred-kilo shells from time to time onto the Mont Saint-Quentin.

We stayed at the Bonfray Farm until October 19. We made profitable use of this time by once again taking up our training of new methods, irresistible ones this time. Now we would show them—a hundred times over!

Each evening, to bolster our morale which might have been weakened by the lamentable sight of the regiments coming back from the trenches, our regimental band played us the most engaging mazurkas and waltzes, right in our cantonment. This made up for the less harmonious sound of the cannon or, even more disagreeable, of the rain which ended up turning the camp into a muddy marsh, after some particularly heavy downpours.

We listened avidly, shivering, to the tales of suffering endured by those who came from the trenches, and who still had the strength to smile. Seeing that there was no way we could escape from this trial, we were impatient to leave, and nothing was more nerve-racking than the false alarms which often came, putting us on alert.

The top brass couldn't comprehend how free men, who had been free right up to the minute the war began, could submit without the slightest murmur, almost voluntarily, to this sacrifice which they knew to be in vain, useless, with more docility than a troop of slaves in ancient Rome heading to some unexpected slaughter.

And our bosses weren't mistaken. They knew quite well that it wasn't the flame of patriotism which inspired this spirit of sacrifice. It was simply a sense of bravado, to not seem more cowardly than one's neighbor. Then there was the presumptuous faith in one's own star; for others it was the secret and futile ambition for a medal, or a sleeve stripe. Finally, for the great mass, it was the uselessness of protesting against an implacable fate.

The fears of our chiefs, that they would see the soldiers waver, then rise up in revolt in an instinctive burst of energy, like the lowest, stupidest beast facing certain death, were therefore groundless. But living too far away from the soldier, and too high above him, to get to know his state of mind, they covered themselves in ridicule by an odious comedy which would have wounded the common soldier's sense of dignity if he'd known about it.

One morning, here is what they dreamed up. A mendacious note announced that the 296th Regiment would not be going up to the front lines. They would simply busy themselves, at night, getting the sector ready to be occupied by the English, who it seemed weren't especially good at this kind of work.

Happy to get out of it so easily, each of us breathed a sigh of relief. But the next day came act two. We learned that a group of young officers, humiliated by this decision which they considered as lack of confidence in the regiment, addressed a plea to the general, asking for the honor of going into combat alongside two other regiments of the division, the 114th Regiment and the 125th Regiment.

The following day came act three. The general hastened to grant us the favor of going to gather up the laurels of victory. It was our turn. Just like that, we had forced the hand of our bosses, to go slog in the mud and have ourselves cut down by the Boche howitzers and riddled by their machine guns.

On October 18, the bombardment reached a hitherto unseen degree of violence. The order came down, to be ready to leave camp at any moment. A cold shower fell, and we shuddered at the thought of leaving camp in such weather. But it wasn't until the next day that we went up to the front lines, to the place of sacrifice for those who would spill their blood and end their lives so miserably.

On October 19, at 1 in the afternoon, the 296th left the barracks of Boufray [Bonfray] in a driving rainstorm, and went up to occupy the front lines near Combles.[2]

We came upon a half-destroyed village, Maricourt. Only the cellars were occupied, by Territorials who watched us march by with an indifferent look. They had seen plenty pass by, over the past four months.

Farther along, we passed through the village of Hardécourt. Few of us even noticed it, because there was hardly anything left other than a few foundations, here and there, ruins and debris of all kinds, torn up, pulverized, with mud and huge chunks of earth churned up by the whirlwind of projectiles.

A kilometer farther along, the road descended into a ravine, at the bottom of which ran the tracks of a narrow-gauge railway where, by night, not without danger, long lines of freight cars brought up to Combles tons of projectiles which our cannon spat out without taking a break.

Where the road crossed the tracks stood what they called the station of Maurepas, named for the village which extended along the opposite slope of the ravine, but whose inhabitants had nothing to make the citizens of Hardécourt envious; they too wouldn't recognize where their houses had stood.

From that point on, we entered the range of fire of enemy artillery, and Maurepas could have been called "Pas de la Mort" ["Death's Straits," as in Pas-de-Calais; a pun on the name Maurepas, in French].

To get to Combles, we abandoned the road, which was used only at night, and we followed the railroad tracks along the ravine.

This ravine must have been the scene of fierce combats: blasted tree trunks pulled out by their roots, shattered wagons and carts, all sorts of debris, rifles, bayonets, grenades, German shells, scattered around or piled up. We marched past in silence, seemingly indifferent, under ceaseless rain which soaked us through and through but which didn't stop the cannonade. It seemed to grow more violent, the farther along we got.

Finally, at nightfall, the battalion gathered in a bend in the ravine, two kilometers from Combles. They were generous enough to grant us two hours of rest, before we renewed our climb to Calvary.

By seven in the evening, the night was dark, the sky seemed to take pity on us because the rain had stopped. Off we go . . .

My little rookies from the former squad came up to greet me. Maybe this is the last time we'll see each other! The little Breton Maurice Yver, to whom I had lent two francs, pressed a forty-sou piece upon me: "Hey," he said to me, "in case they kill me, we're even. Thanks!"

I couldn't care less about forty sous, just then. I refused; he insisted. Did he have a premonition of his impending death, this poor boy who would soon be blown to bits by a German shell? Maybe he did!

Up to that point we'd had mules to haul our little 37mm field guns, but from now on it was upon our shoulders that we had to carry the cannon and the shells. The piece is broken down into two parts, each of which weighs forty kilos! We take turns carrying them, while others carried the munitions.

The team for our gun, composed of six men, had to follow the 4th Machine-Gun Company.

After a hard march of five hours, in the rain, we understood the effort that would be needed for this new foray into impracticable terrain, in an opaque night.

On either side of the widening valley soon appeared the ruins of Combles: a few carcasses of houses were still standing, but probably not for long, because each day the German shells poured down upon these ruins.

After passing through Combles we left the railway line and, crossing the fields, we met the road from Combles to Morval and Sailly-Saillissel.

This was no more than a road dug up by shellfire and full of mud, but protected by an embankment. At the end of a half-hour, no more embankment, no more trace of road—only the dark and sinister plain. We had to follow pathways which snaked around the shell holes, full of water.

Soon we were at the end of our strength. The two men who carried the dismounted cannon had to be relieved every one or two minutes.

Sometimes one would slip and fall, and couldn't get back up. We had to help him, crushed by the weight of his burden, stuck in the mud.

And to think that if a wind of demonic madness hadn't swept across the minds of the people's leaders, we could, at this very hour, be quietly at home, by the fire, with a warm bed awaiting us. How we would mock the rain, the cold, the wind, the night!

Our good Lieutenant Lorius, who had come up with our field gun, begged us, urged us not to stop, not to lose contact with the machine gunners up ahead, whose last stragglers often disappeared from our view.

Several times, he himself went ahead to ask the officers of the machine-gun company to slow their pace.

Finally, we reached a protected road, or a streambed—we couldn't tell which —full of mud, which we could follow only by moving carefully along its edge. They told us that we'd arrived at the commandant's post, and consequently we'd have to wait there until they determined where on the front line our gun would go.

Against the embankment, between the protruding roots of some shattered tree trunks, the men of the team we had just replaced had dug out two holes to squeeze into, but they weren't big enough to hold all of us.

The lieutenant chose two men to accompany me back to Combles, to find the field kitchens and the supply train, and to come back the next day with food and munitions.

It was 10 at night, almost twelve hours after we had left the camp at Boufray. How many more hours did we have to go? And alone, without guides, wouldn't we get lost? I couldn't count on my two comrades, who didn't seem particularly enterprising and were certainly incapable of doing two hundred meters on good road.

We soon met up with a company in relief, heading to the rear. Thinking that it was headed for Combles, we had the bad idea of following them.

I soon realized, from certain landmarks, that we were on the wrong road. I asked those whom we were following. They were from the 77th Regiment and were headed to the Bois des Trônes, to go into reserve duty. We asked them if they had passed by Combles; they had never been there.

We bade them farewell. Now here we were, sitting pretty in the middle of this lugubrious plain, now deserted all around us!

We resigned ourselves to spending the night right there, for fear of getting even more lost, when all of a sudden a battery of 75's started firing a couple of salvos, right nearby.

I dragged my comrades toward this battery. The guards there could tell us the way to Combles. We came upon a miserable road, snarled with heavy caissons and limbers, some of which we saw were completely stuck, being pulled by double and even triple teams of horses, who struggled and themselves got mired in the mud. Ah, what a shame! War is bad for everyone, beasts and men alike.

At one in the morning we arrived at Combles. The town, bombarded around the clock, looked deserted. Only an occasional horse artillery team galloped through, disturbing the fearful silence which weighed down on the ruins.

Completely at the limit of our strength, we decided to lie down in whatever sheltering hole we came across.

We ended up finding, in the middle of the ruins, an orifice, an opening under the corner of one of the few houses still standing. We were already savoring the thought of a few hours of rest and sleep, which we needed so badly, when, entering this space, we were almost suffocated by the unbearable odor of rotting carrion.

To our utter horror, by the gleam of a flashlight, we saw the bodies of six Germans. They had no doubt been killed by the detonation of some enormous shell, because they stood as if petrified, in poses so natural that you'd think they were still alive.

Disgusted and disagreeably impressed, we fled from this tomb.

As we left this inhospitable village we came upon a cylindrical shape, right at ground level. It was one of our big artillery pieces, at rest. It was in a bunker, covered with a canvas tarpaulin painted in neutral colors to camouflage it from the enemy's view.

There was nobody around this gun. The artillerymen, those lucky devils, must have been snoozing away in a fine shelter somewhere. We snuck under the tarpaulin and, rolled up in our damp blankets, stretched out on the cannon's gun carriage, "like Turenne on the eve of battle,"[3] I said to my comrades.

But these poor fellows had never heard of Turenne. They thought he was someone in the company.

"No, you imbeciles," I spat at them, "he was a famous, illustrious general!"

But for these poor young bucks, a general is someone who orders other people to kill one another.

"Ah, the bastard," they said, "I hope he croaked."

By now the sky had cleared and it grew quite cold. We could feel the mud hardening under our feet and cracking as it froze, while in our Midi the nights are still generally mild in October.

Fatigue is a powerful narcotic, and despite the cold and discomfort of our position we fell into a deep slumber, to the point that we didn't hear the explosions of some big shells which fell nearby. But at daylight the cold woke us up. We shivered, and our feet were senseless, numb, so it took us a few minutes to stand up.

We headed toward the place where, the previous evening, the battalion had assembled. We had the good luck of finding there the three caissons of 37mm guns, ready to leave, harnessed to their teams, but the drivers didn't know where the supply trains and the field kitchens were; someone had said they were somewhere near Maurepas.

As we proceeded, we picked up some details which were not encouraging: the field kitchens, which had set up at Combles the evening before, then had to withdraw during the night, nobody knew where, because of the shells falling in and around Combles.

Peyriac's Louis Richardis, cook to His Highness the Commandant Quinze-Grammes and His Eminence the Kronprinz, had one of his comrades killed outright by a shell burst.

A less disturbing detail, but quite bothersome for our daily sustenance: the field kitchen of the 4th Machine-Gun Company was shot full of holes—to its great glory, but a great misfortune for us.

We arrived at Maurepas, or at least what had been Maurepas, because you couldn't find a stone or a brick. The stones and bricks had been gathered up by the Territorials, who used them to pave the roads, at night.

At the center of the village was a jumble of vehicles, caissons, and field kitchens from various regiments, but not the slightest trace of the *Bitterrois* regiment [the 296th; Bitterrois = inhabitant of Béziers].

We had already emptied our mess kits and ration bags that morning. A soggy piece of bread and a chocolate bar transformed into blackish paste by the rain made up my only meal since we had left the Ferme de Bonfray. We were hungry, and for a hungry man the animal instincts take over. Fond yearnings for our cooks and our field kitchens pushed aside those we had for our wives and our children, who couldn't do anything for us. Our thoughts were also with our comrades on the front line, standing in the filthy stream, anxiously awaiting our arrival this evening. They won't get indigestion from overeating!

Helpless, we decided to post ourselves by the side of the road, in hopes that we see someone pass by wearing the fateful "296" patch.

We were in luck, in the form of a horseman, the simple orderly of some brass hat, who had no idea how anxiously we awaited him and how joyfully we spotted him.

He told us that the supply train and the field kitchens had been ordered to Hardécourt. A half-hour later we were at this village. It was three in the afternoon. But the field kitchens had not yet arrived. They were stuck in the mud, up to their axles in a bad stretch of road, and could arrive only much later that evening.

We were lucky enough to discover in Hardécourt the cellar of a vanished house, stuffed with straw—the height of luxury! We took immediate possession of it, by right of first occupancy. But we were barely there a half-hour when a detachment of engineers arrived and, under pretext that this cellar belonged to a detachment which they had just relieved, they ordered us out.

"Messieurs," I told them, "you're too late. Are you the owners of this cellar?

No, I didn't think so. Well, we're here, and we're staying put since we got here first."

They went to look for their officers, but nothing came of it. We declared that we would leave only by force, and we made it clear that this would not be without resistance.

There were no constables, no policemen, no gendarmes in Hardécourt to expel us; they had to abandon this cellar to us, and we had, for this brief relief, a precious refuge against the cold, the rain, and even the shells which fell upon Hardécourt from time to time.

It was much later that night that we were able to resupply our comrades on the front line. It had been two days since they'd had anything to eat or drink. When we had trouble finding them and we called out "Cannon 37! Sergeant Gauthier!" you can imagine how quickly they swarmed out of their mole tunnels.

The truck drivers lent us a hand in the resupply effort, so that we could rest every other night.

Every evening at 5 p.m., as night fell, two of us brought supplies up to our comrades: wine, coffee, letters and packages, and sometimes a sack of shells. This wasn't easy duty; twenty-five kilometers to cover, in moonless nights, on bad roads and invisible pathways which crisscrossed each other, where it was easy to get lost, all the while dodging shellfire.

But what a difference from those who had to stay in the trenches without the slightest shelter, feet in the water, enduring frequent downpours, the cold, and above all the bombardments. The Germans, if they rarely fired on the rear, sent shells in abundance onto the first and second lines of trenches.

Nevertheless, our artillery fired on average four shells for each of the enemy's one. To endure such an avalanche of projectiles the Germans kept only a screen of sharpshooters and machine gunners at their front lines. Those folks were spread out in big shell craters and dug little pits there, where they burrowed down and protected themselves from fragments. Since they brought up enough rations and munitions for the duration of their watch duties, they hardly ever moved out of their holes.

In a war like this one, combat meant mostly being a target for shells. The best leader wasn't the cleverest tactician, but rather the one who knew best how to keep his men alive.

On this subject, our leaders had a lot to learn from the German bosses. It's not that the latter were more humanitarian, but they had the intelligent care to conserve human resources.

One evening, when it wasn't my turn on ration duty, I had already bedded down for a good night's sleep ahead when the sergeant-major of the 4th Machine-

Gun Company made an unlucky appearance, ordering me to carry an urgent dispatch to Lieutenant Lorius, commanding the detachment of a 37mm cannon.

No doubt these were urgent orders for an attack, I thought, but when I indiscreetly read the dispatch I was stunned.

There were, at this time, several models of gas masks in use. They were asking all the unit commanders, like Lieutenant Lorius, for a report stating the number of such-and-such a model being used—pronto!

And that was why I was being ordered, that night, to go out and find our officer, risking death twenty times over, along roads transformed into quagmires.

But you had to obey. What could one say? What would have happened if, tomorrow, our headquarters didn't know how many gas masks of model X or Z there were in our group?

The sergeant-major assured me that I would find Lieutenant Lorius in a fortified bunker near the Combles railway station. Had I been notified earlier, I could have accompanied the ration team, but now I had to make my way alone to Combles. Lucky me—the German guns were unleashing salvos on the town; there were a few moments of ominous silence, then suddenly came the sinister shrieks, and then the massive explosions, the blinding flashes, the sound of falling debris and crumbling walls.

To complete this frightful tableau, two munitions dumps had just blown up. It looked like a fireworks display, with columns of smoke and flame rising to the clouds which reflected them; earth and sky seemed ablaze.

At the risk of being court-martialed for not obeying orders, I was beating a retreat toward Hardécourt when I ran into two engineers who told me that the officer I was looking for must have sought refuge in the "catacombs," like everyone else.

According to them, these so-called catacombs were very easy to find. I had only to climb out of the ravine, take a road which would lead me into the village, and then to the square where I would see the ruins of a château; that's where they were.

I found the road, which was nothing but a muddy quagmire which split into many pathways across the rubble, and while I was wandering in this ghastly solitude the shells began raining down even more abundantly. At each whistling shriek I flattened myself against a bit of crumbled wall or a tree trunk, and I waited for the avalanche of stones and iron to finish cascading down before taking up my course once again.

There was no one from whom I could ask the slightest bit of guidance. What was least reassuring was that I'd be as incapable of finding my way back as I was in finding these famous catacombs.

I was gripped by despair. Ah, I said to myself, sagging against a bit of wall, I might as well die here as anywhere else, right now as well as tomorrow. But at this tragic moment a vision flashed across my mind like a lightning bolt. There, in my distant home, my cherished wife, my two babes with blonde curls, my white-haired mother and father, kneeling at prayer at this very hour, pouring all their hearts, all their souls into it, with grave faces, bent in anguish for the absent one . . . for me.

I don't really believe that prayers, as sincere as they might be, have the power to deflect bullets or shells. But there's something about the mind, detaching itself from all else, concentrating for one moment on one memory, on a single thought of someone dear—that's an act of faith, of love, of hope.

No, I had to escape death as best I could, to get away from this accursed place.

I broke into a run, and found a road in the middle of which an ambulance was ablaze, smelling strongly of gasoline. In the fire's light I saw a field kitchen, which had imprudently come as far as Combles, shattered on the ground. The kitchen's two horses lay moaning on the ground, and nearby were two men, bathed in a puddle of blood, coffee, and wine.

That night, a company in the trenches will await its rations in vain; this will be a day of fast which they will accept without a murmur, without a complaint, once they hear what happened.

I leaned over the two unfortunate ones: one was missing his head, guillotined; the other had a leg blown off at the thigh, and probably other wounds as well.

At this moment a squad of Territorials appeared, nocturnal road workers, peaceable shovels and picks at their shoulders, already going forth at the first pause in the bombardment, to clean up and repair the damage to the roads and the pathways which must be maintained practicable at all costs. If not, tomorrow and the day after, our cannons would be silenced, our wounded couldn't be evacuated, our men in the trenches couldn't be fed.

This duty of the Territorials was not without peril. Often some of them spilled their own blood into the mud which they were cleaning up. Their little crosses lined these roads.

Observing them, I felt like a lost voyager in the desert, coming upon a caravan.

I asked them where I could find the catacombs. "We've just left them," they said. I was just a few steps away. A pile of rubble, a passageway across, an opening, and a gently sloping descent into a long, deep underground passage, with a vaulted ceiling dug into the white-clay earth.

To the right and the left a large corridor led to other, smaller ones. You could see actual chambers, all along the way: offices, telephone centers, first-aid stations, sleeping quarters, mess halls, storage rooms for gas masks, tools, sand bags, weapons, etc.

Down there was a constant coming-and-going, incessant activity. In vain I asked if anyone had seen any officers from the 296th Regiment. I decided to wait for daybreak, and I stretched out on a pile of gas masks belonging to evacuated wounded; although they were both muddy and bloodstained, I stretched out with sheer pleasure, and nothing came along to trouble my sleep.

Who had built this underground complex? Was it the Germans? Had it been there before the war? I couldn't get answers about any of this; in any case, it was a safe harbor, a refuge in the midst of the storm.

At dawn, I went out to the railway station to see if I could find Lieutenant Lorius there, but this was in vain. I then returned empty-handed to Hardécourt, to rejoin my comrades who were wondering about my fate.

Each evening, in the cellar which served as our refuge, we hardly got any sleep since the rationers of the three gun crews hadn't come back. At least we knew what had happened, and we had some assurance that help was on the way.

Each day I went to the field kitchens of my old companies, the 13th and 15th, looking for news. The men were suffering from the bad weather; there were frequent downpours of freezing rain, in the mornings, and naturally there were also wounded and killed; you don't make omelets without breaking eggs.

One of my former little bleus, poor Yver, who had given me back forty sous the day we came up to the front, had burrowed with two of his comrades into a little cavity dug into the trench wall, upon which a big shell landed, pulverizing all three occupants.

Peyriac's Paul Alpech had just left the same shelter, not five minutes earlier, to go for food, and Yver had taken his place.

That's how the war went. Fate determined our life and death in the tiniest circumstances.

October 23, 1916, is a memorable day in the annals of the 296th. The previous night the officers were advised that, the next day, the regiment had to attack, with the objective of taking the first German line.

During the night, the men were kept busy digging parallels—trenches extending ahead of our own front line, to shorten the distance for us to cross at the moment of assault.

It happened that the 4th Battalion, our own, in the darkness pushed this parallel too close to the German trench, and we had to be especially careful that they not discover the work being done right under their noses.

When, the next day, the fog lifted, the Germans were astounded to see the French a few steps away from them.

Since those folks waged war like we did—constrained and forced into it— they judged it useless to defend themselves, and unanimously raised their arms, crying "Comrades! Comrades!"

However, some of them were scared stiff, and profited from the lingering fog and reigning confusion by taking off. As a result there were only fifty-two in our hands.

Various incidents took place. The well-liked Lieutenant Cordier, commanding the 14th Company, marched at the head of his men and was the first to leap into the enemy trench. Seeing a tent cloth covering a dugout, he tossed it aside. A German adjutant, asleep inside, fell out of bed and, when called to surrender, answered with pistol shots at our officer, who was hit by several bullets but who, magnanimously, captured the German and prohibited anyone from harming him.

Farther along, a German soldier couldn't get out of his hole. One of our guys reached a hand out to him, saying "Come on, climb out, lazy-bones." To the Frenchman's surprise the other answered him, in our own language, "I'm not a lazy-bones—you're a Frenchman and I'm a German."

In the area around the trench, they found the body of an enemy officer, his head bashed in, and beside him a shovel covered with blood. It seemed clear that, when he didn't want to surrender, his men had gotten rid of him.

Another officer, haughty and furious about his misfortune, was conducted to the post of the commandant, who was absent. When the latter arrived, the German wouldn't budge. Lieutenant Guillot,[4] commanding the 13th Company, was there, and said in German, "Hey, salute—it's the commandant." The Boche wouldn't move. Second request, same disdainful immobility. Lieutenant Guillot gave him a hard slap on both cheeks. The German went pale, then red, and then he saluted, with rage in his heart.

Meanwhile, at the same hour, the same minute, the 6th Battalion pushed forward, but, put under machine-gun fire, the men flattened themselves in shell holes; otherwise it would have been a total massacre. The losses nevertheless were considerable; they had to be relieved that evening by the 5th Battalion.[5]

On October 25 our 4th Battalion was relieved, and to rest on our laurels we went into reserve in a barren, desertlike ravine to the rear of Combles. But an unfortunate counterorder put our 37mm cannon at the disposal of the commandant of the 5th Battalion.

That same evening, it was my turn to go get the food, with our driver Castet and the ration team from the 5th Battalion's fifth gun, Thoumazou and Fraïssé.

The latter, who had been born in Olonzac, land of good wine, in the middle of the Minervois, had a Rabelaisian face. Blessed with a solid appetite, and fresh-faced, rosy-cheeked, and plump, he breathed joie de vivre from every pore, from the roundness of his belly, the tranquility of his step, his double and even triple chin, to his peaceful and mocking expression.

Philosopher without knowing it, he saw the best side of every occurrence, always ready with a joke or a colorful expression, getting seriously agitated only at the prospect of some sort of day of fast, even at the height of Lent.

The two rationers from the 5th Battalion's field gun had already been in the "Circé" Trench, where we were going, but after we'd gone past the colonel's command post, in front of the dark and gloomy plain where several pathways crossed each other, they hesitated, uncertain about which was the right road to take.

Luckily two liaison men came up, heading for the front line, and were quite willing to serve as our guides, as long as they could lighten our load of food a bit.

They weren't mistaken, because at every moment, in every direction, the German batteries were unleashing frightful volleys of shellfire.

But the two liaison men were carrying only a few scraps of paper. We were carrying bundles of jerricans and musette bags, which made walking difficult.

Fraïssé was especially weighted down, overloaded like a mule; furthermore, the roundness of his belly threw off his center of gravity. Pursued by bad luck, he was always stumbling into one shell hole or another. After each caper he lost his orientation, and we sometimes had to put him back on his feet, which would have given us much to laugh about in another time and place.

The only point of reference in this darkened plain, where no tree, bush, or tuft of grass remained, was a single telephone pole, with two others holding it up (or it was holding them up). From time to time our guides would crouch down and scan the horizon, to seek out these poles outlined by the light of some luminous flare or explosion.

Finally they spotted them. We were a few meters from them when a particularly shrill whistling made us flatten out in a shell hole, without being told to do so.

No one was harmed. And these shells weren't made of chocolate; they were the real thing. It was pure fate.

We got up. "Hurry up," cried our guides. But a second whistle, a second flattening. No damage, again. But the liaison men picked up the pace. We were near the Bois de Morval, a place which usually was quite heavily bombarded.

At that moment I thanked Providence for having blessed me with long legs which allowed me to follow the guides, but it wasn't the same for my three comrades, who called out frantically, "Barthas! Barthas! Wait for us!"

I implored these orderlies to be willing to wait for a minute or two, which they did, not without complaining, while the shells kept raining down. "We're only two hundred meters from the Circé Trench," they said. "We need to get there in one bound. Are you all here? Let's go!"

You'd have thought the German gunners had heard this as a signal to unleash a formidable barrage. Two hundred meters, that's not much, but how long they seemed in those moments! Running, stumbling, sloshing through water, through mud, in the midst of explosions, of flying metal, chunks of clay—you're nothing but a frightened beast, obeying the instinct of self-preservation.

Finally, here is the Circé Trench. It's the safe harbor, salvation; we don't jump in, we fall into it, we collapse; it is deep, with inhabited holes here and there, with solid ladders. We're saved.

But Castet stayed too long in a shell hole; Fraïssé capered about like a clown; Thoumazou, nearsighted by day and blind by night, had wandered off to nobody knew where—I had to gather them up. Castet, half-dead with terror, and Fraïssé, who looks like an enormous block of mud, finally show up. But the *Auvergnat* Thoumazou didn't arrive, and didn't answer our calls. Had he been hit, the unlucky one? Once the bombardment had passed, we looked for him, we called out—nothing!

Here I am, really annoyed. What am I going to say tomorrow when they ask me, "Where did Thoumazou go?"

To hell with this Auvergnat! To hell with my corporal's stripes! How much trouble they've caused me—and to what good?

But no matter whether Thoumazou is alive, lost somewhere, or pulverized out there. We need to find those to whom we are delivering rations.

In this ravine there is an end of the Bois de Morval. In a jumble of half-destroyed trenches are a number of deep, solid shelters built by the Germans. They know right where they are, and at least one enemy battery has its sights fixed right upon these shelters and their surroundings, where salvos of shells fall, day and night.

Our commandant had to give up using these precious shelters, which were crumbling little by little. This sinister corner became a resting place for couriers and signalmen, people used to playing hide-and-seek with falling shells.

But at night our little field guns were useless, and their gun crews as well. So they came to seek refuge in these risky shelters—five minutes of danger for a long night of security.

But just try to discover, in a dark night, and in the midst of landslides, enormous holes, or crevasses, the very shelter where our men are hiding. Nevertheless, at the end of an hour of searching, at the foot of a staircase with muddy steps, booming voices called out in answer to us; it was them.

Our gun crew having received the order to be relieved, we decided to leave at around three in the morning. I led the way, and served as guide, with my sole landmarks a dead body and the three telephone-poles. Nobody got lost, and the return trip was less eventful, but our hands weren't in our pockets; we had to take turns lugging our cannon and our supply of shells.

When we reached Hardécourt, we had hoped to find Thoumazou, but he hadn't come back, which made everyone worried and filled me with anguish.

How the devil had this descendant of the Arverni[6] come to be among us southerners? A mystery; the whim of a rear-echelon recruiting clerk. But he enjoyed himself in our company, and liked and admired the petulance, the glibness, the picturesque expressions, the sonorous curses, all of which characterized the southern spirit and personality.

As he was a cabinetmaker, we had baptized him *Pot á Colle* [Paste-Pot].

Finally, that afternoon, we had the pleasure of seeing Paste-Pot appear, albeit in a pitiful condition, barely recognizable, muddy, covered with dirt and clay. But yes, it was him, without a fingernail or a hair missing.

What a sigh of relief for me! At any moment I had expected an orderly to rise up in front of me and haul me before a scowling brass hat, having to answer this terrifying question: "Corporal Barthas, what have you done with Private Thoumazou?" As if I didn't have to watch out for the blows which might fall upon me, I had to be responsible for those which might fall upon others!

When he had regained his strength, Paste-Pot was called upon to explain his mysterious disappearance.

He'd been carrying containers of wine and coffee for the men of his gun crew. To quench their thirst, those fellows had to drink water swimming with microbes, drawn from a shell hole.

He told us that, just as he reached the Circé shelters along with us, in the midst of frightful shellfire, Fraïssé had taken a particularly bad spill. Thoumazou charitably went to help him get up, but then he himself tumbled into an enormous crater. He called out to Fraïssé as loudly as he could, but was the latter stricken with sudden deafness, or had he simply not heard him, as he claimed? A mystery. In any case, Thoumazou found himself alone, in the middle of a torrent of fire and metal. He dashed off like a madman, wandered all night long in the woods and the deserted ruins of Morval, and ended up, by daylight, finding some shelters occupied by Territorials, who helped him, then made his way back to Hardécourt.

Bad luck rarely arrives alone. The same night that we lost Thoumazou at Morval, somebody stole, or in military terms "pinched," the wheels of our field gun right off their axle, near our shelter in Hardécourt—big iron wheels, upon which we hauled our cannon on the march.

There were no thieves in Hardécourt—nor were there any folks who had come there to kill, or to get themselves killed—but some gun crew of a 37, having lost its own wheels in some morass, made do with ours.

This was no small affair, gunners who let the wheels of their cannon be stolen away. It put the gun crew's driver, two haulers, and me at risk of being sent back to our companies, not to mention disciplinary sanctions. We, the victims of the theft, were going to be punished instead of the thieves.

We lost some sleep and appetite, as a result. From one day to the next, from hour to hour, with the Germans not firing, the encampment at Hardécourt grew in size, expanded wildly, pell-mell, to the delight of everyone there. There were people from all the corners of the universe: Australians, Canadians, Hindus, Negroes, Yellows, Redskins. One could have called it an exodus of peoples, of tribes fleeing before a scourge or departing for some far-off crusade.

There was everything in this polyglot camp which we crisscrossed in every direction—everything, that is, except a pair of wheels for a 37, which we would have snatched away without the slightest scruple. But in vain did we scour all the corners, under trailers, on caissons, around harnesses—nothing, always nothing, and the day of our relief was approaching.

Finally, one night, the rationers of a front-line gun woke us up when they came back and assured us that they had seen, on a trailer at Maurepas, beside the road, a miraculous thing for us—a pair of wheels for a 37.

To be sure, the wheels appeared to be firmly stowed on the trailer, under which stretched a grayish shape which could well be the driver, watching his load and sleeping with one eye open.

But we, the four larceny victims, were determined. I blush with shame to be writing these lines. We armed ourselves with a saw and a hatchet to detach the wheels, and a towel and some rope with which to bind and gag the driver if he tried to interfere.

Like four bandits up to no good, we left at midnight for Maurepas, where we easily found the trailer upon which the enticing wheels were perched.

Climb up onto the vehicle, saw through the cord, carry off the wheels on our shoulders—all this took barely two minutes, without seeing a soul.

We hastened toward Hardécourt, happy as a gang of thieves carrying off a strongbox, without the slightest remorse. And probably none of us had ever stolen even a cherry.

Ah, war—the great moralizer!

One day, unexpectedly, two arms wrapped around my neck and somebody planted kisses on both of my cheeks. It was one of my former little bleus, Victor Grandjean, a young Parisian orphan.

He was my favorite—he called me Papa. The other Peyriac poilus took an interest in him, too. His battalion was in relief near Combles, so he took an excursion to see me.

He told me about the horrible death of the little Breton, Maurice Yver, blown to bits by an enormous shell, along with a comrade and the corporal who had replaced me in the squad, in a hole where the three of them had burrowed.

Peyriac's Paul Alpech had been in this hole right before. It was 9 in the evening; they were calling the rationers to go pick up supplies near Combles. Paul Alpech, who had kept with my successor the functions of rationer, left the hole to gather up pots, pans, and other containers.

Maurice Yver immediately took his place in the hole. Two or three minutes later, the drama occurred.

That is how, in war, fate and luck play out, so that the life and death of a man can hang on the tiniest of circumstances.

He told me about the unspeakable horrors, in the trenches transformed by frequent downpours into muddy open sewers, and the terrible cold which froze always-damp feet.

In the squad Delâtre, who was from Lille and whose lamentable story I will tell, Maurice Jouy, Peyron, and Flammand had been evacuated with frozen feet.

Given our enormous losses, we expected to be brought back to the rear, but alas, on October 31 our 4th Battalion received orders to go back up to the front line, that night, along with our field gun.

When we were getting our mule "Falet" ready to haul our cannon and munitions, the marshal of dragoons who commanded the cavalry detachment declared outright that the road from Maurepas to Combles was too dangerous. No mules could be spared to help us out.

For us simple bipeds, this had no importance. There were endless supplies of men, as many as they could want. But it was getting harder and harder to procure mules; they had to be carefully husbanded.

This would have obliged us to drag along the load with ropes, to push and pull our gun carriage several kilometers, along terrible roads, but necessity breeds boldness. At the moment of our departure, in darkest night, we went and quietly untied our mule, which was kept out in the open under the watch of an inattentive stable guard snuggled comfortably in a nook made of piled-up harnesses and horse collars.

Everything went fine as far as Maurepas. But from there on Falet began to balk at going any farther, slowed his pace, and ended up stopping altogether, in spite of our urgent exhortations and even some caresses from a stout club.

Nobody had ever seen such a stubborn mule. Deep down, maybe he was too intelligent. He sniffed danger from afar.

That night, he wasn't mistaken. The road was bombarded, mainly at certain places which the gun teams crossed at a gallop, even a triple gallop.

All of a sudden, two hundred meters ahead of us, a shell fell upon the road, right in the midst of a group of Territorials going off to work. When we passed by they were taking care of the victims. A dozen of them who showed signs of life were hoisted onto a passing artillery wagon. As for the others, who had breathed their last, we counted eight of them; they weren't worth being hauled off; they were lined up along the roadside for a quick burial. *C'est la guerre!*

An accident like that in peacetime would have taken up plenty of space in the newspapers for several days. But now it was just a simple, everyday accident.

You might say that the impact of this shell made our mule understand that he had to pick up the pace. In fact we now had trouble keeping up with him.

After passing through Combles, when there was no more road to follow, we had to carry the field gun and its accessories up to the front line on our shoulders.

That night, our artillery pounded away with an unusual violence. All of our batteries, and those of the English on our left, threw out an avalanche of iron and fire onto the German lines.

The air was filled with the deafening shrieks of shells and the pulsating vibrations of explosions.

The firing guns and bursting shells made an uninterrupted roar.

No matter how accustomed we were to the cannonade's rumble, a storm like this rattled our brains, burrowed into our skulls, pressed down upon our chests with a pervasive anguish. We were dazed, stumbling around like sleepwalkers.

This frightful bombardment, in which more cannon shots were fired in one night than in a whole campaign of Napoleon's, was in preparation for an offensive which our *corps d'armée* was to undertake the next day.

They had kept this decision under wraps until the very last moment. The men—very tired, badly fed, stuck in muddy trenches—greeted the attack order with grumbling. Many slipped away from the front lines under the pretext of being overwhelmed by shellfire, or falling ill, or having frozen feet, whether true or not. These men, who weren't seduced by the idea of a bayonet charge, chose to stay put once they reached the field kitchens or the first-aid stations, or else they wandered off and were in no hurry to find the right road. Not everyone can be a hero.

At nine in the morning on November 1, the order was given to go forth from the trenches. There was a moment of hesitation, but on our left the 125th Regiment went out with élan and swept right over the first German line.

In the Blood-Soaked Mud of the Somme:
November 1, 1916–January 30, 1917

Seeing that they were being outflanked by the 125th Regiment, the Germans came out of their holes with arms raised, calling out "Comrades! Comrades!" This word is now known in all languages.

Their obliging machine gunners carried their murderous machines across their shoulders.

Some comical scenes occurred. There was rivalry between the 125th and the 296th Regiments over who could gather up the most prisoners. Pulled and tugged first one way, then the other, the prisoners didn't know whom to follow. Dazed, they understood nothing about the animated discussions among ourselves, which sometimes degenerated into quarrels and came close to fisticuffs.

Some Germans, profiting from this confusion, scrambled away, or hid themselves in shell holes.

Finally the prisoners were led to the rear, and we took over the German positions. It was quite a while before the German command noticed the loss of their front line.

Under the cover of thick fog which the sun had not yet penetrated, a leader with any initiative could have taken the second German line even more easily than the first.

But where were our great leaders—the general, or the colonel? Nobody saw them. Prudently they had burrowed into their holes. There was nobody qualified on hand to give orders, to take advantage of circumstances, to alert the artillery to lengthen their range. We stayed in place.

Around noon, the weather cleared. The Germans then saw that their positions were occupied by us, and they organized their second line, now their front line. They didn't counterattack, but they rained shellfire of all calibers onto the lost ground, making us pay rather dearly for the day's success.

On November 2 and 3, some heavy downpours and a cold temperature made the sojourn of the men in these mixed-up positions even tougher. On top of long hours of guard duty and patrol, they were sent out to dig, to undergo work details day and night, without sleep, badly fed. It was with a keen sigh of satisfaction that they welcomed the order for their relief, which took place in the night of the 3rd–4th, by another regiment in our army corps.

At 6 in the morning, the 4th Battalion, to which our group was attached, arrived at Hardécourt. The men's fatigue was extreme, but we had to cover two more hours of marching before reaching Suzanne, where trucks awaited us. The traffic jams were such that they could not have reached Hardécourt without great difficulty.

Suzanne is, or rather was, a nice village grouped around some fine châteaus. German shells had wrought great damage, and still did so, despite our advance.

We had to wait for the lame, the halt, the laggards, those with frozen feet. I took advantage of it to visit the village. The church's steeple was intact, but half of the vaulting had collapsed. With the rubble cleared away, the church was still used for regular services.

In a chapel were buried under the paving stones several generations of counts, dukes, marquis, lieutenants, captains-at-arms of the "most powerful" lords of Suzanne, Cappy, and other places. By fate, up to that time no projectile had profaned this place of burial, which could happen one day or another.

I had the time to visit a magnificent château near the church, with beautiful staircases, galleries, paneling, tapestries, etc.

At 10 o'clock, the trucks headed out, and at three in the afternoon they dropped us off at Aubigny, a little village two kilometers from Corbie beside the Somme.

We had, for our billet, a huge barn which had long served as lodging for troops. The only furniture was, along each side, a camp bed, like in a police station. Upon each plank, some scraps of straw. As always, our accommodation was in the sorriest imaginable state of cleanliness.

The walls, built of *en torchis* [wattle-and-daub], were full of holes, letting in numerous cold drafts, just like a dozen or so ventilators. Even worse, the roof was pierced with openings. Rain falling from the sky had formed a pond in the bottom of the shed. The ground sloped down from the courtyard and its inevitable manure pile. The juice, the extract, the liquid manure from this dung heap seeped into the pond and fed it with germs.

And every day at this time the newspapers stuffed their readers' heads with incessant elegies about the care, the well-being, the hygiene, the comfort which enveloped the poilus when they came back from the trenches.

It must be said that they did give us a second blanket, which made our packs heavier on the march, but which were very useful to us when we shivered from the cold at night. The weather was bad at this time: rain, snow, heavy frosts.

Along one wall in the barn's courtyard were the company's mules. The poor beasts! Without the slightest shelter, submissive, resigned, tethered next to one another, they bore these rigorous conditions, also martyrs to this cataclysm without the means to complain, arousing no sentiment of pity because they were mere beasts—as if the suffering of animals wasn't the same as that of men.

Society for the Protection of Animals—where were you? What were you doing then?

What were the casualty figures of the regiment? Of our battalion? Of our company? They were careful not to say. It wouldn't be an exaggeration to set them at two hundred dead, three hundred wounded, and a hundred evacuated as sick or with frostbitten feet.

From the 7th, the divisional depot sent up all its available replacements. A reinforcement of two hundred men arrived, from the training camp at Troyes. They were made up of bakery workers, pastry chefs, typists, etc., now replaced by people who were lucky enough to have come into the world two or three years earlier than they did.

Of these two reinforcements, few were from the Midi. The regiment therefore lost more and more of its southern character.

For several days, at assembly, it was a downpour of honors and congratulations. General of the division, of the brigade, colonel—each one paying his compliments, exalting our courage, our warlike virtues, our ferocious energy. We were dying with laughter.

"With you, one can, one should, dare all," said one. "With men like you, all hopes are permitted," affirmed another, in all seriousness.

Finally, it was officially recognized and proclaimed that our battalion, the 4th, had made an advance of 1,200 meters, taken 256 prisoners, and seized three machine guns.[1] Our commandant, wishing that this feat of arms be noted for posterity, asked that his battalion be officially cited in the orders of the army. But this would have humiliated the other battalions, so let us shed a tear of regret that history will not record how we had conquered a kilometer of swampy marshland and taken 256 Germans who eagerly awaited our arrival so they could stick up their hands and cry out "Comrades!"

In brief, each of us believed himself to be a hero worthy of the days of Homer.

But our surly colonel [Robert] reminded us of the harsh reality of our servile condition by his draconian prescriptions about our attire, discipline, and training, and brought down our hero's pride. He set down severe measures against those who, in the future, would lose their tools, their weapons, their spare rations, or would themselves get lost, or would leave the trench without authorization, or would report to sick bay and not be recognized as sick. To serve as examples, some unfortunate ones who had committed one of these grave crimes were handed over for court-martial.

But in war, you can't have leaders who are too sensitive, too eager to preserve the lives of their men. Therefore, one morning, a divisional staff car took away, without trumpets or drums, Commandant Cantegril, placed on the inactive list, it was said.

In the 14th Company, Lieutenant Auragne was reduced to sergeant, for rather unclear reasons. It seems he lacked sufficient decisiveness and sangfroid when Lieutenant Cordier, commanding the company, was wounded and he had to take command.

And the training exercises had started up again, with intensity, in all kinds of weather. That was urgently required in order to train, to daze, to stun all these bakers, cooks, orderlies, etc., who had just arrived to take their shares of mud and glory. That's what they really needed. No, they didn't seem to be burning with sacred fire; instead, they had the lugubrious air of folks who were headed for the gallows. For us, it was amusing to see them like this; it's true that distractions were rare in Aubigny. One little tavern into which barely a dozen people could fit, that's all. What was there to do after the evening meal, in our dark, cold billets? Some played cards by the light of a smoky candle; others, to make up for nights spent on watch in the trenches, caught up on sleep.

Most went to spend a few hours in nearby villages which offered, in their restaurants and taverns, a bit more hospitality.

Following the course of the Somme upstream, two kilometers from Aubigny, was the pretty little town of Corbie. But to get there you had to cross the Somme on a bridge upon which several English sentries severely restricted access without authorization from the military authorities.

Corbie was exclusively reserved for the use of the English army. Our allies had put themselves in charge there; the boutiques and shops were stocked with articles from the other side of the Channel, and everywhere you saw signs and billboards in the English language.[2]

We quickly discovered an easy way to get into Corbie. We stationed ourselves two or three hundred meters from the bridge and waited for an English vehicle, either an automobile or a truck, then climbed onto it, concealed ourselves, and the trick was completed. In a few minutes we were in the town. The English drivers willingly went along with this stratagem. Going back the other way was easy; the sentries never even gave us a second glance.

In September 1914 the Germans had occupied Corbie for two weeks, but the inhabitants were unanimous in saying that they had displayed a proper attitude, paying for everything that they acquired.

During the fortnight we were at Aubigny we had the ill luck to find ourselves under a full moon, which earned us nightly visits from the *Taubes*.[3]

Barely had we bedded down when the sinister rumbling of the motors could be heard. They flew overhead, turned, and flew back again, and finally we heard the racket of the bombs they dropped around Corbie or Amiens.

Here and there some cannon shots would be tossed off toward the moon. The spotters played hide-and-seek with the Taubes, which disappeared only when the sun came to relieve the moon in the firmament.

Suddenly, on November 19, the order came down for the 5th and 6th Battalions in the Corbie sector to leave, that very day, for the front line. Our Battalion, the 4th, wouldn't have to leave until the next day.

At roll call, to reassure us, they read out to everyone that the 296th Regiment was going up to the front line just to prepare the sector that the English would henceforth occupy, which was, it seemed, a great honor. But by now we were on to the rude tricks that our big chiefs tried to play on us. Gloomy, resigned to our fates, worn out with anguish, the men took the road toward suffering, peril, horror, and—for many—death, and what a death!

That same day, the chief of our gun team, Sergeant Gauthier, had the coveted good fortune to go home on furlough. Rushing off to Fitou [Aude, on the Mediterranean coast, between Salses and Lapalme], he left me in charge of the [37mm] gun, an honor which was far from flattering to my vanity since I had to go up to the front line with it, instead of staying in the rear echelon.

So on November 20 at 10 in the morning, the trucks carried our battalion toward the trenches. At three in the afternoon we tramped through Suzanne, and at 6 p.m. we set ourselves up in a reserve trench behind Combles.

Being the last to arrive, we couldn't find any shelter for the night—a long, freezing night. Luckily our Lieutenant Lorius authorized us to pull back to Hardécourt until our battalion was called up to the front line.

Around 10 p.m. we reached Hardécourt, where we had to spend the night rolled up in our blankets, under the vans.

The cold roused us early. To warm ourselves up, we dug a hole two meters square and one meter deep, and covered it with tent cloths—a precarious shelter, which a heavy rainstorm would have filled with water. But finally we had a place to sleep, protected from the frigid bise and the damp fog.

One soldier who passed by when we were working asked if we were digging a grave.

In response to our astonished looks, he showed us, a few paces away, six mounds of freshly dug earth, which we hadn't noticed. These were the tombs of six soldiers from the 296th, killed and buried the evening before. We had dug our shelter in the Hardécourt cemetery!

Accursed cemetery! The dead couldn't even sleep there in peace. Enormous shells had torn them up, pulverized them, scattered their bones all around, as if in expiation of some terrible punishment.

They were going to repopulate this cemetery with fresh meat. It would soon be filled up, no doubt, but now there was room for six of us who were still alive. There was no reason to move; we'd be no better or worse off anywhere else.

The proximity of dead men didn't bother us. Weren't we condemned men ourselves, sentenced to death (with a stay of execution)?

Our hole was at the side of a road, across from a flattened house. In the midst of the ruins you could make out a small cellar, which had been a German machine-gun nest. The dugout had only one way in or out, under lock and key. The machine gunners had been locked in there, with no way of getting out. What happened at this strongpoint when Hardécourt was retaken? Had our soldiers rescued the German machine gunners, or massacred them?

A resourceful son of Peyriac, François Maizonnave, a cook at some greasy spoon or other, had discovered this former machine-gun nest and had installed his peaceable field kitchen there.

Exploring the surroundings of the village that same day, prowling among the mounds of earth and the shredded, blasted trees, I saw a thin line of blue smoke curling up into the air. At the same time the appetizing aroma of *civet* [rabbit stew], such as you can smell only in the Midi, caressed my nostrils; intrigued, I approached, and in a half-buried cellar I saw my Peyriac friend Richardis, among his pots and pans, preparing the menu for the highly placed personages to whose gastronomic needs he administered.

To get down into this cellar you had to leap. To get out, you had to clamber up, with your hands and feet grabbing holes and bumps in the wall.

It lacked comfort, for sure, but it was an unexpected opportunity. You had to be enterprising like a son of Peyriac to find such a redoubt in the midst of this complete devastation.

To amuse ourselves, we sometimes went along the road to see the regiments which had been relieved in the night, coming back from the trenches. What a sad spectacle! The men dragged themselves along, singly or in groups. One soldier, crushed with fatigue, crumpled to the ground beside the road, his feet ravaged by the cold. He begged for someone to go to the nearest pump to fill his canteen.

I rushed to carry out his request. During my brief absence, a sergeant-major came up and roundly cursed the unfortunate soldier, ordering him to get back on the march. "I'm sick, my feet are half-frozen, I need to rest for a moment," pleaded the soldier.

This answer, far from softening the officer's heart, only exasperated him even more. Eyes bulging from their sockets, face contorted with anger, he threatened to cite the private for disobedience and shook him by the shoulders.

I couldn't hold back my indignation. "Monsieur," I said to him, "you shouldn't act like this in the middle of a regiment from the Midi. We're too proud to put up with it."

He turned on me in a rage. "Do you know whom you're talking to? You'd better keep your mouth shut."

"Sure, I see your sergeant-major's stripes. But even if you were a general I'd tell you that the military regulations forbid you from laying hands on a subordinate, especially if he claims he's sick. It's the medical officer's business, not yours."

"Is there a police station around here?" was all he responded.

"To take me to? Thanks, but there's no police station in Hardécourt. Here there are only good folks!"

Exasperated, this nasty sergeant-major headed off, not without muttering vain threats toward me and the laggard, with whom I exchanged a fraternal handshake before he moved on, followed closely by his warder.

With our battalion due to head up to the front line on November 24, the preceding evening I made my way to the reserve trench near Combles to get orders from the head of our group, Lieutenant Lorius. Not far from this trench you could see what the English called a tank[4] broken down in the middle of a field. A squad of lucky fellows had found shelter under its carapace. A big howitzer shell had penetrated it without exploding, and the hole served as a chimney for the soldiers who warmed themselves alongside.

Lieutenant Lorius told me that this English tank had contributed to the taking of Combles, but after having sown terror—for this device was something new—and death among the Boches, it broke down on its way back from the enemy lines.

The English tried in vain to rescue their comrades stuck in the tank, who, rather than surrendering and handing over their vehicle and its secrets, must have set the gas tank on fire. Through the slits in the armor you could see tongues of flame and smoke leaping up, and you could smell the odor of grilled flesh. When Combles was finally taken, they pulled four charred bodies out.

Heroes? Martyrs? Or imbeciles?

In reality, perhaps they were involuntary victims of an accident, an explosion in the engine. If they were willing victims, they sure were naïve to think that their fate would prevent the Germans from building tanks of their own.

To spare us further fatigue, Lieutenant Lorius authorized me, for our stint on the front line, to make use of the [37mm] field gun which was already in position, rather than bringing up our own. But unfortunately we wouldn't be occupying the exact same spot. We therefore had to send up the most enterprising guy in our team, to see where the piece was currently positioned and then to see where our battalion would be stationed, so that he could be our guide the next night.

That meant, for this lucky fellow, several hours of scrambling, in daylight, in full view of enemy machine guns and shells. Needless to say, nobody in my team offered to be that enterprising. I finally had to draw lots to see who would carry out this mission.

It was the gun layer Cauneille whom fate selected. He was far from the dumbest, and indeed was one of the cleverest. He investigated the place where the team we were relieving was located, and discovered that the position where we were to link up with our battalion was only a few hundred meters to the left.

At eight in the evening on November 24, without incident, we relieved Sergeant Maury and his men, who left us their field gun with no regrets and quickly hightailed it out of sight.

Loading the cannon and munitions onto our shoulders, we headed to the left, under Cauneille's direction, to rejoin our battalion, or at least to reach a trench. But at the end of an hour's march, slipping, stumbling, paddling through water and mud, we stopped, worn out, not knowing where we had come from or where we were. A thick fog made the night even blacker.

What to do? Wander around on tiptoes like blind men? We could do nothing more than await the arrival of daylight. We sprawled out, immobile, in a shell hole, exchanging no words, no vain condemnations of Cauneille, himself a victim of having completed his mission badly.

We were soaked with sweat, but soon the frigid bise had us shivering, and now the rain took over from the fog. Just what we needed!

Ah, what a night to add to so many others! Lost on this sinister plain, riddled with cold, under a ceaseless rain!

How long it took to appear, this pale, wan, November daylight. Cauneille, to earn forgiveness, went out on patrol, calling to us when he was out of sight. He finally came upon the blasted tree trunks of the Bois de Morval, and a quarter-hour later we reached the Circé dugouts, which we knew from having been there during our previous front-line stint.

We cleaned out the entrance of one shelter which seemed still solid and deep enough, and we installed ourselves inside, where there was a passageway with five wooden bunks, just enough of each of us.

After having dried out and warmed up by the fire we managed to light, rested and fortified ourselves with the contents of our haversacks, we took counsel.

In my capacity as team leader, I had to find Lieutenant Lorius or the battalion command and get their orders. But where were they?

Since our last time at the front the French had gained ground hereabouts, and despite the guides sent to lead us our battalion had wandered off and gotten lost, and hadn't reached its positions until four in the morning.

Parts of front-line units had been relieved and were streaming back. Thanks to them I'd be able to put together some idea of where we were. I asked for one of my comrades to accompany me, but once again no one sought the honor of coming to join me and explore the charming landscape which was before us. We had to draw lots again.

This time it was the gun loader Donadilles, a peasant from Albi, whom fate chose to accompany me. It was now fully daylight, but the rain and thick fog allowed us to move unseen across open country. We followed the course of a rough-hewn boyau which was hemmed in by recent shell holes and dotted with dead bodies abandoned to the voracity of crows. This boyau seemed endless, but in a few minutes we reached a big trench seized from the terrible Hindenburg⁵ a few days ago. We saw solidly built dugouts occupied by units of a neighboring regiment. This was now our second line.

A moment later, by way of the "Michel" boyau, we reached the front line, where we met our Lieutenant Lorius, who was stuck in a little, half-collapsed dugout that was just about ready to cave in.

After consulting with the commandant, he decided that, with this diluvian downpour which risked making the trenches untenable, we'd be best off staying where we were in our shelter until further orders.

Afraid that the commandant would change his mind, we quickly turned on our heels. But this time we had to move along inside the Michel boyau instead of alongside it, because the fog was less thick and we would have been nice targets for the German machine gunners. This boyau, which had seemed to be in good shape the previous evening, was now nothing more than a torrent through which we sometimes had to wade up to our knees. Finally we reached our precious shelter, which we didn't have to leave for the next five days.

During these five days the torrential rain and snow never let up. The walls of the trench were sagging; the precarious shelters which men had dug for themselves collapsed in certain places. Trenches filled with water.

It's useless to try to describe the sufferings of the men, without shelter, soaked, pierced with cold, badly fed—no pen could tell their tale. You had to have lived through these hours, these days, these nights, to know how interminable they were in times like these.

Proceeding in nightly work details or to and from the front lines, men slipped and fell into shell holes filled with water and weren't able to climb out; they drowned or froze to death, their hands grasping at the edges of the craters in a final effort to pull themselves out.

For our part, we were spared all these sufferings, thanks to our precious cannon, which was useless in this storm. Right then the inventor of the 37 had no idea that, huddled at the bottom of a hole somewhere in the Bois de Morval, four enlisted men and a corporal were blessing his name if he was alive, or his memory if dead.

The task of our rationers was harder. We could give them only a vague indication of where we were. The first night, we took turns at the entrance to our dugout standing watch for their arrival or responding to their calls, but it wasn't until the next morning that we spotted them in the Bois de Morval after wandering for hours in search of us.

From then on their task was easier, and we were rationed regularly, except for one night when, surprised by a barrage of cannon fire, they became separated and one of them wandered off and retraced his steps to Hardécourt. Since he was carrying the liquid part, we had to go twenty-four hours with meals without drink. A small matter, in the middle of such big events.

Making my way up to the front lines with some difficulty the next day to get orders from our lieutenant [Lorius], I couldn't find him there; his shelter had completely caved in. He had wisely judged that the place was no longer tenable, and had taken off without leaving a forwarding address.

The commandant had fallen sick and been evacuated, and no one knew who was commanding the battalion. The companies couldn't communicate with each other. Left to our own devices, we could do nothing but wait out the events in our providential shelter.

During our stay at the Circé shelters we had the occasion to put comrades on the right road—or, rather, pathway—and be of help to unfortunate men who had gone astray or were weak with fatigue and cold.

For a day we took care of a stretcher-bearer who had stumbled into our dugout after having taken a bath in a big shell hole. He considered himself quite lucky to have been able to pull himself out on his own. We got him undressed, he wrapped himself in our blankets, and once night fell we lit a nice fire on the landing of our staircase and dried out his clothes.

Another night we welcomed two stretcher-bearers who carried a written order to go identify and bury the bodies which were between the lines.

To carry out a task which required several teams, they sent two men trembling with fear at each shell blast which shook the shelter.

Several times they tried to go out into the dark night, the rain, the fog, but each time they stumbled back precipitately, and finally they decided that they had buried as many of them as they could.

Bah, as [Prussian Chancellor Otto von] Bismarck had said, refusing a ceasefire request to bury the dead the evening after the battle of Champigny.[6] "The dead are as well off on top of the ground as underneath it."

On November 29 our rationers informed us that the battalion was going to be relieved. That very evening, we were to make our way with our field gun back to Hardécourt.

In our last relief, volleys of four shells rained down every five minutes onto the Circé shelters or close by. But this time, instead of a battery, there was now only one cannon which punctually fired its twelve rounds per hour, one every five minutes.

At nightfall, grouped at the top of the staircase, profiting from the armistice of three hundred seconds generously granted us between each falling enemy shell, each of us shouldered our loads and headed out briskly.

At an agreed-upon place our trail boss Castet awaited us with our mule Falet, and spurred on by Jalabert's cudgel we soon crossed the danger zone, and at seven in the evening we made our entry into Hardécourt. There we found our Sergeant Gauthier, not at all annoyed to arrive back from furlough the very day of our relief.

We spent the night under a big tent cloth called a *marabou* [a type of wading bird]. They had put up a large number of them; they were fragile shelter against the cold, and even less effective against shells, but sufficient against rain, night-time dampness, and the bise.

Two days later, December 1, our division was definitively relieved by the English, and the trucks which met us at Suzanne dropped us off at nightfall at Salouel, four kilometers from Amiens, which we marched through.

Salouel could be called a populous suburb of Amiens, which blends into the villages of Saleux and Pont-de-Metz, making up a single agglomeration crossed by a river. There are some factories and manufacturing plants.

The population was gracious. You could supply yourself with all kinds of things, and finally we had good billets with clean straw. We weren't used to such comforts, and we made the best of them.

The day we arrived, they announced that forty percent of us would go on home leave, that very night. There was an explosion of joy. Fatigue, suffering, dangers, all were forgotten. Those who weren't going were also happy; their turns would come sooner than they could have hoped.

Who gave a thought to the dead we left back there in the mud? Since the regiment hadn't attacked, due to the bad weather, we hadn't had high losses like at the time of our first relief. But the shells had claimed victims every day, even in the quietest sectors.

In my old company, the 21st (Hudelle's company), my old active-duty Sergeant Darles had been killed by a shell. His brother, a private in the same unit, went to his aid, but a second shell killed him, two minutes later.

This was a simple fact. What did it matter that it was two brothers, two friends, or two strangers? But think about a father and a mother with two children—their hope, their help in the future, in their old age, upon whom their thoughts settled—who learn, all of a sudden, the brutal news, the horrible death of their two children.

Go talk about glory, victory, the fatherland to these poor old people. They'll ask you not to insult their misery.

In the 23rd Company, where I was sent in disgrace when they took away my measly little corporal's stripes, my comrade Escande had been killed—a chunk of his thigh was torn away by a shell fragment.

Escande was from Citou, a socialist militant of the front rank in a time when that really meant something. How many worthy militants I saw disappear, cut down by machine-gun fire! You could say that war took its vengeance on those who hated it the most and who sought to unite peoples across borders to prevent this monstrous crime.

Someone originally from Peyriac had also found a cruel death during this time on the front lines. His name was François Petit. Up to the age of 12 we played together, as neighbors, and we got our lessons from the same teacher on the benches of our modest schoolhouse. Then he followed his father to [South] America and after almost thirty years of absence he had come back when war was declared.

Petit was not a fervent patriot, and he was more inspired by pacifist sentiments than by warlike ones. It would doubtless have been better for him to have stayed quietly in the Argentine Republic, but he saw an opportunity to return to France, at no cost, thinking that at his age (almost 40) he wouldn't go to the firing line. But he was wrong, and they did him the honor of assigning him to a fighting unit. That's how he fell into the 23rd Company, where my name was duly inscribed next to his on the roster.

Sent out on ration detail for the company, he was killed with four of his comrades, by a barrage of shellfire which took them by surprise.

You can imagine what a sweet death he and his unlucky comrades had. To earn the right and the glory of being a hero killed on the field of honor, you have to pay.

Before his last home leave, which he spent with relatives who had stayed in Peyriac, he told me he intended to slip into Spain and make his way back to peaceful [South] America, where the people weren't caught up in the warlike madness which had poisoned the brains of the inhabitants of the Old World. He had even said farewell and embraced me. But twelve days later he came back to take his place on the front lines, having lacked the decisiveness and the boldness needed to put his plan for flight to Spain into action.

A week later, near Morval, he was blown to shreds by a shell. He'd have been better off staying in [South] America. Who thinks about him now? His name doesn't even appear on the monument erected at Peyriac "to those of its children who died for France," as the epitaph which the patriotic town council had affixed to the monument says so hypocritically.

On December 4, 1916, a corporal named Muller, a Parisian, having all the vices and practicing all the debauches of the capital's lower depths—pervert, lover of cocaine—killed with a revolver a girl of 15 years, whose grandmother ran a tavern and whose father was at the front.

Ah, if in an occupied village a German had killed a young girl! What our newspapers wouldn't have said to inform their readers about this innocent victim, this martyred virgin, this barely budding flower, cut down by a brutal death, etc.

And how they would have described the murderer! Sadistic brute, ferocious barbarian, savage beast, cannibalistic executioner . . . the dictionary couldn't provide enough tarnishing words. The name of this poor girl would have been passed to posterity, and her misery perhaps cited in the history of France, to kindle hatred against the Germans.

But alas—the murderer was a Frenchman, and we have to keep silent about this crime, which was kept out of official dispatches. Many soldiers of the 296th Regiment didn't know what happened, and I wouldn't have known about it if our Lieutenant Lorius hadn't told me, knowing that I was writing the history of our tragic epic.

It was evening, in a tavern. Corporal Muller, drunk, was waving a revolver around and pointed it at the granddaughter of the landlady, saying, "Say *chiche*" [French slang for "I dare you—Bet you can't!"]. The child, thinking it was a joke, called out, "Chiche!" Muller pulled the trigger of his revolver, which he says he thought wasn't loaded, and the bullet tore through the neck artery. Without a cry, a word, the girl fell dead.

You can imagine the emotions aroused in Salouel by this tragic, stupid death. The corporal was arrested right away and brought before a court-martial a few days later. The victim's family had the generosity to intervene on his behalf and sought the indulgence of the judges toward Muller, who was sentenced to just two years in prison.

But this deplorable event had unfortunate consequences for us, as if two thousand men were responsible, in solidarity with the act of one bandit!

All our prowess, all our dazzling actions, for which they couldn't find enough elegiac words to congratulate us, carried no weight in the decision of our big bosses, who chased us out of Salouel and sent us into a tiny village devoid of all comforts.

So on December 6, 1916, the 296th Regiment, in gray weather and a glacial bise, left Salouel with much regret and marched a dozen kilometers to encamp in the village of Briquemesnil (Somme).

296th Infantry Regiment, 1916. Briquemesnil. Aumale. Morvillers. Third home leave. Valmy.

It was nightfall when we made our far-from-triumphal entry into Briquemesnil. An old peasant, three youngsters, and a dozen geese were the sole witnesses to our arrival at this place of exile.

In this little village, with mainly tumbledown houses grouped around a stinking pond, there was no tavern where you could go to sit down, quench your thirst, restore your strength or your spirits. There was only a tiny grocery store run by an ill-tempered gossip, and a single communal well which occupied what appeared to be the public square.

This well was ninety meters deep, and to bring up some of the cloudy, whitish water required no less than a hundred fifty turns of the handle—a two-man operation, if you didn't want to have your shirt soaked through with sweat.

Our cooks lined up early in the morning around the well, to the vexation of the inhabitants, who claimed that the well would soon dry up, forcing them to buy water from neighboring villages.

Our whole 4th Machine-Gun Company was billeted in the upper story of a large barn. To get up there you had to climb up the wall, on the outside, by a ladder which barely reached the window—a simple opening in the wall—and hoist yourself up by sheer arm strength.

For the young guys this was a game, but for those like me who were nearing 40 it was a dangerous exercise. The first time I climbed into our bedroom I almost ended up face-down on the paving stones below. This motivated me to seek lodgings elsewhere. In a corner of the courtyard I was lucky enough to find some pigpens, deemed uninhabitable for those beasts, with unhinged doors, holes in the roof, openings in the crumbling walls, but I rushed to take possession of the least dilapidated of them. Just in time, too—the others were taken by storm, a few minutes later.

Being reduced to the state of disputing with each other over half-demolished pigpens—that's war for you! And we still thought we were lucky to be there, sheltered from the rain, from bullets, from shells, from poison gas. Little by little, we were being taken over by the instincts of primitive men.

I fixed up my precious redoubt the best I could. I stuffed with paper the holes in the wall which the bise blew through. I closed up the rat holes with broken glass. A bit of straw framed with bricks made my bed. A plank stuck to the wall served as my dresser; my knapsack was my pillow, desk, and briefcase; for lighting, I transformed an English hand grenade into a kerosene lamp. In brief, I had a fairly long sojourn there, where I could read, write, and sleep in peace and quiet, far from the noise and hubbub of the main encampment.

From time to time, in the evening, we'd go into the village of Bourgainville [variation of Bougainville], four kilometers away, where it was possible to get provisions and spend a few pleasant moments seated in a warm, well-lit café.

Just think of it: to take a round-trip of eight kilometers, at night, in the dead of winter, to enjoy a bit of warmth, of light, of well-being. That shows how much we wanted to chase away, to dissipate, our boredom and our homesickness.

From the day after our arrival, as if to punish us for the crime at Salouel, the training exercises so detested by the men started up again, despite the cold and occasional rain. Once, when our lieutenant and the three sergeants of our squad had gone off on a mission or on leave, I had to take command of the group.

Since this great honor was accompanied by many worries and few advantages, I cursed this annoying occurrence, despite the fact that they left us pretty much alone. Who would have thought at the end of July 1914 when, in my simple barrelmaker's workshop I handled the peaceful tools of my trade—saws and planes—that one day I would command a group of field guns and their gunners!

Alas, I was no more proud of that than I was of my peacetime tools, and peace itself.

And Christmas arrived. The only difference from other days was that we didn't go out for training. But that day the newspapers, in huge letters, announced the sensational peace proposal of Emperor Wilhelm of Germany.

There was a flash of hope which was soon snuffed out. The servile newspapers, under orders from the madmen who governed us, shouted with joy, with gladness, figuring that if the emperor was making such an offer, it proved he must be running out of everything—money, food, munitions. We must not negotiate, they said, but rather prepare ourselves for the supreme effort, the final death knell, the execution of the exhausted, beaten enemy.

By resisting for two more years, Germany proved that she still had the means to continue the war, and that our governors had lied.

To be sure, I don't seek to defend the odious Kaiser, the living incarnation of haughty, brutal, authoritarian militarism. But he did make a gesture which honors him, by inviting the leaders of the warring peoples to try to meet and reach agreement to stop the shedding of blood.

By refusing to listen to or even acknowledge the Emperor's proposals, under the pretext that they could not be sincere, our leaders assumed an immense responsibility before History, and gave the leading role to the Kaiser.[7]

Around the end of December we learned that our regiment was leaving the Ninth Corps and moving to the Eighth, which left us completely indifferent. Out of twenty men, there were perhaps nineteen who had no idea what corps they belonged to. But this event could not be allowed to pass unnoticed, and on January 6 [1917] a farewell ceremony took place, a few kilometers from the village.

All the troops of the division, with their flags and bands, were there. The weather was freezing, and we had to spend three hours marching, parading, and presenting arms. Finally they formed us up in a square, and the division's general gave a fitting speech, a great elegy, exalting our warlike virtues, and said that our regiment was now a well-tempered weapon of war. He declared that the thought of our departure brought tears to his eyes.

Alas, this war has brought us many more separations, even sadder and more wrenching, for us to be moved by this one.

The next day, January 7, we left Briquemesnil to rejoin our new army corps,[8] and after having marched all day we arrived that night at the village of Morvillers (Somme).

This village was hardly any more attractive than Briquemesnil. It was made up of three hamlets; the church was in the middle of the fields. For our billet our group had a barn with daub-and-wattle walls, that is to say, of straw and hardened earth, riddled with holes. On one side there was a crevice which a man could easily pass through, not to mention the wind, the rain, the bise.

For a mattress there was a sleeping platform, which might as well have been a manure pile, where legions of lice must have swarmed. Clearly my pigpen at Briquemesnil was a villa compared to our new campsite.

I looked all around for some solitary place to bunk, just right for my misanthropy, but hog pens, stables, doghouses, all were occupied by their four-footed inhabitants. Finally I caught sight of some premises being used as a storeroom, right at the edge of a pond. The ground was muddy, and dampness oozed from the walls. Despite these bad hygienic conditions, I took up residence there, in the company of one of our drivers, my friend Vidal, a son of Carcassonne who had lived in Peyriac for some time.

But we had to acquire, whatever the cost, a bit of straw. Even with our billfolds in hand, we couldn't get hold of even an armful. But in a courtyard we spotted a vehicle which had been used to carry some pigs, calves, or sheep to market, in which lay a nice pile of straw. Like thieves making off with a treasure chest, we carried off this straw and spread it out over some planks of wood. The bedding problem was solved.

Oh, how happy I was when I was able to be off by myself, to slip away, to avoid everyone else, to withdraw from that atmosphere of the crowded encampment, from the snoring and the belching of some, from hearing the petty quarrels of irate cardplayers who stayed up half the night, from listening to the rude songs, the stupidities of those who had one too many gulps of pinard. How I preferred the silence, the solitude, away from all this noise, this brouhaha which prevented my spirits from rising above the sad reality.

Those who did not fear the Siberian bise, the gendarmes, and the cost would go in the evenings to the neighboring town of Aumale, where there were stores, cafés, and shops of every sort.

In vain did they tell us every day at assembly that it was forbidden to go there without authorization. The poilus made fun of this, and on Sundays when I would go there with some comrades we would be at least a thousand, strolling the streets with the glorious patch of the 296th right there on our greatcoats.

The gendarmes who guarded the entrances to Aumale were powerless in the face of this invasion. If they hadn't had the prudence to stand aside quietly and if, especially after dark, they had tried to arrest a poilu, they'd have been thrashed and massacred without pity.

There was nothing to be done about it. Such was the attitude of the combatant, who felt pity for the Boche who shared the same sufferings and dangers as he did, but who had sworn ferocious hatred for the gendarme, this slacker who was trying to bother him, keep an eye on him, spoil his rest and his liberty as soon as he got out of the trenches.

On January 13, in freezing cold and fifteen centimeters of snow, we made our way to a spot near Aumale to participate in a review, in which the units of our new division would meet up.

For several hours we had to march and parade like in any respectable review, tramping in the mud and snow, and we got back to Morvillers after dark.

We could have done without this promenade and this parade—I was about to say, or write, "masquerade." But the suffering and the fatigue of thousands of men count for little to the big military chiefs. Tradition and custom must be carried on, rules must be followed, rites must be acted out.

On January 16, at 5 in the morning, in terrible cold, I left Morvillers with a detachment of fellow leave takers to catch the train at Aumale.

The train was supposed to depart, or rather to pass through, at 7 o'clock, but like all the trains full of leave takers it was way behind schedule. Since the station was already overflowing with people who were going to breathe their native air, we had to stay outside and undergo some vigorous calisthenics from time to time against the cold.

On the station platform, in a pile of merchandise, a box had spilled open, and an indiscreet poilu had stuck his hand inside and pulled out a bottle of rum. This produced a mad rush, and in two minutes the case was emptied. War destroys in man, who in uniform becomes an anonymous creature, all sense of honesty.

When killing becomes a duty, a holy thing, then stealing is no more than a peccadillo.

Finally, at 9 o'clock the long-awaited train took us away, and at 10 we were at Beauvais where we had a long wait.

At 9 p.m. we were at the Survilliers switching station [south of Creil]. Because of the congestion of rail lines around Paris it took many long hours to make our way across the metropolitan area, so that it wasn't until 1 a.m. that we arrived at Orléans—too late for the last train to Toulouse. More long hours to wait for another train, in the inhospitable station of Orléans.

But a train for Bordeaux was ready to pull out, and we piled on board. Much better to ride on an express train than to pace back and forth in a station. A detour of two or three hundred kilometers meant little to us. We were traveling for free, and the Boches would pay the bill when the final accounts were settled!

Unfortunately, at that time there was a shortage of window glass, and on trains many windows had only their frames. You can imagine that the compartments available to us were those which had only one pane of glass, at most. That made for rather exaggerated ventilation, especially with a temperature of several degrees below zero. But when you're going home on leave it's as if you are seized with madness; you're indifferent to everything. If it meant leaving sooner, we'd have climbed onto the roofs of the cars.

Naturally, the cars weren't heated. It was necessary to save coal. Despite how tough our hides were, we almost froze during this long January night, shivering as we piled up in the corners, huddled next to one another.

It was with joy that, at 8 in the morning, we put our feet down on the platform of the Bordeaux railway station. A radiant sun warmed our benumbed limbs, and after a couple of hours strolling in the streets of the capital of Gascony, we left at one in the afternoon for Languedoc. Twelve hours later, at one in the morning, I crossed the threshold of my home, where my loved ones, alerted by telegram, awaited me.

I found spirits in the village greatly changed since my last home leave. The disaster in Romania, the dispatch of numerous forces to Salonika, the imminent call-up of the conscript class of 1918, the numbers of those exempted from service who had escaped the net of the recruitment boards, the shortages of sugar, coal, and transport—all those had turned a sunny optimism into somber pessimism, as eyes began to open onto how things really were.[9]

Alas! Seven days passed quickly, and on January 28 it was time to take the road back, with an angry heart.

Having learned from my friends at the front that the regiment had left the Somme and was already at the front lines on the border of Champagne and the Argonne, I figured out that by altering my route slightly I could spend one more day with my family.

Those who read these lines later on will say: "Bah! One day more or less, that's no big deal." True, it was only twenty-four hours of sixty minutes each. But as these hours and minutes were so precious, how we savored them, in spite of the bitterness and the apprehension of our departure.

As we crossed the middle of France by night, the temperature dropped suddenly, and the windows were decorated with arabesques of ice. The countryside was covered with snow. It was sure going to be nice in the Argonne trenches.

Passing through Sens, we saw the firemen putting out a fire in a railway station building, started by a bombardment which had just taken place. There were four victims. The place where the accident happened was covered with shattered rubble and all kinds of debris, still smoking. An agitated crowd pressed forward at the edges, but the soldiers who thronged our train took it all in with an indifferent eye. Ruins, fires, the injured, and the dead—they were utterly blasé at sights like these.

At 4 in the afternoon we passed through Troyes. Night fell, the cold rose up again; we would have liked to get down, to have dinner and spend the night there, but departures were strictly forbidden. Good tables and nice beds weren't for us, the poor pilgrims of death!

At 3 in the morning the train stopped at Valmy, the station where I had to get off. To welcome the leave takers there was a barrack where a glacial cold reigned, despite a smoky stove placed in the middle which no one could get close to, since it was surrounded by twenty poilus vainly trying to gather some bit of warmth from it.

I tried to lie down on one of the wooden benches along the walls, but after a few minutes the cold forced me to pace back and forth in the barrack until dawn.

They granted us a quart of warm drink which they called coffee, and each of us left to join his own unit, guided by the ration squads which had come to the Valmy station.

We passed through the historic village. As we left, I looked for the famous, legendary windmill, but they told me that it had been a long while since any grain had been milled there. Not one stone remained, but a signpost indicated to passersby where it had stood.[10]

With my eyes, I gazed across this battlefield where the fate of France, of the Revolution, and perhaps of all Europe, had played out, and I was astonished.

According to the accounts, the illustrations, the paintings, I had supposed that Valmy was right at the entrance to a gorge, and that there the invasion had been halted like a torrent rushing down a mountainside, and was hurled back right at the point where it would spill forth and spread onto the plain. But the landscape was flat and ordinary—a wide-open plain, with here and there some slight undulations in the terrain.

I stopped at a promontory, from which perhaps Goethe and the Duke of Brunswick had observed the phases of the action, a simple skirmish compared to the titanic battles of the Yser [Flanders], Verdun, or the Somme. The countryside, covered with a blanket of snow, was silent, the roads almost deserted; barely, in the distance, you could hear occasional cannon fire.

This was a calm sector. What a difference from the Somme sector, where the roads were incessantly crowded, day and night, with interminable columns of caissons, trailers, artillery, and vehicles of every sort, not to mention the troops going to and from the trenches.

Seven kilometers from Valmy we came upon a half-demolished village,

Dommartin-sous-Hans. A few tenacious inhabitants still remained, despite the shells which rained down fairly frequently.

I had the happy surprise of finding there the drivers and the crew of a 37 field gun, at rest, well installed in an intact house furnished with tables, chairs, mirrors on the walls, etc. Each trooper slept on a cot or a mattress; we were like real bourgeois, true *embusqués* [shirkers]. My own team was due to come here for their six-day rest break the very next day; all I had to do was wait for them.

That evening, just when we were taking our meal around a big fire, four explosions shook the house, followed by a clattering of broken tiles. It took a few seconds to figure out was going on; then there was a stampede to the basement, but that was all the excitement we had that evening.

A shell had fallen on a nearby house where the food stores were located. Luckily it had exploded when it hit the roof and had made a big hole there, damaging nothing more than a row of sausages, put there by someone with the ill-fated idea of hanging them from an attic rafter to dry.

A second shell had fallen right in front of our lodging, into a corral where about twenty of our horses and mules were tethered. Three of these animals lay on the ground; one of them was headless, while the two others were breathing their last death rattles, and to relieve their suffering someone finished them off with pistol shots.

Fraïssé, whose appetite was always excited by a glacial bise, was elated at the thought of the fine cuts of horse meat which he would enjoy over the next few days.

The 296th Regiment from Béziers in Champagne: January 30–April 26, 1917

Dommartin-sous-Hans. The "Main de Massiges."
The Maisons-Champagne Affair.

From morning to night, our stove and grill were busy transforming the choice cuts of these poor beasts into delicious and savory steaks, which were stuffed into Fraïssé's bottomless belly and expanded his rotundity by several centimeters, enhancing the jowls of his ruddy face.

His belly satisfied, Fraïssé grew more jovial, and by his jokes and colorful and picturesque expressions he cheered up those whose minds were most afflicted by *le cafard* [anxiety].

For variety, he tried to hunt down some harmless sparrows, but all he caught was a scrawny little owl, which he summarily executed and plucked. Alas, it was so skinny that when you pressed on its belly it squeaked like a little baby.

Fraïssé wandered out and, approaching groups of soldiers coming up to their billets, he pressed on the owl's belly and stupefied those who thought they were hearing a newborn's whimpers. After a bit of this entertainment, the little owl went right into Fraïssé's own belly, following the horse- and mule-meat portions which had preceded it.

The next day, my comrades from the gun crew came to spend six days of rest at the billet. The house belonged to a little old lady, still quite alert despite her seventy-five years. She now lived in the village with her son.

Twenty times a day, her hands in a *chauferrette* [hand warmer], she paid us visits, and with her ferret's eye she checked to see that all the furniture, the walls, the windows, the ceiling, and the floor hadn't suffered any damage, because we were threatened with expulsion at the first sign of any harm to the building or the furnishings.

"Old witch! What a leech! Go to hell, you maniac!" we called out in our regional slang at each inspection visit.

One day, she went to the cantonment's duty officer to get us to vacate the premises, because the smoke was blackening her dwelling place.

We had to invoke the impossibility of lodging elsewhere, and to promise to light our fires only in a single, out-of-the-way, cold and shabby room.

This old lady cursed the Germans who had installed themselves as masters of her house for two weeks in 1914. I believe that she would have readily pardoned them for the massacre of Louvain and the destruction of Reims,[1] but not for breaking the front panel of an old armoire and stealing a soup tureen.

Sometime afterward, frequent bombardments forced the inhabitants to evacuate the village. The old lady had her house demolished, and she herself got a German shell fragment in one of her buttocks.

According to the inhabitants, the Germans in 1914 hadn't done any serious damage, and it was almost with pride that they showed us a shed where the Crown Prince—the real one, not our ridiculous adjutant-major—had garaged his motorcar.

During our stay in Dommartin, the thermometer wavered between twelve and fifteen degrees below zero [Celsius] every day. You can appreciate the suffering of the soldiers in the trenches. And to think that in the rear, in Paris above all, they were complaining loudly that they didn't have enough coal to heat their dwellings, the theaters, the cinemas!

These complaints were an insult to those who were condemned by this odious war to live outdoors, so to speak.

On February 6, at nightfall, it was our team's turn to go up to the front line. We passed through the village of Courtémont, less damaged than Dommartin. We passed by the barracks of Cote 202, where our battalion had come to spend six days of rest. Then, close to Minaucourt, we reached a height called "the Promontory," where our brigadier-general had installed himself, facing the opposing escarpment held by the enemy.

We climbed this height by means of a communication trench. Then we headed down the opposite slope, and found ourselves at the foot of another hill, the "Index Finger," one of the "fingers" of the famous "Main [Hand] de Massiges." The ravines separating these "fingers" are dotted with cemeteries where so many fellows from the Midi have come to their final rest, paying the price for the famous victory in Champagne in September 1915.[2]

This Main de Massiges is formed by six hills extending from a little plateau. But since a Christian's hand has only five fingers, one of them was baptized the "Faux Pouce" [False Thumb].[3]

It's there that we came to relieve our comrades, in a very good shelter, with a wire-mesh cot for each one of us.

In the middle of the room, a big iron drum had been made into a stove, fueled by wood that we stole—Fatherland, forgive us—from a neighboring supply depot.

In the morning, we carried our field gun up close to the front lines and set up a battery out in the open, but we had orders not to open fire first unless the enemy attacked, which perfectly suited our pacific temperament.

To get across the Faux Pouce you passed through a tunnel, 150 meters long, through which ran the rails of a Decauville train.

Along either side of this tunnel opened galleries and rooms where whole companies were sheltered, but they were extremely damp and dark.

Half of the team, with Sergeant Gauthier, and the other half, with me, divided the day on the front line with the cannon, and in the evening the piece was brought back to the shelter, where we spread out like embusqués, protected from the rigorous cold of this hard month of February 1917.

During the night of February 14–15, at one in the morning, we were tumbled from our beds by a sudden, violent bombardment which the Germans unleashed on our lines.

Shaken, we got up to see what was happening. Shells were falling all around, even on the edge of our shelter, normally a peaceful corner. It was clear that this bombardment, completely unexpected, was the prelude to a German infantry attack.[4]

At dawn, the cannonade redoubled in fury. The villages in the rear, the roads, the batteries, our rolling field kitchens sheltered behind a hillock called the "Demi-Lune" [Half-Moon] 400 meters away from us, all were heavily shelled. Then, suddenly, the bombardment became very violent on the regiment on our left, the 208th; less intensive on ours, the 296th; and insignificant on the regiment to our right, the 13th.

Since our gun was placed in the 13th Regiment's sector, we could take our usual position. From there we looked down on the ravines and the slopes which were under fire from the German batteries.

The spectacle was impressive, and you had to think back to the tragic days of Lorette, Verdun, and the Somme to conceive of a bombardment like this one.

It lasted until 3 in the afternoon. At precisely that hour, the German artillery lengthened its range, and the earth shook under our feet, rocked by detonation of underground mines which bowled over our front lines. Right away we saw Germans storming the positions occupied by the 208th Regiment. The occupants, holed up in the deepest shelters, barely offered any resistance, and surrendered. We could see them, in bunches, marching away beyond the German trenches, toward exile, forced labor, hunger, fatigue, but far from the zone of death, with the near-certainty of one day seeing their native villages and their familial homes again.[5]

The German communiqués reported the number of prisoners they took from us at 1,050.

Meanwhile, the Germans, having occupied the second line of trenches, pushed no farther, but they tried to widen this breach by attacking from the rear the positions occupied by our regiment, which found itself in a very bad spot by this flank attack. Nevertheless, the Germans made no progress; besides, they didn't appear to be at full strength, only one of their regiments, the 78th, being engaged. For them, it was only a local, limited action, requiring a minimum of preparation, which passed unnoticed by our side and found us completely unprepared for their bombardment.

There were, in the 296th Regiment, some examples of individual heroism:

A machine-gun sergeant, with all his men killed or wounded, stayed alone at his weapon and put the Germans, who got as close as thirty meters to him, to flight.

In a boyau, a corporal, summoned to surrender by a Boche officer, replied with a pistol shot and caused the officer to disappear.

A captain of the 208th Regiment and a few men, including two squads from the 296th, who were completely surrounded, held out behind barricades of sandbags and were able to rejoin our side overnight.

The principal cause of the enemy's halt seems to me to be an error in aiming their artillery, which kept firing violently but did not lengthen its range enough. Its curtain of fire put a barrier in front of the infantry's advance.

In the 208th Regiment was my old comrade, Peyriac's Gabriel Gils, who got out of this scrape safe and sound.

Before the attack, only one battalion out of three was up at the front line. From that day forward, all three battalions were jammed into the trenches without sufficient shelters, obliged to get their rations, do work details, and relieve each other practically in the open, the communication trenches having been leveled at several points or filled with water and mud.

What had been a sector of quiet repose had become, in 24 hours, the scene of exhaustion, suffering, and death, as bombardments and shellings "on the fly" were generously served up to us.

The 37mm field gun to our left was demolished by a 105mm shell, but the crew got out without at scratch, having taken refuge in a deep shelter nearby.

On February 18, our squad was supposed to go for six days of rest. But instead of going to Dommartin, we had to be happy with going one kilometer to the rear, simply in reserve, the whole regiment being up at the front line.

We went to the Index Finger. This hill had the honor of sheltering, in its slope, our Colonel Robert. Having no doubt found the existing dugout unworthy of sheltering such an important personage, the engineers were building another, more spacious one.

"The Index Finger." "The Half-Moon."

There I met Peyriac's Louis Lalaque (later killed, in the final months of the war), who was a corporal in the engineers and who confided in me that the value in material alone—the labor being at no cost—came to at least ten thousand francs.

Inside the Index Finger there were veritable catacombs filled with hundreds of wire-mesh cots, but complete darkness and extraordinary humidity reigned. Water seeped through, dripped from the vaulted ceiling, soaked through the walls, which were sometimes wood-paneled, and formed huge puddles. A bad place for anyone suffering from sciatica or rheumatism.

Outside, there were plenty of airier shelters, open to the elements and with corrugated sheet-metal roofs and terraces, along the twisting road, which snaked down from the summit of the Index Finger to its base.

Unfortunately we were prey to very clever German artillerymen. Through enfilading or plunging fire, they found a way to rain their shells down upon whatever point in the flank was exposed to them. As a result, most of the inhabitants had abandoned the surface shelters and sought refuge underground.

All the way at the end, there was a shelter covered by a large piece of metal— too thin, alas!—which a shell had pierced like an eggshell. Inside were a table, benches, cots; a windowed door, brought from who knows where, kept out the drafts. Finally, a supreme luxury, there was a lamp glowing with light.

One can imagine that this habitation wasn't meant for vulgar poilus from the trenches. If it had been abandoned for the use of whoever came along, that's because several times a day, and even at night, a volley of shells, from less than twenty meters away, fell right in front of the shelter, shattering the crosses in an adjacent cemetery and killing inoffensive frogs which inhabited a pond and a large stream at the end of the ravine.

These shells, it is true, were only puny 77's or 90's. But whether you're killed by a shell the size of your fist or by one as big as a flour sack, you're just as dead.

Despite the danger, four artillerymen, fanatical cardplayers, set up shop in this tempting shelter, seduced by the prospect of interminable card games they could have, day and night.

The rest of us occupied a cabin right near the crest, thinking ourselves to be perfectly secure. But one night, without warning, a 105 shell crashed down, barely a meter from our roof, right onto a neighboring shelter which luckily was empty of any tenants. We saw in this a providential warning, and cursing the Kaiser's gunners we shifted to quarters underground.

Before the business of February 15, the Index Finger enjoyed almost complete calm. It was an important point in the sector. There was a railway station—yes, a railway station—which was filled with all kinds of supplies brought up by trains, called *tacots,* on a 0.6-m gauge rail line. It was even a marshaling yard, because several lines led out from there, going to Beauséjour, the "Half-Moon," and the other fingers of the Main de Massiges.

There was a watering station with a motorized pump. A generator fed electric power to light up the shelters; in an underground stable there was a troop of little donkeys used for ration details and for transporting supplies, and finally three cows furnishing their milk to His Majesty the Colonel and to the sick in the infirmary.

After the Germans had bagged a thousand prisoners on February 15, General Nivelle[6] declared that, whatever the cost (in human lives, except his own), we had to retake the lost ground. Numerous heavy, tractor-mounted artillery pieces quickly were brought up, and on February 23rd they opened a terrible bombardment onto the German positions. Unfortunately some of these pieces aimed too short, and their shells landed right on our lines, claiming victims. I myself heard Colonel Robert declare that if they continued to kill his men he was going to hand in his resignation.

The French attack was to have taken place on the night of February 23–24, but the regiment given that assignment had been decimated in the approach trenches by the enemy barrages. In a pouring rain, what was left of this regiment had to pull back, and the attack was postponed.

During that night, two Germans, for whom the war held no further charms, surrendered. Brought the next day to the colonel's post on the Index Finger by Perier, our lieutenant's aide, they said that the fire from our batteries had made their trenches untenable, and that we would have met no serious resistance.

After having gathered this and other bits of intelligence, our colonel dismissed the prisoners, snarling, "Get this garbage out of here!"

On February 24, our six days of rest having expired, we went up at 9 p.m. to relieve the team at the front line, on the regiment's left.

Six or seven hundred meters from the Index Finger stood another hill, the Half-Moon. Up against this half-moon hill our rolling field kitchens took shelter. It was the terminus of the tacot railway line and the corduroy road by which the ration carts arrived.

Two men from the squad and I stayed at the Half-Moon, lodged like termites in the underground galleries furnished with cots. In front of the entrance, three fresh springs bubbled up and fed a stream which snaked its way toward Massiges.

Our task consisted of sending rations up to our gun team at the front line. Each evening, when the ration squad came back from the gun, I went to the Index Finger to take the report to our lieutenant from Sergeant Gauthier, the gun's commander.

Without the shells which fell upon the Half-Moon, this would have been a leisurely assignment. But since February 15 the enemy gunners paid particular attention to us. This wouldn't have been of particular importance, except that the regiment's field kitchens were set up right there.

The cooks had only the most precarious shelters, and it called for real courage on their part to not quit their posts and throw off their aprons to the devil.

The field kitchen of our 4th Machine-Gun Company was particularly exposed; when shells exploded too nearby, the cooks and their assistants fled into whatever shelter was handy. Only Master Chef Morla stayed at his post, unperturbed. If there was less glory in dying with a ladle than with a rifle in hand, there was still a bit of heroism in it.

For his tranquil courage, his absolute disregard of any danger, he was awarded the Croix de Guerre. Later on, maybe the Worthy Corporation of Cooks of the Great War will be full of pride about this distinction earned by one of their very own.

I'm in the habit of noting down here the characters who offer some sort of originality. I therefore can't leave our own *cordon bleu* in the shadows. He deserves to be remembered in posterity, not so much for the succulence and variety of his menus, no matter how much attention he brought to them, but for other remarkable qualities.

Morla was tall and thin. In his usual pose, holding in one hand the lid of his cooking pot, wreathed in the steam which emerged from it, he evoked the image of the god Vulcan at his forge.

He alone set the menus. He relied solely on his own experience in deciding just how a ragout should taste. Every day he arose well before dawn to make the coffee. He never left to others the task of preparing this sacred potion.

He presided at the smallest distribution, and despite the daily fluctuation of manpower due to arrivals and departures of leave takers, those being evacuated, etc., you wouldn't give a thought to squeezing out an extra serving of meat or pinard. He knew, from memory, without fault, exactly what each squad was due.

He was the sole dispenser of goods from the kitchen. Whoever wanted a clove of garlic, an onion, or a mug of coffee had to present himself to his omnipotent personage, and with the seriousness of a presiding judge he would agree or not agree, with no room for appeal.

He'd gotten the nickname "Paper." I never learned why or how.

One day, having gone to the kitchens to carry back our rations, I was surprised, fifty meters from our shelter, by a volley of four 105mm shells exploding around me. Violently thrown to the ground by the concussion, I thought I was dead, or nearly so. My comrades, who saw this happen to me from the threshold of the shelter, were sure I'd been blown to bits. They rushed to my aid, and were astonished to see me get up on my own. Checking that all my limbs were in working order, I couldn't find a scratch. But all the canteens and pots of food were pounded into marmalade, and we had to go begging to "Paper," who kindly gave us some leftovers for our meal.

Death had brushed right past me maybe twenty times, and turned aside. Once again, a mysterious hand seemed to have saved me from a hideous, certain death.

In the Half-Moon was also stationed Peyriac's own "Vatel," Louis Richardis, master chef, as I've already written, for those two colorless characters: our commandant, and our *capitaine-adjutant-major* Cros-Mayrevielle.

One evening, he had the generous idea of inviting all the sons of Peyriac in the vicinity to a sumptuous feast in his ramshackle cabin, destined any day to be blown to bits by some shell which will find it in its path.

But our friend Richardis was a fatalist. What is written is written, and there's no use fighting against destiny. He cooked away, turning the rotisserie in his cabin as calmly as if he were back in his hotel in Peyriac.

What joy, what happiness to find ourselves around a table, a real table, in places and in times like those, among friends, comrades, compatriots, forgetting the sadness of the present. The conversation turned to our village, to the small everyday events, gossip, tittle-tattle, idle talk, sad stories of dead men—a long list of those who, as the newspapers said, voluntarily offered up the sacrifice of their lives.

Among the Peyriacois guests was Joseph Espanôl, a private in the 13th Regiment of our division, whose shelter was near mine. Late at night, the meal having ended, and having done the honors to a good, hearty wine, even though it wasn't a wine from our Minervois region, Espanôl and I made our way back to our bunkers.

The weather was Siberian cold. There was a thin coat of icy snow, and the slick footing made our progress difficult. My comrade slipped and sprained a leg. Limping along, supported by my shoulder, he reached his mole hill and was evacuated the next day, his leg grossly swollen.

That's one guy who will remember our dinner at the Half-Moon.

Since February 15, the overworked men were in a state of great fatigue. Through his good efforts our colonel was able to get us to change places with a regiment of the division, the 29th, which was occupying the sector of Ville-sur-Tourbe.

On March 2, 1917, at nine in the evening, we left the Main de Massiges to head for Ville-sur-Tourbe.

So at 9 p.m. on March 2, in a driving snowstorm, our group assembled at the Index Finger and headed off toward our new sector, about six kilometers away, dragging our pieces with our own muscle power, which was hard enough, but worse than that was having to walk on a [corduroy] road made with logs placed one next to the other. Some of the logs were splintered, others were pushed down or stuck up. In spite of the bitter cold, our shirts were soaked with sweat. When we left the road we crossed an area of ruins, including the shell of a church; that was Massiges. Further along, other ruins: Virginy. Then other ruins appeared, just as gloomy and forlorn; that was what was left of Ville-sur-Tourbe.

Since it was our team's turn to be in reserve, our guide led us to a shelter, a cellar in the midst of the ruins.

Ville-sur-Tourbe was considered a rest area. Each day the Boches sent a half-dozen shells our way; out of politeness, our artillerymen sent about the same number, that was all.

The village was only a kilometer from the front line. A river, the Tourbe, cut through it, pushing its troubled and muddy waters across swampy areas which we had to cross to get to the trenches.

For a stretch of about four hundred meters, you had to cross on footbridges mounted on pilings, between two rows of *gabions* [wooden cribs, baskets] filled with earth to protect us from being seen and being shot. But these gabions were slowly sinking into the water, almost all the way along the route, so that when it was necessary to venture out onto the footbridges by daylight you had to hurry, and commit your fate to the generosity of the German machine gunners who had their weapons trained on them. During our stay there were some victims, but nevertheless very few. As for me, I went by there maybe a hundred times, and there was only one day when a myopic machine gunner mistook me, with my sergeant's binoculars and my walking stick,[7] for an officer or some other eminent personage, and did me the honor of sending a couple of bullets whistling past my ears.

The Germans occupied the train station, and we the church. When the parishioners return, they'll find their church bells in front of the colonel's billet, hanging from the branches of an apple tree, ready to sound the alarm in case of a poison-gas attack. Those who cast those bells would never have imagined that they would be put to such a use.

The regiment's kitchens were set up a few hundred meters from the village, on the banks of the Tourbe, practically out in the open, barely protected from the enemy's view by a little clump of poplars.

As the Germans had set up their own kitchens near their trenches, it was by reciprocal tolerance that, on each side, in a common interest, we each let the peaceful cooks go about their business in peace at their kettles. If this had happened in the Midi, land of the *mistral* and the *cers* [local names for winds particular to southern France], the Germans could have smelled the aroma of our stews, borne by the wind, and we'd have gotten the vapors of their tasteless *choucroute* [sauerkraut].

In front of the village, separating the opposing lines, there was a *calvaire* [roadside devotional sculpture] still standing, with a tall Christ and a statue of the Virgin.

What a symbol! Between combatants, this Christ and this murdered Virgin, riddled with bullets, seemed to have been put there in mute and tragic protest.

But alas, Christ, called so powerful, let this excruciating torment weigh down on us and limited himself to this mute, platonic protest.

One afternoon I had accompanied the gun-team bosses up to the trenches to reconnoiter the eventual placement of our cannon should an attack or a raid occur. When we came back we ran into Captain Cheffaut of the 4th Machine-Gun Company on the threshold of his shelter.

With a wave of his hand, he stopped me. "Corporal Barthas," he said, "I have to notify you that I'm going to have you court-martialed, for dealings with the enemy."

Captain Cheffaut was a university graduate of some merit, but alas he was an inveterate alcoholic, rather too familiar with his men, sometimes joking with them and then suddenly, for no reason at all, loading them down with inspections, wearing them out on the drill field, imposing a rigorous discipline on them.

Several times he had tried to saddle our group with his despotic authority, but each time he had run up against the resistance of our Lieutenant Lorius defending our autonomy.

The accusation of our captain was so outrageous that at first I didn't take it seriously. He's drunk, I told myself. He's just having fun with me, trying to scare me.

"My captain," I replied with a smile, "is surely joking."

"No, I'm not joking. There are four witnesses ready to testify against you."

"Oh, come on!" I said, with some impatience. "This is the first time today that I've been up to the front lines. This accusation is absurd. You're making a mistake, for sure."

"It's not here at Ville-sur-Tourbe, it's at Cote 193 in Champagne, at outpost number 10, that you had dealings with the Boches."

I felt beads of cold sweat at my temples. I couldn't suppress a trembling of my limbs. Had the secret of outpost number 10 been betrayed? I saw myself lost. In a few seconds I called up the memory of those anguished twenty-four hours, at six paces away from the German outpost. The grenade thrown at the officer who snuck up on us by night, trying to catch us at fault. How he burst in, revolver in hand, yelling threats. Then, in the morning, I myself warning the Germans that we were under a strict watch, and that they shouldn't show themselves or talk to us.

Evidently this was, in the eyes of the brass hats, an unpardonable crime. And four men of my squad were found who would denounce me, after six months, to this authoritarian, mean-spirited captain, loathed by his men.

No, this wasn't possible! But where were my poor little bleus from Champagne? All dead, or shipped out! Delatre had deserted to Switzerland. Having escaped from a German concentration camp and made it back to French lines, he had pleaded not to be sent back up to the front, so he wouldn't fall into German hands again and risk a firing squad. All they were willing to do was to change the name in his pay book. Profiting from a furlough, Delatre took off for a country, Switzerland, where the minds of those in charge had resisted the winds of universal madness.

The only other veteran, the Peyriacois Paul Alpech, was dying in a hospital in the Midi. There was only my little buddy "Big Jean," machine gunner in the 4th Company, who would jump into the fire for me.

I gathered my strength, a bit reassured. "Captain," I said, "who are the witnesses who dare to bring such an accusation against me? I have the right to know their names. Present them to me, and you'll see how I'll prove them wrong."

"Fine," said the drunkard, "I'll see what I can do."

I went to work in search of the one survivor of the squad, Big Jean, whom I found at a crossroads of communication trenches where his machine gun was emplaced. Of course he had never spoken a word to anyone about the outpost affair. He got really worked up at the baseless rumors which had reached the ear of the captain.

"You know," said Big Jean to me, "if anyone causes something bad to happen to you, I'll kill him." Deeply moved, we embraced each other before we parted company.

Nothing further ever came of this business, and Captain Cheffaut never said anything about it to me again.

On March 23, under cover of a very dark night, a German patrol got into our lines and captured three sentries who weren't expecting this kind of nocturnal visit.

The Germans were going to haul away a fourth, and had tied a rope around his neck, but he head-butted a Boche right in the belly and got away, sounding the alarm.

When our side showed up in force, the patrol had disappeared, along with the three prisoners.

This nighttime kidnapping caused a lot of ruckus in our sector. The general and the colonel were furious. For several days, at roll call, there were lamentations, blames, threats, clear instructions about prisoners, friendly sentries, outposts, etc.

The colonel ordered that we, in turn, go and grab up a few Boches from their trenches, to avenge this affront which they had inflicted upon us.

An elite patrol was put together for this purpose. But it failed miserably and came back empty-handed, missing one man who never returned.

All the colonel had to do was to go out and cross through the impenetrable tangle of barbed wire in the darkness. He'd see how easy it was. You had to be as tenacious as a Boche to crawl your way through, carving out a path with a pair of shears.

All this accursed month of March, the weather was terrible, bitterly cold, with fog, rain, and snow squalls. But that didn't stop the firefights or the violent bombardments which rained down upon Maisons-Champagne, to take and retake a few stretches of broken-down trench line.

It wasn't that the possession of these trenches had any capital importance for one adversary or the other. It came from a sense of prestige, of conceit, of glory for the generals responsible, both French and German.

The sufferings and deaths of hundreds and thousands of soldiers counted for little in relation to all that.

Due to more and more frequent bombardments on Dommartin, the supply column had pulled back to Valmy. One by one, the three corporals took turns going to the supply column to report to our liaison; on March 26 it was my turn.

I left Ville-sur-Tourbe at 2 in the afternoon, taking the road to Sainte-Menehould. At three kilometers I passed through the village of Berzieux, completely destroyed and deserted. All by itself, in an underground shelter, an *ambulance américaine* [American volunteer field hospital] was installed.

Leaving this village, there were several forks in the road. I asked a Territorial which one I should take to get to Courtémont, the next village which I was supposed to reach. But he gave me the wrong directions, and the road I took was soon nothing more than a vague, muddy footpath which petered out in unfarmable fields.

I kept on walking, hoping to see the bell tower of Courtémont at any moment. All of a sudden the snow starting coming down heavily, wiping out any trace of a road. Soon I was walking any which way, and I began to get really worried, especially since daylight was already fading, when I happened upon the rails of a narrow-gauge railway. I followed it, thinking that it would surely take me to some inhabited place. Indeed, I soon came upon a wooden structure and a storage dump next to it. On a sign I read: "Point K Station."

A couple of Territorials were inside the station. They told me that I had gone the opposite way from Valmy, and that the station was fifteen kilometers away.

I had to be in Valmy before 6 o'clock to get instructions from the corporal whom I was relieving. A nice bit of bad luck for me!

Meanwhile these good Territorials invited me to approach their roaring fire, obliged me to share their dinner, and gave me a swig of hooch. Finally, an unhoped-for lucky break: a tacot train came down from the trenches at about 5 o'clock, heading for Valmy. I hoisted myself onto the running board, because on these trains there weren't any first- or second-class cars. The empty train moved rapidly downhill and I was thoroughly frozen upon arrival at the Valmy station.

In ordinary times I wouldn't have gotten out of this without some inflammation in the chest, some congestion, or at least a bad cold. But we had grown insensitive, toughened against hardships like savage, primitive men, and the next day I was fresh and healthy as usual.

I profited from my stay in Valmy by climbing the hillock which dominates the village and where the monument to Kellermann stands. On its base I read: "From this place, from this date, a new era begins—Goethe."[8]

There is also a chapel and a funeral mound upon which is inscribed the last wish of the victor of Valmy: that his heart be buried among the soldiers who died on the field of battle. That should give pleasure to those who left their bones on this battlefield!

Finally, on a post I read: "Here stood the mill of Valmy," which appears in paintings and prints depicting the battle.

One morning, the Germans send our way some inoffensive little balloons from which were suspended packets of newspapers. A slow-burning match was attached to the string holding the packet, which allowed it to fall when the match burned through the string.

Two of these fell on the village. It did no good to order us not to open these packets, to hand them over to the military authorities immediately, that anyone found carrying one of these newspapers would be punished. It was no use. There was a rush to snatch up the newspapers. I was lucky enough to put my hands on two or three of these famous *Gazettes des Ardennes.*[9]

There you could read lists of names of French soldiers buried in occupied territory, clippings from French newspapers reprinted without comment, and some anti-English articles.

On the illustrated pages were engravings taken from French newspapers and a photograph of a long column of French prisoners taken last February 15 at Maisons-Champagne, which took up a whole page—nothing sensational about that.

But the Germans sent over other things besides children's balloons. From time to time big projectiles whistled over Valmy, brushing past the hilltop where Kellermann seemed to be trying to catch them with the big hat in his hand, and continued on until they landed two or three kilometers farther, I don't know where. Nevertheless, none of them ever fell on the village; the Germans seemed to want to respect this historic place where their great-grandfathers had fought.

But on March 31 a devil of a Boche gunner, doubtless without meaning to, aimed a bit short, and a nice little 350mm shell, if you please, plummeted down like a race car, barely two meters from the makeshift barn where the company's mules and horses were stabled.

By a stroke of bad luck I was going to visit our mules, along with my friend Castet, the driver of our gun. The shell struck the ground a few steps away from us.

By all logic we should have been pulverized, vaporized into thin air, with no trace of what happened to us. By great luck, landing on damp earth which had been soaked by the daily rains, the shell didn't explode and instead plowed deeply into the ground, digging a hole that a twelve-year-old kid could have easily climbed into.

But the violent shock was such that we were thrown brutally to the ground and terrified by the frightful shriek of the projectile. Covered with mud, we stayed motionless for a moment, without realizing what had happened.

Castet, who had a black terror of shellfire, almost fainted dead away when he saw the terrible danger which we had just escaped, not by a miracle but by flawed manufacture of the shell or other natural cause.

The horses and mules, war-hardened as they were, had been badly shaken up by the monstrous shriek of the shell and the shower of stones and mud which rained down when it fell.

At the same time, the barn was three-quarters demolished, and several of the beasts broke loose and fled in distress, to the great despair of their handlers.

In the churchyard were several hundred graves of military men who had died in the Valmy field hospital. Since the Châlons-Sainte-Menehould rail line passed close by, they had camouflaged the cemetery with tarpaulins and branches to mask the view from impressionable travelers. That's true; rows, ranks, and squares of crosses—how sad, how monotonous. Let's hide them from the happy, satisfied citizens. That's the opposite of glory!

In the church, tourists admire the magnificent stained-glass windows presented by dukes, counts, generals, princesses of the Kellermann family, each one containing a portrait of the donor.

Meanwhile, on April 1 we learned that our division was to be relieved, and at nightfall I went up with the drivers to retrieve our pieces from the front line. One more night of fatigue and danger, of being bombarded, and of treacherous roads, rain and snow.

To get some rest the next day we were going to rejoin the regiment at Braux-Sainte-Cohière, on the road to Sainte-Menehould.

Relieved from the Ville-sur-Tourbe sector.
The 296th Regiment, in stages, comes to billet for several
days at Aulnay-sur-Marne. Unknown destinations. Isse.
Vaudemange. The offensive of April 16, 1917.

They wouldn't even give twenty-four hours of rest to the soldiers coming from the trenches, who had marched all night. They weren't in that much of a hurry. And first of all, where were we going? Nobody knew exactly, but we had a premonition, according to certain rumors, that we were going to take part in an imminent big offensive.

On April 4 we left Braux-Sainte-Cohière and after a twenty-five-kilometer march we billeted at Somme-Yèvre. On the 5th we took up our march again, passing through several small villages which all resembled one another, from "Dommartin-sur-" this to "Somme-sur" that, and after having covered twenty-five kilometers, like the day before, we billeted in the pretty little village of Vésigneul-sur-Marne [southeast of Châlons].

Along our route, when we passed through one village, the population pressed forward to see us go by. On the faces you could read the pity. One woman called out, "Oh, the poor fellows. When will this life of hardships be over?"

Maybe it was a mother whose own son was in the furnace.

In the corner of the village square we noticed a peasant with long hair and a graying beard, standing immobile as if at attention, holding his cap out to us in a broad gesture of salute.

He had a look for each of us, a look of sad farewell. This sincere salute, full of sympathy for the men being led to sacrifice, moved us profoundly.

In another village, there was a group of children marching in formation with a leader at their head, like soldiers, and they made quite a disharmonious racket with their rattles. That's how we learned it was Good Friday; the bell towers were silent, and the children were calling the faithful to church services.

We passed near Châlons-sur-Marne, and finally, after a long and rough march, we reached the momentary goal of our journey, Aulnay-sur-Marne, twelve kilometers [northwest] of Châlons on the road to Epernay.

In this village, the Germans had blown up the bridge in their retreat in September 1914. The inhabitants told us that the French engineers built the very sturdy new bridge out of wood, in twenty-four hours.

The region of Aulnay must be a paradise for hunters. Rabbits and hares are in abundance. As we crossed the countryside we could see them in bands of ten or twelve, running, gamboling, frolicking as if they were far from mankind, in some virgin forest.

Strict orders protected the peace and quiet of these animals. Vigilant gendarmes were on the lookout for those for whom the sight of this game would tempt the appetites and awaken the instincts of the poacher or the hunter.

A poilu who let himself get nabbed by the cops with a hare in hand had to give back his prey, and would get the penalty of a month in prison inscribed into his pay book.

Our 37mm gun crew was lodged, as usual, in a barn. I set myself up in an empty stable stall, with a big horse on one side and a cow on the other as roommates.

One day, I discovered by chance a corner where three careless hens had roosted and laid their eggs.

I shared my discovery with my two buddies Vidal and Castet; honest and scrupulous, we held a sort of council of war to consider what to do next with this find.

It's certain that, had they fallen into the hands of other poilus, these eggs would have disappeared into their pockets and haversacks in less time than it takes to write this down, especially since the farm folk weren't very generous and caring toward us.

But we handed over these eggs without hesitation, asking only that they sell them to us, as a favor. We did the same thing on the following days.

The proprietress and her daughter couldn't get over our unselfishness. In exchange, they rendered us all manner of small kindnesses, to the astonishment of our comrades from whom we kept the news of this little event. All of our comrades would have laughed scornfully at our scruples.

On April 12 our departure was announced for the next day, but at the appointed hour, assembled and ready to go, there was a counterorder. So we unexpectedly earned another twenty-four hours and another good night in a warm stable.

Two days later, the 14th, same orders for departure, and same counterorder, but on the 15th we left Aulnay for good. We passed through Jalons-les-Vignes, where I didn't see even a stump [of *vignes* (vine stocks)], and the regiment came to billet at the village of Isse, where we spent just one night. Finding myself in too tight a space in this encampment, I climbed onto a pile of fodder, where I slept rather badly, because there were thistles in large number and their little barbs pricked my skin disagreeably, which left a piercing recollection of Isse— the only one, by the way.

The next day, April 16, the regiment left Isse at dawn, to head for the front where the cannonade was raging.

April 16—ill-fated day! The unleashing of a fruitless, bloody offensive, the slaughterhouse of the Chemin des Dames,[10] where our regiments were decimated and where all the field stations were overflowing with wounded, who were too numerous to be cared for or evacuated.

To support the head-butting planned for the Chemin des Dames, the offensive had to be extended all along the Champagne front. As usual, our division wasn't part of the shock troops in the front line. Instead, our job was pursuit and mopping up. That's why, at dawn on the 16th, we were spread out along roads and paths instead of charging with fixed bayonets at H hour.

At only three kilometers from Isse we halted in the village of Vaudemange. At a crossroads at the entrance to the village, a dozen "brave ones" from the 1914 Battle of the Marne had found eternal rest in a common grave.

We were warned not to make ourselves too comfortable, because at midnight we would be heading up to the front to begin our pursuit of the enemy.

At roll call, they read us the order-of-the-day from the mass murderer of April 16, General Nivelle, to communicate to the troops—or rather, to the victims—the day before the attack, among other bits of nonsense, that "the hour of sacrifice has sounded, and we can't be bothered by thoughts of home leave."

Alas, it was already almost thirty months that the hour of sacrifice had been sounding, every day, for some poor soul. And as for home leave, in spite of all the orders-of-the-day (or night), that's all the poilus thought about, from morning to evening; everything else was pushed aside.

The reading of this patriotic drivel aroused no enthusiasm at all. To the contrary, it only served to demoralize the soldier who heard in it only a terrible menace, more suffering, great danger, a frightful death—a useless sacrifice, totally in vain. No one had any confidence in this new round of killing leading to any useful result.

In fact, our great leaders didn't doubt for an instant that the Germans would be routed. The most minute preparations had been made for a vigorous pursuit of the enemy.

Each man received rations for several days, enough containers for four liters of drink, grenades by the dozen and cartridges by the hundred, with no thought about whether the soldier could carry such a heavy burden.

As it happened, many threw aside both meals and munitions to lighten their loads. So much waste, due directly to the carelessness of our bosses.

Therefore, at midnight, in a very dark night under a driving rain, bent double under the downpour, we left Vaudemange and headed into the fiery furnace.

After marching a few kilometers on a good road, we headed off on a path across the fields, with muddy ruts where our caissons got stuck and our mules slid and stumbled. The rain kept pouring down. Our feet slopped along in waterlogged shoes.

Finally, at 4 in the morning on the 17th, the dark night began to clear up. They halted us in a wood, a little to the rear of a heavy-artillery battery.

Right then the rain stopped—and was replaced by snow, which fell in big, fat flakes like I'd never seen before.

A blizzard on April 17! While in our Midi, down south, the trees would be already in bloom and the grapevines a sea of green.

But it wasn't a mirage. It was indeed a coating of snow that soon covered everything under a white blanket.

Our fatigue was such that most collapsed at the bases of trees, in groups of three or four, like animals surprised by a storm, even though we were soaked from head to foot and were shivering with cold.

It was just the right time to read and reread General Nivelle's famous order-of-the-day. Now that would have brought forth quite a burst of enthusiasm!

As for me, I slumped down for five minutes, but I got so cold that, despite my fatigue, I made the effort to walk around, just to keep myself warm.

I felt a grumbling in my stomach, reminding me that I'd had only a light supper the day before. I wanted to scrounge around in my mess bag, but my hands were numb with the cold and couldn't work the buttons. In any case, there wasn't much very appetizing inside: the bread, chocolate, cheese—everything was soaked, pulverized, and rendered inedible by the deluge.

Finally, at about 6 a.m., repeated whistle blasts brought all these poor devils, numb with cold, to their feet.

To stimulate the courage and the energy of these men with their haggard, downcast looks, it was quickly announced that, ahead of us, the first and second enemy lines had been taken in a single burst of élan, and that trench warfare was at an end. As a result, we would now be deploying in open formations.

The regiment formed up, and the three battalions, spread out into lines by section, marched off. It was superb. The landscape was covered with pine groves, interspersed with large clearings. We were, it appeared, about four kilometers from the front lines, but we had just covered one kilometer when we got the order to halt.

An hour, two hours, three hours went by, and we were still there.

Evidently something wasn't going right. This something turned out to be a German strongpoint bristling with machine guns, upon which shells were having no effect, and which was holding up our advance.

Luckily the snow had stopped, and no shells were falling in our vicinity. In the afternoon, by an impossible route, our field kitchen caught up to us. A container of bouillon and one of *jus* [coffee] were most welcome.

The cooks told us that on all the roads and byways, the regimental supply trains and other convoys sent up for the pursuit had gotten the order to keep their mule teams harnessed, and they were wandering around this way and that, with no idea where to go. Night fell, and the teams stayed where they were until the next day, awaiting orders that never came. Our great leaders had better fish to fry than to worry about poor beasts of burden and their drivers.

They forgot about us, too. No orders arrived. There was only the night and a chilling breeze. Our tents gave us precarious shelter. To battle the cold we had to light fires, but around there all we could find to burn was damp, green wood, which threw off a thick, suffocating smoke.

Another pretty night, engraved on our memories, to think back on when we're safe at home in our own beds—those whom death will spare, that is.

The next day, April 18, we were constantly on alert, not daring to wander off from our positions. But no orders came our way—only rain, falling in buckets. Then another long night, shivering under our fragile tent cloths, which the rain penetrated with ease.

April 19: the same uncertainty, same waiting. But fate had it that I would witness a conversation between our Colonel Robert and a general on horseback who told him, "Colonel, it's your regiment's turn to move up and attack. Head for the front line right away."

Our colonel yanked the pipe from his mouth, let fly a stream of saliva, and, to my great amazement, replied deliberately in a gruff voice, "General, look at these men and the state they're in. Do you think they don't know they've run into an insurmountable obstacle? The first day, they could have marched ahead. But not now. And me neither."

Not many colonels would have had the courage to make this kind of reply, to spare the lives of his men, but under his rude, brusque, grumpy exterior, Colonel Robert hid a good, generous, and compassionate heart. He was indeed a rare soul.

I thought that the general would be enraged by this formal refusal of an order, but he wasn't at all.

"Oh well, if your men are too tired, go off and let them rest in some nearby village."

Indeed, at three in the afternoon, we marched off happily to the village of Sept-Saux, just three kilometers away.

This was a good-sized village, to the rear of Prosnes, only five kilometers from the front lines. In spite of that, most of the houses were intact and a few inhabitants were still around.

It was one of the quietest sectors. The Russians had occupied it for quite a while. An old woman sowing potatoes in her garden told me that for thirteen months not one shell had fallen on the village, but for the past two weeks they had fallen almost daily.

The day after our arrival, we were taking our evening meal peacefully in the courtyard of our billet when a couple of shells fell on the village. It wasn't our neighborhood which was "watered," so we didn't upset our table for such a minor inconvenience. ("Table" is just a figure of speech, since our table was the pavement of the courtyard.)

We soon learned that these shells had claimed just one victim: Commandant Caussé, killed instantly just as he was dressing down a sentry.

This senior officer, carrying out vague and useless functions, seemed to spend all his time enforcing petty rules and, with mean-spirited tricks, making everyday discipline even more difficult to bear.

Recently, while we were passing through the village, he surprised one of our gunners who had the wild audacity to quit ranks to buy a cigar at a tobacco shop.

He blew this up into a story without end, declaring that it warranted no less than a full week in prison, and the same punishment for the first non-com who followed us for not closing up ranks to fill the space left by our cigar-loving comrade.

The news of his death didn't spark the slightest hint of sympathy among anyone. "So much the worse for him," said one. "If he hadn't stopped to chew out that sentry, this wouldn't have happened to him."

"Good riddance, that's one less," others called out.

It was with just such indifference and scorn that welcomed the news of the death of officers who had made no effort to win the sympathy of the soldiers.

For once, jolly old man Death had spared the little guy and tripped up the proud and arrogant big shot.

Alas, that very evening, at 9 p.m., I was just settling in when a volley of shells crashed down upon the village, and a projectile landed right on the roof of a house where a section of the 22nd Company was billeted. The roof and a section of wall collapsed, burying three soldiers who had already gone to bed. If that shell had fallen a few seconds later, it would have killed as many soldiers as were bunked there.

More volleys landed during the night, troubling our sleep. That soured us, so you can imagine how we welcomed with joy the news that we would be evacuating the village that very day.

At noon, in small bunches, we left Sept-Saux, following the Marne Canal [Canal de l'Aisne à la Marne], where we saw the artillerymen who, during the night, moved up to fire on the enemy's rear lines. After a half-hour's march we reached the main road from Reims to Châlons. Here the canal passed through a tunnel which, I was told, was two and a half kilometers long and so straight that you can see all the way from one end to the other.[11]

We soon left this road to climb up Mont [de] Billy. We passed right next to an immense artillery-ammunition depot. There were thousands and thousands of shells of every caliber, lined up like monstrous insect larvae which one day would burst forth in a blast of fire and brimstone.

It's certain that each new offensive made all the munitions manufacturers even richer. There were several millions francs' worth, right there.

As Anatole France has written: "You may think you're dying for the fatherland, but you're really dying for the industrialists."[12]

What was inconceivable was that the Germans had never fired one cannon shot onto this munitions dump, nor had an airplane dropped a bomb which would have been enough to blow the whole depot sky-high. And it was right in the path of the German planes which often flew over on their way to bombard Châlons-sur-Marne, Mourmelon, etc.

One might have said that in this war of extermination of whole peoples, there was a tacit accord between the warring parties not to destroy munitions.

On the other side of the mountain, or rather the mound, stands the village of Billy-le-Grand, where they billeted us. I don't know if there is a Billy-le-Petit ["Little Billy"] but Billy-le-Grand ["Big Billy"], in spite of its flattering qualifier of "big," wasn't more than a hamlet, and our battalion had a hard time fitting into it.

Our 37mm gun team ended up in a stable, already occupied by some rear-echelon horses.

As was only fair, we put them outside, to make room for us. If the animals were, like us, prone to egoism and meanness, they would have looked at us with hatred, but they didn't even seem to understand. Oh beasts, how superior you are to us, in so many ways!

You'll remember that my team's field gun was smashed to marmalade during the Maisons-Champagne business. On April 25 I got the order to make my way to Châlons-sur-Marne, with the gun's driver, my buddy Vidal, to go to the army's artillery park and get a shiny new 37mm cannon.

Twenty-two kilometers separated Billy-le-Grand from the chief town of the Marne [département; here, Châlons-sur-Marne], where we arrived at 5 in the afternoon.

We went to try out the hospitality of the Chanzy artillery barracks, to spend the night there. They were willing to grant us, for sleeping, a huge stable, empty of horses. But for our supper they wouldn't spare us a bowl of soup or a crust of bread. We had to dig into our pocketbooks and shell out four francs for a meager supper in a restaurant.

To our great astonishment, the town was bursting with soldiers wearing armbands and patches of every color, all manner of képis, sleeve stripes, and service ribbons, silver and gold insignia, shiny shoes and collar tabs . . .

Everyone was strutting about, parading back and forth, crowding the café terraces.

With our mud-stained helmets, our dusty greatcoats and trousers, Vidal and

I looked like vagabonds, mangy dogs, party crashers in the midst of all these fine embusqués. Embarrassed, we slunk along the walls.

The next morning we set out for the artillery park to take delivery of our new cannon. We found the place, but alas—there was only one cannon, without *flèches* ["arrows" or "trails" extending out behind the gun carriage], that is to say, without a gun carriage. A syringe would have been just as useful as this kind of bronze cylinder. "I advise you to take it," said the ordnance officer to me. "As soon as any flèches turn up, we'll send them to you. If not, you run the risk of not having a cannon at all, for a long time."

I resigned myself to taking back this half-cannon. But what would Lieutenant Lorius say when I got back, especially if he had taken a few too many swigs of hooch? He was entirely capable, in a fit of anger, of kicking me off the gun crew. And if I arrived empty-handed, with nothing at all? Wouldn't that be worse?

We set our departure from Châlons for 10 o'clock in the morning. Before leaving, we would have enjoyed a bit of breakfast, but in these strange times an obscure rule authorized soldiers to get food and drink only between 11 a.m. and 1 p.m. The cheapskate restaurateurs, in this era of huge profits, wouldn't run the risk of bending the rules to be nice to two poilus from the trenches.

Having done all we could, we decided to go see the canteen keeper at the Chanzy Barracks. But hardly had we made our request when she responded with astonishment, as if we were asking her for the moon: "Impossible! Don't you know that the canteen is off-limits until 11 a.m.?"

The evening before, we had bought a liter of wine at a bistro across the street, and the proprietress seemed friendly enough. We bought a couple of eggs and went and asked this wine merchant to cook them for us, but alas— we got the same inflexible answer.

The Killing Ground of Mont Cornillet, the 296th Regiment in the Argonne: April 26–July 1, 1917

We were just about resigned to swallowing our eggs raw. But a woman who happened to be at the bistro offered to take us to her place, where—an alluring prospect—we'd be well received and taken care of.

It wouldn't have taken us too much to give this woman a kiss on both cheeks, despite her uncertain age. From the rear she appeared to be around twenty-five; in profile, about thirty; and face to face, at least three dozen. Her hair was a mess—the early morning hour was an excuse, to be sure—and her blouse was far from clean.

Well, those were just minor details. What was important was that we were going to have a nice breakfast.

She led us down a street as narrow as a communication trench, and took us into a low-standing house with gray, cracked walls, made of wobbly, bare stones. This was her abode.

We stepped into a cramped room where hopeless disorder reigned, as well as enough filth to dampen the appetite of even our friend Fraïssé himself.

The table seemed to be perpetually set and never cleared. Glasses, platters, plates were piled up, seemingly unwashed for a fortnight.

This woman picked up a skillet which a mangy dog and a scrawny cat had just licked clean and, without even bothering to wipe it off, cracked our eggs right into it.

At the sight of this, my buddy Vidal declared that he wasn't hungry anymore and felt a bit of indigestion coming on. As for me, I admitted that I too was feeling unwell, which took away my appetite. The woman, dumbfounded, claimed the eggs for herself and her ragged little kid, who had just come in.

Meanwhile she rambled on in friendly banter with us. She confided that she was burdened with an old and bad-tempered husband of sixty who could never bring himself to laugh, while she still felt young, etc.

We couldn't listen to this anymore and we cleared out, not before promising this busybody that we would be happy to be her guests the next time we were in Châlons.

That day, we dined on a piece of bread and a can of sardines. In the evening, without incident, we went back to Billy, where with some worry I presented my half-of-a-cannon to Lieutenant Lorius.

The lieutenant, although furious, was willing to listen to my explanations. On the promise they had given me that, in a short while, they would send us the *flèches* we needed, he didn't find fault with me.

We had hoped that the complete failure of our great offensive of April 16 would have cured our generals of any idea of trying another one. But that was a misunderstanding of their mentality. Our regiment had lost nothing by waiting. We too had to pay our debt in blood.

For eight days, orders and counterorders succeeded each other, proving the incoherence which reigned in the upper ranks. One day we learned that the 296th Regiment was attached to such-and-such an army corps, the such-and-such division, only to hear at roll call the next day that we were replacing another division which was going to the rear to rest.

Abruptly they announced our departure for the front lines that very evening. At the last minute, a telephone call postponed this departure to the next day, and then the next day, and then the day after.

One morning, the squad leaders left in a hurry to reconnoiter a sector that we were to occupy the following night. But the orderlies stumbled over each other to bring them back—we were now assigned to another sector.

This disarray of command, these uncertainties, had a negative effect on the soldiers' spirits, and we were all in a state of depressed morale. But does anyone pay attention to what a soldier thinks and feels? When the order comes to march, to attack, whether you're depressed or not, who would dare to resist, to refuse?

One day, Colonel Robert had assembled his officers for a conference when an officer from headquarters, all buffed, waxed, and polished, dressed to the nines, came up, bringing the latest orders. We were to leave for Mont Cornillet.

When the colonel learned about the mission assigned to his regiment, he rose up, eyes flashing furiously, in front of this parade-ground officer, and with a voice of thunder he roared to him (I have this directly from the mouth of Lieutenant Lorius), "Tell your general that he makes me mad as hell. I've had enough of these orders and counterorders the past week. Tell him that my regiment is not going to attack until the barbed wire has been blown to bits. Yes, and tell him that if I'm holding them up, let them come and tell me!"

On April 27 our battalion left Billy-le-Grand at one in the afternoon, and at nightfall we made camp at the village of Courmelois, completely evacuated, half-destroyed due to the range of the German guns which, that evening, had the good taste to turn their muzzles elsewhere and leave us alone. The next evening [April 28], at twilight, the regiment made its way to the village of Wez, not far from the trenches and completely empty of inhabitants, where shells landed daily.

The next day [April 29] the whole regiment moved up to the front lines. Our group left behind an ammo dump at Wez. I had the unexpected good luck to be assigned by Lieutenant Lorius to stay with Jalabert, from Narbonne, to stand guard over this dump, to assure liaison with field kitchens and our drivers who had halted at Courmelois, and our big caissons stationed with the supply column as well as with all the other embusqués of the regiment stationed far back to the rear, near the Issus [Isse?] bridge.

But this time the Germans played a nasty trick on all these embusqués, because they were even more heavily bombarded than those who were in Courmelois or Wez. Terrified, some of them didn't hesitate to pull back a full league more of road, to go sleep in the long aqueduct tunnel of Mont Billy, in spite of the damp which reigned and the chilly drafts which poured through.

My buddy Jalabert and I were installed in the near-deserted village [Wez], in a house which was miraculously intact, none other than the parsonage. No piece of furniture of any value remained; religious paintings hung on all the walls; crosses, statues of the virgin and saints were stacked in every corner, and a profusion of bibles, books about the lives of saints, etc. Enough to convert an army of pagans.

Installed like a couple of bourgeois, lounging comfortably in the beds of the curate and his housekeeper, was enough to make us feel ashamed, to be so well off when our comrades were doing so badly.

Nevertheless, our repose was disturbed by more and more frequent bombardments which fell upon Wez, where we were soon practically all by ourselves. One night, two shells of respectable caliber landed right on the house next door; that was a bit too close for comfort.

In the middle of the parsonage garden, surrounded by debris and trash, stood the statue of the Virgin, barely grazed by shrapnel.

Was it the Mother of Christ who was protecting this house, where not one shell had yet landed? It was possible, but just to be safe, from this night on, we went to bed prudently in a shelter which some foresighted poilus had set up next to the house, and this in spite of the rats as big as *sabots* [wooden shoes] and lice like grains of wheat which infested this shelter. But you have to choose between the lesser of two evils.

The rolling field kitchens were moving up at night, not without danger, near the trenches. Our roles consisted of, for Jalabert, getting wine, tobacco, and other provisions to the men of our group who were up on the line, which suited Jalabert just fine, as it permitted him to go to the villages in the rear to live it up, drink, and test the virtue of one or another pretty Champagne girl.

As for me, I had only to make my way quietly to Courmelois to gather our provisions, which we then prepared and cooked ourselves.

"Quietly," in a manner of speaking, that is, since sometimes a few shells would fall upon the road where, by daylight, passersby were scarce, and upon Courmelois, which I had to cross through, the field kitchens being stationed in a thickly wooded park at the far end of the village. I then had to cross a marshy area where you could get stuck in the watery mud up to your knees, but where the German gunners, suspecting that only inoffensive toads and frogs were there, would never aim their fire.

But while we were living the easy life, what was our regiment up to?

An offensive, combined with a division which was to engage on our right, was fixed for April 30 at 7 a.m. It was postponed to 12:40 p.m. During the morning, our Colonel Robert, standing in front of his dugout, was mortally wounded in the head by a shell fragment, and died that very day at the field hospital.[1]

This death brought profound emotion in the regiment, but at that time, in such a furnace, we barely had the time to mourn. Everyone was too worried about his own fate.

So at the appointed hour the 296th Regiment surged forward and, with almost no resistance, it reached, in a single bound, the third line of German trenches. But whether the occupants of those trenches had been massacred by our artillery or they had gotten away, we scooped up only about a hundred prisoners who were hiding in the sturdiest shelters.

We would have advanced even farther but, to our right, the 47th Regiment was halted by the machine guns of a strongpoint which could only be taken after several days.

The next day, May 1, the Germans counterattacked several times, led by teams of grenadiers. We had to yield some of the terrain we had gained, and at one point the munitions were starting to run short.

The Germans kept pressing forward, capturing some isolated groups. The situation was becoming serious. In these circumstances, Lieutenant Guillot, commanding the 13th Company, gave proof of sangfroid and coolness bordering on the superhuman.

In the midst of general disarray, he took command of the units at hand, and in shirtsleeves, brandishing a rifle, he led his men, electrifying them, and charged the Germans, pushing them back from position after position.

Finally we stood as masters of the first two enemy trench lines, and the opposing positions were definitively fixed. To the left of Mont Cornillet, the 296th

Regiment had pushed back, or advanced, if you wish, the French border by five hundred meters.

Our generals should have been satisfied. What importance did the loss of human life have? What counted was being able to feed the dispatches, to maintain what they called "the activity at the front," to dazzle the fat-bellied civilian patriots in the rear with the accounts of their exploits. Having pushed the Germans back a few hectometers—that was heroic and brilliant enough, that was a great victory. In reality it was a useless massacre. Oh, what kind of executioner's soul you had to have, to be a general, to order such killings for nothing, for the *amour-propre* of the big bosses, for a trumped-up national pride.

One evening, a sizable work detail from the 14th Company was carrying munitions up to the front line when a shell landed nearby and set off some cases of grenades. There were fifteen men killed or wounded; Captain Miquel, from Béziers, was among the dead.

The Germans, having decimated our troops at the Chemin des Dames, brought up masses of artillery against us. They fired furiously upon our lines. It became worse than Verdun. I saw one soldier carried off, raving mad.

The lieutenant commanding the 17th Company lost his wits and had to be evacuated.

Right beside us, the 47th Regiment, which had ended up taking, or rather encircling, the German strongpoint, wasn't able to capture all the defenders, who sought refuge in the underground corridors, no doubt expecting to be rescued in a counterattack by their own side.

We blocked up all the exits with walls of sandbags and threw asphyxiating grenades into the strongpoint, which henceforth stood as silent as a tomb.

Oh, isn't war fine to behold?

The ones who did that gave it no more thought than would hunters smoking a fox or a marten out of its burrow.

One day, to my bad luck, Sergeant Gauthier, the head of our gun team, fell sick. He had colic, simple colic, indigestion from undercooked beans. When an offensive was on, it wouldn't do for a soldier, not to mention a non-com, to be sick in his belly, stomach, throat, or any other organ. That would be suspicious. So Sergeant Gauthier thought it prudent to not go to sick call, but rather asked Lieutenant Lorius for the authorization, which was granted to him, to go rest up for two or three days back with the field kitchens.

The result: orders for Corporal Barthas, on May 6, to replace Sergeant Gauthier at the [37mm] gun. I had to yank myself away from our tranquil life, our cozy lodgings, and a nice bed, a real bed, to go to the slopes of that sinister Mont Cornillet, which was smoking like a terrible, erupting volcano!

I didn't know the sector, and I received the order to present myself to the dugout of our officer at "Les Marquises." The road that ran in front of the [Wez] parsonage would take me right there. But it was highly imprudent to venture onto the road during the day, at which time it was completely deserted, because it was within easy firing range of the German cannon.

At night, however, or during part of it, at least, you could circulate there in almost complete safety, and this road, crisscrossed by hundreds of vehicles of every kind, was teeming with life, noise, and movement.

The Germans, too, needed to feed themselves, and there was a tacit agreement between the two artilleries that they wouldn't fire on the roads at night. During this time, the cannon weren't idle; they fired without respite upon the enemy trenches, instead of on the roads. Oh, what nights of horror for the poor sacrificial victims, the martyrs who had to live and die there!

By noon, no horseman, or bicyclist, or pedestrian had yet appeared on the road. I had resigned myself to heading out alone, when I finally saw two machine gunners carrying ammunition, and I joined up with them.

As we left Wez, the road crossed an empty, desolate plain, without the slightest rise in ground to take shelter behind, in case of bombardment. That gave you quite a chill, to head out into open country, at the mercy of the simplest "77."

It's true, the road was camouflaged, that's to say that some drapes of gray cloth suspended from telegraph poles protected passersby from the enemy's view. But the shells had, in many places, opened huge gashes and breaches in the cloth, which weren't very reassuring.

At the end of this plain, where the most complete solitude reigned, the road entered a wood where we could see green branches. But we observed with distress that the Germans were bombarding this wood, which seemed to be on fire. There were a number of French batteries hidden in it.

When we arrived at the wood's edge, we stopped, terrified. Enormous, monstrous shells, more terrible than lightning bolts, were tearing up, shredding, decapitating giant, hundred-year-old trees. We saw them wrenched from the ground, twisted, and broken, as if by a giant cyclone.

The whole forest seemed to be complaining, groaning, cracking under the blows of a Titan's cudgel.

Suddenly, from every corner of the wood, we saw artillerymen of the 47/2 [47th Regiment, 2nd Battery] fleeing as if they had the Germans right on their coattails. "We've been sold out, betrayed!" they said. "As soon as we change our positions and camouflage them, they're targeted and bombarded."

Just then, fearing that some shell or other would blow up their ammo supplies, they had given the traditional order of *Sauve-qui-peut!* [Every man for himself!].

Lucky artillerymen, who could skedaddle at the first sign of danger. It wasn't like that for us, the poor infantrymen, who were never granted the right to turn their backs to the enemy.

Nevertheless, these gunners having assured us that, right then, no one was shelling the road itself, we entered the wood. This information wasn't quite true; some fairly recent craters, their edges still black with powder, were somewhat numerous along the sides and even in the middle of the road.

The Territorial road menders would have plenty of work the next night, to put the road back into shape.

Crossing the wood involved a span of barely a kilometer. But we were in such a hurry to get out of there that this kilometer seemed longer than a league. Finally, panting, gasping, out of breath, we reached the other side.

Right there stood a road keeper's cabin torn open by a shell blast. We caught our breaths for a minute in an adjacent pedestrian shelter.

At this place, we left the Prunay road for that of Les Marquises, a hamlet or a château of which nothing more was left than a pile of rubble. We arrived there after a half-hour's suffocating walk along a boyau.

Les Marquises was the terminus for the mobile field kitchens, each evening, and also the site of munitions and equipment depots. There were some reserve units there, as well as the shelter of the colonel, on the doorstep of which Colonel Robert had been killed.

Someone pointed out to me a pile of ruins which, he assured me, belonged to the beautiful and famous Madame Steinheil, in whose arms, so the story went, had died a president of the Republic.[2]

At Les Marquises passed the main road from Reims to Sainte-Menehould and Metz, called the Roman Road. Shelters had been dug under the roadway, and it was in one of them that I found our officer, who had me accompanied up to the emplacement where our team was posted, about five hundred meters toward Mont Cornillet, which looked to me like a whitish shape, the shells having completely overturned and scraped clean the topsoil and laid bare the layer of clay underneath.

I found my comrades entrenched a few meters from our former front line, in a rather deep shelter, at the bottom of which was a little square space filled with mortar rounds that they'd seemed to have forgotten about.

It was nothing more than a simple flight of stairs, down into the ground, where you could very easily be buried alive if a shell collapsed the entryway. This fear wasn't completely imaginary, since a shell exploding nearby had thrown up against the entrance a big pile of dirt and had almost completely blocked it up. Luckily those inside were armed with picks and shovels and could dig themselves out. Nevertheless, even as it was, this shelter was a precious and coveted refuge. With bombardments like these, all the shelters would collapse, one by one, and all the men who were crouched in the bits of boyau waited for nightfall during the day and for daybreak during the night, and always waited for either death or relief.

I've said that, by day, the German batteries fired on the roads, the woods, and the villages, but by night they concentrated their fire on the trench lines, knowing that in nighttime the men were obliged to bring up the rations, go on work details, reliefs, etc.

At any moment, each night, men on work details, liaison duties, ration trips, surprised in our vicinity by frightful barrages, came to seek refuge in our hospitable dugout, bunching up thickly in our staircase. We couldn't even think of getting a minute of sleep there, but it would have been mean-spirited to complain, when others not only weren't getting any sleep but were stuck outside in a storm of steel and fire.

One morning, I saw appear, framed in the doorway of our shelter, the silhouette of our Sergeant Gauthier, who had finally digested his beans and come back to rejoin his post.

On the double-quick I yielded my place back to him and headed out to Wez, with no regrets. Looking back, I had hardly played any sort of glorious role at Mont Cornillet, where our field gun stood mounted in a shell crater, its menacing mouth fixed on the edge of a wood, where those lucky Boches took advantage of the abundant cover these woods provided. Our gun had to fire only when an attack was on.

The Germans much preferred to pound us with their *marmites* [heavy shells] than to undertake bayonet duels with the Frenchmen. So I could spend my sojourn in that area as a simple spectator.

At Wez I met up with my friend Jalabert, who welcomed me with great joy, as complete solitude reigned in the village which was bombarded more and more frequently.

All that remained at Wez was an outpost of two artillery spotters at the top of the church tower. These artillerymen figured that the Germans used this tower as a range-finding reference point. Otherwise they would have already knocked it down like a bowling pin.

Each day the men on the front line anxiously awaited their relief. They were at the limit of their strength. But our implacable bosses didn't want to grant them relief, as long as they had not yet reached, as in all the offensives, the expected percentage of losses.

Exasperated and in despair, some men surrendered to the Germans, and some Germans surrendered to the French.

"What cowards!" say the patriots in the rear. But if all the soldiers, on both sides, had done the same thing, wouldn't that have been sublime? The generals would have had to fight each other. Poincaré could have gone a couple of rounds in the boxing ring with the Kaiser. That would have been hilarious.

My comrade Sabatier, from Rieux-Minervois, whom I've referred to several times in this account, was taken prisoner with a colleague while heading out to occupy a forward listening post.

Poor Sabatier, now dead as I write these lines, illiterate and simple of spirit, had, like so many others, never understood why we were at war. Nobody asked his advice in declaring it, so he didn't ask anyone's permission to slip over to the Germans.

"Your war's over," the Boches told him when Sabatier and his buddy fell into their trench. That's all they were asking for.

Finally, on May 15, the regiment having poured out its share of blood and paid its tribute in suffering to the hydra of war, the 296th was relieved on the night of May 15–16 and went to billets in the village of Isse.

No official numbers of losses, or unofficial ones, were issued, of course, but according to reliable sources the regiment marked its passage by leaving a hundred and fifty dead on the slopes of Mont Cornillet, a hundred more missing, and counted around 350 wounded.

Private Babou of the 13th Company, from Narbonne, had his own son as his sergeant. It took wartime to produce such a paradox, a father forced to passively obey his own son. The very day that the regiment went up to the front line, our Colonel Robert had the generous thought to hold back in reserve the men of the oldest [conscript-year] classes, who would rejoin their units only when any attacks or counterattacks were completed. When Babou senior rejoined his half-section, he no longer found his sergeant—that is, his son, who had been killed in a German counterattack. He didn't even have the consolation of seeing where his son's body had been left in enemy hands.

If our poor colonel had, like all the other colonels, marched everyone forward, the father and son might have both been killed, side by side. Ah, this damned war!

1917. Destination unknown. Compertrix. Daucourt.
The Harazée sector. Sainte-Menehould. The regiment revolts.

At dawn on May 20, the 296th Regiment left Isse and took the road to Châlons-sur-Marne.

This was a Sunday, but those whose slaves we were didn't care about that, the poilus having been forgotten in the list of beneficiaries of a weekly day of rest.

It was pretty hot, following the long, dusty road, and we cast an envious eye on the cool shade of the Marne River valley we were marching along. We were quite worn out when we reached the little village of Compertrix, a few hundred meters outside Châlons.

After the evening meal, with a comrade, I took a walk into Châlons. We could hardly find a glass of beer to drink, with the thousands of embusqués soaking it all up each day.

Lots of activity in the streets, the embusqués showing off their newest képis, their brightest stripes and chevrons.

Most had on their arms their wives or other women, in flowered hats, corsages, dresses with festive colors; all these fine folk strolling around, smiling, gossiping, flirting in perfect ignorance and tranquility.

Nevertheless you could hear in the distance the dull sound of the cannon. Over by Mont Cornillet, the Rocher de Tahure, and the Main de Massiges, human blood was flowing. Ambulances quietly brought wounded flesh to the city's hospitals, next to which the cemeteries grew bigger every day.

We left the town, heartbroken by this indifference, this selfishness, this forgetfulness which insulted those who were dying, who were suffering in the trenches without even knowing why or how.

The next day, at a very early hour, we were on the road, passing through a deserted and silent Châlons. We stopped at the village of Lépine [L'Épine], where we admired a magnificent church, Notre Dame de Lépine, a destination for pilgrims who come to drink the sacred, holy, miracle-working water from a well located inside the church.[3]

Halting in the village right by the walls of this church, quite thirsty and with my canteen dry, I could have easily drunk a whole quart of this precious water, because in the village there was neither a fountain nor a public well.

But the church was prudently locked, and I had to beg a glass of water from a housewife who hastened to give it to me, while telling me that water was very tightly rationed around there.

Around noon, we arrived at our destination, Somme-Vesle.

Next to the church you could see the remains of several burned-out houses. The inhabitants told us that, when troops were recently billeted in the village, there was a big explosion of grenades in one encampment which led to the burning down of a group of houses and a part of the church and the bell tower. Sadly, five soldiers had been killed. The war was over for them, and they rested in the little flower-filled cemetery surrounding the church.

At Somme-Vesle, the war had left its traces of fire and blood.

The next day, May 22nd, after a long march, we billeted at Daucourt, six kilometers from Sainte-Menehould, the last stop in our latest journey on foot.

We stayed at Daucourt for nine days, resting up from the exertions of our latest offensive, with the usual distractions: parades and reviews both big and small, field exercises which were either wearying or boring.

At this time the Russian Revolution broke out. Those Slavic soldiers, only yesterday enslaved and bent double under the weight of iron discipline, unknowingly marching off to massacres like resigned slaves, had thrown off their yokes, proclaimed their liberty, and imposed peace on their masters, their hangmen.

The whole world was stupefied, petrified by this revolution, this collapse of the immense empire of the czars.

These events had repercussions on the Western Front and throughout the French ranks. A wind of revolt blew across almost all the regiments.

There were, besides, plenty of reasons for discontent: the painful failure of the Chemin des Dames offensive, which had no result other than a dreadful slaughter; the prospect of more long months of war ahead, with a highly dubious outcome; and finally, the long wait for home leaves—it's that which bothered the soldiers most, I believe.

I cannot pretend to tell the whole story of what happened almost everywhere just then. I will stick to writing what I know, regarding our regiment and the repression which followed.

There was, at the end of the village, a shopkeeper for whom the war brought only profit. He sold beer, and he had a cute little waitress to serve it to customers —powerful attractions which, every evening after supper, brought a whole crowd of poilus, a well-behaved clientele which plunked down in groups in the big courtyard adjacent to his shop. One evening, some of the soldiers were singing, others were entertaining their fellows with songs and skits, when a corporal began singing words of revolt against the sad life in the trenches, words of farewell to the dear souls whom we might not see again, of anger against the perpetrators of this infamous war, the rich shirkers who left the fighting to those who had nothing to fight for.[4]

At the refrain, hundreds of voices rose in chorus, and at the end fervent applause broke out, mixed with cries of "Peace or revolution! Down with war!," as well as "Home leave! Home leave!"

On another evening—patriots, cover your ears!—the "Internationale" was heard, bursting like a storm.

That time, our chiefs got stirred up. It gave our old friend *Capitaine-adjutant-major* Cros-Mayrevieille such an unbearable itch that he quickly sent a patrol of four men and the inevitable corporal to remind these vile whiners that, 8 o'clock having rung, the men had to hand over the street, the taverns, and the ladies to the officers, and report to their sergeants-of-the-day who were waiting to carry out roll call at the doorways of our empty billets.

The patrol prudently judged that it should beat a hasty retreat, and our *capitaine-adjutant-major*-cop came out himself, escorted by the local police squad.

He tried to speak with moderation, but as soon as the first words left his mouth he was halted by formidable shouting.

Sputtering with rage but powerless, he turned on the unfortunate sergeants, who had unwisely reported that "no one was absent," and forced them to call roll a second time.

A crowd of several hundred soldiers, scorning the roll calls, had massed in front of the police station, where Captain Cros had sought refuge. To give him even more of a scare, one hothead fired a couple of pistol shots into the air.

At noon on May 30, there was even an assembly outside the village, to constitute, following the Russian example, a "soviet" composed of three men from each company, which would take control of the regiment.

To my great astonishment, they came to offer me the presidency of this soviet, that's to say, to replace the colonel—nothing less than that!

That would be quite a sight—me, an obscure peasant who put down my pitchfork in August 1914, commanding the 296th Regiment. That went way beyond the bounds of probability.

Of course I refused. I had no desire to shake hands with a firing squad, just for the child's play of pretending we were the Russians.

But I did decide to give an appearance of legality to these revolutionary demonstrations. I wrote up a manifesto to give to our company commanders, protesting against the delay in furloughs. It began like this: "On the eve of the offensive, General Nivelle had read to the troops an order of the day saying that the hour of sacrifice had rung. . . . We offered our lives and made this sacrifice for the fatherland but, in exchange, we said that the hour of home leaves had also sounded, a while ago . . . ," et cetera.

The revolt was therefore placed squarely on the side of right and justice. The manifesto was read out, in a sonorous voice, by a poilu who was perched astride the limb of an oak tree. Fervent applause underscored his last lines.

My vanity was hardly flattered. If they learned that it was I who had drawn up this protest, moderate as it was, my fate was clear: a court-martial, for sure, and possibly twelve Lebel bullets[5] dispatched to send me off to another world, long before my appointed hour.

Meanwhile the officers had taken note of the call for an enormous assembly of soldiers, out by the Daucourt washhouses. They tried to interrogate some poilus about the purpose of this meeting, but no one was willing to respond, or they answered evasively.

Our commandant tried to block the road by the police station, but the poilus got through by using other routes.

In the afternoon the order was given for immediate departure. It included the formal promise that home leaves would begin again, starting the next day, at a rate of sixteen per one hundred men. The military authorities, so arrogant and authoritarian, had to capitulate. They needed nothing more to reestablish order. In spite of that, there were lively disturbances, especially in the encampments of the 4th Machine-Gun Company, a few moments before departure, and the men headed out only after singing the "Internationale" right in the faces of their stupefied but powerless officers.

At 3 o'clock, under a brilliant sun, we left Daucourt. At 5 o'clock, the regiment marched through Sainte-Menehould, where tragic events had just played out.

Two regiments had just mutinied and seized their barracks, crying "Peace or Revolution!"

General "X," who went to try to harangue the mutineers, was grabbed, slammed against a wall, and was just about to be shot, when a much-beloved commandant succeeded in saving the general and winning the promise that the insurgents be allowed to make their way to the camp at Châlons for a long rest.

Rifle shots were fired on a group of officers who were trying to approach the barracks. The bullets went wild and hit some innocent victims in the town, killing two, it is said.

They judged it prudent to separate the three battalions of the 296th Regiment from one another, and they billeted us fairly far apart. Our battalion was quartered in barracks four kilometers from Sainte-Menehould. It was only when we got there that we learned that the other battalions were elsewhere.

The next day [May 31], at 7 p.m., they assembled us for departure to the trenches. Noisy demonstrations resulted: cries, songs, shouts, whistling; of course, the "Internationale" was heard. I truly believe that, if the officers had made one provocative gesture, said one word against the uproar, they would have been massacred without pity, so great was the agitation.

They chose the wisest path: waiting patiently until calm was restored. You can't cry, shout, and whistle forever, and among the insurgents there was no leader capable of taking decisive direction. We ended up heading for the trenches, not without an undertone of griping and grumbling.

Soon, to our great surprise, a column of mounted cavalry came up and rode alongside us. They accompanied us all the way to the trenches, like convicts being led to forced labor!

Annoyed and suffocated by the dust kicked up by the horses, we didn't have to wait long before scuffles broke out between foot soldiers and cavalrymen, and then some brawls; there were even a few blows from rifle butts, on one side, and from the blunt sides of sabers, on the other. To prevent a real battle from breaking out, they had to move the cavalrymen farther away, which wasn't at all disagreeable to them.

We passed through Moiremont, the final inhabited and civilized place; then Vienne-la-Ville and Vienne-le-Château, two good-sized villages in ruins. Three hundred meters from what had been the village of La Harazée, in the smiling valley of the Biesme River, we relieved the gunners of the 358th Regiment.

We set ourselves up in a veritable little fortress, situated on the flank of a valley, facing the enemy.

In the underground galleries and rooms we could withstand any bombardment, having a hundred meters of bedrock above our heads.

At the ends of two embrasures, two fixed, pivoting naval guns aimed their menacing muzzles at the facing slopes and the ravines which opened into the valley.

The Germans were only a kilometer from our fort, but they couldn't see it because of the oak and pine woods which still covered the steep slopes facing them.

The entrance to our fort, and the terrace in front of it, built in stone and earth excavated when it was dug, were masked from our counterparts, the Kaiser's gunners, by thick bushes and branches which we often had to replenish so that they mingled closely with the surrounding greenery.

Well installed on this terrace for our meals, card games, letter writing, et cetera, we spent happy and peaceful days there.

Below us, a forest with its green and aromatic carpet of flowers, verdure, wild strawberries and raspberries.

Hundreds of birds, drawn by our bread crumbs, dazzled us with their chirping and twittering. A couple of wrens were bold enough to build their nest in the greenery surrounding the embrasure of one of the naval guns.

Beasts and soldiers are made to get along. But what a contrast: the grace, the gaiety of these little birds, right next to a horrible instrument of death!

To remind us that the war wasn't yet finished, the Germans occasionally sent some volleys of shells into the Biesme valley, which obliged us, readers or card-players, to flee into our fortress, like mice chased by a tomcat.

It's also true that, once night fell, our neighbors across the way brought up machine guns onto the "kolossal" plateau[6] over by the "Four de Paris" and swept the valley, which they had in enfilade, and sometimes bullets came and ricocheted off our fortress.

But apart from these little inconveniences, which an embusqué would perhaps have found terrifying, we considered ourselves very lucky, and our fate made others jealous.

In case of an enemy attack, we were supposed to "hold" until the assailants crossed the Biesme, then blow up the works and make our getaway by an underground passage which let out near the summit of the escarpment.

That part of the sector was deserted, and no one except us knew about it or poked around this hidden passageway.

One warm July afternoon, we were all out on the aforementioned terrace of the fort, enjoying ourselves loudly, reinforced by a couple of "watchers" from a nearby surveillance post.

Three or four parties of *bourre* or *manille* [card games] were under way, and a few containers of pinard from the local winegrowers' co-op had served to loosen our tongues—southern tongues so clear and sonorous that you'd have thought yourself on the "Barques" in Narbonne [a riverside promenade] or along the banks of the Garonne in Toulouse.

Bareheaded, in shirtsleeves, untidy, we were taking our ease, when we heard, first in the emergency passageway and then inside the fort, loud voices and a racket. In the darkness inside, someone was crashing and stumbling around.

Qu'es aco? [Occitan for "Who is there?"], cried Simard the Toulousan. But at that very moment, in the entrance to the fort which opened onto the terrace, two men appeared, their uniforms splattered with mud.

The first of these two men was a junior cavalry officer. He stepped aside and then there appeared before our bewildered eyes our divisional general, Elie de Boizière.[7]

If we'd seen the Kaiser himself appear before our eyes, we wouldn't have been more surprised. The general, who had by chance discovered the outlet of our escape route, not knowing where it led, seemed as stupefied as we were.

There was a minute of heavy silence, broken by the dry voice of the general.

"Who commands here?" he said.

The commandant of the fort stood up. His heart was in his boots, this commandant, who was none other than my comrade Sergeant Gauthier.

"It is I, General," he stammered.

"What's going on here?"

For better or worse—more worse than better—the sergeant tried to explain. The general wasn't happy with these vague explanations, and he wanted to know in detail the calibrations of each artillery piece, the distances, the instructions, the reference points, etc.

The sergeant began by mumbling and stammering, but I came to his aid by presenting to the general the panoramas, firing tables, etc., that I had drawn myself and which I had quickly taken down from the walls. That way he could realize the importance of our post, from which, in a minute, we could open fire on any point in front of us.

The general appeared satisfied. He looked at us for a moment longer before leaving, and shaking his head he said to us, "You're like *coqs en pâte*." ["You're in clover; you're sitting pretty"].

So the Harazée sector was a calm one, a place of repose, which only rarely was honored by mention in dispatches. Its tragic, celebrated hour in 1915 had almost been forgotten, the time when terrible combats bloodied this poetic corner of the Argonne.

The army of the German crown prince had given us a real kick in the butt there. Sweeping down the valley from the Font [Fontaine] aux Charmes, the

Germans had even occupied La Harazée, but a French counterattack pushed them out of it. You could still see the shell of a fine house where the crown prince had set up his command post. He was almost collared there by our boys, and owed his salvation to a little door in the rear by which he could flee.[8]

The storm of these fierce combats having passed, the front line was set for the next few years, 700 meters from the village.

The only reminders of the fighting were a few grassy corners transformed into cemeteries, and our dead took their final repose there, in the shade of the lindens, willows, and pines, soothed by the soft murmur of the Biesme.

La Harazée had kept its villagelike appearance; the walls of its little church and a few houses were still standing, since the shells reached them only with some difficulty, the village being strung along the steep slope of the valley.

Among its ruins you could make out the walls of a villa, the country house where the *académicien* André Theuriet,[9] I was told, came to vacation and to breathe the vivifying air.

In the shade of a linden tree, I've written these lines while sitting on a stone bench where perhaps the gifted writer himself wrote those books which tell about the surrounding countryside. One of his books plays out its whole plot in the setting of the Biesme valley.

At La Harazée a rivulet of pure, crystalline water, which nourished Theuriet's garden, flows into the Biesme; it's the water from the Fontaine aux Charmes. This spring was now behind the German lines. At long intervals, on signs nailed to the trunks of pine trees, you could read the words, "Drink at Own Risk."

We stayed in this sector nearly six months. There was never any serious business here, no mine explosions or gas attacks. This tranquility was troubled only by some *coups de main* [trench raids] by one side or the other, which made more noise than they did any harm.

But what is a trench raid?

Any poilu knows about them. But how many civilians have an even approximate idea what they were? Damn few, I'd say.

Their ignorance is excusable, because all the accounts, official or unofficial, even those recounted or written by those who took part, have led them down the wrong path. They talk or write only things that shine light on the courage, the heroism, the disregard for death shown by the French soldier. They're silent about anything that could diminish his glory, his beauty, his valor. One lies— or, if you will, one alters the truth for patriotic reasons, just as one kills, or one lies, "for reasons of state."

First of all, it is generally thought that these trench raids were carried out by elite soldiers, who combined the virtues of a warrior with those of an exemplary citizen. That's the first big error, with few exceptions. These "heroes" were hard cases, unruly, and often had police records which were far from unblemished.

But, you might say, it's surprising that rascals like these would be able to carry out actions requiring great sangfroid and solid courage.

Hold on before deciding. These guys were picked for their weak points: they were obsessed with independence, so the straitjackets of their discipline were loosened a few notches.

Drunk with liberty, they suffocated in the trenches, so they were pulled out and billeted at divisional depots in the rear, and came to the front lines only a few hours before the appointed time of the raid.

At the depot, they were free to have fun, sing, brawl, make a racket, dine, quarrel, brawl among themselves. They were left alone. Relegated to separate barracks, they were treated as indulgently as others were treated severely.

They were compensated, each time, with a few Croix de Guerre, which they were crazy about, and a four- or even eight-day leave for each one, if the group brought back just one prisoner—which was rare.

The day came for one of these adventurous excursions to visit Messieurs les Boches. The "volunteers" were brought up in automobiles or vans close to the trenches, and during the night they installed themselves right up at the forward posts from which they would move out.

Passages through the barbed wire would have been cut in advance, just beyond the forward posts; this was generally done at the first glimmers of dawn's light.

The silence was suddenly broken by the distant firing of a large-caliber artillery piece. This was the signal. The echo wouldn't have finished reverberating through the valleys and ravines before all the batteries of the sector and of neighboring sectors opened up a rolling fire on the point that was going to be attacked. At the same time, all the trench artillery—mortars, bomb throwers, 37mm cannon, "Stokes"[10] guns, etc.—spit out iron and fire on the enemy's forward posts, and beyond. And all this deafening racket was unleashed at one time, as if a single hand had fired a hundred cannon blasts at once.

The "volunteers," piled up in a boyau, their stomachs well fortified with wine and hooch, threw themselves forward at the first cannon shot. The first ones out carried clusters of branches on their heads. Arriving at the Boche barbed wire, the first one tossed his branches and stepped aside; the second climbed onto the first cluster and threw his own ahead, and so forth until they reached the enemy's forward post in two or three minutes.

But while all this was going on, what were the Germans doing, under this deluge of iron falling upon them like an avalanche?

They had a clever tactic. In their forward listening posts they left just two men, whose mission it was to fall back at the first cannon shot, not to the front lines—which were completely deserted—but to the second lines, organized for a solid resistance and which would have been too rash for us to attack.

These forward sentinels, if they hadn't been blown to bits right at their posts, would fall into our hands only if they were wounded while falling back.

Sometimes they disappeared into underground mines or saps linked up by galleries. Most of the time the raiding party ended up empty-handed.

To the French general who waited impatiently at the colonel's command post, the raiders brought back only a pick or spade with the handle broken off, or a tarpaulin or tent cloth picked up in the German trenches.

Eyeing these meager trophies, the general would furrow his brow.

"And the prisoners?" he would say.

With admirable accord, everyone swore that the Boches simply wouldn't surrender, and they were forced to kill every last one of them.

Sometimes they actually succeeded in capturing one or two who were good enough to surrender. That was a real triumph. That meant four days or maybe a week of leave. Starting that very evening. The giddy general would distribute cigarettes, vintage wine, Croix de Guerre, etc.

One day, they brought back a prisoner. While the men of the raiding party crowded around the general who probed them about the perils of the raid, a junior officer [who had not been on the raid] approached the Boche, insulted him and threatened him with a clenched fist right in his face.

A couple of the "volunteers" spotted this and shouted at the officer; they didn't want him to touch their prisoner. "He's ours," they said. "You didn't bring him in, did you?"

And the dumbfounded prisoner found himself plied with cigarettes, coffee, wine, hooch, etc., right in front of the offending officer, who only could stand there in complete silence.

These raids had diverse results. Some had tragic outcomes, others were more like burlesques, bordering on the ridiculous.

Sometimes it happened that the "volunteers," completely drunk, would start arguing, get into brawls, and even wound each other, right in the boyau as they prepared to go over the top, or when they were out on their way to the attack.

There were also mad panics, groups which wandered off and got lost in the tangles of barbed wire. The Boches would never know what happened, but our general would get a full and detailed account of the "successful" action.

Finally the general, a bit skeptical, decided that the raids would take place in broad daylight. But this brought no better results, and so they went back to the predawn hours.

To be fair, it must be noted that, at least one time, the volunteers showed some real courage. Reaching the German trenches, they ran smack into an enemy raiding party which, by bizarre coincidence, was heading for our lines to grab some prisoners. A frightful hand-to-hand combat ensued, and our heroes emerged victorious, killing or chasing off their adversaries.

That's what the raids were all about, so fashionable at the time, and just who they were who carried them out. Some of the raiders were ragged, untidy, like scarecrows. Others were perfumed dandies with long hair, strutting around, indulging in wild bits of apparel for which they sacrificed all economy.

What role did our unit play, during the six months we were in the sector?

First of all, our unit was sharply reduced in size: two men had to leave for the Army of Salonika; another was sent off to be a miner, and a fourth to be a truck driver; there was hardly anyone left at the front but the riffraff of peasants, guys with dirt between our toes.

Comrade Delile had written to his wife and told her about the antimilitarist demonstrations back in June. To teach him to be a little more discreet next time, they sent him off to the divisional disciplinary company.

A third of those who remained left us to go to form a divisional battery of the new English cannon called Stokes.

But the more they shrunk us, the more they increased the number and the variety of hardware to be employed: three 37mm guns, one revolver-cannon, four Brand compressed-air mortars,[11] three 47mm naval guns . . . In brief, there were more cannons than cannoneers.

But our duties nonetheless were not very difficult. On the front line there was only one revolver-cannon and one Brand mortar, served by four gunners; the others were in reserve, in case of attack, in the fortress studded with our five cannons and some machine guns manned by Territorials, who occupied a part of the works.

For the trench raids, which became a nightmare for us, you had to go up to the front line, sometimes as far as the farthest outposts, with our whole arsenal.

We had to fire madly all the while that the raid lasted, for fifteen to twenty minutes, and then quickly scramble to find the nearest shelter, because the volleys of 77mm or 105mm shells soon came crashing down upon the communication trenches.

Our commanding officer, who had served in the artillery, estimated that each trench raid cost, in shells alone, from 300,000 to 500,000 francs! And for what result? Grabbing one or two prisoners! Pulverizing a sentry!

What a waste! But what did money mean to our leaders, for our generals? Germany would pay it all back, one day . . . or the French taxpayer would.

There were, in history, the Red Terror and the White Terror.[12] Now you can add the Militarist Terror. The first made use of the guillotine, the second employed the knife, to teach people how to live. The third used penal companies and the execution post for those who didn't toe the line.

The stirrings of revolt which manifested themselves in May and June in various units had incited our bosses to impose more harsh and severe discipline, we soon noticed.

For some time, most of our mail was opened. Woe to one who voiced approval of the demonstrations, who said he was tired of the war, or who made some other imprudent comment. One subversive word and it's a court-martial, or at least a couple of months of vacation in one of the penal, or "special," companies, which had been hastily put together within each division. No one could be out on the roads, which were lined with gendarmes, without authorization signed by the colonel.

Those going on home leave from the front lines were escorted to Sainte-Menehould like dangerous convicts.

We had to march in ranks of four, on the road, as if in drill, bracketed front and rear, and on the side, by non-coms. As far as Moiremont the leave takers were led by junior officers from the lines. From there, non-coms also going on leave took command of the troops under their charge. It was absolutely forbidden to sing, even "La Madelon,"[13] to break ranks, or to stop individually even to tie a shoelace or obey a call of nature. Either the whole column had to stop at once, or a corporal had to stay behind with the laggard.

In other circumstances there would have been grumbles, and even violent outbursts. But to go on home leave, to escape this atrocious life for just a few days, to see loved ones, we would have walked barefoot, we would have crawled on our knees, we would have endured the kicks of boots and the lashes of riding crops and whips.

From La Harazée to Sainte-Menehould, there were beautiful cherry trees all along the road, almost without interruption, and their interlacing branches formed a fresh arbor over our heads. In June and July these trees were covered with beautiful cherries, red, white, golden, multicolored. But, in yet another torture of Tantalus for the leave takers, there was hell to pay if you got caught pulling down a branch full of cherries. Three-quarters of the fruit rotted on the tree, but too bad for the poilus. That would teach them, once again, not to sing the "Internationale."

Once we reached Sainte-Menehould, they kept us from passing through the middle of town. If we had been lepers, they couldn't have done a better job of preventing any contact between us and the civilian population.

We therefore made a big detour, which allowed us to admire the military cemetery where several thousand "heroes" were buried. Then we reached the barracks outside of town, where a big iron gate closed right behind the last of the leave takers.

We were prisoners, right up to the time the train left, and then we marched no farther than two kilometers from town before getting onto the train, in the middle of the woods.

The return worked the same way. To organize this procedure and to ensure its smooth operation, if one can call it that, they put in place at Moiremont an officer superior in rank if not in qualities. It was a commandant, whose name escapes me. In civilian life he was probably director of an insane asylum or a camp of convicts.

This officer, already on horseback at dawn, scoured all the roads in the sector which brought leave takers back, from morning to night, and fell upon them like a thunderbolt, counting heads, trying to catch them in some misstep.

Watch out, squad leader: the slightest infraction of the rules would lead to your being broken in rank, with no chance for appeal.

Every day he had to claim at least one victim, as testimony to his vigilance.

It mattered little that the soldier or the non-com was a model of courage or bravery. There was no recourse. They needed to make examples. They needed to terrify.

On the day I was leaving for my fourth home leave, we were approaching Sainte-Menehould when one of us stopped to take a leak, then tried to catch up with us. But the terrible commandant surprised him before he regained his place in the ranks.

The End of the 296th Infantry Regiment:
July 1, 1917–January 28, 1918

La Harazée sector. 1917. Argonne.

The situation was very serious, as you will see. A *fourrier* [quartermaster-sergeant] was leading us. He was slapped with eight days of probation; his home leave was suspended, and he could say good-bye to the sergeant's stripes on his sleeve.

The unlucky fourrier tried to explain that he had authorized the man to stop, simply exercising his rights as squad leader.

But the strongest always wins every argument, and the commandant stuck to the punishment he had handed out, calmly warning the non-com not to risk making things worse by protesting further.

This damned commandant accompanied us to the barracks, making us keep in formation and step out like new recruits on the drill field. But once our ranks were scattered, the grumbling arose.

The commandant had returned to the office of the week's adjutant, next to the police station. There he was literally besieged. Everyone called out to him, shouting that if the sergeant wasn't permitted to go on leave, none of us would go.

Seized by a violent rage, the officer appeared at a window, brow furrowed, giving us a look that should have silenced us. But faced with equally fierce expressions, he detected such a level of hostility that he judged it prudent to yield.

"Let him go," he said. "This sergeant will serve his punishment afterward."

Nevertheless, when he came back from leave, the sergeant wasn't bothered at all.

Throughout the companies, battalions, and regiments, there were decent captains, commandants, and colonels who were moved by these arbitrary punishments and demotions for the most petty and ridiculous reasons. They made themselves heard by vigorous complaints, which were mainly useless.

This commandant, our so-called morale booster, was imposed on us by the high command. He was just carrying out the inflexible orders he had received.

Once they decided that we had been sufficiently disciplined, beaten down, choked, they relieved us of this undesirable personage. He was named a lieutenant-colonel somewhere. He had really earned this promotion.

During our stay in this sector, I twice went on "relaxation leave." I noted that, in the rear, the wild enthusiasm of the start of the war had given way to complete indifference.

Each person had arranged his life with the goal of realizing the most well-being and profits.

If you approached a group conversing among themselves, whether in a café, a station, or any other place, you heard talk about everything except the war—everyone was so habituated to it, they had stopped caring about it.

The price of wine soared to new heights, bringing huge profits to those who could till their vineyards.

The war was no longer considered a scourge. From time to time you heard that the son of so-and-so or the husband of what's-her-name had been killed, blown to bits, burned to a crisp, smashed, suffocated, up there in the distant trenches. But these inevitable deaths were considered the price to be paid, in ransom for general prosperity as we awaited the final victory.

Except for home leaves, no one from our group ever left the trenches as part of battalions being sent to the rear for rest, because there weren't enough of us to be relieved. For almost six months we lived in the Argonne woods, cut off from the rest of the world.

These six months of exile were, for me, interrupted by two stints of ten days each, when I went to Camp Soumiat, near Sainte-Menehould, for ballistics training.

For me, my "instruction" consisted of sticking paper on the targets and having them brought and set up on the firing range. That's all I learned how to do.

One November day, we were near our little fortress, busy cutting up an oak tree for firewood, when Sergeant Gauthier, coming back from the kitchens, announced some surprising news: the 296th Regiment was being dissolved, and was going to be dispersed among the units of a Breton regiment which had just been decimated in the Bois le Chaume [north of Verdun].

This news got various welcomes in the regiment. With pleasure by those who for six months had been shuttling between the outposts and the miserable reserve dugouts from which, by night, they went out to place barbed wire and haul other materiel on their shoulders. This dissolution was an unhoped-for windfall, a getaway from the trenches for a few days—who knew for how long? A nice rest before winter's cold set in, perhaps?

But for those who had a comfortable assignment—the dutiful orderly, the greasy cook, the comfortable bicyclist, all the way up to the payroll clerk and the quartermaster—the news brought uncertainty, the fear of losing their cushy jobs.

Clearly there were reasons for this dissolution. The role played by the 296th in the antimilitarist demonstrations of last June was probably not unrelated to the disgrace which fell upon us.

The 296th Regiment was also the regiment headquartered at Béziers. Béziers, where in 1907, at the time of the winegrowers' protests, the regiment had mutinied.

Who didn't know the stirring tale of this regiment, the 17th Infantry which, under the command of a corporal braving the thunderbolts of discipline and the anger of the "Tiger" himself, Clemenceau, then in power, dared to stand in line of battle against the troops of General Lacroisade?[1]

Well, a few days before our dissolution, Clemenceau rose to power again—I should say dictatorial power. Did he fear that, in the 296th Regiment, there were some former mutineers of the 17th Regiment who, like some evil yeast, might stir up some incidents, protests, demonstrations against the return to power of the former butcher of the Midi?

It's possible that such fears inspired in our *Premier Flic* ["top cop"] the idea of getting rid of us, but if that's what he meant to do he was curiously mistaken. The 296th Regiment had become an amalgam, within which were represented almost all of our provincial races. Only a very small number now hailed from the region of Béziers, and even rarer were those who had not forgotten the memory of the tragic events of 1907.

Nevertheless, there was still the corporal who, for a few days back then, had taken the place of the colonel of the 17th Regiment, which didn't keep him from now being signals-sergeant. His name was Fondecave.

On November 16 the news of our dissolution spread widely, and on the 19th our group, with the last remaining elements, left La Harazée, where we had spent such a peaceful six months and where we would have happily remained until the war's end. But now we had to embark on new journeys.

We went to rejoin the regiment near the village of Florent [-en-Argonne], at the Darniéville encampment, made up of barracks hidden in the middle of the woods.

This was a stroll of more than 20 kilometers, because the officer who was guiding us rode a bicycle and preferred riding on the main road to bumping along a country lane, so they had us make a big, useless detour to Moiremont.

This preference cost our legs 4 or 5 more kilometers, but what the hell—foot soldiers are made for walking, just like birds are for flying and fish for swimming.

At Darniéville the first to arrive had, as was their right, occupied the best barracks and even the bad ones, since three battalions had to camp where there was enough room for only one. It was impossible to find even a little bit of room for us, and since there were no hotels at the Darniéville camp we had to find places under the trees to spend the night—a cold, freezing night, but luckily without rain or snow. We could even light some campfires with brush, branches, dead wood and even live wood, which warmed us up a bit.

The next day they handed out flyers with the farewells of our division's general. It was written in emotional terms, recalling all our exploits from Vermelles and Lorette all the way to the Argonne.

There was reference to the events of last June, but the sponge had wiped clean the misdeeds of the 296th Regiment. The general declared himself highly satisfied with its loyal and proper attitude, and said that it had resisted being dragged into the defeatist campaign.

That was a good point. The general couldn't ignore what had happened, but he was politically savvy enough to pretend to ignore it.

Dinner eaten, the regiment assembled for its departure. It was with no regrets that I left this inhospitable camp, where I had shivered all night long under an oak tree.

Trucks came to get us, but because we faced an interminable slope which would no doubt have required too great an expenditure of gasoline, we had to walk for more than an hour to reach them. Covered with sweat, we arrived at the place where the trucks were lined up, right next to Sainte-Menehould.

And by unknown roads we left, a joyless journey because, after having perspired, now we froze, shivering with cold inside the trucks, devoid of any comfort, open to every breeze and cold draft.

Around three in the afternoon the trucks stopped in the middle of the countryside. They made us climb down. Right then, the battalion's leaders, by confidential written orders, got word to convey their units to various surrounding locales.

Why so much mystery, so many precautions, about our moves?

What were they so afraid of, that they didn't dare bring the whole regiment together again, one final time, for a big, sensational parade and review, as is usually done in those situations?

That served to bolster the suspicion that the regiment was in disgrace, and being punished. They treated us like dangerous men, or at least suspects, and that chilled our dignity. We were indifferent to anything that didn't regard home leaves and peace. As for everything else, the soldiers couldn't give a damn.

Our battalion got the order to go to the village of Bassuet, and we set out along the roadway like a flock of sheep heading for the fairground.

Soon there arrived officers from various units, flanked by aides and sergeant-majors, making their choices. In the blink of an eye, by sections, by squads, by whole companies, everything was taken away, disappeared, and only our group remained.

Night fell, and the roadway, where a sharp bise was blowing, sweeping up all the dead leaves, was completely deserted. Nobody wanted us. We were abandoned.

Our Sublieutenant Lorius was furious. He set out to find the colonel of the 248th Regiment,[2] part of which was billeted in the village, and he explained the strange fate of 32 soldiers from the 296th Regiment, in distress, without anything to eat, left on the public highway.

The colonel was willing to take us into his regiment, provisionally. The next day he assigned us to a machine-gun company, and asked the billeting officer to take care of our lodging.

That evening we had to go without supper. What had become of our field kitchen, with its hard-earned battle scars and wounds from Combles, and our number-one chef, Morla, whose portrait I've already sketched in these notebooks, and who was awarded the Croix de Guerre for not having left his station under furious bombardments?

As for our lodging, all the billets being occupied already, we had to resign ourselves to a spot at the edge of the village, in an old coach house which no one else had wanted, because the roof was busted through in twenty places and a hundred drafts seeped through chinks in the wattle-and-daub walls. The flooring consisted of bits of straw made rotten by the rain.

Our blockhouse at La Harazée was a palace compared to this hovel. Although shells and bullets fell upon Bassuet only rarely, the rain and the snow during our stay there came several times each night, forcing us to flee the drainpipes and seek out a drier corner somewhere.

To our great amazement, that very evening, a tailor was sent to cut off the badges of the 296th and to sew on, in their place, those of the 248th Regiment.

Why this haste? Couldn't they wait until the next day?

Was the number 296 so damning that they had to scrub it off, like garbage? If they had known how indifferent we were about it, there would have been less of a rush. No matter what regiment you were in, you were still in the clutches of militarism.

We were thus assigned provisionally to the 4th Battalion of the 248th, awaiting the final determination of our fate at a higher level.

The day after we arrived, the commandant of this battalion felt the need to make our acquaintance, but I'd never seen a review like this one.

We left the billet in single file. The commandant, at the gate, stared at each one of us like a butcher inspects a flock of sheep at his barnyard's gate.

After we'd lined up in front of the billet, he repeated his inspection, stopping at length in front of each man, to whom he posed a few questions about his conscription class, his recruitment, etc.

Why did he look at us like strange beasts? What reputation had they pinned on us?

When he stopped in front of me, he said, "You're a skinny one, you." I kept my mouth shut.

"Why are you so skinny?"

"Commandant, when you don't miss a hitch in the trenches for thirty-six months, you can hardly get fat."

The commandant's voice softened. He turned to our Lieutenant Lorius and said, "All your men look good. But you have this corporal who's worn out. Take care of him."

This certainly wasn't our [former] Commandant Quinze-Grammes, showing interest in whether I was too skinny or too tired! This was the first kindhearted word that a superior officer had said to me since I'd been at the front. That's why I've made note of it.

One evening, in a large structure, a troupe of artists, real artists, came to Bassuet to give a performance. There were female artists in this troupe. That's all that was needed to bring hundreds of poilus running from all the neighboring villages.

The brigadier general himself attended, sitting in the front row, as you'd imagine. It's only in the trenches that the poilu gets a front-row seat. The 248th Regimental Band was the orchestra.

The young, pretty girls were a huge hit. Half-naked, decked out in jewels, they cut capers, danced, sang songs, performed saucy skits. Transported, excited, the poilus stamped, clapped, and roared with laughter.

Ah, this French insouciance, this joy, this laughter, weren't they an insult to the hundreds of dead bodies left by the division in the mud of the sinister Bois le Chaume? The earth hadn't yet soaked up all their blood, and their comrades who had seen them fall were now letting themselves go like this, having fun, getting drunk on songs, music, and off-color jokes?

There were also speeches and patriotic songs, which were a little less well received.

I didn't wait for the end of the performance to return to my hovel. A few comrades who shared my heartache did the same. I even know some who had the dignity not to attend the show at all.

After a week at Bassuet, the fate of our group was finally handed down: we were to be dispersed into various units of the division. As for me, I was kept in the 248th Regiment, which had its headquarters in Guingamp, in the Côtes-du-Nord [Brittany]. I was assigned to the 18th Company, in a battalion located in the village next to Bassuet, which I joined on November 29 with three comrades, including my friend Fraïssé from Olonzac, who were attached to other companies.

Well, we didn't feel like singing "La Madelon" as we marched along.[3] We didn't see anything worthwhile about being incorporated into a regiment of Bretons. "Did anyone think about that," said Fraïssé, usually so jovial, "about putting us with such grumpy, stubborn, buttoned-up, melancholy folks? I'll give them the slip pretty soon."

He was lucky enough to have a patch of chronic eczema on one leg, which had already gotten him evacuated three times. Now, during a rest stop, he showed it to us. It was starting to soften, to scab up, to form a sore. "Soon it will be done just right," he said, "to take to the *major* [medical officer]." In peacetime you would have felt sorry for someone afflicted with such eczema. Now we envied him for it, this lucky Fraïssé. "Convalo"—convalescent hospital— and then a trip back to home base brought the prospect of two or three months of rest.

I had the bad luck to be the only one from our group, and the only one from the 296th, to be assigned to this 18th Company, where I would find only foreign faces. While other companies had been almost completely wiped out, the 18th Company had suffered only a few losses, which had already been made up for with replacements from the rear. The whole 296th Regiment was insufficient to rebuild the division from that disaster which had passed unnoticed in a banal communiqué covering "reciprocal raids, clashes of patrols, major artillery activity in the Bois le Chaume."

In peacetime, a chimney fire would have gotten more notice in local news columns than did this massacre which covered Brittany in mourning.

At the office of the 18th Company where I presented myself, they gave me command of the 15th Squad. Off I went in search of this phantom squad which I couldn't discover in any of the billets occupied by the company.

I immediately found that the Breton soldiers, figuring out from my accent alone that I wasn't one of their own, looked at me with suspicion and weren't at all interested in giving me any information.

I nevertheless learned that the company took its meals in premises converted to a mess hall. This innovation made for a veritable luxury. It was the first time since I'd been at the front, since 1914, that I'd seen benches and tables put to use by poilus for eating their meals.

For sure, this dining room's furniture consisted only of rough, rickety benches, wobbly tables, all as rudimentary as could be. Up on the ceiling were plenty of cobwebs, and this room was well ventilated—too well ventilated, in fact, by numerous drafts. But in the end it made for progress, all the same.

At suppertime it was therefore easy for me to find the 15th Squad, represented by a grand total of two Bretons, who greeted me with unintelligible grunts. They were completely drunk, and had been for three days, it appeared.

They weren't the only ones, and I saw that very first day the passion of the

Bretons for alcohol and wine, which led them to drunkenness every time they had the means and the opportunity.

A Breton would have thought to be dishonoring Brittany if he didn't have a pipe or a quid of tobacco in his mouth.

And I noticed with disgust that almost all of them were covered with vermin.

The ticks don't have a preference, a marked predilection for the skin of a Breton compared to that of a Parisian or an *Auvergnat.* Nevertheless it wasn't completely the men's fault. In the 248th they distributed clean clothes so rarely that most of the men possessed only what they were wearing.

The Bretons are stubborn, quarrelsome, pugnacious, unsociable only when their minds are disturbed by the vapors of wine or other fermented potion. Outside of this abnormal state, the Bretons are as soft as sheep, as valiant and courageous as ancient Gauls, good-hearted and devoted.

The rest of the 15th Squad was either away on leave or had been sent out in agricultural work teams. The higher-ups were starting to understand that it was more useful to put men to work in the fields than parading them around or having them amuse themselves by knocking sticks together or playing leapfrog.

I learned with delight that among the leave takers was a southerner. This was the company's barber; he was from Auch. I would have at least one person with whom I could bond. But while waiting for him I spent several lonely days without a single comrade, in the midst of indifferent if not hostile folks speaking an incomprehensible language.

To make matters worse, the section chief was an old sublieutenant who lived by the rule book and followed it to the letter. Ten times a day he visited our billets, multiplying the inspections, parades, and roll calls.

What a difference from our good old Sublieutenant Lorius who, outside of his duties in the trenches, never bothered us with all the things he could have done to make our lives miserable.

I needed to be brought into line. This maniacal officer saw that right away, and from the first day he was after me. Sometimes it was my shoes not properly shined, or the billet not in order, or the squad not at full strength at roll call. One day I lost my patience and I answered this officer who had just given me a snide comment:

"Lieutenant, I'm asking you to speak to me in a more polite tone. You're my superior, but that doesn't excuse you. You don't have the right to speak to me rudely. Show me some respect, if you want me to respect you."

The officer, to whom I—taciturn and solitary—had spoken only when constrained and forced to do so, no doubt thought I was a near-idiot. He seemed stupefied by my brusque statement.

"But," he said, nonplussed, "the chore that I assigned to you was badly done."

"I've done my best. If you think you have to punish me, that's up to you and your conscience. Go ahead, punish me."

I have to admit that he didn't end up punishing me, and, to tell the truth, he hardly ever punished anyone. He even showed himself to be indulgent and affectionate toward his men. It was said that he had proven his courage and his sangfroid. In my section, the men held him in high regard, and they supported his obsessions without grumbling too much.

Personally, he left me alone from that day on, and subsequently even showed me some kindness.

In spite of the snow covering the ground and the sharp cold, we went out on exercises every day, during which, to amuse us, they had us run races and play games. You can imagine what fun we had.

Meanwhile the division was brought back to strength. We were ready to head back to the trenches. They couldn't let the soldiers spend too much time in the rear, getting soft. On December 5 we left Bassuet, conveyed to the front by automobile.[4]

The cold was downright Siberian. The thermometer hovered around twelve degrees below zero [Celsius]. Traveling in vans covered with canvas full of holes, immobile, tightly packed, we really had to be as hardy as cavemen to not succumb to the cold. But we were immunized. The next day there were no more visitors than usual to sick call.

At nightfall the vans dropped us near the village of Senades, where the regiment was billeted. Our company was billeted in a hamlet with its name inscribed on a Touring Club sign,[5] "La Contrôlerie" [the inspection post]. Funny name. I wonder what they had to inspect in this agglomeration of five or six houses lost in the middle of the woods.

We didn't stay long at La Contrôlerie. The next day, after soup, we headed for the trenches. We passed through Les Islettes, Le Neufour, Le Claon, and La Chalade along the valley of the Biesme, which flowed on to La Harazée at the foot of our sorely missed little fort where we had been barely seventeen days ago.

All these villages we passed through, except the last one, La Chalade, were still partly inhabited despite their proximity to the front lines, because they were protected by the wooded escarpments of the valley.

At nightfall they stuck us in the front lines. This installation consisted of taking possession of a few tiny shelters or individual dugouts carved into the trench walls. They were shored up with wood. Once you got into one you could stretch out but not sit up, because the ceiling was too low. You were well protected from an ordinary shell, but not from the cold, which was so rigorous that it would have been imprudent to let yourself fall off to sleep.

Wandering around a bit, I noted that some sections were better lodged than we were, while others were worse off.

I had to do twelve hours on guard duty out of twenty-four, from noon to midnight, which was fine with me; they kindly let us corporals decide among ourselves. That way each of us had about seven hours of nighttime duty.

Take note of this. Seven hours of walking along the muddy boyaux, a blanket draped over your shoulders, hurried along by a glacial bise or by rain or snow in this chilly Argonne.

Seven hours of tramping the deserted trenches where you might still have an unlucky encounter. Sometimes German patrols infiltrated between listening posts and pounced upon a solitary wanderer.

Or maybe it would be a French officer making his speedy rounds, eagerly telling you that at such-and-such a post the sentinels weren't on the lookout, or catching you taking a break on the steps of some dugout.

You had to go from one outpost to another where, at the end of a sap, two sentinels, huddled, curled up, immobile, waited for the hour of their relief with the passivity of beasts of burden.

Most of the time they weren't even watching. Numbed by the cold, they dozed off.

Every two hours I had to wake up the relief teams. And I had to listen, over and over, to their complaints and their curses against the war. But in the end they got up. Sometimes, chased by the cold or just to shirk their duty, some sought shelter at the mouth of a nearby mine shaft. Then we had to mount a veritable manhunt in the dark shadows.

Those damned corporal's stripes! How I envied the men of the squad—those guys who could, once their two hours of watch were over, burrow into a hole, quietly, without any responsibilities!

This went on for eight days and nights. It would have lasted longer if the men hadn't raised loud complaints which were transmitted to our captain by our sergeant, a lawyer, going to plead our case before courts-martial and earning wide influence in our company command.

They led us 200 meters back from the front line, into a deep and spacious shelter with a wire-mesh cot for each one of us. They were really spoiling us.

As was the rule, we had work details from morning to evening, but at night they were generous enough to leave us alone.

Our main job was to bring rations up to the men on the front lines. The field kitchens were nearby, at the bottom of a ravine, or you could call it a precipice, next to which we were posted.

You reached the bottom by a staircase which counted 500 steps, not one less. And they were "poilu steps"—50 to 80 centimeters, each one. You couldn't be asthmatic and climb this gigantic staircase. It wasn't too hard in dry weather, but when the snow and ice and slick mud covered the steps, watch out for slippery spots! You had to grab onto roots and rocky outcroppings so as not to tumble all the way to the bottom.

And the Boche lines weren't even a hundred meters from the last step of this staircase. Our outposts were only a few steps away from them.

Along the bottom of this deep valley, there was room just for a little tributary of the Biesme and for a road which must have been an enchanting hiking trail up until a certain day in 1915 when the front lines were fixed there.

On this sheltered road, you could have thought yourself perfectly safe. But alas, the Boche gunners found a way, by *tirs plongeants* [plunging fire],[6] to rain their shells right onto the stream or the road, and our field kitchens had to seek shelter in a sharp curve of the valley or in sorts of grottoes which they had to dig. But these artillerymen were wizards. Bombs, shells, mortar rounds often poured down with a thunderous racket, right up to the entrances of these grottoes.

On December 14 our battalion left the front lines and went into reserve one kilometer to the rear, in large shelters, in the middle of the woods, near the "Forester's Cottage," of which not a trace remained. Bloody combats had taken place in this area. Those who had fallen there slept their eternal sleep in a vast cemetery which grew every day with the dead from this sector.

This well-kept cemetery was surrounded by a palisade. At the entrance, on the frontispiece of a triumphal arch constructed skillfully with pine branches, you could read this inscription from the verses of the great Victor Hugo:

Those who piously have died for the fatherland
Deserve to have throngs come and pray at their tomb.[7]

Victor Hugo had no doubt written these sublime and immortal verses for the heroes of the great [French] Revolution, which had freed peoples and spread the ideas of liberty throughout the world.

He could not have imagined that the leaders of nations, seized one day by a monstrous folly, would undertake this killing in which the victims didn't know why they were being driven forward, why they were falling.

If Victor Hugo were alive, he would surely protest the abuse with which they treated his sublime hymn in wartime. He would have found other words to scourge the authors of this war and all those who hadn't made every effort to head it off.

They'd also built a chapel out of pine boughs, with an altar where a priest said mass when a soldier was being buried. In one corner, a few vacant coffins awaited their occupants. They had even been so farsighted as to dig a few graves in advance.

You could call this a deluxe cemetery. In letting us visit there, they thought they were doing us a favor by seeing that the dead were very well received there, and even pampered.

Right near the model cemetery, along the slope of a wooded valley, we set ourselves up in large, spacious shelters, even too spacious, with several entrances and exits, as you'd like, as big as carriage entrances. Of course you couldn't close them, so the bitterly cold Argonne bise swept in, and sometimes snow, too. No need for ventilators here, to refresh the air; it refreshed itself quickly enough.

To help some kitchenware salesman get rid of a collection of outmoded, defective stoves, they had sent some of them to the front, and a few of these were set up in our shelters. This was an unexpected luxury, unknown up to now. *Poêles* [stoves] for the poilus! Naturally the newspapers talked about it, praising the thoughtfulness of our top leaders. But unfortunately we had to fuel these stoves with green or soggy wood. They let off insufficient heat and smoke intense enough to suffocate all the foxes in the Argonne. We had to stop using them. These stoves had served to enrich only their sellers.

There was relatively little snow this December, but it covered the ground. That seemed to provoke famine among the rats, because they arrived, by the ravenous hundreds, in our shelters.

Too bad for him who had forgotten to hang his mess kit up high, or who left in his pack or his cartridge box a piece of soap, or chocolate, or bread, or whatever (except for iron and stones). In the blink of an eye, everything fell to the teeth of these scavengers.

The finest delicacy for them was soap—from Marseille or from the Congo, it mattered little. Since we were given it only very parsimoniously, we held onto bits of soap like precious stones.

If at nighttime you hadn't taken the precaution of covering up your head, you wouldn't be the first to feel—on your nose, your chin, or your ears—the sharp teeth of these accursed beasts.

For beds we had stacked single, wire-mesh bunks in a rather bad condition. That's how the shelters were in the "Basse-Chèvrerie" [Lower Goat Shed]. Commanders who were motivated by a larger spirit of solicitude for the soldiers could have made conditions better with the help of the engineers, at slight expense and minimal effort. But maybe that wasn't what they were looking for. Was it all done on purpose?

They didn't want to give to the soldier who was on rest detail, in reserve, too much well-being, too much comfort, so that he wouldn't find the transition too brutal from the tragic life of the trenches and its unspeakable sufferings.

Even as spread out as these shelters were, the Germans ended up finding them, and to prove it to us they would, from time to time, toss a couple of shells which plowed into the area.

Finally, they had pushed their bad manners to the point of firing poison-gas shells, which had claimed victims among our predecessors. That required us to post vigilant sentinels, day and night, ready to sound the alarm—to leap not to our arms but to our gas masks.

Every day there was a work detail of twenty men, sent out three kilometers to chop down and cut up trees for His Majesty, our brigadier general.

Yes. Read it well. They needed twenty men a day, no matter what the weather was, so that this general and the embusqués who surrounded him wouldn't suffer from the cold. And these twenty men, whom they didn't even compensate with a thank-you, then came back to our shelter, which was as cold as an ice house, to shiver all night long!

However, these twenty men never complained. It didn't make any difference whether they were cutting down trees or digging trenches which other teams of soldiers would occupy. Both tasks were just as difficult.

What would that kind of treatment do to an ox in his yoke, dragging a cart or a wagon?

During our time at the Basse-Chèvrerie, some Boche prisoners, no doubt overcome with bitter nostalgia, escaped from a camp in the rear and tried to cross through our lines to rejoin their comrades. These prisoners must have been fired with zeal to want to resume their lives on the front lines.

It was our bad luck that they chose our sector to cross the lines. All the available troops, in reserve or at rest, were put on alert to stop them. The capture of the Bonnot Gang[8] didn't involve such a marshaling of police forces. No hunter's quarry ever saw on its heels such a pack of bloodhounds. Night and day, all the crossroads were guarded, closely watched. Roads and footpaths were incessantly crisscrossed by patrols of poilus armed to the teeth.

That's fine for daytime. At night, we're walking a beat at a crossroads for three or four hours, or scouring another corner of the forest. Fine if the moon was clear and lit our way, but she proved to be a lazybones, at rest or on furlough. So we slipped and stumbled on the ice, bumped into hidden roots and invisible strands of barbed wire, broken branches, etc. Sprains, scratches, torn clothing and skin—that's what these nocturnal rambles brought us. And there was nothing to show for it. Not the slightest trace of these prisoners who had just disturbed our sleep, disrupted our nights. Couldn't they have waited for the end of the war to see their unhappy Germany again? Or maybe they would decide to stay on our side, let's add egotistically.

But where had they gone, these superpatriotic prisoners who disappeared into thin air as soon as anyone spotted them? You could start to believe that they were ghosts from another world.

Finally, one night, they succeeded in reaching our front lines. But the racket they made while crossing the barbed wire caught the attention of the occupants of a listening post. "Qui vive?" [Who goes there?] came the cry. Not getting a response, they fired on them. There were three of them; not one was hit. Two succeeded in fleeing; they grabbed the third one, who was caught in a tangle of prickly barbed wire, just like a rabbit in a trap.

He stated that he and his comrades had fled from Arcis-sur-Aube [north of Troyes, south of Châlons], that they didn't have anything to complain about but that, as prisoners since 1914, they wanted to see their families again. The unlucky prisoner had to take the road back to his camp the next day, postponing until later the pleasure of kissing his Bertha or his Gretchen.

Finally we were finished with this manhunt and with beating the bushes, day and night.

On December 23 we left the shelters of the Basse-Chèvrerie. We thought we'd be taking the road to the outposts again, but instead they announced that we were going to get two weeks of rest. They led quite a cushy life, this Breton regiment.

Our company went back to billet in the little village of La Contrôlerie. Two days after that was Christmas.

This was the fourth bloodstained Christmas spent far from home and hearth, far from the hometown church tower and the familiar ringing of the bells.

On the night of December 24–25, yesteryear's joyous night of parties, a violent snowstorm struck, whipped up into a blizzard by a big, glacial wind.

In our billet, this was a sad Christmas Eve, as you can well imagine. To defend ourselves from the cold, we all went to bed early, rolled up in our meager blankets, packed tightly against each other.

Oh, the comrades who stood watch out there in the listening posts, on the edge, on the rims of craters which the mine explosions had dug, what did they think about those who, on this very night, in Paris or elsewhere, crowded the cinemas and the theaters, rushing to get seated snugly around well-stocked tables?

A few intrepid poilus made their way to the village of Senades, to attend midnight mass. On the way back they almost got lost. Blinded by the whirlwinds of snow, they thought for a time that they'd never make it back to La Contrôlerie.

The regimental band of the 248th graciously offered its services to this celebration of mass. The war had accomplished this miracle: the army of the secular, anticlerical, free-thinking Republic lent its regimental bands to give more life to religious ceremonies judged to be ridiculous, stupid, contrary to healthy thinking.[9] In return, the French Church offered fervent prayers for the ultimate victory, raised to martyrdom the fallen soldier, promised him paradise, and thus turned this ignominious war into something sacred, sanctified, divine!

The next day, as if by the wave of a magic wand, the wind calmed down completely, but a nice layer of snow brightened the landscape. Upon awakening, I was duly warned that I had to carry out, on this day consecrated to the birth of the Savior, the annoying functions of corporal-of-the-day.

I thought it would be bad enough to have the snow swept away—or to sweep it away myself—from our billet, and to carry it off somewhere nearby. But in addition to these chores, I had to take Private Plumecoq to the village of La Noue.

This soldier had tarried for twenty-four hours too long in the delights of home and hearth. To punish him for this lack of eagerness to rejoin his corps, he had to go spend twenty days in the divisional disciplinary company, which they called the Paté Company, after the name of the general who commanded it.

In the 248th the state of discipline was fairly relaxed. You could get drunk, get into a fight, lose a tool or your gas mask or your rations, wander off from a parade, a drill, or a work detail, all with impunity. But discipline was harsh for the slightest lateness in returning from home leave.

The next day I was on guard detail at the police station with four poilus. It was only a single company, but no matter whether it was a regiment or a squad, there was always a police station. That was the rule.

To add to our bad luck, we got word that a suspected spy, disguised as an infantry non-com, was at large in our sector, who had, so they said, tried to obtain intelligence of a military nature by questioning an artilleryman.

The whole Argonne sector was on alert. A reward was offered for the capture of the spy, search parties were organized, but no one turned up any trace of this mysterious spy. Maybe he existed only in the imagination of an artilleryman who had gone a bit overboard in celebrating the birth of the Savior.

The only result was harsher duty for the listening posts and the sentries, while at night the snow fell thicker and the wind blew harder. The captain of our company took it upon himself to pull the sentries back from the front lines. It sure wasn't our old Captain Cros-Mayrevielle, the Kronprinz, who would never have been so considerate.

Finally, on December 28, I headed off to the nearby station at Les Islettes for my sixth home leave.

By a singular stroke of fate, in my village of Peyriac-Minervois, right next to my house, a family of refugees from Les Islettes, the "X____" family, were lodged in an old farmhouse.

I pass over the joy of spending time once again in the midst of my loved ones, and the sadness of returning to duty. I was completely discouraged, broken in body and spirit, when I found myself once again at Les Islettes station, the morning of January 14 [1918].

Sad and alone, under a gray sky in which a few snowflakes swirled, I made my way to the trenches.

At the village of [Le] Neufour, where the company sergeant-majors were encamped, I hoisted my pack, my weapons, and all the gear with which a poilu was loaded down, and I headed off briskly because I had a dozen kilometers to cover, through the woods, along bad roads unknown to me, as the regiment had by now taken up front-line positions near Vauquois.

After the village of Le Claon I had to climb a steep hill which forced me to stop a dozen times to catch my breath. The road, now leading through thick forest, was almost deserted. As the snow fell it hardened on the ground and got slippery, which made walking quite difficult.

At the Croix de Pierre crossroads, I had to leave the road and follow footpaths. Night was falling and, despairing of being unable to arrive before daylight's end, I looked for some sort of shelter in which to spend the night.

Luckily a sergeant of the 248th Regiment came along, whom I only had to follow to finally reach the ravine where our field kitchens were hidden.

Then I just had to tag along with my squad's *homme de soupe* [rationer] up to the place where the section was posted in reserve, about two hundred meters back from the front line. The men had come there that very morning, having spent four days in the forward outposts. I had the unexpected luck of getting some rest that night. For sure, the shelter lacked any comfort, but when you were expecting to spend a long night outdoors, contemplating the stars (when they are visible), you count yourself lucky and privileged. The four days spent in the hollow of the ravine where our shelter was located cured me of the fatigues of my journey.

Each day we would put back into shape the boyaux which had been blocked by some shellfire or by landslides brought on by the heavy frosts. Each evening, after supper, we would spend two or three hours placing barbed wire between the lines or carrying up heavy *chevaux de frise* [portable wire entanglements] already wrapped with wire. I assure you that it's much sweeter to spend an evening by a crackling fire, in the warmth of family life. But it was with some regret that we left behind this shelter and these chores, once our four days were up, to go up and occupy the forward outposts.

The squad had to furnish two sentries for a listening post perched on the lip of a gigantic mine crater. The earth that had been thrown up by the explosion formed a rim which you reached by climbing a ladder.

All the listening posts were similarly placed, and on the opposite side were the Germans.

From the height of these lookouts, the surrounding landscape was frightful. All you could see were enormous blisters and scars, as if the earth had undergone chaotic convulsions.

The opposing front lines were now separated by an uninterrupted row of gigantic mine craters, transformed by the rain into muddy lakes.

How can one describe the melancholy, the sadness which weighed upon these places, most notably at times of calm when the heavy silence was disturbed only by the cawing of a famished crow!

About 200 meters to the left there was a mound, a little higher than the others, thrown up by the explosion of a deep mine which had literally split the hill in two.

This elevation was the "Fille Morte" [Dead Girl] often mentioned in dispatches. I don't know whether there had ever been a dead girl in the vicinity. But there were quite a few young fellows who found their tombs there.

For quite a while now the echoes of the Argonne had been only rarely disturbed by the thunderous detonation of underground mines.

Mine warfare was dying out. Gunpowder was growing more and more costly, and the timbers needed to shore up the mines were growing scarce. Lastly, the results were mediocre because, on both sides, we had pulled back and abandoned a large expanse of terrain in which only a few listening posts were scattered.

Here and there, you'd hear the explosion of a *camouflet,* so deep underground that sometimes the surface wasn't even disturbed.

These camouflets were intended to destroy the enemy's approach tunnels by means of clusters of explosives sent into the mine shafts by a sort of motorized drill.

Woe to anyone who happened to be in a mine when one of these explosions took place. You'd be buried alive, or suffocated by the gases.

For those who worked day and night deep in the mines, these camouflets were a terrible danger. But following a tacit accord between the French and German engineers there were rarely any victims.

For a while mines and camouflets were set off only between 2 and 6 in the morning. At 10 minutes to 2, every night, on both sides, the listening posts and front lines were evacuated, then reoccupied quietly at six o'clock in the morning.

Since that time, there were hardly ever any casualties from these mines, which before had been so murderous. On both sides, the sacred flame of patriotism was burning out. The war was lasting too long. But war is meant to waste money, and that's why they still kept digging, at great cost, the expensive and useless mines.

The tunnels were lit with electricity. Ventilators, pumps, drills, winches, all were run by electric power produced by a veritable underground factory, set up at the second line of defense, right in the trenches, which fed the whole sector.

Power stations in the trenches! But then they were thinking that the war would go on for years and years.

Our squad, lost in the midst of these chaotic upheavals, was connected to the outside world only by the *homme de liaison,* who came every day at 4 o'clock, bringing letters, packages, newspapers, and what we had ordered the day before: tobacco, candles, etc.

How impatiently we waited for his arrival, at the turn of the boyau!

As chief of the outpost, I had to see to the relief of sentries, walking all night long from one listening post to the other, while staying in contact with neighboring outposts. This would have worn out the legs of the Wandering Jew!

Those who gave out these impossible orders—were they unconscious? Or did they have the souls of executioners?

But no order can overcome the laws of nature. When fatigue and weariness weighed down too heavily, you collapsed even in the most miserable hole.

As a result, when the sentries at a listening post didn't see their relief detail arriving, one of them scrambled back into the dugout to wake them up, and sometimes both sentries left the listening post at the same time, leaving surveillance completely to chance. But whose fault was that?

On January 27, it was someone else's turn to come and contemplate the peaceful landscape of the mine craters, and having become a "reserve section" we went to occupy shelters in wooded terrain. That meant we actually saw some trees which had not been ripped up, guillotined, mutilated.

The whole section packed into a deep but damp shelter, so damp that it would have filled up with water if they hadn't pumped it out from time to time. It was a breeding ground for rheumatism, bronchitis, and tuberculosis.

We were all the way at the end of this grotto, piled up with two levels of wire-mesh bunks. It wasn't unusual that, in the morning, those in the lower bunks felt water lapping against their backsides.

The lack of space forced us to take our meals out in the boyau, in all kinds of weather. Oh, you didn't have to blow on your soup or your rata to cool it down, the January bise took care of that. In two or three minutes your meal would be finished.

One day, with my squad, I was ordered to go to the colonel's command post to pick up some oilskin or waxed jackets. This was an event, a special day. After three and a half years of war, someone seemed to have finally noticed that the poilu didn't have anything to keep off the rain, water being considered as an unimportant element which didn't deserve worrying about.

Here we are, then, en route to picking up these precious raincoats. After having followed the boyau for about four hundred meters, we had in front of us a wide open space crossed by the Varennes road and a narrow-gauge railroad track. Beyond was the colonel's dugout, prudently hidden away.

For several days a German battery had fixed its sights on this road, the tacot railway line, and the clearing. Just when anyone was least expecting it, without warning, a volley of shells would crash down like a thunderbolt, and almost every day there were some victims.

We doubtless could have escaped this trap by making a detour of five or six hundred meters. But the soldier never fears a danger which isn't apparent. He has faith in his own star, and almost everyone imprudently crossed the clearing which served as a target for the Germans.

After a quick consultation, by four votes against one and one abstention—mine—we decided to cross, which we did at full speed, with no accidents. The return trip went off just as peacefully. We carried oilskin jerseys, but only two per squad, only a sampling.

We also brought fine rubber boots, a sure way to keep the feet dry—but again, only two pair per squad.

We brought all this to the captain's command post, which was in a tunnel at least five hundred meters long. This tunnel was spacious, two meters high, solidly shored up with timber. It opened near the front line, and there were numerous rooms to the right and left. In one of them our captain was installed, spending his nights snoring away and his days playing cards, drinking, and eating. The rooms and the tunnel were lit by the fairy Electricity.

In anticipation of the expected big German offensive, the sappers had dug, here and there, *fourneaux de mine* [mine stoves] to blow up the tunnel in case of retreat.

The captain, eyes shining, face flushed with drink, cast a disdainful look on the oilskin jerseys. But right away he took hold of a pair of rubber boots.

It was no doubt the praiseworthy intention of those who had sent these boots that they be destined, first and foremost, to the sentries who had to stand immobile, for hours on end, at the listening posts, feet stuck in the mud or the snow. But officers, adjutants, sergeants, orderlies, etc., pounced upon these boots like a flight of crows upon prey, under the complicit eye of the captain who had himself set a scandalous example.

On January 29, work details completed, we were bedding down in our damp shelter at 11 p.m. when the sudden sound of a barrage broke out like a clap of thunder.

This was the German riposte to the last trench raid, which the French had carried out on January 21 at the Four de Paris.

I scrambled up the muddy and narrow staircase to find out what was going on. I noticed with a selfish satisfaction that it was "going on" at least two kilometers to our left, probably on top of the regiment next door, the 202nd Regiment. There was nothing to worry about. We could go back to sleep. In front of us, all was calm.

I started going down the stairs, to reassure my comrades. I had put my foot on the first step when I heard someone arriving at full speed. It was our sub-lieutenant, "X," the section chief—agitated, crazed, seemingly gone mad.

"Hey," he shouted when he saw me, "You haven't heard the barrage? Let's go, grab your rifles! Everybody up and outside!"

"But lieutenant," I said to him, "the firing isn't in front of us. See, our sector is completely quiet, nothing abnormal."

But the officer would hear none of it. He called us out in full gear as if the Germans were right there, and posted us haphazardly along the abandoned boyau. We were stationed there at the ready. He kept us there a full hour, stomping in the freezing mud and blowing on our fingers until the last cannon shot was heard.

Basic common sense, even if the shells were falling right onto us, would be to stay in the dugout, with just one sentry posted at the top of the staircase, because we're at least one kilometer back from the front line and we had an advance section posted five hundred meters in front of our shelter.

Trench raids were preceded by sudden, violent bombardments, trying to catch anyone who had the bad luck to be outside at the moment. Leaving shelters to take up positions in the wide open, in a boyau, just because an enemy patrol was going to pay a visit to a distant listening post—that was risking men's lives through sheer stupidity. It's true that the officer stayed out there with us. For him it was an extenuating circumstance.

18th Notebook

The Last Year of Martyrdom:
January 29–August 11, 1918

The "Fille Morte" sector, Argonne, 1918

Of course, for anyone else but us, the show would have been worth watching: white, red, and green rockets lighting up the night sky, blending together, giving to the heavens unexpected colors and reflections, accented with the flashes of cannon fire and explosions of projectiles which seemed to burst out of the very earth. It was terrifying, hallucinating, phantasmagorical.

And along with it a racket which would cover the noise of ten simultaneous thunderbolts. Blasé as we were, we hardly paid any attention to it, but waited impatiently for the calm to return so that we could reclaim our hole in the ground.

This time, the Germans didn't succeed in taking any prisoners—the main goal of any trench raid—but their bombardment produced twenty casualties (killed and wounded) in the ranks of the 202nd Regiment. Not many for a bombardment like that one, for such an avalanche of projectiles. But always too many for those who lost their lives.

After four days of so-called rest, we came back up to the front lines, more tired than before we came away from them. In our lodgings we were badly allotted; we had to pile up two squads in a redoubt where one squad would have had trouble fitting.

In the middle of this so-called redoubt, which was nothing more than a roofed-over crossroads of trenches, there was a big barrel of gasoline which poilu ingenuity had turned into a stove. It was central heating of sorts. Only four men could stand around it at one time and benefit from the soothing heat that it emitted. These four privileged places were reserved for the sentries, chilled to the bone, who had just come back from spending two hours of suffering at the listening posts.

One day the sergeant-major made his twice-a-month appearance in the trench, to pay off our pittances of salaries. He came only for that opportunity.

For him, there was a lot of money to be made in this. In a calm sector, he even pushed boldness and imprudence as far as coming to pay the poilus at the farthest outposts.

That same day, some of the Bretons, whom I believe would have sold their souls for a cask of wine, decided to transform their pay into *bidons* [containers] of pinard, which the rationers went to seek at the "co-op" without a care for the shells that often rained on the Varennes road they had to follow and the clearings they had to cross.

In the afternoon, the drinking bout began. A Breton declared that if someone would bet him a few liters of wine he would shave off his mustaches, fine mustaches like those which "our Gallic ancestors" wore. The bet was made, and in the midst of the joy, of general hilarity, the face of the Breton was changed into that of a coachman or a Benedictine friar.

A second Breton offered his mustaches up in sacrifice for some jugs of grape-arbor juice, then a third, then a fourth . . . I lost count. It was such a large number of bidons of pinard consumed that almost all of them were drunk, and two or three were dead-drunk.

They fell into arguing, shouting, singing, all at once, just as if they were in a peaceful corner of their Brittany.

The sergeant who was with us was in despair at not being able to quiet them down, fearing an officer making his rounds or a German patrol coming to see what was happening.

In this sector, the terrain was riddled with mine shafts. It was like being on top of a volcano, always ready to blow its top. For the reasons I mentioned above, we were under orders to pull back to the second lines, at two in the morning.

It was no small task to gather up all these drunkards. At a forward listening post, two sentries had passed out and refused to come along. Others wandered in the labyrinth of boyaux. With the terror-stricken sergeant we really had to beat the bushes to try to find them, which didn't work.

If by misfortune a mine had gone off that night, what would have been our responsibility, humble *gradés* [non-coms], to have left men up at the front line despite formal orders. Luckily that night there was neither a mine detonation nor an officer's rounds, and the next day we were all together again. The drunks were ashamed of their conduct and promised never to do that again . . . until the next opportunity, no doubt.

On February 5 a company of the 248th Regiment was given orders to make an incursion into the German lines. We couldn't just sit there twiddling our thumbs, and we had dispatches to feed.

This company was the 15th, commanded by young Captain Guillot, who had acquired a well-deserved reputation for bravery in the 296th. Almost all of the men had followed him to the 15th Company of the 248th, which had been practically wiped out at the Bois le Chaume. It was now a company made up of southerners within a Breton regiment.

Guillot's company appeared to be the elite unit of the regiment. In fact, it was capable of carrying out difficult missions where others had failed.

Why so? Were its men handpicked to be the bravest, the most devoted? No, there was no warrior quality which distinguished them from the masses of poilus. But they loved their young captain, who treated them all like comrades, who indulged them in their peccadilloes, who kept them out of whatever drudgery he could—work details, parades, drills, all those things that soldiers hate.

He was no prouder of his medals and his stripes than the lowliest private was of the unadorned sleeves of his coat. When he was the first to leap over the parapet and dash toward the enemy lines, he didn't need to look back to see if he was being followed. Not one man stayed back in the trench.

All morning long our big-caliber batteries, hidden in the woods, rained destructive fire on the German lines and their batteries, which kept silent.

At noon the firing from our artillery redoubled in violence. The assault company, Guillot at its head, following the edges of the shell holes, reached the German forward listening posts in a few bounds. We saw men, bent double in the nearly filled-up boyaux, infiltrating toward the enemy's second trench lines; then they were lost from our view.

They all came back, with not one killed or wounded, having scooped up twenty-five prisoners and five machine guns. The Germans had offered no resistance to speak of. Their subsequent artillery fire was very feeble. In the regiment there were only two victims: two rationers, inoffensive and peaceable, were utterly blown to bits while bringing up food for the squads.

This lucky trench raid cost us only two dead—for nothing.

The next day, February 6, the regiment left the trenches for two weeks. Our company set itself up near the mobile field kitchens in the Meurissons ravine, where we spent only one night.

1918. Argonne. Work in the forest.
Up to the lines again. Incidents and accidents.

A few days earlier, the dictator Clemenceau had spoken about calling up some older conscript classes to undertake various defensive works, in anticipation of a big German offensive everyone was talking so much about.

Due to the deplorable effect produced across the country by this announcement, he had decided, instead, to get this work done by poilus already spending the winter on the front lines, under the heading of "relaxation."

That is how, the very day after our arrival at the Meurissons ravine, our captain called us together and gave each section its work assignment. He, alone, had nothing to do. The section I was assigned to was charged with cutting down trees in the woods near Neufour. They didn't ask if this was our profession, but it is understood that a soldier should know how to do everything, at least in theory.

We traversed a dozen kilometers of muddy, barely passable roads, accompanied by chilly rain showers. After three or four hours walking we arrived at the village of Les Petites-Islettes, where we were posted in support of an artillery unit.

These artillerymen who formed the garrison of Petites-Islettes were surprised by our arrival, which hadn't been announced to them. The consequence of this oversight was that nothing had been foreseen about where we would lodge or what we would eat.

We had to wait a couple of hours before somebody decided to give us a few cans of sardines, along with, for dessert, a bucket of jam to dip a piece of bread into. Then they conducted us to some cabins made of planks, built at the edge of the forest.

What did this group of artillerymen—without cannon—do in this village of around fifty inhabitants?

This group was called a "section of infantry munitions." Its role consisted of bringing up supplies from a nearby station to the neighboring village of Neufour, where the ammunition depot of our regiment could be found.

And for this ridiculous assignment there were, in this village, a good sixty horses and 150 men, with, at their head, a big-bellied captain, a pomaded lieutenant, adjutants, sergeant-majors, quartermaster-sergeants, billet-assigners, miscellaneous employees, all of them plump, fresh, and rosy-cheeked.

The simple mortals of the artillery, enjoying more meager fare, had a less flowery look about them. From morning to evening, they took care of their horses and those of the numerous striped-sleevers, or carried out work details.

For three and a half years of war, this privileged group hadn't had one casualty, despite their village being within easy reach of German cannon. Not a shell, not a piece of shrapnel had fallen on them. These embusqués died only of sickness.

The next day, two forest guards, young and vigorous, who looked down on us and spoke dryly, spelled out our duties.

We had to cut down trees and transform them, on the spot, into logs, fence posts, mine shaft walls, firewood, etc., all tallied up, measured, down to the smallest twig or stick or wood, not for us to be paid—we worked gratis—but to quantify each day's work, which they never found to be sufficient.

During our stay in this place, I can tell you that the isolated Bretons, far from any officers or non-coms, indulged in drunken binges which could only lead to tragic consequences.

One night, one of them fired all the cartridges in his revolver, at the risk of wounding some comrade, and struck terror in the village where the firing could be heard.

The captain of the embusqués, who perhaps hadn't heard the gunshots closely enough, spoke the next day only about sending the drunkard in front of a court-martial.

One evening, two Bretons who bunked with me in the same cabin left for Neufour to go drinking.

At midnight I was tossed out of bed by the noise of the door opening loudly. At the same time someone stumbled on top of me, uttering Breton curse words: *Fil d'en Dou!* [Son of God], *Mou mame!* [My soul], *Ma Doué!* [My Lady]. I rolled the drunkard to the other end of the barrack. He tripped over sleepers, who gave him a warm welcome.

I lit my candle.

"Where did you leave your comrade?" I asked him.

"I dunno . . . I dunno," he stammered.

And he passed out in a corner like an inert mass.

An hour later, some artillerymen living in a shelter halfway from the village came to tell us that they heard some moaning and groaning in the area. That couldn't be anyone but our second drunkard.

Carrying a lantern, there we were in the dark of night, very cold, drowned in fog, searching for this boozer who, no doubt having fallen asleep, gave no signs of life. We couldn't find him.

The next day, at dawn, he showed up, and in what a state! He'd been rolling around in muddy potholes, then had fallen asleep according to the natural laws of drunkenness, protected from the cold by Bacchus, the god of drunkards.

This quiet and solitary life in the middle of the woods pleased me greatly. Only in the evenings did sadness overcome me, alone, without a comrade. In the dark, cold cabin which the Bretons had abandoned in search of pinard, it was no fun.

Sometimes I went to spend the evening at the *foyer du soldat* [soldier's re-treat] in Les Islettes. There, for three sous, you could drink a mug of café au lait or hot chocolate. There was a fireplace, books, and newspapers.

I would spend two or three hours there, in the warmth and the light, but it was a seven-kilometer trip each way to cover in the nighttime.

But our apprenticeship as woodcutters was coming to an end. The 248th Regiment had to go back up to the front lines, and on February 21 after supper we left to rejoin the 18th Company at the Meurissons ravine.

A van carried our packs, and I had the good luck to be picked to accompany the driver, who didn't know the route. The others had to take the connecting roads. It was somewhat moving to follow this route across the dark Argonne forest which, more than a century before, the unlucky fugitive King Louis XVI had followed.

But unlike him, we couldn't reach Varennes.[1] Our friends the Germans had established themselves solidly there. We stopped at the dugouts which the 18th Company occupied, where we spent only one night. The next day we went to occupy reserve shelters built into the slopes of one of the *mamelons* [nipples] which bordered the valley of the Biesme. This place was called Le Chalet. There was a real little village: dugouts, cabins, hangars, little chalets, supply dumps, and a tacot train station. Night and day there was an intense level of activity, and this just a few hundred meters from the German listening posts! But the sharp declivities of the valley's terrain didn't permit the German gunners, clever as they were, to drop a shell on us.

But one detail was hardly reassuring: all the trees were dead. A hideous yellow coating covered their trunks, clearly indicating that a deadly cloud of poison gas had passed by there.

Our section was exclusively devoted to making *ribards*. The war will have had this one good result: enriching the dictionary with new words. Those who will look up the definition will learn that a ribard is composed of prickly barbed wire rolled around iron loaf-shaped cores. After dark, you'd go out by moonlight and toss these ribards between the lines.

In summertime this work duty was somewhat entertaining. But handling this prickly barbed wire with fingers blue with cold—several degrees below zero, if you please—we would have preferred to be standing guard at the outposts.

There are folks who find the eight-hour day too short. I'd like to see them rolling ribards in the Argonne in the dead of winter.

On March 9 we moved out, still in reserve, and headed for "Les Sapins" [Pine Trees] position. This was now the fourth winter I'd spent in the trenches. I was more and more worn out, bone-tired. I looked so bad that the captain and my section chief, taking pity, exempted me from daily work details. Along with some pip-squeaks and other worn-out guys, we did our chores in the shelters and peeled potatoes with the cooks.

Every morning I mustered the sick, including some who were better off than I was, and led them to sick bay under a big, comfortable tent. There was an infirmary where they took care of the slightly wounded and the sick who were under observation. At that time it cost you plenty in order to be evacuated altogether from the trench lines. You had to have broken legs or arms, or a fever like a horse.

The height of comfort: a board-certified dentist, with stripes on his sleeves, gave dental care. This tooth puller had plenty of work. First of all, it was free of charge, and then, for those chosen as patients, there was the precious opportunity to miss a morning of work.

During our sojourn at Les Sapins there was a tragic series of accidents. In a long, tunnellike shelter, a hundred men slept on iron-frame bunk beds, in two tiers. On the iron-mesh bed frames everyone spread out armfuls of ferns and straw. One night a drunken Breton lit his bunk on fire, which spread to adjacent ones. The tunnel filled with flames and a lot of smoke. All the occupants of the tunnel were able to get out, except for the guy who had started the fire. They found him dead of smoke inhalation.

The next day, our *caporal d'ordinaire* and our *sergent-fourrier* [quartermaster-sergeant], on a spree fueled by the company's pinard, were playing around with a revolver when all of a sudden it went off, and the bullet went through the caporal d'ordinaire's arm and he was evacuated.

A few days later, a guy was cleaning his automatic revolver when it went off, and the bullet—he didn't know it was in the gun—struck a corporal in the belly. He died the next day at the field hospital. This was Corporal Mons, one of my old comrades from the 296th Regiment, a husband and father. He was from Ornaisons [Aude].

Clearly these automatic pistols were dangerous toys for their owners. They probably killed more Frenchmen than Germans during this war.

At Les Sapins they set up a very well-stocked co-op. There you could buy fresh fish, coquillages, shrimp, oysters, and escargots as well as lots of other things to eat. They even sold *marrons* [chestnuts], which a clever poilu with an *Auvergnat* accent and appearance was roasting in a perforated tin can and offering to everyone, "Hot marrons! Hot marrons! Six for a sou!"

On the night of March 20–21, the division was relieved and pulled back from the sector. The companies had to be dispersed farther back from the front, on a large expanse, to carry out defensive works.

We were under the threat of a major German offensive. But we didn't know where the onslaught of fire and steel would fall upon us. We lived in anxiety, like a scrawny little bird sitting under a leaf, waiting for the onset of a violent storm.

Our company was picked to be stationed in the village of Les Islettes, wielding picks and shovels while awaiting the big blow.

Argonne 1918. Les Islettes. The final German offensive. Departure. Sainte-Menehould. Auve.

My strength was diminishing day by day, and each relief was a nightmare because often I couldn't keep up with my comrades. That evening, I made a great effort to arrive at the same time as they did, because it wasn't any fun to be looking for your squad's campsite in the dark, and you were sure to have the worst spot if you arrived last.

At midnight we entered Les Islettes. They ordered us to form up in bunches.

To my astonishment, I noticed that I didn't have my rifle. I had left it at Les Petites-Islettes where we had taken our last rest break.

What a warrior I was! Forgetting my sacred weapon in a ditch beside the road!

Without breathing a word to anyone, I made my way back to Les Petites-Islettes, under a magnificent full moon. I ran into a group of non-coms from the company who had stayed back to give guidance to our replacements. Among them was my section chief, Sublieutenant "X," who recognized me and said, "Where are you going, Barthas?"

"To our last rest stop. I forgot something, and I'm going back to get it."

"So what is it?"

Might as well speak frankly, I thought.

"It's my rifle that I forgot."

"Your rifle! My God," said the officer, sputtering with surprise. "How did you manage to do that?"

"I was so tired, Lieutenant, that I wasn't thinking when I got back on the road."

"Well, go find it, at least," said the lieutenant, with more solicitude than menace in his voice.

My rifle was right where I had left it. Quietly, with barely enough strength in my legs to carry me the four kilometers, I rejoined my comrades, who had been worried about my disappearance, at the campsite.

There were only a few inhabitants left at Les Islettes. The village was frequently bombarded, but there must have been some pretty lackluster gunners on duty, because very few of the houses were struck by shells.

Every day the company went out to dig trenches. To stimulate the workers' zeal we were paid at a fixed rate for the job, but nobody made a fortune. The strongest ones earned only fifteen sous a day!

Clemenceau sure got up early for the poilus.

Next day, my lieutenant was up early to see if I had found my *flingot* [rifle; literally, peashooter]. It had been bothering him all night long. Basically he was a good man, and seeing me wasting away he exempted me from going on work details. All I had to do was to accompany the sick to sick bay.

Meanwhile the war had ended on the Russian front. Germany was marshaling all its forces for a supreme effort on our front. It was around Amiens that the main hammer blow fell, but from the North Sea to the Vosges the Germans unleashed an impressive effort. Every night their planes bombed railway stations near the front. Their batteries fired on roads and villages incessantly. Shells fell on Paris. Mine explosions, gas attacks—nothing was spared to sow terror, fear, discouragement.

One day at roll call they said to us: "All leaves are canceled."

How heavy with menace that sentence was for all of us, so laconic yet such a blow for those who were going on home leave that very day or the next day!

I know some who had given their families such joy in announcing their impending leave, and who only got home, once the war ended, between four pinewood boards!

On March 23 and 24 the village of Les Islettes was heavily shelled. All of the units based in the village were quickly moved out.

In the night of the 24th–25th, blessed with an accursed full moon, the Gothas[2] flew over several times and dropped their bombs, trying to destroy the railway and the station.

Two or three bombs fell barely a hundred meters from our billet, which we had to abandon and then spend the night outdoors. Better to risk a touch of bronchitis than to be guillotined, disemboweled, or blown to bits.

On March 27 we were put on alert. We spent the whole day at the ready, our arms stacked. Finally, about 5 p.m. we got our orders setting our departure on foot for 6 the next morning.

At 8 a.m. on March 28 we marched through Sainte-Menehould, which offered a sad spectacle. This city had been spared by the Germans up to this point, by a strange whim, but for five or six days now volleys of shells had fallen. The inhabitants scrambled to get away, like fleeing a cataclysm, some with wagons, some with handcarts or wheelbarrows, or some just carrying on their own backs what they considered most indispensable.

In streets and neighborhoods not yet shelled, the inhabitants hesitated to leave. It's not easy to quit your home, your work, your daily routine, to head out into adventures and misadventures. The fact that we were leaving made an impression on the civilians, and bothered them. "Why are you leaving us? Why are you abandoning us?" they said. To the contrary, our departure should have reassured them. If we were being sent elsewhere, it was because our bosses didn't think there'd be an attack right here.

As we left the village, an old lady came up to us, carrying something in her apron. They were some eggs which she handed out to us. As I passed by I managed to snatch one. It's a small thing, an egg, but we were very touched by it. This poor old lady was giving up something necessary for her, to give us this offering. How a gift is made is more important than the gift itself.

This was a tough march. Around noon, despite my comrades from time to time carrying my rifle for me, I had to fall out of rank. Our lieutenant told me to keep up as best I could, simply suggesting that I take charge of the laggards at the rear, who were becoming more and more numerous. They were counting on me to buck up the laggards!

About 4 p.m., after ten hours of marching without much of a break, we arrived in a village called Auve [on the Auve river, southwest of Sainte-Menehould].

We were lodged in wood-plank barracks. When I got there I collapsed in a heap, without having the strength to take off my gear. My comrades had to pull the pack off my aching shoulders.

The captain came to tell us that we had to get to bed early. Next day's march would be even longer. This hardly encouraging news spurred me to go to sick call, to try to get exempted from carrying a pack, the next day.

Just as I got there, the *major* [medical officer] was just closing up. At the sight of me he got angry.

"Another one of them? Why didn't you get here earlier?"

"*Monsieur le Major,* I couldn't keep up with my comrades. I've only just arrived in Auve."

"Hold on," he said to his *caporal infirmier* [medical corporal]. "Let's evacuate this one, too. Otherwise he'll be nagging us every day. But I'm sure there's nothing wrong with him. It's just that we have to get rid of these people who don't want to do anything," he said in rising anger.

My self-interest should have led me to keep quiet and play the idiot, but I was stung and I responded:

"Monsieur le *Major,* since 1914 I've never been evacuated, but now I'm at the end of my strength."

"And what about me?" shouted the *toubib* [doctor]. "I've been at it since 1914! I've been in Belgium and everywhere else!"

He didn't even ask what was wrong with me. To his scribe, when he asked what he should put down on my card, he said: "He's got nothing wrong. Put down whatever you want," and turning to me, "Be back here in twenty minutes with all your gear, or else I'm not evacuating you. Do you hear?"

Yes, I heard just fine. Despite his unjustified anger toward me, despite his insults, I would have hugged this man's knees, kissed his hands. With wobbly legs I stumbled back to the cantonment.

The squad was eating dinner. The old-timer Sonnes, from the Gers [département, west of Toulouse], grumbled to me, "Well, where've you been hanging out? Too bad for you, we couldn't wait for you."

"Eat up, friends. Don't worry about me. I'm leaving right away. I'm being evacuated."

At these words, forks hung suspended in mid-air. Dumbstruck, the men gazed at me, then their hands reached out to me, I saw their eyes get moist, their voices trembled a little. Would we ever see each other again? Had I really won a bit of esteem, of affection, from these gloomy Bretons, always aloof from those who aren't of their race?

For as long as I'd been among them I'd given them all my tobacco and my ration of *gniole* [hooch]—precious gifts for the Bretons. That might have had something to do with their regret at my departure. The most afflicted was my friend Sonnes, the only one of the squad from the Midi; same age as me, just as worn out, my companion bringing up the rear in all the relief details, all the marches.

"So," he said to me in a reproachful tone, "you're abandoning me? Tomorrow I'll be the only laggard?"

Deeply moved, I embraced him, and not finding the words to say I left, without a look back, and joined the lame and the halt at the police post.

There were ten of us. By a curious twist of fate, two were old comrades from my very first squad when I arrived at the front in 1914. They were Donadilles from the Tarn, who had just pulled a lucky sprain while horsing around with a comrade, and Sajus from Toulouse, whose feet had gotten bloody the previous winter.

They led us to an *ambulance* [field hospital] which was near the village. It was made up of about fifty barracks buildings capable of housing more than two thousand wounded, but at that time there were more doctors and nurses than sick. It was farther away from where the storm was bursting and human flesh was being shredded.

They gave me a nice, soft bed which I stretched out on with delight. It's not that I was spoiled. This was the first time on the front lines since 1914 that I slept in a real bed.

In the morning, I heard the regiment waking up in the village, getting ready to leave. In a driving rain they marched out on the road alongside the barracks. I pitied my poor comrades. That spoiled my happiness.

At 8 o'clock the *major* showed up. Nothing in common with the brute who'd evacuated me. A sympathetic look, a soft word. He asked about my family, and was visibly moved when I told him I'd been manning the trenches since 1914. He prescribed rest and a fortifying diet for me. That's all that I was asking for.

In the barracks we were forty or so of us on sick leave. Every part of the world, every race, every color was represented. Moroccans, Annamites, Americans both white and black, Italians, etc., and five or six Frenchmen. When the conversations flowed you heard quite a cacophony.

No poilus right from the trenches, though. They had been snagged in the fishnet, held back in regimental and divisional field stations which sent them back to their front-line squads as soon as they were healed, without a single day of leave.

Farther to the rear, behind a capriciously drawn line parallel to the front, the sick and the wounded benefited from at least ten days of convalescence. Happily for me, the Auve field hospital was on the right side of the demarcation line and you could get ten days of convalescence at home, with the condition that you had to have been there at the hospital at least ten days. That's what everyone hoped for, and it was rare that the medical officers sent them away without granting the full ten days—except for the Americans and the Annamites, whom they couldn't exactly send to San Francisco or Hanoi for ten days.

On April 6 they decided to evacuate me to Châlons-sur-Marne.

My buddies treated me like a lucky devil. It seemed I had a stroke of rare good luck. I was following the right path, the one that took me away from the front lines. I owed this happy decision to my skeletal skinniness and the help of the head corpsman for whom I'd done some small favors (updating his logbook, cleaning the room, etc.).

That same day, at noon, I embarked from the Auve train station with two big Moroccan troopers evacuated like me and put in my charge.

This was easy duty, since these two lascars weren't about to escape. For them, a stay in hospital was a pasha's life. I was supposed to drop one of them off along the way, at the village field hospital in Saint-Hilaire-au-Temple.

At the Saint-Hilaire station I gave him his papers and asked him to get off the train, but he didn't understand a word of French, nor did his comrade, and it took a long time for him to comprehend. When he finally got it, he refused to get off. He didn't want to leave his compatriot. Luckily, two gendarmes who were on duty there succeeded in getting him out of the compartment. The train left ten minutes late.

At 3 p.m. the train entered the station at Châlons. It gave me goose bumps to see what condition the station was in, since from the start of the German offensive the Gothas came almost every night and dropped a few bombs right on it.

I had to present myself at the first-aid station. It took a while to find it because it had helpfully moved its location. During the half-hour it took me to ferret it out, in a *guitoune* [hide-away] dug into the railway embankment, some *pandores* [military policemen], intrigued by the distracted air of my Moroccan companion, hauled him off to the police station, despite his vain and unintelligible protests.

I freed him from the clutches of the gendarmes who had taken him for a deserter. A minute later we made our entrance to the Février hospital.

A paper scratcher put me through an interrogation worthy of a prosecutor. He even asked me what religion I professed, in case I left the hospital in a pine box, so they'd know who to send along with me—a priest, a pastor, a rabbi, or maybe I wanted to take the journey all by myself. They planned ahead at this hospital!

I was then led to a building called "Pavilion B" and pushed into a room where I barely had time to read on the door the not-very-reassuring label saying "Bronchitis Patients." All those with tuberculosis went by this name of bronchitis patients—less frightening, they supposed.

Next morning, 9 a.m., we had a visit from a vulgar-looking medical officer with a scowling face, stingy with his words (which were often harsh and hurtful), also stingy with medication.

"He's a scab!" my bunk mates often said. "He hates poilus, and thinks we're all liars. If he alone were in charge, nobody would spend any time here at all."

He hardly deigned to look at me and hear my story. He moved on to the next one.

"What shall I put down for him?" asked the head nurse who followed him, notebook in her hand.

"Why, nothing at all," said this poor excuse for a medical officer, optimistically. "He isn't sick."

"Since he doesn't seem to be digesting well, we could give him a little *Eau de Vals* [brand of mineral water]," the nurse insisted.

"Not at all. I've told you, he isn't sick. Just put him on a light diet."

Now there was a good prescription for fattening me up. I guess he didn't think I was skinny enough.

Nevertheless, the nurse whispered to me, "I'll get you something."

In this hospital we were taken care of by nurses most of whom were young and pretty. There was also a swarm of housekeepers, cooks, laundresses, etc. The menial jobs were done by Annamites. I guess the bosses thought they were doing them a favor and an honor, and giving them a sense of doing something worthwhile, by making them empty the spittoons and clean the latrines.

Our ward nurse looked to be about 25. I don't know whether she was reserving all her warmth and kindness for the love of her life, but she was somewhat cold and distant to the patients. She showed up in the ward only to make her rounds, and then she disappeared right away.

One day the doctor, making his rounds, roughly yanked the bedding off a patient and yanked his nightshirt up. The nurse had been looking elsewhere but when her eyes suddenly fell upon this specimen of a man in the state of Adam she turned bright red with embarrassment and did a quick pirouette, just as if a snake had bitten her on the heel.

This didn't go down well with the patients, who criticized her when she left the ward. They said that a nurse doing her duty with true heart and devotion shouldn't show any repugnance.

One morning we had a visit to the ward from the hospital's chief doctor, Dr. Dejonc, who before the war had run a clinic in Paris, a venerable figure radiating intelligence, with sparkling, gimlet-sharp eyes. He gave everyone a good, hard look, stopping here and there to find out what was up.

"And this one, what's wrong with him?" he said, pointing to a new arrival proposed for noncombat service.

"*Basta!* [Enough!]" replied our ward's *major*. "Nothing at all, I don't see anything wrong with him."

But the doctor was already bending over, tapping the patient on the chest.

"What?" he said, standing up straight. "You don't find anything? Give him a tap, here and here."

But the other one persisted in hearing nothing, understanding nothing. With a dry tone, the doctor said to his colleague, who was turning from red to deep crimson: "I don't want to make this one out to be sicker than he really is, but there is something wrong with him. As for you, I think you're going deaf."

If we had dared, we would have applauded these words with all our hearts, but the mocking looks we exchanged with each other were full of significance.

Every Saturday the *médecin-chef* himself examined in his office the sick men who had arrived during the week and passed judgment on their fates.

That's how I got my turn to appear before this eminent person, at whose side stood our ward's *major*, who declared, as soon as he saw me, that I had nothing wrong with me, that I was "complaining about vague aches and pains," he didn't know precisely where, nor apparently did I know . . .

I protested, thin as I was, that I was on my last ounce of strength, worn out by uninterrupted duty in the trenches since 1914.

"Come on," the médecin-chef said to me soothingly, "you haven't saved France all by yourself, you haven't spent three and a half years at the *petit-poste*."

"No, Monsieur le *Major*, but three-and-a-half years in a regiment holding the front lines, where I spent four long winters."

He got me to undress, to lie down on a table, then he listened to my chest.

"Yes," he said, "this man is worn out. We're going to send him to the rear."

Then I just had to wait my turn to depart, the *trains sanitaires* [hospital trains] being infrequent. I wouldn't have been in a particular hurry to leave Châlons except for the nocturnal visits by the sinister Gothas, which were destroying the city bit by bit. The tenacious inhabitants who nevertheless remained were obliged to seek shelter, every evening, in underground cellars two kilometers from the city.

This daily exodus of people, of women, old men, children, carrying their blankets, their mattresses, their pillows, their cradles, was truly lamentable.

With the arrival of night, a gloomy solitude, a deathly silence, weighed down upon the city, which seemed altogether dead.

But the hospitals couldn't be evacuated and nothing could protect us. We were at the mercy of the Gothas. Doors and windows were locked to keep us from fleeing. You can imagine our fright, our anguish when we heard the sinister birds of death droning over our heads. But during my stay there no bomb fell on the hospital or the immediate neighborhood.

One night I felt my blanket being pulled off me. I lit a match and shuddered with horror: my neighbor was vomiting gobs of blood from his mouth and his nose which gushed out onto my bunk. It was a young Parisian with lungs burned by poison gas. He couldn't speak, and pulled my blanket off to wake me up.

I quickly ran to the ward's office where an Annamite guard was on duty—or rather was dozing—and after five minutes of wild gestures to get him to understand, sent him to find the night duty nurse.

Very soon a nurse and a *major* were at the sick man's bedside. A few injections, a few compresses stopped the hemorrhaging for now. But every day thereafter he spat up blood, and when I left Châlons he was dying.

Finally, April 21, it was my turn to leave Châlons, destination unknown. The next day the train was in the Brotteaux station [in Lyon], where we were served a meal. We were very happy to be hospitalized in this big city where we thought a bevy of beautiful ladies and ravishing young girls would be clamoring to take care of us. But we had to be disabused of these notions. Our meals digested, we got back on the train, which headed for Grenoble.

Before we left Châlons they gave each of us an envelope to be handed over when we got to our destination, containing our diagnosis. This envelope was sealed, but naturally every one of us broke his open without the slightest scruple. I read on my card: "General fatigue. Suspicious rattles in the upper right lung." Well! This diagnosis wasn't very reassuring. Neither was that of most of my comrades. But it didn't seem possible to us that, after all the bursting shells, machine guns, poison gas, exploding mines, etc., one could die just from getting sick. That was just too silly. Joy was on all our faces. You'd have thought we were just ordinary folks leaving on a holiday train trip and not a train of tubercular, hernia, or cardiac patients.

In the afternoon our train dropped us off in the little town of Bourgoin, in the Isère [département]. We were driven to a convalescent hospital installed within the buildings of a mill and foundry where several hundred men and women were employed, right beside the vast park and château of the proprietor, M. Diederichs.[3]

We were the guests of one of the biggest war profiteers. At his own expense, he funded this hospital as a deduction from his profits.

At Châlons we'd been shut up like prisoners. Here, in contrast, complete freedom to wander around town or the countryside, any time between the morning rounds and the evening roll call at 9 p.m.

Like at Auve, like at Châlons, and doubtless like everywhere else, I observed that out of a hundred patients, at least fifty had nothing wrong with them, or hardly anything. They exploited or exaggerated some little fault in their wellbeing, or faked or pretended some small illness, using techniques which were whispered along by word of mouth, from "coming down with a fever" and "rattling the bronchial tubes" to making your eyes red or making pus come out of your ears—at the risk of going deaf or blind.

I'd have been curious to know how many dressing stations, field hospitals, and clinics functioned during the war, and how many patients—or pseudopatients—they sheltered, along with legions of nurses, orderlies, stretcher-bearers, medical officers, pencil pushers.

And out there, in the forward observation posts, there often weren't enough men to relieve the sentries who had to do double shifts, watching from their firing steps.

But you'd have to admit that there were plenty who really were sick: the gassed, the tubercular, the weak-hearted—they formed the majority.

I had as my bunk mate a fellow who had epileptic seizures resulting from shellfire. These attacks would seize him suddenly, when he least expected them, while playing cards, or in bed, or in the middle of a quiet conversation. He rolled on the floor like a madman, eyes bulging out of their sockets, teeth clattering, foaming at the mouth. Once back to his senses, he didn't remember what had happened. He didn't once dare to venture into town. He would walk only in the park of the château, where I would accompany him.

In my ward there was also a young man named Joseph whom you could have called Joséphine because practically everything about him was ladylike: high voice, round breasts, beardless face, curvy hips. Only about a tenth of him was male—the part that would permit him to exercise his masculine duties.

The *major* had said to him, "I don't know why they called you up. I can't tell if you're a man or a woman!"

This poor Joseph (we called him Jojo) told me that he was worried about being sent home on convalescent leave. His parents were dead, and his two sisters made clear that it would be a big bother for them to take him in.

He also had a brother who was a priest, but who didn't want him around because he had a young niece at home. "As if I'd be any danger," he said with tears in his eyes, "me—almost a woman myself!" The truth was that in their household, growing up, Jojo was mama's and papa's favorite, and the others were jealous and had no love for him.

I told him about the work of the *parrains* [godfathers] of Neuilly.[4] I wrote up a request for him, which was accepted, and he was able to have his convalescence in a place like that.

In any hospital, those who were merely sick, whether cured or not, soon had to make room for new arrivals, more and more numerous in these months of steadily worse and worse combat, before the war's end. But anyone who could make himself useful doing any kind of chores could stay the maximum length of time, that's to say two months, followed by a long convalescent leave. As for myself, I made myself useful in the hospital office. That's how I was able to meet the section's chief medical officer, a redoubtable person who could determine your fate with the stroke of his pen.

"What?" he said to me. "You haven't had a day of sick leave since 1914? That's not possible."

"Monsieur le *Major,* I've had a couple of little discomforts. But I was determined not to be evacuated."

This bombastic statement pleased him no end, and he told me, "Well, we're going to give you the nice long rest you deserve."

He first wanted to send me to a sanatorium. I made a face. Sure, it would be better to live with unfortunate people coughing out their lungs, than to die alongside the able-bodied in the trenches. Nevertheless, what I really wanted, not having seen my loved ones in six months, was to leave right away for home.

I explained to the *major* that I lived in the country, and the fresh air and the care of my family would restore me completely in no time. This considerate *major* recommended two months of convalescence which the medical board approved two days later.

With a heart full of joy, I left Bourgoin on June 8, having spent a month and a half of quiet rest, away from the horrors of the front.

1918. Convalescence. Paris. Guingamp. Garrison life.

I left Bourgoin at 8 in the evening. At 10 I was in Lyon, at the Gare Perrache, where there was a huge crowd of military men of all branches and all colors, despite home leaves having been suspended. It was hard to find a place in the huge dining hall where, for modest prices, you could get food, fruit, and drink at the *guichets* [shop windows].

No train for poilus until 7 in the morning. But at 1 a.m. a first-class train was due to pass through, bound for the Côte d'Azur, which wouldn't even pick up civilian passengers at the Lyon station.

I overheard some Marseillais plotting to work their way onto this train of privileged types. I joined in with them. As soon as the train started to pull out we threw ourselves against the platform gates just as if we were storming an enemy position. And there we were, on the train, before the station employees could stop us.

The strict conductors took down our names and numbers, and vowed we'd be put off at the next stop, Valence, and be handed over to the military authorities.

At Valence we disembarked quietly. But just like at Lyon, as soon as the train started up again we made a dash for the gates. This time most of us were held back by the station crews repulsing the assailants.

I managed to fly through a gate which wasn't guarded and plunked myself down quietly at the end of a railway-car corridor.

I was duly warned that I would be put off at Avignon and handed over to the station police there, which left me utterly cold. I offered to pay my way; they refused. Even paying poilus weren't welcome on this train. It just would not do to have crude, dusty, muddy creatures like us offending the fine messieurs and their *belles dames* lounging on the soft banquette cushions.

You should have seen the disdain with which they looked at me, crouched in my corner. Several times the conductors swore at me, threatened me. They were sturdy, healthy lads, and you'd be amazed to see such slackers. I wasn't shy about telling one of them so.

Then came time for the *déjeuner*. From the *wagon-restaurant* the obsequious waiters brought trays of plates to the pampered passengers.

What a contrast between the luxury, the well-being of the insolent rich pursuing their pleasures, having a whole train to themselves, a few dozen parasites, and this soldier chewing on a crust of brown bread, viewed as an intruder, a mangy dog, a beggar.

I could see for sure that my presence bothered them, spoiled their appetite, troubled their digestion. That's understood. For them I was a living reproach, though mute. I represented those who suffered, who were being tortured, who were dying in a hellish place, to protect their property, their fortunes, their privileges . . .

Here we are at Avignon. As soon as the train stopped a conductor marches me toward the police station. But here's a long freight train stopped in our path. While he's asking a yard worker if there's an underground passage, I sneak between two freight cars and hightail it away at full speed.

I never saw that conductor again. An hour later I left Avignon on an express train and was home that very evening.

I'll skip over the two months I spent with my loved ones. Sometimes I went so far as to believe it was all over, that I had taken up my former life again, forever.

But alas—August 10—I had to put on my uniform once again—I'd thrown it in a corner—and tear myself away from the affection of my family. But this time the separation wasn't as cruel as before, because I wasn't going straight back to the front.

I was taking the garrison route. This mysterious garrison duty—full of unknowns, object of the dreams of every poilu on the front lines. But often it was only a short step to the training companies where there was no rest. Three weeks later, you're on your way back to the trenches.

The next day, at 10 a.m., I left for Paris, or "Paname" as it was called by the Parisian poilus who never called anything by its real name.

At the station which bears the name of the massacre of Austerlitz, I wanted to take the *métro* which would get me to the Gare Montparnasse. I was amazed to be climbing a staircase. The métro ran right on top of the roof of the station. Funny!

There I was, en route—or rather, en métro. We went along a viaduct overlooking a boulevard, then we barreled underground. I discovered that this train didn't go to the Gare Montparnasse. They advised me to get off at a stop which brought me to an almost deserted boulevard. I had to ask ten times for directions to the Gare Montparnasse.

Once I got there I had to climb a big staircase to reach the waiting room on the first floor, at the same level as the tracks.

I saw written on a big board that the first train for Brest wouldn't be leaving until 8 p.m. I decided to explore the capital. After stowing my gear I hopped on the first tram I saw leaving, which took me first to the Place de la Bastille—noteworthy only for the gloomy, bloody—or, if you like, glorious—memories it evokes. There I jumped on another tram, and then another one.

By chance in my wanderings, I saw the law-making factory—the Chambre des Députés, which didn't seem to deserve the pompous title of "palace."⁵ You'd think you were looking at a district court or a modest subprefecture, with its pillars. I passed near the Eiffel Tower with its admiring crowds of American soldiers, and the Big [Ferris] Wheel which seemed like an enormous toy.

I saw the towers of Notre Dame in profile, and the front of the aristocratic Madeleine church.

I paraded indifferently through the Arc de Triomphe, walked down the Champs-Elysées and crossed the Place de la Concorde. I passed in front of the *cagna* [hangout] of patriotic President Poincaré, the Elysée palace. Its exterior appearance disappointed me. It reminded me of a convent, a barracks, a prison surrounded by walls and low buildings.

I'm sure I passed by many places worthy of being admired, but alone, without a guide, I had to be happy with seeing whatever fate had me come upon.

Finally I got lost, and I was going to miss my train. In fact it left without me. Luckily there was a "half-train" leaving twenty minutes after.

These few hours of sightseeing in Paris allowed me to see the friendliness of Parisians, all very eager to offer directions. At the doors of shops where people were waiting in line, the poilu went right to the front and was helped right away. Two or three times, the lady tram conductors pretended not to see me. One of them said to me, "Keep your three sous. My brother's a soldier, too."

I was shocked by what some Parisian women wore. Were they part of high society, or respectable folk, or the demimonde [courtesans]? I couldn't tell. Unbuttoned, hardly covered at all, bare arms and shoulders, their sole purpose seemed to be to please, to be noticed, to attract attention, to spark the desire of passersby. And this at the time when anguish that was afflicting so many hearts, when so many eyes that were weeping, hung in the balance!

This left me scandalized, but nobody around me seemed to be bothered by it. Everyone seemed to find this perfectly natural.

This was when the "Big Bertha"[6] shells were falling on Paris, but I don't think any struck during the day I was there. Here and there I saw a few damaged buildings.

They lasted for a few days and ended long before Paris was turned into a pile of ruins. Besides, a falling shell didn't make a very big impression, due to the incessant street noise in that huge city.

The next day, at dawn, I was in Brittany. My eyes saw a rather monotonous landscape: woods, pastures, fields, succeeding each other, in the middle of which popped up, here and there, some farms with gray walls and thatched roofs. An indefinable melancholy pervaded this ancient terrain.

At six in the morning I was at Guingamp, a city of twelve thousand inhabitants. It stretched out in a long line, the train station at one end and the barracks, where I was headed, at the other. The walk was about two kilometers.

The barracks looked just like any other. That's not where you find any marvels of architecture.

Above the main entrance was inscribed, "Caserne (de) la Tour d'Auvergne." I wasn't particularly flattered to enter this place where such a great hero was honored.[7] I look on heroes with horror. Their hands are stained with blood.

The End of the Nightmare:
August 11, 1918–February 14, 1919

After signing in on the official register—the true cogwheel of militarism—I went to the garrison, which was the headquarters of the three regiments of infantrymen of which the city of Guingamp was so proud.

The barracks was reserved for the future heroes of the conscript class of 1920, which was finishing up its apprenticeship in the noble profession of arms. As for us, the graybeards, the leather-skins, the tough old guys of every shade and hue, we had to be content being housed in what had been the stables for remounts. There were no more than a half-dozen stallions still there—the care of which required the presence of three or four dozen embusqués.

I didn't receive a very warm welcome at the office. It seemed that I was arriving three days late. I had left home the day after my convalescence leave had expired. But there were several days which the dictator Clemenceau, to get the sick and the wounded back to the front lines more quickly, had decreed that any delays in travel would henceforth be included in the home leave or convalescence.

I didn't know that. But no one is allowed to be ignorant of the law, even a decree. So they told me that I would be called before the generalissimo of all the troops in Guingamp, who would decide whether or not I'd be considered a deserter!

Next day I was sent to the barracks for the obligatory medical exam. Despite a gruff exterior and sour manner, the *major* [medical officer] harbored a kind heart and did everything in his power to help the poilus. Observing my skinny body, my haggard features, the bags under my eyes, and learning that I'd been evacuated for the first time in four years, he said to me, "Good man! Go get your gear, you're coming to the infirmary, you'll help work in the garden."

The next day I began my peaceful duties as assistant gardener, watering the cabbages and lettuce, pulling up potatoes, all kinds of things which appealed much more to my pacifist temperament than handling a rifle, grenades, and other homicidal devices.

But, back at the barracks, where my transfer to the infirmary had at first gone unnoticed, they looked for me everywhere, calling Barthas to appear before the commandant.

They ended up deciding that I had indeed deserted for good, and they were about to alert all the police stations in the vicinity when finally some clerk discovered on the sick roster that I'd gone back to the infirmary.

The hospital or infirmary is a sacred temple, at the threshold of which the external power and discipline cease. I was saved. They didn't bother me anymore about this.

At the infirmary there reigned as absolute authority a young and pretty nurse called *La Blanchette* because she was dressed in white from head to toe.

Every morning she would get all the patients to work, washing, scraping, sweeping the staircases, corridors, lavatories, etc. Nobody even thought of sleeping in. Anyone who tried to sneak out of these chores or question her authority didn't last long at the infirmary. But if you knew how to get into her good graces you could spend two quiet months there. That's all the rules allowed.

We were prisoners, in a way. Only on Sunday, from noon to 4 p.m., we were driven to the edge of Guingamp by a non-com and allowed to wander around the countryside.

But this had less appeal than a nice afternoon spent at a bistro. But woe to anyone who had the bad luck of finding La Blanchette in his path. The next day the doors of the infirmary would be wide open for you. You were free to go. But from the infirmary-prison the only place you'd go would be a retraining camp, leading right to the hell of the front lines.

One day an order was posted that all *gradés* [non-coms] in the garrison could, upon request, be assigned to Vitré to train the group of instructors of the conscript class of 1920, just about to be called up. This was like tossing up a lifesaver—three or four months assured, far from the bad stuff.

I declared to the *major* that I was healed and I signed up.

To be sure, I wasn't happy about learning how to teach a profession that I abhorred. But saving my life imposed this sacrifice. And then there was the attraction of a home leave of seven days granted to all those who took up this assignment.

I left that very evening. This time passing through Paris I visited the Palais des Invalides, but I couldn't see the red marble tomb of that great battler Napoleon I because it was covered with sandbags to protect it from enemy bombs.

That would have been quite a paradox, if the murderer who had never suffered a scratch during more than a hundred battles would have been touched by a piece of metal, a century later, in his coffin.

On September 8, in the morning, I was back at Guingamp.

That September 8, the same day I got back from home leave, along with thirty corporals, sergeants, and adjutants, I took the train to Vitré.

At Saint-Brieuc, the station crew told us there was a forty-minute stop. I shared my compartment with two corporals whose names I've forgotten. These two decided to take a little tour of the town. Tired out, I decided not to join them. It's a good thing I didn't, because the train left sooner than we'd been told—before the return of my two companions.

Arriving at Vitré, I reported this to the section chief, who gathered up all the gear of the two missing persons, who were coming along on the next train, and took it off the train.

Nothing happened as a result. But what if I had followed my two comrades in Saint-Brieuc, and all three of us had missed the train?

No one would have missed us at Vitré, in the middle of the night, in a pouring rain, under nobody's authority, since *Messieurs les officiers* had granted themselves the right to get off at Rennes. Where would our knapsacks, canteens, and weapons have gotten to?

We would have been in a fine mess.

At nine in the evening we showed up at La Trémoille barracks, where our arrival took the guard detail completely by surprise and disturbed their sleep.

The teams of instructors weren't supposed to arrive until the next day. As a result, we didn't get a very warm welcome. We had to skip supper, and slept on beds without mattresses. We consoled ourselves with the thought that we'd seen plenty of those.

The day after, our apprenticeship in the noble profession of soldiering began. From dawn to twilight, we were either in the barracks courtyard or snaking our way across the training field, with barely an hour of rest, hardly enough time to wolf down something to eat, write a letter, look at a newspaper—all at full gallop.

We spent hours doing to-the-left-march, right-face, showing off for a boss who was never satisfied with how smartly we clicked our heels, marching past him in full salute twenty times in a row, while he shouted commands to us so loudly as to burst a vein in his neck. It's tough enough to take these monkey-shines when you're twenty. What about at forty—after already doing your three years of military service, and then three years on the front lines.

I'd get red in the face with shame, but I did the best I could, so as not to be sent back for being an inept instructor. But from my very first days there it was clear that I didn't have the proper military attitude. The officers reproached me for the lack of energy in my gestures, suppleness in my movements. But to fix those I'd need to change my wobbly legs and my aching back.

Nevertheless, I got my revenge. Nature, in one of her rare gifts to me, had blessed me with a good memory. As daunting as I found the study of these stupidities and ineptitudes of military theory, I could spew out all the nonsense to the astonishment of the officers who couldn't have recited them to save their lives, and to that of my comrades, most of whom couldn't put three words together without looking like idiots.

Every day there were choral sessions, and we sang going to and from the training field. It was forced cheerfulness. We had two priests with us who sang "La Madelon," "Margoton," "La Boulangère" so often as to give you a headache. That didn't keep them from singing Mass every morning at a church in Vitré—and getting paid for it.

Vitré is a city of about ten thousand inhabitants. The people are Bretons because they're part of Brittany. But they aren't Breton in their customs or their language.

They speak only French. And it would be a pretty good French if they didn't say, for example, "Vitren" for "Vitré," "marchen" for "marché," "Sévignen" for "Sévigné," etc., for every word ending in "é." Right in the city is the ancient, admirably conserved castle of the Seigneur de la Trémoille, the big brawler whom Vitré holds dear to its heart.[1] At the base of this castle flows the Vilaine river, which deserves its name [*vilain:* ugly, nasty]. It's not pretty to look at, with its muddy water, dirtied, they say, by factories located upstream.

Vitré's local celebrity is Madame de Sévigné,[2] who lived in the Château des Roches-Noires [Black-Rock Castle], a few kilometers outside town, a place of excursion and even pilgrimage for any traveler passing by.

In the public garden at Vitré they've raised a statue of Madame de Sévigné. She's shown with an inoffensive pen in her hand. I much prefer that to a brandished sword, battle-ax, or rifle.

One day our officers were nice enough to drive us to the former Château des Roches-Noires. We could see the writing room of the person who made this place famous. Everything was exactly the same as she left it. In one corner, her tiny wooden shoes were there to show how small her feet were. In the park there was a sort of grotto which produced unexpected echoes. I shouted *Vive la paix!* [Long live peace!] May this cry echo around the world and reach the ears of the people's false shepherds.

One afternoon we were driven to the theater of Vitré, not to see a performance but to hear a speech about American war aid, so as to boost our morale which risked being sapped by the pacifist or, as they called it, defeatist, campaign which was rife at this time.

So here was this young officer, embusqué, this charlatan of morale, pouring into our ears fantastic numbers of cannon, airplanes, tanks, Yankees armed to the teeth flooding in. At the end of each tirade, to conclude it, he cried out two or three times, *C'est formidable! C'est formidable!* [It's terrific!]

First came the smiles, then the muffled laughter, then the guffaws bursting forth irreverently. The officers had a hard time keeping a straight face, and the successor to de la Trémoille himself, the military governor of Vitré, chewed on his big gray mustaches. At the end, the speaker himself was caught up in the laughter which rocked the hall, and the conference ended in the midst of general hilarity. The funniest thing was that this emissary of Clemenceau had no idea about the reason for this hilarity and continued to punctuate each of his sentences, full of conviction, with "C'est formidable! C'est formidable!"

1918. Armistice! Liberation!

Meanwhile the great drama was reaching its conclusion. Alone against twenty nations baying after her in a fantastic clamor, Germany, so proud in 1914, now on its knees, asked for mercy, asked for armistice.

But this way of fleeing the war didn't appeal to the striped sleeves, who didn't have their fill of crosses, medals, stars, stripes, ribbons, honors and glories.

For these folks, war had to end with total disaster for the German army, against which Jena, Waterloo, and Sedan[3] would be mere skirmishes. Thousands of captured cannon, hundreds of thousands of captured Boches, shattered enemy forces streaming back across the Rhine bridges, pursued with bayonets at their backs by our soldiers, our regiments entering the great cities beyond the Rhine, flags fluttering, bands playing—here was the apotheosis dreamed of not only by our great warriors but also by the government, almost all the press, all the embusqués, and, back in the rear, all those who had nothing more to lose, or who had more to gain by continuing the war.

What did a hundred thousand, two hundred thousand more cadavers matter, a few more months of unimaginable suffering to bear?

Did that matter for those who were far from the slugfest?

And to accomplish this monstrous dream, the so-called Allied governments sought to delay for as long as possible the hour of the last cannon shot, by requiring Germany to repeat its demand for armistice several times, for simple questions of form and formulas.

During this time, in an orgy of murder, bloodletting, and burning, the whole front was in flames, from Ypres to Belfort. Without exception, all the regiments were thrown into the assault on German machine guns.

The German armies bent back on all the points of contact, without letting their line be broken, and their retreat didn't turn into a rout.

They had to cede the floor to the diplomats. But I'm not going to pretend to write history here, by recounting the dramatic, agonizing twists and turns which led to the signing of the Armistice, November 11, 1918, at five in the morning.

The big bosses themselves didn't believe that things would end so soon. Evidence: two days before the Armistice, we arrived at the barracks at 11 a.m., our appetites sharpened by three or four hours of exercise. We believed we were going to eat our meager meal, when we had the disagreeable surprise of discovering in our courtyard the commander of the military district, the famous General d'Amade, renowned for his exploits in the colonies.[4]

The general had no doubt dined well. He was in no hurry. He had us assemble, he congratulated the officers, stopped here and there before some poilus, asked various questions, then finally gave us the patriotic sales pitch. Finishing up, no doubt believing this would please us, he assured us that "victory is certain, but the war isn't over, and we still have laurels to gather up!" Thanks to these laurels, this end of the speech spoiled our appetites, and we went back to our rooms pensive and care-worn.

It was noon when the news reached us in the Vitré barracks. There wasn't a single soldier left in the rooms. It was a devilish stampede down the corridors and down to the police station, where they had just posted a telegram announcing, in two laconic lines, the deliverance of millions of men, the end of their tortures, the imminent return to civilized life.

How many times had we thought about this blessed day, which so many did not live to see. How many times had we peered into the mysterious future, looking for this star of salvation, this invisible lighthouse in the dark night.

And now this forever immortal day had arrived!

This happiness, this joy, overwhelmed us. We couldn't keep it in our hearts. We stood there looking at each other, mute and stupid.

But we were called back to reality by the cries of *Rassemblement* [Assembly]! and the whistle blasts of the adjutants on duty, to head out for exercises as usual.

What, to exercises? On such a solemn day, which will be unforgettable in future centuries—that was a joke. Grumbling, we set out for the training field, and the next day, too. Finally some striped-sleeve type, less stupid than the others, put an end to these exercises which had lost their purpose. Three days later we were in Guingamp. But for our trip there someone had the intelligence to put us on a train which wasn't direct, and we had to spend the night on the benches of the waiting room at Rennes.

I soon obtained a leave of fifty days—as a barrelmaker—and returned to duty at the garrison on 10 January 1919.

Passing through Paris, I visited the Jardin des Plantes and walked past the Opéra and the Louvre.

One more month separated me from my liberation. I spent it standing guard at the 48th Regiment's barracks [at Guingamp] and at a hospital where German prisoners from all over the region were being cared for.

They were installed by themselves in two big tents at the end of the hospital's garden. If you were too sick, you died, and there's one less Boche.

No daily examination rounds for them. Just once a week, a *major* would pass by and decide, based on appearance, those who were ready or who looked to be ready to rejoin the prison camp they'd come from.

One day I was assigned to go with four soldiers to take a dozen of these "cured" prisoners to their cantonment in Saint-Brieuc.

Their prison was a school in town. We arrived there at the moment they were serving a meal, made up only of rice cooked in water with a few pieces of low-grade meat floating in it—bits of skin, tendon, fat, etc. You could have as much rice as you wanted. Those who liked this *plat du jour* could have as much as they wanted.

Others who had some money could buy some delicacies. In one corner of the courtyard a profiteer had set up a table loaded with cans of preserves, chocolate, etc. All the sous from the meager purses of the prisoners went right to the pockets of this profiteer.

We spent the rest of the day visiting Saint-Brieuc, which was separated from the sea by steeply embanked ravines.

On one square stands the statue of a former town mayor killed by the Chouans[5] who, one night, took over Saint-Brieuc and opened the gates of prisons, releasing men who were condemned to die the very next day.

Finally my long-awaited day arrived: February 14, 1919.

That day, at Narbonne, after multiple formalities imposed upon the demobilized and visits from one office to another, a desk-bound adjutant handed me my discharge papers with the words, as long awaited as the Messiah, "Go, you're free."

I was free, after fifty-four months of slavery! I was finally escaping from the claws of militarism, to which I swore such a ferocious hatred.

I have sought to inculcate this hatred in my children, my friends, my neighbors. I will tell them that the fatherland, glory, military honor, laurels—all are only vain words, destined to mask what is frighteningly horrible, ugly, and cruel about war.

To keep up morale during this war, to justify it, they lied cynically, saying that we were fighting just for the triumph of Right and Justice, that they were not guided by ambition, no colonial covetousness or financial or commercial interests.

They lied when they said that we had to push right to the end, so that this would be the last of all wars.

They lied when they said that we, the poilus, wanted to continue the war in order to avenge the dead, so that our sacrifices would not be useless.

They lied . . . but I'm not going to write anymore about the lies which came out of the mouths or the pens of our governors or journalists.

Victory has made us forget everything, absolve everything. Our leaders needed it, at all cost, to save themselves. And to get it, they would have sacrificed the whole human race, as General Castelnau said.[6]

In the villages they're already talking about raising monuments of glory, of apotheosis, to the victims of the big butchery, to those, as the phony patriots say, who "have voluntarily made the sacrifice of their lives," as if those unfortunate ones could have chosen to do otherwise.

I'll contribute my penny only if the monuments symbolize a vehement protest against war and the warrior spirit, and do not exalt or glorify such a death so as to incite future generations to follow the example of these reluctant martyrs.

Ah, if the dead of this war could come out of their tombs, how they would shatter these monuments of hypocritical pity, because those who are erecting have sacrificed these dead without pity. Who has dared to cry out: "Enough blood spilled! Enough dead! Enough suffering!"

Who has refused to turn in his gold, his silver, his paper money, publicly, in the war-bond drives, to keep the war going?

Returned to the bosom of my family after the nightmare years, I taste the joy of life, or rather of new life. I feel tender happiness about things which, before, I didn't pay attention to: sitting at home, at my table, lying in my bed, putting off sleep so I can hear the wind hitting the shutters, rustling the nearby plane trees, hearing the rain strike the windows, looking at a starry, serene, silent night or, on a dark, moonless night, thinking about similar nights spent up there . . .

Often I think about my many comrades fallen by my side. I heard their curses against the war and its authors, the revolt of their whole beings against their tragic fate, against their murder. And I, as a survivor, believe that I am inspired by their will to struggle without cease-fire nor mercy, to my last breath, for the idea of peace and human fraternity.

February 1919

Rémy Cazals

"Do you know a work on the life of Louis Barthas?"

When a work speaks for itself, you should let it speak. [In the present edition] I have not touched my very brief introduction to the 1978 edition. It was sufficient to situate the author and to describe the conditions in which the work was written. But a reader wrote to the publisher: "Do you know a work on the life of Louis Barthas? The preface written by Rémy Cazals seems to me— no offense to Rémy Cazals—insufficient. If, in my first letter, I called the *Carnets de guerre* [War Notebooks] of Louis Barthas 'moving,' now I have to say something more—it grabs you right in the guts! That's why I'd like to know more about the life of Louis Barthas, whose *Carnets de guerre* occupy the highest place of honor in my library."

Needless to say, this comment delighted me. I love producing books which occupy the highest place of honor in libraries!

Louis Barthas wrote only about the war of 1914–18. Barrelmaker (*tonnelier*) by trade both before and after the First World War, he died in his village of Peyriac-Minervois on May 4, 1952. No written work has ever been devoted to this "ordinary man." And here I can only offer, as new information, one anecdote and the contents of two letters. On August 10, 1915, from "the front-line trenches near X . . . ," Barthas wrote to Marcel Sembat, at the request of his comrades, to draw the Socialist minister's attention to the faulty organization of the distribution of bread to the soldiers. In 1920, he wrote to the [National Assembly] deputy from the Aude [Barthas' home *département*], Milhet, and we have the latter's reply, dated May 15: He would employ Barthas' arguments to obtain suspension of a penalty imposed on the deserter Gontran (see 8th Notebook, pp. 144–45). Then the anecdote, told me by Abel Barthas, elder son of Louis: "One evening, after school, I had to write a history lesson, a description in a few lines of the work of [historian and politician Adolphe] Thiers, under the heading 'Thiers, liberator of our territory.' My father told me, 'Wait, I'll give you the description myself.' And he wrote: 'Thiers, hangman of the Commune, assassin of the working class.' I was shaking on my way to school, the next day. The teacher took my notebook, turned red, then pale; he closed it, and didn't mention it again." Abel was eight years old in 1914. This anecdote would therefore have taken place a little before the First World War.

I can't offer anything else. It's not for me to tell the reader what he has already discovered in the *Carnets*. This afterword will just be an echo of the welcome received by the book in its first twenty years of publication.[1]

"A veritable gold mine"

Let's first take a look at some of the comments in the press: "A veritable gold mine" (*Les Nouvelles Littéraires*). "An exceptional document" (*Le Matin de Paris*). "Here is a great book" (*L'Humanité*). "Authentic and irreplaceable" (*Témoinage Chrétien*). "An eyewitness account of the first order" (*L'Histoire*). "Precious" (*Le Canard Enchaîné*). In *La Liberté-Dimanche* (Fribourg, Switzerland), Alain Favarger wrote: "The verve and the simplicity which run throughout this book put it in the first rank of great testimonies of humanity against stupidity and barbarity." And Bruno Villien, in *Le Nouvel Observateur:* "Louis Barthas is an especially qualified witness: a pitiless eye, a sharp ear, a sense of humor full of irony, searing, bracing." In *Le Monde,* Gilbert Comte makes a comparison: "The barrelmaker [Barthas] and the bourgeois [French Holocaust survivor André Kahn] in the same fierce storm." *Lire* gave twelve pages to Barthas in March 1979, and *Télérama* two more in March 1982 in advance of a telecast of [Stanley Kubrick's] *Paths of Glory.* I could add favorable reviews in numerous other periodicals, numbers of letters from readers, and the statement of President François Mitterand during a visit to Carcassonne: "Ah, the *Carnets* of Louis Barthas! This book has great historical value, and it's also a true work of literature."

Some rank Barthas with [Henri] Barbusse [author of *Le feu*, "Under Fire," considered the greatest French novel of the First World War]. Some put him above. I'm frankly of the latter opinion, without claiming any objectivity and without forgetting the impact of *Le feu* when it was published in 1916 and its thunderous success. It seems to me that Barthas' talent is characterized by the absence of literary effects and artifices. And also by a great authenticity, but here we're touching on the value of eyewitness testimony, and we need to factor in the opinion of veterans and that of historians.

"I wept several times while reading it"

The reactions of veterans of the war of 1914–1918 to Barthas' book have not been systematically solicited. But I can report several letters of support, among them one from Jacques Meyer, himself the author of a number of books of quality.[2] Auguste Bastide, with political ideas the opposite of those of Barthas, wrote to me: "[The story of] the trenches, and in fact that of the whole war, is written in a simple and totally authentic way by Louis Barthas, barrelmaker. This book is a marvel, a veritable fresco of '14–'18 by a *poilu* who lived through it. This book is so beautiful and so true that I wept several times while reading it." Adrien Benizat: "I read the whole work from start to end in one day. I will read it again, often, because it represents a whole period of my life. . . . I find myself in the same situations, because I (like Barthas) was a foot soldier and I've drunk from the same cup, as they say." And the widow of Fernand Tailhades: "See what Barthas writes. They were all the same. All said the same thing."

Likewise for many notebooks, diaries, or letters from working-class veterans, which have been either not published or published only recently.[3] The account of Léopold Noé (*Nous étions ennemis sans savoir pourquoi ni comment,* Carcassonne, n.d.) is particularly interesting because at the start of the war this electrician from Corbières [Aude] was in the same regiment as Barthas (but not in the same battalion, and they didn't know each other). Without exchanging words, the two *Audois* wrote practically the same things about the behavior of certain officers, "stupid in their men's eyes," and on the rank and file's rejection of the war. "The war we fought can't be described as a series of painful episodes. I have a son. I tell him right now that when he's old and he sees that war is about to break out, he should sell everything and move to a neutral country, to escape such suffering and horrors." Like Barthas, Noé talks about the rain, about fraternization and desertion in December 1915. Before that, on September 23, Barthas and Noé heard the same patriotic speech. "An impressive silence greeted the colonel's final words," wrote Barthas (see 6th Notebook, p. 107). And Noé: "A gloomy silence followed the end of his speech." The sentence "We were enemies without knowing why or how," which was used as the title for Noé's published memoir, appears almost identically in Barthas' *Carnets* (see 16th Notebook, p. 325).

"I have drawn heavily on the diary of Barthas"

Several renowned historians have issued positive judgments on Barthas' book. "One of the best firsthand accounts," said Annette Becker at a recent colloquium in Perpignan (1996). Earlier, Richard Cobb noted that he had drawn heavily from the *Carnets* in writing his book *French and Germans, Germans and French: A Personal Interpretation of France Under Two Occupations, 1914–1918, 1939–1945* (University Press of New England, 1983). Let us also mention Jules Maurin (Montpellier), John Horne (Dublin), Madeleine Rebérioux (Paris), Rémy Pech (Toulouse), Len Smith (Ohio), Marc Ferro, and Pierre Vilar (Paris). Antoine Prost quotes Barthas in her text on Verdun in *Les lieux de mémoire;* Maurice Agulhon in his *La république.*[4] After having quoted it in his paper "Mémoire paysanne de la Grande Guerre" at the Verdun colloquium in 1986, Pierre Barral delivered "Les cahiers de Louis Barthas" at the Carcassonne colloquium in 1992, posing the question: Knowing the rigorous requirements of Jean Norton Cru, what would he have thought of Barthas? His clear answer:

"Its quality and its originality, which have struck all its readers, place it at the level of those accounts recognized as the most accurate, and give it a general value of the first rank. . . . The barrelmaker from Peyriac expresses with accuracy just what his colleagues were feeling viscerally, not knowing how to articulate it."[5]

Numerous school textbooks include excerpts from *Carnets* of Barthas, and in 1981 the national *baccalauréat* [high-school honors] exam, when it still included a section on the First World War, provided a quoted passage for comment.

"The author pushes to paroxysm the deformation of memory"

Is the praise for Barthas' *Carnets* unanimous? No. They bother some adulators of the army and its hierarchy, as well as the historian Stéphane Audoin-Rouzeau. To be sure, Barthas is harsh toward many officers. But he judges them on their acts, not on their standing. Could anyone respect the maniac of the latrines (see 5th Notebook, p. 74), the one obsessed by the tailflaps of coats (see 11th Notebook, pp. 226–27), the cowards of Cote 304 (see 11th Notebook, pp. 217–18)? In contrast, Commandant Garceau, Lieutenants Lorius and Cordier, and others merit a positive appreciation, and Captain Guillot is a model officer, for he was the first out of the trenches when the order was given to attack, and he treated his men as comrades, sparing them "inspections, parades, exercises, chores, all the things the soldier hates" (see 18th Notebook, p. 359). The opinions of the unconditional defenders of the officer corps have little scientific weight; let's not talk about them.

In his book *A travers leurs journaux, 14–18. Les combattants des tranchées,*[6] Audoin-Rouzeau cites Barthas among the "major works" in his bibliography, but only to put forward this peremptory claim: "The author has written his *carnets de guerre* from personal notes taken down during the conflict. By its antimilitarism, the work is revelatory: the author pushes to paroxysm the deformation of memory." I have written to Audoin-Rouzeau to further discuss this summary execution. He has not responded. Without animosity, and because he fired the first shot, I owe it to myself to defend Louis Barthas.

Let me say first that the book of Audoin-Rouzeau on trench newspapers was a youthful work, sometimes naïve. It introduced its subject by affirming that, up until now, the soldiers of the Great War were "unknown to history." He was "introducing them to the present day" by going directly to "the primary sources, eyewitness accounts written on the spot, raw documents," by using the trench newspapers as his sources. To validate his sources and his own premise, the historian clearly would have a vested interest in denigrating any documents which risked undermining his conclusions.[7]

Let's go back and read Barthas again! Does he give us "deformed memories?" Not at all. Veterans and historians have recognized the viability of his eyewitness account. Were his war memories "deformed"—let's not even discuss "paroxysm"—by the antiwar sentiments of the twenties and thirties? If the definitive editing was done, painstakingly in the nineteen notebooks, after the war and the barrelmaker's demobilization, most of the text was already there, entirely written during the war. In fact, on several occasions, the author mentions comrades or officers who know that he has written not brief notes but "the life we're leading" (see 5th Notebook, p. 83), "the true story of our doleful calvary" (see 5th Notebook, p. 114), "the history of our tragic saga" (see 15th Notebook, p. 286). In the summer of 1917, at La Harazée, not far from the house of *académicien* André Theuriet, Barthas tells us (see 16th Notebook, p. 331), "In the shade of a linden tree, I've written these lines while sitting on a stone bench where perhaps the gifted writer himself wrote those books which tell about the surrounding countryside." "I've written these lines"—weren't all these lines written on the spot, all these pages brimming with details, dates, precise locations, portraits, conversations? The few sentences added after the war are immediately evident and don't lead us into error (such as the comrade who died subsequently, the war-memorial project). The last page is a judgment on the totality of the war, delivered in February 1919. There was no need to wait for years to deliver it.

I've noted the weak points in Barthas' text, and I don't think there are many more than these three: The announcement of mobilization is set on August 2, while it really took place on the 1st. Barthas says that it "inspired more enthusiasm than desolation," but we know that he was confined to his sickroom that day. He surely did not witness firsthand the first reaction of the Peyriacois, more likely one of sadness and resignation than of enthusiasm.[8] Second weakness: an anecdote is repeated (see 4th Notebook, pp. 70–71, and 5th Notebook, p. 90). Let's add that evoking the hatred of Clemenceau for the Béziers regiments (see 17th Notebook, p. 339) is no doubt excessive, but it, along with other, similar examples on other pages, is revealing of widespread sentiment in the Midi.

Barthas cites numerous episodes which bear witness to "war culture" (*culture de guerre*): the arrival of the first war-wounded at Narbonne, the passage of prisoner-of-war convoys, a jingoistic newspaper, etc. But he himself, thoughtful, with a past as a labor militant, represented another culture, a countercurrent quite small in August 1914 but which grew in the course of the interminable conflict.[9] Barthas proclaims his disgust for war. But how to escape from the "massive grinding wheel" that threatened to crush him? Revolt would work only if it were widespread, and if it failed the immediate consequences would be terrible. To win, the Germans would have to be drawn in. The tragedy, for men like Barthas, is that the workers and their organizations were not capable of preventing the war by an international agreement. So when you're at war, the only thing to do is to endure it (Leonard Smith), to bend your backs in submission to circumstances (Jules Maurin), to do your duty, the duty of a citizen (without forgetting to write to the government minister, or to draw up a manifesto claiming the right of home leaves), and duty to comrades, too (this "small-group loyalty" which Wilhelm Deist cites among German soldiers).[10]

"Enough"

Those who haven't read Barthas but only the comment by Audoin-Rouzeau might tend to reject the barrelmaker's account as after the fact or distorted. Jay Winter, professor at Cambridge, delivered a strong response in 1996 with a big "BBC Book"[11] and a television series broadcast in the United States and Great Britain. Louis Barthas occupies a large part of it: pages 233 to 239 of the book; the reproduction of his portrait photograph and a notebook page; and other references throughout the text.

Barthas is in the front rank of those who say "Enough!" alongside the English writers Siegfried Sassoon and Wilfred Owen and the German sailor Richard Stumpf—men who suffered imprisonment in the midst of war, in the midst of carnage. The reflections of Barthas allow us to understand the soldiers' condemnation of the military tactic of attack-at-all-costs.[12] They affirm that soldiers are citizens in uniform who retain the right to think freely and who deserve to be treated like free men. In contrast, Jay Winter underscores the capacity for military life to produce what the English soldiers of the Second World War called "chickenshit"—the petty attempts at humiliation of soldiers by their officers. The *Carnets* of Barthas illustrate, on several occasions, these clashes between citizen soldiers and infantile officers. Isn't that right, *Monsieur capitaine-adjutant-major?*

"I propose building this monument right here"

On November 11, 1992, at Neuville-Saint-Vaast, France, Marie-Christine Blandin, president of the Conseil Régional Nord-Pas-de-Calais, ended her speech honoring Armistice Day by reading the famous passage from Louis Barthas about the fraternization of December 1915 (see 8th Notebook, p. 144), noting the concluding words: "Who knows—maybe one day in this corner of Artois they will raise a monument to commemorate this spirit of fraternity among men who shared a horror of war and who were forced to kill each other against their wills."

"Well," she added, "I propose building this monument right here, on the very spot where, seventy-seven years ago, in the space of a few hours, humanity triumphed over folly. Life won out over death."

To end these brief notes, it seems appropriate to give to readers, who have just spent four years with Corporal Barthas, some news about several consequences of this book, such as the project of a monument to fraternization. Will it ever be built? There already exists, at Pontcharra-sur-Brede (département of the Isère), a Peace Monument upon which are inscribed the final words of the book: "Often I think about my many comrades fallen by my side. I heard their curses against the war and its authors, the revolt of their whole beings against their tragic fate, against their murder. And I, as a survivor, believe that I am inspired by their will to struggle without cease-fire nor mercy, to my last breath, for the idea of peace and human fraternity.—Louis Barthas, February 1919, *Carnets de guerre.*"

A 1981 song by Marcel Amont, "Lo caporau Bartàs," was sung in the Occitan of Gascony. Since 1983 the actor Philippe Orgebin has been crisscrossing France (with detours into Germany) with his stage adaptation of the *Carnets de guerre,* titled *Caporal tonnelier* (Corporal Barrelmaker).

Following its participation in the publication of Barthas' notebooks, the *Fédération audoise des œuvres laïques* (FAOL), based in Carcassonne,[13] has launched a series of publications called "La Mémoire de 14–18 en Languedoc," which today numbers a dozen titles, including among its projects an analysis of the 214 articles submitted by Léon Hudelle, Barthas' captain in the 280th, to his newspaper *Le Midi Socialiste.* In addition the FAOL has participated in the publication of several works related to Barthas: the *Carnets de guerre de Gustave Folcher paysan languedocien 1939–1945,* considered one of the best eyewitness accounts of combat in the 1940 fall of France and subsequent forced labor by prisoners-of-war in Nazi Germany;[14] *Le jeune homme qui voulait devenir écrivain,* by Albert Vidal, a contemporary of Barthas, also born in 1879, combat veteran of the First World War, author of an original memoir which might become even better known than that of the barrelmaker, since it extends to the arrival of wounded Spanish Republican refugees in 1939 and the French Resistance in 1940;[15] and the proceedings published in 1997 of the 1996 international colloquium in Carcassonne, a scholarly conference which was a further homage to the work of the barrelmaker from the Aude.[16]

Notes

Introduction to the English Translation (2014) / R. Cazals

1. Jean Norton Cru, professor of French at Williams College, Massachusetts, was the author of *Témoins, Essai d'analyse et de critique des souvenirs de combattants édités en français de 1915 à 1928* (Paris: Les Étincelles, 1929; reissued by Les Presses Universitaires de Nancy in 1993 and in 2006 with a critical essay by Frédéric Rousseau).

2. See Marc Ferro, Malcolm Brown, Rémy Cazals, and Olaf Mueller, *Frères de tranchées,* (Paris: Perrin, 2005); in English, *Meetings in No Man's Land, Christmas 1914 and Fraternization in the Great War* (London: Constable and Robinson, 2007).

3. Jacques Meyer, *La vie quotidienne des soldats pendant la Grande Guerre* (Paris: Hachette, 1966). This book cites authors whose works had appeared up to that date. The subject was revisited, with numerous new contributions, by Rémy Cazals and André Loez, *Dans les tranchées de 1914–18* (Pau: Cairn, 2008); published as *14–18 Vivre et mourir dans les tranchées* (Paris: Taillander, 2012).

4. Pierre Barral, "Les cahiers de Louis Barthas," in *Traces de 14–18,* ed. Sylvie Caucanas and Rémy Cazals (Carcassonne: Les Audois, 1997), 21.

5. See, notably, Romain Ducoulombier, "La Sociale sous l'uniforme: obéissance et résistance à l'obéissance dans les rangs du socialisme et syndicalisme français, 1914–1916," in *Obéir/désobéir, Les mutineries de 1917 en perspective,* ed. André Loez and Nicolas Mariot (Paris: La Découverte, 2008).

6. Space does not permit citation of all notable works; see the CRID 14–18 website: www.crid1418.org.

7. *Un long dimanche de fiançailles, Album souvenir* (Paris: Les Arènes, 2004), 27.

Introduction (1978) / R. Cazals

1. *Fédération audoise des œuvres laïques,* 22, rue Antoine-Marty, 11000 Carcassonne, France.

2. *Témoins,* by Jean Norton Cru, 1929, and, more accessibly by the same author, *Du témoinage,* 1939, partly reissued in the "Libertés" collection, J.-J. Pauvert, 1967.

3. Jacques Meyer, *La vie quotidienne des soldats pendant la Grande Guerre* (Paris: Hachette, 1966).

4. Ibid.

5. This observation is not fully satisfying. But in this instance, there is a certain community of shared opinion among the members of the squad, drawn from the working classes. On the other hand, *Capitaine-Adjutant-Major* Cros-Mayrevielle, although an Occitan speaker, is detested because of his haughty attitude and the harassment which he makes his soldiers undergo. No wonder they called him *"le Kronprinz"* (the Crown Prince).

1st Notebook: Garrison Duty

1. A bacterial infection of the skin and underlying tissue.

2. "Narbonne (population 28,273) . . . lies in a dusty plain, 5 miles from the Mediterranean. . . . It carries on various industries (distilling, coopering, etc.) and is noted for its honey." Karl Baedeker, *Southern France . . . Handbook for Travellers,* 6th ed. (Leipzig, 1914), 104.

3. French army regiments in 1914 were grouped into four categories, based on the age of the soldiers and reservists: *Active* (for example, the 80th Infantry Regiment), *Réserve de l'Active* (for example, the 280th Infantry Regiment, numbered beginning with "2"), *Territoriale* (where Barthas' unit was at mobilization), and *Réserve de la Territoriale,* or R.A.T. Due to heavy casualties suffered on the front lines in the war's early months, many Territorial regiments, like Barthas' 280th, moved up from *Territoriale* to *Réserve de l'Active.*

4. The Capuchins, a Roman Catholic religious order of friars and one of the independent orders of Franciscans, were expelled from France in 1903.

5. Standard French infantry uniforms dating back sixty years, to the Crimean War.

6. Falet's actual surname.

7. Dr. Ernest Ferroul (1853–1921) was a medical doctor, editor, deputy to the National Assembly, and mayor of Narbonne (1891–1921), the first Socialist mayor in France; in June 1907 he was leader of a winegrowers' protest movement (he resigned from office, was arrested, and was reinstated).

8. Zouaves, renowned for their colorful uniforms and ferocity, were originally Berber tribesmen encountered by the French when they conquered Algeria in the 1830s. By mid-century, Zouave units were made up of European colonists in French North Africa; indigenous, non-European troops were known as *Tirailleurs.*

9. Famous boulevard-promenade in Marseille.

10. Units of the British Indian Army, on their way to the Western Front.

11. Baedeker, *Southern France* (1914), 193: "a small town on a plateau (5,135 feet), was once an important fortress built by [renowned French military engineer] Vauban in 1681."

12. Worn by French soldiers away from the front lines.

13. "Beyond Mont-Louis we cross the Col de la Perche (5,175 feet, view), a slight depression, where the Spaniards were defeated by the French in 1793." Baedeker, *Southern France,* 193.

14. "Llivia, the centre of a Spanish enclave of 4 sq. mi. in area (population 1,000). This was the Roman Julia Livia and was the capital of the Cerdagne down to the 11th cent., but is now both uninteresting and unsavory. Being styled a 'town,' it was excluded by the Treaty of the Pyrenees in 1659 from the cession by Spain to France of 33 villages of the Cerdagne. . . . A neutral road, on French soil for nearly 1 mi., connects Llivia with the Spanish frontier." Ibid., 193.

15. "Puycerda, Span. Puigcerdá (3,905 feet, population 2500), the capital of the Spanish Cerdagne . . . now a favorite summer resort of wealthy Barcelonians (two casinos)." Ibid., 194.

16. Barthas did his compulsory military service at Narbonne, with the 15th Infantry Regiment, from November 1900 (his conscription "class" year) to September 1903. He was promoted to corporal in September 1901. He subsequently undertook sessions of training duty, several weeks in length, also at Narbonne, in August–September 1906; with the 80th Infantry Regiment, May 1909 and June 1914. My thanks to Rémy Cazals for providing this information.

2nd Notebook: To the Killing Fields

1. Saint-Pol: "An old market town . . . developed importance as a railway junction during the War . . . frequently bombed." Findlay Muirhead, ed., *The Blue Guides: Belgium and the Western Front* (London: Macmillan and Co., and Paris: Librairie Hachette, 1920), 74.

2. Nœux-les-Mines: "A mining town . . . shelled with regularity. . . . A large slag-heap, the most favored target, dominates the station. . . . 'Nuxley's Mines' to the British." Ibid., 89.

3. 75-millimeter cannon, the mainstay of French field artillery.

4. Léon Hudelle (1881–1973), journalist and socialist militant, served on the front lines throughout the war until he was wounded in February 1918. See http://www.crid1418.org/temoins/2008/02/18/hudelle-leon-1881-1973/.

5. At this time, the infamous Western Front trench line, from the North Sea to the Swiss border, had not yet been established. It would soon take its familiar shape. "The basic frontline systems ordinarily consisted of three trenches. The first one was called the fire trench. . . . A support trench formed the second line. . . . Counterattacks would issue from the support trench if the first line was overrun. . . . Finally . . . was a reserve trench. . . . Communication trenches—*boyaux*—completed the effect of a demented spider's web. They zigzagged cross-country, roughly at right angles to the frontline system . . . dug at intervals of about seventy-five yards." Robert Cowley, "The Unreal City," *MHQ: The Quarterly Journal of Military History* 6, no. 2 (Winter 1994): 14.

6. Slang for Parisian street gangs of the early 1900s, whose ferocity contemporary journalists likened to that of Apache Indians of the American Southwest.

7. The 296th Regiment's attack on Vermelles is recounted in a regimental history: *Historique du 296e Régiment d'Infanterie* (Béziers, 1919). At the end of 1915, elements of the 280th Regiment, including Barthas' unit, would be absorbed into the 296th.

8. Gustave Hervé (1871–1944), a fiercely anarchist and antimilitarist editor who in 1914 became an ardent supporter of the French war effort (his newspaper *La Guerre Sociale*, founded in 1907, became *La Victoire*).

9. Quote from Pierre Corneille, French dramatist (1608–1684).

3rd Notebook: Massacres

1. From the British Indian army; see 1st Notebook, note 10.

2. Rosalie: slang for bayonet. The term was popularized by songwriter Théodore Botrel (1868–1925), whose song "Rosalie" was dedicated "to the glory of the little French bayonet." See "Botrel, the Trench Laureate, France's Unique Poet, Who Is at the Front Singing His Patriotic Songs to the Soldiers," *New York Times,* July 18, 1915.

3. Here and at other times infrequently throughout the notebooks Barthas opted not to identify an individual by name.

4. Joseph Jacques Césaire Joffre (1852–1931), commander in chief of the French army, 1911–16.

5. In reality, between 580,000 and 600,000, according to Odon Abbal, *Soldats oubliés, Les prisonniers de guerre français* (E and C, 2001). My thanks to Rémy Cazals for providing this source.

6. Although the front cover of the 3rd Notebook has the concluding date of May 4, 1915, the narrative does not extend beyond December 1914.

4th Notebook: Toward the Lorette Charnel House

1. Although the front cover of the 4th Notebook has the date of May 4, 1915, the narrative content of this notebook begins in December 1914.

2. Here Barthas had stuck a newspaper clipping into the notebook. It has unfortunately been lost. See Tony Ashworth, *Trench Warfare 1914–1918: The Live and Let Live System* (London: Pan Books, 1980, 2000); Malcolm Brown and Shirley Seaton, *Christmas Truce: The Western Front, December 1914* (London: Pan Books, 1984, 2001); Marc Ferro, Malcolm Brown, Rémy Cazals, and Olaf Mueller, *Meetings in No Man's Land, Christmas 1914 and Fraternization in the Great War* (London: Constable and Robinson, 2007; first published in French in 2005). My thanks to Rémy Cazals for the information regarding the lost clipping and for providing these sources.

3. "[N]arrow saps were thrust out into no-man's land, like suckers sprouting from a gnarled branch. At their ends were listening posts, often uncomfortably close to the enemy wire (and to his own saps). They were usually occupied only at night." Robert Cowley, "The Unreal City," *MHQ: The Quarterly Journal of Military History* 6, no. 2 (Winter 1994): 14.

4. Chevalier d'Assas: young nobleman (1733–1760), captain of *chasseurs* in the Auvergne Regiment in the Seven Years' War, who on night patrol discovered an enemy force hiding in ambush and called out, "*À moi, Auvergne, ce sont les ennemis!*" ("Over here, Auvergne, it's the enemy!"); he was then bayoneted to death.

5. Actually the British had taken Neuve-Chapelle in March. May 9 was the date of a genuine British disaster: eleven thousand casualties at Aubers Ridge, in front of Neuve-Chapelle. My thanks to Rob Cowley for this clarification.

6. Maurice Sarraut, editor of the Toulouse newspaper *La Dépêche*. Socialist leader Jean Jaurès wrote more than 1,300 articles in *La Dépêche* from 1887 to his assassination in 1914. My thanks to Rémy Cazals for providing this information.

5th Notebook: The Lorette Charnel House

1. A fable by Jean de La Fontaine (Book 7, Fable 1, 1678–1679), in which the plague-stricken animals select one among themselves to be sacrificed to appease the gods, based upon who has committed the most heinous offenses. The lowly donkey, whose confessed transgressions are relatively modest, becomes the chosen victim of the more powerful beasts: "Thus human courts acquit the strong, / and doom the weak, as therefore wrong."

2. Raymond Poincaré (1860–1934), president of France, 1913–20.

3. The flamethrower, or *Flammenwerfer,* was a German invention—though the notion of pyrotechnic projection goes back at least as far as the so-called Greek fire, which the Byzantine navy successfully used to turn away Muslim flotillas in 678. The first recorded flamethrower attack of the Great War occurred on February 26, 1915, at Malancourt Woods, west of Verdun. The Germans, employing stationary devices, took 220 acres and two lines of French trenches, a substantial gain in Western Front terms. They continued their experiments, and Barthas found himself on the receiving end of a flamethrower attack early in June 1915, memorably recorded here. The Germans next directed liquid fire at the British on July 30, at Hooge, near Ypres, this time trying out portable backpack versions of the projector. "Jets of flame as if from a line of powerful fire-hoses," said the British Official History, "spraying fire instead of water, shot across the front trenches."

The fire-hose simile was particularly apt. In one of those ironies of which history is so fond, the special detachment of combat engineers that operated the devices were mostly firemen-turned-soldiers under the command of the former fire chief of Leipzig. My thanks to Rob Cowley for providing this information.

4. Both Liévin and Lens were German-occupied towns.

6th Notebook: The Accursed War

1. A figure from medieval folklore, popularized in France by novelist Eugène Sue's *Le Juif Errant* (1844).

2. A series of anticlerical laws passed under the governments of Emile Combes and Aristide Briand, 1902–5, culminating in the *Loi du 9 décembre 1905 concernant la Séparation des Eglises et de l'Etat.*

3. Anthem of the international socialist movement since the late nineteenth century, with original French words (1871) by Eugène Pottier (a veteran of the Paris Commune) and music by Pierre Degeyter (1888).

4. General Henri Albert Niessel (1866–1955), who subsequently commanded an army corps in the 1917 Chemin des Dames offensive, and later led French and Allied missions to Russia and the nascent Baltic states. In 1920 he advised the Polish army in its battles against the Bolshevik Red Army (Charles de Gaulle served as his aide). He wrote several books about the war's aftermath in northeastern Europe.

5. My thanks to Rémy Cazals for providing this translation.

6. In the epic French victory over Austrian and Russian armies at Austerlitz, December 2, 1805, the morning sun pierced through thick clouds, unveiling the vast extent of Napoleon's forces.

7th Notebook: The Bloody and Futile Offensive of September 25, 1915

1. First lines of the poem "Le Clairon" ("The Bugler," 1872) by Paul Déroulède (1846–1914), hero of the Franco-Prussian War, irredentist writer, founder of the right-wing *Ligue des Patriotes,* anti-Dreyfusard, leader of an abortive putsch (1899), exiled to Spain (1899–1905). "Le Clairon" was set to music in the 1870s and became a popular patriotic anthem: "*L'air est pur, la route est large / Le Clairon sonne la charge/ . . .*"

2. The Abbaye de Royaumont is the site of a large military hospital in the Oise valley, north of Paris.

8th Notebook: The Neuville-Saint-Vaast Sector

1. In Greek mythology, the fifty daughters of Danaus, who, as punishment in Hades for murdering their cousins, the fifty sons of Aegyptus, were "compelled everlasting to pour water into a sieve." *Smith's Smaller Classical Dictionary* (New York: Dutton, 1958), 102.

2. The 296th Infantry Regiment was based in Béziers, near Narbonne on the Mediterranean seaboard, in the département of Hérault. In August 1914 the regiment, part of the 66th Reserve Division, entered German-occupied Alsace, engaged in combat outside Mulhouse, then fell back to the frontier passes in the Vosges Mountains. In mid-October the regiment was attached to the 58th Reserve Division, part of the 10th Army (under de Maud'huy), and sent to the Artois front. (Barthas' 280th Regiment was also in this division.) The 296th joined in the sustained attack on Vermelles until the town was taken in early December. The regiment and its division consolidated their positions during the winter months before ceding the sector to the British and moving south, in early June, to the Lorette front (along with the 280th Regiment). On June 5–7 it engaged in fierce fighting in the Fond de Buval, near Noulette. For the rest of the summer the regiment rotated in and

out of the front lines; at the end of August and into September it was detailed, along with the 280th, to training duties in Flanders (Bergues, West-Cappel). The regiment returned to Artois, stood in reserve on the Scarpe river for the September 25 offensive, then rotated with the 280th between Marœuil and the trenches of the Neuville-Saint-Vaast sector, weathering the same miserable conditions (rain, mud) described by Barthas. On December 20 the regiment incorporated the 6th Battalion of the 280th Regiment, then was reassigned from the 58th Division to the 152nd Division along with two regular regiments, the 114th and the 125th, still within the 10th Army (under the command of Victor-Louis-Lucien d'Urbal; see note 3 below). *Historique du 296e Régiment d'Infanterie* (Béziers, 1919), passim.

3. Victor-Louis-Lucien d'Urbal, 1858–1943, born in Sarreguemines, Lorraine; cavalry commander, 1912–1914; general commanding the 8th Army, Nov. 1914-Apr. 1915; general commanding the 10th Army, Apr. 1915-Apr. 1916; inspector-general of cavalry, 1916–1918.

4. Arcola (1796), Austerlitz (1805), and Jena (1806) were French victories won by Napoleon. General d'Urbal may have misspoken: the Hôtel des Invalides, in Paris, built by Louis XIV to house wounded soldiers, displays captured enemy flags, not French regimental flags, in its Church of Saint-Louis.

5. Barthas means that Sabatier speaks Occitan—the language of Languedoc—but not French.

6. Guillaume Marie Anne Brune (1763–1815), born in Brive-la-Gaillarde; an early comrade of Bonaparte in the Italian Campaigns, 1796–97. Brune became one of Napoleon's less-distinguished marshals, and was lynched by a royalist mob in Avignon after Waterloo.

7. "1915 had been a year in which mining operations, as a routine part of trench warfare on the Western Front, had reached a degree of intensity which continued until the early summer of 1916. Mines were used as part of a general offensive . . . but more often they were used for highly localized attacks. These attacks often had the objective of securing a particularly valuable piece of ground, offering good views over the enemy lines, and thereby denying a similar advantage to the foe. . . . Mines were often blown to provide the basis of an earthwork which could be fortified and manned and therefore dominate part of the line or of No Man's Land. Sometimes they were simply blown to create an obstruction to the enemy's view." Nigel Cave, *Battleground Europe: Arras, Vimy Ridge* (London: Leo Cooper, 1996), 36–38.

8. See 2nd Notebook, note 6.

9. "Mont St. Eloi (400 feet) was a French observation post during the battles of Souchez in May–June 1915. The Augustinian abbey, founded by St. Eloi in the 7th cent., is now in ruins, but the famous 17th cent. towers, though battered, are still standing." Findlay Muirhead, ed., *The Blue Guides: Belgium and the Western Front* (London: Macmillan and Co., and Paris: Librairie Hachette, 1920), 74.

9th Notebook: Toward the Hell of Verdun

1. *Mourir pour la Patrie / C'est le sort le plus beau, le plus digne d'envie* (To die for the fatherland / That's the finest fate, the most worthy of envy). Refrain from "Le chant des Girondins," French national anthem under the Second Republic (1848–52), words by Alexandre Dumas fils.

2. See 4th Notebook, note 3.

3. "In February [1916], the regiment was assigned to a sector at Mont Saint Eloi, in shattered trenches which were subjected to continual bombardment. The snow joined the party; some men had their feet frozen. This painful period ended on March 9, when the English

came to relieve us so that we could prepare for our participation in the battle of Verdun."
Historique du 296e Régiment d'Infanterie (Béziers, 1919), 8.

4. "Crécy-en-Ponthieu, famous for the victory of Edward III [of England] over Philip VI
of France in 1346." Findlay Muirhead, ed., *The Blue Guides: Belgium and the Western Front*
(London: Macmillan and Co., and Paris: Librairie Hachette, 1920), 9.

5. Militia units created in the 1860s to supplement the regular army of the French Second Empire. While some fought well in the 1870 Franco-Prussian War, few had received
sufficient training and equipment to be effective.

6. This nickname refers to Crown Prince Friedrich Wilhelm, the Kaiser's son, who led
the German Fifth Army attacking Verdun. He commanded little respect on either side.
"Friedrich Wilhelm certainly appeared the very model of the playboy soldier. His youth (he
was 34 at the time of Verdun) put it beyond doubt that he owed his rank to his position in
the imperial family. . . . His habit of conducting indiscreet affairs with French women from
German-occupied regions several times threatened embarrassment. Even in uniform his
bearing let him down. . . . His lean, gangling body and wizened schoolboy face [made him]
a gift to hostile cartoonists." Ian Ousby, *The Road to Verdun* (London: Jonathan Cape,
2002), 42.

7. Allegorical personification of French republican virtue. Her depiction as a young
woman coiffed in a Phrygian cap hangs in town halls throughout France.

8. Georges Courteline (1858–1929), pseudonym of Georges Moinaux, popular French
playwright, humorist, and novelist who satirized bureaucrats, government officials, military
officers, policemen, and the bourgeoisie and petite-bourgeoisie, based on his personal experience as a civil servant. The comical character Adjutant Flick, a petty tyrant in uniform,
appeared in his first published work, *Les gaîetés de l'escadron* (1886), drawing on the author's
own military service in a cavalry unit.

9. "From their first distant prospect of the battle [of Verdun], men commonly spoke of
it as a furnace, or called it a hell, an inferno." Ousby, *The Road to Verdun*, 9.

10. "Revigny . . . Zeppelin L.Z. 77 was shot down here in Feb. 1916." Findlay Muirhead,
ed., *The Blue Guides: North-Eastern France* (London: Macmillan and Co., and Paris: Librairie
Hachette, 1922), 148.

11. From the Polish *ulan*, term for a German cavalryman.

10th Notebook: The Verdun Charnel House

1. Four-handed card game, played with a deck of thirty-two cards.

2. Palace built by Louis XIV in the 1680s, west of Paris, as a retreat from the court life
of Versailles; demolished during the French Revolution. Pond, gardens, and park have
survived.

3. Henri-Philippe Pétain (1856–1951), since February 1916 the commander of the French
Second Army defending Verdun.

4. The 114th Line (Regular) Regiment was based at Parthenay, Deux-Sèvres, in the Ven-
dée-Poitou region; the 125th was based at Poitiers. Both had fought at the Marne in 1914
and in Artois in 1915.

5. Town in Belgium, near the French border, evacuated by the French Fifth Army after
fierce fighting, August 21–23, 1914.

6. "On May 5, picked up in automobiles and thrown into the furnace, [the regiment]
is going to take its glorious part in the defense of Verdun." *Historique du 296e Régiment
d'Infanterie* (Béziers, 1919), 8.

7. Avocourt was actually to the left (west) of Mort Homme and Cote 304, and Chattancourt was slightly to their right (southeast).

8. The villages of Damloup and Fleury, located respectively to the east and west of the fort of Vaux, were taken by the Germans after heavy bombardments; the fort of Vaux fell to the Germans on June 7.

9. The ancient Greek philosopher Diogenes of Sinope, famous for his disregard of material comforts, lived in a barrel.

10. Menthol lozenges, developed in 1905 by pharmacist Henri-Edmond Cannone, who first sold them in his Paris pharmacy and on trains.

11. *Vae Victis* ("Woe to the conquered"), quoted by Livy (59 BC–17 AD) in his *History* (5.49). Gauls had invested and sacked Rome, ca. 386 BC, and entered into negotiations with the Senate to abandon the siege. "Together they agreed upon the price, one thousand pounds' weight of gold. . . . The weights which the Gauls brought for weighing the metal were heavier than standard, and when the Roman commander objected the insolent barbarian flung his sword into the scale, saying 'Woe to the vanquished!'—words intolerable to Roman ears." Before negotiations were completed, the Roman general Camillus relieved the city and drove away the Gauls. *Livy: The Early History of Rome,* trans. A. de Sélincourt (New York: Penguin Classics, 1960), 395.

12. "On May 18, the 3rd Mixed [Regiment of North African Zouaves and *Tirailleurs*] proceeds to an attack which, on its right, Captain Barbier supports with 7 sections and 2 machine-gun sections of the 296th. With one burst of élan, the Zouaves gain their first objective, but a German barrage is immediately unleashed, which cuts off all communication with the rear. The Zouaves repulse the violent counterattacks and Captain Barbier cooperates in the resistance. Without interruption, Boche reinforcements pour out of the village of Béthincourt. No matter how violent their efforts against the 3rd Mixed, particularly at its point of junction with the 296th, all the positions taken remain in our hands." *Historique du 296e Régiment d'Infanterie,* 8–9.

13. *Les derniers jours du fort de Vaux. 9 mai–7 juin 1916* (Paris: Plon-Nourrit, 1916). Henry Bordeaux (1870–1963), a successful lawyer, novelist, essayist, and member of the *Académie Française,* France's elite scholarly body, was mobilized as a captain of reserves in 1914 and served throughout the war at General Headquarters. "Before the war he had made his reputation with novels set in the countryside of his native Savoie. Serving nominally as a staff officer at Verdun, he in fact became the semi-official historian of the battle even while it was still being fought. Indeed, he appointed himself the laureate of Verdun." Ian Ousby, *The Road to Verdun* (London: Jonathan Cape, 2002), 11. Bordeaux was elected to the Académie Française in 1919.

11th Notebook: The 296th Regiment in Champagne

1. A tributary of the Aude river, the Argent-Double river runs through Barthas' hometown, Peyriac-Minervois.

2. General François Andrieu had taken command of the 152nd Reserve Infantry Division on January 27, 1916.

3. In Charles Perrault's fairy tale *Barbe-Bleu* (Bluebeard), the murderous husband has threatened to kill his too-curious young wife, as he has all her predecessors. She wins a ten-minute reprieve and secretly asks her sister Anne to be on the lookout, from a high tower, for the anticipated arrival of their two brothers. "Anne," she cries out repeatedly, "Don't you see anyone coming?" Anne replies that she sees nothing, until finally she can report that she sees two horsemen coming; they arrive just in time to dispatch Bluebeard and free their sisters.

4. François Vatel, renowned French chef of the seventeenth century.

5. The regimental history of the 296th Regiment chronicles the fierce fighting May 20–23 at Cote 306 and the adjacent Mort Homme by the Fifth and Sixth Battalions, including poison-gas and flamethrower attacks. "One company, the 23rd, reduced to less than 30 rifles, repulsed an attack and was wiped out on the spot rather than fall back. . . . The Regiment gave manifest proof of its solidity and its gallantry. 13 officers and 650 men—those are losses of these two days [May 21–22] for the two battalions and the two machine-gun companies which took part in the combat." *Historique du 296e Régiment d'Infanterie,* 9–11.

6. "Two days later [May 24] the regiment embarked for Champagne (La Cheppe and the Camp de la Noblette), where it would reconstitute itself while occupying, from time to time, a sector alternating between the encampments of the Ferme du Piémont and of Vadenay." *Historique du 296e Régiment d'Infanterie,* 11.

7. There is a lack of consensus about where the battle of Châlons (AD 451) was actually fought. "Even its exact location is in doubt. In that general area of modern France, it has been a favorite occupation of retired colonels to spend their weekends looking for evidence of the battlefield." Arther Ferrill, "Attila at Châlons," in *MHQ: The Quarterly Journal of Military History* 1, no. 4 (Summer 1989): 54.

8. "Cuperly stands on the S. outskirts of the entrenched Camp de Châlons (47 sq. m.; aerodromes, manœuvre grounds), created in 1857 by Napoleon III." Findlay Muirhead, ed., *The Blue Guides: Belgium and the Western Front* (London: Macmillan and Co., and Paris: Librairie Hachette, 1920), 180.

9. A sixty-centimeter-gauge light railway system developed by Paul Decauville (1846–1922), the tracks of which could be laid without ties. It served factories, mines, agricultural complexes, and rural transportation lines throughout France and its colonies.

10. In Perrault's fairy tale, Tom Thumb and his brothers and sisters have been abandoned deep in a dark forest by their parents, who cannot afford to keep them. Tom climbs a tall tree to look for light, and eventually leads his siblings home to their repentant parents and a happy ending.

11. Polichinelle's secret was no secret at all; delivered as a stage whisper, it was therefore known to everyone. Polichinelle (in Italian *Pulcinella* and in English *Punchinello,* from which "Punch" is derived) is a stock character of Italian commedia dell'arte folk theater.

12. Character in Victor Hugo's *Les Misérables,* the quintessential street-smart, wisecracking urchin of Paris.

13. See 2nd Notebook, note 6.

14. Literally, "war godmothers." "The *marraines de guerre* began as a scheme for women to adopt an unknown soldier, keeping him supplied with woolen comforters, and had grown into a powerful propaganda instrument." Alistair Horne, *The Price of Glory: Verdun 1916* (New York: St. Martin's, 1963), 64.

15. "On June 14, Lieutenant Colonel Douce, who, since October 1914, had led the regiment in so many engagements, was named to the command of the 58th Infantry Division; he left only regrets in the 296th. He was replaced on June 27 by Colonel Robert." *Historique du 296e Régiment d'Infanterie,* 11.

16. In early 1916 two brigades of Russian soldiers, about twenty thousand men, were sent to fight alongside their French allies on the Western Front. "With their training complete in July 1916, the First Brigade went into battle in the Champagne sector east of Paris, fought extremely well in various engagements, and won the French authorities' praise for their valor." Jamie Cockfield, "Sold for Shells," *MHQ: The Quarterly Journal of Military History* 12, no. 1 (Autumn 1999): 68. The Russian Expeditionary Force performed creditably in fur-

ther combat in Champagne that autumn and in the Chemin des Dames offensive in April 1917, but the divisive effects of the Russian Revolution led to its withdrawal from the front lines, partial mutiny, and internal conflict—"the first battle of the Russian Civil War" (ibid., 72). Most survivors were eventually repatriated to Soviet Russia after the war, but several thousand chose to remain in France. There is a Russian military cemetery at Mourmelon-le-Grand.

12th Notebook: The 296th Regiment in Champagne

1. The French 37mm infantry field cannon was introduced in 1916. It could be disassembled into three pieces and had detachable wheels and sometimes an armored shield. "To clear away machine-gun nests, the infantry companies were to carry forward their own artillery in the form of the lightweight 37-mm. cannon which would be handled by only two men." Richard M. Watt, *Dare Call It Treason: The True Story of the French Army Mutinies of 1917* (New York: 1969, repr. Dorset Press, 2001), 157.

2. *Mourir pour la patrie est le sort le plus beau, le plus digne d'envie* (To die for your country is the finest fate, most worthy of envy).

3. After the fall of the Roman Empire in the West, the territory of Gaul was roughly divided between the kingdom of the Franks in the north and that of the Visigoths in the south.

4. Henri Joseph Etienne Gouraud (1867–1946). After service in Morocco, he was placed in charge of the French expeditionary force in the 1915 Dardanelles Campaign. There, on June 30, Gouraud was severely wounded by a shell burst, losing an arm and breaking both legs. After less than six months' recuperation he returned to active service, in early 1916, to lead the Fourth Army in Champagne. That December he was appointed resident general in Morocco, but he returned to command the Fourth Army in July 1917, where he distinguished himself in repulsing German attacks, earning the nickname "the Lion of Champagne." After the war Gouraud served in the Levant and in senior army staff positions, retiring in 1937.

5. "On June 17 [*sic*] the regiment changes sectors and heads off to Perthes-les-Hurlus [five kilometers south of the Butte de Tahure], a relatively calm sector which it could occupy while pursuing its reorganization. The Germans nevertheless did not stay inactive and dug numerous mine shafts under our listening posts, leading to some skirmishes, mainly with grenades, and some probing attacks which were easily repulsed and during which we took some prisoners, from whom we obtained some intelligence." *Historique du 296e Régiment d'Infanterie* (Béziers, 1919), 11.

6. "To the E. of Rheims is the region still known as '*Champagne Pouilleuse*' (lousy Champagne) for the poverty of its soil; here in 1915–1917 were delivered the greatest French attacks of the war." Findlay Muirhead, ed., *The Blue Guides: North-Eastern France* (London, Macmillan and Co., and Paris: Librairie Hachette, 1922), 114.

7. The so-called Wallace fountains, which dispensed free drinking water along the sidewalks of Paris, were a gift from British philanthropist Sir Richard Wallace, who donated fifty of them to the city of Paris in 1872 (to which the city later subsequently added another thirty-six fountains of identical design).

8. Site of particularly savage combat during the First and Second Battles of Champagne, February–March and September 1915.

9. Canal system connecting the Mediterranean and the Atlantic. The seventeenth-century Canal du Midi, from Toulouse to Sète on the Mediterranean, passes not far from Barthas' hometown, Peyriac-Minervois.

10. Léon Daudet (1867–1942), vocal critic of the Third Republic and democracy in general, son of the novelist Alphonse Daudet. In 1907 he co-founded, with Charles Maurras, the right-wing periodical *Action Française*. Georges Clemenceau (1841–1929) first served as prime minister from 1907 to 1910, during which time the government ruthlessly suppressed winegrowers' strikes in the Languedoc, including shootings of demonstrators in Narbonne. For Hervé, see 2nd Notebook, note 8.

11. August 15 is the feast day of the Assumption of the Virgin Mary.

13th Notebook: The Somme Offensive

1. Moux (Aude) is the railway station nearest Peyriac-Minervois, on the main Narbonne-Carcassonne line.

2. "On the 19th [October 1916] the 296th relieved elements of the 18th Division in its sector of Combles; the relief proved to be difficult due to a pounding rain [and] fields churned up by shellfire." *Historique du 296e Régiment d'Infanterie* (Béziers, 1919), 11.

3. Henri de la Tour d'Auvergne, vicomte de Turenne (1611–1675), famous seventeenth-century French general. As a youth in Sedan, "he showed a very decided taste for the profession of arms. . . . One winter evening, to prove to his friends that he was stout enough to undergo the fatigues of war, he went out secretly and passed the night on the ramparts; they found him in the morning asleep on a gun platform." General Maxime Weygand, *Turenne, Marshal of France,* trans. George B. Ives (Boston and New York: Houghton Mifflin, 1930), 10.

4. Spelled "Guillaut" in the *Historique du 296e Régiment d'Infanterie,* 11.

5. The *Historique du 296e Régiment d'Infanterie,* 11–12, describes the attack as beginning on October 21, with the 13th Company under Lieutenant Guillaut advancing 250 meters, and continuing on October 22 and 23, with Lieutenant Cordier being grievously wounded; the 4th Battalion (under Commandant Ducombeau) captured two machine guns and sixty prisoners; and the 5th Battalion wavered under heavy enemy machine-gun fire.

6. Gallic people of the present-day Auvergne region, who took a leading role in resisting Roman rule; their nobleman Vercingetorix led a revolt against Julius Caesar in 52 BC.

14th Notebook: In the Blood-Soaked Mud of the Somme

1. The regimental history *Historique du 296e Régiment d'Infanterie* (Béziers, 1919), 12, places this attack on November 2: "The 4th Battalion displayed an admirable tenacity; by 1400 hours all the objectives had been reached. The 13th and 14th Companies had seized a machine-gun and taken 117 prisoners."

2. "Corbie . . . a market town . . . lies between the branching valleys of the Somme and the Ancre. . . . Crowded by troops during the Somme battles of 1916, and the headquarters of many auxiliary services." Findlay Muirhead, ed., *The Blue Guides: Belgium and the Western Front* (London: Macmillan and Co., and Paris: Librairie Hachette, 1920), 121.

3. *Tauben* is the German word for doves. Although the *Tauben* were a specific type of swept-wing German monoplane used for training and observation, the word was commonly used in Allied slang to refer to any German aircraft, especially those dropping bombs.

4. On the Somme battlefield, "on September 15 [1916], tanks were used for the first time in battle. Forty-nine tanks took part in the attack, moving forward on a wide front. Ten of the tanks were hit by German artillery fire, nine broke down with mechanical difficulties, and five failed to advance. But those that did manage to go forward were able to advance more than 2,000 yards. . . . Recognising the potential of the new weapon, [British commanding General Sir Douglas] Haig asked the war office for a thousand of them." Martin Gilbert, *The First World War* (New York: Henry Holt and Company, 1994), 286.

5. Field Marshal Paul von Hindenburg (1847–1934), named chief of the German General Staff in August 1916.

6. Champigny-sur-Marne, east of Paris, where, during the Franco-Prussian War, the French counterattacked against the German army investing the capital, November 30, 1870.

7. "On December 12 [1916], the German Chancellor, [Theobald von] Bethmann-Hollweg, in a speech to the Reichstag, offered to open negotiations with the [Allied] Entente in a neutral country. . . . On December 20, before the Entente had replied to Bethmann-Hollweg's suggestion for negotiations, President [Woodrow] Wilson asked each of the Allied powers to formulate its own peace conditions. . . . . The official British answer came on the day after Wilson's note, and was made by [David] Lloyd George, who had become Prime Minister twelve days earlier. 'We shall put our trust rather in an unbroken army than in broken faith,' he declared. . . . On December 30 the Entente powers formally rejected Bethmann-Hollweg's suggestion for negotiations as 'empty and insincere.'" Gilbert, *The First World War*, 303–4.

8. "On 7 January 1917, [the regiment] passed from the 152nd to the 169th Infantry Division (Eighth Army Corps) and went into encampment at Morvillers. . . . The 169th Infantry Division established itself in this region, under the orders of Gen. Serot-Almeris-Latour. It was made up of the 13th, 29th, and 296th Infantry Regiments. The division's infantry was under the orders of Col. Denis Lecomte." *Historique du 296e Régiment d'Infanterie*, 13.

9. On October 5, 1915, the British and French reached agreement with the Greek government to occupy the northern port city of Salonika (today Thessaloniki), to bolster their ally Serbia against Austria-Hungary and Bulgaria. However, troops landed too late to prevent a disastrous Serbian defeat. The Allies were stalemated in Salonika until mounting a victorious offensive into Macedonia in 1918.

Romania had declared war on Austria-Hungary on August 27, 1916, invading Transylvania. Germany came to the aid of its ally and by December had occupied Romania's capital, Bucharest, and much of the country. The Romanian government formally surrendered in May 1918.

10. In the battle of Valmy, September 20, 1792, a French revolutionary army under Dumouriez and Kellermann repulsed invading Prussian, Austrian, and émigré French forces led by the Duke of Brunswick. A tall wooden windmill figured prominently and memorably at the center of the French line of artillery. The German poet Goethe was present at the battle and left an account of his observations.

15th Notebook: The 296th Regiment from Béziers in Champagne

1. On August 25–29, 1914, German troops occupying the university town of Louvain, Belgium, "burned buildings and executed civilians. . . . About a fifth of Louvain's houses were gutted. . . . These episodes not only shocked the British and French public, they also gave the Entente propagandists an early triumph." Martin Gilbert, *The First World War, A Complete History* (New York: Henry Holt, 1994), 42–43. "The destruction of the famous University Library [at Louvain] was perhaps, after that of Rheims Cathedral, the greatest act of vandalism committed by the Germans." Findlay Muirhead, ed., *The Blue Guides: Belgium and the Western Front* (London: Macmillan and Co., and Paris: Librairie Hachette, 1920), 311. "Shattered by four years' constant bombardment, Rheims has earned the first place of honour among the martyred towns of France." Ibid., 173.

2. "The Allied offensive on the Western Front . . . began on 25 September 1915. . . . The French attacked the German trench lines in Champagne . . . [and] made a two-mile dent

in the German line along a fifteen-mile front and took 1,800 Germans prisoner." Gilbert, *The First World War,* 196.

3. "This natural fortress which dominates the valley of the Aisne, and is situated to the north of the village of Massiges, owes its name to the contour lines on the military maps, which take the form of a left hand. The fingers are separated by deep indentations, which the combatants, seeing them from the depth of their trenches, called ravines. The Hand of Massiges marked the eastern limit of the Champagne Front. . . . It was the object of incessant attacks, particularly in 1914 and 1915, but in spite of the bravery of the [attackers] it was never totally overrun." http://perso.wanadoo.fr/champagne1418/circuit/circuitmassiges/massiges/massiges.htm (English text).

4. "From the 25th [January 1917], the regiment occupied the Massiges West sector, of which Colonel Robert took command, and which needed to be put back into good repair, because the trenches were in bad condition. German artillery, mines, and mortars of all caliber disturbed our work. The bombardment reached as far as the Dammartin [*sic*] cantonments. . . . The situation continued until mid-February, the battalions taking turns in the trenches. On February 15, the German artillery was more active, and the enemy launched an attack on the neighboring regiment, which gave up a bit of terrain. The 296th consolidated its links with adjacent units. The 15th and 18th Companies supported the machine gunners, who inflicted serious losses on the enemy and pushed them back to the west." *Historique du 296e Régiment* (Béziers, 1919), 13.

5. This mass surrender is referred to as *L'Affaire de Maisons-Champagne* in reference to where it took place. See page 299 for further mention of this event.

6. Robert Nivelle (1856–1924) succeeded Joffre as commander in chief of the French army in December 1916. After the failure of the Chemin des Dames offensive in April 1917 led to army mutinies, he was succeeded by Henri-Philippe Pétain on May 15 and was subsequently posted to North Africa.

7. Binoculars and a walking stick typically were an officer's accoutrements, but Barthas had obtained a pair of binoculars in 1915 (see 7th Notebook), and Rémy Cazals notes that Barthas began to use an improvised walking stick because, by this point, he was starting to feel the ill effects of his years on the front lines.

8. Goethe wrote: *Von hier und heute geht eine neue Epoche der Weltgeschichte aus und ihr könnt sagen, ihr seid dabei gewesen.* The monument to the Strasbourg-born general François Etienne Christophe Kellermann (1735–1820), Napoleonic marshal and Duc de Valmy, was erected in 1892 to commemorate the battle on its centennial. See 14th Notebook, note 10.

9. "In the [German-]occupied territories the local inhabitants had no access to information about their loved ones or the fate of the French Army. The Germans controlled the flow of news and to this end they started publishing the paper *La Gazette des Ardennes* in November 1914 (it was printed in Charleville-Mézières). Distributed by the *Kommandanturen* [German command posts], it was originally a weekly publication with a small circulation (4,000 copies) whose sole purpose was to publish translations of official German communiqués. Conscious of the general hostility towards *La Gazette des Ardennes* the German Army attempted to solve the problem by recruiting a French journalist by the name of Prévost, and the choice turned out to be a good one. Prévost hit upon the idea, in April 1915, of publishing the names of the latest French soldiers to have been taken prisoner or to have died in the prison camps (in all more than 250,000 names would be published) and by October 1917 they were printing 175,000 copies of every edition. Although the people of Nord

[département] despised the paper, nicknaming it the paper of lies (*journal des minteux*), it was the only source of information available to them. The last edition came out on 2 November 1918." http://www.remembrancetrails-northernfrance.com/history/the-department -of-nord-and-the-coal-basin-under-german-occupation/the-german-press-la-gazette-des -ardennes-and-the-liller-kriegszeitung.html.

10. "The famous ridge traversed by the *Chemin des Dames* (650 feet). . . . The 'Ladies' Road' was constructed for the journeys of the daughters of Louis XV. . . . The ridge was repeatedly attacked by the French, who gained a footing on the middle part of the ridge during Nivelle's unsuccessful offensive (April 17th–20th, 1917) and secured the E. heights after bitter fighting (May 4–10th, 1917)." Findlay Muirhead, ed., *The Blue Guides: North-Eastern France* (London: Macmillan and Co., and Paris: Librairie Hachette, 1922), 107.

11. Today the Autoroute de l'Est and the N44 highway go through this tunnel, between Châlons and Reims.

12. *On croit mourir pour la Patrie et on meurt pour les industriels.* A famous quote by novelist and Nobel Prize–winner Anatole France (1844–1924).

16th Notebook: The Killing Ground of Mont Cornillet

1."On April 30 the 5th Battalion was due to launch the attack. . . . Soon after 6 in the morning Colonel Robert, coming out of his command post, was gravely wounded by a shell. At H-hour, 12:40, the first waves go over the top, followed by the rest of the three assault companies who rush forward with admirable spirit and enthusiasm. . . . The news of the death of Col. Robert, wounded on the 30th and made *Commandeur de la Légion d'Honneur,* spreads through the regiment and provokes general consternation, so beloved was this brave and generous man. The regiment is in mourning. . . ." *Historique du 296e Régiment d'Infanterie* (Béziers, 1919), 14–15.

2. Marguerite Jeanne Steinheil (1869–1954) was the mistress of François Félix Faure (1841–1899), president of France from 1895 until his death, which allegedly occurred in her company.

3. "L'Épine, or Notre-Dame de l'Épine, a small town on the Vesle (burned in 1914), with a beautiful Gothic church of 1410–1600, surmounted by two elegant openwork spires of unequal height." Findlay Muirhead, *The Blue Guides: North-Eastern France* (London: Macmillan and Co., and Paris: Librairie Hachette, 1922), 138.

4. The song of revolt sung by the corporal and echoed in refrain is known as the "Song of Craonne." Its authorship is unknown. My thanks to Rémy Cazals for providing this information.

5. Bolt-action repeating rifle, since 1887 the standard weapon of the French infantry, named after Lieutenant Colonel Nicolas Lebel, who devised its distinctive, full-metal-jacket 8mm ammunition.

6. Barthas mockingly employs a German word to indicate "massive, oversized." My thanks to Rémy Cazals for providing this information.

7. Probably General Alexis Roger Hely d'Oissel (1859–1937), who commanded the 8th Army Corps in the Champagne and eastern France in 1917. http://www.military-photos. com/helydoissel.htm.

8. The savage fighting in this area from December 1914 to the end of 1915 is recounted in *The Americans in the Great War, Volume 3: The Meuse-Argonne Battlefields* (Paris and London: Michelin, 1919, repr. G. H. Smith and Son, 1994), 8–10 and 98–105: "From June 20 to July 14 [1915] the Crown Prince launched an offensive in great force, employing as much as an entire army corps for a single thrust. . . . The Crown Prince had expected to cross the

Argonne, but after sacrificing thousands of soldiers, he was unable to break down the French resistance. . . . In 1917, the fighting consisted almost entirely of hand-to-hand struggles for outposts or trenches. The French, who excelled in this kind of warfare, constantly destroyed the enemy mines and brought back numbers of prisoners from more or less extensive raids."

9. André Theuriet (1833–1907); novelist and poet of provincial rural and woodland life, became a member of the Académie Française in 1896.

10. Three-inch trench mortar firing an eleven-pound shell, counterpart to the German *minenwerfer;* introduced by the British in September 1916, invented by Sir Wilfred Scott-Stokes.

11. Type of pneumatic mortars, introduced by the French in 1915; the compressed air (generated by gas canister or foot pedal) that propelled the 60mm shell was noiseless and smokeless, thereby enabling it to avoid detection.

12. Historians of the French Revolution refer to "Red Terror" Jacobin repression of internal enemies (1792–94) and subsequent "White Terror" repression of Jacobins by their opponents (1794–99).

13. Popular song, also known as "Quand Madelon," about a favorite barmaid in a soldiers' café, written in 1914 by "Bach" (Charles-Louis Pasquier, 1882–1953).

17th Notebook: The End of the 296th Infantry Regiment

1. In the early twentieth century the wine-growing region of Languedoc was greatly affected by a severe slump that produced a catastrophic drop in growers' prices. Massive demonstrations took place in 1907, and in Narbonne troops killed six people. The killings took place while Georges Clemenceau was prime minister, and he was referred to by many in the Midi, including Barthas, as the "gunman of Narbonne," the "hangman of the Midi." During this period, the 17th Regiment, based in Béziers, mutinied, and armed conflict between the mutineers, led by Corporal Fondecave, and the troops of General Lacroisade was narrowly avoided. The mutineers ultimately surrendered and as punishment were sent to southern Tunisia. The newly re-formed Béziers regiments took the numbers 96 (regulars) and 296 (reserves). While in office (1906–9) Clemenceau embraced the title of "top cop of France." His ferocity against his political adversaries also earned him the nickname "the Tiger." He returned as prime minister in November 1917, serving until January 1920. (My thanks to Rémy Cazals for providing this information.)

2. "On November 20 [1917], the 4th battalion of the 296th Infantry Regiment, which had just been dissolved, is assigned to the 248th and divided among the three battalions which are thus restored to strength." *Historique Sommaire du 248e Régiment d'Infanterie, Aôut 1914–Avril 1919* (Rennes, 1920), 24. The 248th had been raised in Guingamp (Brittany) in August 1914 and fought at the Marne, in Champagne, at Verdun, in Champagne again, and most recently at Bois le Chaume, near Verdun, where it suffered terrible losses. The regiment had encamped at Bassuet on November 12.

3. See 16th Notebook, note 13.

4. "On December 5, the regiment is sent [from Bassuet] to a sector in the Argonne; until December 23 it occupies the section of front line situated to the east of the Four de Paris." *Historique Sommaire du 248e Régiment,* 24.

5. Founded in 1890 to promote tourism in France, the Touring Club de France had by 1914 installed more than thirty thousand road signs throughout the country. See: http://tcf-randonnee.com/fr/qui-sommes-nous/randonnee-ile-de-France.

6. Gunfire directed toward a target at a steeply elevated angle so as to strike difficult-to-reach enemy positions such as a narrow valley or ravine.

7. First two lines of the poem "Hymne," by Victor Hugo (1802–1885): *Ceux qui pieuse-ment sont morts pour la Patrie / Ont droit qu'à leur cercueil la foule vienne et prie.*

8. Notorious gang of homicidal, anarchist bank robbers led by Jules Bonnot (1876–1912); its crimes and its downfall were closely followed by the popular press in France, from 1911 to 1913.

9. Since before the war, under the anticlerical Third Republic, which had imposed the separation of church and state.

18th Notebook: The Last Year of Martyrdom

1. In June 1791 King Louis XVI and Queen Marie-Antoinette secretly fled Paris, travel-ing east to reach Austrian territory. "[At] Sainte-Ménehould, on the evening of June 21, the king was recognized. Drouet, the local postmaster . . . made a dash to Varennes, the next town on the route. Here the party was stopped, the whole town turned out. . . . On the morning of the twenty-second messengers arrived from Paris with orders to bring the would-be es-capers back." William Doyle, *The Oxford History of the French Revolution* (Oxford and New York: Oxford University Press, 1989), 151.

2. The Gotha G.[I-]V was a heavy bomber used by the *Luftstreitkräfte* (Imperial German Air Force) during World War I. http://en.wikipedia.org/wiki/Gotha_G.V

3. Southeast of Lyon; today, Bourgoin-Jallieu. See http://www.bourgoinjallieu.fr/decouvrir -la-ville/office-de-tourisme/patrimoine for more information about the town's history and Théophile Diederichs.

4. Like the *marraines de guerre* (see 11th Notebook, note 14), this charitable organization of "godfathers" undertook sponsorship of needy soldiers.

5. The building which housed the Chambre des Députés, the French legislature of the Third Republic, is called the Palais [palace] Bourbon.

6. "[In 1918 the Germans deployed] a long-range gun, known to the Allies as 'Big Ber-tha,' which dropped shells into the city [Paris], psychologically if not objectively to consid-erable effect, from a range of seventy-five miles." John Keegan, *The First World War* (New York: Knopf, 1998), 406.

7. Théophile Malo Corret de la Tour d'Auvergne (1743–1800), Breton-born hero of the French Revolutionary and early Napoleonic Wars, killed in battle in Bavaria, called by Bonaparte "the first grenadier of France."

19th Notebook: The End of the Nightmare

1. There are several members of the de la Trémoille family who had notable military careers, but Barthas is probably referring to Antoine Philippe de La Trémoïlle, Prince of Talmont (1765–1794), a leader of anti-Jacobin rebels in the Vendée-Maine region who was captured by Revolutionary forces and guillotined in Laval. The Château de Vitré became the property of the de la Trémoille family in the 1600s.

2. The letters of Madame Marie de Sévigné (1626–1696), widow of a Breton marquis killed in a duel, written to her daughter form an invaluable literary tapestry of aristocratic life in the reign of Louis XIV.

3. Each of these battles brought an empire to an end: Jena, the Prussian Empire (1806); Waterloo, Napoleon's First Empire (1815); and Sedan, Napoleon III's Second Empire (1870).

4. Albert Gérard Léo d'Amade (1856–1941), French general with a distinguished career in North Africa and Indochina; commanded French forces in the Gallipoli landings, April 1915, but returned to France due to illness after a few weeks; ended World War I as com-mander of the Tenth Military District, based in Rennes.

5. Breton antigovernment rebels during the French Revolution and subsequent years.

6. Noël Marie Joseph Édouard, vicomte de Curières de Castelnau (1851–1944), army commander, led French successes at Le Grand Couronné (August–September 1914) and Champagne (September–November 1915); he was an initial defender of Verdun (February 1916), and was appointed by Pétain to command the city's defense. He lost three sons in the war.

Afterword to the 1997 Edition / R. Cazals

1. Every reader of the *Carnets* will note Barthas' remarkable breadth of knowledge [*culture*]. I have contributed an article, "La culture de Louis Barthas, tonnelier," in *Pratiques et cultures dans la France contemporaine. Hommage à Raymond Huard* (Montpellier: Université Paul-Valéry, 1995), 425–35.

2. Co-author with Andre Ducasse and Gabriel Perraux, *Vie et mort des Francais 1914–1918* (Paris: Hachette, 1959).

3. Ferdinand Tailhades, *Ils m'appelaient tout le temps "Camarade";* Léopold Noé, *Nous étions ennemis sans savoir pourquoi ni comment;* Auguste Bastide, *Tranchées de France et d'Orient* (three titles from the collection *La mémoire de 14–15 en Languedoc,* published by the *Fédération des œuvres laïques de l'Aude;* see below, note 12); similarly: *Poilus Savoyards,* collection *Gens de Savoie,* (Chambéry: 1981), etc.

4. Pierre Nora, ed., *Les lieux de la mémoire,* book 2, "La Nation," vol. 3 (Paris: Gallimard, 1984), 111–41; Maurice Agulhon, *La république,* 2d ed. (Paris: Hachette, 1992), vol. 1.

5. Gérard Canini, ed., "Mémoire de la Grande Guerre, Témoins et témoinages,*" Proceedings of the Verdun Colloquium* (Nancy: PUN, 1989), 131–39, and "Traces de 14–18," *in Proceedings of the Carcassonne Colloquium,* ed. Sylvie Caucanas and Rémy Cazals (Carcassonne: Les Audois: 1997), 21–30. As for Jean Norton Cru, everyone agrees about his originality and the rigor of his working methods, as well as about the enormous amount of work involved in producing *Témoins: Essai d'analyse et de critique des souvenirs de combattants édités en français de 1915 à 1928* (Paris: Les Étincelles, 1929, repr. Nancy: PUN, 1993). But reading this book from the first to the last line with careful attention, one also sees the sophistication of his analysis and his sense of nuance.

6. Paris: Armand Colin, 1986.

7. An attentive reading of the documentation marshaled by Audoin-Rouzeau shows that the so-called trench newspapers were often produced in the rear echelon, under the control of military authorities, and that some of them participated in *bourrage de crane*. See my remarks in "Editer les carnets de combattants," in "Traces de 14–15," op. cit.

8. The works of Jean-Jacques Becker (*1914: Comment les Français sont entrés dans la guerre,* 1977) have clearly shown this for the rural world. His conclusions are fully confirmed by an in-depth study carried out in a dozen villages of the Aude département (but not Peyriac). See *La vie des Audois en 14–18,* Archives de l'Aude, 1986.

9. After Louis Barthas, who represents a countercurrent of opinion in August 1914, I have discovered Albert Vidal, a bourgeois republican from the provinces, openly hostile to Pétain in 1940. See Albert Vidal and Rémy Cazals, *Le jeune homme qui voulait devenir écrivain* (Toulouse: Privat, 1985).

10. It is not possible to develop and discuss here the themes of "consent," "revolt," "being caught up in the system," "sense of duty," which would require a lengthy analysis of firsthand testimonies left by soldiers of several countries. The three works cited are: Leonard V. Smith, *Between Mutiny and Obedience: The Case of the French Fifth Infantry Division During World War I* (Princeton: Princeton University Press, 1994); Jules Maurin, *Armée—Guerre—Société—Soldats languedociens (1889–1919)* (Paris: 1982); Wilhelm Deist,

"Le Moral des troupes allemandes sur le front occidental à la fin de l'année 1916," in *Guerres et Cultures 1914–1918,* ed. Jean-Jacques Becker et al. (Paris: 1994). On the coexistence between sense of duty and temptation to desert, see Dominique Richert, *Cahiers d'un survivant: un soldat dans l'Europe en guerre, 1914–1918* (Strasbourg: 1994), translated from the German.

11. Jay Winter and Blaine Baggett, *1914–1918: The Great War and the Shaping of the 20th Century* (London: BBC Books, 1996).

12. On combatants' reflections on the war they're being asked to fight, and on "negotiation" between officers and their troops, see the work of Leonard Smith already cited (see note 10). Smith has studied the case of the Fifth Infantry Division (Normandy). The *Carnets* of Barthas offer multiple confirmations of his thesis.

13. FAOL, 22 rue Antoine-Marty, BP 24, 11001 Carcassonne, France.

14. French edition by Maspero, Paris, in 1981 in the collection Actes et Mémoires du peuple. English edition by Brassey's (London, 1996), with the title *Marching to Captivity: The War Diaries of a French Peasant 1939–1945,* translated by Christopher Hill, preface by R. Cazals and C. Hill.

15. Published by Privat in 1985.

16. "Traces de 14–18," op. cit. (contributors include Sylvie Caucanas, Pierre Barral, Rémy Cazals, Leonard V. Smith, Thomas Ferenczi, Claude Sicard, Patrick Cabanel, Patrick Ourednik, Michel Cadé, Natacha Laurent, John Horne, J. S. Cartier, Jean-Charles Jauffret, Jean-Claude Sangoï, Pierre Guibbert, Rémy Pech, Nicolas Brejon de Lavergnée, Éric Vial, Pierre Laborie, and conclusions by Marc Ferro).

Chronology

FRANCE AND ALLIES AT WAR: WESTERN FRONT*		LOUIS BARTHAS AT WAR	

1914

August 2	**Announcement of mobilization**	*Notebook 1:* August 2	Peyriac-Minervois: announcement of mobilization
August 3	Germany declares war on France		
August 4	Germans invade neutral Belgium		
August 7–25	French invade German-occupied Alsace, take Mulhouse, withdraw	August 6– October 1	To Narbonne; garrison duty
August 11–25	"Battles of the Frontiers" (Battles of Morhange, Sarrebourg, Charleroi, Mons, Maubeuge, Saint-Quentin / Guise)		
August 20	Germans occupy Brussels		
September 4–13	Battle of Grand Couronné, Lorraine		
September 5–12	Battle of the Marne (Battles of the Ourcq, the Morins, the Marshes of Saint-Gond)		
September 13– November 3	"Race to the Sea"	October 2–30	Mont-Louis (Pyrenees): guarding German prisoners
October 16–31	Battle of the Yser	*Notebook 2:* November 4–11	Via Narbonne to Flanders; Barlin, Annequin
October 19– November 22	First Battle of Ypres	November 12–30	To trenches in coalfields
December 1–7	**Battle of Vermelles**	December 1–14	Attack on Vermelles; "Tranchée de la Mort"; Annequin
December 14– January 15, 1915	**First Battle of Artois**	*Notebook 3:* December 15–23	Attack on Auchy-lez-la-Bassée; first combat
December 18–22	Battle of Givenchy-lez-la-Bassée		
December 20– March 17, 1915	First Battle of Champagne		
December 24–25	**Reports of "Christmas Truce"**	*Notebook 4:* December 23	Rumors of "Christmas Truce"

*__Bold__ denotes events in which Louis Barthas participated.

FRANCE AND ALLIES AT WAR: WESTERN FRONT		LOUIS BARTHAS AT WAR	

1915

January 19–March 26	Battle for Hartmannswillerkopf, Vosges Mountains, Alsace	January 1–May 16	Annequin, Vermelles
February 17–April 30	Battles of Vauquois, Les Éparges		
March 10–13	Battles of Neuve-Chapelle, Aubers Ridge		
		April 12	Easter Mass at "The Washbowl"
April 22–May 25	Second Battle of Ypres; first use of poison gas	May 4	To trenches
May 9–June 18	**Second Battle of Artois (Vimy Ridge, Notre-Dame-de-Lorette)**	May 17–28	Nœux-les-Mines, Mazingarbe-les-Brébis; new uniforms
May 15–25	Ypres salient: First Battle of Festubert	May 29–June 1	To Lorette sector (Houdain, Sains-en-Gohelle)
		Notebook 5: June 2–4	Artois, Notre-Dame-de-Lorette: to trenches; Aix-Noulette
		June 5–6	Fond de Buval; bombardment, flamethrower attack
		June 13	Bombardment, death of Mondiès
		June 14–July 1	Sains-en-Gohelle
		Notebook 6: July 1–2	Death of Marty
		July 3–August 27	Hersin-Coupigny, Bully-Grenay, Tranchée Carbonnière, Sains-en-Gohelle
September 15–November 4	**Third Battle of Artois**	August 27–September 19	Across Flanders; training exercises
		September 20–27	Return to Artois front (Habacq, Marœuil)
September 25–28	Battle of Loos	*Notebook 7:* September 27–October 4	Lorette sector (Neuville-Saint-Vaast, "Boyau des Morts")
September 25–November 6	Second Battle of Champagne	October 5–November 15	Artois front (Marœuil, Agnez-lès-Duisans); bombardments; to Tranchée du Moulin
		Notebook 8: November 15–December 19	Marœuil, Agnez-lès-Duisans; Mercier and Moulin trenches; flight of Private Gontran
		December 19–28	Fraternization with enemy; Beaudricourt; part of 280th Regiment merged into 296th

FRANCE AND ALLIES AT WAR: WESTERN FRONT		LOUIS BARTHAS AT WAR

1916

		December 28, 1915–January 21, 1916	Hersin-Coupigny; with new regiment to Queux; home leave
February 21	**Battle of Verdun begins**	January 22–February 28	Return to regiment in Artois (Bailleul-les-Cornailles, Béthonsart, Mont-Saint-Eloi)
February 25	Verdun: Germans take Fort Douaumont	*Notebook 9:* February 29–April 14	Trench duty; broken in rank; across Picardy to English Channel coast and back
		April 15–26	En route to Verdun: across Champagne to Condé-en-Barrois
		Notebook 10: April 27–May 19	To Verdun (Hill 304, Mort Homme); week in "The Furnace"
June 9	Verdun: Germans take Fort Vaux	*Notebook 11:* May 19–25	Bois Saint-Pierre, Bethancourt
		May 26–July 12	Corporal again; across Champagne (Cuperly, Vadenay, Suippes, Camp de Châlons)
July 1–November 18	**Battle of the Somme** (Battles of La Boisselle, Mametz Wood, Ovillers, Contalmaison, Bazentin Ridge, Trônes Wood, Longueval, Delville Wood, **Morval,** Thiepval)	*Notebook 12:* July 13–30	Artillery training, Ferme de Bouy; trench duty, Butte de Tahure; "Camp A"
		July 31–August 29	Fraternization with Germans; "Camp I"
		Notebook 13: August 29–September 13	En route to the Somme
September 15–22	Somme, Flers-Corcelette; first use of tanks in battle	September 14–24	Home leave
		September 24–October 22	To the Somme (Hamelet, Ferme de Bonfray, Combles, Hardécourt)
		October 23–November 1	In front-line trenches of the Somme; Circé Trench, Bois de Morval
November 2	Verdun: French retake Fort Vaux	*Notebook 14:* November 1–December 1	The Somme (Suzanne, Aubigny, Corbie, Hardécourt, Bois de Morval, Circé Trench)
December 13	Nivelle replaces Joffre as French commander-in-chief	December 1–January 15, 1917	Amiens sector (Salouel, Briquemesnil, Morvillers, Aumale)

FRANCE AND ALLIES AT WAR: WESTERN FRONT		LOUIS BARTHAS AT WAR	

1917

		January 16–28	Home leave
		January 28–30	To Champagne / Argonne fronts (Valmy, Dommartin-sous-Hans)
		Notebook 15: January 30– February 14	Dommartin to "Main de Massiges"
February 23– April 5	Germans withdraw to Hindenburg Line of defenses	February 15– March 1	Bombardment; mass surrender at Maisons-Champagne; "Half-Moon" and "Index Finger"
		March 2– April 1	Ville-sur-Tourbe, Valmy
April 9–25	Canadians take Vimy Ridge, Artois	April 2–15	To Champagne front (Braux-Sainte-Cohière, Aulnay)
April 9–May 17	Battles of Arras, Artois		
April 16–May 9	**Chemin des Dames / Nivelle offensive; Battle of the Monts-de-Champagne**	April 16–25	Supporting Chemin des Dames / Nivelle offensive; Sept-Saux, Mont de Billy, Châlons
		Notebook 16: April 26–30	Monts-de-Champagne (Billy-le-Grand, Wez)
		April 30	Death of Colonel Robert
May 3–June 30	**Mutinies in French army**	May 1–21	Monts-de-Champagne (Mont Cornillet, Wez, Isse)
May 15	Nivelle dismissed, replaced by Pétain; offensive halted	May 22–31	Daucourt: 296th Regiment mutinies
June 7–14	British attack Messines Ridge, Ypres sector	June 1–30	To Argonne sector (Biesme valley, La Harazée); trench raids
July 31– November 10	Battle of Passchendaele / Third Ypres	*Notebook 17:* July 1– November 18	La Harazée sector
November 20– December 3	Battle of Cambrai; first use of massed tanks in battle	November 19–29	296th Regiment merged into 248th; Florent-en-Argonne, Darniéville
		November 29– December 5	Bassuet
		December 5–23	To Argonne trenches, Biesme valley; "Lower Goat Shed"
		December 28– January 14, 1918	Home leave; return to trenches

FRANCE AND ALLIES AT WAR: WESTERN FRONT		LOUIS BARTHAS AT WAR	

1918

		January 15–28	Argonne front: bombardments, trench raids
		Notebook 18: January 28–February 6	Trench raids in "Fille Morte" sector
March 3	Treaty of Brest-Litovsk; Russia withdraws from war	February 7–March 21	Les-Petites-Islettes; woodcutting, digging trenches; drunken Bretons
		March 22–28	To Les Islettes; bombardments
March 26	Foch appointed supreme commander of Allied forces	March 28	Final march, to Auve; evacuation order
April 5–29	German Spring Offensive	April 6	Evacuated from Auve to Châlons, for exhaustion; Février hospital
		April 23–June 8	To convalescent hospital at Bourgoin (Isère)
May 28	Battle of Cantigny; first U.S. combat		
June 1–26	Battle of Belleau Wood; U.S. Marines in combat	June 8–August 10	Convalescent home leave, two months
July 15–August 6	Second Battle of the Marne (last German offensive on Western Front); Battles of Château-Thierry, Soissons		
August 8–November 11	Allied "Hundred Days" offensive: Battles of Noyon, Second Somme, Second Arras, Saint-Mihiel, Hindenburg Line	August 10–11	Via Paris to Guingamp, Brittany (248th Regiment headquarters)
		Notebook 19: August 11–September 8	Guingamp: infirmary and gardening; home leave
		September 8–February 14, 1919	Vitré, Brittany: training conscripts
November 11, 1918	**Armistice**	November 11	Armistice
		November 22–January 10, 1919	Fifty-day home leave

1919

		January 10–February 12	Guingamp hospital: guarding German prisoners
		February 14	Mustered out, Narbonne; home to Peyriac-Minervois

Index